MW01009251

Software Design Methods for Concurrent and Real-Time Systems

Hassan Gomaa
George Mason University

ADDISON-WESLEY PUBLISHING COMPANY

Reading, Massachusetts
Menlo Park, California ■ New York
Don Mills, Ontario ■ Wokingham, England
Amsterdam ■ Bonn ■ Sydney ■ Singapore
Tokyo ■ Madrid ■ San Juan ■ Milan ■ Paris

Software Engineering Institute

The SEI Series in Software Engineering

Editor-in-Chief
Nico Habermann, *Carnegie Mellon University*

Associate Editors
Peter Freeman, *Georgia Institute of Technology*
John Musa, *AT&T Bell Laboratories*

Editorial Advisors
Roger Bate, *Software Engineering Institute*
Laszlo Belady, *Mitsubishi Electronic Research Laboratory*
Barry Boehm, *University of Southern California*
John Ellis, *Xerox Corporation*
Robert Goldberg, *IBM Corporate Technical Institutes*
Harlan D. Mills, *Software Engineering and Technology Institute*
William E. Riddle, *Software Design and Analysis, Inc.*
William A. Wulf, *University of Virginia*

Library of Congress Cataloging-in-Publication Data

Gomaa, Hassan.
    Software design methods for concurrent and real-time systems / by
Hassan Gomaa.
        p.   cm.— (SEI series in software engineering)
    Includes bibliographical references (p.) and index.
    ISBN 0-201-52577-1
        1. Computer software—Development.   2. Parallel processing
(Electronic computers)   3. Real-time data processing.   I. Title.
    II. Series
    QA76.76.D47G65   1993
    005.1'1—dc20   92-23216
                                                          CIP

Copyright © 1993 by Addison-Wesley Publishing Company, Inc.

1 2 3 4 5 6 7 8 9 10-MA-959493

To Gill, William, Alexander, Amanda, Edward,
and my mother, Johanna.

Preface

This book describes the concepts and methods used in the software design of concurrent and real-time systems. It outlines the characteristics of concurrent and real-time systems, describes important concepts in the design of these systems, discusses the role of software design in software development, and surveys and compares a number of software design methods for concurrent and real-time systems, with the aid of examples. It then describes two related software design methods for these systems in more detail and illustrates them with a number of case studies.

With the massive reduction in the cost of microprocessors over the last few years and the large increase in their performance, concurrent, real-time, and distributed real-time microcomputer-based systems have become a cost-effective solution to many problems. Nowadays, more and more commercial, industrial, consumer, medical, and military products are microcomputer based and either are software controlled or have a crucial software component to them. These systems range from microwave ovens to video cassette recorders, from telephones to television sets, from automobiles to aircraft, from submarines that explore the depths of the oceans to spacecraft that explore the far reaches of space, from automated vending machines to automated teller machines, from patient monitoring systems to factory monitoring systems, from robot controllers to elevator controllers, from city traffic control to air traffic control, from "smart" transportation highways to "smart" information highways—the list is continually growing. These systems are concurrent, and they are real-time. Many of them are also distributed.

There are few books oriented towards the design of large-scale concurrent and real-time software systems. This book is a result of the author's experience in developing concurrent and real-time systems in industry, in developing and applying software design methods, and in teaching courses on software engineering in general and software design in particular, both in academia and in industry. The book is intended for software professionals and students who intend to design, implement, evaluate, or understand how to design the software for these concurrent, real-time, and distributed applications.

The book is divided into four parts. Part I describes overall concepts for the design of concurrent and real-time systems. In Chapter 2, software life cycle considerations specific to concurrent and real-time systems are surveyed. Chapter 3 focuses on design concepts that are of particular importance to concurrent and real-time system design, such as concurrent tasks, information hiding, object-oriented concepts, and finite state machines. Environments for concurrent processing and operating system support for concurrent processing are described.

Part II starts with an overview of software design and software design methods in Chapter 4. It then surveys several software design methods for concurrent and real-time systems. The methods surveyed are Real-Time Structured Analysis and Design (Chapter 5), the Design Approach for Real-Time Systems - DARTS (Chapter 6), Jackson System Development (Chapter 7), the Naval Research Laboratory Software Cost Reduction Method (Chapter 8), and Object-Oriented Design (Chapter 9). In each of these chapters, the concepts on which each method is based are described first so as to show what the method is attempting to achieve. After a brief description of the notation used by the method, the steps involved in using the method are described to give an appreciation of the method. A list of the products of each method are also given. Since the methods are best understood by studying an example, an example is given of applying each design method to solve the same real-time problem, namely an automobile cruise control and monitoring system. This is followed by an assessment of the method and a summary of the extensions and/or variations of the method.

The methods are then compared in Chapter 10 from the perspective of how they address the important design concepts introduced in Chapter 3. Chapter 11 describes the performance analysis of concurrent and real-time software designs, and introduces the subject of real-time scheduling, an important consideration in real-time design.

Part III provides a detailed description of two related software design methods for concurrent and real-time systems, ADARTS (SM) (Ada-based Design Approach for Real-Time Systems) and CODARTS (COncurrent Design Approach for Real-Time Systems), which build on the methods described in Part II. ADARTS is a proven method, which is currently in active use by several aerospace companies. CODARTS, which is based on ADARTS, contains the author's latest ideas on software analysis and design.

Part III is structured as follows. Chapter 12 provides an overview of ADARTS and CODARTS and describes the notation used by them. Chapter 13 describes the COncurrent Object-Based Real-Time Analysis (COBRA) method used in CODARTS, which is an alternative to Real-Time Structured Analysis (used by ADARTS) for developing a behavioral model. The next five chapters from Chapter 14 through 18 provide detailed descriptions of the subsequent steps in the ADARTS and CODARTS methods. Chapter 19 describes how a performance analysis of an ADARTS or

CODARTS design may be carried out, applying real-time scheduling theory and event sequence analysis. Chapter 20 describes the aspects of CODARTS that deal with the design of distributed concurrent and distributed real-time applications.

Part IV presents a number of ADARTS and CODARTS case studies. These are an Automobile Cruise Control and Monitoring System (Chapter 22), a Robot Controller (Chapter 23), an Elevator Control System (Chapter 24), and finally a distributed Factory Automation System (Chapter 25).

Readers familiar with software life cycle issues and software design concepts may skip Chapters 2 and 3. Readers familiar with software design methods may skip the survey in Part II and begin with the comparison in Chapter 10. Readers particularly interested in ADARTS and CODARTS may proceed directly to Parts III and IV. Readers particularly interested in real-time scheduling and its application should read Chapters 11, 19, and the case studies in Chapters 22 through 25.

Acknowledgements

The author gratefully acknowledges the reviewers of earlier drafts of the manuscript for their constructive comments; in particular, David Weiss, Peter Freeman, Harlan Mills, Melody Eidbo, Jeff Magee, and Peter Bailor. Ragunathan Rajkumar provided valuable comments on the sections on real-time scheduling. Gary Ford provided helpful overall comments. The author is also indebted to his students on his Software Requirements and Design courses at the Wang Institute of Graduate Studies and George Mason University for their enthusiasm, dedication, and valuable feedback.

The author gratefully acknowledges the Software Engineering Institute for sponsoring the development of the curriculum module on "Software Design Methods for Real-Time Systems," which was the first step in writing this book. The author also gratefully acknowledges the SEI for the material provided on real-time scheduling, on which parts of Chapter 11 are based.

The author also gratefully acknowledges the Software Productivity Consortium's sponsorship of the development of the ADARTS method, as well as the contributions of Mike Cochran, Rick Kirk, and Elisa Simmons, particularly during the ADARTS validation exercise [Cochran & Gomaa91]. Acknowledgements are also due to David Weiss for his thoughtful comments during the formative stages of ADARTS.

The author is also grateful to John Brackett who provided the problem definition for the Automobile Cruise Control and Monitoring System, and to Elizabeth O'Hara-Schettino who helped with the details of several solutions to that problem. He also thanks Robbie Gosner, Vijayan Sugumaran, Iraj Tavakoli, Raghu Ram, and Jaime Iribarren for their hard work producing earlier versions of the figures. Thanks are also due to Richard Evans for his considerable assistance with the glossary. The Software through Pictures CASE tool, used for earlier versions of the data flow diagrams, was donated to George Mason University by Interactive Development Environments, Inc.

Last, but not least, I would like to thank my wife, Gill, for her encouragement, understanding, and support.

Contents

PART ONE

Concepts

1

Introduction

1.1 A Wide Range of Applications

With the massive reduction in the cost of microprocessor and semiconductor chips and the large increase in microprocessor performance over the last few years, real-time and distributed real-time microcomputer-based systems are a very cost-effective solution to many problems. Nowadays, an increasing number of industrial, military, medical, and consumer products are microcomputer based and either are software controlled or have a crucial software component to them.

This book describes the design of concurrent systems as well as two important categories of concurrent systems: real-time systems and distributed applications. This first chapter introduces and discusses the characteristics of concurrent systems, real-time systems, and distributed applications.

1.2 Concurrent Systems

1.2.1 Concurrency

Most early computer systems were batch programs. Each program was sequential and ran off-line. Today, with the proliferation of interactive systems and the tendency towards distributed microcomputer systems, many systems are concurrent in nature. A concurrent system typically has many activities (or tasks) occurring in parallel. Often the order of incoming events is not predictable and these events may overlap.

The concept of concurrent tasks, which are frequently referred to as concurrent processes, is fundamental in these systems' design. The design concepts for concurrent systems are generally applicable to real-time systems and distributed applications as well.

1.2.2 Concurrent Tasks

A task represents the execution of a sequential program or a sequential component in a concurrent program. Each task deals with one sequential thread of execution. Thus no concurrency is allowed within a task. However, overall system concurrency is obtained by having multiple tasks executing in parallel. The tasks often execute asynchronously (i.e., at different speeds), and are relatively independent of each other for significant periods of time. From time to time, the tasks need to communicate and synchronize their operations with each other.

The body of knowledge on cooperating concurrent tasks has grown substantially since Dijkstra's seminal work [Dijkstra68]. Among the significant early contributions were those of Brinch Hansen [Brinch-Hansen73], who developed an operating system based on concurrent tasks that incorporated semaphores and message communication, and Hoare [Hoare74], who developed the monitor concept that applies information hiding to task synchronization. Several algorithms were developed for concurrent task communication and synchronization, such as the multiple readers/multiple writers algorithm, the sleeping barber algorithm, the dining philosophers algorithm, and the banker's algorithm for deadlock prevention.

The concurrent tasking concept has been applied extensively in the design of operating systems, database systems, real-time systems, interactive systems, distributed systems, and in simulation programs. Key issues for developing concurrent systems include providing a capability for structuring a system into concurrent tasks, providing a capability for tasks to communicate with each other, to synchronize their operations, and to provide synchronization of access to shared data. In addition, it is highly desirable to provide support for concurrent execution in the programming language and/or operating system. The concurrent tasking concept is described in more detail in Chapter 3.

1.2.3 Advantages of Concurrent Tasking

The advantages of using concurrent tasking in software design are:

1. Concurrent tasking is a natural model for many real-world applications since it reflects the natural parallelism that exists in the problem domain, where there are often several activities happening simultaneously. For these applications, the target system is best designed with concurrency explicitly defined at the outset. A design emphasizing concurrent tasks is clearer and easier to understand, since it is a more realistic model of the problem domain than a sequential program.

2. Structuring a concurrent system into tasks results in a separation of concerns of what each task does from when it does it. This usually makes the system easier to understand, to manage, and to construct.

3. A system structured into concurrent tasks can result in an overall reduction in system execution time. On a single processor, concurrent tasking results in improved performance by allowing I/O operations to be executed in parallel with computational operations. With the use of multiple processors, improved performance is obtained by having different tasks actually execute in parallel on different processors.

4. Structuring the system into concurrent tasks allows greater scheduling flexibility since time critical tasks with hard deadlines may be given a higher priority than less critical tasks.

5. Identifying the concurrent tasks early in the design can allow an early performance analysis of the system. Many of these tools and techniques use concurrent tasks as a fundamental component in their analysis.

However, whereas concurrent tasking is recommended for many real-world applications, having too many tasks in a system can unnecessarily increase complexity and overhead because of the additional intertask communication and synchronization involved.

1.3   Real-time Systems

Real-time systems have widespread use in industrial, commercial, and military applications. These systems are often complex because they deal with multiple independent streams of input events and produce multiple outputs. These events often have unpredictable arrival rates, although they must be responded to in a manner subject to timing constraints specified in the software requirements. Furthermore, the input load may vary significantly and unpredictably with time.

A feature of most real-time systems is concurrent processing; that is, there are many activities that need to be processed in parallel. Thus real-time systems are concurrent systems with timing constraints.

Real-time systems are frequently classified as hard real-time systems or soft real-time systems. A hard real-time system has time critical deadlines that must be met, otherwise a catastrophic system failure could occur. In a soft real-time system, it is considered undesirable but not catastrophic if deadlines are occasionally missed.

Real-time software systems have several characteristics that distinguish them from other software systems. These characteristics include:

1. *Embedded systems.* A real-time system is often an embedded system, i.e., component of a larger hardware/software system. An example is a robot controller

that is a component of a robot system consisting of one or more mechanical arms, servomechanisms controlling axis motion, and sensors and actuators for interfacing to the external environment. A computerized automobile cruise control system is embedded in the automobile.

2. *Interaction with external environment.* A real-time system typically interacts with an external environment that is to a large extent non-human. For example, the real-time system may be controlling machines or manufacturing processes, or it may be monitoring chemical processes and reporting alarm conditions. This often necessitates a sensory interface for receiving data from the external environment and actuators for outputting data to and controlling the external environment.

3. *Timing constraints.* Real-time systems have timing constraints; that is, they must process events within a given time frame. Whereas in an interactive system, a human may be inconvenienced if the system response is delayed, in a real-time system a delay may be catastrophic. For example, inadequate response in an air traffic control system could result in a mid-air collision of two aircraft. The required response time will vary by application, ranging from milliseconds to seconds or even minutes.

4. *Real-time control.* A real-time system often involves real-time control, where the system makes control decisions based on input data without any human intervention. An automobile cruise control system adjusts the throttle based on measurements of current speed to ensure that the desired speed is maintained.

   A real-time software system may also have non–real-time components. For example, real-time data collection necessitates gathering the data under real-time constraints, otherwise the data could be lost. However, once collected the data could be stored for subsequent non–real-time analysis.

5. *Reactive systems.* Many real-time systems are reactive systems [Harel88a]. They are event driven and must respond to external stimuli. In reactive systems the response made by the system to an input stimulus is usually state dependent; that is, the response depends not only on the stimulus itself but also on what has previously happened in the system.

1.4 Distributed Applications

A distributed application is a concurrent application that executes in an environment consisting of multiple nodes, which are in geographically different locations. Each node is a separate computer system; the nodes are connected to each other by means of a local or wide area network. Because the system software required to support distributed applications is so complex, the term distributed system is often used to refer to distributed operating systems, distributed file systems, and distributed databases. Since the emphasis in this book is on designing applications using these services, the term *distributed application* is used.

The advantages of distributed processing are:

1. *Improved availability.* Operation is feasible in a reduced configuration in cases where some nodes are temporarily unavailable. There is thus no single point of failure.

2. *More flexible configuration.* A given application can be configured in different ways, by selecting the appropriate number of nodes for a given instance of the application.

3. *More localized control and management.* A distributed subsystem, executing on its own node, can be designed to be autonomous, so that it can execute in relative independence of other subsystems on other nodes.

4. *Incremental system expansion.* If the system gets overloaded, the system can be expanded by adding more nodes.

5. *Reduced cost.* Frequently a distributed solution is cheaper than a centralized solution. With the rapidly declining costs and rapidly increasing performance of microcomputers, a distributed solution can be significantly more cost effective than an equivalent centralized solution.

6. *Load balancing.* In some applications, the overall system load can be shared among several nodes.

7. *Improved response time.* Local users on local nodes can have their requests processed in a more timely fashion.

2

Software Life-cycle Considerations for Concurrent and Real-time Systems

2.1 Introduction

As with any software system, concurrent and real-time systems should be developed using a software life cycle, which is a phased approach to developing software. The "Waterfall" Model [Boehm76, Fairley85] is the most widely-used software life-cycle model. This section gives an overview of the Waterfall Model. Alternative software life-cycle models are then outlined, which have been developed in order to overcome some of the Waterfall Model's limitations. The three models are the Throwaway Prototyping Model, the Incremental Development Model (also referred to as Evolutionary Prototyping), and the Spiral Model. Finally, the important activity of design verification and validation is discussed.

2.2 The Waterfall Life-cycle Model

2.2.1 Overview

In the last twenty years, the cost of developing software has grown steadily, while the cost of developing and/or purchasing hardware has rapidly decreased. Software now typically accounts for 80 percent of total project costs.

In the 1960s, the problems of developing software were not clearly understood, but it was realized that a software crisis existed. The term software engineering was coined to refer to the management and technical methods, procedures, and tools required to develop a large-scale software system effectively. With the application of software engineering concepts, many large-scale software systems have been developed using a software life cycle. The most widely-used software life-cycle model is often referred to as the Waterfall Model, generally considered the conventional or "classical" software life cycle.

2.2.2 Requirements Analysis and Specification

In this phase of the Waterfall Model, the user's requirements are identified and analyzed. The software requirements are specified in a Software Requirements Specification [SRS]. The goal of the SRS is to provide a complete description of *what* the system's external behavior is without describing *how* the system works internally. The issues of what constitutes a SRS are described lucidly in [Davis90].

Since a real-time software system is often part of a larger embedded system, it is likely that a systems requirements analysis and specification phase precedes the software requirements analysis and specification. With this approach, system functional requirements are allocated to software and hardware before software requirements analysis begins [Brackett89, Davis90].

2.2.3 Architectural Design

During this phase of the model, the system is structured into its constituent components. An important factor frequently differentiating concurrent and real-time systems from other systems is addressing the issue of structuring the system into concurrent tasks. Depending on the design method used and/or the designer's decisions, the emphasis may be on decomposition into tasks, modules, or both. Another important factor is consideration of the behavioral aspects of the system (i.e., the sequences of events and states that the system experiences). This action provides valuable insights into understanding the dynamic aspects of the system.

2.2.4 Detailed Design

During the Detailed Design phase, the algorithmic details of each system component are defined, using a Program Design Language (PDL) notation (also referred to as structured English or pseudocode). In concurrent and real-time systems, particular attention needs to be paid to algorithms for resource sharing and deadlock avoidance, as well as interfacing to hardware I/O devices.

2.2.5 Coding

During the coding phase, each component is coded in the programming language selected for the project, adhering to a set of coding and documentation standards.

For concurrent systems, either a concurrent language (e.g., Ada or Modula 2) or a sequential language supported by a multi-tasking operating system or kernel is chosen.

2.2.6 Software Testing

Some aspects of testing concurrent and real-time systems are no different than those for testing other systems [Beizer84, Myers79]. Most of the differences are either because the software system consists of several concurrent tasks or because the system interfaces to several external devices.

A major problem in testing concurrent systems is that execution of such systems is non-deterministic (i.e., the response of the system to its inputs varies in a way that is difficult to predict). An approach for the deterministic testing of concurrent systems is described in [Tai91].

Since real-time systems are often embedded systems, testing is often more complex, possibly requiring the development of environment simulators [Gomaa86a]. Furthermore, the performance of the system needs to be tested against the requirements.

Because of the difficulty of detecting errors and then locating and correcting them, software systems are usually tested in several stages. Unit and integration testing are "white box" testing approaches, requiring knowledge of the internals of the software, while system testing is a "black box" testing approach, based on the software requirements specification.

2.2.7 Unit Testing

Unit testing consists of testing an individual component before it is combined with other components. A minimum test coverage criterion is each statement should be executed at least once (referred to as statement coverage), and that every possible outcome of each branch should be tested at least once (referred to as branch coverage).

2.2.8 Integration Testing

Integration testing involves combining tested components into progressively more complex groupings of components, and testing these groupings until the whole software system has been put together and the interfaces tested.

A distinguishing feature of integration testing for concurrent systems is that concurrent task interfaces need to be tested. A systematic method for the integration testing of concurrent tasks is described in Chapter 18 and in [Gomaa86a].

2.2.9 System Testing

System testing is the process of testing an integrated hardware and software system to verify that the system meets the specified requirements [IEEE83] as described in the Requirements Specification. To achieve greater objectivity, it is preferable if system testing is performed by an independent test team.

Statistical usage testing [Cobb90] has been advocated for both integration and system testing, where "black-box" test scenarios are developed by an independent test team based on the expected usage profile of the system.

During system testing several aspects of a concurrent and/or real-time system need to be tested [Beizer84, Myers79]. These include:

1. Functional testing, to determine that the system performs the functions described in the requirements specification;

2. Load (stress) testing, to determine whether the system can handle the large and varied workload it is expected to handle when operational;

3. Performance testing, to determine that the system meets its response time requirements.

System testing of real-time systems can be greatly assisted by the construction of environment simulators which simulate the behavior of the external environment. This allows the creation of a controlled reproducible environment that can greatly assist in software regression and performance testing [Gomaa82b, Gomaa86a].

2.2.10 Acceptance Testing

Acceptance testing is usually carried out by the user organization or its representative, typically at the user installation, prior to acceptance of the system. Most of the issues relating to system testing also apply to acceptance testing.

2.3 Limitations of the Waterfall Model

The Waterfall Model is a major successful improvement over the undisciplined approach used on many early software projects. In practice, it is often necessary to have some overlap between successive phases of the life cycle and some iteration between phases when errors are detected. However, there are significant problems with the Waterfall Model:

1. Software requirements are not properly tested until a working system is available to demonstrate to the end users. In fact, several studies [Boehm76] have shown that errors in the requirements specification are usually the last to be detected, often not until system or acceptance testing, and are the most costly to correct;

2. A working system only becomes available late in the life cycle. Thus a major design or performance problem may go undetected until the system is almost operational, at which time it is usually too late to take effective action.

For software development projects with a significant risk factor (e.g., due to requirements that are not clearly understood), variations or alternatives to the Waterfall Model have been proposed.

Two different software prototyping approaches used to overcome some of the limitations of the Waterfall Model are throwaway prototypes and evolutionary prototypes. While throwaway prototypes can help resolve the first problem of the Waterfall model outlined above, evolutionary prototypes can help resolve the second problem.

2.4 Throwaway Prototyping

A throwaway prototype is a working system developed rapidly and at low cost, which is used to help clarify user requirements [Agresti86, Gomaa81a]. A throwaway prototype may be developed after a preliminary requirements specification. By giving users the capability of exercising the prototype, much valuable feedback can be obtained. Based on this feedback, a revised requirements specification can be prepared. Subsequent development proceeds following the conventional software life cycle.

Throwaway prototypes can also be used for experimental prototyping of the design, determining if certain algorithms are logically correct or if they meet their performance goals.

Throwaway prototyping, particularly of the user interface, has proved to be an effective solution to the problem of specifying requirements for interactive information systems. For example, [Gomaa81a] described how a throwaway prototype was used to help clarify the requirements of a highly interactive manufacturing application. The biggest problem it helped overcome was the communications barrier that existed between the users and the developers.

2.5   Evolutionary Prototyping by Incremental Development

The evolutionary prototyping approach is a form of incremental development, in which the prototype evolves through several intermediate operational systems into the delivered system [McCracken82, Gomaa86b]. This approach can help in determining whether the system meets its performance goals for testing critical components of the design and for reducing development risk by spreading the implementation over a longer time frame. Event sequence diagrams may be used to assist in selecting system subsets for each increment [Gomaa86a].

One objective of the evolutionary prototyping approach is to have a subset of the system working early that is then gradually built upon. It is advantageous if the first incremental version of the system tests a complete path through the system from external input to external output.

An example of evolutionary prototyping by means of incremental development is described in [Gomaa86b]. Using this approach on a real-time robot controller system [Gomaa86a] resulted in an early operational version of the system being available. This had a big morale boosting effect on both the development team and management, and also had the important benefits of verifying the system design, establishing whether certain key algorithms met their performance goals, and spreading system integration over time.

2.6   Combining Throwaway Prototyping and Incremental Development

With the Incremental Development Life-Cycle Model approach, a working system, in the form of an evolutionary prototype, is available significantly earlier than with the conventional Waterfall Model. Nevertheless, greater care needs to be taken in developing this kind of prototype than with a throwaway prototype since it forms the basis of the finished product. Thus software quality has to be built into the system from the start; in particular, the software architecture needs to be carefully designed and all interfaces specified.

The conventional Waterfall Model is impacted significantly by the introduction of throwaway prototyping or incremental development. It is also possible to combine the two approaches. A throwaway prototyping exercise is carried out to clarify the requirements. Once the requirements are understood and a specification is developed, an incremental development life cycle is pursued. Further changes in requirements may be necessary due to changes in the user environment after subsequent increments.

2.7 Spiral Model

Another approach for integrating prototyping and incremental development with the Waterfall Model is called the Spiral Model [Boehm88]. The Spiral Model is an iterative life cycle in which each loop of the spiral represents one iteration. The radial coordinate represents cumulative cost. An important aspect of each iteration is a risk assessment of the project. The areas of greatest uncertainty and potentially significant problems are identified. Prototypes are developed and evaluated to help alleviate the areas of greatest risk. For example, if user requirements are not clearly understood, a throwaway prototype is developed. During design, a prototype could be developed to assess areas of greatest performance risk. Implementation only begins when the risks have been substantially reduced to a level considered acceptable by management.

2.8 Design Verification and Validation

According to Boehm [Boehm81], the goal of software validation is to ensure that the software development team builds the right system; that is, that the system conforms to what the user needs. Software verification is to ensure that the software development team builds the system right; that is, that each phase of the software system is built according to the specification defined in the previous phase.

Software quality assurance is a name given to a set of activities whose goal is to ensure the quality of the software product. Software verification and validation are important goals of software quality assurance. Software technical reviews can help considerably with software verification and validation [Fagan76].

For validation of the system before it is developed against the user requirements, throwaway prototyping is one of the approaches that is most helpful in ensuring that the team builds the right system. Another important activity is testing the fully integrated system against the software requirements (carried out during system testing).

In software verification, it is important to ensure that the design conforms to the software requirements specification. Requirements tracing and technical reviews of the software design help with this activity. Throwaway prototypes can also be used for experimental prototyping of the design. Once the design of the system has been completed, simulation can be used to verify that the design is sound and that it meets its timing requirements.

3

Software Design Concepts

This chapter describes key concepts in the software design of concurrent and real-time systems. The concurrent processing concept, first introduced in Chapter 1, is described in more detail, in particular the issues of communication and synchronization between concurrent tasks. This is followed by a description of system environments and operating system support for concurrent processing. The information hiding concept is introduced from the perspective of decomposing a system into modules. Object-oriented concepts are discussed with the role of information hiding in object-oriented design, as well as an introduction to the concepts of classes and inheritance. Finally, the role of finite state machines in concurrent and real-time system design is described.

3.1 Concurrent Processing

3.1.1 Cooperation Between Concurrent Tasks

Several problems that do not arise when designing sequential systems need to be considered in the design of concurrent systems. In most real-time and concurrent applications, concurrent tasks must cooperate with each other in order to perform the services required by the application. Three common problems that arise when tasks cooperate with each other are:

1. *The mutual exclusion problem.* This problem occurs when tasks need to have exclusive access to a resource, such as shared data or a physical device. A variation on this problem, where the mutual exclusion constraint can be relaxed in certain situations, is the multiple readers/multiple writers problem.

2. *The task synchronization problem.* Two tasks need to synchronize their operations with each other.

3. *The producer/consumer problem.* This problem occurs when tasks need to communicate with each other in order to pass data from one task to another.

These problems and their solutions are described in the next three subsections.

3.1.2 Mutual Exclusion Problem

Mutual exclusion arises when it is necessary for a shared resource to be accessed by only one task at a time. With concurrent systems, more than one task may simultaneously wish to access the same resource. Consider the following situations:

☐ If two or more tasks are allowed to write to a printer simultaneously, then output from the tasks will be randomly interleaved and a garbled report will be produced; and

☐ If two or more tasks are allowed to write to a data store simultaneously, then inconsistent and/or incorrect data will be written to the data store.

To solve these problems, a synchronization mechanism must be provided ensuring that access to a critical resource by concurrent tasks is mutually exclusive.

A task must first acquire the resource (that is, get permission to access the resource) use the resource, and then release the resource. When a task A releases the resource, task B may then acquire the resource. If the resource is in use by A when task B wishes to acquire it, then B must wait until the resource is released by A.

The classical solution to the mutual exclusion problem was first proposed by Dijkstra [Dijkstra68] using binary semaphores. A binary semaphore is a boolean variable that is only accessed by means of two atomic (i.e., indivisible) operations, Wait(s) and Signal(s), where s is the semaphore. Dijkstra originally called these the P (for Wait) and V (for Signal) operations.

The indivisible Wait(s) operation is executed by a task when it wishes to acquire a resource. The semaphore s is initially set to 1, meaning that the resource is free. As a result of executing the Wait operation, s is decremented by 1 to 0 and the task is allocated the resource. If the semaphore s is already set to 0 when the Wait operation is executed by task A, this means another task already has the resource. In this case, task A is suspended until task B signals that it is releasing the resource by executing a Signal(s) operation. This results in task A being allocated the resource. It should be noted that the task executing the Wait operation is only suspended if the resource has already been acquired by another task. The code executed by a task while it has access to the mutually exclusive resource is referred to as the critical region or critical section.

An example of mutual exclusion is a shared sensor data store, which contains the current values of several sensors. Some tasks read from the data store in order to process or display the sensor values, while other tasks monitor the external environment and update the data store with the latest values of the sensors. To ensure mutual exclusion in this example, each task must execute a Wait operation before it starts accessing the data store and execute a Signal operation after it has finished accessing the data store. The Pseudocode for acquiring the sensor data store resource to enter the critical section and releasing the resource is as follows:

```
Wait (Sensor_data_store_semaphore)
Access sensor data store [critical region]
Signal (Sensor_data_store_semaphore)
```

The solution assumes that during initialization, the initial values of the sensors are stored before any reading takes place.

In some concurrent applications, it may be too restrictive to allow only mutually exclusive access to a shared resource. Thus, in the sensor data store example described previously, it is essential for a writer task to have mutually exclusive access to the data store. However, it is permissible to have more than one reader task concurrently reading from the data store, providing no writer task writes to the data store simultaneously. This is referred to as the Multiple Readers/Multiple Writers Problem [Courtois71]. This problem may also be solved using semaphores and is described further in Chapter 16.

3.1.3 Task Synchronization Problem

Event synchronization is used when two tasks need to coordinate their operations without data being communicated between the tasks. Events are used to synchronize the operations of the two tasks. The source task executes a Signal (Event) operation, which signals that an event has taken place.

The destination task executes a Wait (Event) operation, which suspends the task until the event has been signalled by the producer. If the event has already been signalled, then the destination task is not suspended. Event synchronization is described in more detail in Chapter 14. Task synchronization may also be achieved by means of message communication as described next.

3.1.4 Producer/Consumer Problem

A common problem in concurrent systems is that of producer and consumer tasks. The producer task produces information which is then consumed by the consumer task. For this to happen, data needs to be passed from the producer to the consumer. In a sequential program, a calling procedure also passes data to a called procedure. However, control passes from the calling procedure to the called procedure at the same time as the data.

In a concurrent system, each task has its own thread of control and the tasks execute asynchronously. It is therefore necessary for the tasks to synchronize their operations when they wish to exchange data. Thus the data must be produced by the producer before the consumer can consume it. If the consumer is ready to receive the data but the producer has not yet produced it, then the consumer must wait for the producer. If the producer has produced the data before the consumer is ready to receive it, then either the producer has to be held up or the data needs to be buffered for the consumer, thereby allowing the producer to continue.

A common solution to this problem is to use message communication between the producer and consumer tasks. Message communication between tasks serves two purposes:

1. Transfer of data from a producer (source) task to a consumer (destination) task; and

2. Synchronization between producer and consumer. If there is no message available, then the consumer has to wait for the message to arrive from the producer. In some cases, the producer waits for a reply from the consumer.

Message communication between tasks may be loosely or tightly coupled. The tasks may reside on the same node or be distributed over several nodes in a distributed application.

With loosely-coupled message communication, the producer sends a message to the consumer and continues without waiting for a response. Loosely-coupled message communication is also referred to as asynchronous message communication.

With tightly-coupled message communication, the producer sends a message to the consumer and then immediately waits for a response. Tightly-coupled message communication is also referred to as synchronous message communication and in Ada as a rendezvous. Message communication is described in more detail in Chapters 14 and 20.

3.2 Environments for Concurrent Processing

In a concurrent system, the concurrency is real if each task executes on a different processor. Alternatively, the concurrency is virtual if the tasks are interleaved. There are three main environments for concurrent systems:

1. *Multiprogramming environment.* In this environment, there are multiple tasks sharing one processor. Virtual concurrency is achieved by having the operating system control the allocation of the processor to the individual tasks, so that it appears as if each task has a dedicated processor. The multiprogramming environment, illustrated in Fig. 3.1, is typical for mini- and microcomputers. The

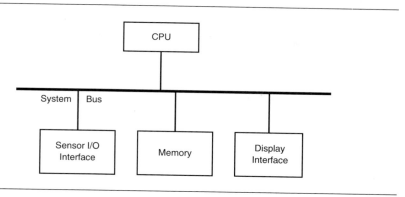

FIGURE 3.1 Multiprogramming (single CPU) Environment

hardware components reside on printed circuit cards (also referred to as circuit boards), which are connected to each other via the system bus. For example, in Fig. 3.1, there is a CPU card and a memory card, where the code and data for each task are stored, as well as the operating system software. The system interfaces to two I/O devices, a display and sensor input device, via the device interface cards. There is a device controller on each device interface card.

2. *Multiprocessing environment.* The multiprocessing environment is illustrated in Fig. 3.2. In this environment there are two or more processors with shared memory. There is one virtual address space that is common to all the processors. All the tasks reside in the shared memory. In a multiprocessing environment, real concurrency is supported as the processors are executing concurrently. The tasks

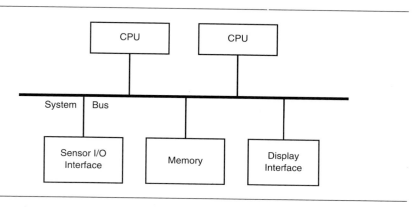

FIGURE 3.2 Multiprocessing Environment

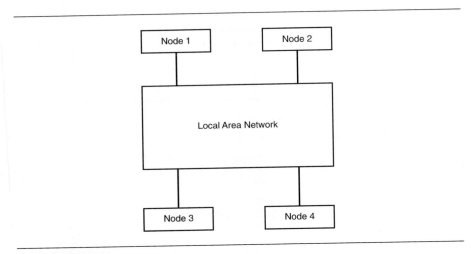

FIGURE 3.3 Distributed Processing Environment

executing on different processors can communicate with each other via the shared memory.

3. *Distributed processing environment.* In this environment, there are two or more computers connected to each other by a communications network or high speed bus. Each computer has its own local memory and there is no shared memory between the processors. Thus a distributed application consisting of concurrent tasks can have the tasks distributed over the network communicating via messages. The distributed processing environment is illustrated in Fig. 3.3. Each node typically consists of a multiprogramming system as shown in Fig. 3.1 or a multiprocessing system as shown in Fig. 3.2. In addition each node needs to have a network interface card.

3.3   Run-time Support for Concurrent Processing

3.3.1   Run-time Support Services

Run-time support for concurrent tasks may be provided by either a real-time multi-tasking executive (also referred to as a kernel of an operating system) or the run-time support system for a concurrent language. With sequential languages such as C, Pascal, and Fortran, there is no support for concurrent tasks. To develop a concurrent tasking application using a sequential language, it is necessary to use a multi-tasking kernel. Examples of multi-tasking kernels are DEC's VAX/ELN and Ready System's VRTX. Typical services provided by a multi-tasking kernel are:

□ Priority pre-emption scheduling (i.e., the highest priority task executes as soon as it is ready);

□ Intertask communication using messages;

□ Mutual exclusion using semaphores;

□ Intertask synchronization using events. Alternatively messages may be used for synchronization purposes;

□ Interrupt handling and basic I/O services; and

□ Memory management. In hard real-time systems, it is usually the case that all concurrent tasks are memory resident. The reason for this is to eliminate the uncertainty and variation in response time introduced by paging overhead.

With a multi-tasking kernel, the Send Message and Wait Message operations for message communication, and the Signal Event and Wait Event operations for event synchronization are direct calls to the multi-tasking kernel. Mutually-exclusive access to critical regions is ensured using the Wait and Signal semaphore operations, which are also provided by the multi-tasking kernel.

With a concurrent language, the language supports constructs for task communication and synchronization. In this case, the language's run-time system handles task scheduling and provides the services and underlying mechanisms to support task communication and synchronization.

Concerns are sometimes expressed about the overhead of the Ada run-time system in real-time applications. In such situations, it is possible to use a multi-tasking kernel instead of the multi-tasking features of the concurrent language and its run-time system.

3.3.2 Task Scheduling

On a single processor (CPU) system, the multi-tasking kernel has to schedule concurrent tasks for the CPU. The kernel maintains a Ready List of all tasks that are ready to use the CPU. Various task scheduling algorithms have been designed to provide alternative strategies for allocating tasks to the CPU. For a time-sharing system, where multiple users are interactively accessing the system, round-robin scheduling is often used.

The goal of the round-robin scheduling algorithm is to provide a fair allocation of resources. Tasks are queued on a first-in/first-out (FIFO) basis. The top task on the Ready List is allocated the CPU and given a time slice. If the time slice expires before the task has blocked, the task is preempted, which means that the task is suspended by the kernel and placed on the end of the Ready List. The CPU is then allocated to the task at the top of the Ready List.

However, in real-time systems, round-robin scheduling is not satisfactory. A fair allocation of resources is not a prime concern and tasks need to be assigned priorities according to the importance of the operations they are executing. Thus time-critical tasks need to be certain of executing before their deadlines elapse. A more satisfactory scheduling algorithm for real-time systems is priority pre-emption scheduling. Each task is assigned a priority and the Ready List is ordered by priority. The task with the highest priority is assigned the CPU. It executes until it either blocks or is pre-empted by another higher priority task that has just become ready after being blocked. Tasks with the same priority are assigned the CPU on a FIFO basis. It should be noted that priority pre-emption scheduling does not use time slicing. The issue of what priorities to assign the concurrent tasks in a real-time design is discussed in more detail in Chapter 11.

When a task is suspended, its current context or processor state must be saved. This involves saving the contents of the hardware registers, the task's program counter (which points to the next instruction to be executed), and the program status information. When a task is assigned the CPU, its context must be restored so that it can resume executing. This whole process is referred to as context switching. In real-time systems, it is essential that context switching be fast.

In a multiprocessing environment, a copy of the multi-tasking kernel executes on each processor. Each processor selects the task at the top of the Ready List to execute. Mutually exclusive access to the Ready List is achieved by means of hardware semaphores typically implemented by means of Test and Set Lock instructions. Thus the same task can execute on different processors at different times.

3.3.3 Input/Output Considerations

Input/output considerations are important for real-time systems that frequently have to interface to special purpose I/O devices. There are two general mechanisms for performing input/output. These are interrupt driven I/O and polled I/O. With interrupt driven I/O, an interrupt is generated when the input arrives or after an output operation has been completed. With interrupt driven I/O, there are many different approaches available. Two widely-used approaches on mini- and microcomputers are interrupt driven program controlled I/O and interrupt driven program initiated I/O. In the former case an interrupt is generated after each character has been read or written. In the latter case, a direct memory access (DMA) device is placed between the I/O device and main memory. The DMA device controls the transfer of a block of data between the I/O device and main memory. When the transfer has completed, the DMA device generates an interrupt.

Arrival of the interrupt results in the CPU immediately suspending the executing task, saving its context, and invoking an interrupt handler to process the interrupt. After the interrupt has been serviced, the interrupted task's context is restored so that it can resume execution.

I/O devices interface with the system via device controllers, which reside on the device interface cards shown in Figs. 3.1 and 3.2. The multi-tasking kernel interfaces with the device controller rather than the I/O device itself. A controller has some registers that are used for communicating with the CPU. On some computers, there are separate instructions for accessing the controller's registers. With memory mapped I/O the controller's registers are part of the regular memory address space.

Device drivers, which execute on the CPU, are responsible for communicating with the I/O devices via the device controllers. Usually there is one device driver for each device type. The multi-tasking kernel supports the device drivers for the standard I/O devices such as keyboards, displays, disks, and line printers. However the device drivers for special purpose I/O devices, which are frequently necessary in real-time systems, are usually developed as part of the application software.

In the I/O subsystem of the kernel, interrupt handlers are low-level routines. The job of the interrupt handler is to determine which task should be activated when the interrupt occurs and then activate it using one of the task synchronization mechanisms supported by the multi-tasking kernel, such as a semaphore or event. With this approach, the device driver can be implemented as a concurrent task. The device driver has to know the specific details of how to interface to the device controller of the I/O device. In the case of input, the input device driver sends the device controller a command to read the input and then suspends itself waiting to be activated by the interrupt handler. When the input is received, the device controller generates the interrupt which results in the device driver being awakened. The device driver task can then communicate with the device controller via the controller's registers. In the case of output, the output device driver initiates the output and then usually suspends itself. It is awakened when the output has been completed.

In some systems, the arrival of the interrupt results in the device driver task being activated directly without the intervention of the low-level interrupt handler. In this case, the device driver task does its own interrupt handling.

With polled I/O, the system must periodically sample an input device to determine whether any input has arrived and periodically sample an output device to determine whether an output operation has completed. In the case of polled I/O, the device controller sets a flag when there is input available or when the output operation has completed. This allows a polling task, which executes on the CPU, to determine later that the I/O operation has been completed.

3.4   Information Hiding

3.4.1   Modularity

Modularity provides a means of decomposing a system into smaller, more manageable units with well-defined interfaces between them. However, there are many definitions of the term "module." A module often means a function, procedure, or subroutine. A module can also mean an information hiding module (IHM), which contains the hidden information as well as the access procedures to it.

3.4.2   Information Hiding Concept

Information hiding is a fundamental software design concept and is relevant to the design of all classes of software systems, not just concurrent and real-time systems. Early systems were frequently error-prone and difficult to modify because they made widespread use of global data. Information hiding was proposed by Parnas [Parnas72] as a way of making systems more modifiable by greatly reducing or ideally eliminating global data. Parnas advocated Information Hiding as a criterion for decomposing a software system into modules. Each module should hide a design decision that is considered likely to change. Each changeable decision is called the secret of the module.

With information hiding, the information that could potentially change is encapsulated (i.e., hidden) inside a module. External access to the information can only be made indirectly by invoking operations (e.g., access procedures or functions) that are also part of the module. Only these operations can access the information directly. Thus the hidden information and the operations that access it are bound together to form an Information Hiding Module. The specification of the operations (i.e., the name and the parameters of the operations) are called the virtual interface of the module. The virtual interface is also referred to as the abstract interface or external interface of the module. The virtual interface represents the visible part of the module.

The reasons for applying information hiding are to provide modules that are modifiable and understandable and hence maintainable. Because information hiding modules are often self-contained, they have a much greater potential for reuse than modules developed using other techniques. There has been much experience with information hiding [Parnas72, Parnas79] to support the view that it can lead to more self-contained and hence more modifiable and maintainable systems. Several design methods based on information hiding have been developed [Parnas84, Booch91, Gomaa89b]. Information hiding is in fact a basic concept of Object-Oriented Design.

3.4.3   Information Hiding Applied to Internal Data Structures

A potential problem in application software development is that an important data structure, which is accessed by several modules, may need to be changed. Without information hiding, any change to the data structure is likely to require changes to all the modules that access the data structure. Information hiding can be used to hide the design decision concerning the data structure, its internal linkage, and the details of the operations that manipulate it. The information hiding solution is to encapsulate the data structure in a module. The data structure is only accessed directly by the operations provided by the module.

Other modules may only indirectly access the encapsulated data structure by calling the operations of the module. Thus if the data structure changes, the only module impacted is the one containing the data structure. The external interface supported by the module does not change. Hence the modules that indirectly access the data structure are not impacted by the change. This form of information hiding is called data abstraction.

3.4.4   Information Hiding Applied to Access Synchronization

The solutions to the mutual exclusion and multiple readers/multiple writers problems (described in Section 3.1.2) are error prone. It is possible for a coding error to be made in one of the tasks accessing the shared data, which would then lead to serious synchronization errors at execution time. Consider, for example, the mutual exclusion problem described in Section 3.1.2. If the Wait and Signal operations were reversed by mistake, the pseudocode would be:

```
Signal (Sensor_data_store_semaphore)
Access sensor data store [should be critical section]
Wait (Sensor_data_store_semaphore)
```

This error means that the task would enter its critical section without doing a Wait. As a result, it is possible to have two tasks executing in a critical section, thereby violating the mutual exclusion principle. If instead the following coding error is made

```
Wait (Sensor_data_store_semaphore)
Access sensor data store [should be critical section]
Wait (Sensor_data_store_semaphore)
```

the task would enter its critical section the first time but then would not be able to leave it. Furthermore, it would prevent any other task from entering its critical section, thus provoking a deadlock where no task is able to proceed!

These potential problems are caused by making synchronization a global problem that every task has to be concerned about. Using information hiding, the global synchronization problem can be reduced to a local synchronization problem, in which only one information hiding module need be concerned about synchronization. An information hiding module that hides details of concurrent access to data is also referred to as a monitor [Hoare74].

For example, the sensor data store could be encapsulated in a sensor information hiding module, which supports Read and Update operations. These operations would be called by any task wishing to access the data store. The internals of the operations would synchronize access to the data store, thereby hiding these details from the calling tasks. This example is described in more detail in Chapter 16.

3.4.5 Information Hiding Applied to I/O Devices

Information hiding can be used to hide the design decision of how to interface to a specific I/O device. The solution is to provide a virtual interface to the device that hides the device specific details. If the device is replaced by a different one with the same overall functionality, the internals of the module would need to change, in particular, since they must deal with the precise details of how to interface to the real device. However, the virtual interface, represented by the specification of the operations, remains unchanged. Hence the modules that use the device interface would not need to change.

As an example of information hiding applied to I/O devices, consider an output display used on an automobile to display the average speed and fuel consumption. A virtual device can be designed that hides the details of how to format data for and how to interface to the mileage display.

The operations supported are: `Display_Average_Speed (Speed)`, and `Display_Average_MPG (Fuel_consumption)`.

Details of how to position the data on the screen, special control characters to be used, and other device specific information, are hidden from the users of the module. Thus if this device is replaced by a different device with the same general functionality, the internals of the operations will need to change, but the virtual interface remains unchanged. Thus users of the module are not impacted by the change to the device.

3.5 Object-Oriented Concepts

3.5.1 Introduction

In a taxonomy of languages supporting objects, Wegner [Wegner87, Wegner90] refers to languages that support objects (information hiding modules) but not inheritance (e.g., Ada and Modula-2) as object-based languages and languages that support classes as well as objects (e.g., Clu) as class-based languages, while languages that support objects, classes, and inheritance (e.g., Smalltalk, C++, and Eiffel) as object-oriented languages. Thus

Object-oriented = Objects + Classes + Inheritance

The term object-oriented was first introduced in conjunction with object-oriented programming in Smalltalk, although the concepts of information hiding and inheritance have earlier origins. Information hiding dates back to Parnas [Parnas72]. The concepts of classes and inheritance were first used in Simula67.

This section discusses the object-oriented concepts of objects, classes and inheritance.

3.5.2   Information Hiding in Object-based Design

Information hiding is used in designing the object, in particular when deciding what information should be visible and what information should be hidden by the object. Thus those aspects of a module that need not be visible to other objects are hidden. Hence, if the internals of the object change, only this object is impacted. The term encapsulation is also used to describe hiding information inside an object. The hidden data cannot be accessed directly by users (also referred to as clients) of the object. The data is updated indirectly by calls to the operations. Operations are also referred to as methods in object-oriented programming. However, use of the term method to mean operation is avoided in this book, since it can be confused with a software design method.

3.5.3   Active and Passive Objects

An object may be active or passive. Whereas objects are often passive and never initiate any actions, some object-oriented approaches support active objects (i.e., asynchronous objects that are autonomous and can initiate actions of their own).

Active objects are concurrent tasks [Wegner90]. A task has its own thread of control (sometimes referred to as its own "life") and can execute independently of other tasks. A passive object is an information hiding module and has no thread of control. Its operations are called by active objects. A called operation executes within the thread of control of the calling active object.

In many versions of object-oriented design and programming, objects conceptually communicate by means of messages. For each kind of message sent to an object, there is an operation to support the message. The name of the message corresponds to the name of the operation and the parameters of the message correspond to the parameters of the operation. In many object-oriented languages, this form of message passing is quite restrictive, being synchronous (tightly coupled) and actually corresponds to a procedure call. With this approach, objects are passive and always inactive when a message is received. On the other hand, an active object can be busy when a message arrives. It accepts the message when it has completed processing the previous one.

Since objects are usually passive, in the remainder of this discussion the term object is used to refer to a passive object.

3.5.4   Classes

A class is a an object type and can thus be considered a template for objects [Wegner87, Wegner90]. The class concept is usually associated with abstract data types; thus Meyer [Meyer88] defines a class as an implementation of an abstract data type. As (passive) objects are information hiding modules, a class is a module type.

An object is an instance of a class. Whereas in a language like Pascal, a record type can be defined, from which actual record instances can be created (instantiated), a class-based language extends the concept to support object types consisting of encapsulated data and operations on that data. Individual objects, which are instances of the class, are instantiated as required at execution time.

For example, a stack class can be created defining the data structure to be used for the stack, and the operations that manipulate it. Individual stack objects are instantiated as required by the application. Each stack object has its own name and has its own local copy of the stack data structure, as well as a local copy of any other instance variables required by the stack's operations.

3.5.5   Inheritance

Classes may be specialized using inheritance. Inheritance is a mechanism for sharing and reusing code between classes. A child class can adapt the structure (i.e., data encapsulated) and behavior (i.e., operations) of its parent class for its own use by adding new operations and instance variables, or by redefining existing operations. The parent class is referred to as a super-class and the child class is referred to as a sub-class. Inheritance is often referred to as an "is-a" relationship; that is, if a class C inherits from class B, then C "is-a" B.

The concept of inheritance has been applied very effectively in object-oriented programming. Inheritance is used as a code sharing and adaptation mechanism, where a new class is based on the definition of an existing class, without having to copy the actual code manually. Used in this way, the biggest benefit is in detailed design and coding, where substantial gains can be obtained from code sharing [Meyer88].

Inheritance can be used when designing two similar (but not identical) module types during design. It can also be used when adapting a design either for maintenance or reuse purposes. Used in this way, the biggest benefit is from using inheritance as an incremental modification mechanism [Wegner90].

3.6   Finite State Machines

3.6.1   Concepts

Finite state machines may be used for modeling the behavioral aspects of a system. Many real-time systems (in particular real-time control systems) are highly state dependent. That is, their actions depend not only on their inputs, but also on what has previously happened in the system. The state dependent aspects of a real-time system may be defined by means of one or more finite state machines.

A finite state machine is a conceptual machine with a given number of states. It can be in only one of the states at any specific time. State transitions are changes in state that are caused by input events. In response to an input event, the system may transition to the same or to a different state. Furthermore, an output event may be optionally generated. In theory, a state transition is meant to take zero time to occur. In practice, the time for a state transition to occur is negligible compared to the time spent in the state.

Notations used to define finite state machines are the state transition diagram and the state transition table or matrix. A state transition diagram is a graphical representation of a finite state machine in which the nodes represent states and the arcs represent state transitions. A state transition table or matrix is a tabular representation of a finite state machine. More information on finite state machines, as well as their notations and implementations, is given in [Allworth87].

3.6.2   Use of Finite State Machines in Real-time System Design

Since large real-time systems are typically highly state dependent, state transition diagrams or tables/matrices can help substantially by providing a means of understanding the complexity of these systems. When a system (or subsystem) is modeled by means of a finite state machine, it has a finite number of states and transitions between them. A state represents a mode of behavior of the system. Frequently, in real-time system design, the state is an externally visible mode of behavior. Since a system can only be in one state at a time, a state represents what is currently happening in the system.

A state transition diagram for a complex system is liable to be complex also. Instead of trying to model the whole system with one state transition diagram, a good way to simplify the finite state machine representation of the system is to use separate state transition diagrams to model different aspects of the system.

Another notation for state dependent systems is that of **statecharts** [Harel88a, Harel88b, Rumbaugh91], whose objective is to exploit the basic concepts and visual advantages of state transition diagrams. The statechart notation supports hierarchical decomposition of states, aggregation of state transitions, and concurrent statecharts.

3.6.3   Example of State Transition Diagram

As an example of a state transition diagram consider the different states of a concurrent task. These states are maintained by a multitasking kernel that uses the priority pre-emption scheduling algorithm described in Section 3.3.2. The different states for a task can be depicted on a state transition diagram (Fig. 3.4) in which states are represented by boxes and transitions are represented by arcs.

When a task is first created it is placed in Ready State, during which time it is on the Ready List. When it reaches the top of the ready list, it is allocated the CPU, at which time it transitions into Executing state. The task may later be pre-empted by

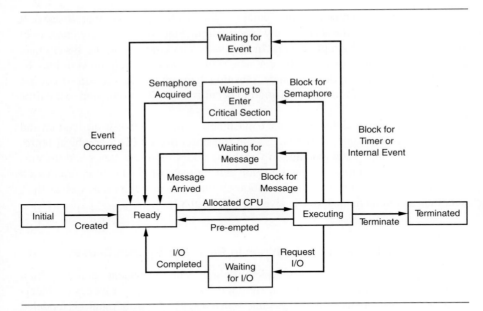

FIGURE 3.4 State Transition Diagram for Concurrent Task

another task and re-enter Ready state, at which time the kernel places it on the Ready List in a position determined by its priority.

Alternatively, while in Executing state, the task may block, in which case it enters the appropriate blocked state. A task can block waiting for I/O, waiting for a message from another task, waiting for a timer event or an event signalled by another task, or waiting to enter a critical section. A blocked task re-enters Ready state when the reason for blocking is removed; in other words, when the I/O completes, the message arrives, the event occurs, or the task gets permission to enter its critical section.

3.6.4   Events and Conditions

One way of simplifying state transition diagrams is to allow conditions as well as events. A condition defines some aspect of the system which can be true or false for some finite period of time. It thus represents the value of a boolean variable. It is possible for a condition to represent the state of some other aspect of the system. A condition is sometimes referred to as a state variable.

Events and conditions may be combined in defining a state transition. The notation used is that of Event (Condition). Thus an event is allowed to cause a transition providing the condition given in parentheses is True. For example the transition Block for Message in Fig. 3.4 could have a condition associated with it called Message Unavailable. Thus the transition would be labelled Block for Message (Message Unavailable). If at the time of blocking no message was available for the task, the condition Message Unavailable would be true and so the task would transition into the Waiting for Message state as before. However if there was a message available, the condition Message Unavailable would be false and so the transition would not occur. Instead, the task would remain in Executing state, receive the message and continue processing.

3.6.5 Output Events

Associated with a transition is an optional output event. The output event usually initiates some action in the system, as a result of receiving the input stimulus. For example, whenever a task blocks and transitions into one of the Waiting states, an output event Switch Context is generated to initiate context switching.

PART TWO

Survey of Software Design Methods

4

Overview of Software
Design Methods

4.1 Introduction

This chapter provides an overview of software design methods by introducing terminology used in describing software design methods, giving a brief description of the evolution of software design methods, and discussing the boundary between requirements and design. Next, the criteria and rationale used for selecting the design methods surveyed in Part II are given, followed by an outline of the strategies used by these methods. The overall structure of Part II is then presented. Finally, the informal problem description is given for the case study of an automobile cruise control and monitoring system, which is used to illustrate the application of each of the design methods described in Part II of this book.

4.2 Software Design Terminology

A **software design** defines how a software system is structured into components and defines the interfaces between the components. The nature of the component depends on the concepts and strategies employed by the method; for example, they may be tasks or modules.

A **software design strategy** is an overall plan and direction for performing a design. For example, functional decomposition is a software design strategy.

A **software design concept** is a fundamental idea that can be applied to designing a system. For example, information hiding is a software design concept.

Software structuring criteria are heuristics or guidelines used to help a designer in structuring a software system into its components (i.e., for decomposing the system).

A **software design notation** (or **representation**) is a means of describing a software design. It may be graphical, symbolic or textual. For example, structure charts are a graphical design notation and pseudocode is a textual design notation.

A **software design method** is a systematic approach for creating a design. While not providing a cookbook approach for creating a design, a software design method helps identify the design decisions to be made, the order in which to make them, and the criteria to use in making them. A design method usually describes a sequence of steps for a designer or design team to follow when creating a design, given the software requirements of the application. A design method is based on a set of design concepts, employs one or more design strategies, and documents the resulting design using one or more design notations. During a given design step, the method may provide a set of structuring criteria to help the designer in decomposing the system into its components. For example, Structured Design is a software design method. It is based around the concept of functional modules. It employs the Transform and Transaction Analysis design strategies. It provides the module cohesion and module coupling structuring criteria to assist the designer with decomposing the system into modules. The design is documented using the structure chart graphical notation and the detailed design of each module is described in a textual notation, using Program Design Language (PDL) or pseudocode.

Design is a highly creative intellectual exercise. Due to differences in software requirements and execution environments, designs vary widely. Consequently a designer must use skill and judgement in applying a software design method to solve a problem. When a method is deficient in a certain aspect, it is often the case that an experienced designer will compensate for this by developing an ad hoc solution. More information on the software design process is given in [Freeman83a, Freeman83b].

4.3   Evolution of Software Design Methods

In the 1960s, programs were often implemented with little or no systematic requirements for analysis and design. Graphical notations, particularly flowcharts, were often used, either as a documentation tool or as a design tool for planning a detailed design prior to coding. Subroutines or subprocedures, originally created as a means of allowing a block of code to be shared by calling it from different parts of a program, were recognized as a means of constructing modular systems and were adopted as a project management tool. A program could be divided up into modules, where each module could be developed by a separate person and implemented as a subroutine or function.

With the growth of structured programming in the early 1970s, the ideas of top down design and stepwise refinement gained prominence as program design methods, with the goal of providing a systematic approach for structured program design. One of the first system design methods was developed by Dijkstra with the design of the THE operating system [Dijkstra68]. This was a hierarchical design method, introducing the idea that software could be structured into several levels with modules at one level providing services for modules at higher levels. This was the one of the first design methods to address the design of a concurrent system, namely an operating system. Dijkstra's goals were to provide an approach for designing, coding, and testing a hierarchical system in a systematic way.

In the mid- to late 1970s, two different software design strategies gained prominence, data flow oriented design and data structured design. The data flow oriented design approach, as used in Structured Design, was one of the first comprehensive and well documented design methods to emerge. The view was that a better understanding of the functions of the system could be obtained by considering the flow of data through the system. It provided a systematic approach for developing data flow diagrams for a system and then mapping them to structure charts. Structured Design introduced the coupling and cohesion criteria for evaluating the quality of a design. This approach emphasized functional decomposition into modules and the definition of module interfaces. The first part of Structured Design, based on data flow diagram development, was refined and extended to become a comprehensive analysis method, Structured Analysis [DeMarco78, Gane79].

An alternative software design approach was that of data structured design. This view was that a full understanding of the problem structure is best obtained from consideration of the data structures. Thus the emphasis is on first designing the data structures and then designing the program structures based on the data structures. The two principle advocates of this strategy were Jackson Structured Programming [Jackson 75] and the Warnier/Orr method [Orr77].

In the data base world the concept of separating logical data and physical data was key in the development of data base management systems. Various approaches were advocated for the logical design of data bases, including the introduction of entity-relationship modeling by Chen [Chen76].

A great contribution to software design was made by Parnas with his advocacy of information hiding [Parnas72]. A major problem with early systems, even in many of those designed to be modular, resulted from the widespread use of global data. This made these systems error prone and difficult to change. Information hiding provided an approach for greatly reducing, if not eliminating, global data.

For the design of concurrent systems, a major contribution came in the late 1970s with the introduction of the MASCOT notation [Simpson79], which suggested an approach for designing concurrent and real-time systems although it did not go so far as to provide a systematic design method for doing so. However, using the notation forced designers to think about important issues such as task structuring and designing task interfaces. Based on a data flow approach, the MASCOT notation formalized the

way tasks communicate with each other, either via channels for message communication or pools, which are information hiding modules that encapsulate shared data
structures. The data maintained by a channel or pool is only accessed by a task
indirectly by calling access procedures provided by the channel/pool. The access
procedures also synchronize access to the data, typically using semaphores, so that all
synchronization issues are hidden from the calling task.

In the 1980s there was a general maturation of software design methods. Several
system design methods were introduced. Parnas's work with the Naval Reseach Lab
in which he explored the use of information hiding in large scale software design led
to the development of the Naval Research Lab software cost reduction method (NRL)
[Parnas84]. Work on applying Structured Analysis and Structured Design to concurrent and real-time systems led to the development of the Real-Time Structured
Analysis and Design (RTSAD) [Ward85, Hatley88] and the Design Approach for
Real-Time Systems (DARTS) [Gomaa84] methods. Another system development
method to emerge was Jackson System Development (JSD) [Jackson83], with its view
of a design as being a simulation of the real-word and its emphasis on modeling entities
in the problem domain using concurrent tasks.

The popularity and success of object-oriented programming led to the emerging
of several object-oriented design methods, including Booch [Booch86, Booch91],
Wirfs-Brock et al [Wirfs-Brock90], Rumbaugh et al [Rumbaugh91], and Coad/Your-
don [Coad91, Coad92]. The emphasis in these methods was on modeling the problem
domain, information hiding, and inheritance.

4.4   The Boundary Between Requirements and Design

It is often argued that a requirements specification should only define the external
behavior of the system; that is, it should view the system as a black box. An excellent
example of a black box specification method is the NRL software requirements
specification method [Heninger80]. While a specification should indeed reflect the
external behavior of the system, others argue that it is desirable for the specification
to be potentially executable, so that a prototype of the system may be developed. In
order to satisfy this goal, the specification should be operational (i.e., a problem-oriented specification that is potentially executable [Zave84]).

A characteristic of the operational specification is that, in order to be executable,
it needs to reflect the requirements (external behavior) as well as the internal structure
needed to support these requirements. Jackson System Development [Cameron86] is
an example of a method that reflects the operational viewpoint. A JSD specification
is in principle executable.

Most analysis methods (e.g., Real-Time Structured Analysis (RTSA) and Object-
Oriented Analysis (OOA)) take a problem-oriented perspective. Problem domain
components and the interfaces between them are determined. Many object-oriented

analysis methods claim that they provide a smoother path from analysis to design. The problem domain objects determined in the analysis are mapped to solution domain objects in the design. In Structured Analysis and Design, the goal is to map problem domain functions, determined during analysis, to functional modules in design.

In both RTSA and OOA, decisions made during analysis often have a strong influence on the subsequent design. Even though the components determined during analysis are problem oriented, design decisions need to be made relating to the scope of each component and how it interfaces to other components.

Thus for many design methods, it is necessary to consider the analysis method that precedes it. This book therefore considers the problem oriented analysis to be part of the design process, usually being the first phase of the design. The design methods described here have an analysis phase that either precedes them or is part of the method. JSD does not differentiate between analysis and design. The other methods all have an analysis phase that precedes the design. RTSAD and DARTS start with Real-Time Structured Analysis. The Object-Oriented Design method (OOD) starts with either RTSA or OOA. The analysis done in the NRL method in order to develop a black box software requirements specification helps in the subsequent design by indicating aspects of the requirements that should be encapsulated as separate information hiding modules.

4.5   Criteria for Selecting Software Design Methods

Part II of this book surveys several software design methods for real-time systems. In selecting the design methods to be included in this survey, the following criteria for selection were used:

1. The method must be published in the literature and not be proprietary.
2. The method must have actually been used on a real world real-time application.
3. The method must not be oriented to a specific language.
4. The method must be a design method and not a design notation. A design notation suggests a particular approach for performing a design, but does not provide a systematic approach describing the steps for performing a design.

4.6   Rationale for Methods Selected

As pointed out in Chapter 3, key concepts for designing concurrent and real-time systems are concurrent processing, finite state machines, information hiding and object-oriented concepts. The survey of design methods addresses methods that are based on one or more of these concepts.

Real-Time Structured Analysis and Design is selected for two main reasons. Apart from being a widely-used method, Real-Time Structured Analysis emphasizes the use of finite state machines and integrating them with the data flow analysis to provide the control and sequencing. The chapter on RTSAD discusses in particular how finite state machines are used in a real-time design method. The study of Structured Design is instructive because it shows how an inherently concurrent problem can be solved using a sequential design method.

The Design Approach for Real-Time Systems method is chosen because it specifically addresses the design of concurrent systems. It places great emphasis on task structuring and defining the interfaces between tasks. As an extension of RTSAD, it also shows how a sequential design method can be extended to become a concurrent design method by inserting the steps for task structuring between Real-Time Structured Analysis and Structured Design.

Jackson System Development is chosen because it also places great emphasis on task structuring. It takes a different approach for structuring tasks by modeling entities in the problem domain. It also has an interesting systematic approach (task inversion) for mapping a highly concurrent design to a less concurrent, or even sequential, design for optimization purposes.

The NRL method is chosen because of its great emphasis on information hiding. Although not widely used at present, its pioneering application of this concept influenced several of the object-oriented design methods.

Of the several emerging object-oriented design methods, Booch's version of OOD is chosen. It has evolved over several years and now includes the concepts of information hiding, classes, and inheritance. It is also appropriate for concurrent systems as it considers issues concerning concurrent objects.

4.7 Software Design Strategies for Concurrent and Real-time Systems

The software design methods described in Part II of this book use different strategies and emphasize different design concepts in structuring the system into its components. Some design methods employ more than one strategy. A classification of the methods, based on the strategy used, follows:

1. *Design methods based on functional decomposition.* This strategy is used by Real-Time Structured Analysis and Design [Ward85, Hatley88]. The system is decomposed into functions (called transformations or processes) and interfaces between them are defined in the form of data flows or control flows. Functions

(i.e., data or control transformations) are mapped onto processors, tasks, and modules [Ward85].

2. *Design methods based on concurrent task structuring.* This strategy is emphasized by DARTS [Gomaa84]. Concurrent tasking is considered a key aspect in concurrent and real-time design. DARTS provides a set of task structuring criteria to assist the designer in determining the concurrent tasks in the system and also provides guidelines for defining task interfaces.

3. *Design methods based on information hiding.* This strategy aims at providing software components that are modifiable and maintainable, as well as being potentially more reusable. This is achieved through the use of information hiding in the design of components. This strategy is used by the Naval Research Lab software cost reduction method [Parnas84] and the Object-Oriented Design method [Booch91].

4. *Design methods based on modeling the problem domain.* This strategy is emphasized by the Jackson System Development method [Jackson83, Cameron86, Cameron89]. With this strategy, the objective is to model entities in the problem domain and then map these entities onto software processes (tasks). OOD employs this strategy to a lesser extent, relying on OOA approaches (e.g., [Shlaer88]) to help determine objects in the problem domain or by applying object structuring criteria to a RTSA specification.

4.8   Problem Description for Cruise Control and Monitoring System

This section presents the problem description for the Cruise Control and Monitoring System case study used to illustrate each of the design methods described in this book.

The informal problem description, in the form of a memo from Marketing to Engineering, is the starting point for the analysis and design of the Cruise Control and Monitoring System:

```
To:        Vehicle Systems Engineering Division
From:      GMU Product Line Marketing Group
Subject:   Cruise Control and Monitoring System
```

As you may already know, we have decided to incorporate a combined cruise control and monitoring system in next year's Grand Motoring Unit (GMU) model. None of our subcompact models have previously offered such features as standard equipment, but we believe that by doing so on the sports version of next year's model, its perceived value will increase far more than the incremental cost to build it. The system will be an option on the economy model.

This memo summarizes the key features that Marketing wants the system to have. However, we are leaving the specification of the detailed requirements to Vehicle Systems, subject to our review. Engineering continues to insist that the design of both the hardware and the microcomputer software is its domain.

Please avoid the problem we had with the cruise control system on earlier models. As you recall, someone assumed that all models would come with the same size of tires, and when they didn't, the cruise control did not work accurately in all the models with the optional handling and tire package.

The cruise control system has a control lever with four switch positions: ACCEL, RESUME, and OFF (two positions), as shown below. It also has a neutral position. The required cruise control functions are:

1. *Automatic Cruise Control* For additional driving comfort, the car is equipped with an automatic cruise control system. The automatic cruise control system is activated and controlled by a lever at the right-hand side of the steering wheel column. The control lever has four switch positions. The following functions are activated in the individual switch positions.

   □ *Accel* Cruising speed is set and memorized. By holding the lever in this position, the car accelerates without using the accelerator pedal. After releasing the lever, the achieved speed is maintained and also memorized. The cruising speed control is automatically switched off in any operation when using the footbrake.

   □ *Off (two positions)* By moving the control lever either in a downward or upward direction, the cruise control can be switched off in any driving and operating condition.

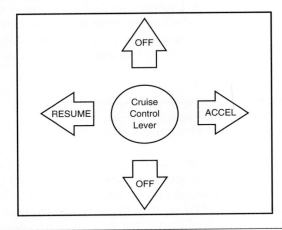

□ *Resume* The last memorized speed can be resumed by moving the lever to "Resume." The memorized speed is cancelled by switching off the ignition.

There should be no unpredictable interaction between the use of the cruise control system and the use of the monitoring functions. Next year, we may decide to include just the cruise control as standard equipment on some models.

2. *Monitoring Functions* The required vehicle monitoring functions are:

□ Display of average speed from the start of a trip on a mileage display screen. The driver may reset the trip start mileage;

□ Display of average fuel consumption for a trip on a mileage display screen. The driver may reset the trip start mileage;

□ Driver notification of required vehicle maintenance as follows:

5,000 miles for oil service and oil filter change.

10,000 miles for air filter change.

15,000 miles for major service.

Three reset buttons are to be available for the maintenance technician to reinitialize the maintenance indicators after a service has been carried out.

The maintenance messages are to be displayed on a maintenance display screen. When the car is within 250 miles of a maintenance threshold, there should be an intermittent message given. When the car is within 50 miles of the maintenance threshold, the message should be on constantly. Multiple messages can be on at the same time if the car has not been properly serviced.

5

Structured Analysis and Design for Real-time Systems

5.1 Overview of RTSAD

Real-Time Structured Analysis and Design (RTSAD) is an extension of Structured Analysis and Structured Design (RTSA) that addresses the needs of real-time systems. Real-Time Structured Analysis (RTSA) is viewed by many of its users as primarily a specification method addressing the software requirements of the system being developed. Two variations of RTSA have been developed, the Ward/Mellor [Ward85, Ward86] and Boeing/Hatley [Hatley88] approaches. A third variation, the Extended System Modeling Language (ESML) [Bruyn88], is an attempt to merge the Ward/Mellor and Boeing/Hatley methods for Real-Time Structured Analysis.

The extensions to Structured Analysis address the need to represent more precisely the behavioral characteristics of the system being developed. This is achieved primarily through the use of state transition diagrams, control flows, and integrating state transition diagrams with data flow diagrams through the use of control transformations (Ward/Mellor) or control specifications (Boeing/Hatley).

In the RTSA phase of RTSAD, an essential model (Ward/Mellor) is developed. This essential model is also referred to as a requirements model (Boeing/Hatley). There are three related views of an essential model: the functional view, the behavioral view, and the informational view. For a real-time system, the primary emphasis is usually placed on the functional and behavioral views. In fact, the Boeing/Hatley approach does not support the informational view.

Structured Design [Myers78, Page-Jones88, Yourdon79] is a program design method which uses the criteria of module coupling and cohesion in conjunction with the Transform Analysis and Transaction Analysis strategies to develop a design starting from a Structured Analysis specification.

44

5.2 Basic Concepts

During analysis, the system is decomposed into **functions** (called transformations or processes) and the interfaces between them are defined in the form of data flows or control flows. Transformations may be data or control transformations. During design, the functions are mapped to **modules.**

Finite state machines, in the form of state transition diagrams, are used to define the behavioral characteristics of the system. The major extension to Structured Analysis is the introduction of control considerations, through the use of state transition diagrams. A control transformation represents the execution of a state transition diagram. Input event flows trigger state transitions and output event flows control the execution of data transformations [Ward85].

In the Boeing/Hatley and ESML methods, it is also possible for a control transformation to be described by means of a decision table. Process activation tables are also used in Boeing/Hatley to show when processes (transformations) are activated.

Entity-relationship (E-R) models are used to show the relationships between the data stores of the system [Yourdon89]. They are used for identifying the data stores (either internal data structures or files) and for defining the contents (attributes) of the stores. These are particularly useful in data intensive systems. E-R models are not used in the Boeing/Hatley approach.

Module cohesion is used in module decomposition as a criterion for identifying the strength or unity within a module [Myers78, Page-Jones88, Yourdon79].

Module coupling is used in module decomposition as a criterion for determining the degree of connectivity between modules [Myers78, Page-Jones88, Yourdon79].

5.3 Notation

Data flow/control flow diagrams are used in Real-Time Structured Analysis [Ward85, Hatley88]. They are an extension to data flow diagrams to include event flows and control transformations.

The Ward/Mellor notation for data flow/control flow diagrams is shown in Fig. 5.1. Data transformations are identical to those used in Structured Analysis [De Marco 79]. They are also referred to as bubbles or processes. A control transformation, shown by the dashed circle, is used to represent a control activity in the system and is defined by means of a state transition diagram. Data flows may be either discrete or continuous. Discrete data arrives at specific time intervals and so is similar to a message. Continuous data is the conventional data flow. Real-time systems typically deal with discrete data more often than continuous data. An event flow (or control flow) is a

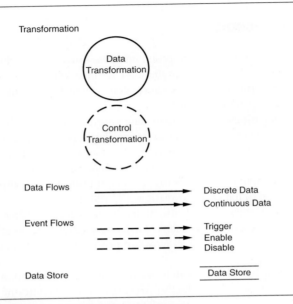

FIGURE 5.1 Real-time Structured Analysis Notation

discrete signal and has no data value. It is used to signal that some action has happened or to initiate a command. There are three kinds of event flow: trigger, enable, and disable.

State transition diagrams are a graphical representation of finite state machines in which the nodes represent states and the arcs represent state transitions [All-worth87].

Entity-relationship diagrams, a graphical notation for E-R models, are used for depicting the entities in the system, the attributes of each entity, and the relationships between the entities.

Structure charts are used in Structured Design [Page-Jones88, Yourdon79] to show how a program is decomposed into modules, where a module is typically a procedure or function, and to show the interfaces between modules.

5.4   Steps in Method

5.4.1   Real-time Structured Analysis

Using RTSA, an essential model is built that is intended to reflect the requirements of the system. During the Real-Time Structured Analysis stage, the following activities take place. (It should be noted that these steps are not necessarily sequential and that the steps are usually applied iteratively).

1. *Develop the system context diagram.* The system context diagram defines the boundary between the system to be developed and the external environment. The context diagram shows all the inputs to the system and outputs from the system. The terminators, which represent the sources and sinks of data, are shown explicitly on the diagram. The system to be developed is shown as one data transformation. The diagram defines the interfaces between the system data transformation and the terminators.

2. *Perform data flow/control flow decomposition.* The system is structured into functions (called transformations or processes) and the interfaces between them are defined in the form of data flows or control flows. Transformations may be data or control transformations. The system is structured as a hierarchical set of data flow/control flow diagrams that may be checked for completeness and consistency.

   The Boeing/Hatley approach emphasizes hierarchical decomposition of both function and data, starting from the system context diagram. A hierarchical data flow diagram decomposition is performed in which the data transformation on the context diagram is decomposed into a data flow diagram consisting of a number of data transformations connected by data flows and data stores, which are repositories of data. This decomposition may proceed to several levels, depending on the complexity of the system and is based on functional decomposition. Thus each data transformation on a data flow diagram may be decomposed into a lower-level data flow diagram. The contents of the data flows and stores are defined in a data dictionary.

   The Ward/Mellor approach starts with an event list (a list of inputs to the system) and then determines the system response to each event. Frequently this response is state dependent and hence necessitates the construction of one or more state transition diagrams. A control transformation is defined to execute each state transition diagram and to control the execution of certain data transformations. Data transformations are defined to perform the required, and in some cases state dependent, functions. With this approach the initial data flow/control flow diagram is non-hierarchical. Consequently, the data and control transformations are then grouped to achieve a top-level data flow diagram and, if necessary, decomposed further to determine lower-level data flow diagrams.

3. *Develop Control Transformations (Ward/Mellor) or Control Specifications (Boeing/Hatley).* The major real-time extension to Structured Analysis is the introduction of control considerations to define the behavioral characteristics of the system. This is achieved through the use of finite state machines, in the form of state transition diagrams or tables. Each state transition diagram shows the different states of the system (or subsystem). It also shows the input events (or conditions) that cause state transitions, and output events resulting from state transitions.

In the Ward/Mellor approach, a control transformation represents the execution of a state transition diagram. Input event flows trigger state transitions and output event flows control the execution of data transformations [Ward85]. A control transformation is a leaf node (i.e., may not be decomposed further) in the data flow/control flow hierarchy.

In the Boeing/Hatley approach, a control specification may be defined by means of one or more state transition diagrams, state transition tables, decision tables, and process activation tables. The process activation table shows the activation of data transformations resulting from the output events of the state transition diagram or decision table. A control specification is associated with a data flow diagram at any level of the hierarchy and is not confined to leaf nodes.

4. *Define mini-specifications (process specifications).* Each leaf node data transformation on a data flow diagram is defined by writing a mini-specification (or process specification), usually in Structured English. Other notations for describing mini-specifications are considered acceptable as long as the specification is a precise and understandable statement of requirements [Yourdon89].

5. *Develop data dictionary.* A data dictionary is developed that defines all data flows, event flows, and data stores.

5.4.2   Real-time Design

Following the RTSA phase, the Ward/Mellor and Boeing/Hatley approaches diverge. The Boeing/Hatley approach uses system architecture diagrams [Hatley88]. The Ward/Mellor approach continues as follows [Ward85, volume 3]:

6. *Allocate transformations to processors.* The RTSA transformations are allocated to the processors of the target system. If necessary the data flow diagrams are redrawn for each processor.

7. *Allocate transformations to tasks.* The transformations for each processor are allocated to concurrent tasks. Each task represents a sequential program.

8. *Structured Design.* Transformations allocated to a given task are structured into modules using the Structured Design method. Structured Design uses the criteria of module coupling and cohesion in conjunction with two design strategies, Transform and Transaction Analysis, to develop a program design starting from a Structured Analysis specification.

Transform Analysis is a strategy used for mapping a data flow diagram into a structure chart whose emphasis is on input-process-output flow [Myers78, Page-Jones88, Yourdon79]. Thus the structure of the design is derived from the functional structure of the specification. The input branches, central transformations and output branches are identified on the data flow diagram and structured as separate branches on the structure chart.

Transaction Analysis is a strategy used for mapping a data flow diagram into a structure chart whose structure is based on identifying the different transaction types [Myers78, Page-Jones88, Yourdon79]. The processing required for each transaction type is identified from the data flow diagram and the system is structured such that there is one branch on the structure chart for each transaction type. There is one controlling transaction center module.

Module cohesion is used in module decomposition as a criterion for identifying the strength or unity within a module [Myers78, Page-Jones88, Yourdon79]. Functional cohesion and informational cohesion are considered the strongest (and best) form of cohesion. In the early practice of Structured Design [Yourdon79], functionally cohesive modules in the form of procedures were emphasized. The informational cohesion criterion was added later by Myers [Myers78] to identify information hiding modules.

Module coupling is used in module decomposition as a criterion for determining the connectivity between modules [Myers78, Page-Jones88, Yourdon79]. Data coupling is considered the lowest (and best) form of coupling, in which parameters are passed between modules. Undesirable forms of coupling include common coupling, where global data is accessed by several modules.

5.5   Products of RTSAD

1. *Real-time Structured Analysis* The result of applying RTSA is a specification that consists of:

   a. System context diagram;

   b. Hierarchical set of data flow/control flow diagrams;

   c. Data dictionary (also referred to as the requirements dictionary in Boeing/Hatley);

   d. Mini-specifications. A Structured English mini-specification is used to describe each primitive transformation (i.e., one that is not decomposed further); and

   e. A state transition diagram defining each control transformation (Ward/Mellor) or a control specification (Boeing/Hatley) defining one or more state transition diagrams (tables), decision tables, and process activation tables.

2. *Structured Design* For each program, there is a structure chart showing how it is decomposed into modules. Each module is defined by its external specification,

namely input parameters, output parameters, and function. The internals of the module are described by means of pseudocode.

5.6   Cruise Control and Monitoring System Case Study

5.6.1   Real-Time Structured Analysis

The Real-Time Structured Analysis specification includes the system context diagram, a hierarchical set of data flow/control flow diagrams, and state transition diagrams, as shown in Figs. 5.2–5.11. The Ward/Mellor notation (Fig. 5.1) is used for this solution, although the solution could easily be mapped to the Boeing/Hatley notation.

5.6.2   Develop System Context Diagram

Figure 5.2 shows the system context diagram, each external entity is represented by a terminator.

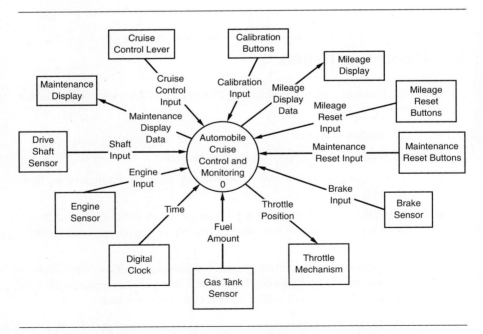

FIGURE 5.2 Cruise Control and Monitoring System Context Diagram

5.6.3   Decompose System Context Diagram

Functional decomposition is used for structuring a real-time application into the major functions. An analysis of the Cruise Control and Monitoring System given in the problem definition shows that there are two relatively independent functions. Figure 5.3 shows the top-level data flow/control flow diagram (DFD), in which the system context diagram is decomposed into the two major functions, the Cruise Control function and the Monitoring function. Because of the RTSA convention that the name of a data transformation should start with a verb, the data transformations are called Perform Automobile Cruise Control and Perform Automobile Monitoring, respectively.

5.6.4   Perform Automobile Cruise Control

Perform Automobile Cruise Control (Fig. 5.3) is decomposed as shown on the DFD in Fig. 5.4. Three data transformations monitor the automobile sensors. Monitor Engine reads the engine sensor and sends the Engine On and Engine Off event flows to Control Speed. Monitor Brake reads the brake sensor and sends the Brake Pressed and Brake Released event flows to Control Speed. Monitor Cruise Control Input reads inputs from the cruise control lever and sends these as Cruise Control Request event flows to Control Speed.

Control Speed computes the throttle value when cruise control is active. It passes the throttle value to Output to Throttle, which outputs the actual throttle position to the real-world throttle. Measure Distance and Speed computes Current Speed and Cumulative Distance. It also performs the measured mile calibration.

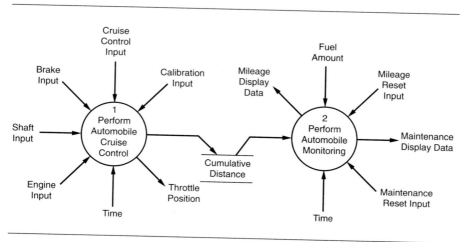

FIGURE 5.3 Decomposition into Subsystems

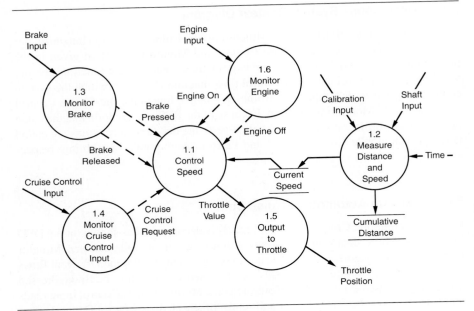

FIGURE 5.4 Perform Automobile Cruise Control

5.6.5 Cruise Control State Transition Diagram

The Control Speed data transformation (Fig. 5.4) is decomposed into a data flow/control flow diagram. The Cruise Control state transition diagram, shown in Fig. 5.5, is executed by the Cruise Control control transformation shown in Fig. 5.6.

Using the Real-Time Structured Analysis conventions in Fig. 5.5, states are represented by rectangles while labeled arrows represent state transitions. Above the straight line is the input event that causes the state transition. Below the straight line is the output event(s) that is generated when the transition occurs. The output event triggers (T), enables (E), or disables (D) a data transformation, which then performs a specified action. The output events are numbered for conciseness, and preceded by a letter identifying the type of event.

The different states of the car, from a cruise control perspective, are:

- □ Idle. In this state, the engine is switched off;
- □ Initial Not Braking. When the driver turns the engine on, the car enters Initial Not Braking state. The car stays in this state as long as no attempt is made to engage cruise control. In Initial Not Braking state, there is no previously stored cruising speed;
- □ Initial Braking. This state is entered if the brake is pressed while in Initial Not Braking state;

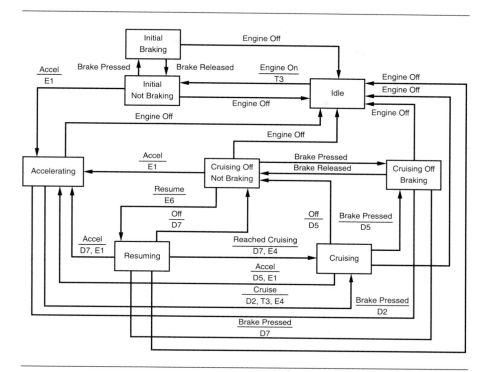

FIGURE 5.5 Cruise Control State Transition Diagram

□ Accelerating. When the driver engages the cruise control lever in the ACCEL position (transition Accel), the car enters Accelerating state and accelerates automatically;

□ Cruising. When the driver releases the lever (transition Cruise), the current speed is saved as the cruising speed and the car enters Cruising state. In this state, the car speed is automatically maintained at the cruising speed;

□ Cruising Off Not Braking. When the driver engages the lever in the OFF position, cruise control is deactivated and the car returns to manual operation;

□ Cruising Off Braking. This state is entered if the brake is pressed while in Accelerating, Cruising, Resuming, or Cruising Off Not Braking State. In the first three cases, automated control of the vehicle is immediately disabled. From this state, when the brake is released, Cruising Off Not Braking state is entered;

□ Resuming. When the driver engages the lever in the RESUME position while in Cruising Off Not Braking state (transition Resume), the car automatically accelerates or decelerates to the last cruising speed. When the car reaches the cruising speed, it enters Cruising state.

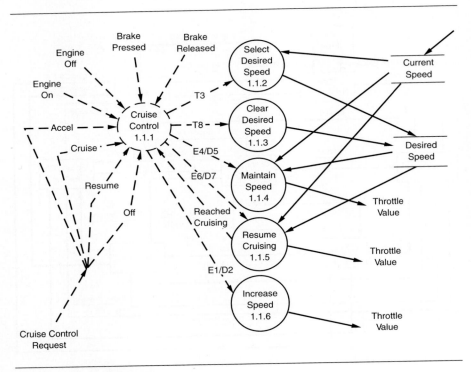

FIGURE 5.6 Control Speed

The output events are as follows:

E1	Enable "Increase Speed"	D5	Disable "Maintain Speed"
D2	Disable "Increase Speed"	E6	Enable "Resume Cruising"
T3	Trigger "Select Desired Speed"	D7	Disable "Resume Cruising"
E4	Enable "Maintain Speed"	T8	Trigger "Clear Desired Speed"

5.6.6 Control Speed

The data transformations on the DFD for Control Speed (Fig. 5.6) are triggered, enabled, or disabled at state transitions. A triggered transformation is a one-shot function. For example, Select Desired Speed is triggered when Cruise Control transitions into Cruising state. It then sets the desired speed, which is the speed the car is to cruise at, equal to the current speed. Clear Desired Speed clears this value.

A transformation that is enabled for the duration of the entire state is likely to be cyclic. For example, Maintain Speed is enabled when Cruise Control enters cruising state and is disabled when Cruise Control leaves cruising state. Thus Maintain Speed is active throughout Cruising state. It periodically reads Current Speed and Desired Speed, and adjusts the throttle value so that the cruising speed is maintained. Increase Speed is active during Accelerating state; it periodically adjusts the throttle value so that the speed of the vehicle is gradually increased. Resume Cruising is active in Resuming state; it periodically reads the Current Speed and Desired Speed data stores, and adjusts the throttle value so that the speed of the vehicle is increased or decreased to reach the cruising speed. When the cruising speed is reached, Resume Cruising sends the Reached Cruising event flow to Cruise Control.

5.6.7 Measure Distance and Speed

The Measure Distance and Speed data transformation of Fig. 5.4 is decomposed into the DFD shown in Fig. 5.7. Monitor Shaft Rotation increments the shaft rotation count, once for each rotation.

Determine Distance is activated periodically to compute the incremental distance travelled, given the current value of the Shaft Rotation Count, Last Distance (the value of the Shaft Rotation Count when incremental distance was last computed), and the Calibration Constant (the shaft rotation count per mile). Determine Distance then adds

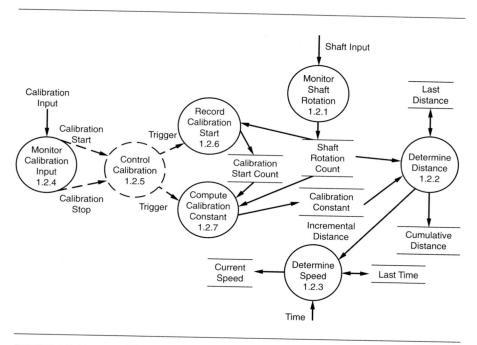

FIGURE 5.7 Measure Distance and Speed

the Incremental Distance to the Cumulative Distance. Determine Speed receives the Incremental Distance and computes Current Speed given the incremental time.

Four transformations are required to compute the value of the calibration constant. Monitor Calibration Input reads the calibration buttons and sends Calibration Start and Calibration Stop event flows to the control transformation Control Calibration. Control Calibration is defined by means of the state transition diagram shown in Fig. 5.8.

When the driver pushes the Start Measured Mile Calibration button, Monitor Calibration Input sends the Calibration Start event flow to Control Calibration. Control Calibration then transitions from Not Measuring state to Measuring Mile state (Fig. 5.8) and triggers Record Calibration Start, which then reads the shaft rotation count and stores it in Calibration Start Count.

When the driver pushes the Stop Measured Mile Calibration button, Monitor Calibration Input sends the Calibration Stop event flow to Control Calibration. Control Calibration then transitions back to Not Measuring state (Fig. 5.8) and triggers Compute Calibration Constant. Compute Calibration Constant then reads the shaft rotation count and the Calibration Start Count. It computes the difference, the shaft rotation count per mile, which is the Calibration Constant. As a safety check, if this count is not within predefined upper and lower limits, then the Calibration Constant is set to a default value.

5.6.8   Perform Automobile Monitoring

Perform Automobile Monitoring (Fig. 5.3) is decomposed further in Fig. 5.9. Monitor and Display Averages computes and displays average miles per gallon and average

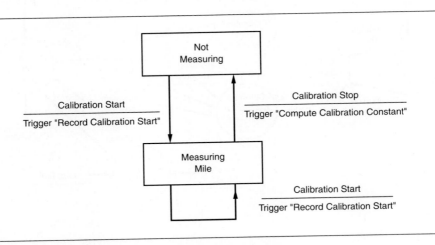

FIGURE 5.8 Control Calibration State Transition Diagram

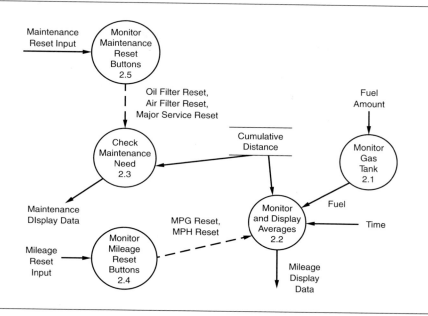

FIGURE 5.9 Perform Automobile Monitoring

miles per hour. Check Maintenance Need determines whether maintenance is required on the car and if so lights up the maintenance display. Monitor Mileage Reset Buttons checks whether the driver has pressed the buttons to reset the MPH and MPG trip averages. Monitor Maintenance Reset Buttons checks whether the maintenance technician has reset any of the maintenance buttons.

5.6.9   Monitor and Display Averages

The Monitor and Display Averages data transformation of Fig. 5.9 is decomposed into the DFD shown in Fig. 5.10. It computes and displays the average miles per gallon and miles per hour.

When Initialize MPH is activated by the MPH Reset event flow, it records the start of the trip by capturing the current distance and time and storing them in the Initial Distance and Time data store. Compute Average MPH periodically reads the current values of distance and time, subtracts the initial values to obtain the distance travelled and time elapsed, computes the average miles per hour, and then passes this data to Display Averages.

Initialize MPG and average MPG operate in a similar way except that the distance and fuel level are read, the average miles per gallon is computed and then displayed.

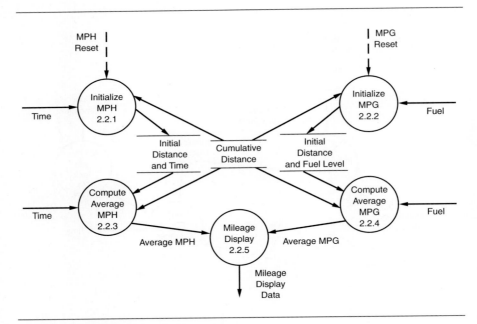

FIGURE 5.10 Monitor and Display Averages

5.6.10 Check Maintenance Need

The Check Maintenance Need data transformation of Fig. 5.9 is decomposed into the DFD shown in Fig. 5.11. Three kinds of maintenance service are performed at regular intervals, oil filter, air filter, and major service maintenance. Each is handled in a similar way.

For example, consider oil filter maintenance. On completing the oil filter service, the maintenance technician pushes the oil filter reset button. Initialize Oil Filter receives the Oil Filter Reset event flow, and then reads the current value of Cumulative Distance and stores it in the Miles at Last Oil Filter Maintenance data store. Check Oil Filter Maintenance periodically reads Cumulative Distance and compares it with the mileage value in the Miles at Last Oil Filter Maintenance data store to determine the distance travelled since the last service, and hence whether a new service is required. If it is, Check Oil Filter Maintenance sends an Oil Filter Status message to Display Maintenance Lights, which outputs the message to the maintenance display.

5.6.11 Structured Design

Next the RTSA specification is mapped to Structured Design. As Structured Design provides no guidance with structuring a system into concurrent tasks, the system is

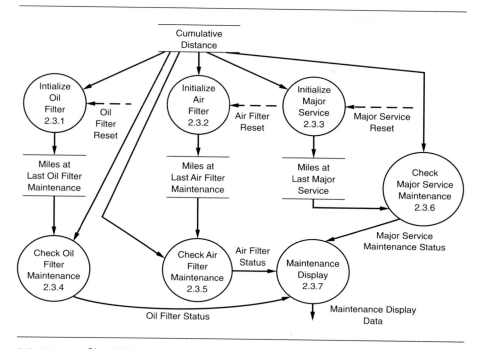

FIGURE 5.11 Check Maintenance Need

structured as one program, and hence one task, as shown in Figs. 5.12–5.18. Where tasks are required, they are designed outside the context of Structured Design.

The modules on the structure chart are primarily functional modules (i.e., consist of one procedure), although some are information hiding modules. Most of the functional modules are functionally cohesive. The main module, Cruise Control and Monitoring System (Fig. 5.12), has a cyclic loop in which it determines when to call its subordinate modules: Perform Automobile Cruise Control and Perform Automobile Monitoring.

5.6.12   Perform Automobile Cruise Control

Perform Automobile Cruise Control has four subordinate modules, corresponding to the four major functions it performs. Consider Get Cruise Control Input, which is decomposed further in Fig. 5.13. If the I/O devices were asynchronous, i.e., interrupt driven, then a separate asynchronous I/O task would usually be needed for each asynchronous device. As Structured Design provides no guidance with structuring a system into concurrent tasks, asynchronous I/O tasks cannot be determined in the Structured Design context. The options are to use polled I/O or, in cases where the

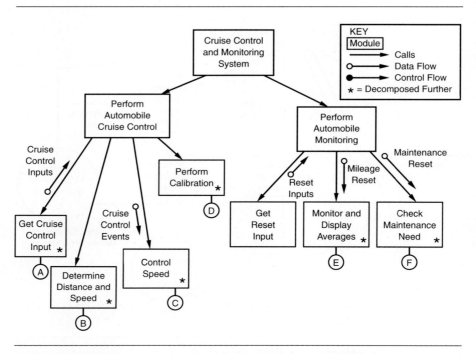

FIGURE 5.12 Structure Chart for Cruise Control and Monitoring System

constraints of the application make asynchronous I/O necessary, to design a task outside the context of Structured Design.

Using the polled I/O approach, the cruise control lever, engine, and brake inputs are sampled on a periodic basis by the modules called by Get Cruise Control Input. For example, Read Cruise Control Lever Input returns the appropriate cruise control request if a request has been received since the last time it was called. Otherwise, it returns a null request.

In cases where use of an interrupt handler is essential to avoid loss of data, a separate interrupt handler task is designed. However the design of this task and its interface to the Cruise Control task is outside the SD context. (This is an example of an ad hoc design decision compensating for a limitation in a design method.) The interrupt handler approach has been taken for the Shaft Interrupt Handler, which receives an interrupt every shaft rotation. Since it is essential to record every time a shaft rotation is completed, the shaft interrupt handler updates an internal variable, the Shaft Rotation Counter, which is then accessed by the Determine Distance module (Fig. 5.14) in order to compute the Cumulative Distance travelled. To ensure mutually exclusive access to the Shaft Rotation Counter, particularly if access to the variable consists of more than one CPU operation, a semaphore is used.

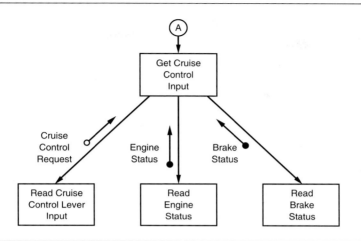

FIGURE 5.13 Structure Chart for Get Cruise Control Input

Whenever there is new cruise control input, Perform Automobile Cruise Control calls the Control Speed module (Fig. 5.15). Control Speed calls the Cruise Control module, which encapsulates the Cruise Control state transition table (derived from the state transition diagram), and passes to it the cruise control event. Cruise Control uses the input event as an index to the state transition table in order to determine the new state and return the appropriate cruise control action(s). Based on the desired cruise control action, Control Speed calls the appropriate subordinate module.

Although each subordinate module is functionally cohesive, there is an issue concerning the data coupling. One option is to have common coupling, where the Current Speed and Desired Speed data items are global, so that they can be accessed by more than one module. In Structured Design, information hiding can be introduced to alleviate the undesirable use of global data. In particular, information hiding modules (IHMs) can be used to encapsulate data stores. With this approach, IHMs are created to encapsulate the contents of the Current Speed and Desired Speed data stores (Fig. 5.6) respectively, as shown in Fig. 5.15. These IHMs, Current Speed and Desired Speed, each consist of the hidden data as well as the operations used to access the data. In Structured Design, information hiding modules are typically at a low level of abstraction and are thus often the lowest-level modules on a structure chart.

As an example, consider Maintain Speed. Its function is to ensure that the current speed of the vehicle is equal to the desired cruising speed. Maintain Speed calls Get Current Speed and Get Desired Speed. If these two speeds are equal, then there is no action to be taken. Otherwise Maintain Speed computes the adjustment required to the throttle and calls Output to Throttle passing to it the Throttle Value.

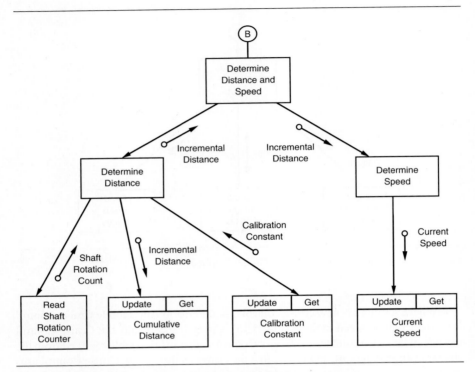

FIGURE 5.14 Structure Chart for Determine Distance and Speed

5.6.13 Timing Issues

Since the whole system is treated as one sequential program, the timing aspects of the program have to be carefully considered. Initially, we may determine that the cruise control functions should be performed every 100 milliseconds, while the monitoring functions need only be done every second. This means that the main module, Cruise Control and Monitoring System (Fig. 5.12), executes a cyclic loop in which it calls Perform Automobile Cruise Control 10 times a second and Perform Automobile Monitoring once a second. This may be achieved by using a timer event, which awakens the main module every 100 milliseconds. Each time it is awakened, it calls Perform Automobile Cruise Control, while every tenth time it is awakened, it also calls Perform Automobile Monitoring.

On each cycle, Perform Automobile Cruise Control calls Get Cruise Control Input to determine if there is any new input. It then calls Determine Distance and Speed to update the cumulative distance and compute the current speed. It then calls Control Speed to process the next cruise control event and/or perform any state dependent

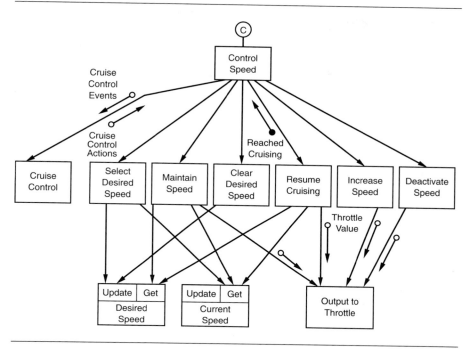

FIGURE 5.15 Structure Chart for Control Speed

function. Finally, it calls Perform Calibration (Fig. 5.16) to check if there is a calibration event, and if so to process it.

If there is a new Cruise Control event, then this may cause the vehicle to start increasing speed, to start resuming speed, or to start maintaining speed. Even if there is no new cruise control event, it is still necessary for Perform Automobile Cruise Control to call Control Speed, which then checks the current cruising state. If the vehicle is under automated control, Control Speed must call the appropriate action routine to compute the necessary periodic adjustment to the throttle. Thus as long as the vehicle is in Cruising state, the module Maintain Speed must be periodically called in order to compute the throttle adjustment. As long as the vehicle is in Accelerating state, the module Increase Speed must be periodically called. As long as the vehicle is in Resuming state, the module Resume Cruising must be periodically called. However, since any new input could potentially change the vehicle's state, each time the throttle adjustment has been computed, it is necessary to return to the main module, which will on its next cycle call Get Cruise Control Input, via Perform Automobile Cruise Control, to check if there is any new input. Thus the concurrent activities of getting cruise control in-

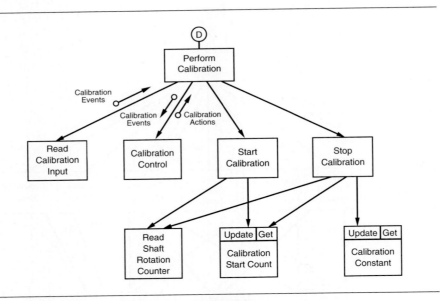

FIGURE 5.16 Structure Chart for Perform Calibration

put and outputing to the throttle have to be explicitly interleaved in a sequential program.

5.6.14 Perform Automobile Monitoring

Perform Automobile Monitoring calls Get Reset Input (Fig. 5.12) to determine if one of the mileage or maintenance reset buttons has been pressed. For example, if the MPH reset button was pressed, Perform Automobile Monitoring calls Monitor and Display Averages (Fig. 5.17), which in turn calls Initialize MPH. Initialize MPH reads the current time and calls Get Cumulative Distance to get the current distance. It then stores these trip start values by calling Update Initial Distance and Time.

Assuming that the average MPH and MPG are to be computed every second, then Monitor and Display Averages calls the Compute Average MPH and Compute Average MPG modules respectively, followed by Display Averages. If these values are only to be computed every five seconds, then Monitor and Display Averages calls these modules once every five times it is called. Compute Average MPH reads the current time and calls Get Cumulative Distance to get the current distance. It calls Get Initial Distance and Time to obtain the values at the start of the trip. Given the initial and

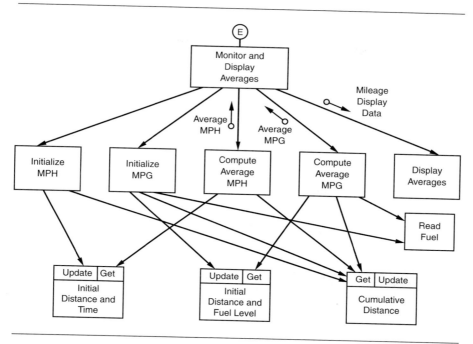

FIGURE 5.17 Structure Chart for Monitor and Display Averages

current values, it computes the Average MPH and returns this value to Monitor and Display Averages, which then calls Display Averages to display it.

If one of the maintenance buttons has been pressed, Perform Automobile Monitoring calls Check Maintenance Need (Fig. 5.18), which in turn calls the appropriate initialization module to store the current distance as Miles at Last Maintenance. Check Maintenance Need also periodically calls each of the Check Maintenance modules to determine whether it is time for an oil filter service, air filter service, or major service respectively.

5.7   Assessment of Method

The **strengths** include:

1. Structured Analysis and the real time extensions to it have been used on a wide variety of projects and there is much experience in applying the method;

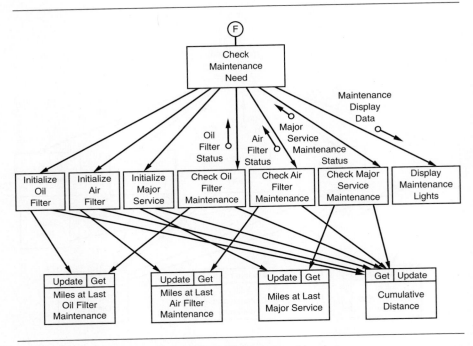

FIGURE 5.18 Structure Chart for Check Maintenance Need

2. There are a wide variety of CASE tools to support RTSA;

3. The use of data flow and control flow diagrams can assist in understanding and reviewing the system. For example, a good overview of the system can be obtained;

4. Emphasizes the use of state transition diagrams/tables, which is particularly important in the design of real time control systems, as they are usually state dependent; and

5. The Structured Design module decomposition criteria of cohesion and coupling help in assessing the quality of a design.

The **weaknesses** include:

1. There is not much guidance on how to perform a system decomposition. Consequently different developers could structure the system in substantially different ways;

2. RTSA is usually considered a requirements specification method. However, unlike the NRL requirements specification method that treats the system to be developed as a black box, RTSA addresses system decomposition. Hence there

is a tendency in many projects to make design decisions during this phase, particularly if the specification gets detailed. This makes the boundary between requirements and design fuzzy;

3. Although Structured Design can be used for designing individual tasks, it is limited for designing concurrent systems, and hence real time systems, because of its weaknesses in the areas of task structuring. Thus Structured Design is a program design method leading primarily to functional modules and does not address the issues of structuring a system into concurrent tasks; and

4. In its application of information hiding, Structured Design lags behind the Naval Research Lab and Object-Oriented Design methods.

5.8   Extensions and/or Variations

ESML, the Extended System Modeling Language [Bruyn88], is an attempt to merge the Ward/Mellor and Boeing/Hatley methods for Real-Time Structured Analysis. The COBRA analysis and modeling method, described in Chapter 13, uses the same notation as RTSA but uses an alternative strategy for developing a behavioral model. For developing state transition diagrams, the Ward/Mellor approach supports events but not conditions, whereas the Boeing/Hatley approach supports conditions but not events. Each of these restrictions is overcome in both ESML and COBRA, which support both events and conditions, in common with the NRL method [Parnas86] and the statechart notation [Harel88a, Harel88b].

6

DARTS (Design Approach for Real-Time Systems)

6.1 Overview

The Design Approach for Real-Time Systems (DARTS) method emphasizes the decomposition of a real-time system into concurrent tasks and defining the interfaces between these tasks. The method originated because of a perceived problem with a frequently-used approach for developing real-time systems. This involved using Structured Analysis and, more recently, Real-Time Structured Analysis (RTSA), during the analysis phase followed by Structured Design during the design phase. The problem with this approach is that it does not take into account the characteristics of real-time systems, which typically consist of several concurrent tasks.

The DARTS design method addresses these issues by providing the decomposition principles and steps for allowing the software designer to proceed from a Real-Time Structured Analysis specification to a design consisting of concurrent tasks. The Design Approach for Real-Time Systems [Gomaa84, Gomaa86a, Gomaa87] provides a set of task structuring criteria for structuring a real-time system into concurrent tasks, as well as guidelines for defining the interfaces between tasks. Each task, which represents a sequential program, is then designed using Structured Design.

The Design Approach for Real-Time Systems (DARTS) method has evolved over time. Initially the method started with a Structured Analysis specification [Gomaa84]. Later, after the introduction of Real-Time Structured Analysis (RTSA) [Ward85], it was extended to start with a Real-Time Structured Analysis specification [Gomaa87].

6.2   Basic Concepts

A set of **task structuring criteria** is provided to assist the designer in structuring a real-time system into concurrent tasks. These criteria are a set of heuristics derived from experience obtained in the design of concurrent systems. The main consideration in identifying the tasks is the concurrent nature of the functions within the system. In DARTS, the task structuring criteria are applied to the transformations (functions) on the data flow/control flow diagrams developed using RTSA. Thus a function is grouped with other functions into a task, based on the temporal sequence in which the functions are executed.

Guidelines are provided for defining the interfaces between concurrent tasks. **Task interfaces** are in the form of message communication, event synchronization, or information hiding modules (IHMs). Message communication may be either loosely coupled or tightly coupled. Event synchronization is provided in cases where no data is passed between tasks. Access to shared data is provided by means of information hiding modules.

Information hiding is used as a criterion for encapsulating data stores. Information hiding modules (IHMs) are used for hiding the contents and representation of data stores and state transition tables. Where an IHM is accessed by more than one task, the access procedures must synchronize the access to the data.

Finite state machines, in the form of state transition diagrams, are used to define the behavioral characteristics of the system. State transition diagrams are an effective tool for showing the different states of the system and the transitions between them.

Evolutionary prototyping and **incremental development** are assisted by the identification of system subsets using event sequence diagrams. These diagrams identify the sequence of execution of tasks and modules that are required to process an external event. System subsets form the basis for incremental development.

6.3   Notation

Data flow/control flow diagrams are used in RTSA [Ward85, Hatley88]. They are an extension to data flow diagrams to include event flows and control transformations. Event flows represent discrete signals that carry no data. Control transformations control the execution of data transformations and are specified by means of state transition diagrams or decision tables.

State transition diagrams are a graphical representation of finite state machines in which the nodes represent states and the arcs represent state transitions [Allworth87].

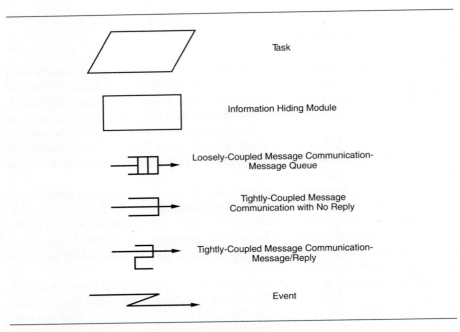

FIGURE 6.1 Task Architecture Diagram Notation

Task architecture diagrams are used by the DARTS design method to show the decomposition of a system into concurrent tasks and the interfaces between them in the form of messages, events, and information hiding modules. The notation used by task architecture diagrams is shown in Fig. 6.1.

Structure charts, which originated in Structured Design [Page-Jones88, Yourdon79], are used in DARTS to show how a task (which executes a sequential program) is decomposed into modules, where a module is typically a procedure or function.

6.4 Steps in Method

The steps in the method are as follows:

1. *Develop system specification using Real-Time Structured Analysis.* The system context diagram and state transition diagrams are developed. The system context diagram is decomposed into hierarchically structured data flow/control flow

diagrams. The relationship between the state transition diagrams and the control and data transformations (functions) is established. This step is similar to RTSA steps 1 through 5, described in Chapter 5.

2. *Structure the system into concurrent tasks.* The task structuring criteria are applied to the leaf nodes of the hierarchical set of data flow/control flow diagrams. A preliminary task architecture diagram is drawn showing the tasks identified using the task structuring criteria. I/O data transformations that interface to external devices, are mapped to asynchronous I/O tasks, periodic I/O tasks, or resource monitor tasks. Internal transformations are mapped to control, periodic, or asynchronous tasks and may be combined with other transformations according to the sequential, temporal, or functional cohesion criteria.

3. *Define task interfaces.* Task interfaces are defined by analyzing the data flow and control flow interfaces between the tasks identified in the previous stage. Data flows between tasks are mapped to either loosely-coupled or tightly-coupled message interfaces. Event flows are mapped to event signals. Data stores form the basis of information hiding modules. The task architecture diagram is updated to show the task interfaces.

   At this stage, a timing analysis may be performed. Given the required response times to external events, timing budgets are allocated to each task. Event sequence diagrams [Gomaa86a] can help in this analysis by showing the sequence of task execution from external input to system response.

4. *Design each task.* Each task represents the execution of a sequential program. Using the Structured Design method, each task is structured into modules. Either Transform Analysis or Transaction Analysis is used for this purpose. The function of each module and its interface to other modules are defined. The internals of each module are designed.

6.5   Products of Design Process

There are three products of design process:

□ RTSA specification;

□ Task structure specification. Defines the concurrent tasks in the system. The function of each task and its interface to other tasks are specified;

□ Task decomposition. The decomposition of each task into modules is defined. The function of each module, its interface, and detailed design in PDL are also defined.

6.6   Cruise Control and Monitoring System Case Study

6.6.1   Real-Time Structured Analysis

The first stage in applying DARTS is to develop a RTSA specification. This is similar to the RTSA phase of RTSAD and is described in Section 5.6.

6.6.2   Task Structuring

After developing the RTSA specification, DARTS uses the task structuring criteria for determining the concurrent tasks in the system. Figures 6.2 and 6.3 shows the task architecture diagrams for the Cruise Control and Monitoring subsystems.

In the Cruise Control subsystem (Fig. 6.2), the tasks Monitor Cruise Control Input and Monitor Shaft Rotation are asynchronous device input tasks. Each task is activated by an external interrupt when there is input available for it. Monitor Auto Sensors and

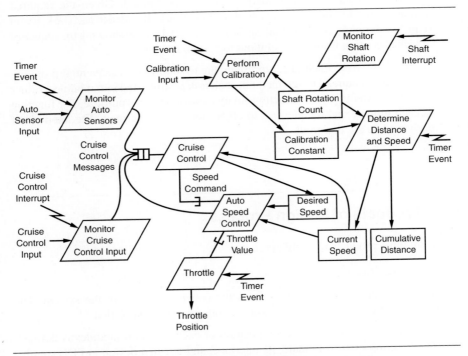

FIGURE 6.2 Task Architecture Diagram for Cruise Control Subsystem

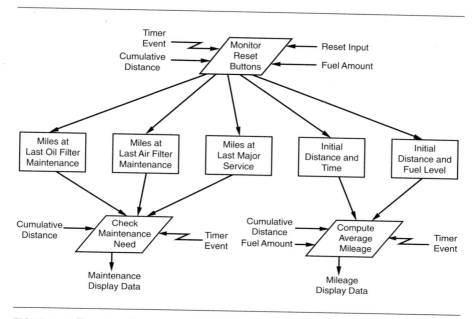

FIGURE 6.3 Task Architecture Diagram for Monitoring Subsystem

Perform Calibration are both periodic input tasks. Monitor Auto Sensors, which is also temporally cohesive, samples the brake and engine sensors at regular intervals to determine if there is any change in their status. Cruise Control is a high priority control task that executes the state transition diagram. Auto Speed Control is a task which is both sequentially and functionally cohesive (its functions are all related to speed control and they are constrained to execute sequentially because they execute in different states). Throttle is a periodic output task. Determine Distance and Speed is a periodic sequentially cohesive task, which computes the cumulative distance travelled and the current speed at regular intervals.

In the Monitoring Subsystem (Fig. 6.3), Monitor Reset Buttons is a periodic temporally cohesive input task. It periodically checks to see if any of the reset buttons have been pressed. Check Maintenance Need and Compute Average Mileage are periodic temporally cohesive tasks. Compute Average Mileage periodically computes the average MPH and MPG, and outputs their values to the mileage display.

6.6.3 Task Interfaces

These tasks communicate via messages or IHMs.

Data stores that are accessed by more than one task are mapped to IHMs. Thus, in the Cruise Control subsystem, the Current Speed, Desired Speed, Cumulative Distance, Shaft Rotation Count, and Calibration Constant data stores are all mapped to information hiding modules. In the Monitoring subsystem, the interfaces between the three tasks are all via data stores, which are mapped to IHMs. Since more than one task can access the data, it is up to the access procedures to ensure that access to the data is mutually exclusive. This is achieved using semaphores.

The interface to the Cruise Control task is a loosely-coupled FIFO queue. This is to ensure that the I/O tasks are not held up by Cruise Control and that if input events arrive in quick succession, none of them are lost. The interface between Cruise Control and Auto Speed Control is tightly coupled without reply.

6.6.4   Structured Design

Once the tasks have been designed and the interfaces between them defined, the next step is to design each task, which represents the execution of a sequential program, by decomposing it into modules using the Structured Design method. The modules are primarily functional modules, although there are some IHMs. In Structured Design, the IHMs are usually at the lowest level of the hierarchy.

Figure 6.4 shows the structure of the Cruise Control Task. By convention, the main module (procedure) is also called Cruise Control. Cruise Control calls Receive

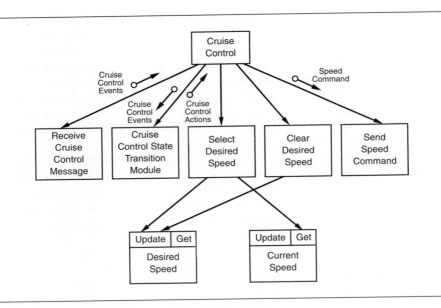

FIGURE 6.4 Structure Chart for Cruise Control Task

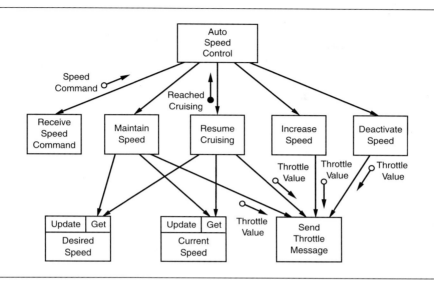

FIGURE 6.5 Structure Chart for Auto Speed Control Task

Cruise Control Message to wait for an input message. The task is suspended waiting for a message. When a message arrives, the task is re-activated. Receive Cruise Control Message returns the incoming event to Cruise Control. Cruise Control calls the Cruise Control State Transition Module, passing it the event. The STM looks up the State Transition Table to determine what the next state should be (if any), given the current state and the incoming event. The action to be performed (if any) is returned to Cruise Control. If the action is Select Desired Speed or Clear Desired Speed, Cruise Control calls the appropriate procedure. Other actions are sent as speed command messages to Auto Speed Control.

Two encapsulated IHMS, Current Speed and Desired Speed, are shown in this figure. These IHMS are also accessed by other tasks. Hence the Update and Get access procedures must ensure properly synchronized access to the data. This can be done using semaphores.

The structure of the Auto Speed Control is shown in Fig. 6.5. It receives speed commands by calling Receive Speed Command and waiting for the message. The design of Auto Speed Control is an example of Transaction Analysis. Depending on the command received (the transaction), Auto Speed Control (the transaction processor) calls the appropriate transaction handling procedure to execute the transaction. Thus if the incoming speed command is to maintain cruising speed, Auto Speed Control calls the transaction handling procedure Maintain Speed.

Figure 6.6 shows the structure chart for Perform Calibration. Perform Calibration calls Read Calibration input to receive an input. Since the task is periodic, Read

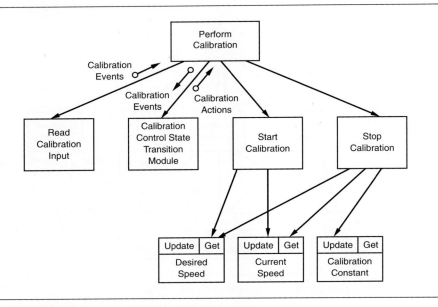

FIGURE 6.6 Structure Chart for Perform Calibration Task

Calibration Input periodically samples the calibration buttons to determine if a button
was pressed. If so, it returns the calibration event to Perform Calibration. The rest of
this task is structured in the same way as Cruise Control, since it is also a control task.

6.7   Assessment of Method

The **strengths** of this method are as follows:

1. Emphasizes the decomposition of the system into concurrent tasks and provides
    criteria for identifying the tasks, an important consideration in concurrent and
    real-time system design;

2. Provides detailed guidelines for defining the interfaces between tasks;

3. Emphasizes the use of state transition diagrams, which is particularly important
    in the design of real-time control systems; and

4. Provides a transition from a RTSA specification to a real-time design. Real-Time
    Structured Analysis is probably the most widely-used analysis and specification
    method for real-time systems. Its use is being encouraged by the proliferation of

CASE tools supporting the method. However, many designers then find it difficult to proceed to a real-time design. DARTS directly addresses this issue by providing the decomposition principles and steps for allowing the software designer to proceed from a RTSA specification to a design consisting of concurrent tasks.

The **weaknesses** of this method are as follows:

1. Although DARTS uses information hiding for encapsulating data stores, it does not use it as extensively as the NRL and OOD methods. Instead, it uses the Structured Design method for structuring tasks into procedural modules.

2. A potential problem in using DARTS is that if the RTSA phase is not done well, task structuring could be more difficult. Another problem of RTSA is that it does not provide many guidelines on how to perform a system decomposition. The approach recommended with DARTS is to develop the state transition diagrams before the data flow diagrams (i.e., pay attention to control considerations before functional considerations).

6.8 Extensions and Variations

In large systems, it is usually necessary to structure a system into subsystems before structuring the subsystems into tasks. One approach for structuring a system into subsystems is an extension to DARTS to support distributed real-time applications called DARTS/DA [Gomaa89a]. Subsystem structuring is also addressed in Chapter 13. Distributed application design is described in Chapter 20.

The DARTS weakness in information hiding is addressed by the ADARTS[SM] [Gomaa89b, Gomaa89c] and CODARTS methods. ADARTS and CODARTS use the DARTS task structuring criteria for identifying tasks but replace Structured Design with an information hiding module structuring phase in which modules are identified using a set of module structuring criteria. These criteria are based on the Naval Research Laboratory method [Parnas84] module structuring criteria, supported by the Object-Oriented Design [Booch86] object structuring criteria. ADARTS and CO-DARTS designs may be described using a graphical notation similar to Buhr diagrams [Buhr84]. ADARTS and CODARTS are described in more detail in Part III of this book.

The potential problem with using RTSA is addressed in the CODARTS method by using the COBRA analysis and modeling method instead of RTSA. COBRA, described in Chapter 13, uses the same notation as RTSA but uses an alternative strategy for developing a behavioral model.

7

Jackson System Development (JSD)

7.1 Overview

Jackson System Development (JSD) is a modeling approach to software design. A JSD design models the behavior of real world entities over time. Each entity is mapped onto a concurrent task (referred to as a process in JSD). JSD is an outgrowth of Jackson Structured Programming (JSP), which is a program design method [Jackson75].

Although JSD is in principle applicable to concurrent and real-time systems, the emphasis of earlier work [Jackson83, Cameron86] has been on data processing applications. More recently, however, a number of papers have directly addressed the issue of applying JSD to concurrent and real-time systems [Renold89, Cameron89, Sanden89]. Renold described mapping JSD designs to concurrent implementations. One paper in [Cameron89] describes mapping a JSD design to the Mascot3 notation [Allworth87], which specifically addresses concurrent processing, while another paper describes mapping JSD designs to Ada. Sanden [Sanden89] describes a variation on JSD that is oriented toward the needs of concurrent and real-time systems and which also maps to Ada.

7.2 Basic Concepts

A fundamental concept of JSD is that the design should model reality first [Jackson83] before considering the functions of the system. The system is considered a simulation of the real world. The functions of the system are then added to this simulation.

Each real world entity is modeled by means of a concurrent task called a model task. This task faithfully models the entity in the real world. Since real world entities usually have long lives, each model task typically also has a long life.

The model of reality in terms of potentially large numbers of logical concurrent tasks is transformed in a series of steps to an implementation version that consists of one or more physical concurrent tasks.

7.3   Notation

Entity structure diagrams are used in JSD to show the structure of a real-world entity, in the form of the time ordered sequence of events received by it [Jackson83, Cameron86, Cameron89]. The graphical notation is similar to that used in JSP structure diagrams [Jackson75]. The order of events shown on an entity structure diagram are depicted in terms of three basic constructs—sequence, selection, and iteration—as shown in Fig. 7.1. The incoming events are the leaf nodes of the entity structure diagram. Non-leaf nodes represent structured combinations of these events.

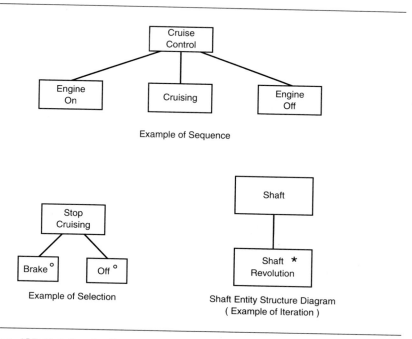

FIGURE 7.1 JSD Notation for Entity Structure Diagrams

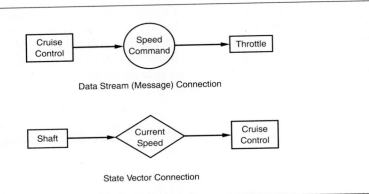

FIGURE 7.2 JSD Notation for Data Streams and State Vectors

For example, in Fig. 7.1, Cruise Control consists of a sequence of three events: Engine On, Cruising, and Engine Off. Stop Cruising consists of a selection (indicated by the "o" in the top right-hand corner of the box) of either a Brake event or an Off event. Shaft is an iteration (indicated by the "*" in the top right-hand corner of the box) of Shaft Revolution events.

JSD network diagrams are used to show all the tasks in a JSD design and the interfaces between them. Each task is shown as a box in the JSD notation. Interfaces are represented in the form of data stream communication or state vector inspections [Jackson83, Cameron86, Cameron89], as illustrated in Fig. 7.2. Data streams (shown as circles) correspond to message queues between tasks. A state vector (shown as a diamond) corresponds to internal data maintained by a task. Only the task that maintains its state vector can write to it, but other tasks may read from it. In the example shown in Fig. 7.2, the Cruise Control task sends Speed Command messages to the Throttle task. The Cruise Control task also reads the Shaft task's state vector, called Current Speed.

7.4 Steps in Method

There are three major steps in this method. They are as follows:

1. *Modeling phase* During the modeling phase [Cameron89], the real world entities are identified. The entity is defined in terms of the time ordered sequence of events (referred to as actions in JSD) it receives. The attributes of each event received by the entity are defined. Furthermore, the attributes of the entity itself are also defined. An entity structure diagram is developed in which the sequence of events

received by the entity is explicitly shown. A software model task is created for each entity and has the same basic structure as the entity.

2. *Network phase* During the network phase, the communication between tasks is defined, function is added to model tasks, and function tasks are added.

Communication between tasks is in the form of data streams (where producer tasks send messages to consumer tasks), or by means of state vector inspections (where tasks may read data maintained by other tasks). An initial network diagram is developed showing the communication between the model tasks.

The functions of the system are considered next. Some simple functions are added to the model tasks, providing they can be directly associated with an event received by the task. Other independent functions are represented by function tasks. Typical function tasks are input data collection tasks, error handling tasks, output tasks, and interactive tasks. The network diagram is updated to show the function tasks and their communication with other function or model tasks.

After the network diagram has been established, the timing constraints of the system are considered. Thus, it can be specified that certain system outputs must be generated within a specified time from the arrival of certain inputs.

3. *Implementation phase* During the implementation phase, the JSD specification consisting of a potentially very large numbers of logical tasks is mapped onto a directly executable implementation version. Originally, with the emphasis on data processing, the specification was mapped onto one program using the concept of program inversion [Jackson75]. Each task is transformed into a subroutine; a scheduler (supervisory) routine decides when to call the task routines.

During the implementation phase, JSD specifications can be mapped to concurrent and real-time implementations. Mappings have been defined from JSD to Mascot3 subsystems, activities, channels, and pools [Cameron89]. With this approach, there is little or no need for program inversion. Mappings to Ada implementations have also been defined [Cameron89].

7.5   Products of Design Process

One product of this design process is the definition of each task in the form of structure diagrams and structure text. In the case of a model task, this also includes the definition of the attributes of the entity, as well as a definition of each input event and its attributes. Another product is a system network diagram showing the concurrent model and function tasks in the system and their data stream and state vector interfaces. A third product is a system implementation diagram showing the physical implementation of the system as well as structure text for the system implementation.

7.6   Cruise Control and Monitoring System Case Study

7.6.1   Modeling Phase

During the modeling phase of JSD [Cameron89], the real world entities are determined. The entity is defined in terms of the events it receives. A model task is created to model the life of the entity.

In JSD, events can only be system inputs, and entities are those objects that receive a time ordered sequence of events or those for which it is necessary to maintain data. Thus system input is emphasized over system output. In the Cruise Control and Monitoring system, the entities that receive external events are Cruise Control, Calibration, Shaft, and Buttons.

The Cruise Control entity models all automobile cruise control related events initiated by the driver, receiving all mutually-constrained events that impact the vehicle cruise control. The events are:

Engine on: Switch engine on.

Accel: Initiate automatic controlled acceleration of car.

Cruise: Stop automatic acceleration and start cruising at constant speed.

Brake: Driver presses brake pedal.

Off: Switch off cruise control mechanism.

Resume: Initiate automatic acceleration (or deceleration) to cruising speed.

Engine off: Switch engine off.

The calibration entity models the calibration buttons used by the driver to perform a measured mile calibration. The events are:

Start calibration: initiate measured mile calibration.

Stop calibration: stop measured mile calibration.

The shaft entity models the drive shaft from which measures of vehicle speed and distance travelled are derived. Shaft receives the following event:

Shaft revolution: event generated each time drive shaft completes one revolution.

The buttons entity models the buttons used by the driver for automobile monitoring events related to average speed, average fuel consumption, and automobile maintenance. The events received by the Buttons entity are:

MPG Reset: Reset average miles per gallon computation and display.

MPH reset: Reset average speed computation and display.

Oil filter maintenance reset: Reset oil filter maintenance computation and display.

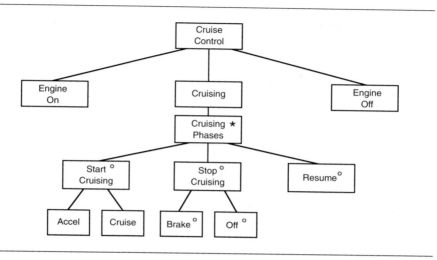

FIGURE 7.3 Cruise Control Entity Structure Diagram

Air filter maintenance reset: Reset air filter maintenance computation and display.

Major service maintenance reset: Reset major service maintenance computation and display.

An entity structure diagram is developed in which the sequence of events received by each entity is explicitly shown. A software model task is created for each entity and has the same basic structure as the entity.

Figure 7.3 shows the entity structure diagram for the Cruise Control entity and model task. Each leaf node of the tree corresponds to an event that the entity can receive. The non-leaf nodes of the tree represent relationships between events or groups of events. Thus Cruise Control is a sequence of Engine On, Cruising, and Engine Off. Cruising in turn is an iteration of Cruising Phases. Each Cruising Phase consists of a selection of a Start Cruising event, a Stop Cruising event, or a Resume event. Start Cruising consists of an Accel event followed by a Cruise event. Stop Cruising consists of either a Brake event or an Off event.

Figure 7.4 shows the calibration entity structure diagram. Calibration is a sequence of a Start Calibration event followed by a Stop Calibration event.

Figure 7.1 shows the shaft entity structure diagram. Shaft consists of an iteration of Shaft revolution events, one for each revolution of the shaft.

Figure 7.5 shows the buttons entity structure diagram. Buttons consists of an iteration of Button Presses. Each Button Press consists of a selection of one of the reset buttons being pressed. There are two mileage reset buttons and three maintenance reset buttons.

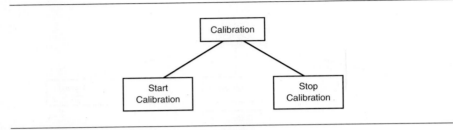

FIGURE 7.4 Calibration Entity Structure Diagram

Figure 7.6 shows the system structure at the end of the modeling phase. At this stage, there are four independent model tasks that are not connected. Input events from the real world are modeled as input messages, referred to as data streams in JSD.

7.6.2 Network Phase

During the network phase, the communication between tasks is defined, function is added to model tasks and function tasks are added.

The initial network diagram (Fig. 7.7) shows the four model tasks—Cruise Control, Calibration, Shaft, and Buttons—and their interfaces in the form of data streams and state vectors. Consider first the functionality that is added to the model tasks. Each time the Shaft task receives a Shaft Revolution event, it increments the state vector Shaft Rotation Count, and computes the current values of the state vectors Current Speed and Cumulative Distance, making use of the Calibration Constant.

The Cruise Control task receives an input stream of Cruise Control events.

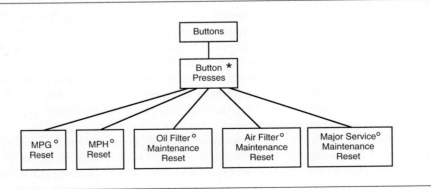

FIGURE 7.5 Buttons Entity Structure Diagram

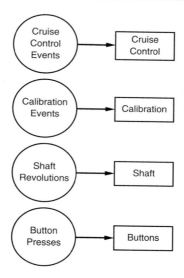

FIGURE 7.6 System Structure at End of Modeling Phase

When it receives the Cruise event, it reads Current Speed and sets its value to Desired Speed.

The Calibration task computes the value of the Calibration Constant state vector. Each time a Start Calibration event is received, it reads the current value of the state vector Shaft Rotation Count. When it receives the Stop Calibration event, it reads Shaft Rotation Count again and the difference between the two readings corresponds to the value of the Calibration Constant. Because these functions can be associated directly with an event, they can be incorporated directly into the Calibration task.

When the Buttons task receives a button press, it reads the current value of the Cumulative Distance state vector and stores it as the Initial Distance Value. In the case of MPG reset, it also reads the Fuel Level state vector, corresponding to the fuel in the gas tank.

Some functions cannot be associated directly with an event received by a model task, and so cannot be incorporated into a model task. These functions need to be supported by function tasks, which are added to the network diagram. Further data stream and state vector interfaces are added to the network diagram as required.

Figure 7.8 shows the network diagram with function tasks added. Three input function tasks are added to read inputs from the real world and pass them on to the Cruise Control task as messages. These tasks are Cruise Control Lever, Brake, and Engine. It is assumed that the cruise control lever is an asynchronous input device and so generates an interrupt when input is available, while the brake and engine are

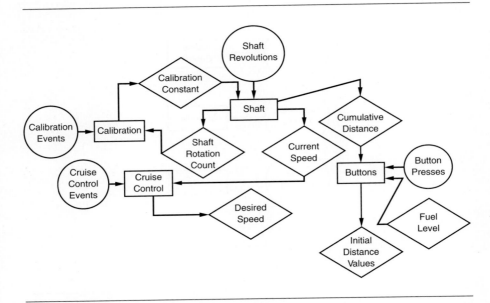

FIGURE 7.7 Initial Network Diagram

passive input devices. The Cruise Control Lever task receives Lever Event inputs directly from the real world cruise control lever, shown as a data stream input. However, the passive devices need to be polled, which is depicted by means of state vector inspections carried out by the Brake and Engine tasks.

Two output function tasks are added, one for each output device, namely Throttle and Display. Throttle receives Speed Commands from Cruise Control to accelerate, cruise, and resume. After receiving a speed command, it periodically reads the Current Speed and Desired Speed state vectors, and computes the required throttle adjustment. Display periodically computes the average MPH and average MPG, and displays these values. It also checks to see if any of the maintenance services is required and if so outputs the appropriate message.

7.6.3   Implementation Phase

In the implementation phase, the network diagram is mapped to an implementation. There are many possible implementations for a JSD network, ranging from a highly concurrent version, where each model task and function task is implemented as a concurrent task, to a highly sequential implementation, where the whole network diagram is implemented as one sequential task (i.e., one program). In this section, two cases are considered. First, a task inversion, where the concurrent solution is mapped to a sequential solution. Second, mapping the specification to Ada is addressed.

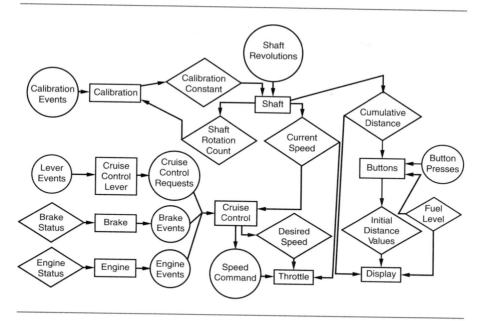

FIGURE 7.8 Revised Network Diagram

Consider first the case where a sequential solution is required; that is, the implementation consists of one task. This case uses program inversion and is illustrated in Fig. 7.9. The approach used is to have a main procedure, the Scheduler, which reads all system inputs. Each task that receives input events from the outside world is implemented as a procedure, which is called by the Scheduler when there is input for it. Thus Cruise Control Lever, Brake, Engine, Shaft, Calibration, and Buttons are called by the Scheduler when there is an input for them.

Any consumer task that receives a message from a producer task can be inverted with respect to the producer. Inversion of the Consumer with respect to the Producer means that the Consumer is mapped to a procedure that is called by the Producer, when there is a message for it. Instead of receiving a message from the Producer, the contents of the message are passed as parameters of the call. For example, as Cruise Control receives messages from Cruise Control Lever, Brake, and Engine, in the inverted solution Cruise Control is called by any of these procedures when there is a message for it. Similarly since Cruise Control sends messages to Throttle, in the inverted solution it calls Throttle and passes to it the Speed Command as a parameter. Finally, Display (a periodic output function task) is mapped to a procedure, which is called periodically by the Scheduler. State vectors are mapped to global data and are therefore not explicitly shown in Fig. 7.9.

As a second example of implementation, consider the mapping of a JSD specification to Ada. One approach is to have one Ada task for each JSD task, one Ada

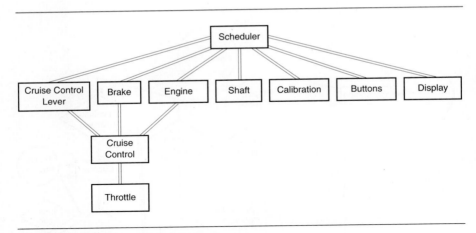

FIGURE 7.9 Example of Task Inversion

task to buffer each of the JSD task's input streams, and one Ada task to manage accessing the state vector. The JSD task calls entries provided by the buffer tasks to get a message and entries provided by the state vector task to update the state vector. The tasks are all encapsulated in a package, so that other tasks interact with the JSD task via access procedures provided by the package. There is one access procedure to write to each data stream, and another access procedure for each state vector inspection.

This approach leads to a proliferation of Ada tasks, and consequently is inefficient if there are large numbers of JSD tasks. If loosely-coupled message communication is not needed, another approach is to eliminate the buffer tasks and have tightly-coupled message communication. With this option, there is an accept statement in the JSD task for each data stream to receive input messages. In addition, the model task can encapsulate the state vector and provide an entry for reading the contents of the state vector. A third option is to map each JSD task to a procedure using the task inversion technique.

7.7 Assessment of Method

This assessment is made in terms of how applicable JSD is to the design of concurrent and real-time systems. The **strengths** include:

1. The emphasis on modeling real world entities is a theme that has since been adopted by several of the object oriented analysis and design methods;

2. Modeling each real world entity by emphasizing the sequence of events received by the entity is especially relevant in real-time system design;

3. Concurrent processing is a central theme of the method; and

4. Clear steps are provided for mapping a JSD design to an implementation using the inversion technique.

The **weaknesses** include:

1. Since the entity structure, and consequently the task structure, models the sequence of events in the real world so faithfully, relatively small real world changes can impact the software structure. This could make maintainability more difficult and is a potential hindrance to reuse as recognized in [Cameron89];

2. It is often easier to model event sequences in a complex entity using a state transition diagram than an entity structure diagram. This is particularly the case in real-time systems where complex event sequences are not unusual, a fact recognized by some real-time system advocates of JSD [Renold89, Sanden89];

3. The differentiation between model tasks and function tasks is often difficult to make. They are determined during different phases of JSD. Not all entities in the problem domain are mapped to model tasks; for example, entities that provide outputs are usually mapped to function tasks;

4. Defining the internal structure of the model tasks in the modeling phase can lead to overemphasis on detailed design before the architectural design is completed in the network phase; and

5. JSD does not emphasize data abstraction and information hiding. For example, tasks can read each other's state vectors. This is likely to have a negative impact on maintainability.

7.8   Extensions and Variations

Sanden [Sanden93] describes a variation on JSD that is oriented towards the needs of concurrent and real-time systems and also maps directly to Ada. The approach, called Entity-Life Modeling, eliminates the distinction between model and function tasks, maps JSD tasks directly onto Ada tasks, uses state transition diagrams instead of entity structure diagrams when this is considered desirable, and uses information hiding modules to encapsulate data structures and state vectors.

8

Naval Research Laboratory Software Cost Reduction Method

8.1 Overview

The Naval Research Laboratory software cost reduction method (NRL) originated to address the perceived growing gap between software engineering principles advocated in academia and the practice of software engineering in industry and government [Parnas84]. These principles formed the basis of a design method that was first applied to the development of a complex real-time system: namely the Onboard Flight Program for the U.S. Navy's A-7E aircraft. Several principles were refined as a result of experience in applying them in this project.

Application of the design method is preceded by a specification phase in which a black box requirements specification is produced [Heninger80]. During the requirements phase, consideration is given to factors that could have a profound effect on the future evolution of the system, specifically the desirable system subsets, which are used during the design phase in developing the uses hierarchy, and the likely future changes to the system requirements, which are used during the design phase in developing the information hiding module hierarchy.

The software structure of a system is considered as consisting of three orthogonal structures, the module structure, the uses structure, and the task (referred to as process in the NRL method) structure [Parnas74, Parnas84]. The module structure is based on information hiding. Each module is a work assignment for a programmer or team of programmers. The uses structure determines the executable subsets of the software. The task structure is the decomposition of run-time activities of the system.

8.2 Basic Concepts

The NRL method applies the **information hiding concept** to the design of large-scale systems [Parnas84]. The use of information hiding emphasizes that each aspect of a system that is considered likely to change (e.g., a system requirement, a hardware interface, or a software design decision) should be hidden in a separate information hiding module. The changeable aspect is called the secret of the module. Each module has an abstract interface that provides the external view of the module to its users.

To manage the complexity of handling large numbers of information hiding modules, the NRL method organizes these modules into a tree-structured **information hiding module hierarchy** (also referred to as the module structure) and documents them in a module guide. Criteria are provided for structuring the system into modules.

An **abstract interface specification** defines the visible part of an information hiding module. It is a specification of the operations provided by the module. The abstract interface to a module is intended to remain unchanged, even if the module's internals do change.

Design for extension and contraction is achieved by means of the uses hierarchy, which is a hierarchy of operations (access procedures or functions) provided by the information hiding modules. An operation A uses an operation B if and only if A cannot meet its specification unless there is a correct version of B present. By considering subsets and supersets, designing systems is considered a process of designing program families [Parnas79].

The concurrent task (process) structure is the decomposition of the run-time activities of the system. Tasks synchronize their operations by means of events.

Errors are referred to as **undesired events.** The undesired events that each module has to deal with, and the response to each undesired event, are explicitly addressed in an NRL design.

8.3 Notation

The NRL method does not use a graphical notation; rather, it uses tables extensively. In an NRL design, state transition tables are used to represent the states in the system (referred to as modes) and the transitions between them. Tables are also used to summarize the information about each module, in particular the design decision hidden in each module.

8.4 Steps in Method

The following steps in the NRL method are based on [Parnas86]. Reviews are considered an integral part of the method and are conducted for each work product [Parnas85].

1. *Establish and document the requirements.* The software requirements specification is a black box specification of the system. The method emphasizes the outputs of the system over its inputs. The system is viewed as a finite state machine whose outputs define the system outputs as functions of the state of the system's environment.

   The method uses separation of concerns in organizing the specification document. Sections are provided on the computer (hardware and software) specification, the input/output interfaces, specification of output values, timing constraints, accuracy constraints, likely changes to the system, and undesired event handling. Decisions made during specification influence the subsequent design as illustrated in the Cruise Control example (Section 8.6).

2. *Design and document the module structure.* To manage the complexity of handling large numbers of modules, the NRL method organizes information hiding modules into a tree-structured hierarchy and documents them in a module guide. The guide defines the responsibilities of each module by describing the design decisions that are to be encapsulated in the module. The objectives of the module guide are to provide structure, to check on completeness, and to avoid duplication of function. The guide allows modules to be referenced more easily during the subsequent development and maintenance phases of the project.

   The information hiding module hierarchy is an "is composed of" relation. Each non-leaf module is composed of lower-level modules. Only leaf modules contain executable operations. The main categories of modules, as determined on the A7 project, are:

   a. *Hardware hiding modules.* These modules are categorized further into extended computer modules and device interface modules. Extended computer modules hide the characteristics of the hardware/software interface that are likely to change. Device interface modules hide the characteristics of I/O devices that are likely to change.

   b. *Behavior hiding modules.* These modules hide the behavior of the system as specified by the functions defined in the requirements specification. Thus changes to the requirements impact these modules.

   c. *Software decision modules.* These modules hide decisions made by the software designers that are likely to change.

      Further categorization of modules may be carried out, although this is likely to be application dependent. Module structuring is described in more detail in [Parnas84].

3. *Design and document module abstract interfaces.* Here the abstract interface specification for each leaf module in the module hierarchy is developed. This specification defines the external view of the information hiding module. It is intended to contain just enough information for the programmer of another module to be able to use it effectively.

   The interface specification includes the operations provided by the module, the parameters for these operations, the externally visible effects of the module's operations, timing and accuracy constraints, assumptions that users and implementers can make about the module, and definition of undesired events raised.

4. *Design and document uses hierarchy.* The uses hierarchy defines the subsets that can be obtained by deleting operations and without rewriting any operations. This is important for staging system development and for developing families of systems, where a family of systems is a collection of systems that have common characteristics and components. During this stage, the operations used by each operation (an operation is provided by a module) are determined. By this means a hierarchy of operations is developed. The "allowed-to-use structure" defines the possible choices of operations, while the "uses structure" specifies the choice of operations for a particular version (member of the family).

5. *Design and document module internal structures.* After designing the module abstract interface, the internal design of each module is developed. This includes designing the internal data structures and algorithms used by the modules. In some cases, the module may be decomposed further into submodules.

   During this phase the task structure of the system is developed [Faulk88]. Tasks may be either demand or periodic tasks. They are usually relatively small, consisting of single functions. Intertask synchronization is achieved by means of event synchronization.

8.5   Products of Design Process

The products of the design process are described above and consist of a module guide, module abstract interface specifications, a uses hierarchy, module internal structures, and a task structure.

8.6   Cruise Control and Monitoring System Case Study

8.6.1   Introduction

The NRL design of the Cruise Control and Monitoring System is presented using the three views: the information hiding module view, the uses hierarchy view, and the task structuring view. The input to this design is the NRL Software Requirements Specification (SRS). Since some of the NRL information hiding modules are derived from the SRS, this section first outlines some of the information that is in the SRS for the Cruise Control and Monitoring System for the purposes of showing how the design is derived from it.

8.6.2   Software Requirements Specification

The Software Requirements Specification provides information on specifying the interface to each input/output device. The characteristics of the input and output devices are defined. The inputs received by the system from each input device and the outputs sent by the system to each output device are also specified. Additional information is provided on mode determination tables used to define the different externally visible modes (states or superstates) and the transitions between them. Information is also provided on specifying the functions of the system. Functions are defined as being output generating functions. Functions are classified as being demand or periodic functions. The frequency with which these functions need to be performed is also defined. If the function is periodic, the frequency of activation is given.

8.6.3   Information Hiding Module Hierarchy

The module hierarchy consists of three main categories of modules and is shown in Table 8.1. The first main category is hardware hiding modules. Hardware hiding modules are divided into two subgroups. The first of these subgroups is device interface modules (DIM). Following the NRL approach, there is one DIM for each I/O device, hiding the characteristics of the device. These modules are derived from the SRS, by mapping each I/O device defined in the SRS to a DIM. For the Cruise Control and Monitoring system, the DIMs are shown in Table 8.2, together with their secrets (what information they hide). A DIM hides how an input is read and how an output is written. The notation is to show inputs as /cruise control input/ and outputs as //oil message//.

The second subgroup is extended computer modules. The only extended computer module for the Cruise Control and Monitoring System is the System Clock, which hides the characteristics of the real-time clock.

The second main category is Behavior Hiding modules. There are several categories of Behavior Hiding modules, with three being the most typical. The first of these three is Function Driver modules. Each Function Driver module controls a set of closely related outputs. The module determines the values to be sent to a given virtual output device supported by a DIM. The primary secret of a Function Driver module is the rules determining the values of these outputs.

There are several Function Driver modules in this application. These modules are also derived from the SRS, which has a section on the output functions of the system.

TABLE 8.1 NRL MODULE HIERARCHY FOR CRUISE CONTROL AND
MONITORING SYSTEM

Hardware Hiding Modules

Device Interface Modules
   Engine Sensor
   Brake Sensor
   Cruise Control Input
   Calibration Input
   Drive Shaft Sensor
   Throttle
   Gas Tank Sensor
   Mileage Reset
   Maintenance Reset
   Mileage Display
   Maintenance Display

Extended Computer Modules
   Clock

Behavior Hiding Modules

Function Driver Modules
   Auto Speed Control
   Average MPH
   Average MPG
   Oil Filter Maintenance
   Air Filter Maintenance
   Major Service Maintenance

Mode Determination Modules
   Cruise Control
   Calibration Control

System Value Modules
   Current Speed
   Desired Speed
   Distance

Software Decision Modules

Data Abstraction Modules
   Calibration
   Shaft Rotation Count

The Function Driver modules are outlined in Table 8.3. Each Function Driver module outputs to one device via the operations of the DIM that encapsulates the device. For example the Auto Speed Control function driver module encapsulates the algorithm for computing the degree to which the throttle needs to be adjusted and supports operations to Increase Speed, Maintain Speed, Resume Speed, and Deactivate. The actual output to the throttle is performed by the Throttle DIM.

The second typical module type is Mode Determination modules. There is one

TABLE 8.2 DEVICE INTERFACE MODULES

Virtual Device	Secret (How to . . .)
Cruise Control Input	read /cruise control input/
Calibration Input	read /calibration input/
Mileage Reset	read /mph reset/ read /mpg reset/
Maintenance Reset	read /maintenance reset/

Mileage Display	write the following outputs:
	//average mpg display//
	//average mph display//

Maintenance Display	write the following outputs:
	//oil message//
	//air message//
	//service message//

Gas Tank Sensor	read /fuel amount/
Brake Sensor	read /brake engaged/
Throttle	write //throttle//
Engine Sensor	read /engine running/
Drive Shaft Sensor	read /shaft rotation/

Key:
  /system input/
  //system output//

Mode Determination module [Parnas84] for each mode determination table in the SRS. A mode determination table in the NRL method is equivalent to a state transition table, as a mode is a state or superstate.

In the Cruise Control and Monitoring System, there are two Mode Determination modules. Cruise Control hides the Cruise Control mode determination table; in particular, it hides the states, the transitions between the states, and the current state. Calibration Control hides the Calibration Control mode determination table.

The third typical module type is System Value modules. A System Value module computes a set of values, some of which are used by more than one Function Driver.

Three system value modules are identified: Current Speed, Desired Speed, and Distance. These modules compute values that are described in the SRS and are used by the function driver modules. System value modules support operations to update and read the system value. For example, the Current Speed system value module encapsulates the current speed of the vehicle and supports operations to update and read the current speed.

The Auto Speed Control function driver module uses the value of current speed by calling the Read Current Speed operation provided by the Current Speed module. The Average MPG, Average MPH, and Maintenance function driver modules all use the value of the cumulative distance by calling the operation Read Cumulative Distance provided by the Cumulative Distance system value module.

TABLE 8.3 FUNCTION DRIVER MODULES

Function Driver	Secret (How to . . .)
Auto speed control	How to determine what the value of //throttle// should be: Increase Speed Maintain Speed Resume Speed Deactivate
Oil filter maintenance	How to determine when the oil message status light should be on, off, or blinking.
Air filter maintenance	How to determine when the air message status light should be on, off, or blinking.
Major service maintenance	How to determine when the service message status light should be on, off, or blinking.
Average MPH	How to determine what the value of //average mph display// should be.
Average MPG	How to determine what the value of //average mpg display// should be.

The third and final main category is Software Decision modules. These tend to be the most difficult modules to identify, since they generally are not related directly to the SRS. Two data abstraction modules are determined, Calibration and Shaft Rotation Count.

8.6.4   Module Abstract Interfaces

The Module Abstract Interface defines the external view of the information hiding module. It includes the operations provided by the module and the parameters for these operations. Table 8.4 shows the operations provided by each module.

8.6.5   Uses Hierarchy

In order to derive the Uses Hierarchy, it is necessary to determine the operations used by each of the operations (which are provided by modules). Thus, the Uses Hierarchy is actually a hierarchy of operations.

The operations used by each of the operations are shown in Table 8.4. It should be noted that the Uses Hierarchy shows the relationship "requires the presence of." In most cases, the Uses Hierarchy is similar to the Calling Hierarchy. However, there are cases when the two hierarchies differ. For example, although Read Incremental Distance is at the bottom of the calling hierarchy, it is not at the bottom of the Uses Hierarchy. Thus, Read Incremental Distance uses Compute Distance, which in turn uses Read Shaft Rotation Count, since if shaft rotation interrupts are not received, the distance traveled by the vehicle cannot be computed, and hence the value cannot be read correctly. An example of the Uses Hierarchy for the operation Maintain Speed,

TABLE 8.4 CRUISE CONTROL AND MONITORING SYSTEM OPERATIONS
PROVIDED AND USED BY MODULES

Module	Provides	Uses
Hardware Hiding Modules		
Engine Sensor	Read Engine Status	
Brake Sensor	Read Brake Status	
Cruise Control Input	Read Cruise Control Input	
Calibration Input	Read Calibration Input	
Drive Shaft Sensor	Read Shaft Rotation	
Throttle	Output to Throttle	
Gas Tank Sensor	Read Fuel	
Mileage Reset	Reset MPH Reset MPG	
Maintenance Reset	Reset Oil Filter Reset Air Filter Reset Major Service	
Mileage Display	Display MPH Display MPG	
Maintenance Display	Display Oil Message Display Air Message Display Service Message	
Clock	Read Clock	
Behavior Hiding Modules		
Cruise Control	Process Cruise Control Event	Read Engine Status Read Brake Status Read Cruise Control Input
	Read Cruise Control State	
Calibration Control	Process Calibration Event	Read Calibration Input
	Read Calibration State	
Auto Speed Control	Increase Speed	Output to Throttle Process Cruise Control Event
	Maintain Speed	Output to Throttle Read Current Speed Read Desired Speed Process Cruise Control Event
	Resume Cruising	Output to Throttle Read Current Speed Read Desired Speed Process Cruise Control Event
	Deactivate	Output to Throttle Process Cruise Control Event

TABLE 8.4 (continued)

Module	Provides	Uses
Average MPH	Initialize MPH	Read Cumulative Distance Display MPH Reset MPH Read Clock
	Compute MPH	Read Cumulative Distance Display MPH Read Clock
Average MPG	Initialize MPG	Read Cumulative Distance Display MPG Read Fuel Reset MPG
	Compute MPG	Read Cumulative Distance Display MPG Read Fuel
Oil Filter	Initialize Oil Filter	Read Cumulative Distance Display Oil Filter Message Reset Oil Filter
	Check Oil Filter	Read Cumulative Distance Display Oil Filter Message
Air Filter	Initialize Air Filter	Read Cumulative Distance Display Air Filter Message Reset Air Filter
	Check Air Filter	Read Cumulative Distance Display Air Filter Message
Major Service	Initialize Major Service	Read Cumulative Distance Display Major Service Message Reset Major Service
	Check Major Service	Read Cumulative Distance Display Major Service Message
Current Speed	Update Current Speed	Read Incremental Distance Read Clock
	Read Current Speed	Update Current Speed
Desired Speed	Select Desired Speed	Read Current Speed Process Cruise Control Event
	Clear Desired Speed	Process Cruise Control Event
	Read Desired Speed	Select Desired Speed
Distance	Compute Distance	Read Shaft Rotation Count Read Calibration Constant
	Read Cumulative Distance	Compute Distance
	Read Incremental Distance	Compute Distance

TABLE 8.4 (continued)

Module	Provides	Uses
Software Decision Modules Calibration	Start Calibration	Read Shaft Rotation Count
	Stop Calibration	Read Shaft Rotation Count
	Read Calibration Constant	
Shaft Rotation Count	Update Shaft Rotation Count	
	Read Shaft Rotation Count	Update Shaft Rotation Count

which is at the top of the hierarchy and hence not used by any other operation, is shown in Table 8.5.

An operation A may use an operation B several ways—by calling it, by being dependent on an event signalled by it, by relying on some input or output data processed by it, or by some combination of the above. Thus Maintain Speed calls the operations Read Desired Speed and Read Current Speed. It is activated and deactivated by events signalled by Process Cruise Control Event. It also signals events to Output to Throttle, passing throttle value data to it via a buffer.

8.6.6 Task Structuring

The NRL method leads to a relatively large number of tasks, with the objectives of separation of concerns and maximizing scheduling flexibility. Tasks perform single

TABLE 8.5 USES HIERARCHY

Maintain Speed

Process Cruise Control Event
   Read Cruise Control Input
   Read Engine Status
   Read Brake Status

Read Desired Speed
   Select Desired Speed

Read Current Speed
   Update Current Speed
      Read Incremental Distance
        Compute Distance
          Read Shaft Rotation Count
            Update Shaft Rotation Count
          Read Calibration Constant
      Read Clock

Output to Throttle

TABLE 8.6 NRL CONCURRENT TASKS

Periodic I/O Tasks	Periodic Non-I/O Tasks
Read Engine Status	Compute Distance
Read Brake Status	Update Current Speed
Reset MPH	Compute MPH
Reset MPG	Compute MPG
Reset Oil Filter	Check Oil Filter
Reset Air Filter	Check Air Filter
Reset Major Service	Check Major Service
Demand I/O Tasks	**Demand Non-I/O Tasks**
Read Cruise Control Input	Process Cruise Control Event
Read Calibration Input	Process Calibration Event
Read Shaft Rotation	Select Desired Speed
Output to Throttle	Clear Desired Speed
	Increase Speed
	Maintain Speed
	Resume Cruising
	Start Calibration
	Stop Calibration
	Initialize MPH
	Initialize MPG
	Initialize Oil Filter
	Initialize Air Filter
	Initialize Major Service

functions, and are demand (asynchronous) or periodic tasks. Thus tasks are primarily determined by analyzing the operations provided by each module. Intertask synchronization is achieved by means of events.

The NRL method provides few guidelines for task structuring. Hence the following example of task structuring uses additional information derived by analyzing the problem. For the purpose of the cruise control example, four categories of tasks are determined: demand I/O tasks, demand non-I/O (internal) tasks, periodic I/O tasks, and periodic non-I/O tasks. The characteristics of each I/O device, whether asynchronous or passive, need to be known in order to make the decision about the kind of I/O task. The concurrent tasks are shown in Table 8.6, using the categories described here.

All operations that are at the top of the Uses Hierarchy are likely to be structured into separate tasks. Thus function driver operations are potential tasks. For example, Maintain Speed is a function driver operation, which is at the top of the Uses Hierarchy, and is structured as a demand non-I/O task. Each function that is activated periodically is also a potential task (e.g., Compute Distance). Each input device potentially has a task associated with it. This is either a periodic task, if the I/O device is passive (e.g., Read Engine Status task), or a demand task if the device is asynchronous, that is the I/O device generates interrupts (e.g., Read Cruise Control Input task).

Synchronization between tasks is achieved by means of events. Thus an input task signals an event when there is new input, for example, Read Brake Status sends a Brake Pressed event when it detects a change in brake status. The task waiting on the event, in this case Process Cruise Control Event, is activated by the event and processes it. If the cruise control state is Cruising, then Process Cruise Control Event changes the state to Cruising Off and signals a Disable event. This signal is received by Maintain Speed, which then deactivates automated control of the vehicle.

8.7   Assessment of Method

The **strengths** of this method are as follows:

1. Emphasis on information hiding leads to modules that are relatively modifiable and maintainable;

2. In addition to the emphasis on information hiding, the module hierarchy provides a means of managing large numbers of modules by organizing them into a tree-structured hierarchy;

3. Emphasis is placed on designing for change. This starts during the requirements phase when likely changes in requirements are considered. It continues into design with the module structure, where each module hides an independently changeable aspect of the system;

4. Emphasis is placed on identifying system subsets. This starts during the requirements phase when desirable subsets are identified. It continues in the design phase with the Uses Hierarchy;

5. There is a clear separation between requirements and design. The requirements present a black box view of the system, emphasizing inputs, outputs, externally visible states and their transitions, as well as output-oriented functions; and

6. Emphasizes the use of finite state machines, which is particularly important in the design of real-time control systems, which are frequently state dependent.

The **weaknesses** of this method are as follows:

1. It is usually difficult to get an overview of the system. In particular, it is often difficult to see how the major components of the system fit together. This is compounded by the lack of any graphical notation;

2. There is less emphasis on task structuring. Although recognized as an important software structure, little guidance is given on how to identify the tasks in the system; and

3. Proceeding from the software requirements specification to the module structure is often a big step. There is little guidance provided for making this transition.

9

Object-Oriented Design

9.1 Overview

Object-Oriented Design (OOD) is a design method based on the concepts of abstraction and information hiding. Two views on whether inheritance is an essential feature of OOD are to be found. The first is in the Ada world [Booch87a] and views inheritance as a desirable—but not essential—feature of OOD. The second view, originating in the object-oriented programming area (as illustrated by Smalltalk [Goldberg83], C++ [Stroustrup86] and Eiffel [Meyer88]), states that inheritance is an essential feature of OOD.

This section gives an overview of Booch's view of OOD because it lends itself more readily to the design of concurrent and real-time systems. Initially, Booch's version of OOD supported objects through information hiding, but did not support classes or inheritance [Booch86]; his later version of OOD supports all three [Booch91]. Other views of OOD are outlined in Section 9.8.

9.2 Basic Concepts

Abstraction is used in the separation of an object's specification from its body. The specification is the visible part of the object and defines the operations that may be performed on the object (i.e., how other objects may use it). The body of the object, or its internal part, is hidden from other objects.

Information hiding is used in structuring the object, deciding what information should be visible and what information should be hidden. Thus, those aspects of an object that need not be visible to other objects are hidden.

Objects are based on the information hiding concept. The characteristics of an object [Booch86] are that it has state, or internal data, which can only be modified by calling the operations provided by the object. An object also provides operations, which can be used by other objects; uses operations provided by other objects; is a unique instance of some class; has restricted visibility of and by other objects. Thus an object's visible part is given by its external specification. Its implementation (internals) are hidden. Similarly its view of other objects is limited to those objects' external specifications; and is viewed by either its specification or its implementation.

A **class** is an object type, it can be considered to be a template for objects. An object is an instance of a class.

Inheritance is a relationship among classes where a child class can share the structure and operations of a parent class and adapt it for its own use.

9.3   Notation

Class diagrams are used in OOD to show the relationships between classes in the logical design of a system [Booch91]. One or more diagrams are used to show the class structure of the system. A class diagram (Fig. 9.3) is intended to show the static structure of a system, particularly the inheritance and uses relationships between classes.

Object diagrams are used in OOD to show both the objects in the system and the relationships between objects [Booch91]. Each object in an object diagram is an instance of a class. Object diagrams are intended to show the dynamic aspects of a system. Thus a diagram may show a snapshot in time of a group of communicating objects. Objects communicate with each other by means of messages.

A **state transition diagram** shows the states of an object and the events that cause transition between these states.

Timing diagrams are used to show the dynamic interaction of a group of objects by showing the time-ordered sequence of execution of operations provided by the objects.

Module diagrams show the allocation of classes and objects to modules in the physical design of a system [Booch91]. In Ada, modules correspond to packages.

Process diagrams show the allocation of concurrent processes (tasks) to processors in the physical design of a system.

9.4 Steps in Method

Booch's approach to OOD (referred to in [Booch91] as "Round-trip Gestalt Design") is highly iterative and consists of the following steps:

1. *Identify the classes and objects.* The designer attempts to identify the key abstractions in the problem domain: classes and objects. Objects are identified by determining the entities in the problem domain. Each real word entity is mapped onto a software object.

   An informal strategy is used for identifying objects. Initially Booch [Booch87a] advocated identifying objects by underlining all nouns (candidates for objects) and verbs (candidates for operations) in the specification. However, this was not practical for large-scale or even medium-size systems.

   Booch later advocated the use of Structured Analysis as a starting point for the design, and then identifying objects from the data flow diagrams by applying a set of object structuring criteria [Booch86, Booch87b], which are based on information hiding. For each external entity (source or sink of data) on the system context diagram, there is a corresponding software object that hides device specific details. For each data store on the data flow diagrams, there is a corresponding software object that hides the structure and content of the data store.

   Most recently, Booch [Booch91] has advocated determining classes and objects directly by analyzing the problem domain and applying object structuring criteria such as those described in [Coad91, Shlaer88], which model objects in the problem domain using information modeling techniques. Thus each class or entity is defined by means of its attributes and its relationships to other classes. In addition, objects provide operations and objects may communicate with each other using messages.

2. *Identify the semantics of the classes and objects.* Each object's interface is determined. The operations provided by each object, which are used by other objects, are determined. The operations this object uses, which are provided by other objects, are also determined. This step is likely to be iterative as designing one object's interface may impact the design of an object that it interfaces to. Preliminary class and object diagrams are developed.

3. *Identify the relationships among classes and objects.* This step is an extension of the second one. The static and dynamic dependencies between objects are determined. Visibility is considered on a class and object basis. A decision might be made to create a new class that defines the common behavior of a group of similar objects. The inheritance and uses structures are defined; the class and object diagrams are refined; and preliminary module diagrams are developed.

   Three kinds of objects are possible: servers (which provide operations for other objects but do not use operations from other objects); actors (which use operations from other objects but do not provide any); and agents (which provide operations and also use operations from other objects).

4. *Implement classes and objects.* Design decisions are made concerning the representations of the classes and objects. Classes and objects are allocated to information hiding modules (packages in Ada) and programs are allocated to processors. The internals of each object are developed. This involves designing the data structures and internal logic of each object.

9.5   Products of Design Process

There are six products of the design process. The first is class diagrams. Associated with each class diagram is the specification of the individual classes, including each of the operations supported by the class. The second product is object diagrams. Associated with each object diagram is the specification of the individual objects. The third and fourth products are state transition diagrams and timing diagrams. The fifth product is module diagrams, with which the specification of the individual modules is associated. And the final product is process diagrams, with which the specification of the individual processes and processors is associated.

9.6   Cruise Control and Monitoring System Case Study

In applying Object-Oriented Design to the Cruise Control case study, four primary steps are followed.

9.6.1   Identifying Classes and Objects

In this step, the designer attempts to identify the key abstractions—classes and objects—in the problem domain. Objects are identified by determining the entities in the problem domain. Each real word entity is mapped onto a software object. The objects and their informal descriptions are given in Table 9.1.

For most classes there is only one object that is an instance of the class; in the cruise control case study, there is only one brake and one engine.

Initially tangible or concrete objects in the problem domain are determined. There is one tangible object for each external device (each source of data and each sink of data). Examples of tangible objects that represent external devices that are sources of data are the Brake, the Engine, and the Shaft. The Mileage Display and the Maintenance Display are examples of tangible objects that represent external devices that are

TABLE 9.1 OBJECTS IN CRUISE CONTROL AND MONITORING SYSTEM

Objects	Informal Description
Cruise Control Input	Interfaces to the real world cruise control lever
Calibration Input	Interfaces to the real world calibration buttons
Maintenance Display	Interfaces to the maintenance display
Mileage Display	Interfaces to the mileage display
Driver Reset	Interfaces to the mileage and maintenance reset buttons
Gas Tank Sensor	Interfaces to the real world gas tank sensor
Brake	Interfaces to the real world brake and provides the brake status
Throttle	Interfaces to the real world throttle device and controls throttle position
Engine	Interfaces to the real world engine and provides the engine status
Shaft	Interfaces to the real world drive shaft
Current Speed	Maintains the car's current speed
Desired Speed	Maintains the car's desired cruising speed
Cruise Control	Encapsulates the cruise control state transition diagram
Calibration Constant	Maintains the calibration constant, the number of shaft rotations per mile
Distance	Maintains the incremental distance and cumulative distance travelled
Average MPH	Maintains the trip average MPH
Average MPG	Maintains the trip average MPG
Oil Filter Maintenance	Determines the need for an oil filter maintenance
Air Filter Maintenance	Determines the need for an air filter maintenance
Major Service Maintenance	Determines the need for a major service
Shaft Rotation Count	Maintains the count of shaft rotations
Clock	Provides the stimulus for periodic actions

sinks of data, while an example of a tangible object that is both a source and sink of data is the Throttle. Next, abstract objects are determined. Examples of abstract objects that encapsulate data stores are Distance, Current Speed, and Desired Speed.

9.6.2 Identifying Semantics of Classes and Objects

Here, each object's interface is determined. The operations provided by each object (Table 9.2), and the operations used by each object (Table 9.3) are determined. Preliminary class and object diagrams are developed.

TABLE 9.2 OPERATIONS PROVIDED BY EACH OBJECT

Objects	Operations Provided
Cruise Control Input	None
Calibration Input	None
Maintenance Display	Display Oil Filter Message Display Air Filter Message Display Major Service Message
Mileage Display	Display Average MPH Display Average MPG
Driver Reset	None
Gas Tank Sensor	Read Gas Tank
Brake	None
Throttle	Maintain Speed, Resume Cruising Increase Speed, Deactivate Speed
Engine	None
Shaft	None
Current Speed	Get Current Speed, Determine Speed
Desired Speed	Select Desired Speed, Clear Desired Speed, Get Desired Speed
Cruise Control	Process Cruise Control Event
Calibration Constant	Start Calibration, Stop Calibration, Get Calibration Constant
Distance	Determine Distance, Get Cumulative Distance, Get Incremental Distance
Average MPH	Initialize Average MPH, Compute Average MPH
Average MPG	Initialize Average MPG, Compute Average MPG
Oil Filter Maintenance	Initialize Oil Filter, Check Oil Filter
Air Filter Maintenance	Initialize Air Filter, Check Air Filter
Major Service Maintenance	Initialize Major Service, Check Major Service
Shaft Count	Increment Shaft Rotation Count, Get Shaft Rotation Count
Clock	Read Clock

9.6.3   Identifying Relationships Among Classes and Objects

The static and dynamic dependencies between objects are determined, inheritance and uses structures are defined, and the class and object diagrams are refined.

In the cruise control example (except for the Maintenance class, which is described later), each class has only one instance (object). Furthermore, these objects exist for the lifetime of the system. The object diagram for the Cruise Control subsystem is given in Fig. 9.1 and for the Monitoring subsystem is given in Fig. 9.2. The objects Engine, Brake, and Cruise Control Input send messages to Cruise Control whenever there is an input from the external devices that they encapsulate. Thus if the

TABLE 9.3 OPERATIONS USED BY EACH OBJECT

Object	Operations Used
Cruise Control Input	Process Cruise Control Event
Calibration Input	Start Calibration, Stop Calibration
Maintenance Display	None
Mileage Display	None
Driver Reset	Initialize Oil Filter, Initialize Air Filter, Initialize Major Service, Initialize MPH, Initialize MPG
Gas Tank Sensor	None
Brake	Process Cruise Control Event
Throttle	Get Current Speed, Get Desired Speed, Process Cruise Control Event
Engine	Process Cruise Control Event
Drive Shaft	Increment Shaft Rotation Count
Current Speed	Get Incremental Distance, Read Clock
Desired Speed	Get Current Speed
Cruise Control	Select Desired Speed, Maintain Speed, Clear Desired Speed, Resume Cruising, Increase Speed, Deactivate Speed
Calibration	Get Shaft Rotation Count
Distance	Get Shaft Rotation Count, Get Calibration Constant
Average MPH	Get Cumulative Distance, Display Average MPH Read Clock
Average MPG	Get Cumulative Distance, Display Average MPG, Monitor Gas Tank
Oil Filter Maintenance	Display Oil Filter Message
Air Filter Maintenance	Display Air Filter Message
Major Service Maintenance	Display Major Service Message
Shaft Count	None
Clock	Determine Speed, Compute Average MPH, Compute Average MPG, Determine Distance, Check Oil Filter, Check Air Filter, Check Major Service

driver engages the cruise control lever in the Resume position or presses the brake, a corresponding message is sent to Cruise Control. Cruise Control is a control object that executes the cruise control state transition diagram conceptually. As a result of the state transitions that take place, cruise control invokes operations in other objects. For example, it sends messages to invoke operations in Throttle to Maintain Speed, Resume Cruising, and Increase Speed. Throttle in turn invokes operations to read the values of Current Speed and Desired Speed.

The Brake, Engine, and Cruise Control Input objects are all examples of actor

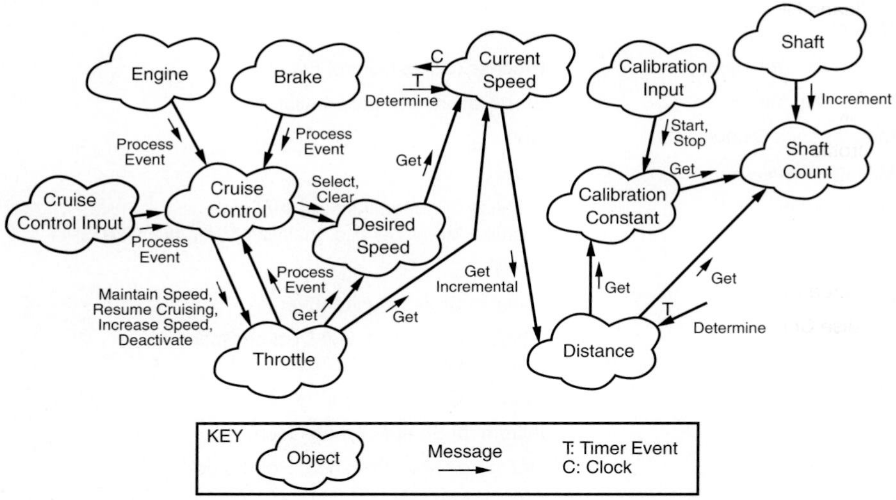

FIGURE 9.1 Object Diagram for Cruise Control Subsystem

objects, for they operate on other objects but are not operated upon by them. Shaft Count is an example of a server object as it is operated on by other objects but does not operate upon other objects. Cruise Control is an example of an agent object as at times it operates on other objects and, at different times, it is operated on by other objects.

The Class diagram shown in Fig. 9.3 is for that part of the system that deals with automobile maintenance. This diagram is of particular interest, as it demonstrates how the inheritance and uses relationships are employed on the same diagram. Oil Filter, Air Filter, and Major Service are all subclasses of the Maintenance class. Thus they have the same overall structure as Maintenance but also they also introduce some changes through inheritance. In addition, each of these subclasses uses the class Maintenance display to output a maintenance message to the driver. Not shown on Fig. 9.3, but shown on Fig. 9.2, is that the three maintenance subclasses also use the class Distance to read the cumulative distance. In addition the class Driver Reset uses each of the three maintenance sub-classes for initialization after a service has been carried out.

9.6.4   Implementing Classes and Objects

If the design is to be mapped to Ada, the OOD objects are mapped to Ada packages and tasks. Component Interface Specifications are given in the form of Ada package specifications, and the Maintenance class is implemented as a generic package.

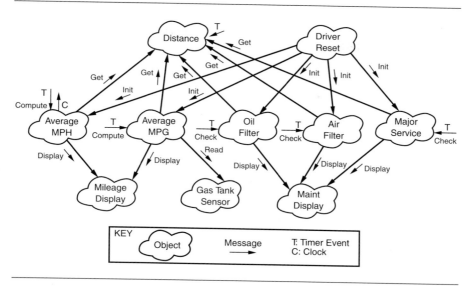

FIGURE 9.2 Object Diagram for Modeling Subsystem

9.7 Assessment of Method

In terms of how applicable OOD is to the design of concurrent and real-time systems, the **strengths** of this method are as follows:

1. The method is based on the concepts of information hiding, classes, and inheritance, which are key concepts in software design.

2. Structuring of a system into objects to make the system more maintainable and components potentially reusable.

3. Providing inheritance allows components to be modified in a controlled manner where necessary.

4. Maps well to languages that support information hiding modules (such as Ada and Modula-2), and to languages that support classes and inheritance (such as C++, Smalltalk, and Eiffel).

The **weaknesses** of this method are as follows:

1. Does not adequately address the important issues of task structuring, which is an important limitation in real-time design, as it assumes that the same criteria may be used for identifying tasks as information hiding modules.

2. The method assumes a very iterative procedure in developing a design. As a result, it is not specific as to what procedures should be applied at each step.

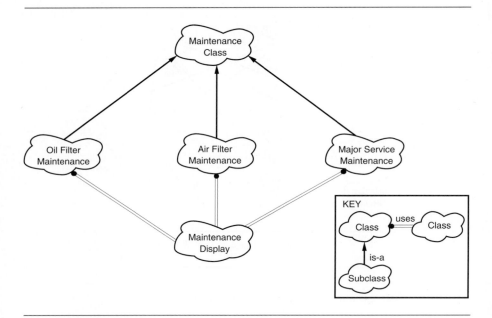

FIGURE 9.3 Class Diagram

3. The object structuring criteria are not as comprehensive as the NRL module structuring criteria.

4. Although it uses timing diagrams, the method does not adequately address timing constraints.

9.8   Extensions and Variations

The emerging Object-Oriented Analysis methods [Coad91, Shlaer88, Rumbaugh91] use information modeling techniques for identifying objects in the problem domain, as does the General Object-Oriented Design (GOOD) method [Seidewitz89]. In addition, GOOD provides techniques for mapping from problem domain objects to solution domain objects. Other object-oriented analysis and design methods that have emerged recently are described in Wirfs-Brock et al [Wirfs-Brock90], Rumbaugh et al [Rumbaugh91], Hood [Hood89], and Coad/Yourdon [Coad91, Coad92]. The ADARTS and CODARTS methods provide a set of information hiding module structuring criteria that incorporate some of the OOD object structuring criteria. The COBRA analysis method provides a set of object structuring criteria oriented to identifying objects in the problem domain.

10

Comparison of Concurrent and Real-Time Software Design Methods

10.1   Introduction

When comparing the concurrent and real-time software design methods, the approach taken is to evaluate how they address those design concepts outlined in Chapter 3: concurrent tasks for defining the concurrency in the system; information hiding/object structuring for defining modifiable and potentially reusable software components; and finite state machines for defining the control aspects of a system. A fourth criterion for comparison is how they handle timing constraints, an important characteristic of real-time systems. The comparison uses the examples from the Cruise Control and Monitoring system to illustrate the issues raised.

10.2   Concurrent Tasks Comparison

Although all the methods address concurrent tasks to some extent, there is a wide variation in the emphasis placed on them. Concurrent tasks are fundamental to two of the methods, DARTS and JSD. The NRL and OOD methods place less emphasis on task structuring.

The Ward/Mellor [Ward85, Vol. 3] version of RTSAD addresses structuring the system into concurrent tasks but provides few guidelines for this purpose. Structured Design (SD) is a program design method and hence does not address the issue of task structuring. However, SD can be used for designing individual tasks, as is done in the DARTS method.

In the Cruise Control problem, the SD solution takes an inherently concurrent problem and maps it to a sequential solution. This leads to an awkward situation, where control has to be returned periodically to the input modules to determine whether there is any new input. In addition, to handle asynchronous shaft rotation inputs, a task had to be designed outside the SD context.

DARTS addresses the weaknesses of RTSAD in the task structuring area by introducing the task structuring criteria for identifying concurrent tasks in the system and by providing guidelines for defining task interfaces.

Comparing the DARTS solution to the Cruise Control problem with the SD solution, a naturally concurrent problem is mapped to a concurrent solution. Each task can wait for its input (either external or internal in the form of a message or event), without constantly checking to see if some input has occurred in some other part of the system. Instead of the whole system having to be controlled by a cyclic executive as in SD, the DARTS tasks are much more independent. Periodic tasks are activated on a regular basis to perform an activity. All other (aperiodic) tasks are activated on demand. Thus they wait for input indefinitely, and are only activated when there is work for them to perform.

Concurrent processing plays an important role in JSD since each external entity is mapped onto a model task in the Modeling phase. Function tasks are then added in the Network phase. JSD model tasks are similar to control tasks in DARTS. Many of the other DARTS task structuring criteria are similar to the criteria for the definition of function tasks in JSD, an observation also made in [Renold89]. For example, JSD input and output function tasks are similar to DARTS device input and output tasks. The DARTS task cohesion criteria for grouping potential tasks into the same actual task for performance reasons is addressed in JSD during the implementation phase, where tasks are combined using task inversion. Thus task structuring, which is carried out in one task structuring phase in DARTS, is spread over all three phases of JSD.

In the JSD solution to the Cruise Control problem, only four tasks are determined in the Modeling phase. The JSD Cruise Control and Calibration model tasks are respectively similar to the DARTS control tasks Cruise Control and Perform Calibration. The JSD Shaft task is equivalent to the DARTS device input task Monitor Shaft Rotation, while the Buttons task is equivalent to the DARTS Monitor Reset Buttons task. Three of these JSD tasks receive inputs directly from the external environment. However, other input tasks (Cruise Control Lever, Brake, and Engine) are considered input function tasks and hence not determined until the Network phase. Output tasks in JSD (e.g., Throttle and Display) are usually determined in the Network phase and considered output function tasks, as they do not receive events from the external environment. Any attempt to combine Brake and Shaft into one task, as with the DARTS task cohesion criteria, is carried out in the implementation phase.

The NRL method views the task structure as an important software structure that is orthogonal to the module and uses structures. However, task structuring is carried out comparatively late in the NRL method and few guidelines are provided for identifying the tasks. Each periodic or demand function is mapped to a task. This leads to a proliferation of simple tasks. There is no concept of task cohesion as in DARTS or task inversion as in JSD to group functions together when mapping to tasks.

Unlike the DARTS and NRL methods, the OOD method assumes that the same object structuring criteria can be used for identifying tasks (active objects) and information hiding modules (passive objects). The OOD object structuring criteria are based on information hiding and do not take into account concurrency and timing issues. Thus no criteria are given for distinguishing between active and passive objects. If all objects were mapped to tasks, this would lead to a proliferation of tasks and to a high system overhead for many systems. Object-Oriented Design has no strategy for optimizing the design, as DARTS has with the task cohesion criteria and JSD has with task inversion.

10.3   Information Hiding and Objects Comparison

Information hiding is the fundamental underlying principle in two of the methods, NRL and OOD. It is also addressed by the DARTS and RTSAD methods but not by JSD.

Both the NRL and OOD methods emphasize the structuring of a system into information hiding modules (objects). As OOD emphasizes determining objects from the problem domain, OOD objects are generally similar to NRL device interface modules and behavior hiding modules, which are determined from the Software Requirements Specification.

In general, the NRL module structuring criteria are more comprehensive than the OOD object structuring criteria. Thus, there is also a whole category of modules identified in the NRL method (software decision modules) that is not addressed directly by OOD. These modules are not related to the problem domain and are hence not determined from the Software Requirements Specification.

In addition, the NRL method is more concerned about each module hiding a secret or a decision that could change independently. Thus in the NRL method, a module can hide the details of an algorithm that could potentially change. For example, in the NRL Cruise Control design, the Auto Speed Control IHM hides the algorithm for computing the desired speed of the vehicle and the necessary adjustments to the throttle to achieve that speed.

In comparison with the NRL method, less attention is paid to having each object/module hide one design decision during object structuring in OOD; thus an object could hide more than one design decision. Consequently, OOD-derived components may not be as modifiable and reusable as NRL-derived components. For example, in the NRL Cruise Control design, the Auto Speed Control IHM is structured separately from the Throttle IHM, which hides the interface to the real-world throttle. This is because the design decision concerning the speed control algorithm could change independently of the design decision concerning the interface to the real-world throttle. However, in OOD the object Throttle encapsulates both the interface to the device and the algorithm used for computing the throttle value, which is considered an operation of the object. Thus decisions concerning the algorithm could be intertwined with decisions concerning the interface to the real world throttle, making the object more difficult to modify.

RTSAD is weak in the area of information hiding. In its application, Structured Design lags behind the NRL method and OOD. Although the concept of informational strength (information hiding) modules was added by Myers [Myers78], the design strategies of Transform and Transaction Analysis do not address information hiding. In fact, information hiding modules are typically determined very late in the design process. Thus the decision in the SD cruise control design to support IHMs such as Current Speed and Desired Speed is done after the overall structure of the system has been determined, unlike OOD and NRL where the determination of objects/modules is one of the first decisions made. Hence a designer using this method is liable to arrive at a design that is mainly functional. Because of this, requirements and design changes are likely to have a more severe effect on systems developed using RTSAD.

Although DARTS uses information hiding for encapsulating data stores and state transition tables, it does not use information hiding as extensively as NRL and OOD. Thus it uses the Structured Design method, and not information hiding, for structuring tasks into what are primarily functional modules.

10.4   Finite State Machines Comparison

The use of finite state machines is a major consideration in three of the methods: RTSAD, DARTS, and NRL. It is a secondary consideration in OOD. In JSD, a different approach is taken with event sequences depicted using entity structure diagrams.

The major extension to Structured Analysis for real-time applications is to address the control aspects of a system, primarily through the use of finite state machines. The use of state transition diagrams and tables has been well integrated into the method through the use of control transformations and specifications. Thus the Cruise Control state transition diagram and the control transformation that executes it are key components of the RTSA solution. However, the Ward/Mellor version of RTSA only allows events but not conditions on state transitions. The Boeing/Hatley allows conditions but not events. The NRL method supports both events and conditions, allowing more concise state transition tables.

State dependency is not handled well in Structured Design, where [Yourdon 79] goes so far as to say that the "difficulty with state-dependent decision procedures is a fundamental defect in the transaction centered structure," because system outputs depend entirely on the inputs to the system and are not state dependent. This problem was solved in DARTS by introducing state transition modules to encapsulate state transition tables, thereby allowing system responses to be state dependent. The SD solution to the Cruise Control problem borrowed this idea from DARTS, with the introduction of the Cruise Control state transition module.

Finite state machines are an important feature of the DARTS method, which advocates analysis of the control aspects of the system before the functional aspects. DARTS uses RTSA as a front end to the design method. Control tasks execute finite state machines and state transition tables are encapsulated into information hiding modules. Thus the Cruise Control control transformation is mapped to the Cruise Control task and the state transition table is mapped to a state transition module inside the task.

Finite state machines are also an important aspect of the NRL method. A key feature of the specification method is the identification of system modes (superstates) and the transitions between them. In the design phase, each mode transition table is encapsulated in a mode determination module.

In OOD, an object may be defined by means of a finite state machine that is encapsulated within the object. However, OOD does not give as much prominence to finite state machines as the previous three methods.

In JSD, entities in the problem domain are modeled using entity structure diagrams that show the sequence of events experienced by the entity. The regular expression notation used by entity structure diagrams is mathematically equivalent to finite state machine notation. However, for complex entities where there are comparatively many transitions in relation to the number of states, it is frequently more concise to use a finite state machine notation rather than entity structure diagrams.

The Cruise Control entity structure diagram corresponds to the state transition diagram for the control transformation Cruise Control described in the Real-Time Structured Analysis solution. However, the Cruise Control entity structure diagram is actually substantially simplified to make it readable. It only handles the straightforward cases and does not address the more complicated cases addressed in the state transition diagram.

10.5   Timing Constraints

Each of the methods described addresses timing constraints to some extent. The required system response times are defined during system specification. During design, the timing requirements for each task are determined.

RTSAD addresses timing constraints during the analysis and design phases. During analysis, the response time specification is developed. This includes response times to external events, sampling times of external inputs, required frequency of periodic outputs, and response times to user inputs [Hatley88]. During design, the timing requirements of each task are determined. Frequency of task activation and context switching overhead are also considered in arriving at a timing estimate [Ward85].

DARTS uses the RTSA timing specification to allocate time budgets to each task. Event sequence diagrams [Gomaa86a] are used to show the sequence of tasks executed from external input to system response. Percentages of this response time are then allocated to each task in the sequence and to system overhead.

In the NRL method, timing constraints are specified at the requirements stage for periodic and demand functions that generate system outputs. During design, the timing requirements for each task are specified, including its deadline and worst case execution time [Faulk88].

In JSD, timing requirements in the form of system responses to external inputs are analyzed. Network diagrams are used to determine the timing constraints for individual tasks, which are executed to generate the response to the external input [Jackson83]. This approach is similar to the use of event sequence diagrams in DARTS.

In OOD [Booch91], timing diagrams are used to show timing dependencies among objects. However, the issue of using timing diagrams to help analyze performance is only mentioned briefly.

In conclusion, however, it is clear that despite the importance of timing constraints in real-time systems, it is a characteristic (and limitation) of most software design methods for real-time systems that the methods tend to emphasize structural and behavioral aspects of real-time systems and generally pay significantly less attention to timing constraints. This issue is addressed further in the next chapter.

11

Performance Analysis of Concurrent and Real-time Software Designs

11.1   Introduction

The quantitative analysis of a software design is for the software design conceptually executing on a given hardware configuration with a given external workload applied to it. This is useful for the early detection of any potential performance problems, allowing alternative software designs and hardware configurations to be investigated. Performance analysis of software designs is particularly important for real-time systems.

This chapter presents an overview of performance analysis of software designs through performance modeling and by applying real-time scheduling theory. A performance model is developed of the software design, whose performance is then analyzed. Real-time scheduling is an approach that is particularly appropriate for hard real-time systems that have rigid deadlines [Sha90].[1]

11.2   Performance Models

11.2.1   Concepts

A performance model of a computer system is an abstraction of the real computer system behavior, developed for the purpose of gaining greater insight into the performance of the system, whether the system actually exists or not. This abstraction may be in the form of a mathematical model or a simulation model. A mathematical

1. A comprehensive reference book on performance analysis and modeling is [Smith90].

model is a mathematical representation of the system. Queueing models, Petri net models, and regression models are examples of mathematical models. A simulation model is an algorithmic representation of the system reflecting system structure and behavior.

A model of a computer system may be static or dynamic. Static models either omit the recognition of time altogether or model the steady state situation. A regression model is an example of a static model which does not recognize time. Many queueing models describe steady state situations. Dynamic models explicitly recognize the passage of time. A simulation model is an example of a dynamic model.

Some performance modeling techniques are more appropriate for modeling existing systems, for which much data can be collected from performance measurements. In particular, empirical techniques, such as regression modeling, can provide useful insights into system performance of existing systems. Regression models are constructed by statistical curve fitting, in particular by applying least squares fitting techniques to the performance data [Gomaa77]. As regression models do not attempt to model the structure and behavior of the system being modeled, they are of less value in analyzing the software designs of systems that do not yet exist.

11.2.2   Queueing Models

Queueing models are analytical models of computer systems used to analyze contention for limited resources and for predicting system performance [Kleinrock75]. In an analytical model, it is possible to deduce a solution to the problem under study directly from its mathematical representation.

Queueing models of computer systems usually involve a number of simplifying assumptions that make the model more amenable to mathematical analysis. The most common assumption is that the probability of getting a new request does not depend on how long ago the last request was made, sometimes called the "memory-less" property. As a consequence of this assumption, the request interarrival time distribution follows an exponential distribution, which assigns the highest probability density to the smallest time interval of length zero. In many computing environments, short values of interarrival times between requests are unlikely. A further simplifying assumption sometimes used is that of only analyzing the steady state environment.

These assumptions mean that the greatest value of queueing models is usually as high-level models of computer system performance to get an overall view of whether a system can meet its performance goals. However, for a more detailed performance analysis, other modeling techniques are needed.

11.2.3   Simulation Models

Simulation can be an effective way of verifying that the design is sound and meets its timing requirements. With this approach, the software system under development, as well as the environment it is to operate in, are simulated. To be of greatest value, the simulation should be performed before system development is started. Although much useful information can be obtained from a simulation exercise, simulation models are often very detailed and hence the time to develop them can be considerable. Care must also be taken to ensure that the assumptions made in the model are realistic.

A simulation model of a software design models the system's real world behavior by means of an algorithmic abstraction of the system, reflecting system structure and behavior. A simulation model is dynamic (i.e., it deals explicitly with the passage of time), and simulating a system provides a means of analyzing the behavior of the system over a period of time.

In a discrete event simulation model, changes in the state of the system are represented by a collection of discrete events. Changes of state only take place when a discrete event occurs. Thus the simulation can skip over the time between events and is able to "compress" time.

A computer system simulation model models the behavior of the "real" computer system, or the software design executing on the computer hardware. The model requires an abstraction of the workload as input. The model produces a record of estimated computer system behavior as output.

Workloads have sometimes been modeled using probability distributions, which often make unjustified assumptions about the workload. Alternatively, the workload may be modeled by means of an event trace. An event trace consists of a description of each event and the time at which the event occurred. The trace is ordered by arrival time. On an existing system, an event trace may be derived by monitoring the actual computer system. However, when modeling a design for a system that does not yet exist, the event trace will need to be derived from observations of the real-world environment in which the system is intended to operate.

11.2.4 Problems in Modeling Computer Systems

A number of factors need to be considered in developing a model. Factors of prime importance are the cost of developing a model, the level of detail incorporated into a model, the speed of the completed model, and its degree of accuracy.

Although simulation can provide the greatest level of detail and potentially the greatest accuracy, the principle drawback to simulation modeling is its high cost, which is closely linked to selecting the right level of detail to be included in the model. In general, there is a tradeoff between a model's speed and its degree of realism. If the level of detail is too gross, the model may be unrealistic because important details have been aggregated to such an extent that their effect is lost. On the other hand, if the model is too detailed, it may be too expensive to develop and to use.

One approach that has been attempted to help overcome these problems is the use of hybrid models, which combine more than one modeling technique, such as hybrid queueing/simulation models or hybrid simulation/regression models [Gomaa81]. With this approach, simulation is used for modeling those aspects of a system of particular interest at a greater level of detail, while other aspects of the system, which are of less interest, are modeled in less detail using queueing or regression techniques.

Another problem in modeling computer systems is that of calibrating and validating the model against the real world. With a performance model of an existing computer system, the calibration and validation process uses data obtained by measuring the performance of the real system. The calibration and validation process is usually an iterative statistical procedure which attempts to ensure that the predictions of the model are not significantly different from the real world performance [Beilner72, Gomaa78]. Once this has been achieved, the model may be used for estimating the impact of changes to the system, by playing "what if" scenarios.

The calibration and validation process for a performance model of a system that does not yet exist is much more error-prone. Certain parameters, such as operating system overhead (e.g., for context switching and servicing task communication requests), can be obtained by performance measurement of the actual target system. However, many other parameters, such as task execution times, have to be estimated. Thus the accuracy of the model predictions are highly dependent on the accuracy of the estimates of the performance parameters.

11.3   Petri Nets

Finite state machines have been used to model systems in which the sequence of events plays an important role; that is, the response to a given input event depends not only on the type of event but also on what has happened previously in the system. However, finite state machines are strictly sequential and thus they cannot be used to model parallelism.

An alternative modeling approach to finite state machines is that of Petri nets [Peterson81]. Petri nets can model concurrent systems directly, so they are a more powerful tool than finite state machines. Indeed, the finite state machine is a sequential subset of the Petri net.

A Petri net is represented as a directed graph. The two types of nodes supported are called places (depicted by circles) and transitions (depicted by bars). The execution of a Petri net is controlled by the position and movement of markers called tokens. Tokens are depicted by black dots that reside in the places of the net. Tokens are moved by the firing of the transitions of the net. A transition is enabled to fire when all its input places have a token in them. When the transition fires, a token is removed from each input place and a token is placed on each output place.

Various extensions have been proposed to Petri net models. In particular, Timed Petri nets are particularly useful for modeling real-time systems. Whereas a basic Petri net has no times associated with it, Timed Petri nets allow finite times to be associated with the firing of transitions [Coolahan83], allowing a Petri net model to be analyzed from a performance perspective.

Petri nets can be used as analysis tools as well as modeling tools. Petri nets have been used successfully to model hardware systems, communication protocols, and software systems. In the latter case, Petri nets have been used to model task synchronization [Peterson81], message communication between tasks [Peterson81], and Ada concurrent tasking applications.

The analysis capability of Petri nets is very powerful; for example, they can be used to detect reachability and deadlocks. Furthermore, a stochastic Petri net model can be used to analyze throughput of the proposed system. Thus Petri nets are an attractive proposition for real-time and distributed systems, where throughput and response times are important considerations.

11.4   Real-time Scheduling Theory

11.4.1   Introduction

Real-time scheduling theory addresses the issues of priority-based scheduling of concurrent tasks with hard deadlines. The theory addresses how to determine whether a group of tasks, whose individual CPU utilization is known, will meet their deadlines. The theory assumes a priority pre-emption scheduling algorithm, as described in Chapter 3. This section is based on the reports on real-time scheduling produced at the Software Engineering Institute [Sha90, SEI93], which should be referenced for more information on this topic.

As real-time scheduling theory has evolved, it has gradually been applied to more complicated scheduling problems. Problems that have been addressed include scheduling independent periodic tasks, scheduling in situations where there are both periodic and aperiodic (asynchronous) tasks, scheduling in cases where task synchronization is required, and scheduling concurrent tasks in Ada.

11.4.2   Scheduling Periodic Tasks

Initially, algorithms were developed for independent periodic tasks, which do not communicate or synchronize with each other [Liu73]. Since then, the theory has been developed considerably so that it can now be applied to practical problems, as will be illustrated in the examples. In this chapter, it is necessary to start with the basic rate monotonic theory for independent periodic tasks in order to understand how it has been extended to address more complex situations.

A periodic task has a period T, which is the frequency with which it executes, and an execution time C, which is the CPU time required during the period. Its CPU utilization U is the ratio C/T. A task is schedulable if all its deadlines are met (i.e., the task completes its execution before its period elapses). A group of tasks is considered to be schedulable if each task can meet its deadlines.

For a set of independent periodic tasks, the rate monotonic algorithm assigns each task a fixed priority based on its period, such that the shorter the period of a task, the higher its priority. Thus, if there are three tasks t_a, t_b, and t_c with periods 10, 20, 30 msec respectively, then the highest priority is given to the task with the shortest period

t_a, the medium priority is given to task t_b, and the lowest priority is given to the task t_c with the longest period.

11.4.3   Utilization Bound Theorem

According to the rate monotonic scheduling theory, a group of n independent periodic tasks can be shown to always meet their deadlines providing the sum of the ratios C/T for each task is below an upper bound of overall CPU utilization.

The Utilization Bound Theorem [Liu73], which is also referred to as Theorem 1, states that

UTILIZATION BOUND THEOREM (THEOREM 1)

A set of n independent periodic tasks scheduled by the rate monotonic algorithm will always meet its deadlines, for all task phasings, if

$$\frac{C_1}{T_1} + \cdots + \frac{C_n}{T_n} \le n(2^{1/n} - 1) = U(n)$$

where C_i and T_i are the execution time and period of task t_i, respectively.

The upper bound U(n) converges to 69% (ln 2) as the number of tasks approaches infinity. According to Theorem 1, the utilization bounds for up to nine tasks are given in Table 11.1. This is a worst case approximation and for a randomly chosen group of tasks, [Lehoczky89] showed that the likely upper bound is 88%. For tasks with harmonic periods (i.e., with periods that are multiples of each other), the upper bound is even higher.

The rate monotonic algorithm has the advantage of being stable in conditions where there is a transient overload. In other words, a subset of the total number of tasks, namely those with the highest priorities (and hence shortest periods), will still meet their deadlines if the system is overloaded for a relatively short time. The lower priority tasks may occasionally miss their deadlines as the processor load increases.

As an example of applying the Utilization Bound Theorem, consider three tasks with the following characteristics, where all times are in msec and the utilization $U_i = C_i/T_i$:

Task t_1: $C_1 = 20$; $T_1 = 100$; $U_1 = 0.2$
Task t_2: $C_2 = 30$; $T_2 = 150$; $U_2 = 0.2$
Task t_3: $C_3 = 60$; $T_3 = 200$; $U_3 = 0.3$

It is assumed that the context switching overhead, once at the start of the task's execution and once at the end of its execution, is included in the CPU times.

The total utilization of the three tasks is 0.7, which is below Theorem 1's upper bound for three tasks of 0.779. Thus the three tasks can meet their deadlines in all cases.

TABLE 11.1 UTILIZATION BOUND THEOREM (THEOREM 1)

Number of Tasks n	Utilization Bound U(n)
1	1.000
2	0.828
3	0.779
4	0.756
5	0.743
6	0.734
7	0.728
8	0.724
9	0.720
Infinity	0.690

However, if task t_3's characteristics are instead as follows:

Task t_3: $C_3 = 90$; $T_3 = 200$; $U_3 = 0.45$

The total utilization of the three tasks is 0.85, which is higher than Theorem 1's upper bound for three tasks of 0.779. Thus Theorem 1 indicates that the tasks do not meet their deadlines. Next, a check is made to determine whether the first two tasks can meet their deadlines.

Given that the rate monotonic algorithm is stable, the first two tasks can be checked using Theorem 1. The utilization of these two tasks is 0.4, which is well below Theorem 1's upper bound for two tasks of 0.828. Thus the first two tasks always meet their deadlines. Given that Theorem 1 is pessimistic theorem, a further check can be made to determine whether Task 3 can meet its deadlines, by applying the more exact Theorem 2.

11.4.4   Completion Time Theorem

If a set of tasks have a utilization greater than Theorem 1's upper bound, then Theorem 2, which gives a more exact schedulability criterion [Lehoczky89], can be checked. For a set of independent periodic tasks, Theorem 2, also referred to as the Completion Time Theorem, provides an exact determination of whether the tasks are schedulable. It assumes a worst case of all the periodic tasks ready to execute at the same time. It has been shown [Liu73, Lehoczky89] that in this worst case, if a task completes execution before the end of its first period, then it will never miss a deadline. Theorem 2 therefore checks if each task ti can complete execution before the end of its first period.

COMPLETION TIME THEOREM (THEOREM 2)

For a set of independent periodic tasks, if each task meets its first deadline when all tasks are started at the same time, then the deadlines will be met for any combination of start times.

To do this, it is necessary to check the end of the first period of a given task t_i, as well as the end of all periods of higher priority tasks. Following the rate monotonic theory, these tasks will have shorter periods than t_i. These periods are referred to as scheduling points. Task t_i will execute once for a CPU amount of C_i during its period T_i. However, higher priority tasks will execute more often and can pre-empt t_i at least once. It is therefore necessary to consider the CPU time used up by the higher priority tasks as well.

Theorem 2 can be illustrated graphically using a timing diagram. Consider the example given earlier of the three tasks with the following characteristics:

Task t_1: $C_1 = 20$; $T_1 = 100$; $U_1 = 0.2$
Task t_2: $C_2 = 30$; $T_2 = 150$; $U_2 = 0.2$
Task t_3: $C_3 = 90$; $T_3 = 200$; $U_3 = 0.45$

The execution of the three tasks is illustrated using the timing diagram shown in Fig. 11.1.

Given the worst case of the three tasks being ready to execute at the same time, t_1 executes first because it has the shortest period and hence the highest priority. It completes after 20 msec after which the task t_2 executes for 30 msec. On completion of t_2, t_3 executes. At the end of the first scheduling point, $T_1 = 100$, which corresponds to t_1's deadline, t_1 has already completed execution and thus met its deadline. t_2 has also completed execution and easily met its deadline, and t_3 has executed for 50 msec out of the necessary 90.

At the start of t_1's second period, t_3 is pre-empted by task t_1. After executing for 20 msec, t_1 completes and relinquishes the CPU to task t_3 again. Then t_3 executes until the end of period T_2 (150 msec), which represents the second scheduling point due to t_2's deadline. As t_2 was completed before T_1 (which is less than T_2) elapsed, it easily met its deadline. At this time, t_3 has used up 80 msec out of the necessary 90.

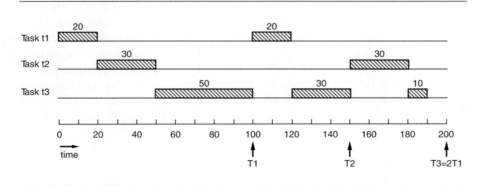

FIGURE 11.1 Timing Diagram

Task t_3 is pre-empted by task t_2 at the start of t_2's second period. After executing for 30 msec, t_2 completes relinquishing the CPU to task t_3 again. Task t_3 executes for another 10 msec, at which time it has used up all its CPU time of 90 msec, thereby completing before its deadline. Figure 11.1 shows the third scheduling point, which is both the end of t_1's second period ($2T_1 = 200$) and the end of t_3's first period ($T_3 = 200$). It also shows that each of the three tasks completed execution before the end of its first period and thus successfully met its deadline.

Figure 11.1 shows that the CPU is idle for 10 msec before the start of t_1's third period (also the start of t_3's second period). It should be noted that a total CPU time of 190 msec was used up over the 200 msec period, giving a CPU utilization for the above 200 msec of 0.95, although the overall utilization is 0.85. After an elapsed time equal to the least common multiple of the three periods (600 msec in this example) the utilization averages out to 0.85.

11.4.5 Mathematical Formulation of Completion Time Theorem

The Completion Time Theorem can be expressed mathematically in Theorem 3 [Sha90] as follows:

THEOREM 3

A set of n independent periodic tasks scheduled by the rate monotonic algorithm will always meet its deadlines, for all task phasings, if and only if:

$$\forall i, 1 \le i \le n, \quad \min \sum_{j=1}^{i} C_j \frac{1}{pT_k} \left\lceil \frac{pT_k}{T_j} \right\rceil \le 1$$

$$(k, p) \in R_i$$

where C_j and T_j are the execution time and period of task t_j respectively and $R_i = \{(k, p) \mid 1 \le k \le i, p = 1, \cdots, \lfloor T_i/T_k \rfloor\}$.

In the formula, t_i denotes the task to be checked and t_k denotes each of the higher priority tasks that impact the completion time of task t_j. For a given task t_i and a given task t_k, each value of p represents the scheduling points of task t_k. At each scheduling point, it is necessary to consider task t_i's CPU time C_i once, as well as the CPU time used by the higher priority tasks, and hence to determine whether t_i can complete its execution by that scheduling point.

Consider Theorem 3 applied to the three tasks, which were illustrated using the timing diagram in Fig. 11.1. The timing diagram is a graphical representation of what Theorem 3 computes. Once again the worst case is considered of the three tasks being ready to execute at the same time. The inequality for the first scheduling point, $T_1 = 100$, is given from Theorem 3:

$$C_1 + C_2 + C_3 \le T_1 \quad 20 + 30 + 90 > 100 \quad p = 1, k = 1$$

For this inequality to be satisfied, all three tasks would need to complete execution within the first task t_1's period T_1. This is not the case as t_3 is pre-empted before it completes by t_1 at the start of t_1's second period.

The inequality for the second scheduling point, $T_2 = 150$, is given from Theorem 3:

$$2C_1 + C_2 + C_3 \le T_2 \quad 40 + 30 + 90 > 150 \quad p = 1, k = 2$$

For this inequality to be satisfied, task t_1 would need to complete execution twice, while tasks t_2 and t_3 would each need to complete execution once within the second task t_2's period T_2. This is not the case as t_3 is preempted by task t_2 at the start of t_2's second period.

The inequality for the third scheduling point, which is both the end of t_1's second period ($2T_1 = 200$) and t_3's first period ($T_3 = 200$), is given from Theorem 3:

$$2C_1 + 2C_2 + C_3 \le 2T_1 = T_3 \quad 40 + 60 + 90 < 200 \quad p = 2, k = 1 \text{ or } p = 1, k = 3$$

This time the inequality is satisfied and all three tasks meet their deadlines. As long as all three tasks meet at least one of the scheduling point deadlines, then the tasks are schedulable.

11.4.6   Scheduling Periodic and Aperiodic Tasks

When dealing with aperiodic (asynchronous) tasks as well as periodic tasks, the rate monotonic theory is extended. An aperiodic task is assumed to arrive randomly within some period T_a, which represents the minimum interarrival time of the event which activates the task. The CPU time C_a used by the aperiodic task to process the event is reserved as a ticket of value C_a for each period T_a. When the event arrives, the aperiodic task is activated, claims its ticket, and consumes up to C_a units of CPU time. If the task is not activated during the period T_a, the ticket is discarded. Thus, based on these assumptions, the CPU utilization of the aperiodic task is C_a/T_a. However, this represents the worst case CPU utilization since, in general, reserved tickets are not always claimed.

If there are many aperiodic tasks in the application, the sporadic server algorithm [Sprunt89] can be used. From a schedulability analysis viewpoint, an aperiodic task is equivalent to a periodic task whose period is equal to the minimum interarrival time of the events that activate the aperiodic task. Hence T_a, the minimum interarrival time for an aperiodic task t_a, can be considered the period of an equivalent periodic task. Each aperiodic task is also allocated a budget of C_a units of CPU time, which can be used up at any time during its equivalent period T_a. In this way, aperiodic tasks can be placed at different priority levels according to their equivalent periods and treated as periodic tasks.

11.4.7   Scheduling with Task Synchronization

Real-time scheduling theory has also been extended to address task synchronization. The problem here is that a task that enters a critical section can block other higher priority tasks that wish to enter the critical section. The term **priority inversion** is used to refer to the case where a low priority task prevents a higher priority task from executing, typically by acquiring a resource needed by the latter.

Unbounded priority inversion can occur because the lower priority task, while in its critical section, could itself be blocked by other higher priority tasks. One solution to this problem is to prevent pre-emption of tasks while in their critical sections. This is only acceptable if tasks have very short critical sections. For long critical sections, lower priority tasks could block higher priority tasks that do need to access the shared resource.

The priority ceiling protocol [Sha90] avoids mutual deadlock and provides bounded priority inversion; that is, at most one lower priority task can block a higher priority task. Only the simplest case of one critical section is considered here.

Adjustable priorities are used to prevent lower priority tasks from holding up higher priority tasks for arbitrarily long periods of time. If, while a low priority task t_p is in its critical section, other higher priority tasks become blocked by it because they wish to acquire the same resource, t_p's priority is increased to the highest priority of all the tasks blocked by it. The goal is to speed up the execution of the lower priority task so that blocking time for higher priority tasks is reduced.

The priority ceiling P of a binary semaphore S is the highest priority of all tasks that may acquire the semaphore. Thus a low priority task that acquires S can have its priority increased up to P, depending on what higher priority tasks it blocks.

Another case that could occur is deadlock, where two tasks each need to acquire two resources before they can complete. If each task acquires one resource, then neither will be able to complete since each one is waiting for the other to release its resource, leading to a deadlock situation. The priority ceiling protocol handles this problem [Sha90].

The rate monotonic scheduling theorems need to be extended to address the priority inversion problem, as described in the next section.

11.4.8   Generalized Real-time Scheduling Theory

In real-world problems, situations often arise where the rate monotonic assumptions do not hold. There are many practical cases where tasks have to execute at actual priorities different from their rate monotonic priorities and it is therefore necessary to be able to extend the basic rate monotonic scheduling theory in order to address these cases. One case is given in the previous section concerning lower priority tasks blocking higher priority tasks from entering critical sections.

A second case often happens when there are aperiodic tasks. As discussed in Section 11.4.6, aperiodic tasks can be treated as periodic tasks with the worst case interarrival time considered the equivalent periodic task's period. Following the rate monotonic scheduling algorithm, if the aperiodic task has a longer period than a periodic task, it should execute at a lower priority than the periodic task. However, if the aperiodic task is interrupt driven, it will need to execute as soon as the interrupt arrives, even if its worst case interarrival time, and hence equivalent period, is longer than that of the periodic task.

The term priority inversion is given to any case where a task cannot execute because it is blocked by a lower priority task. In the case of rate monotonic priority inversion, the term "priority" refers to the **rate monotonic priority;** that is, the priority assigned a task based entirely on the length of its period and not on its relative importance. A task may be assigned an actual priority that is different from the rate monotonic priority. In this situation, **rate monotonic priority inversion** is used to refer to a task A pre-empted by a higher priority task B, where in fact task B's rate monotonic priority is lower than A's.

This is illustrated by the following example of rate monotonic priority inversion, in which there is a periodic task with a period of 25 msec and an interrupt driven task with a worst case interarrival time of 50 msec. The periodic task has the higher rate monotonic priority since it has the shorter period. However, in practice, it is preferable to give the interrupt driven task the higher actual priority so that it can service the interrupt as soon as it arrives. Whenever the interrupt-driven task pre-empts the periodic task, this is considered a case of priority inversion, relative to the rate monotonic priority assignment, since if the interrupt driven task had been given its rate monotonic priority, it would not have pre-empted the periodic task.

It is necessary to extend the basic rate monotonic scheduling theory in order to address these practical cases of rate monotonic priority inversion. This has been achieved [SEI93] by extending the basic algorithms to take into account the blocking effect from lower priority tasks as well as pre-emption by higher priority tasks which do not observe rate monotonic priorities. As rate monotonic scheduling theory assumes rate monotonic priorities, pre-emption by higher priority tasks that do not observe the rate monotonic priorities is treated in a similar way to blocking by lower priority tasks.

Consider a task t_i with a period T_i during which it consumes C_i units of CPU time. The extensions to Theorems 1–3 mean that it is necessary to explicitly check each task t_i to determine whether it can meet its first deadline by considering:

a. Pre-emption time by higher priority tasks with periods less than t_i. These tasks can pre-empt t_i many times. Call this set H_n and let there be j tasks in this set. Let C_j be the CPU time for task t_j and T_j the period of task t_j, where $T_j < T_i$, the period of task t_i. The utilization of a task t_j in the H_n set is given by C_j/T_j.

b. Execution time for the task t_i. Task t_i executes once during its period T_i and consumes C_i units of CPU time.

c. Pre-emption by higher priority tasks with longer periods. These are tasks with nonrate monotonic priorities. They can only pre-empt t_i once as they have longer periods than t_i. Call this set H_1 and let there be k tasks in this set. Let the CPU time used by a task in this set be C_k. The worst case utilization of a task t_k in the H_1 set is given by C_k/T_i, since this means that t_k pre-empts t_i and uses up all its CPU time C_k during the period T_i.

d. Blocking time by lower priority tasks, as described in the previous section. These tasks can also only execute once as they have longer periods. Blocking delays have to be analyzed on an individual basis for each task ti to determine the worst case blocking situation for it. If B_i is the worst case blocking time for a given task t_i, then the blocking utilization for the period T_i is B_i/T_i.

Since for any given task t_i, cases a and b are taken care of by Theorems 1–3, the generalization of Theorems 1–3 is to take into account cases c and d. Theorem 1, the Utilization Bound Theorem, is extended to address all four cases above as follows:

$$U_i = \left(\sum_{j \in H_n} \frac{C_j}{T_j} \right) + \frac{1}{T_i} \left(C_i + B_i + \sum_{k \in H_1} C_k \right)$$

The Generalized Utilization Bound Theorem is referred to here as Theorem 4. U_i is the utilization bound during a period T_i for task t_i. The first term in Theorem 4 is the total pre-emption utilization by higher priority tasks with periods less than t_i. The second term is the CPU utilization by task t_i. The third term is the worst case blocking utilization experienced by t_i. The fourth term is the total pre-emption utilization by higher priority tasks with longer periods than t_i.

By substituting in the above equation the utilization U_i can be determined for a given task. If U_i is less than the worst case upper bound (Table 11.1), this means that the task t_i will meet its deadline. It is important to realize that the utilization bound test needs to be applied to each task, since in this generalized theory, where rate monotonic priorities are not necessarily observed, the fact that a given task meets its deadline is no guarantee that a higher priority task will meet its deadline.

Once again if the utilization bound test fails, a more precise test is available, which verifies whether or not each task can complete execution during its period. This is a generalization of the Completion Time Theorem, and assuming all tasks are ready for execution at the start of a task t_i's period, determines whether t_i can complete execution by the end of its period, given pre-emption by higher priority tasks and blocking by lower priority tasks. Pictorially, this can be illustrated by drawing a timing diagram for all the tasks up to the end of task t_i's period T_i.

11.4.9   Real-time Scheduling and Design

Real-time scheduling theory can be applied to a set of concurrent tasks at the design stage or after the tasks have been implemented. In this book, the emphasis is on applying real-time scheduling theory at the design stage. During design, as all CPU times are estimates, it is best to err on the side of caution. For real-time tasks with hard deadlines, it is therefore safer to rely only on the more pessimistic Utilization Bound Theorem, with its worst case upper bound utilization of 0.69, even though the real-time scheduling theory frequently predicts upper bounds higher than this. If this worst case upper bound cannot be satisfied, then alternative solutions should be investigated. From a pessimistic designer's perspective, having a predicted upper bound utilization higher than 0.69 is acceptable providing the utilization above 0.69 is entirely due to lower priority soft real-time or non–real-time tasks. For these tasks to miss their deadlines occasionally is not serious.

It is also the case that at design time, the designer has the freedom to choose the priorities to be assigned to the tasks. In general, wherever possible priorities should be assigned according to the rate monotonic theory. This is most easily applied to the periodic tasks. Estimate the worst case interarrival times for the aperiodic tasks, and attempt to assign the rate monotonic priorities to these tasks. Interrupt driven tasks will often need to be given the highest priorities to allow them to quickly service interrupts. This means that an interrupt driven task may need to be allocated a priority that is higher than its rate monotonic priority. If two tasks have the same period and hence the same rate monotonic priority, it is up to the designer to resolve the tie. In general, assign the higher priority to the task that is more important from an application perspective.

11.4.10   Example of Applying Generalized Real-time Scheduling Theory

As an example of applying the generalized real-time scheduling theory, consider the following case. There are four tasks, of which two are periodic and two are aperiodic. One of the aperiodic tasks t_a is interrupt driven and must execute within 200 msec of its interrupt arriving or else data will be lost. The other aperiodic task t_2 has a worst case interarrival time of T_2, which is taken to be the period of the equivalent periodic task. The detailed characteristics are as follows, where all times are in msec and the utilization $U_i = C_i/T_i$:

> Periodic task t_1: $C_1 = 20$; $T_1 = 100$; $U_1 = 0.2$
> Aperiodic task t_2: $C_2 = 15$; $T_2 = 150$; $U_2 = 0.1$
> Interrupt driven aperiodic task t_a: $C_a = 4$; $T_a = 200$; $U_a = 0.02$
> Periodic task t_3: $C_3 = 30$; $T_3 = 300$; $U_3 = 0.1$

In addition, t_1, t_2, and t_3 all access the same data store, which is protected by a semaphore s. It is assumed that the context switching overhead, once at the start of a task's execution and once at the end of its execution, is included in the CPU times.

If tasks were allocated priorities strictly according to their rate monotonic priorities, t_1 would have the highest priority followed respectively by t_2, t_a, and t_3. However, because of t_a's stringent reponse time need, it is given the highest priority. The priority assignment is therefore t_a highest followed respectively by t_1, t_2, and t_3.

The overall CPU utilization is 0.42, which is below the worst case utilization bound of 0.69. However, it is necessary to investigate each task individually because rate monotonic priorities have not been assigned. First consider the interrupt driven task t_a. Task t_a is the highest priority task and always gets the CPU when it needs it. Its utilization is 0.02 and so will have no difficulty meeting its deadline. Next consider the task t_1, which executes for 20 msec during its period T_1 of duration 100 msec. Applying the Generalized Utilization Bound Theorem, it is necessary to consider

a. Pre-emption time by higher priority tasks with periods less than T_1. There are no tasks with periods less than T_1.

b. Execution time C_1 for the task $t_1 = 20$. Execution utilization $= U_1 = 0.2$.

c. Pre-emption by higher priority tasks with longer periods. The task t_a falls into this category. Preemption utilization during the period $T_1 = C_a/T_1 = 4/100 = 0.04$.

d. Blocking time by lower priority tasks. Both t_2 and t_3 can potentially block t_1. Based on the priority ceiling algorithm, at most one lower priority task can actually block t_1. The worst case is t_3 since it has a longer CPU time of 30 msec. Blocking utilization during the period $T_1 = B_3/T_1 = 30/100 = 0.3$.

Worst case utilization = Pre-emption utilization + Execution utilization + Blocking utilization = $0.04 + 0.2 + 0.3 = 0.54 <$ worst case upper bound of 0.69. Consequently t_1 will meet its deadline.

Next consider task t_2, which executes for 15 msec during its period T_2 of duration 150 msec. Again applying Theorem 4, it is necessary to consider

a. Pre-emption time by higher priority tasks with periods less than T_2. Only one task, t_1, has a period less than T_2. Its pre-emption utilization during the period $T_2 = U_1 = 0.2$.

b. Execution time C_2 for the task $t_2 = 15$. Execution utilization $= U_2 = 0.1$.

c. Pre-emption by higher priority tasks with longer periods. The interrupt driven task t_a falls into this category. Pre-emption utilization during the period $T_2 = C_a/T_2 = 4/150 = 0.03$. Total pre-emption utilization by t_1 and $t_a = 0.2 + 0.03 = 0.23$.

d. Blocking time by lower priority tasks. The task t_3 can block t_2. In the worst case, it blocks t_2 for its total CPU time of 30 msec. Blocking utilization during the period $T_2 = B_3/T_2 = 30/150 = 0.2$.

Worst case utilization = Pre-emption utilization + Execution utilization + Blocking utilization = $0.23 + 0.1 + 0.2 = 0.53 <$ worst case upper bound of 0.69. Consequently t_2 will meet its deadline.

Finally consider task t_3, which executes for 30 msec during its period T_3 of duration 300 msec. Once again, applying Theorem 4, it is necessary to consider

a. Pre-emption time by higher priority tasks with periods less than t_3. All three higher priority tasks fall into this category. So total pre-emption utilization $= U_1 + U_2 + U_a = 0.2 + 0.1 + 0.02 = 0.32$.

b. Execution time C_3 for the task t_3. Execution utilization = U_3 = 0.1.

c. Pre-emption by higher priority tasks with longer periods. There are no tasks that fall into this category.

d. Blocking time by lower priority tasks. There are no tasks that fall into this category.

Worst case utilization = Pre-emption utilization + Execution utilization = 0.32 + 0.1 = 0.42 < worst case upper bound of 0.69. Consequently t_3 will meet its deadline. In conclusion, all four tasks will meet their deadlines.

11.4.11   Real-time Scheduling in Ada

There are some aspects of the Ada conceptual model that raise concerns about its suitability for real-time systems that support tasks with hard deadlines. For example, tasks are queued FIFO rather than by priority, task priorities cannot be dynamically changed at run-time, and priority inversion can lead to high priority tasks being delayed indefinitely by lower priority tasks.

These problems are being addressed by proposing changes to the Ada run-time system to support the priority ceiling protocol and by providing a comprehensive set of guidelines for Ada real-time programming together with an "enlightened interpretation of Ada's scheduling rules [Sha90]."

11.5   Performance Analysis Using Event Sequence Analysis

During the requirements phase of the project, the system's required response times to external events are specified. After task structuring, a first attempt at allocating time budgets to the concurrent tasks in the system can be made. Event sequence analysis is used to determine the tasks that need to be executed to service a given external event. An event sequence diagram is used to show the sequence of internal events and tasks activated following the arrival of the external event. The approach is described next.

Consider an external event. Determine which I/O task is activated by this event, and then determine the sequence of internal events that follow. This necessitates identifying the tasks that are activated and those I/O tasks that generate the system response to the external event. Estimate the CPU time for each task. Estimate the CPU overhead, which consists of context switching overhead, interrupt handling overhead, and intertask communication and synchronization overhead. It is also necessary to consider any other tasks that execute during this period. The sum of the CPU times for the tasks that participate in the event sequence, plus any additional tasks that execute, plus CPU overhead, must be less or equal to the specified system response time. If there is some uncertainty over the CPU time for each task, then allocate a worst case upper bound.

To estimate overall CPU utilization, it is necessary to estimate, for a given time interval, the CPU time for each task. If there is more than one path through the task, then estimate the CPU time for each path. Next, estimate the frequency of activation of tasks. This is easily computed for periodic tasks. For asynchronous tasks, consider the average and maximum activation rates. Multiply each task's CPU time by its activation rate. Sum all the task CPU times, and then compute CPU utilization. (An example of applying the event sequence analysis approach is given in Chapter 19.)

11.6   Performance Analysis Using Real-time Scheduling Theory and Event Sequence Analysis

This section describes how the real-time scheduling theory can be combined with the event sequence analysis approach. Instead of considering individual tasks, it is necessary to consider all the tasks in an event sequence. The task activated by the external event executes first and then initiates a series of internal events, resulting in other internal tasks being activated and executed. It is necessary to determine whether all the tasks in the event sequence can be executed before the deadline.

Initially attempt to allocate all the tasks in the event sequence the same priority. These tasks can then collectively be considered one equivalent task from a real-time scheduling viewpoint. This equivalent task has a CPU time equal to the sum of the CPU times of the tasks in the event sequence, plus context switching overhead, plus message communication or event synchronization overhead. The worst case interarrival time of the external event that initiates the event sequence is then made the period of this equivalent task.

To determine whether the equivalent task can meet its deadline, it is necessary to apply the real-time scheduling theorems. In particular it is necessary to consider pre-emption by higher priority tasks, blocking by lower priority tasks, as well as the execution time of this equivalent task. An example of combining event sequence analysis with real-time scheduling using the equivalent task approach is given in Chapter 19 for the cruise control problem.

In some cases, the approach of assuming that all the tasks in the event sequence can be replaced by an equivalent task cannot be used (e.g., one of the tasks is used in more than one event sequence, or executing the equivalent task at that priority would prevent other tasks from meeting their deadlines). In that case, the tasks in the event sequence need to be analyzed separately and assigned different priorities. In determining whether the tasks in the event sequence will meet their deadline, it is necessary to consider pre-emption and blocking on a per task basis. However, it is still necessary to determine whether all tasks in the event sequence will complete before the deadline.

PART THREE

ADARTS (Ada-based Design Approach for Real-Time Systems) and CODARTS (COncurrent Design Approach for Real-Time Systems)

12

Overview of ADARTS and CODARTS

12.1 Introduction

Part III of this book describes two related methods, ADARTS (Ada-based Design Approach for Real-Time Systems) and CODARTS (COncurrent Design Approach for Real-Time Systems). Both these software design methods are based on the concepts described in Part II of this book and build on those methods.

This chapter describes the origins of the ADARTS and CODARTS methods. It also describes the conceptual foundation for ADARTS and CODARTS, including the features of other software design methods that influenced the development of these methods. Finally, the steps to be followed in using these methods are described.

12.2 Origins of ADARTS and CODARTS

The origins of ADARTS and CODARTS go back to the early 1980s, to an industrial real-time system development project, namely an industrial robot controller system.

DARTS (Design Approach for Real-Time Systems) originated because of a perceived problem with a frequently-used approach for real-time system development involving the use of Structured Analysis [De Marco79]—and, more recently, Real-Time Structured Analysis (RTSA)—during the analysis phase, followed by Structured Design during the design phase. The problem with this approach is that it does not take into account the characteristics of real-time systems, which typically consist of several concurrent tasks. The DARTS design method addresses these issues by providing the decomposition principles and steps for allowing the software designer to proceed from a RTSA specification to a design consisting of concurrent tasks.

DARTS was later extended to address the needs of distributed real-time applications. DARTS/DA (DARTS for Distributed Applications) provides a set of subsystem structuring criteria for identifying distributed subsystems [Gomaa89a]. Real-time subsystems are then developed using DARTS. DARTS/DA was used to develop a distributed system architecture for computer integrated manufacturing systems.

Another important issue in real-time design is the need for analyzing the behavioral characteristics of a real-time system. State transition diagrams are an excellent tool for modeling these behavioral characteristics. In the 1984 version of DARTS [Gomaa84], this was achieved by having a transformation on a data flow diagram execute the state transition diagram. This concept was later formalized by Ward [Ward85] and Hatley [Hatley88] in the real-time extensions to Structured Analysis, where control transformations execute state transition diagrams and control data transformations by means of event flows. To take advantage of this, DARTS was extended to start with a specification developed using Real-Time Structured Analysis instead of Structured Analysis, as described in [Gomaa87].

DARTS was later extended to support Ada-based design. This version of DARTS is known as ADARTS. CODARTS is the latest refinement of the DARTS and ADARTS methods.

12.3   Features of ADARTS and CODARTS

ADARTS is oriented towards the design of Ada-based concurrent and real-time systems, although the first four steps of ADARTS are language-independent. In the fifth step, a language-independent design is mapped to an Ada-based design. In addition to supporting mapping to Ada, a goal of ADARTS is to provide more maintainable and potentially reusable designs through greater use of information hiding than DARTS. This is achieved by replacing the Structured Design step of DARTS with an Information Hiding Module Structuring step. After integrating the task and module structures, a step to map the design to Ada follows. The first two steps, developing a Real-Time Structured Analysis specification and Task Structuring, are similar to DARTS.

CODARTS provides two major extensions to ADARTS. It is also a general purpose design method that is not oriented toward a particular language. The first extension is that it provides an alternative approach to RTSA for analyzing and modeling the system. This approach is COBRA (Concurrent Object-Based Real-Time Analysis), which addresses the limitations of RTSA. COBRA emphasizes the decomposition of a system into subsystems that provide a set of services supported by objects and functions. A behavioral analysis strategy is provided that emphasizes the control and sequencing aspects of the problem. The second extension provided by CODARTS is the support for the design of distributed applications. Thus CODARTS provides criteria for structuring a system into subsystems that can execute on geographically distributed nodes and communicate over a network. In doing this, CODARTS builds on and substantially refines and extends the ideas from DARTS/DA. Furthermore, ADARTS and CODARTS both address the issue of analyzing the performance of real-time designs.

12.4 Conceptual Foundations for ADARTS and CODARTS

This section describes how ADARTS and CODARTS build on the methods described in Part II and how they address the limitations of these methods.

12.4.1 Real-Time Structured Analysis and Design (RTSAD)

RTSA is used as the first step of ADARTS. CODARTS uses the COBRA method, which provides an alternative decomposition strategy to RTSA for analyzing and modeling the problem domain.

From RTSA, the features used in COBRA include the RTSA notation, which is used for modeling the problem domain. This notation is widely used and is supported by several CASE tools. Use of state transition diagrams to model control and sequencing within one control component is also a feature, as is the integration of state transition diagrams with data flow diagrams. COBRA addresses the limitations of RTSA by providing guidelines for developing the environmental model, guidelines for decomposing a system into subsystems, which may potentially be distributed, structuring criteria for determining the objects and functions within a subsystem, and a behavioral approach for determining how the objects and functions within a subsystem interact with each other.

With RTSAD there is a lack of emphasis on task structuring and information hiding. Both these limitations are addressed by ADARTS and CODARTS.

12.4.2 DARTS

From the DARTS method, the features used in both ADARTS and CODARTS include an emphasis on task structuring, where the provision of task structuring criteria helps identify concurrent tasks, an emphasis on designing task interfaces, and the use of event sequence diagrams for consideration of sequencing in the system, for supporting the performance analysis of the design, and for supporting incremental development of the software.

ADARTS and CODARTS replace the Structured Design method for designing individual tasks with a much greater emphasis on information hiding by providing structuring criteria to determine the information hiding modules in the system.

In addition, CODARTS builds on the ideas of DARTS/DA in addressing the design of distributed applications. It provides criteria for structuring a system into subsystems which potentially can execute on multiple nodes in a distributed environment, guidelines for defining the message interfaces between the subsystems, and guidelines for designing configurable distributed subsystems.

12.4.3   Jackson System Development (JSD)

From the JSD method, the features used in CODARTS include the concept of real-world entities being modeled by means of concurrent objects, which are designed as concurrent tasks, the use of functional tasks to support the functional aspects of the problem, and an emphasis on sequencing in developing the design.

The limitations in JSD addressed by CODARTS are a lack of emphasis on information hiding, the use of state transition diagrams, which are frequently more effective than entity structure diagrams for depicting highly state-dependent objects, and the lack of criteria to assist in determining the components to be included in the design. COBRA provides object structuring criteria to determine the concurrent objects in the system.

12.4.4   Naval Research Lab Method (NRL)

From the NRL method, the features used in both ADARTS and CODARTS include information hiding as a fundamental design concept, the concept of design for change, information hiding module structuring criteria, or the idea of each module hiding a secret, an aspect of the system that can change independently of the other aspects of the system, and the categorization of IHMs to handle the issue of complexity in large scale systems.

In comparison with the NRL method, ADARTS and CODARTS provide task structuring criteria for determining the concurrent tasks, a hierarchical decomposition approach for defining the structure of the system, and a graphical notation so that the overall structure of the system can be documented and reviewed.

12.4.5   Object-Oriented Design (OOD)

From OOD, the features used in both ADARTS and CODARTS include the use of information hiding as a fundamental design concept, the need for object structuring criteria, and the use of inheritance as a means of providing code sharing and code adaptation, allowing passive objects to provide similar though not identical services, and use of inheritance as a means of adapting objects for reuse.

The limitations of OOD addressed by ADARTS and CODARTS include the fact that for real-time systems, it is necessary to clearly distinguish between tasks and information hiding modules, as described in the next section. It is also necessary to address the performance analysis of real-time designs.

12.5   Integration of Concepts

Concurrency and timing issues need to be considered in task design, while information hiding needs to be considered in module design. Thus tasks can be considered as active objects and information hiding modules as passive objects. Two different sets of criteria are needed. Information hiding module structuring criteria are used for determining modules, while task structuring criteria are used for determining tasks.

Of the five methods compared in Part II, only DARTS and JSD address task structuring in considerable detail. Both the NRL and OOD methods emphasize the structuring of a system into information hiding modules but place less emphasis on task structuring. ADARTS and CODARTS attempt to build on the strengths of the other methods by emphasizing both information hiding module structuring and task structuring.

To achieve the objective of developing maintainable and reusable software components through information hiding, ADARTS and CODARTS incorporate a blend of the NRL module structuring criteria and the OOD object structuring criteria. To achieve the objective of structuring a system into concurrent tasks, ADARTS and CODARTS use a set of task structuring criteria that is a refinement of that originally developed for the DARTS design method.

The first step in both methods is to develop a behavioral model. ADARTS uses RTSA while CODARTS uses COBRA. When performing task and module structuring, the behavioral model is viewed from two perspectives, the dynamic and the static structuring views. The dynamic view is provided by the concurrent tasks, which are determined using the task structuring criteria. The static view is provided by the information hiding modules, which are determined using the module structuring criteria. Guidelines are given for integrating the dynamic and static views.

The task structuring criteria are applied first, followed by the module structuring criteria, although it is intended that applying the two sets of criteria should be an iterative exercise. The reason for applying the task structuring criteria first is to allow an early performance analysis of the concurrent tasking design to be made, an important consideration in real-time systems.

12.6   Steps in Using ADARTS

The first four steps of ADARTS are language-independent. The fifth step maps the design to Ada.

1. *Develop Real-Time Structured Analysis Specification.* The system context diagram and state transition diagrams are developed. A hierarchical data flow/control flow decomposition is performed. The relationship between the state transition diagrams and the control and data transformations is established.

2. *Structure the system into concurrent tasks.* Determine the concurrent tasks in the system by applying the task structuring criteria to the Real-Time Structured Analysis Specification. The intertask communication and synchronization interfaces are determined.

3. *Structure the system into information hiding modules.* Determine the information hiding modules in the system by applying the module structuring criteria. A module aggregation hierarchy is created in which the information hiding modules are categorized.

4. *Integrate the task and module views.* Tasks are determined using the task structuring criteria. Information hiding modules are determined using the module structuring criteria. These two views are now integrated to produce a software architecture.

5. *Develop an Ada-based architectural design.* Add Ada support tasks and define Ada task interfaces. Additional tasks are usually required in an Ada application to address loosely-coupled intertask communication and synchronization of access to shared data.

6. *Define component interface specifications.* The component interface specifications are defined for tasks and modules. These specifications represent the externally visible view of each component.

7. *Develop the software incrementally.* The detailed design, coding, and testing of the software is done in stages. This requires the identification of system subsets to be used for each increment.

12.7   Steps in Using CODARTS

Seven steps are necessary in using CODARTS as well.

1. *Develop environmental and behavioral model of system.* The COBRA method is used for analyzing and modeling the problem domain. COBRA provides an

alternative decomposition strategy to RTSA for concurrent and real-time systems. It provides guidelines for developing the environmental model based on the system context diagram and structuring criteria for decomposing a system into subsystems that may potentially be distributed. It also provides criteria for determining the objects and functions within a subsystem. Finally, it provides a behavioral approach for determining how the objects and functions within a subsystem interact with each other using event sequencing scenarios.

2. *Structure the system into distributed subsystems.* This is an optional step taken for distributed concurrent and distributed real-time applications. CODARTS provides criteria for structuring and configuring a distributed application into subsystems, which communicate by means of messages.

3. *Structure the system (or subsystem) into concurrent tasks.* Determine the concurrent tasks in the system (or subsystem of a distributed application) by applying the task structuring criteria. The intertask communication and synchronization interfaces are determined. Task structuring is applied to the whole system in the case of a non-distributed design. In the case of a distributed design where the subsystems have already been defined, task structuring is applied to each subsystem.

4. *Structure the system into information hiding modules.* Determine the information hiding modules in the system by applying the module structuring criteria. A module aggregation hierarchy is created in which the information hiding modules are categorized.

5. *Integrate the task and module views.* Tasks are determined using the task structuring criteria. Information hiding modules are determined using the module structuring criteria. These two views are now integrated to produce a software architecture.

6. *Define component interface specifications.* The component interface specifications are defined for tasks and modules. These specifications represent the externally visible view of each component.

7. *Develop the software incrementally.* The detailed design, coding, and testing of the software, is done in stages. This requires the identification of system subsets to be used for each increment.

12.8   ADARTS and CODARTS Notation

12.8.1   Real-Time Structured Analysis Notation (RTSA)

Figure 12.1(a–c) shows the notation used in the Ward/Mellor version of Real-Time Structured Analysis (RTSA). This notation is also used by COBRA.

Figure 12.1(a) shows the notation used for the system context diagram. A rectangle represents an external entity that the system has to interface to. An external entity is also referred to as a terminator. It can be a source of data or a sink of data. The system to be developed is shown as one data transformation, by means of a circle or "bubble." The system interfaces to the external entities via data flows and event flows.

Figure 12.1(b) shows the notation for data flow/control flow diagrams. Data transformations are identical to those used in Structured Analysis [De Marco79]. They are also referred to as bubbles or processes. The term process is not used in this context as it can be confused with concurrent task. A control transformation, shown by the dashed circle, is used to represent a control activity in the system and is defined by means of a state transition diagram. Data flows may be either discrete or continuous. Discrete data arrives at specific time intervals and so is similar to a message. Continuous data is the conventional data flow; that is, data is continuously flowing in the direction of the data flow. An event flow is a discrete signal and has no data value. It is used to indicate that some event has happened or to indicate a command.

Figure 12.1(c) shows the RTSA notation for state transition diagrams, which is the Ward/Mellor notation with one extension. States are represented by rectangles while labeled arrows represent state transitions. Associated with the transition is the input event that causes the state transition (shown above the line). The one extension to the Ward/Mellor notation is the use of conditions, in addition to events. This is in common with the NRL method, Statecharts, and ESML (Extended System Modeling Language), all of which allow events and conditions. Conditions are used as follows:

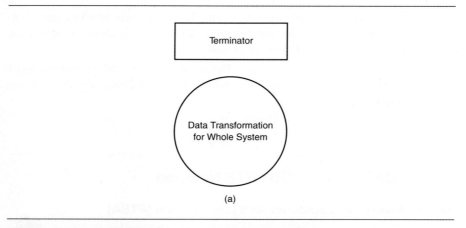

FIGURE 12.1 (a) RTSA Notation: System Context Diagram

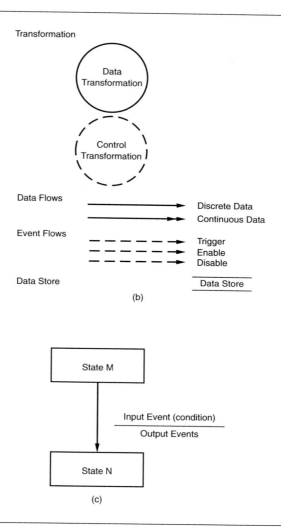

FIGURE 12.1 (b) RTSA Notation: Transformations, Flows, and Stores (c) RTSA Notation: State Transition Diagram

optionally after the input event (and shown in parentheses) is a condition that must be true, when the input event arrives, for the state transition to take place. Below the line is the output event(s) that is generated when the transition occurs. The output event triggers (T), enables (E) or disables (D) a data transformation, which performs the desired action.

12.8.2   Task Architecture Diagram Notation

The notation for task architecture diagrams is shown in Fig. 12.2. A task is indicated by a parallelogram. An information hiding module is shown by a box. Tasks interface to each other by means of messages, events, or information hiding modules. Several examples of uses of this notation follow. In the notation for loosely-coupled message communication, a message queue is used to show a loosely-coupled interface where messages may be queued up between a producer task and a consumer task. In the notation for tightly-coupled message communication with reply, the producer task sends a message to the consumer task. The consumer task then sends a reply back to the producer. This form of communication is shown by means of a message in each direction. The messages are joined showing the tight coupling. In the notation for tightly-coupled message communication without reply, the producer task sends a message to the consumer task and waits for acceptance of the message by the consumer. This form of communication is shown by means of a single message sent from producer to consumer. In the notation for event synchronization, a dormant task is awakened by an event. An event may be an external, an internal, or a timer event. An external event is an event from an external entity, typically an interrupt from an I/O

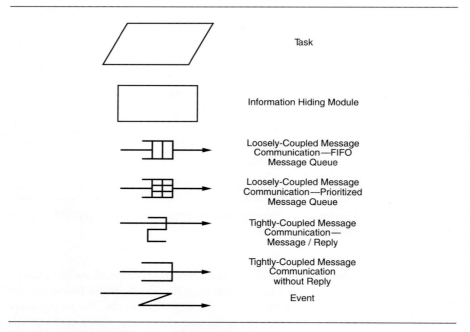

FIGURE 12.2 Task Architecture Diagram Notation

device. An internal event represents internal synchronization between a source task and a destination task. A timer event represents a periodic activation of a task. Finally, in the notation for task communication via an information hiding module, the direction of the data flow between task and module represents the direction in which the data travels, as in data flow diagrams.

12.8.3   Software Architecture Diagram Notation (SAD)

The notation for SAD is shown in Fig. 12.3. As in task architecture diagrams, a task is shown by means of a parallelogram and an information hiding module is shown by means of a rectangle. However, the notation is extended for information hiding modules. In particular, the operations of the module (procedures or functions) are explicitly shown on a SAD. The directions of the arrows on lines connected to the operations represent control flow and not data flow. Thus they represent the direction of the call from the calling task to an operation provided by the called information hiding module.

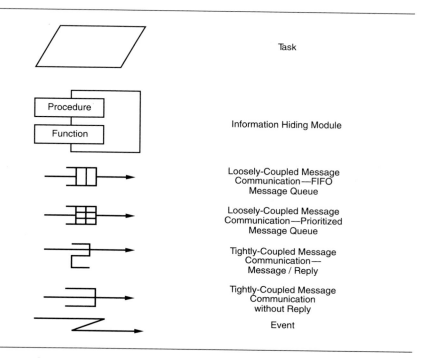

FIGURE 12.3 Software Architecture Diagram Notation

12.8.4   ADA Architecture Diagram Notation (AAD)

The notation for AAD is shown in Fig. 12.4. The AAD uses the notation used by the software architecture diagram for the information hiding module (package). However, it introduces Ada specific tasking notation. On AADs, task entries are explicitly shown. The directions of the arrows on lines connecting two tasks represent control flow and not data flow. Thus they represent the direction of the call from the calling task to an entry provided by the called task.

12.8.5   Notation for Distributed Applications

The notation for distributed applications is shown in Fig. 12.5. A distributed subsystem consists of one or more tasks that execute on the same node. Tasks in different subsystems communicate with each other by means of loosely-coupled or tightly-coupled message communication. Loosely-coupled message communication is either by means of multiple message FIFO queues, where several messages may be queued up, or single message queues, where only one message is queued up. Tightly-coupled message communication is either in the form of single client/server communication (identical to tightly-coupled message communication with reply described earlier) or multiple client/server communication. In the latter case, each client sends a message to the server and waits for a response: a queue may build up at the server.

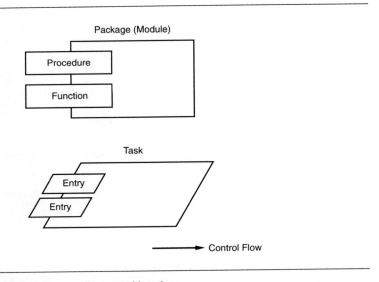

FIGURE 12.4 Ada Architecture Diagram Notation

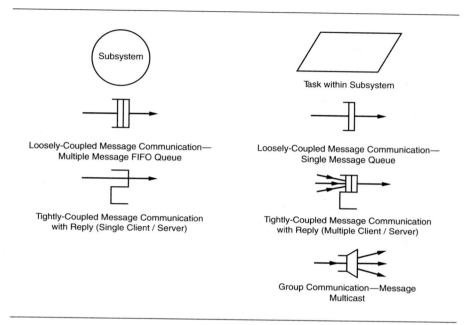

FIGURE 12.5 Notation for Distributed Applications

In distributed environments, loosely-coupled message communication is used wherever possible for greater flexibility. Group communication, where the same message is sent from a source task to all destination tasks who are members of the group (referred to as multicast communication), is also supported.

13

Analysis and Modeling for Concurrent and Real-time Systems

13.1 Introduction

Concurrent Object-Based Real-Time Analysis (COBRA) is an alternative approach to Real-Time Structured Analysis (RTSA) for analyzing and modeling the problem domain. It uses the same notation as RTSA. Subsequent CODARTS steps start with a behavioral model developed using COBRA.

As with RTSA, an environmental model and a behavioral model are developed. The environmental model describes the environment within which the system has to operate, and the inputs to the system and outputs from the system. The behavioral model describes the behavior of the system (i.e., the responses of the system to the inputs it receives from the external environment). In real-time systems, these responses are frequently state-dependent.

COBRA provides an alternative decomposition strategy for concurrent and real-time systems. The main features of COBRA are, first, its guidelines for developing the environmental model (based on the system context diagram) for concurrent and real-time systems. Second, its decomposition approach for decomposing a system into subsystems that may potentially be distributed. This is required for large systems and is based on object decomposition. A set of subsystem structuring criteria are provided. The third feature is its structuring criteria for determining the objects and functions within a subsystem. This approach is oriented towards real-time and concurrent systems by modeling each object and function as a potentially concurrent task. Finally, its behavioral approach, called behavioral analysis, for determining how the objects and functions within a subsystem interact with each other and with other subsystems. The approach uses event sequencing scenarios and may be either state-dependent or nonstate-dependent. The scenarios show the system response to incoming events from the external environment.

13.2 Developing the Environmental Model

13.2.1 Developing the System Context Diagram

The environmental model defines the boundary between the system to be developed and the external environment. It is described by means of the system context diagram, which shows the external entities that the system has to interface to, as well as the inputs to the system and outputs from the system. In concurrent and real-time systems, it is usually the case that input from and output to the external entities is via discrete data flows.

In developing the system context diagram, a key issue is that of identifying the terminators, which represent the external entities to which the system has to interface. A terminator usually represents a source of data or a sink of data. A terminator can sometimes be both a source and a sink of data. Three kinds of terminator are described in this section: terminators that represent I/O devices; terminators that represent users of the system; and terminators that represent other systems (or subsystems) to which this system has to interface.

For a real-time system, it is desirable to identify low-level terminators corresponding to the physical I/O devices to which the system has to interface. A general guideline is that a human user should only be represented as an external entity if the user interacts with the system via standard I/O devices, such as a keyboard/display. Furthermore, for those users who interact with the system via a keyboard/display, there should be one terminator for each category or type of user. On the other hand, if the user interacts with the system via system specific I/O devices, then it is these I/O devices that should be represented by terminators.

For example, in the cruise control problem, many of the inputs are initiated by the driver. One option would be to make the driver a terminator and have one data flow from the driver to the system called Driver Input. However, the driver is not a good choice for a terminator, as the driver actually interacts with the system via several I/O devices: the cruise control lever (to enter cruise control requests), the engine sensor (to switch the engine on and off), the brake sensor (to press and release the brake), calibration buttons, mileage reset buttons, and maintenance reset buttons. Consequently, each of these I/O devices should be modeled as a separate terminator. Thus there should be terminators on the context diagram for cruise control lever, brake sensor, engine sensor, calibration buttons, mileage reset buttons, and maintenance reset buttons. A complete system context diagram for the Cruise Control and Monitoring system is given in Fig. 13.1.

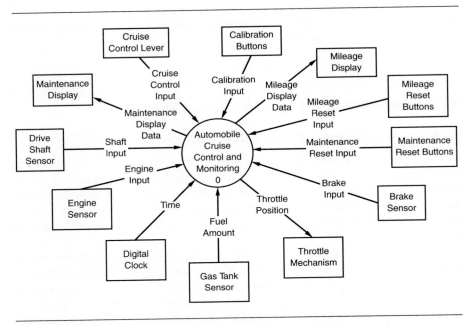

FIGURE 13.1 Cruise Control and Monitoring System Context Diagram

As an example of users interfacing to the system, consider the system context diagram for the factory automation system. There are three types of users who interact with the system via a keyboard/display: process engineers, factory operators, and production managers. Consequently, each type of user is viewed as an external entity and is represented by a terminator on the context diagram. Thus there are terminators for Process Engineer, Factory Operator, and Production Manager.

A terminator may also be used to represent an external system to which this system has to interface. For example, in the factory automation system the Assembly Robot and the Pick and Place Robot represent external systems to which the system has to interface. Communication with external systems is usually through messages.

13.2.2 Subsystem Context Diagrams

In some cases, the system to be developed is actually a large subsystem that has to interface to other subsystems. In this situation, the context diagram actually represents the boundary between the subsystem and the other subsystems and external entities it interfaces to. If a context diagram is used to represent a subsystem, then any external subsystem that this subsystem has to interface to should be shown as a terminator.

Consider the case where the Cruise Control subsystem is to be developed by a separate development team. The subsystem context diagram showing the scope of this subsystem is given in Fig. 13.2. The Monitoring subsystem, which Cruise Control has to interface to, is a subsystem terminator. The data flow, Cumulative Distance, represents the interface between the Cruise Control and Monitoring subsystems. All other terminators represent external entity terminators. Conversely, the subsystem context diagram for the Monitoring subsystem has the Cruise Control subsystem as a subsystem terminator that interfaces to the Monitoring subsystem by means of the data flow, Cumulative Distance. All other terminators represent external entity terminators.

In some cases, the subsystem represented by a terminator on the system context diagram may be developed by a different organization or may represent some existing software package that has to be interfaced to. It is particularly useful to show subsystem context diagrams when the subsystems are being developed by separate organizations and it is necessary to define precisely the interfaces between the subsystems.

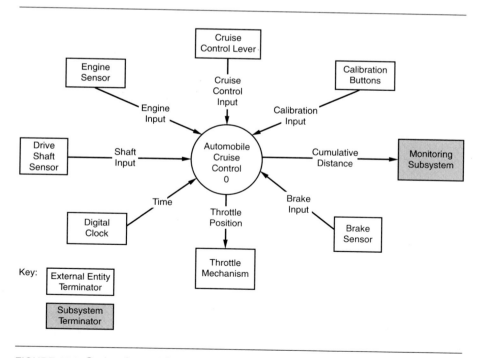

FIGURE 13.2 Cruise Control Subsystem Context Diagram

13.3 System Decomposition into Subsystems

13.3.1 Introduction

This section describes a decomposition approach for decomposing a large scale system into subsystems. A set of subsystem structuring criteria is provided to help determine the subsystems. In cases where the subsystems are part of a distributed application, additional criteria are provided for mapping to distributed nodes.

13.3.2 System Decomposition Issues

To manage the inherent complexity of large-scale software systems successfully, it is necessary to provide an approach for decomposing them into subsystems. After performing this decomposition and then carefully defining the interfaces between the subsystems, each subsystem can be designed independently. This section provides some guidelines for subsystem structuring by giving a set of subsystem structuring criteria. Here only decomposition related to the problem domain is considered. Mapping subsystems to distributed nodes is addressed later.

In analyzing the problem domain and decomposing a system into subsystems, the emphasis is on separation of concerns. Each subsystem performs a major service, which is relatively independent of the services provided by other subsystems. A subsystem may be decomposed further into smaller subsystems, consisting of a subset of the services provided by the parent subsystem.

Subsystems are relatively independent of each other and loosely coupled. Once the interface between subsystems has been defined, subsystem design can proceed independently. A subsystem performs a well-defined major service (or group of related services) of the system. A service consists of a closely related group of functions, which are supported by a collection of objects and the operations provided by these objects. Subsystems can also be decomposed further into lower-level subsystems. Eventually a subsystem is decomposed into simple (i.e., leaf-level) objects and supporting functions.

13.3.3 Characteristics of Subsystems

Although structured analysis often encourages the specifier to decompose a transformation into 7 +/– 2 lower-level transformations, for subsystem decomposition this structuring criterion is often not appropriate. Thus it is quite possible to identify only two or three subsystems when decomposing the context diagram into subsystems. In performing this decomposition, it may be necessary to iterate a few times.

A subsystem should be relatively independent of other subsystems and should therefore have low coupling with other subsystems. On the other hand, cohesion or unity between the components of the system should be high. Thus the data traffic within a subsystem may be high.

In order to ensure that there is strong cohesion within a subsystem and loose coupling between subsystems, there are certain guidelines that should be observed in decomposing the system into subsystems. The first four guidelines apply to subsystem structuring in general, whereas the fifth guideline applies if the subsystems are to be mapped to distributed nodes in a distributed environment.

1. *Aggregate object.* A subsystem supports information hiding at a more abstract level than an object. A software object can be used to model an entity in the problem domain. An aggregate object models an aggregate entity in the problem domain and is typically composed of a group of related objects that work together in a coordinated fashion, analogous to the assembly structure in manufacturing. The relationship between an aggregate object and its constituent objects is the IS-PART-OF relationship. It is often the case that multiple instances of the aggregate object (and hence multiple instances of each of the constituent objects) are needed in an application. The relationship between an aggregate object and its constituent objects can be illustrated using entity-relationship diagrams.

   An example of an aggregate object is the elevator subsystem. Each elevator aggregate object is composed of n elevator button objects, n elevator lamp objects, one elevator motor object, one elevator door object, and one floor arrival sensor object. There can be several instances of the elevator subsystem, one for each elevator.

2. A subsystem deals with a subset of the external entities shown on the context diagram. An external entity should only interface to one subsystem.

3. A data store should be encapsulated within one subsystem, which is responsible for managing the data store. Other subsystems may read or update the data store. However the data store is never at an interface between subsystems. A subsystem may encapsulate more than one data store.

4. A control object (transformation) and all the data transformations that it directly controls are all part of one subsystem and are not split between subsystems.

5. In a distributed environment, communication between distributed subsystems is only by means of discrete data flows, which represent messages that can be sent from one subsystem to another. Data stores cannot be read directly. A request must be made for the data. If an event is to be sent from subsystem to another, it is carried by a message. This guideline applies to subsystems that are to be mapped to a distributed environment, in which case communication between subsystems is restricted to messages.

13.3.4 Subsystem Structuring Criteria

The decomposition of a system into subsystems is based on the nature of service provided by the subsystem. It may be possible to recognize major subsystems by looking for major services to be provided in the user requirements document. For example, it is possible to recognize from the problem definition for the Cruise Control and Monitoring system that there are two major services to be performed: Automobile Cruise Control and Automobile Monitoring (Fig. 13.3).

In general, however, it is preferable to provide criteria for determining subsystems. Although subsystems are likely to be application dependent, some of the services that are provided by subsystems in concurrent, real-time, or distributed application domains are described next. For a given application, there may be several instances of a given subsystem.

Real-time Control.   In this kind of subsystem, the subsystem controls a given aspect of the system. The subsystem receives its inputs from the external environment and generates outputs to the external environment, usually without any human intervention. In some cases, it is possible that some input data may be gathered by some other subsystem(s) and used by this subsystem. Alternatively, this subsystem may provide some data for use by other subsystems.

An example of a real-time control subsystem is the Automobile Cruise Control subsystem (Fig. 13.3). This subsystem receives its inputs from the cruise control lever, brake, and engine. Its outputs control the throttle. Decisions about what adjustments should be made to the throttle are made without human intervention.

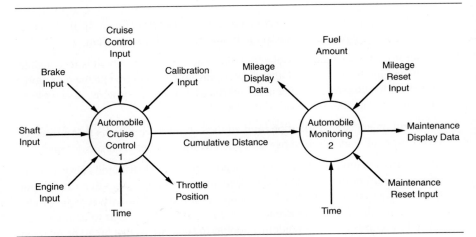

FIGURE 13.3 Cruise Control and Monitoring System: Decomposition into Subsystems

Real-time Coordination.   In cases where there is more than one real-time control subsystem, it is sometimes necessary to have a real-time coordination subsystem, which coordinates the real-time control subsystems. If the multiple real-time control subsystems are completely independent of each other, then no coordination is required. Another possibility is for the real-time control subsystems to coordinate activities among themselves. This is usually possible if the coordination is relatively simple. However, if the coordination activity requires some relatively complex algorithm, then it is often more advantageous to have a separate real-time coordination subsystem. For example, the real-time coordination subsystem may decide what item of work a real-time control subsystem should do next.

An example of a real-time coordination subsystem is the Scheduler subsystem in the Elevator Control system. In this system, any service request made by a passenger in a given elevator has to be handled by that elevator. However, when a service request is made by a prospective passenger at a floor, a decision has to be made concerning which elevator should service that request. If there is an elevator already on its way to this floor and moving in the desired direction, then no special action is required. However, if this is not the case, then an elevator needs to be dispatched to this floor. The decision made about this will usually take into account the proximity of the elevators to this floor and the direction in which they are heading. This decision can be handled by a Scheduler subsystem, as shown in Fig. 13.4, which receives a Service Request from the Floor subsystem, decides whether an elevator should be dispatched to the floor, and if so, sends a Scheduler Request to the selected Elevator.

Data Collection.   This kind of subsystem collects data from the external environment. In some cases, it stores the data, possibly after collecting, analyzing, and reducing it. Depending on the application, the subsystem responds to requests for values of the data. Alternatively the subsystem passes on the data in reduced form; for example, it might collect several raw sensor readings and pass on the average value converted to engineering units. In other cases it might output results directly to the external environment. Some combination of the above is also possible.

An example of a data collection subsystem is the Sensor Data Collection subsystem (Fig. 13.5), which collects raw data from a variety of digital and analog sensors in real-time. The frequency with which the data is collected depends on the characteristics of the sensors. Data collected from analog sensors is converted to engineering units. Processed sensor data is sent to consumer subsystems such as the Sensor Data Analysis subsystem.

Data Analysis.   This kind of subsystem analyzes data and provides reports and/or displays for data collected by another subsystem. It is possible for a subsystem to provide both data collection and data analysis, as is the case with the Automobile Monitoring subsystem (Fig. 13.3). In some cases data collection is done in real-time, whereas data analysis is a non–real-time activity.

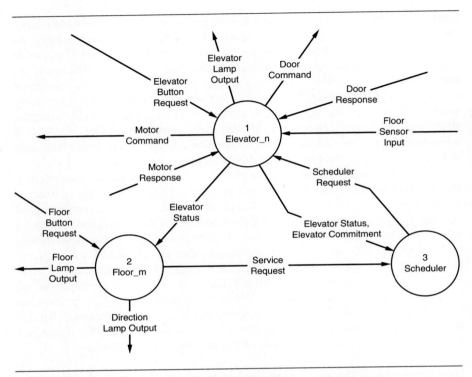

FIGURE 13.4 Elevator Control System: Decomposition into Subsystems

An example of a data analysis subsystem is the Sensor Data Analysis subsystem, shown in Fig. 13.5, which receives sensor data from Sensor Data Collection subsystem. The Sensor Data Analysis subsystem analyzes current and historical sensor data, performing statistical analysis such as computing the means and standard deviations, produces trend reports, and generates alarms if disturbing trends are detected.

Server.   This kind of subsystem provides a service for other subsystems. It responds to requests from client subsystems. It does not, however, initiate any requests. Frequently, the server provides services that are associated with a data store or set of related data stores. Alternatively, the server may be associated with an I/O device or set of related I/O devices.

An example of a data store server is the Sensor Data Server, shown in Fig. 13.5, which stores current and historical sensor data. It receives new sensor data from the Sensor Data Collection subsystem. Sensor data is requested by other subsystems such as the Operator Services subsystem, which displays the data. Other examples of servers are File Servers and Line Printer Servers. Server subsystems are frequently used in distributed applications.

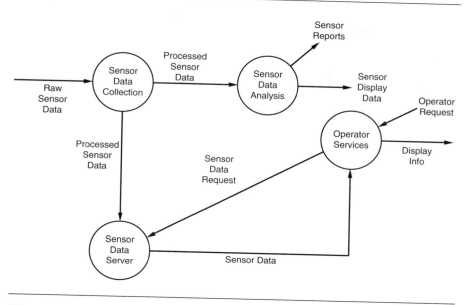

FIGURE 13.5 Example of Subsystems

User Services.   This kind of subsystem provides the user interface and a set of services required by a group of users. There may be more than one User Services subsystem, one for each category of user. An example of a user services subsystem for factory operators is Operator Services, as shown in Figure 13.5.

System Services.   Certain services are not problem domain specific, but provide system level services, such as file management and network communications management. Although these subsystems are not usually developed as part of the application, it should be recognized that they exist, as system level services are provided by these subsystems and are used by the application subsystems.

13.3.5   Examples of System Decomposition

In the Cruise Control and Monitoring system, an analysis of the problem indicates that there are two relatively independent and loosely-coupled subsystems: the Cruise Control subsystem and the Monitoring subsystem (Fig. 13.3). The Cruise Control subsystem is a real-time control subsystem, while the Monitoring subsystem provides data collection and analysis. By analyzing the problem further, the interface between the two subsystems can be determined. Thus, the only data item needed by both subsystems is Cumulative Distance, which is computed by Cruise Control and used by Monitoring.

Once the two subsystems have been determined, each of the data transformations on the subsystem data flow diagram represents the context for that subsystem. In fact, it is possible to draw a context diagram for each of the subsystems. These subsystem context diagrams represent a decomposition of the system context diagram and represent the division of responsibility among the subsystems. The development of each subsystem may then proceed independently. Thus two subsystem context diagrams may be drawn for the Cruise Control and Monitoring subsystems. In the Cruise Control subsystem context diagram in Fig. 13.2, the Monitoring subsystem is a terminator, while the Monitoring subsystem context diagram has the Cruise Control subsystem as a terminator. It should also be noted that each external entity terminator only interfaces to one subsystem (apart from the Digital Clock, which is actually a system service provided by the operating system).

As another example, consider the elevator control system (Fig. 13.4). By analyzing the problem, it is determined that elevators and floors are separate aggregate objects. Each elevator aggregate object is composed of n elevator button objects, n elevator lamp objects, one elevator motor object, one elevator door object, and one floor arrival sensor object. Furthermore, each elevator aggregate object is composed of the same objects. On the other hand, a floor aggregate object consists of two floor buttons (up and down requests), two floor lamps, and two direction lamps, except for the top and bottom floors, which only have one of each. The number of floors is usually different from the number of elevators, but each floor has the same constituent objects. Thus in the elevator system, the system is decomposed into a Floor subsystem and an Elevator subsystem. The Elevator subsystem is a real-time control subsystem, while the Floor subsystem is a data collection subsystem. There is one instance of the Floor subsystem for each floor and one instance of the Elevator subsystem for each elevator. With multiple elevators, it is necessary to coordinate the activities of the elevators, in particular when a floor request is made, it has to be serviced by a specific elevator. A real-time coordination subsystem (the Scheduler) is therefore needed, which schedules each floor request to a given elevator.

13.4   Notation for Behavioral Model

13.4.1   Real-Time Structured Analysis Notation

This section describes the notation used by COBRA. The behavioral model consisting of objects and functions is represented using the Ward/Mellor Real-Time Structured Analysis (RTSA) notation. The behavioral model is represented by a hierarchical set of data flow/control flow diagrams. At non-leaf levels of the hierarchy, a data transformation is used to represent a subsystem, which may in turn be decomposed into lower-level subsystems, or consist of objects and functions supported by the subsystem. At the leaf levels of the hierarchy, control transformations are used to represent control objects, while data transformations are used to represent non-control objects and functions. The products of a COBRA specification are similar to those for an RTSA specification, consisting of a system context diagram, a hierarchical set of data flow/control flow diagrams, a data dictionary, mini-specifications for the lowest-level data transformations, and state transition diagram defining each control trans-formation.

This section emphasizes the control aspects of the notation, which is represented by means of state transition diagrams, event flows, and integrating state transition diagrams with data flow diagrams through the use of control transformations.

13.4.2   State Transition Diagrams

As the RTSA solution to the Cruise Control problem showed, only having events and no conditions resulted in more states. Using the approach of allowing a state transition to have an optional condition associated with it, can result in a significant reduction in the number of states.

A simplified state transition diagram using the Ward/Mellor RTSA notation, with the one extension of allowing conditions as well as events, is shown for the Cruise Control system (Fig. 13.6). States are represented by rectangles while labeled arrows represent state transitions. Associated with the transition is the input event that causes the state transition. Optionally, there may be a boolean condition, which must be true when the event occurs for the state transition to take place.

For example, if the Accel event arrives when the current state is Initial, the transition to Accelerating state only occurs if the condition (Brake=Off) is true. An optional output event is generated when the transition occurs. The output event triggers (T), enables (E), or disables (D) a data transformation, which then performs a specific action.

13.4.3   Event Flows

An event flow is a discrete signal and has no data value. It is used to indicate that some event has happened or to indicate a command. RTSA supports three types of event flows (indicated by dashed arcs between nodes) to represent control flow. The first type is trigger. A **trigger event flow** represents a stimulus that occurs at a specific instant. (Examples are Brake Pressed and Brake Released.) Trigger event flows may originate from the external environment or be generated by data transformations or control transformations. Trigger event flows generated by control transformations can be used to activate a data transformation to perform a specific action. A trigger event flow can be used also to control the external environment; for example, to switch an external device on or off. The second type of event flow is enable. An **enable event flow** also activates a data transformation. However, the transformation remains

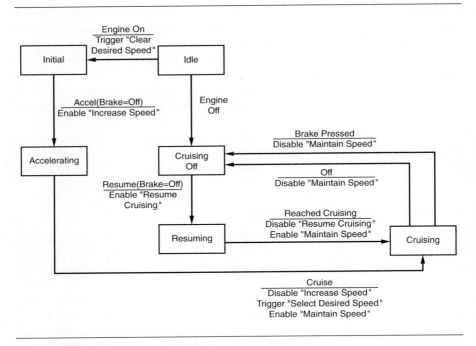

FIGURE 13.6 State Transition Diagram

enabled until it is disabled by a subsequent disable event flow. Enable event flows are only generated by control transformations. The third type of event flow is disable. A **disable event flow** deactivates a previously-enabled data transformation. Disable event flows are only generated by control transformations. Enable and disable event flows are always used in pairs.

13.4.4 Control Transformations

A control transformation is defined by means of a state transition diagram and it is represented by a dashed circle. In the Ward/Mellor approach, only event flows are inputs to or outputs from a control transformation. Input event flows to a control transformation may be trigger event flows from the external environment or from data transformations. They also be trigger, enable, or disable event flows sent by other control transformations. An input event flow into a control transformation can cause a state transition. For example, in Fig. 13.6, if the state transition diagram is in Accelerating state, the input event flow Cruise into the Cruise Control control transformation (Fig. 13.7), which corresponds to the Cruise event on the state transition diagram, will cause a state transition to Cruising state.

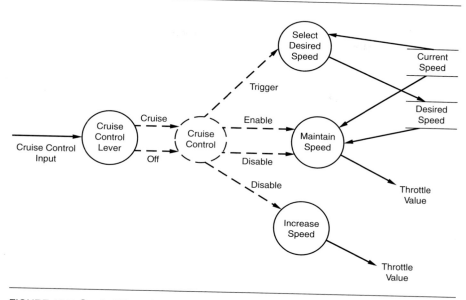

FIGURE 13.7 Control Transformation and Controlled Data Transformations

Output event flows from a control transformation may be trigger event flows to the external environment (e.g., to switch devices on or off). They may also be trigger, enable, or disable event flows to data transformations or other control transformations. An output event flow can trigger a data transformation, so that the data transformation is activated to perform a specific action and then it voluntarily terminates; enable a data transformation, so that the data transformation is activated to perform a cyclic action; or disable a previously enabled data transformation.

It is possible to have more than one output event flow associated with a transition. It is usually the case that the actions activated by the output event flows are independent of each other. However, if the actions are related, then it is important to ensure that certain conventions are observed as events occur in a certain sequence, although the time to perform them is considered negligible. Thus it is necessary to consider events associated with leaving the old state, events associated with the transition to the new state, and events associated with entering the new state:

a. Disable event flows are sent first, since they deactivate actions that were active in the previous state;

b. Trigger event flows are sent next, since they cause actions that take place during the state transition; and

c. Enable event flows are sent last, since they activate actions that are initiated on entry into the next state.

Thus it is possible to interpret a Disable, a Trigger, and an Enable event flow associated with one state transition in an unambiguous way. For example, the state transition diagram in Fig. 13.6 shows that in the transition from Accelerating State to Cruising state, Increase Speed is disabled (it was active throughout Accelerating State), then Select Desired Speed is triggered, then Maintain Speed is enabled (it will remain active throughout Cruising state).

13.4.5 Data Transformations

Unlike Structured Analysis, a control transformation may control the execution of a data transformation. in RTSA. These controlled data transformations are initially inactive. A control transformation activates a data transformation either by a trigger event flow or by an enable event flow.

In RTSA and COBRA, a data transformation is inactive unless there is some specific action for it to perform. A data transformation may be activated by a trigger or enable event flow from a control transformation, a discrete data flow or event flow from another data transformation, or a timer event if the data transformation is to perform a periodic action.

An example of a data transformation, Select Desired Speed, triggered by the control transformation Cruise Control, is shown in Fig. 13.7. An example of a data transformation, Maintain Cruising Speed, which is enabled by the control transformation Cruise Control and subsequently disabled, is shown in Fig. 13.7.

It should always be clear from the data flow/control flow diagram which inputs can activate a data transformation. For this reason, timer events that activate data transformations should always be shown explicitly. Continuous data flow inputs and data flow inputs from a data store cannot activate a data transformation. They correspond to read operations.

13.4.6 Mini-specifications

Like RTSA, in COBRA leaf-level data transformations are defined by means of mini-specifications. A control transformations does not need a mini-specification as it is fully defined by means of a state transition diagram or table. An example of a mini-specification for a triggered data transformation, Select Desired Speed, follows:

```
FUNCTION Select Desired Speed
a. Inputs:
Event flow input: Trigger
Data store input: Current Speed
b. Outputs:
Data store output: Desired Speed
c. Pseudocode:
LOOP
```

```
WHEN TRIGGER EVENT Received
   Read Current Speed
   Set Desired Speed = Current Speed
END LOOP
```

An example of a mini-specification for an enabled/disabled data transformation, Maintain Speed, is given next:

```
FUNCTION Maintain Speed
a. Inputs:
Event flow input: Enable/Disable
Data store inputs: Current Speed, Desired Speed
b. Outputs:
Data flow output: Throttle Value
c. Pseudocode:
LOOP
WHEN Enable Event Received
DO PERIODICALLY UNTIL DISABLED
   Read Current Speed
   Read Desired Speed
   Delta Speed = Current Speed - Desired Speed
   Compute Throttle Value given Delta Speed
   If Absolute Value (Throttle Value) > Minimum Value
      THEN Output Throttle Value
END DO
END LOOP
```

13.4.7   Data Definition

Other aspects of the RTSA notation are also used by COBRA. Thus a data dictionary is used to define all data and event flows. For those applications that have complex data relationships, entity-relationship diagrams are used to show the relationships between the data stores of the system [Yourdon89]. They are used for identifying the data stores (either internal data structures or files) and for defining the contents (attributes) of the stores.

13.5   Modeling Objects in the Problem Domain

13.5.1   Introduction

This section describes criteria for determining concurrent objects in a behavioral model of the problem domain. The goal is to assist the designer in structuring a system or subsystem into objects and related functions. The objective is to first determine the objects in the problem domain, then to determine the functions that interact with these objects.

In order to give maximum flexibility to the designer at the modeling phase, each leaf-level object and function is viewed as being potentially concurrent; that is, it can execute concurrently with other objects or functions. However, no concurrency is allowed within a leaf-level object or function. Thus the behavioral model is highly concurrent.

The approach used for identifying objects is to look for real-world objects in the problem domain and then design corresponding objects in the software system that models the real world. To avoid confusion between real-world objects (real "things") and software objects (software "things"), the term entity is used to describe a real-world "thing." The term object is only used to describe a software "thing" that models a real-world entity. Thus for each real-world entity in the problem domain, there should be a corresponding software object in the model of the real world.

Some object-oriented analysis methods provide criteria for determining objects in the problem domain [Coad91, Shlaer88], which are mostly oriented toward information systems. For the domain of concurrent and real-time systems, the following criteria are considered most useful for determining objects in the problem domain.

13.5.2   External Device I/O Objects

A concrete entity in the application domain is an entity that exists in the real world and has some physical attributes. For every concrete entity in the real world that is relevant to the application domain, there should be a corresponding software object in the system. For example, in the cruise control system, the drive shaft, brake, engine, and cruise control lever are all relevant real-world concrete entities since they impact the cruise control system, whereas the wheels do not. In the software system, the relevant concrete entities are modeled by means of drive shaft, brake, engine, and cruise control lever software objects respectively.

In concurrent real-time systems, it is often the case that real-world concrete entities interface to the system via sensors and actuators. These entities provide inputs to the system via sensors or are controlled by the system via actuators. Thus to the software system, the concrete entities are actually I/O devices that provide inputs to and receive outputs from the system. As the concrete entities correspond to I/O devices, the software objects that model these entities are often referred to as external device I/O objects or device I/O objects.

For example, in the cruise control system, the drive shaft, brake, engine, and cruise control lever are all real world entities that have sensors (input devices), which provide inputs to the system. The throttle is a real world entity that is controlled by the system via an actuator (output device) and receives outputs from the system.

Each software objects hides the details of the interface to the real world entity that it receives input from or provides outputs to. However, a software object models the events experienced by the concrete entity to which it corresponds. The events experienced by the entity are inputs to the system, particularly to the software object that models the entity. In this way, the software object can simulate the behavior of the entity. In the case of a concrete entity that is controlled by the system, the software object that models the entity outputs an event that constrains the behavior of the entity.

In some applications, there may be many concrete entities of the same type. These are modeled by means of one device I/O object for each concrete entity, where all the objects are of the same type. For example in the elevator control system, there are many button objects of the same type and many lamp objects of the same type.

As concrete real world entities interface directly to the system, they should appear as terminators on the system context diagram. The external events are generated by the source terminators and are inputs to the system. Sink terminators receive outputs from the system.

For each terminator on the context diagram that represents an I/O device, there should be a corresponding external device I/O object that interfaces to that terminator. A device is usually an input or an output device. However, a complex I/O device may support both input and output. An external device I/O object is represented by a data transformation on a data flow diagram. The data transformation represents both the object and the operations it supports.

An example of external device I/O objects is given in Fig. 13.8 for the engine and brake sensors. The engine sensor and brake sensors are each represented by a terminator on the context diagram. Each input device also has a concurrent object to

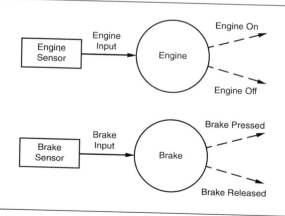

FIGURE 13.8 Device I/O Objects

interface to it. Thus the Engine object reads inputs from the engine sensor, while the Brake object reads inputs from the brake sensor.

As the system context diagram is used as a means of depicting the physical entities that interface to the system, and these real-world physical entities are modeled by means of software objects, deriving the system context diagram is an important activity. Thus developing the system context diagram and deriving the external device I/O objects in the system is often an iterative activity.

13.5.3   User Role Objects

A user role object models a role played in the application domain, typically by a user. A role is a sequence of related actions performed sequentially by a user. For example in a factory automation system, there are roles played by the operator, process engineer, and manufacturing engineer. If a user can play two or more independent roles, then this may be represented by a different object for each role. For example, it is possible for the same user to play both a factory supervisor role and an operator role. It is also possible to have multiple users, each playing the same role. For example, there may be several operators in the factory automation domain. In that case, there are multiple objects of the same type.

In addition to terminators that represent I/O devices on the system context diagram, there are terminators that represent type of users who interface to the system. There should be a terminator for each type of user who interfaces to the system. For each user I/O terminator on the system context there is a corresponding user role object (or potentially user services aggregate object reflecting a whole subsystem), which defines the role of the user. The user role object interacts with the real-world user to perform some user requested service. An example of a user role object is Operator Interface, which accepts operator commands, reads from the sensor data store, and displays data to the operator.

13.5.4   Control Objects

A control object is an active abstract object in the problem domain that has different states and controls the behavior of other objects and functions. A control object is defined by means of a finite state machine, which is represented by a state transition diagram or state transition table. State transitions may have optional conditions associated with them. A control object receives incoming events that cause state transitions. It generates output events that control other objects or functions. An example of a control object is the Cruise Control object, which is defined by means of the Cruise Control state transition diagram (Fig. 13.6).

In a real-time control system or subsystem, there are usually one or more control objects. If there are several different control objects, then each control object is defined by a state transition diagram and represented by a control transformation. In the cruise control example there are two control objects, Cruise Control and Calibration Control. Each is defined by its own state transition diagram.

It is also possible to have multiple control objects of the same type. Each object executes an instance of the same finite state machine (state transition diagram), although each object is likely to be in a different state. An example of this is from the elevator control system, where the control aspects of each elevator are modeled by means of a control object, Elevator Control, and defined by means of a state transition diagram. Consequently, each elevator has an Elevator Control object.

A control object is represented by means of a control transformation and defined by means of a state transition diagram. The inputs to the control object are input event flows, which correspond to the events that cause state transitions on the state transition diagram. Output events that result from state transitions are represented by output event flows leaving the control transformation. For example, the control transformation for the Cruise Control object is depicted in Fig. 13.7, which executes the state transition diagram shown in Fig. 13.6.

Concurrent finite state machines are addressed in COBRA by having one control object for each finite state machine. The finite state machines may communicate indirectly by having their control objects send events to each other.

13.5.5 Data Abstraction Objects

For every entity in the application domain that needs to be remembered, there should be a corresponding data abstraction object. These objects model the real world entities by encapsulating the data that needs to be remembered as well as supporting the operations on that data. Locations and organizations are examples of objects that need to be remembered.

A data abstraction object is a passive object. The basis for a data abstraction object is a data store, which is a repository of data, typically shown on a data flow diagram. Examples of data stores that form the basis for data abstraction objects are the Current Speed and Desired Speed data stores shown in Fig. 13.7.

The basic operations required to access the data store, such as read and write operations, are associated with the data store. However, it is often the case that more complex operations can be provided by a data abstraction object, which is sometimes more difficult to determine. This is described further in Chapter 15.

It should be noted that, as server subsystems encapsulate data stores, they are actually composed of data abstraction objects. In the simplest case, a server subsystem could consist of a single data abstraction object. In the example given in Fig. 13.5, the sensor data server subsystem contains two data abstraction objects, a digital sensor data abstraction object, and an analog sensor data abstraction object.

In applications with complex data relationships, entity-relationship modeling may be used to determine the relationships between the entities (i.e., the data abstraction objects) and the attributes of each data abstraction object. This is described in more detail in several textbooks including [Rumbaugh91, Shlaer88].

13.5.6 Algorithm Objects

An algorithm object encapsulates an algorithm used in the problem domain. This kind of object is more prevalent in real-time domains. For example, in the Elevator Control system, there is an algorithm object, the Scheduler object, which encapsulates the algorithm used for determining what elevator should service a given floor request (Fig. 13.4). It should be noted that the Scheduler subsystem consists of a single object, the Scheduler object.

13.6   Modeling Functionality in the Problem Domain

13.6.1 Introduction

In addition to modeling objects in the problem domain, it is necessary to model the functions that are supported by these objects or alternatively interact with these objects. Certain functions can be immediately associated with objects. However, with other—usually internal—functions, it is often not obvious which object or objects they should be associated with. In state-dependent systems, it is the functions that are activated as a result of state transitions. Furthermore, in real-time systems, there is the added complication that timing considerations are usually associated with functions and only indirectly with objects.

Once the objects have been determined using the object structuring criteria, the next step is to determine the functions that the system has to perform. Each function is a sequential activity that potentially may execute concurrently with other objects and functions. These functions are represented by means of data transformations on the data flow /control flow diagrams. The following sections provide a taxonomy of the functions that are typically needed in a behavioral model.

13.6.2 Functions Supported by Objects

The functions associated with an object are eventually mapped to the operations supported by the object. In COBRA, an object represented by a data transformation can be decomposed to show the functions it supports, which are also represented by data transformations.

Thus, in the case of a device I/O object, the functions that deal with reading from or writing to the device are supported by that device I/O object. For example, the Motor device I/O object shown in Fig. 13.9(a) supports three operations: Start Moving Up, Start Moving Down, and Stop Motor. These three functions represent the decomposition of the Motor object and are shown explicitly in Fig. 13.9(b). Figures 13.9(a) and (b) are two alternative ways of depicting Motor, the first an object perspective and the second a functional perspective.

The Motor object receives trigger event flows from Elevator Control. When the functions being triggered are not shown explicitly [as in Fig. 13.9(a)], the convention is to name the event flows (e.g., Up, Down, and Stop). When the functions being triggered are described explicitly, the event flow names could be omitted and replaced by "Trigger," as shown in Fig. 13.9(c).

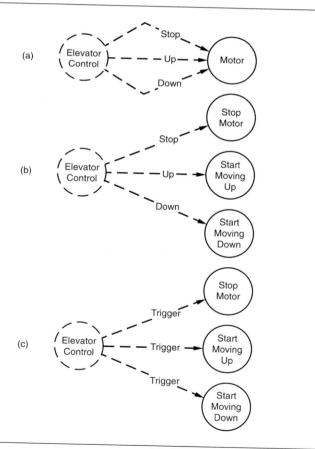

FIGURE 13.9 Functions Provided by Object

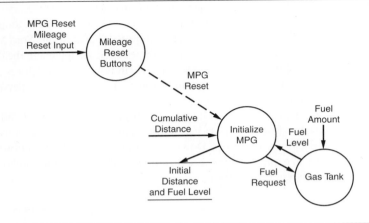

FIGURE 13.10 Asynchronous Function

13.6.3 Asynchronous Function

An asynchronous function is activated by another object or function to perform some action. Often it is activated by a device input object. It can be activated by either a discrete data flow or an event flow from another data transformation representing an object or function. An example of an asynchronous function is the Initialize MPG function (Fig. 13.10), which is activated on demand whenever there is a MPG Reset event flow sent by the Mileage Reset Buttons object.

13.6.4 Asynchronous State Dependent Function

An asynchronous state-dependent function is activated by a control object to perform a given action. Usually this is a "one-shot" action; that is, it performs the action once and then voluntarily stops. Conceptually, such a function executes during the transition from one state to another. An asynchronous state-dependent function is represented by a data transformation on a data flow/control flow diagram, which is triggered by an event flow arriving from a control object (transformation).

An example of an asynchronous state-dependent function is Selected Desired Speed, shown in Fig. 13.7. Select Desired Speed is initially inactive. It is activated by the trigger event flow from the control object Cruise Control. Select Desired Speed then performs a one-shot action, which consists of it reading the Current Speed data store and storing its value as Desired Speed. It then voluntarily stops. This function is executed during the transition from Accelerating state to Cruising state on the Cruise Control state transition diagram (Fig. 13.6).

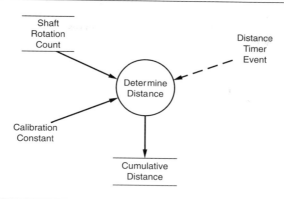

FIGURE 13.11 Periodic Function

13.6.5   Periodic Function

A periodic function is activated at regular intervals to perform some action. The frequency with which a periodic function is activated is application dependent. A periodic function is represented by a data transformation, which is activated periodically by a timer event.

An example of a periodic function is Determine Distance (Fig. 13.11), which is periodically activated by a timer event and then computes the distance travelled by the vehicle. It should be noted that timer events that cause a data transformation to be activated should always be shown explicitly on a data flow diagram.

13.6.6   Periodic State-dependent Function

A periodic state-dependent function is activated by a control object to perform some action that needs to be done at regular intervals. It is activated on entry into a state and de-activated on leaving a state, usually the same state. Normally such a transformation is enabled but in some cases it may be triggered. In most cases, the periodic state-dependent function performs its actions while the system or subsystem is in a given state or group of states. The difference between the periodic function and the periodic state-dependent function is that the latter only performs its action periodically in one (or more) state(s), while the former is activated periodically independent of state.

An example of a periodic state-dependent transformation is Maintain Cruising Speed, shown in Fig. 13.7. Maintain Speed is initially inactive. It is activated by the Enable event flow, which is sent by the Cruise Control object when it transitions into

Cruising state. Maintain Cruising Speed then periodically adjusts the throttle value in order to maintain the current speed of the vehicle at the cruising speed. This requires it to periodically read the Current Speed and Desired Speed data stores and to adjust the throttle value so as to maintain the cruising speed. Maintain Cruising Speed is deactivated by a Disable event flow, which is sent by the control object Cruise Control when it leaves Cruising state (Fig. 13.6).

13.7   Behavioral Analysis

13.7.1   Introduction

Behavioral analysis is a strategy used to help determine how the objects and functions within a subsystem interact with each other. Scenarios are developed for sequences of external events. A scenario shows a sequence of external events, as well as the sequence of internal events that result from the arrival of each external event. It also shows the eventual system response, which is frequently state dependent.

The behavioral analysis approach is iterative. After a first attempt at determining subsystems, an attempt is made at determining the objects and functions within the subsystem. An analysis is then made of how the objects and functions interact with each other. Behavioral analysis may show that there is a need for further objects and functions. It may also show that certain events are so loosely coupled that they should be handled by a different subsystem. Alternatively, the analysis may reveal that other events, initially handled by a different subsystem, may be tightly coupled with this subsystem and therefore should be part of it. Behavioral analysis may be either state dependent or non-state dependent.

13.7.2   Scenarios

A scenario is developed by identifying a typical sequence of external events that the system experiences. The scenario is manually executed (i.e., by walking through it) to determine the sequence of internal events that are initiated by the arrival of each external event. The sequence of events are numbered and shown on a version of the data flow/control flow diagram, which is referred to as an event sequence diagram. In behavioral analysis, an event is considered to be any discrete input to a control or data transformation. Thus an event can be an event flow or a discrete data flow. A discrete data flow corresponds to a message, and it is the event representing the arrival of the data flow that is of primary importance in an event sequence diagram, rather than the data associated with it.

13.7.3 State Dependent Behavioral Analysis

In state dependent behavioral analysis, the objective is to determine the interaction between the device I/O objects, the control objects and the state transition diagrams they execute, and the objects and functions whose execution is controlled (i.e., triggered, enabled, and disabled) by the control object.

There are three main steps in the state dependent behavioral analysis strategy. The first, **build the scenarios,** includes the four following steps:

a. Initial object determination. Using the object structuring criteria, a first attempt is made at determining the objects in the system or subsystem;

b. Develop state transition diagram for the system or subsystem. This necessitates determining the externally visible states of the system/subsystem, and the events that arrive directly or indirectly from the external environment to cause the system/subsystem to change state. Develop a control object to execute the state transition diagram;

c. Define external events. Consider each external entity that interfaces to this subsystem and define the external events that it generates or outputs that it receives. Primary emphasis is placed on source entities since they generate events that potentially cause the system to change state. Each external entity should generate at least one external event that causes some state change or receive some output generated by the subsystem. If not, then the entity probably does not have a role to play in this subsystem; and

d. Develop scenarios. Use the state transition diagram and the list of external events to develop one or more scenarios. Each scenario consists of a sequence of external events that the system experiences.

In the second main step, **execute each scenario.** The scenario is executed. As each external event is executed in sequence, the following steps are performed:

a. For each event that leads to a state transition, determine the input from the external environment that is required to generate this event. Determine the device I/O object needed to read this input and generate the appropriate trigger event flow to the control object, which executes the state transition diagram;

b. For each state transition, determine all the actions that result from this change in state. Determine all objects and/or state dependent functions required to perform these actions. In the case of an object, it is necessary to consider which of the functions it supports is to perform the action. In the case of a function being activated, it is necessary to determine whether the function should be triggered or enabled. It is also necessary to determine if any function(s) should be disabled;

c. For each triggered or enabled object or function, determine what outputs it generates and whether these outputs are written to a data store for later use, output to the external environment, or passed on to another object or function; and

d. Show the external event and the subsequent internal events on both the state transition diagram and a partial data flow/control flow diagram, which is referred to as an event sequence diagram. The events are numbered to show the sequence in which they are executed.

The third and final step is **completing the scenarios.** It is necessary to ensure that the executed scenarios have driven the state transition diagram through every state and every state transition at least once, and that each action has been performed at least once, so that each state dependent function has been either triggered, or enabled and subsequently disabled.

13.8   Example of State Dependent Behavioral Analysis

The behavioral analysis strategy is best illustrated by means of a detailed example showing several intermediate steps, rather than just the final solution. The following Cruise Control subsystem example shows the main points of this strategy.

13.8.1   Initial Object Determination

An initial attempt is made at determining the objects in the Cruise Control subsystem. A control object Cruise Control is required, which will execute the controlling state transition diagram for the subsystem. Device input objects are Cruise Control Lever, Engine, and Brake. Each of these objects corresponds to a concrete entity in the real world. In each case, the name of the object reflects the fact that the object hides the interface to the real-world entity and supports the function(s) to read inputs from the real-world entity. These inputs could potentially cause the Cruise Control object to change state.

The Throttle is also required since the whole purpose of this subsystem is to control the output to the throttle. It is also apparent that a Shaft object is needed for computing speed and distance travelled. However, whether it influences the Cruise Control object directly is not clear at this stage, so it is initially omitted. Other objects are to be determined later.

13.8.2   Develop State Transition Diagram

After the initial attempt at determining the objects in this subsystem, the next step is to develop the state transition diagram for the control object Cruise Control. A simplified state transition diagram is shown in Fig. 13.12, which shows the main states of the cruise control object, the most frequently used transitions, and the events that

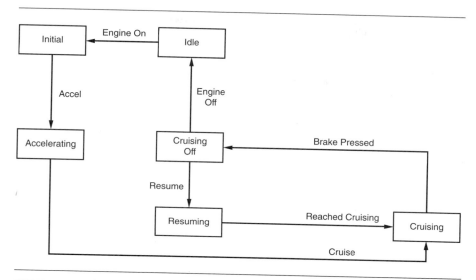

FIGURE 13.12 Cruise Control System: Simplified State Transition Diagram

cause these transitions. However, at this stage the actions that result from state transitions are not yet determined.

The states of the Cruise Control object are all externally visible states; that is, the driver of the vehicle is aware of each of these states. In fact the states represent consequences of actions taken by the driver, either directly or indirectly. A brief description of the Cruise Control states follows:

1. *Idle.* The engine is switched off;
2. *Initial.* When the driver turns the engine on, the car enters Initial state;
3. *Accelerating.* When the driver engages the cruise control lever in the ACCEL position (transition Accel), the car enters Accelerating state and accelerates automatically;
4. *Cruising.* When the driver releases the lever (transition Cruise), the current speed is saved as the cruising speed and the car enters Cruising state. In this state, the speed of the car is automatically maintained at the cruising speed;
5. *Cruising Off.* When the driver presses the brake (transition Brake Pressed), the car enters Cruising Off state and returns to manual operation, with automatic control suspended; and
6. *Resuming.* When the driver engages the cruise control lever in the RESUME position (transition Resume), the car automatically accelerates or decelerates to the last cruising speed. When it reaches the cruising speed, the car returns to Cruising state (transition Reached Cruising).

13.8.3 Define External Events

After developing the state transition diagram, it is necessary to consider the inputs from the external environment that cause the state transition diagram to change state. The input events from each real-world physical entity, represented by a source terminator on the system context diagram, are defined.

For example, for the Cruise Control problem, the source terminators represent the Cruise Control Lever, Brake, and Engine external entities. The events generated by the software objects that interface to these real-world entities are defined. The input events from the Brake object are Brake Pressed and Brake Released, while the input events generated by the cruise control lever object are Accel, Cruise, Resume, and Off.

13.8.4 Develop Scenario

Based on the state transition diagram and the list of external events, one or more scenarios, each consisting of a sequence of external events, are developed for the subsystem. A typical scenario consists of the following sequence of external events:

1. Driver engages the cruise control lever in the ACCEL position;
2. Driver releases the cruise control lever in order to cruise at a constant speed;
3. Driver presses the brake to disable cruise control; and
4. Driver engages the cruise control lever in the RESUME position to resume cruise control.

In addition, assume that the state transition diagram is in Initial state at the start of the scenario.

13.8.5 Executing the Scenario

The scenario is now executed. By manually executing this scenario, determine the device I/O objects that provide input event flows to the Cruise Control control object and the state dependent functions whose execution is controlled (i.e., triggered, enabled, and disabled) by Cruise Control. The sequence of events are numbered and shown on a version of the data flow/control flow diagram called an event sequence diagram, as shown in Fig. 13.13. The event sequence numbering is also shown on the state transition diagram (Fig. 13.14).

Consider the first external event (i.e., the driver engages the cruise control lever in the ACCEL position). The device input object, Cruise Control Lever, reads this input (event 1 on Fig. 13.13). The Cruise Control Lever object sends the Accel event flow to the Cruise Control object (event 2 on Fig. 13.13). The Cruise Control object conceptually executes the Cruise Control state transition diagram. The Accel event

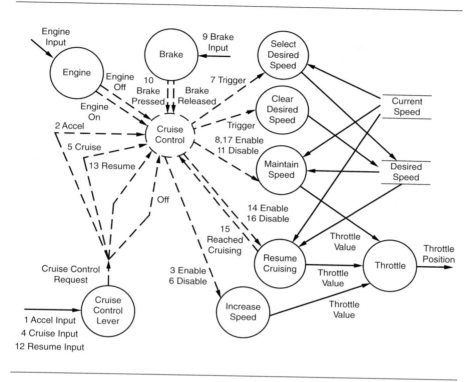

FIGURE 13.13 Event Sequence Diagram Based on Data Flow/Control Flow Diagram

flow into Cruise Control corresponds to the Accel event on the state transition diagram (STD) that causes a transition from Initial state to Accelerating state (Fig. 13.14).

Next consider what actions result from this transition. In Initial state, the car is under driver control. However, in Accelerating state, the car is under automatic control and should accelerate automatically. Thus, as a result of the transition, the state dependent function Increase Speed must be activated. To determine whether the transformation should be triggered or enabled, it is necessary to consider whether the Increase Speed transformation should be active as long as the STD is in Accelerating state or not. In fact, Increase Speed should be continuously active while the vehicle is automatically accelerating. Its function is to adjust the throttle value periodically so that the speed of the vehicle gradually increases. Increase Speed should therefore be enabled when the STD transitions from Initial to Accelerating state. This is shown as event 3 on Figs. 13.13 and 13.14. Increase Speed is thus a periodic state dependent function.

The next external event results from the driver deciding to release the cruise control lever. Cruise Control Lever reads this external input (event 4 in Fig. 13.13)

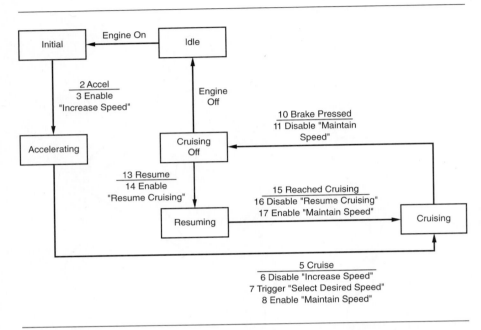

FIGURE 13.14 Cruise Control System Event Sequence Diagram Based on State Transition Diagram

and sends the Cruise event flow to Cruise Control (event 5 in Fig. 13.13). This input event causes Cruise Control to transition into Cruising state (event 5 in Fig. 13.14). Consider the actions that now need to take place, as shown on Figs. 13.13 and 13.14. The first output event flow disables Increase Speed (event 6), since the vehicle must no longer accelerate. The second action is to record the cruising speed; since this is a one shot action, it is achieved by triggering Select Desired Speed (event 7), which reads the Current Speed data store and stores this value as the Desired Speed. The third output event flow enables the function Maintain Speed (event 8), which periodically reads Current Speed and Desired Speed and adjusts the throttle value to maintain the cruising speed. In summary, the actions associated with the Cruise transition are to disable Increase Speed, trigger Select Desired Speed, and enable Maintain Speed.

The next external event occurs when the driver presses the brake because of some obstacle ahead. The Brake device input object is needed to read Brake Input (event 9 on Fig. 13.13) and generate a Brake Pressed event flow (event 10). As a result, the STD transitions from Cruising to Cruising Off state (event 10 on Fig. 13.14). The action associated with this transition is to disable the Maintain Speed transformation (event 11 on Figs. 13.13 and 13.14). The vehicle is now back under driver control.

At some later time, the driver wishes to resume cruising. The driver engages the cruise control lever in the RESUME position (event 12 on Fig. 13.13). The Cruise Control Lever object sends the Resume event flow to Cruise Control (event 13 on Fig. 13.13). As a result, the STD transitions from Cruising Off state to Resuming state (event 13 on Fig. 13.14).

The action associated with this transition is to enable the transformation Resume Cruising (event 14 on Figs. 13.13 and 13.14). Resume Cruising reads the Current Speed and Desired Speed data stores, and periodically adjusts the throttle value so that the speed of the vehicle increases or decreases to reach the cruising speed. When the car reaches cruising speed, Resume Cruising sends the Reached Cruising event flow to Cruise Control (event 15 on Fig. 13.13).

The Reached Cruising event causes the STD to transition from Resuming state back to Cruising state (event 15 on Fig. 13.14), to disable the transformation Resume Cruising (event 16 on Figs. 13.13 and 13.14), and to enable the transformation Maintain Speed (event 17 on Figs. 13.13 and 13.14).

The event sequence diagram shows the response of the system to external events, except for one where the response is to an internal event. The internal event Reached Cruising results indirectly from the previous external event, the driver engages the cruise control lever in the RESUME position.

Continuing with the scenarios, it is necessary to ensure that all states are entered and all state transitions are taken. Further analysis would lead to the addition of the Engine object and the Clear Desired Speed function. Based on this analysis, the event sequence diagram showing all the objects and functions that participated in the scenario is shown in Fig. 13.13. The device input objects are Cruise Control Lever, Brake, and Engine; the control object is Cruise Control; the device output object is Throttle; and two data stores, Current Speed and Desired Speed, form the basis of two data abstraction objects.

In addition, there are five state dependent functions, all represented by data transformations. Two of the functions, Select Desired Speed and Clear Desired Speed, are triggered and conceptually execute during a state transition. Thus they are asynchronous state dependent functions. The other three functions, Increase Speed, Maintain Speed, and Resume Cruising, are all periodic state dependent functions. Each function is enabled on entry to a given state (e.g., Maintain Speed in Cruising state), performs a periodic function while in that state (e.g., adjusting the throttle as required) until it is subsequently disabled on leaving the state.

At this stage, the transformations represent objects and functions that are all at the same level of decomposition, and are leaf transformations (i.e., are not decomposed further). As this is only part of the cruise control subsystem, it is necessary to introduce additional objects and functions, which in turn leads to a single large data flow/control flow diagram. Now that the behavioral analysis has led to a clearer understanding of the problem, the behavioral model can be restructured so that it consists of two or more levels of decomposition. Introducing additional levels of decomposition can clarify the presentation of the model, although it does not necessarily correspond to the way the problem was solved.

13.9   Non-state Dependent Behavioral Analysis

In a non-state dependent subsystem, the events generated by the external entities that interface to the subsystem are determined. For each event, the objects and functions required to process the event are considered. A device I/O object is needed for each external entity. On receipt of the external input, the device I/O object either writes the data to a data store or sends it to an internal object or function for further processing.

In the case of periodic activities (e.g., reports that are generated periodically), it is necessary to consider the timer events that lead to system outputs being generated. Each significant system output, such as a report, requires an object or function to produce the data, and then typically sends the data to a device output object.

13.10   Example of Non-state Dependent Behavioral Analysis

An example is now given of non-state dependent behavioral analysis. This is for the Average Mileage subsystem in the Monitoring subsystem. For each real-world entity that interfaces to this subsystem, a software device I/O object is needed. For this subsystem, the device input objects are Mileage Reset Buttons and Gas Tank. There is one device output object, Mileage Display.

Since this is not a state dependent subsystem, there is no control object. Consider the external events. There are two aperiodic events from the Mileage Reset Buttons: MPH reset and MPG reset. When the MPG reset button is pressed, indicating a new trip mpg computation is required, the object Mileage Reset Buttons is activated (Fig. 13.15). It sends the MPG Reset event to activate the asynchronous function Initialize MPG, which reads the current value of the Cumulative Distance data store and the current value of Fuel Level (provided by the Gas Tank device input object), and stores these values in the Initial Distance and Fuel Level data store. For MPH reset, a similar initialization is carried out except that current time is stored instead of current fuel level.

In this subsystem there are also two periodic events, MPG timer event and MPH timer event. Consider the MPG timer event. When this timer event occurs, the periodic function Compute Average MPG is activated (Fig. 13.16), which reads the current value of the Cumulative Distance data store and the current value of Fuel Level, reads the initial values from the Initial Distance and Fuel Level data store, and then computes the Average MPG. Compute Average MPG then outputs the Average MPG to the

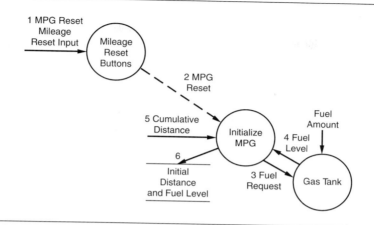

FIGURE 13.15 Behavioral Analysis: Aperiodic Event

Mileage Display device output object, which in turn outputs the data to the real-world display.

The complete picture for Average MPG is derived by combining Figs. 13.15 and 13.16 resulting in the data flow diagram shown in Fig. 13.17.

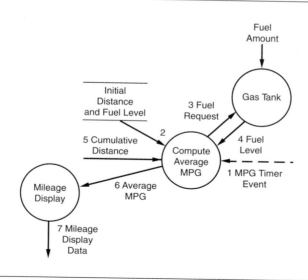

FIGURE 13.16 Behavioral Analysis: Periodic Event

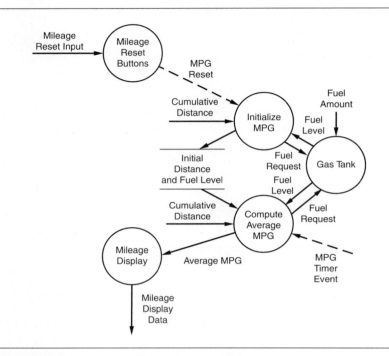

FIGURE 13.17 Initial Data Flow Diagram for Average MPG

13.11   Comparison with Other Methods

COBRA uses the RTSA notation and emphasizes the use of state transition diagrams. However, it differs from RTSA [Yourdon89] in its emphasis on concurrency and on identifying objects in the problem domain. COBRA is similar to Jackson System Development (JSD) [Cameron86] in that it models the problem domain using concurrent objects and concurrent functions. However, it provides criteria for identifying the objects in the problem domain and defines control objects by means of state transition diagrams, which are often more useful for real-time systems than JSD entity structure diagrams. As with Object-Oriented Analysis (OOA) [Shlaer88, Coad91], COBRA uses object structuring criteria. However, unlike OOA, it emphasizes concurrency and finite state machines rather than information modeling, and hence is more applicable to real-time systems. In addition, COBRA provides a comprehensive approach for behavioral analysis.

14

Task Structuring

14.1 Introduction

During the task structuring phase, the system is structured into concurrent tasks and the task interfaces are defined. In ADARTS, task structuring starts with a behavioral model developed using RTSA. In CODARTS, task structuring starts with a behavioral model developed using COBRA. The task structuring step is common to the DARTS, ADARTS, and CODARTS methods.

To help determine the concurrent tasks, task structuring criteria are provided that assist in mapping a behavioral model of the system into a concurrent-tasking architecture. These criteria are a set of heuristics, which have been determined through experience with the design of concurrent and real-time systems.

The task structuring criteria were first introduced in the DARTS design method [Gomaa84, Gomaa86] and later refined in earlier papers on ADARTS [Gomaa89b, Gomaa89c]. In this chapter, the description of the task structuring criteria is expanded substantially to provide more information on how to use them. The task structuring criteria are categorized into four broad categories. Guidelines are provided, together with examples, on how the criteria should be applied and the order in which they should be applied. The rationale for the task structuring criteria is also given.

After introducing some general aspects of Task Structuring, the task structuring categories are described, followed by a detailed description with examples of the criteria within each category (i.e., I/O task structuring criteria, internal task structuring criteria, task cohesion criteria, and task priority criteria). This is followed by some guidelines on the order of applying the task structuring criteria. Next, defining task communication and synchronization interfaces is described. Finally, guidelines are given for restructuring the design in situations where there are performance problems due to task overhead.

14.2   Concurrent Task Structuring Issues

Many advantages to having a concurrent tasking design exist. However, the designer must be careful in designing the task structure; too many tasks in a system can unnecessarily increase complexity and overhead because of the additional intertask communication and synchronization involved. The system designer therefore has to make tradeoffs between, on the one hand, introducing tasks to simplify and clarify the design and, on the other hand, not introducing too many tasks, which could make the design too complex. The task structuring criteria are intended to help the designer make these tradeoffs. They also allow the designer to experiment with different tradeoffs by trying alternative task structures.

The concurrent structure of a system is best understood by considering the dynamic aspects of the system. In the behavioral model, the system is modeled as a collection of concurrent objects and/or functions, which communicate by means of discrete event flows and data flows (messages). During the task structuring phase, the concurrent nature of the system is formalized by defining the concurrent tasks and the communication/synchronization interfaces between them.

The main consideration in decomposing a software system into concurrent tasks concerns the asynchronous nature of the objects and functions in the system, as represented by the data and control transformations on the data flow/control flow diagrams that comprise the behavioral model. The term transformation in the behavioral model refers to either an object or function. The data and control transformations of the behavioral model are analyzed to determine which may run concurrently and which needs to execute sequentially. Transformations that execute concurrently are structured into separate tasks. A set of transformations that is constrained to execute sequentially is grouped into the same task. Thus a task may encompass one or more transformations.

The behavioral model is viewed from two perspectives: the dynamic and the static. Each task, determined by using the task structuring criteria, sequentially executes a set of functions. However, the information hiding modules that contain the functions (operations) are determined using the module structuring criteria described later.

The decomposition of the behavioral model should end with sequential objects and/or functions as the lowest-level data and control transformations. If concurrency within a transformation is discovered during Task Structuring, then the transformation should be decomposed further.

14.3   Task Structuring Categories

The task structuring criteria are grouped into four main categories based on how they are used to assist in task structuring. The four task structuring categories are:

1. *I/O task structuring criteria.* Addresses how physical device I/O objects and functions are mapped to I/O tasks and when an I/O task is activated.

2. *Internal task structuring criteria.* Addresses how internal objects and functions are mapped to internal tasks and when an internal task is activated.

3. *Task cohesion criteria.* Addresses whether and how transformations should be grouped into concurrent tasks.

4. *Task priority criteria.* Addresses the importance of executing a given task relative to others.

Tasks are activated either periodically or aperiodically, i.e., on demand. A task may exhibit more than one of the task structuring criteria.

14.4   I/O Task Structuring Criteria

14.4.1   Characteristics of I/O Devices

Certain hardware related information concerning I/O devices is typically not provided with a behavioral model. Nevertheless, this information is essential to determine the characteristics of tasks that interface to the devices. Before the I/O task structuring criteria can be applied, it is necessary to determine the hardware characteristics of the I/O devices that interface to the system as well as the nature of the data being input to the system by these devices or being output by the system to these devices. The I/O considerations were introduced earlier. In this section, I/O issues specific to task structuring are described. The first issue is **characteristics of I/O devices.** It is necessary to determine whether the I/O device is asynchronous (active) or passive. Two major classes of I/O devices are asynchronous (interrupt driven) and passive. An asynchronous input device generates an interrupt when it has produced some input that requires processing by the real-time system. An asynchronous output device generates an interrupt when it has finished processing an output operation and is ready to perform some new output. A passive device does not generate an interrupt on completion of the input or output operation. Thus the input from a passive input device needs to be read either on a polled basis or on demand. In the case of a passive output device, output needs to be provided on either a regular (periodic) basis or on demand.

The second issue is **characteristics of data.** It is necessary to determine whether the I/O device provides discrete data or continuous data. Discrete data is either boolean or has a finite number of values. Analog data is continuous data and can in principle have an infinite number of values. An I/O device that provides analog data will almost certainly have to be polled. If an analog device generated an I/O interrupt every time there was a change in its value, it would probably flood the system with interrupts.

The third issue is the **characteristics of passive devices.** If the device is polled, it is necessary to determine whether it is sufficient to sample the device on demand, in particular when some consumer needs the data. Alternatively, the device needs to be polled on a periodic basis so that any change in value is sent to a consumer without being explicitly requested, or is written to a data store with sufficient frequency so that the data does not get out of date.

The fourth and final issue is the **polling frequency for passive devices.** If the device is to be polled on a periodic basis, it is necessary to determine the polling frequency. The polling frequency depends on how critical the input is and how frequently it is expected to change. In the case of an output device, the polling frequency depends on how often the data should be output in order to prevent it from getting out of date.

14.4.2   Asynchronous Device I/O Task

Asynchronous device I/O tasks are needed when there are one or more asynchronous I/O devices to which the system has to interface. For each asynchronous I/O device, there needs to be an asynchronous device I/O task to interface to it. During task structuring, each device I/O object in the behavioral model, which interfaces to an asynchronous I/O device, needs to be mapped to an asynchronous device I/O task. Asynchronous tasks are also referred to as aperiodic tasks.

An asynchronous device I/O task is constrained to execute at the speed of the asynchronous I/O device it is interacting with. Thus an input task may be suspended indefinitely awaiting an input. However, once activated, the input task often has to respond to an interrupt within a few milliseconds in order to avoid any loss of data. Once the input data is read, the input task may send the data to be processed by another task. This releases the input task to respond to another interrupt that may closely follow the first.

The concept of one task for each asynchronous I/O device was originally proposed by Dijkstra [Dijkstra68] in his early work on cooperating sequential processes and used by Brinch Hansen [Brinch Hansen73] in his work on operating system design based on concurrent processes.

An asynchronous device I/O task is a device driver task. It is typically activated by either a low-level interrupt handler or in some cases directly by the hardware. As

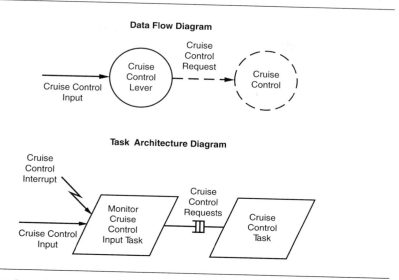

FIGURE 14.1 Asynchronous Device I/O Task

an example of an asynchronous device I/O task, consider the Cruise Control Lever object in the data flow diagram in Fig. 14.1. The Cruise Control Lever object reads each Cruise Control input, converts the input to an internal format, and sends it as a cruise control request to the Cruise Control transformation. As the cruise control lever is an asynchronous input device, the Cruise Control Lever object is mapped to an asynchronous device input task. When the task is activated by the Cruise Control interrupt, it reads the Cruise Control input, converts the input to an internal format, and sends it as a Cruise Control request message to the Cruise Control task.

14.4.3   Periodic I/O Task

Periodic I/O Tasks.   While asynchronous device I/O tasks deal with asynchronous I/O devices, periodic I/O tasks deal with passive I/O devices, where the device is polled on a regular basis. In this situation, the activation of the task is periodic but its function is I/O related. The periodic I/O task is activated by a timer event, performs an I/O operation, and then waits for the next timer event. The task's period is the time between successive activations.

Periodic I/O tasks are often used for simple I/O devices that, unlike asynchronous I/O devices, do not generate interrupts when I/O is available. Thus they are often used for passive sensor devices that need to be sampled periodically.

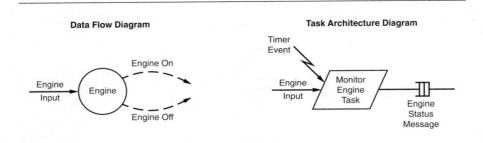

FIGURE 14.2 Periodic I/O Task

Sensor-based Periodic I/O Tasks. The concept of a periodic I/O task is used in many sensor-based industrial systems. Such systems often have a large number of digital and analog sensors. A periodic I/O task is activated on a regular basis, scans the sensors, and reads their values.

Consider a passive digital input device (e.g., the engine sensor). This is handled by a periodic I/O task. The task is activated by a timer event and then reads the status of the device. If the value of the digital sensor has changed since the previous time it was sampled, then the task indicates the change in status. In the case of an analog sensor (e.g., a temperature sensor), the device is sampled periodically and the current value of the sensor is read.

As an example of a periodic I/O task, consider the Engine object shown in Fig. 14.2. It periodically reads the current value of the engine sensor and sends changes in status by means of the Engine On and Engine Off event flows. This case is handled by a periodic input task, Monitor Engine. The task is activated by a timer event. It samples the sensor and if there is a change in status, it sends a message to the consumer task containing the new value. It then waits for the next timer event.

Timing Considerations for Periodic I/O Tasks. The frequency with which a task samples a sensor depends on the frequency with which the sensor's value is expected to change. It also depends on the delay that can be tolerated in reporting this change. For example, ambient temperature varies slowly and so can be polled with a frequency in minutes. On the other hand, to provide a fast response to the automobile brake being pressed, the brake sensor may need to be polled every 100 milliseconds, assuming the brake is a passive device.

Although digital input can be supported by means of an asynchronous input device, it is rare for analog input to be supported by means of an asynchronous input device. If an analog input device generated an interrupt every time there was a change in its value, it would very probably impose a heavy interrupt load on the system. The higher the sampling rate of a given task, the more the overhead that will be generated. For a digital input device, a periodic input task is likely to consume more overhead than the equivalent asynchronous input task. This is because there will probably be times when the periodic input task is activated and the value of the sensor being monitored will not have changed. If the sampling rate chosen is too high, then significantly unnecessary overhead could be generated. The sampling rate selected for a given task depends on the characteristics of the input device as well as the characteristics of the environment external to the application.

14.4.4 Resource Monitor Task

An input or output device that receives requests from multiple sources should have a resource monitor task to coordinate these requests, even if the device is passive. A resource monitor task has to sequence these requests in order to maintain data integrity and to ensure that no data is corrupted or lost. For example, if two or more tasks are allowed to write to a line printer simultaneously, then output from the tasks will be randomly interleaved and a garbled report will be produced. To avoid this problem, it is necessary to design a line printer resource monitor task, which receives output requests from multiple source tasks and has to deal with each request sequentially. Since the request from a second source task may arrive before the first task has finished, having a resource monitor task to handle the requests ensures that multiple requests are dealt with sequentially.

14.5 Internal Task Structuring Criteria

Whereas the I/O task structuring criteria are used to determine I/O tasks, the internal task structuring criteria are used to determine internal tasks.

14.5.1 Periodic Task

Many real-time and concurrent systems have functions that need to be executed on a periodic basis. These periodic functions are typically handled by means of periodic tasks. While periodic I/O transformations are structured as periodic I/O tasks, periodic internal transformations are structured as periodic tasks. In some cases, periodic transformations are grouped into a single temporally cohesive task.

Each transformation that executes a function periodically (i.e., at regular, equally spaced intervals of time) is structured as a separate periodic task. The task is activated by a timer event, performs the periodic function, and then waits for the next timer event. The task's period is the time between successive activations.

An example of a periodic task is the periodic function Determine Distance shown in Fig. 14.3. When activated, it reads the shaft rotation count and calibration constant,

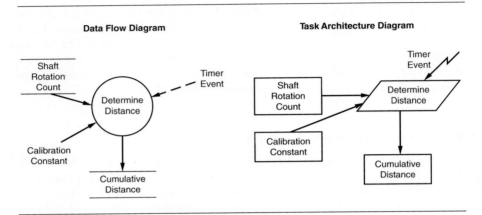

FIGURE 14.3 Periodic Task

and computes the cumulative distance travelled. Determine Distance is structured as a periodic task that is activated periodically by a timer event.

14.5.2 Asynchronous Task

Many real-time and concurrent systems have transformations that need to be executed on demand. These asynchronous transformations are typically handled by means of asynchronous tasks. Whereas asynchronous I/O tasks deal with I/O transformations that are activated by external interrupts, asynchronous internal tasks (often referred to as asynchronous or aperiodic tasks) address internal transformations that are activated by internal events or messages.

A transformation that executes on demand (i.e., when activated by an internal event or message sent by a different task) is structured as a separate asynchronous task. The task is activated on demand by the arrival of the event or message sent by the requesting task, performs the demanded action, and then waits for the next event or message.

An example of an asynchronous task is given in Fig. 14.4. The Scheduler algorithm object receives service requests from Floor Buttons and outputs Scheduler Requests. The Scheduler object is structured as an asynchronous task called the Scheduler, which is activated by the arrival of Service Request messages.

14.5.3 Control Task

In a behavioral model, a control object is represented by a control transformation, and executes a state transition diagram. By definition, the execution of a state transition

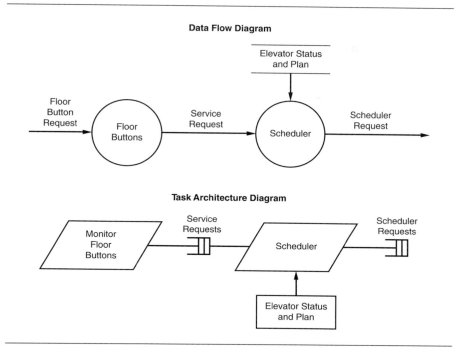

Data Flow Diagram

Task Architecture Diagram

FIGURE 14.4 Asynchronous Task

diagram is strictly sequential. Hence a task, whose execution is also strictly sequential, can perform the control activity. A task that executes a state transition diagram (mapped to a state transition table) is referred to as a control task. An example of a control task is shown in Fig. 14.5. The control object Cruise Control, which is represented by the control transformation and executes the Cruise Control state transition diagram, is structured as the Cruise Control task because execution of the state transition diagram is strictly sequential.

14.5.4   User Role Task

A user typically performs a set of sequential operations. Since the user's interaction with the system is a sequential activity, this can be handled by a user role task. The speed of this task is frequently constrained by the speed of user interaction. As its name implies, a user role object in the behavioral model is mapped to user role task.

A user role task usually interfaces with various standard I/O devices, such as the input keyboard and output display, which are typically handled by the operating system. Since the operating system provides a standard interface to these devices, it is usually not necessary to develop special purpose device I/O tasks to handle them.

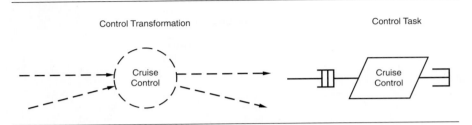

Control Transformation

Control Task

FIGURE 14.5 Control Task

The concept of one task per user is typical in many multi-user operating systems. For example in the VAX/VMS and UNIX operating system, there is one task (process) per user. If, on the other hand, the user can play two or more independent roles, then one user role task is allocated for each sequential activity. Thus, in the UNIX and VAX/VMS operating systems, it is possible for the user to spawn background tasks. All the user role tasks belonging to the same user execute concurrently.

The concept of one task per sequential activity is also used on advanced workstations (e.g., the HP and Sun workstations) with multiple windows. Each window executes a sequential activity and so there is one user role task for each window.

As an example, the object Operator Interface accepts operator commands, reads from the sensor data store, and displays data to the operator. Since all operator interactions are sequential in this example, the Operator Interface object is structured as a user role task.

In a multiple windows workstation environment, a factory operator may view factory status in one window (supported by one user role task) and acknowledge alarms in another window (supported by a different user role task).

14.5.5   Multiple Tasks of Same Type

As pointed out earlier, it is possible that there are many objects of the same type. Each object is mapped to a task, where all the tasks are instances of the same task type. In the case of a control object, each object executes an instance of the same state transition diagram, although each object is likely to be in a different state. This is addressed by having one control task for each control object, where the control task executes the state transition diagram.

It may be that, for a given application, there are too many objects of the same type to allow each to be mapped to a separate task. This issue is addressed using task inversion, as described in Section 14.10.

An example of multiple control tasks of the same type comes from the Elevator Control system, as shown in Fig. 14.6. The control aspects of a real-world elevator are modeled by means of a control object, Elevator Control, and defined by means of

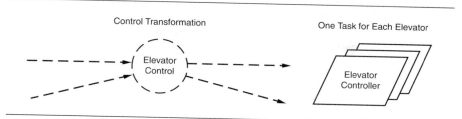

FIGURE 14.6 Multiple Control Tasks of the Same Type

a state transition diagram. During task structuring, the Elevator Control object is mapped to an Elevator Controller task. In a multiple elevator system, there is one elevator task for each Elevator Control object (one per elevator). The tasks are identical and each task executes an instance of the same state transition diagram. However, each elevator is likely to be in a different state on its state transition diagram.

14.6   Task Cohesion Criteria

14.6.1   Introduction

The module cohesion concept is used in Structured Design [Page-Jones88] as a criterion for identifying the strength or unity of the functions contained in a module. In ADARTS/CODARTS, the term cohesion is used differently. The ADARTS/CODARTS task cohesion criteria are used to determine which objects and/or functions (as shown by the transformations in a behavioral model) could be grouped into a single task.

The hierarchical decomposition reflected in the behavioral model potentially leads to a large number of objects and/or functions at the lowest level of decomposition, each of which is potentially concurrent. This high degree of concurrency in the behavioral model provides considerable flexibility in the design. However, if each of these transformations becomes a task, this could lead to a large number of small tasks, potentially resulting in increased system complexity and execution overhead.

In ADARTS/CODARTS, the asynchronous nature of the transformations is analyzed. The task cohesion criteria provide a means of analyzing the concurrent nature of the transformations and hence a basis for determining whether two or more transformations should be grouped into a single concurrent task and, if so, how. Thus, if two transformations are constrained so that they cannot execute concurrently and hence must execute sequentially, then there is no advantage to having them in separate tasks.

14.6.2 Temporal Cohesion

Temporal Cohesion Criterion. Certain transformations may perform operations that are activated by the same event. If there is no sequential dependency between the transformations (i.e., no required sequential order in which the transformations must execute), then the transformations may be grouped into a task based on the temporal cohesion criterion, so that they are all executed each time the task receives a stimulus.

It is frequently the case that transformations activated by the same periodic event may be grouped into a task according to the temporal cohesion criterion. The functions may be executed in any order, since there is no sequential dependency in their relationship. Hence an arbitrary execution order needs to be selected by the designer.

Temporal cohesion may be used for transformations that are activated asynchronously as well as for transformations that are activated periodically. However, temporal cohesion is more frequently applicable to periodic transformations.

Example of Temporal Cohesion. An example of temporal cohesion is given in Fig. 14.7. The data flow diagram shows two data transformations, each of which monitors a different input sensor, namely the brake and engine sensors. If these were asynchronous I/O devices, then each device would be handled by a separate asynchronous device I/O task, which would be activated by a device interrupt every time there was an input from the device. However, if the two sensors are passive, then the only way for the system to be aware of a change in sensor status is for it to sample the sensors periodically.

For example, Monitor Engine periodically reads the current value of the engine sensor and sends changes in engine status by means of the Engine On and Engine Off

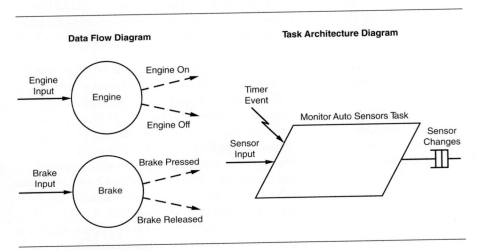

FIGURE 14.7 Temporal Cohesion

event flows. Similarly, Monitor Brake periodically reads the current value of the brake sensor and sends changes in brake status by means of the Brake On and Brake Off event flows. Furthermore, assume the sensors are to be sampled with the same frequency (e.g., every 100 milliseconds). Consequently, the Monitor Engine and Monitor Brake transformations are grouped into a task called Monitor Auto Sensors based on the temporal cohesion criterion. This task displays both temporal and functional cohesion, since the two monitoring transformations are also functionally related. Monitor Auto Sensors is activated periodically by a timer event and then samples the status of the brake and engine sensors. If there is a change in status in either of the sensors, it sends a Sensor Change message. If coincidentally there is a change in both sensors, then it sends two Sensor Change messages.

It should be noted that from the consumer task's perspective, it has no knowledge of whether a message it receives was sent by an asynchronous device I/O task, by a periodic device I/O task, or by a temporally cohesive I/O task. Thus any change to the characteristics of a producer I/O task(s) is hidden from the consumer task.

Issues in Temporal Cohesion.   When deciding whether to structure candidate transformations into a temporally cohesive task, there are some tradeoffs that need to be considered. First, if one function is more time critical than the other, then these functions should be mapped to separate periodic device I/O tasks, since this gives the additional flexibility of allocating different priorities to the two tasks. Second, if it is considered likely that two functions that are candidates for temporal cohesion could be executed on separate processors, then these functions should be mapped to separate tasks. Third, preference should be given in temporal cohesion to transformations that are functionally related and likely to be of equal importance from a scheduling viewpoint. Finally, the period or sampling rate needs consideration. An issue is whether it is possible to group two periodic transformations, which are functionally related to each other but have different periods, into a temporally cohesive task. This approach can be used providing the periods are multiples of one another. However, this form of temporal cohesion is weaker than if the periods are identical. For example, two periodic I/O transformations may be grouped into one task if one transformation samples a sensor A every 50 msec, while the second transformation samples another sensor B every 100 msec. The temporally cohesive task has a period of 50 msec, samples sensor A every time it is activated and sensor B every second time it is activated.

An important issue to consider in combining temporal transformations is that one group of temporal transformations may be more important than another and should be in a higher priority task in that case. This issue is illustrated by means of another example from the cruise control problem. Check Maintenance Need is a periodic temporally cohesive task. However, it is not desirable to group Monitor Brake and Check Maintenance Need into one task based on temporal cohesion. It is very likely that monitoring the brake is a more important function than checking if auto maintenance is required. In fact, there is a difference of at least two orders of magnitude in the frequency with which these operations need to be performed. Thus the brake may need to be sampled every 100 msec, whereas checking for auto maintenance could be done every 10 secs.

It is therefore recommended that temporal cohesion be used for related functions (i.e., a combination of temporal and functional cohesion). Grouping temporal transformations that are not functionally related into one task is not considered desirable from a design viewpoint, although it may be done for optimization purposes if the tasking overhead is considered too high, as described in Section 14.10.

Taking temporal cohesion to an extreme would result in one temporally cohesive task executing all periodic functions. This approach is similar to the cyclic executive style of programming [Glass83], which has been shown to be very difficult to maintain. With the cyclic executive approach, all periodic transformations are grouped into one task, with different periodic events activating different transformations. This approach requires a supervisory procedure, which has to be activated with a period that is the highest common factor of the periods of all the functions handled by the task. Each time it is activated, the supervisory procedure has to decide which function(s) to execute. For example, if there are three periodic functions with periods of 15, 20, and 25 msec, the supervisory procedure has to be activated every 5 msec. One disadvantage is that the supervisory procedure duplicates the services provided by a multitasking executive or in the case of an Ada environment, the services provided by the Ada run-time system. Consequently, this approach is not considered desirable because it increases the complexity of the system and hence is likely to result in increased maintenance costs.

14.6.3   Sequential Cohesion

Sequential Cohesion Criterion.   Certain transformations perform operations that must be carried out in a sequential order. The first transformation in the sequence is triggered by an asynchronous or periodic event. The other transformations are then executed sequentially after it. These sequentially dependent transformations may be grouped into one sequentially cohesive task.

Example of Sequential Cohesion.   As an example of sequential cohesion, consider the two transformations shown in Fig. 14.8. The transformation Determine Distance, which is activated periodically, computes the incremental distance traveled since it was last activated. It adds this to the Cumulative Distance data store and then passes the Incremental Distance to Determine Speed, which then computes the value of Current Speed. Thus the first transformation, Determine Distance, is activated periodically and since it computes Incremental Distance that is used by Determine Speed, there is a sequential dependency between the two transformations. Thus the two transformations may be grouped into one task, Determine Distance and Speed, based on sequential cohesion.

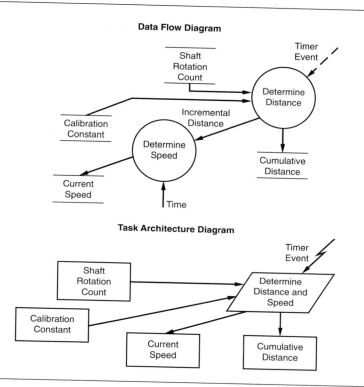

FIGURE 14.8 Sequential Cohesion

Issues in Sequential Cohesion.   When combining successive transformations using sequential cohesion, the following guidelines apply.

- If the last transformation in a sequence writes to a data store, then this terminates the group of transformations to be considered for sequential cohesion. This happens with Determine Speed, in Fig. 14.8, which ends a sequence of two sequentially connected transformations by updating the Current Speed data store.

- If the next transformation in the sequence also receives inputs from another source and therefore can also be activated by receiving input from that source, then this transformation should be structured as a separate task. This happens in the case of the Cruise Control transformation (Fig. 14.1), which can receive inputs from several device I/O transformations, and so is structured as a separate task, the Cruise Control task.

- If the next transformation in the sequence is likely to hold up the preceding transformation(s) such that they could either miss an input or a state change, then the next transformation should be structured as a separate lower priority task. This is what happens with Scheduler (Fig. 14.4), which receives Service Requests from Floor Buttons. Floor Buttons must not miss any floor button requests, so it is structured as a separate task from the Scheduler task.

□ If the next transformation is of a lower priority and follows a time-critical transformation, then the two transformations should be in separate tasks.

14.6.4   Control Cohesion

Control Cohesion Criterion.   Control cohesion can potentially occur whenever there is a control object (transformation), which executes a state transition diagram. In certain cases, the control object may be grouped with the data transformations it activates into a task based on the control cohesion criterion.

In the behavioral model, a control object is defined by means of a state transition diagram. The control object should be structured as a separate task because, by definition, the execution of a state transition diagram is strictly sequential. Furthermore, the control object may be grouped with other state-dependent data transformations, which it triggers, enables, or disables, based on the control cohesion task structuring criterion. It may be grouped with other non-state dependent data transformations based on the sequential cohesion criterion. Consider the following cases:

1. *State dependent data transformations that are triggered by the control transformation as a result of a state transition.* Consider a data transformation that is triggered at the state transition and both starts and completes execution during the state transition. Such a data transformation does not execute concurrently with the control transformation. Consequently, it should be grouped with the control transformation into a task based on the control cohesion criterion.

2. *State dependent data transformations that are either enabled or disabled by the control transformation as a result of a state transition.* Consider a data transformation that is enabled at a state transition and then executes continuously until disabled at a subsequent state transition. This data transformation should be structured as a separate task, since both the control transformation and data transformation will need to be active concurrently. This is particularly the case if the data transformation does not determine the event that causes the next change of state in the control transformation. So the control transformation has to be in a separate concurrent task to receive the event from some other source, so that it can then disable the data transformation executing in a different task.

3. *State dependent data transformations that are triggered by the control transformation as a result of a state transition and execute for the duration of the state.* This case has to be analyzed carefully. If the data transformation is deactivated by the control transformation, then it should be structured as a separate task, since both the control transformation and data transformation will need to be active

concurrently. However, if it is the data transformation that recognizes it is time for a state change, it will send an event to the control transformation to trigger the state change. Furthermore, if this is the *only* event that causes a state change (while the state transition diagram is in this state), then the data transformation may be grouped with the control transformation into one task according to the control cohesion criterion. This is because only this data transformation can activate the control transformation. On the other hand if the control transformation could also be activated by an event from another source, then it must be structured as a separate task.

4. *Non-state dependent data transformations that send events to the control transformation, which cause it to change state.* If these events are the only events that cause the control transformation to change state, then the data transformation may be grouped with the control transformation into one task according to the sequential cohesion criterion.

Example of Control Cohesion. An example of control cohesion is given from the Cruise Control problem. Figure 14.9 shows a data flow diagram in which the control object Cruise Control executes the state transition diagram. Actions resulting from different state transitions include the triggering and execution of the Select Desired Speed and Clear Desired Speed data transformations. Each of these data transformations performs a function that starts and completes execution during a state transition.

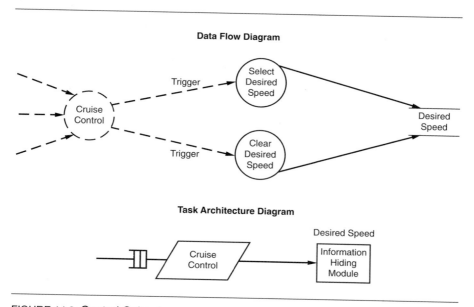

FIGURE 14.9 Control Cohesion

Consequently, the control transformation Cruise Control and the data transformations Select Desired Speed and Clear Desired Speed are grouped into the Cruise Control task based on the control cohesion criterion. However, it should be noted that other data transformations, which execute for the duration of a given state, are not placed into the Cruise Control task because they are both enabled and disabled by it and consequently need to execute concurrently with it.

14.6.5 Functional Cohesion

Functional Cohesion Criterion. Functional cohesion occurs when there are one or more functions that are closely related. In addition, because of the constraints of the application, only one function may be executed at any one time. These functions may be grouped into a task according to the functional cohesion criterion.

A functionally cohesive task also often displays temporal or sequential cohesion. In general, the functional cohesion criterion is the weakest form of task cohesion. It should be used primarily when it supports the other forms of cohesion. Categories of functional cohesion are sequentially related functional cohesion, clustered functional cohesion, and temporally related functional cohesion.

In the first, the data traffic between two functions may be high, in which case having them as separate tasks could increase the system overhead. In this case the transformations also satisfy the sequential cohesion criterion. In the second case a group of functions all operate on the same data structure or the same I/O device. This structuring criterion is analogous to the information hiding structuring criterion for modules. It is considered a stronger module structuring criterion than task structuring criterion (i.e., always desirable for modules but only in certain cases for tasks). In the third case transformations are related both temporally and functionally. For example, consider the temporally cohesive task shown in Fig. 14.7. The functions of monitoring the engine and brake are functionally related since they all relate to monitoring the auto sensors. Thus this task is functionally cohesive as well as being temporally cohesive.

Example of Functional Cohesion. In the robot controller system, there is one transformation Process Program Statement that reads the robot program, as shown in Fig. 14.10. Depending on the kind of statement—motion command, sensor command, arithmetic statement, or decision statement—the statement is passed to the appropriate transformation.

These five transformations are closely related because they are all part of the program interpreter. In addition, because program statements are executed sequentially, these transformations can never execute in parallel. Consequently, the five transformations are grouped into one functionally cohesive Interpreter task, which is also sequentially cohesive.

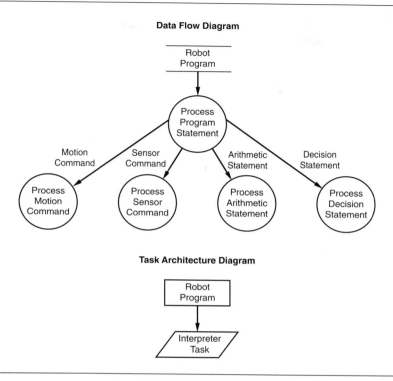

Data Flow Diagram

FIGURE 14.10 Functional Cohesion

14.6.6   Task Inversion Criteria

The task inversion criteria are used for merging tasks to reduce task overhead. Task inversion may be used either during initial task structuring or during design restructuring as described in Section 14.10.

14.7   Task Priority Criteria

Task priority criteria take into account priority considerations in task structuring; in particular, high and low priority tasks are considered. Task priority is often addressed late in the development cycle. The main reason for considering it during the task structuring phase is to identify any time-critical or non–time-critical computationally intensive transformations that need to be treated as separate tasks.

Most tasks have their priorities determined based on real-time scheduling considerations.

14.7.1 Time-critical Tasks

A time-critical function is one that needs to meet a hard deadline. Such a function needs to run at a high priority and is therefore structured as a separate high priority task. High priority time-critical tasks are needed in most real-time systems. For example, the execution of a time-critical function may be followed by a non–time-critical function. One option is to group these functions together according to the sequential cohesion criterion. However, to ensure that the time-critical function gets serviced rapidly, it may be better to allocate it to its own high priority task. This is typically the case with an asynchronous I/O task, where I/O interrupt handling is time critical.

An example of a time-critical task is the Furnace Temperature Control transformation monitoring the temperature of the furnace. If the temperature is above 100 degrees Centigrade, then the furnace must be switched off. Furnace Temperature Control is mapped to a high priority task called Furnace Control. It must execute within a pre-defined time, otherwise the contents of the furnace could be damaged. Other examples of time-critical tasks are control tasks and asynchronous device I/O tasks. A control task executes a state transition diagram and needs to execute at a high priority since state transitions must be executed rapidly. An asynchronous device I/O task needs to have a high priority so that it can service interrupts quickly, otherwise there is a danger that it might miss interrupts.

14.7.2 Non–time-critical Computationally Intensive Tasks

A non–time-critical computationally intensive function may run as a low priority task consuming spare CPU cycles. The concept of a low priority computationally intensive task executing as a background task, which is pre-empted by higher priority foreground tasks, has its origins in early multiprogramming systems and is typically supported by most modern operating systems.

An example of a non–time-critical computationally intensive task is given in Fig. 14.11. A data transformation Compute Sensor Statistics reads from a sensor data store and computes the mean and standard deviation of temperature and pressure. It then passes this data to Display Sensor Statistics. Compute Sensor Statistics is a low priority function, so it is mapped to a low priority background task that uses up spare CPU time. Since the statistics computed are for information purposes only, it does not matter if the information displayed is slightly out of date.

It is not always the case that a computationally intensive function can be mapped to a low priority task. The priority of a function is application dependent. It is thus

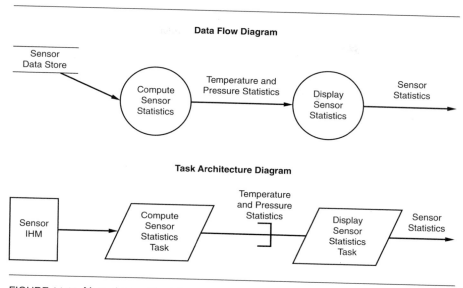

Data Flow Diagram

Task Architecture Diagram

FIGURE 14.11 Non–time-critical Computationally Intensive Task

possible in some applications for a computationally intensive function to be time critical and thus need to be executed at a high priority.

14.8 Developing the Task Architecture

14.8.1 Guidelines for Applying Task Structuring Criteria

The task structuring criteria may be applied to the data and control transformations of an RTSA or COBRA behavioral model in the following order:

1. *I/O transformations.* Start with the transformations that interact with the outside world. Structure these into asynchronous device I/O, periodic I/O, resource monitor, or temporally cohesive periodic I/O tasks.

2. *Control transformations.* Analyze each control transformation and the data transformations that interface to it. Structure each control transformation into a control task. Any data transformations that it triggers can often be structured into the same task based on the control cohesion criterion. Any data transformations that it enables should be structured into separate tasks. Analyze the enabled transformations to determine if any can be grouped with the control transformation into a task based on the cohesion criteria.

Use the same approach for multiple control objects of the same type. Check whether each object can be mapped to a separate task or whether it is necessary to use task inversion, particularly if there are a large number of tasks of the same type and task switching overhead is a concern.

3. *Periodic transformations.* Analyze the internal periodically activated transformations. Determine if any periodic transformations are triggered by the same event. If they are, they may grouped into the same task based on the temporal cohesion criterion. Other functions that execute in sequence may be structured according to the sequential cohesion criterion.

4. *Other internal transformations.* For each internal transformation activated by an internal event, identify whether any adjacent transformations on the data flow diagram may be grouped into a task with it according to the temporal, sequential, or functional cohesion criteria.

Since a task may fall into more than one task structuring category, using the above guidelines, a task will be identified by the first criterion applied successfully to it. Subsequent criteria that apply to it should either confirm the initial structuring decision or indicate that it should be revisited. For example a transformation may be structured as an I/O task but also be activated by a control transformation. If it transpires that the I/O operation is always performed synchronously during a state transition, then the initial task structuring decision should be questioned.

14.8.2 Task Architecture Diagram

After structuring the system into concurrent tasks, a preliminary task architecture diagram is drawn showing all the tasks in the system. On this preliminary diagram, the interfaces between the tasks are still those shown on the data flow/control flow diagrams. An example of a preliminary task architecture diagram is given in Fig. 14.12.

14.9 Task Communication and Synchronization

14.9.1 Introduction

After structuring the system into concurrent tasks, the next step is to define the task interfaces. At this stage the interfaces between tasks are in the form of data flow/control flow diagram interfaces; that is, data flows, event flows, and data stores. It is necessary to map these data flow/control flow diagram interfaces to task interfaces in the form of message communication, event synchronization, or information hiding modules. This chapter describes how these data flow diagram interfaces are mapped to task interfaces.

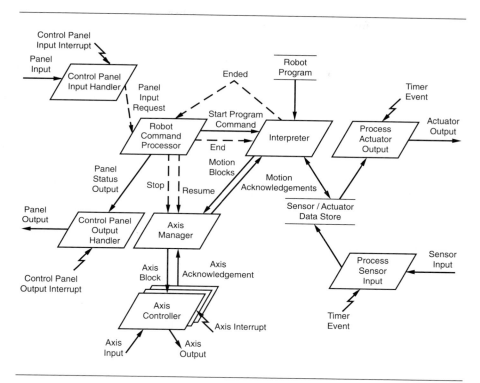

FIGURE 14.12 Preliminary Task Architecture Diagram: Data Flow/Control Flow
Diagram Interfaces

14.9.2 Message Communication

Concepts. A discrete data flow interface between two tasks is mapped to a message
interface. Message interfaces between tasks are either loosely coupled or tightly
coupled. With tightly-coupled message communication, the producer sends a message
to the consumer and then immediately waits for a response. The semantics of
tightly-coupled message communication are similar to those of the Ada rendezvous.
For tightly-coupled message communication, two possibilities exist: tightly-coupled
message communication with reply and tightly-coupled message communication
without reply.

Loosely-coupled Message Communication. With loosely-coupled message
communication, the producer sends a message to the consumer and either does not
need a response or has other functions to perform before receiving a response. Thus
the producer sends a message and continues without waiting for a response. The
consumer receives the message. As the producer and consumer tasks proceed at

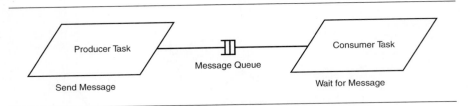

FIGURE 14.13 Loosely-coupled Message Communication

different speeds, a first-in/first-out (FIFO) message queue can build up between producer and consumer. If there is no message available when the consumer requests one, then the consumer is suspended. The notation for loosely-coupled message communication is shown in Fig. 14.13.

An example of loosely-coupled message communication in the Elevator Control system is given in Fig. 14.14. A partial preliminary task architecture diagram showing the data flow diagram interfaces is shown in Fig. 14.14(a). The Elevator Manager task receives discrete data flows from the Monitor Elevator Buttons and Scheduler tasks. Monitor Elevator Buttons sends Elevator requests, which are requests from passengers in the elevator, to the Elevator Manager task. The Scheduler task sends Scheduler requests, which are requests to stop at certain floors to pick up passengers, to the

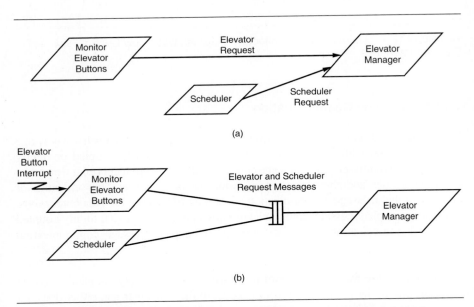

FIGURE 14.14 Loosely-coupled Message Communication (a) Preliminary Task Architecture Diagram: Data Flow Interfaces (b) Revised Task Architecture Diagram: Message Communication Interface

Elevator Manager task. This interface to the Elevator Manager task is mapped to a loosely-coupled message communication interface in which the Elevator Manager supports one input message queue, allowing it to receive messages from both Monitor Elevator Buttons and the Scheduler tasks, as shown in Fig. 14.14(b). Messages from the two producer tasks are interleaved, and the Elevator Manager task services messages in the order they arrive. After servicing a message, the task loops back to wait for the next message on its queue.

The pseudocode for the Elevator Manager task is as follows:

```
LOOP
WAIT MESSAGE from Elevator and Scheduler Request Queue
CASE Message OF
. . . .
Elevator Request Message:
  Service Elevator Request Message
  . . . .
Scheduler Request Message:
  Service Scheduler Request Message
  . . . . .
ENDCASE
ENDLOOP
```

Tightly-coupled Message Communication with Reply.   In the case of tightly-coupled message communication with reply, the producer sends a message to the consumer and then waits for a reply. When the message arrives, the consumer accepts the message, processes it, generates a reply, and then sends the reply. The producer and consumer then both continue. The consumer is suspended if there is no message available. For a given producer/consumer pair, no message queue develops between the producer and the consumer. The notation for tightly-coupled message communication with reply is shown in Fig. 14.15.

An example of tightly-coupled message communication with reply is given in Fig. 14.16. The data flow interface, which consists of the producer, the Axis Manager

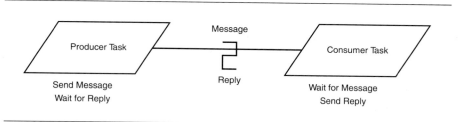

FIGURE 14.15 Tightly-coupled Message Communication with Reply

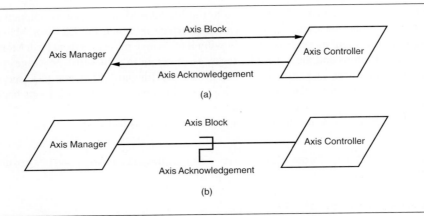

FIGURE 14.16 Tightly-coupled Message Communication Interfaces (a) Preliminary Task Architecture Diagram: Data Flow Interfaces (b) Revised Task Architecture Diagram: Message Communication Interfaces

task, sending an axis block to the consumer, the Axis Controller [Fig. 14.16(a)]. Since the Axis Manager task cannot proceed until it has received a reply from the Axis Controller, the interface between the two tasks is mapped to a tightly-coupled message interface with reply [Fig. 14.16(b)]. The Axis Manager task sends the axis block message to the Axis Controller and then waits for the reply. The Axis Controller waits for a message from the Axis Manager. After receiving the message, the Axis Controller processes the message, performs the desired action, and sends a reply (an axis acknowledgement) to the Axis Manager. On receiving the reply, the Axis Manager resumes execution.

Tightly-coupled Message Communication without Reply.   In the case of tightly-coupled message communication without reply, the producer sends a message to the consumer and then waits for acceptance of the message by the consumer. When the message arrives, the consumer accepts the message, thereby releasing the producer. The producer and consumer then both continue. The consumer is suspended if there is no message available. For a given producer/consumer pair, no message queue develops between the producer and the consumer. The notation for of tightly-coupled message communication without reply is shown in Fig. 14.17.

An example of tightly coupled message communication without reply is shown in Fig. 14.11. The data flow interface, which consists of the producer task, Compute Sensor Statistics, sending Temperature and Pressure Statistics to the consumer task, Display Sensor Statistics, which then displays the information. In this example, the decision made is that there is no point in Compute Sensor Statistics computing temperature and sensor statistics if the Display Sensor Statistics cannot keep up with displaying them. Consequently, the interface between the two tasks is mapped to a

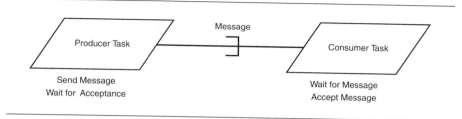

FIGURE 14.17 Tightly-coupled Message Communication without Reply

tightly-coupled message communication without reply interface. Compute Sensor Statistics computes the statistics, sends the message, and then waits for the acceptance of the message by Display Sensor Statistics before resuming execution. Compute Sensor Statistics is held up until Display Sensor Statistics finishes displaying the previous message. As soon as Display Sensor Statistics accepts the new message, Compute Sensor Statistics is released from its wait and computes the next set of statistics while Display Sensor Statistics displays the previous set. By this means, computation of the statistics, a compute bound activity, can be overlapped with displaying the statistics, an I/O bound activity, while preventing an unnecessary message queue of statistics building up at the display task.

Message Communication with Priority Message Queues. The FIFO message queue does not recognize the relative importance of messages being sent to a task. For example, a given consumer task may receive messages from three producer tasks. Furthermore, it is required that messages from producer A must always be handled first, while messages from producer B must be handled before messages from producer C. This situation cannot be handled using a FIFO message queue and instead requires a priority message queue.

With a priority message queue, each message has a priority associated with it. The consumer always accepts higher priority messages before lower priority messages. The notation for a priority queue is shown in Fig. 14.18.

Continuing with the example of the three producers, it is necessary to have three priority levels in the priority message queue. Messages from producer A have the highest priority level, messages from producer B have an intermediate priority level, and messages from producer C have the lowest priority level. Messages at any given priority level are handled on a FIFO basis. It should be pointed out that, in general, the number of message priority levels is independent of the number of producers.

14.9.3 Event Synchronization

Concepts.   Three types of event synchronization are possible, an external event, a timer event, and an internal event. An external event is a stimulus from an external

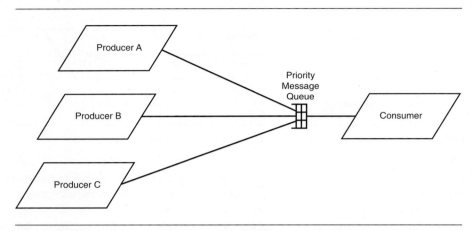

FIGURE 14.18 Message Communication with Priority Message Queue

entity, typically an interrupt from an external I/O device. An internal event represents internal synchronization between a source task and a destination task. A timer event represents a periodic activation of a task.

Internal event synchronization is used when two tasks need to coordinate their operations without data being communicated between the tasks. The source task signals the event. The destination task waits for the event and is suspended until the event is signalled. It is not suspended if the event has previously been signalled.

An example of event synchronization is shown in Fig. 14.19. An external event, typically a hardware interrupt from an I/O device, activates the source task. The source task then signals an internal event to the destination task. The destination task waits for the internal event, is activated, and then performs a periodic function, during which it is activated periodically by a timer event. The timer event only occurs while the periodic function is active.

Mapping Event Flows to Task Interfaces.   In most cases, an event flow sent from one data or control transformation to another transformation on a data flow diagram is mapped to an internal event signalled from a source task to a destination task on a task architecture diagram. An example of this is the End event flow from the Robot Command Processor to the Interpreter task, which signals that the robot program should terminate execution, as shown in Fig. 14.20. This is mapped to an internal event sent by the Robot Command Processor task to the Interpreter task. Similarly the Ended event flow from the Interpreter to the Robot Command Processor, which signals that the robot program has terminated, is mapped to an internal event sent by the Interpreter task to the Robot Command Processor task. In both cases, the

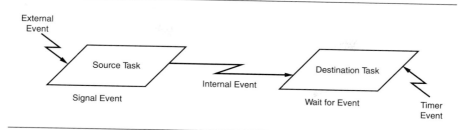

FIGURE 14.19 Event Synchronization

event represents a way in which the two tasks can synchronize their operations with each other. No data is actually passed between the two tasks.

There are also several cases where an event flow between data transformations may be mapped to a message communication interface between tasks. The first case is when the destination task is on a different processor in a distributed environment. In this case an event flow is mapped to a loosely-coupled message communication interface, in which a message is sent containing the event.

The second is when the destination task can receive several different event flows from the source task. Although the event flows could be mapped to several different internal events between the two tasks, this can sometimes be cumbersome. In fact, it is often easier to map this kind of interface to a message communication interface, in which the arrival of the message signals the event and the contents of the message identify which event it is.

An example of this is given in the Cruise Control problem, where Cruise Control sends Speed Command event flows to the Auto Speed Control task. Speed

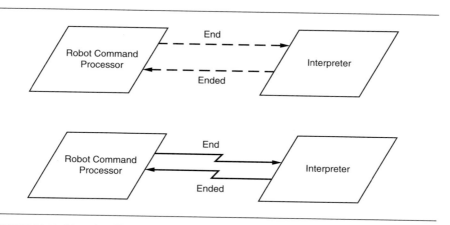

FIGURE 14.20 Mapping Event Flow Interfaces to Inter-task Event Synchronization

Command is an aggregate event flow consisting of four simple event flows: Increase Speed, Maintain Speed, Resume, and Deactivate. As events carry no data, these four event flows could be mapped to four corresponding intertask events, as shown in Fig. 14.21.

In the interface between the Cruise Control and Auto Speed Control tasks, it is simpler to map the four event flows to one message communication interface called Speed Command, where the message parameter identifies which of the four events has arrived (Fig. 14.21). Since a command sent from Cruise Control to Auto Speed Control occurs at a state transition, it is desirable for the message to be accepted at the transition and there is no possibility of a message queue. The interface between the two tasks is therefore tightly coupled. As there is no response from Auto Speed Control, the interface is tightly coupled without reply.

The third case is when the destination task can receive several events from source producer tasks and it is important for the task not to miss any events. Furthermore, the tasks must receive the events in the order they were sent. In such situations, it is more appropriate to use a FIFO message queue for the events.

An example of this is given in the Cruise Control problem. The preliminary task architecture diagram (Fig. 14.22) shows that the Cruise Control task receives event

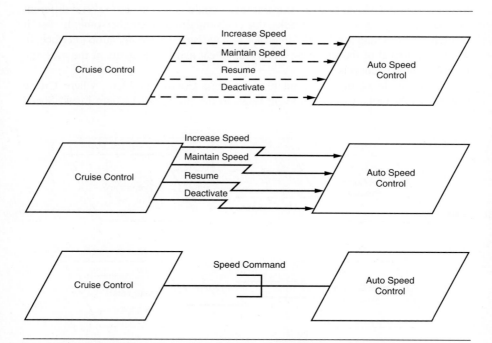

FIGURE 14.21 Mapping Event Flow Interfaces to Tightly-coupled Message Communication

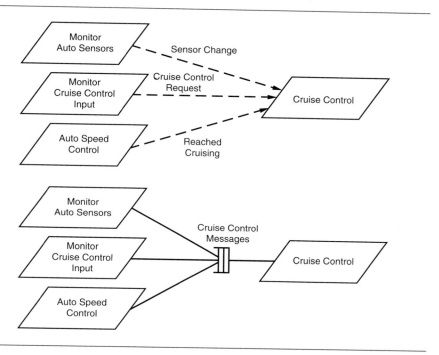

FIGURE 14.22 Mapping Multiple Event Flows to Loosely-coupled Message Communication

flows from three tasks: Monitor Cruise Control Input, Monitor Auto Sensors, and Auto Speed Control. Since it is crucial that the Cruise Control task not miss any incoming events and it is important to receive the events in the order they were sent, the interface to Cruise Control is mapped to a loosely-coupled message communication interface, the Cruise Control message queue, where the parameter of the message identifies the event being carried. Most of the time, the queue will be empty. However, in periods where there are bursts of activity, there can be more than one message in the queue. The Cruise Control task will receive them FIFO and no message will be lost.

14.9.4 Information Hiding Modules (IHMs)

Information hiding modules (IHMs) are used for encapsulating (i.e., hiding the contents and internal representation of) data stores. A task accesses the data store indirectly via operations, which manipulate the contents of the data store. Where an IHM is accessed by more than one task, the operations must synchronize the access to the data. For example, an information hiding module is accessed by two tasks. Task A reads from and updates the IHM, while task B reads from the IHM (Fig. 14.23).

IHM structuring is described in the next chapter.

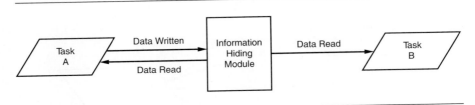

FIGURE 14.23 Task Communication with Information Hiding Module

14.10   Design Restructuring Using Task Inversion

14.10.1   Task Inversion

Task inversion is a concept that originated in Jackson Structured Programming and Jackson System Development [Jackson83], whereby the number of tasks in a system can be reduced in a systematic way. At one extreme, a concurrent solution can be mapped to a sequential solution. In this section, the task inversion concept is applied to the tasks determined using the task structuring criteria. It is viewed as a design restructuring technique in situations where there are concerns about high tasking overhead. In particular, task inversion can be used if a performance analysis of the design indicates that the tasking overhead is too high. Three forms of task inversion are described here: multiple instance task inversion, sequential task inversion, and temporal task inversion. The task inversion criteria, and in particular multiple instance task inversion, may be also used during initial task structuring if high task overhead is anticipated.

14.10.2   Multiple Instance Task Inversion

Handling multiple control tasks of the same type was described earlier in this chapter. With this approach, several objects of the same type can be modeled using one task instance for each object, where all the tasks are of the same type. The problem is that, for a given application, the system overhead for modeling each object by means of a separate task may be too high.

With multiple instance task inversion, all identical tasks of the same type are replaced by one task that performs the same service. For example, instead of each control object being mapped to a separate task, all control objects of the same type are mapped to the same task. The different states of each of the objects are captured by having a separate data record for each object, which maintains all the necessary state information for that object.

As an example of multiple instance task inversion, consider the Elevator Control System, where each elevator object is mapped to a separate Elevator Controller task.

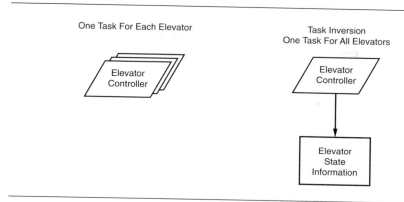

FIGURE 14.24 Multiple Instance Task Inversion

If the system overhead is too high to allow this, then an alternative solution is to have only one Elevator Controller task for the whole system and to have a separate data record for each elevator containing all the state information for that elevator (Fig. 14.24). The state information for the elevators is contained in an information hiding module. With task inversion, the main procedure of the task is a scheduling procedure, which reads all inputs to the task and decides for which elevator the data is intended, thereby ensuring that the appropriate elevator record is used.

14.10.3   Sequential Task Inversion

Sequential task inversion is used primarily in cases where there is tightly-coupled communication between two or more tasks. The tasks are combined such that the producer task calls an operation provided by the consumer task rather than send it a message. This is referred to as inversion of the consumer with respect to the producer. Each message type that can be sent from the producer to the consumer is replaced by a consumer operation that is called by the producer. The parameters of the message become the parameters of the call.

As an example of sequential task inversion, consider the three task sequence from the Cruise Control problem where the Cruise Control task sends a Speed Command message to the Auto Speed Control task, which in turn sends Throttle value messages to the Throttle task. All message communication is tightly coupled without reply. These three tasks may be combined into one task using sequential task inversion, the Inverted Cruise Control task, as shown in Fig. 14.25. Whenever this task receives a Cruise Control message, it "executes" the state transition diagram. If there is an action to be performed, it calls the appropriate speed control procedure, rather then sending a message to the Auto Speed Control task. If the action procedure involves updating of the throttle position it calls a Throttle procedure instead of sending a message to the Throttle task.

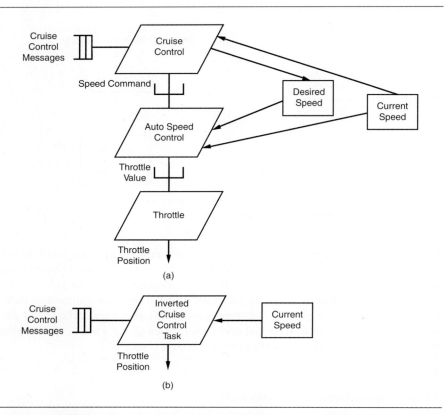

FIGURE 14.25 Sequential Task Inversion (a) Message Communication between Tasks (b) Inverted Task

14.10.4   Temporal Task Inversion

In temporal task inversion, which is similar to the weak forms of temporal cohesion, two or more periodic, periodic I/O, and/or periodic temporally cohesive tasks are combined into one task. The task has a timer event driven main scheduling procedure, which determines when it is time to call a particular operation to execute.

Grouping temporal transformations that are not functionally related into one task is not considered desirable from a design viewpoint. However, with temporal task inversion, this is done for optimization purposes in situations where the tasking overhead is considered too high.

An example of temporal task inversion is when two periodic tasks—the temporally cohesive periodic I/O task, Monitor Auto Sensors and the periodic I/O sequentially cohesive task, Perform Calibration—are combined into one task (Fig. 14.26), the Inverted Periodic Task, for optimization reasons. This task is activated periodically

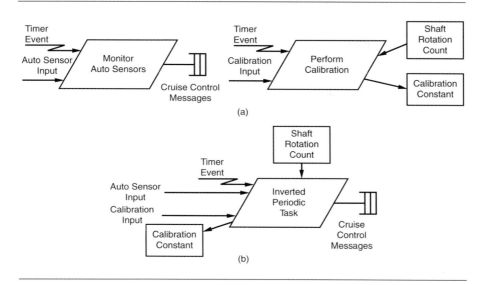

FIGURE 14.26 Temporal Task Inversion (a) Periodic Tasks (b) Inverted Periodic Task

by a timer event, and monitors the auto sensor (brake and engine) inputs as well as the calibration inputs, although with different frequency. Each time the main scheduling procedure is activated by the timer event, it determines whether it is time to check the auto sensors or calibration inputs, or both. In the former case, it outputs Cruise Control messages if there is a change in brake or engine status. In the latter case it updates the Calibration Constant data store.

14.11   Task Behavior Specifications (TBS)

14.11.1   Task Behavior Specification for Task Architecture Diagram

A task behavior specification (TBS) describes a concurrent task's interface, structure, timing characteristics, relative priority, event sequencing logic, and errors detected. It is a task's version of a behavioral model mini-specification. The task's interface defines how it interfaces to other tasks. The task's structure describes how its structure is derived using the task structuring criteria. The task's timing characteristics addresses frequency of activation and estimated execution time. This information is used for real-time scheduling purposes. The task's event sequencing logic describes how it responds to events and messages it receives.

The TBS evolves as the design of the task is refined. It is introduced with the task architecture diagram (TAD) to specify the characteristics of each task on the TAD. During task structuring, the TBS emphasizes the relationship between the task inputs and its outputs. The TBS is refined during the development of the software architecture diagram and the Ada architecture diagram. The TBS consists of

a. The **task interface** should include a definition of message inputs and outputs. For each message interface (input or output) there should be a description of the type of interface (loosely coupled, tightly coupled with reply, or tightly coupled without reply), and for each message type supported by this interface (message name and message parameters). Also to be defined is events signalled (input and ouput), including the name of event and the type of event (external, internal, timer). The third definition is of external inputs or outputs. Define the inputs from and outputs to the external environment.

b. The **task structure** information consists of the task structuring criterion used to design this task, and the behavioral model data/control transformations mapped to this task.

c. **Timing characteristics** include frequency of activation. For example, if periodic task: period T_i of task; if aperiodic task: estimated average and maximum frequency of activation by aperiodic events. Also included is the estimated execution time C_i for the task. If the task has more than one path through it, the estimated execution time for each of the major paths is added.

d. The task's relative **priority** is determined in relation to the other tasks in the system.

e. The task's **event sequencing logic** describes how the task responds to each of its message or event inputs, in particular what output is generated as a result of each input. Thus the TBS provides the necessary information in order to be able to define an event sequence diagram. The TBS is described informally in pseudo-code or in precise English, and may be supplemented by a diagram (e.g., to define a state transition diagram for a control task).

f. Possible **errors detected** during execution of this task are also defined.

14.11.2   Example of Task Behavior Specification

This example of a task behavior specification is from the robot controller case study presented later in this book. (The task architecture diagram for the robot controller system is shown in Fig. 23.9.)

```
TASK: Interpreter
A) TASK INTERFACE:
```

TASK INPUTS:

Event Inputs:

1) End (internal event) - Signals program is to be terminated

Message Inputs:

1) Start Program - identifies program to be interpreted
   Parameter: program id

2) Motion Acknowledgements Queue - identifies that motion block has been processed
   Parameter: motion block id

TASK OUTPUTS:

Event Output: Ended (internal event) - program has terminated

Message Outputs:

Motion Blocks Queue - three motion block types exist:

1) Move linear
   Parameter - destination point.

2) Move joint
   Parameter - destination point.

3) Move circular
   Parameters - destination point and intermediate point.

IHMS REFERENCED:

Sensor / Actuator IHM - Encapsulates Sensor / Actuator data store.

Robot Program - Contains contents of robot programs

B) TASK STRUCTURE:

Criterion: Functional and Sequential Cohesion

Data Transformations: Interpret Program Statement, Process Motion Command, Process Sensor / Actuator Command

C) TIMING CHARACTERISTICS:

Activation: Aperiodic - indirectly by operator. Worst case inter-arrival time = 125 msec. Average inter-arrival time 10 minutes. Required robot program statement interpreting rate = 8 statements / minute.

Execution time C_i: 10 ms for 1 robot program statement

D) PRIORITY: Medium - lower than I/O tasks

```
E) TASK EVENT SEQUENCING:
LOOP
WAIT MESSAGE (Start Program)
WHEN Start Program (x) message received
  Initialize robot program x
WHILE NOT End signalled LOOP
Read next program statement from Robot Program
IF motion command
  THEN Create motion block
  SEND MESSAGE (motion block) to Motion Blocks Queue
ELSIF sensor input command
  THEN wait for Motion Acknowledgements
  read sensor value from Sensor/Actuator IHM
ELSIF actuator output command
  THEN wait for Motion Acknowledgements
    update actuator value in Sensor/Actuator IHM
END IF
END LOOP
Wait for Motion Acknowledgements
Signal (Ended) to notify of program termination
END LOOP
F) ERRORS DETECTED:
   - Error in Robot Program
   - Illegal sensor id
   - Illegal actuator id
```

15

Information Hiding Module Structuring

15.1 Introduction

After determining the concurrent tasks in the system and defining the task interfaces, the next stage is to define the information hiding modules, as described in this chapter. The objective is to provide modules that are more self-contained and hence potentially more reusable, and to provide a system that is more easily maintained.

The objects and functions from the behavioral model, defined using Real-Time Structured Analysis (RTSA) or Concurrent Object-Based Real-Time Analysis (COBRA), are mapped to information hiding modules using a set of information hiding module structuring criteria. The approach is to use a blend of the module structuring criteria from the Naval Research Lab software cost reduction (NRL) method supported by the object structuring criteria from Booch's version of Object-Oriented Design (OOD).

Objects determined using Concurrent Object-Based Real-Time Analysis are mapped directly to information hiding modules. Functions determined using Concurrent Object-Based Real-Time Analysis or Real-Time Structured Analysis are grouped into information hiding modules by applying the module structuring criteria. The operations of each module are also defined.

This chapter describes the Ada-based Design Approach for Real-Time Systems (ADARTS) and COncurrent Design Approach for Real-Time Systems (CODARTS) module structuring criteria in detail. The categorization of information hiding modules is also described. Finally, the use of inheritance in design is discussed.

15.2   Information Hiding Module Structuring Categories

The ADARTS/CODARTS information hiding module structuring criteria are based primarily on the NRL module structuring criteria, supplemented by the OOD object structuring criteria. The ADARTS/CODARTS module structuring criteria are categorized as device interface modules, behavior hiding modules, and software decision modules. Device interface modules are similar to the NRL method and combine the OOD data source and destination objects. Behavior hiding modules hide system requirements. These are categorized further as data abstraction modules, state transition modules, function driver modules, and algorithm hiding modules. Software decision modules hide decisions made by the software designers that are likely to change.

In ADARTS/CODARTS, device interface modules and behavior hiding modules are determined from the behavioral model by applying the module structuring criteria. Software decision modules cannot usually be identified from the behavioral model and instead are determined later in the design process.

ADARTS/CODARTS do not use the extended computer module structuring criterion used by the NRL method because ADARTS/CODARTS designs are intended for execution in an environment where either a combination of the multi-tasking executive and the compiler for the high-level system implementation language hide the machine-specific details from the application, or an Ada environment where the Ada virtual machine hides the machine-specific details. Thus a combination of the Ada compiler, Ada run-time system, and underlying operating system manage machine resources and thereby hide the machine-specific details from the application.

15.3   Device Interface Modules (DIM)

15.3.1   Criterion

An important objective in developing a real-time system is to insulate users from changes to real-world I/O devices. A typical change to a real-world I/O device is to replace it with a different model of device that performs the same function. It is clearly undesirable for such a change to impact all users of the device. The solution is to use a device interface module (DIM). A DIM provides a virtual interface that hides the actual interface to the real-world I/O device.

With a device interface module, the information hiding concept is used to hide the design decision of how to interface to a specific I/O device. This is achieved by providing a virtual interface to the device and hiding the device-specific details inside the module. Thus, the DIM hides the details of the actual interface to the real world device, as shown in Fig. 15.1.

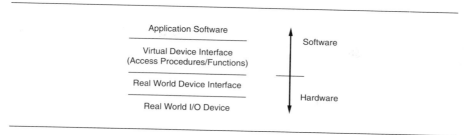

FIGURE 15.1 Device Interface Module

Users only access the device by means of the virtual interface. The virtual interface consists of a set of operations in the form of access procedures and/or functions. When a change to the real-world device is made that impacts the real-world interface, this change is hidden from the device users. This is achieved by keeping the virtual interface unchanged. The impact of the change is limited to the internals of the operations. By this means, users of the module are insulated from changes to the real-world device.

15.3.2   Deriving Device Interface Modules

During the analysis and modeling phase, external device I/O objects are determined using the COBRA object structuring criteria. These objects correspond to the physical entities in the real world that interface to the system. During module structuring, each external device I/O object is mapped to a DIM. The DIM hides the actual interface to the real-world device by providing a virtual interface to it.

In addition, it is necessary to determine the operations provided by each DIM. An external device I/O object interfaces to the real-world device and supports the functions that read from and/or write to the device. During the analysis phase, it is optional whether the data transformation representing the external device I/O object is decomposed further to show the actual functions supported by the object. In this phase, these functions need to be determined and mapped to the operations of the DIM.

If the behavioral model was developed using RTSA, the functions that input data from or output data to the I/O devices are shown on the data flow diagrams. During module structuring, an I/O DIM is created for each I/O device and the functions on the data flow diagram are mapped to the operations provided by the DIM.

15.3.3   Example of Device Interface Module

As an example of a device interface module, consider a data flow diagram shown in Fig. 15.2. Two data transformations representing the functions, Display Average Speed and Display Average MPG (which could have resulted from the decomposition of the device output object Mileage Display), both output data to the Mileage Display.

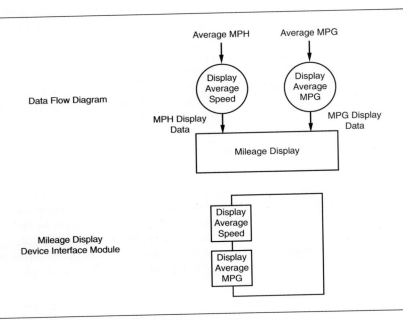

FIGURE 15.2 **Example of Device Interface Module**

Applying the information hiding module structuring criteria, a device interface module is created called Mileage Display, as shown on Figure 15.2. The Mileage Display module supports two operations, Display Average Speed and Display Average MPG. The information hidden is the details of how to format data for and interface to the real-world Mileage Display.

15.4 Behavior Hiding Modules

15.4.1 Data Abstraction Modules (DAM)

Criterion.   Each data store in the behavioral model potentially forms the basis for a data abstraction module (DAM). The DAM is used to encapsulate the data store, thereby hiding the internal structure of the data store.

The operations of the DAM (i.e., the access procedures and/or functions) are determined by analyzing the transformations on the data flow diagram that access the data store. There are several cases to be considered. First, if the whole transformation operates on the data store, then the transformation represents an operation of the DAM.

Second, if part of the transformation operates on the data store, then the operation can be determined by inspecting the mini-specification for the transformation. Thus simple operations, such as read and update, may not be explicitly shown on the data flow diagram but would instead appear in the mini-specifications. Third, if the transformation reads from one data store and updates a second data store, then the operation should be associated with the data store it updates, since an operation that changes the contents of the module is considered more important than one that does not. The data store that is read should be encapsulated in a different DAM that supports a read operation. Finally, if a transformation updates more than one data store, then the update operations are actually contained in the mini-specification. In this case, the transformation is not associated directly with either data store but uses operations that are associated with the data stores. The operations are designed as access procedures or functions, whose internals are also hidden.

Example of Data Abstraction Module.   As an example of a data abstraction module, consider the data flow diagram, shown in Fig. 15.3, which consists of three transformations and two data stores. The data stores Current Speed and Desired Speed form the basis of data abstraction modules with the same names.

Next, the transformations are analyzed to determine which DAM they should be associated with. Read Desired Speed and Clear Desired Speed are associated with

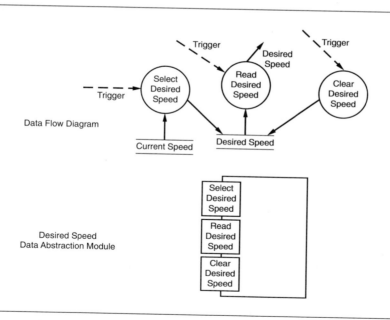

FIGURE 15.3 Data Abstraction Module

the Desired Speed DAM, as they operate wholly on the data store. However, Select Desired Speed manipulates two data stores; it reads Current Speed and updates Desired Speed. The decision is made to associate the Select Desired Speed operation with the Desired Speed DAM. This is because the update operation on Desired Speed is more important than reading Current Speed, as it changes the contents of the module. In addition, a separate Read Current Speed operation is required that operates on the Current Speed data store and is packaged with the Current Speed data abstraction module.

The Desired Speed Data Abstraction module is shown in Fig. 15.3. The specification of the module consists of one operation for each transformation: Select Desired Speed, Read Desired Speed, and Clear Desired Speed. Furthermore, the Read Current Speed operation, which is provided by the Current Speed DAM, is used by Select Desired Speed. The contents of the Desired Speed data store, as well as the internals of the operations, are hidden by the Desired Speed DAM. The synchronization of access to the data store is also hidden by the Desired Speed DAM and is a concern of the internals of the operations, as described in the following chapter.

15.4.2   State Transition Modules (STM)

A state transition module (STM) is a behavior hiding module. During module structuring, a control object in the behavioral model is mapped to a STM. The state transition diagram executed by the control object is mapped to a state transition table. Thus the STM hides the contents of the state transition table and maintains the current state of the module. It typically has operations to process an event and to reveal the current state.

An example of a state transition module from the Cruise Control and Monitoring system is the Cruise Control State Transition module. The data flow diagram in Fig. 15.4 shows the control object Cruise Control, which is represented by a control transformation. From a module structuring perspective the control transformation Cruise Control is structured as a state transition module also called Cruise Control. The STM hides the contents of the state transition table and supports two operations, Process Event and Current State. Process Event is called when there is a new event to process. Current State is an optional operation, which returns the cruise control state. It is only needed in applications where the current state needs to be known by clients of the STM. When called to process a new event, the Process Event operation may change the state of the module, depending on the current state of the module and any specified conditions that must hold. Optionally, it may return one or more actions to be performed.

A STM is a generic module type in that it can be used to encapsulate any state transition table. The contents of the table are application dependent and are defined at the time the STM is instantiated and/or initialized.

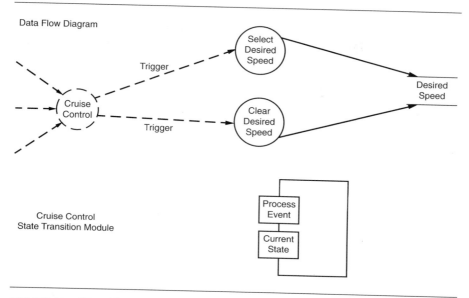

Data Flow Diagram

Cruise Control
State Transition Module

FIGURE 15.4 State Transition Module

15.4.3 Function Driver Modules

A function driver module is also a behavior hiding module [Parnas84]. It controls a set of closely related outputs to a virtual I/O device, which is supported by a device interface module. A function driver module hides the rules to determine the values of these outputs.

The data flow diagram for a function driver module from the cruise control and monitoring system shows the three transformations, Increase Speed, Maintain Speed, and Resume Cruising (Fig. 15.5). Each of these transformations is active during a different state of the system and computes the throttle value of the vehicle.

These three transformations are combined into a behavior hiding function driver module, Speed Control. The reason for this is that these functions all deal with automatic speed control and compute the throttle value, which is then passed to the Throttle device interface module. The Speed Control module supports these three operations plus a fourth operation, Deactivate.

15.4.4 Algorithm Hiding Modules

An algorithm hiding module is a behavior hiding module that hides an algorithm used in the application domain as well as any local data used by the algorithm. Algorithm hiding modules are typically found in real-time systems, as well as in

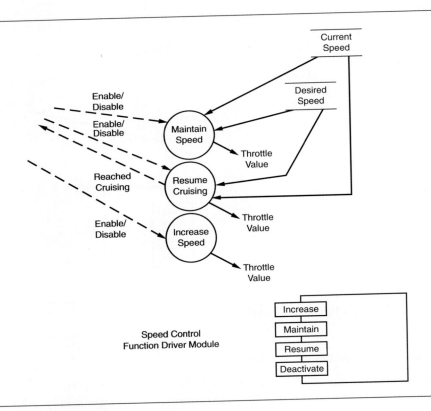

FIGURE 15.5 Function Driver Module

scientific and engineering applications. An example of an algorithm hiding module is the Elevator Scheduler module, which hides the algorithm used in the Elevator Control system for deciding which elevator should be selected to service a passenger request.

15.5   Software Decision Modules

Software decision modules hide design decisions made by the software designer that are considered likely to change. Software decision modules are usually developed later in the design process. They are not determined from the behavioral model, which relates to the problem domain. Examples of software decision modules are encapsulated data structures, such as stacks, queues, and data tables chosen by the designer.

15.6 Information Hiding Module Aggregation Hierarchy

The information hiding modules determined during the module structuring phase are categorized in an information hiding module aggregation hierarchy. As this hierarchy represents an approach for categorizing information hiding modules, only the leaf modules are actually executable. This is analogous to the decomposition hierarchy used in the behavioral model, where only the leaf nodes are described by means of mini-specifications. The information hiding modules are described in informal module specifications.

The information hiding module aggregation hierarchy has three main categories of modules. Device interface and behavior hiding modules are determined from the behavioral model. Software decision modules are developed later as required by the developers. An example of an information hiding module aggregation hierarchy for the Cruise Control and Monitoring system example is given in Table 15.1.

15.7 Inheritance in Design

15.7.1 Concepts

Inheritance is a mechanism for sharing and reusing code between classes (object types). A child class can adapt the structure (i.e., data encapsulated) and behavior (i.e., operations) of its parent class for its own use by adding new operations and instance variables or by redefining existing operations. The parent class is referred to as a superclass and the child class is referred to as a subclass. The adaptation of a parent class to form a child class is referred to as specialization. Child classes may be further specialized allowing the creation of class hierarchies, which are also referred to as generalization/specialization hierarchies.

Inheritance can be used in software design even though the target programming language may not support inheritance. Inheritance can be used when designing two similar—but not identical—module types during design. During architectural design, the modules need to be designed with inheritance in mind, so that code sharing and adaptation can be exploited in detailed design and coding. This is illustrated by means of a simple example in the next section.

TABLE 15.1 INFORMATION HIDING MODULE AGGREGATION HIERARCHY

Device Interface Modules
  Engine
  Brake
  Cruise Control Lever
  Calibration Input
  Shaft
  Throttle
  Gas Tank
  Mileage Reset
  Maintenance Reset
  Mileage Display
  Maintenance Display

Behavior Hiding Modules
  Data Abstraction Modules
    Shaft Rotation Count
    Calibration
    Current Speed
    Desired Speed
    Distance

  State Transition Modules
    Cruise Control
    Calibration Control

  Function Driver Modules
    Speed Control
    Average MPH
    Average MPG
    Oil Filter Maintenance
    Air Filter Maintenance
    Major Service Maintenance

15.7.2   Example of Inheritance in Design

As an example of inheritance in design, consider the automobile maintenance class from the cruise control and monitoring system. Although Oil Filter Maintenance, Air Filter Maintenance, and Major Service Maintenance could all be designed as separate modules, greater code sharing can be obtained by designing them as subclasses of the Maintenance class.

The class Maintenance is defined with two Operations: Initialize Maintenance and Check Maintenance. There is an encapsulated data item shared by both operations (Initial Mileage), which is the cumulative distance travelled when the previous maintenance service was carried out. When called, the Initialize Maintenance operation calls Read Cumulative Distance, an operation provided by the Distance module, and assigns the current cumulative distance to Initial Mileage. Using a concept from the Eiffel language [Meyer88], the Check Maintenance operation is deferred (i.e., its

TABLE 15.2 EXAMPLE OF GENERALIZATION/SPECIALIZATION HIERARCHY

Maintenance
  Oil Filter Maintenance
  Air Filter Maintenance
  Major Service Maintenance

specification is defined in the Maintenance class but the definition of its body is deferred to the subclasses).

A maintenance subclass (e.g., Oil Filter Maintenance) inherits the overall structure from the maintenance class including the type definition of Initial Mileage and the full definition (specification and body) of the Initialize Maintenance operation, as well as the specification of the deferred Check Maintenance operation. The Oil Filter Maintenance subclass now needs to add the definition of the body of the Check Maintenance operation. This would need to define the mileage at which oil filter maintenance is needed, the message that needs to be output when this mileage is exceeded, as well as the operation to be called from the Maintenance Display module (in this case Display Oil message). The Check Maintenance operation also calls the Read Cumulative Distance operation to determine the current cumulative distance travelled. It subtracts from this value the Initial Mileage to determine whether the prescribed number of miles have elapsed and hence whether it is time for an oil filter maintenance to be carried out on the vehicle. The generalization/specialization hierarchy for the maintenance class is given in Table 15.2.

15.7.3   Mapping to Object-based Implementation

There are few languages available at this time that support information hiding, inheritance, and concurrency. Consequently, when mapping the concurrent object-oriented design to an implementation, it is often the case that the object-oriented design will need to be mapped to an object-based language such as Ada. The developer needs to do by hand what an object-oriented compiler does automatically, and this can be achieved by manually "flattening" the inheritance hierarchy when mapping from design to code. This means that inherited operations will need to be explicitly duplicated in each subclass. Techniques for mapping object-oriented designs to non–object-oriented languages are described in [Rumbaugh91].

An example is now given of mapping the Maintenance generalization/specialization hierarchy to an object-based language. When mapping to code, the three maintenance subclasses, Oil Filter Maintenance, Air Filter Maintenance, and Major Service Maintenance, are designed as three separate information hiding modules. Consider the Initialize operation, which is only defined once in the maintenance superclass and then inherited by the three subclasses. When mapped to code, each module has to have its own copy of the Initialize operation.

15.8   Informal Specification of Information Hiding Modules

15.8.1   Documentation

An informal module specification defines the external view of the information hiding module, including the operations provided by the IHM. It specifies the following information:

- Information hidden by IHM. For example, data store(s) encapsulated in the case of DAMs or device interfaced to in the case of DIMs.

- Module structure. Module structuring criterion used to design this module.

- Assumptions made in specifying the module. For example, whether or not the operations of the module can be concurrently accessed by more than one task.

- Anticipated changes.

- Operations provided by the IHM. For each operation, define function performed, input parameters, output parameters, and operations used from other modules.

The information in the informal module specification may be documented in narrative or tabular form. The informal module specification is refined during the component interface specification step, where the module interface is formally defined.

15.8.2   Example of Informal Module Specification

An example of an informal module specification for an information hiding module is given for the sensor/actuator data abstraction module, which is taken from the robot controller case study.

```
IHM: Sensor/Actuator_DAM
Information Hidden: Encapsulates Sensor / Actuator
    data store. Stores current values of robot
    controller sensors and actuators.
Module Structure: Data Abstraction Module.
Assumptions: Operations may be concurrently accessed
    by more than one task.
Anticipated changes: Currently support boolean
    sensors and actuators only. Possible extension to
    support analog sensors and actuators.
Operations:
1) Read_Sensor
```

Function: Given the sensor id, returns the
   current value of the sensor.
Input parameters: Sensor_id
Output parameters: Sensor_value
Operations used: None

2) Update_Actuator
   Function: Used to update the value of the
      actuator in preparation for output.
   Input parameters: Actuator_id
      Actuator_value
   Output parameters: None
   Operations used: None

3) Update_Sensor
   Function: Used to update sensor value with new
      reading from the external environment.
   Input parameter: Sensor_id
      Sensor_value
   Output parameters: None
   Operations used: None

4) Read_Actuator
   Function: Used to read the new value of the
      actuator to output to the external environment.
   Input parameters: Actuator_id
   Output parameters: Actuator_value
   Operations used: None

16

Integration of Task and Information Hiding Module Views

16.1 Concepts

After structuring the system into tasks (Chapter 14) and into information hiding modules (Chapter 15), this chapter describes how the task and module views are integrated. Several examples are given to illustrate the approach.

Both the task structuring criteria and the module structuring criteria are applied to the objects and/or functions of the behavioral model, which are represented by data and control transformations on the data flow/control flow diagrams. When performing task and module structuring, the behavioral model is viewed from two perspectives, the dynamic and the static views. The dynamic view is provided by the concurrent tasks, which are determined using the task structuring criteria. The static view is provided by the information hiding modules, which are determined using the module structuring criteria. This chapter provides guidelines for integrating the task and module views.

A task is considered an active component while a module is considered a passive component. The structuring criteria for tasks and modules are generally different, although they sometimes coincide; that is, they lead to the same component being determined. For example, the task structuring criterion of asynchronous device I/O coincides with the module structuring criterion of device interface module.

The relationship between tasks and modules is handled as follows. The active component, the task, is activated by an external, internal, or timer event. It then calls an operation provided by the passive component. A software architecture diagram is a refinement of the task architecture diagram, which explicitly shows the relationship between tasks and modules. It shows a network of concurrent tasks and IHMs, explicitly showing the operations provided by the IHMs. Intertask interfaces, in the form of message communication and event synchronization, are shown in the same way as on task architecture diagrams.

16.2 Asynchronous Device I/O

Consider the case of asynchronous device I/O from both the task structuring and module structuring perspectives. Structure the task as an asynchronous device I/O task. Structure the module as a device interface module. Define the operations of the module. Place the DIM inside the task, since no other task calls it. An asynchronous I/O task is activated by an interrupt. Once activated, the task calls an operation provided by the DIM to read the input from the device.

An example of asynchronous device I/O is given in Fig. 16.1. The data flow

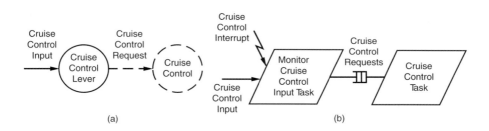

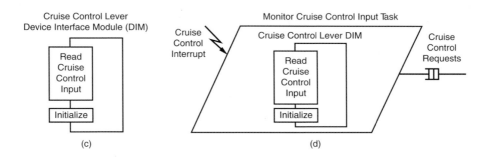

FIGURE 16.1 Asynchronous Device I/O (a) Data Flow Diagram (b) Task Structuring View (c) Module Structuring View (d) Integrated Task and Module Structuring View

diagram [Fig. 16.1(a)] shows that the Cruise Control Lever device input object reads cruise control inputs from the cruise control lever and sends them as cruise control requests to the Cruise Control control object.

From a task structuring perspective, as the cruise control lever is an asynchronous input device, the object Cruise Control Lever is structured as an asynchronous device input task called Monitor Cruise Control Input [Fig. 16.1(b)]. When the task is activated by the cruise control interrupt, it reads the input and then sends this as a Cruise Control Request message to the Cruise Control task.

From a module structuring perspective, the Cruise Control Lever device input object is structured as a Cruise Control Lever device interface module [Fig. 16.1(c)]. The DIM hides the specific I/O details of the cruise control lever. The DIM supports two operations, Read Cruise Control Input and Initialize. Initialize is called at system startup to initialize the DIM's internal data structures and perform any necessary device initialization.

From a combined task and module structuring perspective, the Cruise Control Input device interface module is placed inside the Monitor Cruise Control Input task [Fig. 16.1(d)], as no other tasks call the Read Cruise Control Input access procedure. When the Monitor Cruise Control Input task is activated by a cruise control interrupt, it calls the Read Cruise Control Input access procedure to read the input, and then sends this as a message to the Cruise Control task.

16.3   Polled I/O

Consider the case of polled I/O from both the task structuring and module structuring perspectives. With polled I/O, structure the task either according to the periodic I/O (for one I/O device) or periodic I/O–temporal cohesion (for two or more I/O devices) criteria. Each passive I/O device is encapsulated in a DIM. The operations provided by the DIM are defined and the DIM is placed inside the task. In either case, the task is activated by a timer event. It then calls the operations provided by each DIM to obtain the latest status of each device.

An example of polled I/O is given in Fig. 16.2. The data flow diagram shows the two device input objects, Brake and Engine [Fig. 16.2(a)], which monitor the brake and engine sensors respectively. The brake and engine sensors are sampled periodically and with the same frequency.

From a task structuring perspective, the Engine and Brake device input objects are grouped into a task called Monitor Auto Sensors based on the periodic I/O and temporal cohesion criteria.

Monitor Auto Sensors [Fig. 16.2(b)] is activated periodically by a timer event at

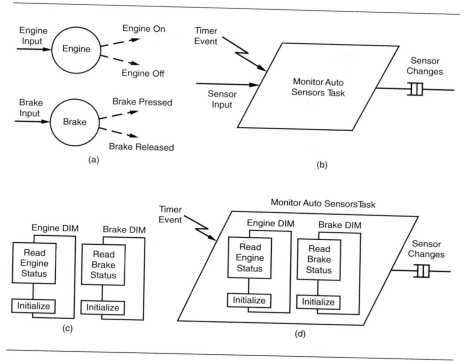

FIGURE 16.2 Polled I/O (a) Data Flow Diagram (b) Task Structuring View (c) Module Structuring View (d) Integrated Task and Module Structuring View

which time it reads the current values of the sensors. If there is a change in the engine and/or brake sensor status, it sends a message(s) to the Cruise Control task.

From a module structuring perspective, two separate device interface modules are created for the engine and brake sensors [Fig. 16.2(c)]. Each DIM supports two operations. For the engine sensor, the operations are Read Engine Status and Initialize. For the brake sensor, they are Read Brake Status and Initialize.

From a combined task and module perspective [Fig. 16.2(d)], the Monitor Auto Sensors task is activated periodically by a timer event, at which time it reads the current values of the sensors by calling each of the access procedures, Read Engine Status and Read Brake Status. If there is a change in the engine and/or brake sensor status, it sends a message(s) containing the new value(s) to the Cruise Control task.

By separating the concerns of how a device is accessed into the device interface module from the concerns of when the device is accessed into the task, greater flexibility and potential reuse is achieved. Thus, for example, the brake DIM could be used in different applications by an asynchronous I/O task, a periodic I/O task, or by a temporally cohesive periodic I/O task. Furthermore, the characteristics of different brake sensors could be hidden inside the DIM, while preserving the same virtual device interface.

16.4   Internal Tasks and Modules

The next case to be considered is that of internal tasks and modules. An internal task is activated either periodically or aperiodically. It calls operations provided by one or more modules. Internal tasks typically access behavior hiding modules; for example, data abstraction modules or state transition modules.

An example is given in Fig. 16.3 of a control task and the modules it interfaces to. The data flow diagram [Fig. 16.3(a)] shows that the control object Cruise Control triggers two data transformations at different state transitions, Select Desired Speed and Clear Desired Speed.

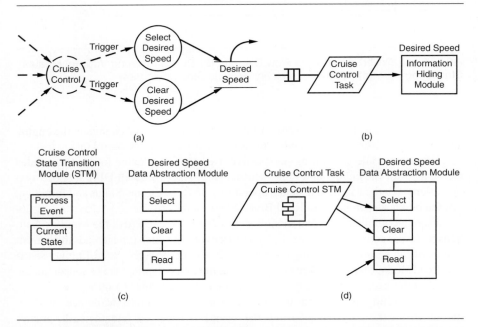

FIGURE 16.3 Control Task and Modules (a) Data Flow Diagram (b) Task Structuring View (c) Module Structuring View (d) Integrated Task and Module Structuring View

From a task structuring perspective, the control object Cruise Control is structured as a control task because, by definition, the execution of its state transition diagram is strictly sequential. Furthermore, the control object may be combined with other data transformations that it interacts with based on the control cohesion criterion. This applies in the case of a data transformation that is triggered by the state transition and performs a function that starts and completes execution during the state transition. Thus the transformations Select Desired Speed and Clear Desired Speed are combined with Cruise Control according to the control cohesion criterion [Fig. 16.3(b)].

From a module structuring perspective [Fig. 16.3(c)] the data store Desired Speed forms the basis of a data abstraction module that supports three access procedures, Select Desired Speed, Clear Desired Speed, and Read Desired Speed. The control object Cruise Control is structured as a state transition module that hides the structure and content of the Cruise Control state transition table.

From a combined task and module structuring perspective [Fig. 16.3(d)], there is one task, the Cruise Control task, and two modules, the Cruise Control state transition module and the Desired Speed data abstraction module. The Cruise Control state transition module is placed inside the Cruise Control task since no other task uses it.

The Desired Speed data abstraction module is not placed inside a task as it is accessed by more than one task. The access procedures Select Desired Speed and Clear Desired Speed are actually part of the Desired Speed module but are executed by the Cruise Control task. The third procedure, Read Desired Speed, is executed by a different task, Auto Speed Control. Because the DAM is accessed by more than one task, it is important for the operations to synchronize access to the data.

16.5   Concurrent Access to Modules

A module whose operations are used exclusively by one task can reside inside that task. A module whose operations are called by more than one task must reside externally to the tasks. If a module is accessed by more than one task, then the module's operations must synchronize the access to the data it encapsulates. Mechanisms for providing this synchronization are discussed later.

Because the internals of a module's operations are designed differently depending on whether the module is accessed by one task or several tasks, it is important to define clearly the context in which the module is to be used. Document this information in the assumptions section of the informal module specification.

For packaging reasons, it may be undesirable to place a module that is accessed by only one task inside the task. However, it must be clearly stated that this module is designed to be only accessed by one task.

A DIM that is only accessed by one task does not need to provide any synchronization of access to the device. If the device is to be accessed by more than one task, then the internals of the DIM have to be redesigned to allow this. Alternatively, sequential access to the DIM can be ensured by ending all device I/O requests to a resource monitor task, which is then the only task that calls the operations of the DIM.

16.6   Example of Synchronization of Access to Modules

16.6.1   Operations Provided by IHM

As an example of synchronization of access to an information hiding module, consider the sensor data store example. During module structuring, this data store is mapped to a sensor data abstraction module. In designing this module, one design decision relates to whether the sensor data structure is to be designed as an array or a linked list. Another design decision relates to the nature of the synchronization required, whether the module is to be accessed by more than one task concurrently; and if so, whether mutual exclusion or the multiple readers/writers algorithm is required. These design decisions relate to the design of the information hiding module and need not concern users of the module.

By separating the concerns of *what* the module does—namely the specification of the operations—from *how* it does it—namely the internal design of the module—then any changes to the internal data structure (e.g., from array to linked list), and changes to the internal synchronization of access to the data (e.g., from mutual exclusion to multiple readers/writers), has no impact on users of the module. The impact is only on the internals of the module, namely the internal data structure and the internals of the operations that access the data structure.

For the same external interface of this DAM, consider two different internal designs for the synchronization of access to the sensor data store, mutual exclusion and multiple readers/multiple writers.

In the sensor data store example, the operations provided by the sensor data abstraction module are (see Fig. 16.4):

```
Read_Analog_Sensor (Sensor_id, Sensor_Value,
   Upper_Limit, Lower_Limit, Alarm_Condition)
```

This operation is called by reader tasks who wish to read from the sensor data store. Given the sensor id, this operation returns the current sensor value, upper limit, lower limit, and alarm condition to users of this module, who may wish to manipulate or display the data. The range between Lower Limit and Upper Limit is the normal range

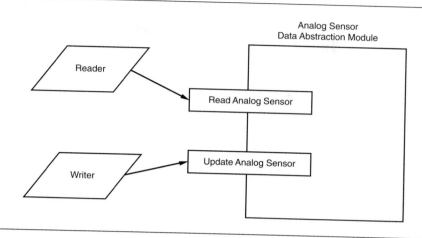

FIGURE 16.4 Task Synchronization via Information Hiding Module

within which the sensor value can vary without causing an alarm. If the value of the sensor is below the lower limit or above the upper limit, the boolean variable Alarm_Status is equal to Low or High respectively.

Update_Analog_Sensor (Sensor_id, Sensor_Value)

This operation is called by writer tasks who wish to write to the sensor data store. It is used to update the value of the sensor in the data store with the latest reading obtained by monitoring the external environment. It checks whether the value of the sensor is below the lower limit or above the upper limit; and if so, it sets the value of Alarm_Status to Low or High respectively. If the sensor value is within the normal range, the Alarm_Status is set to OK.

16.6.2 Example of Mutual Exclusion

Consider first the mutual exclusion solution. To ensure mutual exclusion in the sensor data store example, each task must execute a Wait operation on the semaphore Sensor_data_store_semaphore (initially set to 1) before it starts accessing the data store and execute a Signal operation on the semaphore after it has finished accessing the data store. The pseudocode for the Read and Write operations is as follows:

Read_Analog_Sensor (Sensor_id, Sensor_Value,
    Upper_Limit, Lower_Limit, Alarm_Condition)

```
— Critical section for read operation.
Wait (Sensor_data_store_semaphore)
  Sensor_Value := Sensor_data_store (Sensor_id, Value)
  Upper_Limit := Sensor_data_store (Sensor_id, Up_Lim)
  Lower_Limit := Sensor_data_store (Sensor_id, Lo_Lim)
  Alarm_Condition := Sensor_data_store (Sensor_id,
    Alarm)
Signal (Sensor_data_store_semaphore)
```

In the case of the Update operation, in addition to updating the value of the sensor in the data store, it is also necessary to determine whether the sensor's alarm condition is High, Low, or Normal.

```
Update_Analog_Sensor (Sensor_id, Sensor_Value)
— Critical section for write operation.
Wait (Sensor_data_store_semaphore)
  Sensor_data_store (Sensor_id, Value) := Sensor_Value
  IF Sensor_Value ≥ Sensor_data_store (Sensor_id,
    Up_Lim)
    THEN Sensor_data_store (Sensor_id, Alarm) :=
      High_Alarm
  ELSIF Sensor_Value ≤ Sensor_data_store (Sensor_id,
    Lo_Lim)
    THEN Sensor_data_store (Sensor_id, Alarm) :=
      Low_Alarm
    ELSE Sensor_data_store (Sensor_id, Alarm) := Normal
  ENDIF;
Signal (Sensor_data_store_semaphore)
```

16.6.3 Example of Multiple Readers/Multiple Writers

With the multiple readers/multiple writers solution, multiple reader tasks may access the data store concurrently, while writer tasks have mutually exclusive access to it. Two binary semaphores are used, Reader_semaphore and Sensor_data_store_semaphore, which are initially set to 1. A count of the number of readers, number_of_readers, is also maintained, which is initially set to 0. The Reader_semaphore is used by readers to ensure mutually exclusive updating of the reader count. The Sensor_data_store_semaphore is used to ensure mutually exclusive access to the sensor data store by writers. This semaphore is also accessed by readers. It is acquired by the first reader prior to reading from the data store and released by the last reader after having finished reading from the data store. The pseudocode for the Read and Write operations is as follows:

```
Read_Analog_Sensor (Sensor_id, Sensor_Value,
  Upper_Limit, Lower_Limit, Alarm_Condition)
— Read operation called by reader tasks. Several
— readers are allowed to access the data store
— providing there is no writer accessing it.
Wait (reader_semaphore)
  Increment number_of_readers
  IF number_of_readers = 1
    THEN Wait (Sensor_data_store_semaphore)
Signal (reader_semaphore)
  Sensor_Value := Sensor_data_store (Sensor_id, Value)
  Upper_Limit := Sensor_data_store (Sensor_id, Up_Lim)
  Lower_Limit := Sensor_data_store (Sensor_id, Lo_Lim)
  Alarm_Condition := Sensor_data_store (Sensor_id,
    Alarm)
Wait (reader_semaphore)
  Decrement number_of_readers
  IF number_of_readers = 0
    THEN Signal (Sensor_data_store_semaphore)
Signal (reader_semaphore)
```

The pseudocode for the Update operation is similar to that for the mutual exclusion example, as it is necessary to ensure that writer tasks who call the Update operation have mutually exclusive access to the sensor data store.

```
Update_Analog_Sensor (Sensor_id, Sensor_Value)
— Writer tasks calling this operation have mutually
— exclusive access to the sensor data store.
Wait (Sensor_data_store_semaphore)
  Sensor_data_store (Sensor_id, Value) := Sensor_Value
  IF Sensor_Value ≥ Sensor_data_store (Sensor_id,
    Up_Lim)
    THEN Sensor_data_store (Sensor_id, Alarm) :=
      High_Alarm
  ELSIF Sensor_Value ≤ Sensor_data_store (Sensor_id,
    Lo_Lim)
    THEN Sensor_data_store (Sensor_id, Alarm) :=
      Low_Alarm
    ELSE Sensor_data_store (Sensor_id, Alarm) := Normal
```

```
  ENDIF;
Signal (Sensor_data_store_semaphore)
```

16.7   Example of Resource Monitor Task and Device Interface Module

An example of concurrent access to modules is given from the Elevator Controller case study (Fig. 16.5). The Direction Lamps output device is encapsulated in a DIM of the same name, which provides two operations, Set and Clear. The DIM is designed to be accessed by only one task. As the device is passive, an asynchronous output task is not required. Furthermore, output to the task is on demand, so a periodic output task is not required. For a single elevator, the Elevator Controller task calls the Set and Clear operations directly [Fig. 16.5(a)].

In the multiple elevator case, it is possible to have multiple instances of the

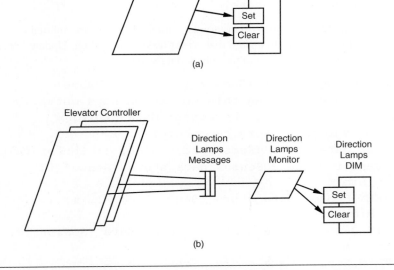

FIGURE 16.5 Device Interface Module for Passive Device (a) Accessed by One Task (b) Accessed by Multiple Tasks via the Resource Monitor Task

Elevator Controller task attempting to output to the Direction Lamps concurrently. The Direction Lamps DIM is not designed to handle this. A solution is to provide a Direction Lamps resource monitor task, which ensures that output requests are handled sequentially [Fig. 16.5(b)]. Instead of calling the Set and Clear operations, the Elevator Controller tasks send direction lamp messages to the Direction Lamps resource monitor task. The Direction Lamps resource monitor waits for incoming messages and processes each message by calling the appropriate Set or Clear operation for the desired lamp. Furthermore, by supporting a loosely-coupled message communication interface, the Elevator Controller tasks are not held up by the Direction Lamps resource monitor task.

16.8   Task Behavior Specification (TBS) for Software Architecture Diagram

16.8.1   Introduction

During the development of the software architecture diagram (SAD), the task behavior specification (TBS) is refined to include the calls to the operations supported by the IHMs. Thus certain operations executed by the task may actually be provided by an IHM and called by the task, rather than be contained within the body of the task. The task behavior specification defines when the operations provided by an IHM are called by the task. The IHMs referenced section of the TBS is also refined to show all new IHMs referenced by the task.

16.8.2   Example of Updated Task Behavior Specification

The task behavior specification for the Interpreter task is updated to correspond to the SAD. (The SAD for the Robot Controller system is shown in Fig. 23.10.)

```
LOOP
WAIT MESSAGE (Start Program)
WHEN Start Program (x) message received
   Robot Program.Initialize (x)
WHILE NOT End signalled LOOP
Robot_Program.Read_next_statement (statement)
IF motion command
   THEN Create motion block
   SEND MESSAGE (motion block) to Motion Blocks Queue
```

```
ELSIF sensor input command
  THEN wait for Motion Acknowledgements
  Sensor/Actuator_DAM.Read_Sensor (Sensor_id,
    Sensor_value)
ELSIF actuator output command
  THEN wait for Motion Acknowledgements
  Sensor/Actuator_DAM.Update_Actuator (Actuator_id,
    Actuator_value)
END IF
END LOOP
Wait for Motion Acknowledgements
Signal (Ended) to notify of program termination
END LOOP
```

17

Ada-based Architectural Design

17.1 Mapping Design to Target System Environment

After completing the module structuring stage, the design is thus far independent of target language and target environment. It is also consistent with the Ada programming language as it supports tasks and packages (information hiding modules).

The next step is to map the design to the target system environment. If the design is to be mapped to a sequential language, there is no language support for concurrent tasks. In this case, support for the concurrent tasks has to be provided by a multi-tasking kernel. The message communication and event synchronization interfaces, are typical of those provided by multi-tasking kernels. Mapping them to the intertask communication and synchronization primitives provided by the multi-tasking kernel should therefore be relatively simple. Refer back to Chapter 3 for more information on run-time support for concurrent tasks and multi-tasking kernels.

With Ada-based Design Approach for Real-Time Systems (ADARTS), Ada is the target language and the main activity in this step is to develop the Ada-based architectural design by addressing Ada-specific issues. In particular, these are to add Ada support tasks, to address loosely-coupled intertask communication and access synchronization to shared data, and to define the Ada task interfaces.

An Ada architecture diagram (AAD) is used to display graphically an Ada-based architectural design. The AAD notation is based on the Buhr diagram notation [Buhr84]. It shows a network of concurrent tasks and packages, explicitly illustrating the task and package interfaces, and is a further refinement of the task architecture diagram and the software architecture diagram.

17.2   Ada Support Tasks

With ADARTS, tasks are categorized as being either application tasks or support tasks. Application tasks relate directly to the application and are identified by the task structuring criteria. Support tasks are also usually required in a real-time Ada application because of restrictions in the Ada language (not because of application needs). If the application were developed using a different language, the support tasks would probably not be required.

A typical Ada multi-tasking application requires these additional support tasks to ensure the appropriate communication and synchronization between tasks. Synchronizing tasks are required where information maintained by a package is concurrently accessed by more than one task. In this case, access to the information needs to be synchronized. Message buffering tasks are needed to relieve the constraints of the Ada rendezvous, which only supports tightly-coupled communication between tasks.

17.3   Synchronized Access to Data Stores

Each data abstraction package that may be concurrently accessed by more than one task may need to have access to the hidden data synchronized, in particular if one or more tasks update the data. This is handled by means of a nested synchronizing task.

The nature of the synchronized access to the data varies with the application. In some cases, for example, it may be desirable to provide mutual exclusion by having the critical sections implemented inside the nested task. Thus only one application task at a time may access the data by making an entry call to the synchronizing task. In other cases, it may be desirable to support multiple concurrent readers but only one writer to the data store. In this situation, the nested task acts as a resource manager, controlling which tasks access the data and when. Ada solutions to these classical problems in concurrent processing are described by Buhr [Buhr84] and Gehani [Gehani84]. There are also cases where access to more than one data store may need to be synchronized. For example, a task may need to have mutually-exclusive access to two data stores. A solution to this problem is to encapsulate each data store in a package and then to embed the two packages within a synchronizing task.

If mutually-exclusive operations are required on a shared variable rather than a data structure, then an alternative to using a synchronizing task is to use Ada's pragma SHARED capability [Gehani84]. This ensures that reads or updates to the shared variable are indivisible and hence mutually exclusive.

In an example of a data abstraction package with a nested synchronizing task (Fig. 17.1), the critical sections are executed by the synchronizing task, which ensures that only one application task may access the data at a time. Consider the case when a reader task wishes to read data. It calls the Get procedure of the data abstraction

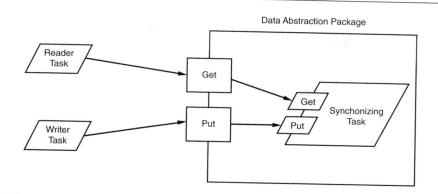

FIGURE 17.1 Synchronizing Task

package, which in turn makes a Get entry call to the synchronizing task. The synchronizing task is waiting to accept either a Get or Put entry call. Assume that when the reader task makes the Get entry call, the synchronizing task is idle. Hence the synchronizing task accepts the call, thereby establishing the rendezvous. Assume that the Writer task now calls the Put access procedure of the data abstraction package, which in turn calls the Put entry of the synchronizing task. As the synchronizing task is still servicing the Get entry call, the writer task is temporarily suspended. On completing the rendezvous with the reader task, the synchronizing task returns the requested data to the reader task. The synchronizing task can now service the Put entry call from the writer task. Thus mutual exclusion is ensured by the fact that the synchronizing task only accepts one entry call at a time.

17.4   Message Communication

The intertask communication and synchronization interfaces were determined earlier; in this section, the Ada designs required to support these interfaces are described.

17.4.1   Ada Rendezvous

In Ada, tightly-coupled message communication can be handled directly by means of the Ada rendezvous. In the tightly-coupled situation, a producer task sends a message to the consumer task and then waits for the rendezvous with the consumer. In Ada, the producer makes an entry call to the consumer and the parameters of the message become the input parameters of the entry call. The producer is suspended for the

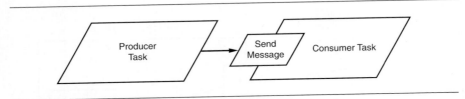

FIGURE 17.2 Tightly-coupled Message Communication: Ada Rendezvous

duration of the rendezvous. The consumer accepts the call and executes the sequence of statements associated with the accept statement. If the producer needs a reply, the consumer computes the reply and then passes the reply back to the producer as an output parameter. This completes the rendezvous, so that the producer and consumer may continue executing concurrently.

Two examples are used to illustrate the two cases of tightly-coupled message communication. The task interface for tightly coupled message communication without reply is mapped directly to an Ada rendezvous [Fig. 17.2]. The consumer task supports a Send Message entry for receiving the message. The task interface for tightly-coupled message communication with reply is also mapped directly to an Ada rendezvous [Fig. 17.2].

17.4.2   Message Buffering Tasks

Loosely-coupled message communication, where a message queue can build up between the producer and consumer tasks, cannot be handled directly by the Ada rendezvous. This case is handled by introducing a message buffering task, which is used to buffer a message queue.

Figure 17.3 shows an example of a message buffering task introduced between the producer and consumer. Messages are queued FIFO in a buffer maintained by the task. The message buffering task provides two entries, a Send Message entry and a Receive Message entry. The Send Message entry is called by the producer to send a message to the message buffering task. The parameters of the message become the

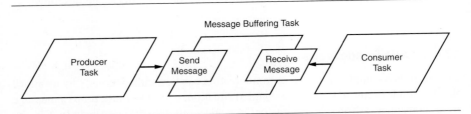

FIGURE 17.3 Loosely-coupled Message Communication with Message Buffering Task

input parameters of the entry call. The message is stored at the end of the queue in the message buffer. The Receive Message entry is called by the consumer to receive a message from the message buffering task. The first message in the queue is extracted from the message buffer. The parameters of the message become the output parameters of the entry call.

Guards [Buhr84] may be used to prevent the producer from sending a message when the buffer is full and the consumer from receiving a message when the buffer is empty. The message buffering task should be idle most of the time, so the producer and consumer tasks should not be held up except for the buffer full and buffer empty cases, respectively. Problems with delays in message communication using message buffering tasks are discussed later.

17.4.3   Message Buffering Tasks with Priority Queues

A more complex situation is that of the priority message queue. This situation is handled by a more complex message buffering task, which buffers all the messages for the consumer task. The consumer task receives messages from the message buffering task in priority order, with messages at the same priority level queued on a FIFO basis.

Consider three producer tasks connected to a consumer task by means of a priority message queue, where messages from producer A have the highest priority and messages from producer C have the lowest priority. The Ada solution in Fig. 17.4 has a priority message buffering task introduced between the producer and consumer. The

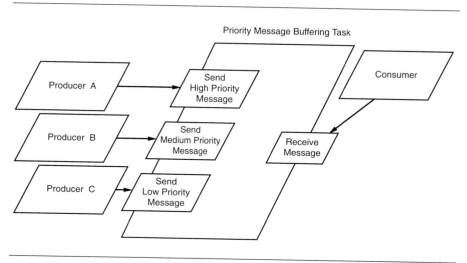

FIGURE 17.4 Loosely-coupled Message Communication with Priority Message Buffering Task

priority message buffering task provides a Send Message entry for each priority level and one Receive Message entry. A given producer X calls the appropriate Send Priority Message entry to send a message to the message buffering task. Messages are queued by priority inside the task. The consumer waits for a message by calling the Receive Message entry. There is a guard associated with this entry, so as long as there are no messages for the consumer, it is suspended at the rendezvous. If there is a message, the consumer receives the highest priority message.

An alternative solution is to have the same structure for the message buffering task as that shown in Fig. 17.3 with only one Send Message entry, but with a parameter added containing the priority of the message.

17.5   Event Buffering Task

Tightly-coupled event synchronization between tasks is handled directly by means of the Ada rendezvous. This is handled in the same way as tightly-coupled message communication. Loosely-coupled event synchronization is handled by means of an event buffering task, which buffers events sent from a source task to a destination task. The structure of an event buffering task is similar to that of a message buffering task. An event buffering task is particularly useful for buffering events sent by different producer tasks which are destined for the same consumer task.

17.6   Other Support Tasks

Other types of support tasks have been proposed by Buhr [Buhr84] and Neilsen [Neilsen88], such as transporter and relay tasks. Neilsen also proposes relay buffers that need two support tasks and transporter buffers that need three tasks. These support tasks are all aimed at preventing the producer and consumer from being delayed at a rendezvous and at allowing them to respond to other requests.

ADARTS discourages the proliferation of support tasks, which can cause bottle-necks and additional overhead. Instead, ADARTS advocates using the message communication paradigm, where message buffering tasks are used to support loosely-coupled message communication between tasks. As described earlier, message buffering tasks may be used to buffer one or more message queues.

A key point to realize is that if all requests to the consumer task come through a single message buffering task, then if the consumer is suspended at the Receive Message rendezvous, the buffer is empty and consequently there is no work for the consumer.

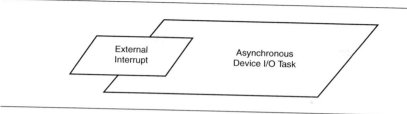

FIGURE 17.5 Mapping External Events to Ada

In the case of the producer, it is only in danger of being suspended for a significant period of time if the buffer is full. If it is considered undesirable for the producer to be held up when the buffer is full, then the message buffering task should accept the message immediately and either overwrite the oldest message in the buffer or throw away the new message. Another alternative to discarding a message is for the message buffering task to return a negative response to the producer task and let it decide what to do.

17.7   Defining Task Entries

At this stage, after addressing all task interfaces, either directly by means of a rendezvous or via a message buffering interface, most task entries will have been defined. One additional important case in real-time systems is that of tasks activated by hardware interrupts. This applies in particular to an asynchronous device I/O task activated by means of an external interrupt. In Ada, this is handled by means of an entry which is called by the hardware, as shown in Fig. 17.5.

A timer event is usually mapped to an Ada Delay statement. In cases where a more accurate measure of time is required, a real-time clock interrupt may be used. In this case, the periodic task is activated by an entry call from the real-time clock.

17.8   Packaging the Tasks

There are two reasons for packaging tasks. The first is to make the components more reusable, in which case the task is embedded in a package. The second reason is implementation related. In Ada, a task is not a library unit but packages are. It is therefore necessary to package the tasks into library units such as packages.

17.9   Task Behavior Specification for Ada Architecture Diagram

17.9.1   Documentation

During the development of the Ada architecture diagram (AAD), additional information needs to be provided about the support tasks introduced (i.e., message buffering tasks and synchronizing tasks), as well as the definition of all task entries. Informal task and package specifications are produced. The task behavior specifications are updated to include the Ada specific aspects of the design, and hence to be consistent with the AAD. The task and package interface specifications are formally defined in the component interface specifications. Task behavior specifications need to be created for the newly identified support tasks.

17.9.2   Example of Updated Task Behavior Specification

The task behavior specification (TBS) for the interpreter task is updated to correspond to the AAD. (The AAD for the Robot Controller System is shown in Fig. 23.11.)

```
TASK Interpreter
Number_of_motion_blocks_sent := 0
Number_of_Motion_Acknowledgements := 0
LOOP
Interpreter_Message_Buffer.Receive_Interpreter_
   Message (Message)
IF Message = Start_Program (x)
   THEN Robot Program.Initialize (x)
   ELSE Error condition
END IF
WHILE NOT End_signalled LOOP
Robot_Program.Read_next_statement (Statement)
IF Statement = motion_command
   THEN Create motion_block
   Motion_Block_Buffer.Send (motion_block)
   Increment Number_of_motion_blocks_sent
ELSIF Statement = sensor_input_command
   THEN Wait_for_Motion_Acknowledgements
   Sensor/Actuator_DAM.Read_Sensor (Sensor_id,
      Sensor_value)
ELSIF Statement = actuator_output_command
   THEN Wait_for_Motion_Acknowledgements
```

```
    Sensor/Actuator_DAM.Update_Actuator (Actuator_id,
      Actuator_value)
  END IF
  — Read next message - do not wait if no message
  SELECT
  Interpreter_Message_Buffer.Receive_Interpreter_
    Message (Message)
  ELSE
  — Continue without waiting
  END SELECT
  IF Message = Motion_Acknowledgement
    THEN Increment Number_of_Motion_Acknowledgements
  ELSIF Message = End_ Event THEN End_signalled :=
    TRUE
  END IF
  END LOOP
  Wait_for_Motion_Acknowledgements
  — Notify of program termination
  Robot_Command_Buffer.Send(Ended_Signal)
  END LOOP
  END Interpreter
```

Wait_for_Motion_Acknowledgements is designed as a procedure, as follows:

```
  PROCEDURE Wait_for_Motion_Acknowledgements
  WHILE Number_of_Motion_Acknowledgements < Number_
    of_motion_blocks_sent LOOP
  Interpreter_Message_Buffer.Receive_Interpreter_
    Message (Message)
  IF Message = Motion_Acknowledgement
    THEN Increment Number_of_Motion_Acknowledgements
  END LOOP
  END Wait_for_Motion_Acknowledgements
```

18

The Later Phases of
Software Development in
ADARTS and CODARTS

18.1   Define Component Interfaces

Having previously identified the components of the system (i.e., the tasks and information hiding modules), the component interface specifications are now defined. The component interface specification—also known as the abstract interface specification [Parnas84, Lamb88]—represents the externally visible view of the component.

During task structuring, tasks were defined informally in task behavior specifications, which were refined later. During module structuring, modules and the operations they support were defined informally. During this current stage, the component interface specifications are defined formally. The component interface specification can be defined by means of the task or module (package in Ada) specification of the component together with additional information that can be stored as comments.

The specification for a component is given by the following elements.

1. Name of the component (task or package);

2. Brief description of the features provided by the component;

3. Assumptions made in specifying the component (e.g., if the operations of a module can be concurrently accessed by more than one task);

4. Description of the visible operations supported by the component, including access procedures and/or functions, task entries, parameters, and parameter types;

5. Description of externally visible effects of component's operations, including any external I/O and any operations used from other modules;

6. Changes to the module that are anticipated at the time the specification is developed;

7. Timing characteristics (for tasks only), including frequency of activation of task and estimated execution time of task; and

8. Errors detected by this component.

In an ADARTS design, it is also necessary to specify the component interface specifications for all tasks that are hidden inside package bodies, because they contain important design information.

Usually, each software organization has its own standards for defining component interface specifications, so this topic is not addressed further.

18.2 Incremental Development

Once the architectural design of the system has been completed using ADARTS or CODARTS, subsequent software development can be carried out using the software life cycle in practice at the software organization. However, ADARTS/CODARTS can be used in conjunction with an incremental development approach for the detailed design, coding, and testing of the software. For an ADARTS design, the inputs to this step are the component interface specifications, as well as the AADs and Ada-based task behavior specifications described earlier. For a CODARTS design, the inputs to this step are the component interface specifications, as well as the SADs and language independent task behavior specifications described earlier.

If the software is to be developed incrementally, it is necessary to have a strategy for identifying system subsets. Event sequence diagrams (ESD) can be used for this purpose. ESDs, initially introduced in [Gomaa86], help in analyzing the behavioral characteristics of a system by showing the sequence of actions graphically that take place in the system when an external event occurs. Event sequence diagrams can be used with data flow diagrams, state transition diagrams, task architecture diagrams, software architecture diagrams, or Ada architecture diagrams.

Event sequence diagrams provide a means of identifying system subsets. During incremental development, the ESD is based on the TAD, SAD, or AAD, depending at what stage planning for incremental development is taking place. ESDs are particularly effective for identifying subsets in concurrent systems. Thus an event can be handled by message passing between two tasks or by a procedure call within a task. An ESD defines:

□ The state of the system before the arrival of the external event,

□ The external event that initiates the event sequence,

□ Subsequent internal events that result from the external event, and

□ The expected output, either to the external environment or an update to a data store via a data abstraction module.

In the event sequence diagram, the events are numbered sequentially in the order in which they are processed. They may be also be labelled with the specific event being performed. After completing the architectural design, the system can be implemented in stages. A system increment is determined by considering what external events the increment should process. The tasks and modules required to support these events are identified from the ESDs and then implemented. For a given module, only those operations needed for the increment need be implemented. Other operations can be implemented as stubs, and replaced with the operation body when required in a subsequent increment.

ESDs can also be used to help determine the integration test cases for each incremental build of the system. Tests are created based on each external event the increment must process. The state of the system prior to the arrival of the event needs to be defined. The expected system response to the external event in the form of subsequent internal events are defined before the test and then compared with the actual test results.

An example of using event sequence diagrams to help identify system subsets is given for the Cruise Control and Monitoring system case study.

19

Performance Analysis of ADARTS and CODARTS Designs

19.1 Introduction

The quantitative analysis of a real-time system design allows the early detection of potential performance problems. The analysis is for the software design executing on a given hardware configuration with a given external workload applied to it. Early detection of potential performance problems allows alternative software designs and hardware configurations to be investigated.

This section applies two approaches, described earlier in Chapter 11, for analyzing the performance of a design. The first approach uses event sequence analysis while the second uses real-time scheduling theory. The two approaches are then combined. Both event sequence analysis and real-time scheduling theory are applied to a design consisting of a set of concurrent tasks. Consequently, the performance analysis can start as soon as the task architecture has been designed.

19.2 Example of Performance Analysis Using Event Sequence Analysis

As an example of event sequence analysis, consider the Cruise Control subsystem of the cruise control and monitoring problem. The event sequence diagram in Fig. 19.1, which is based on the task architecture diagram for the Cruise Control subsystem, is used to assist in this analysis. Assume that all the tasks in the Monitoring subsystem

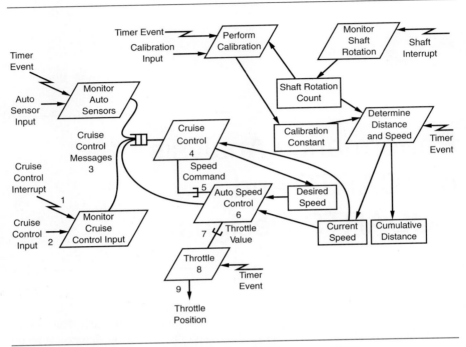

FIGURE 19.1 Cruise Control Subsystem: Event Sequence Diagram

as well as the Perform Calibration task in the Cruise Control subsystem have lower priorities and can therefore be ignored to a first approximation.

Assume that the first case to be analyzed is that of the driver engaging the cruise control lever in the ACCEL position, resulting in controlled acceleration of the car. A performance requirement is that the system must respond to the driver's action within 250 milliseconds. The sequence of internal events following the driver's action is shown on the event sequence diagram in Fig. 19.1.

Assume that the Cruise Control subsystem is in Initial state. Consider the case of the ACCEL cruise control input. The event sequence is as follows, with the CPU time to process each event given in parentheses (where C_n is the CPU time required to process event n):

1. Cruise control interrupt arrives. (C_1)

2. Monitor Cruise Control Input reads the ACCEL input from the cruise control lever. (C_2)

3. Monitor Cruise Control Input sends a cruise control request message to Cruise Control. (C_3)

4. Cruise Control receives the message, executes its state transition diagram, and changes state from Initial to Accelerating. (C_4)

5. Cruise Control sends an Increase Speed Command message to Auto Speed Control. (C_5)

6. Auto Speed Control executes the command and computes the throttle value. (C_6)

7. Auto Speed Control sends a Throttle Value message to the Throttle task. (C_7)

8. Throttle computes the new throttle position. (C_8)

9. Throttle Position is output to the Throttle.

This event sequence diagram shows that four tasks—Monitor Cruise Control Input, Cruise Control, Auto Speed Control, and Throttle—are required to support the ACCEL external event. There is also a minimum of four context switches required, $4*C_x$, where C_x is the context switching overhead.

The total CPU time for the tasks in the event sequence (C_e), which is the sum of the CPU time for all the tasks in the event sequence plus CPU time for message communication and context switching overhead, is given by:

$$C_e = C_1 + C_2 + C_3 + C_4 + C_5 + C_6 + C_7 + C_8 + 4*C_x.$$

Assume that message communication overhead C_m is the same in all cases, in which case the times C_3, C_5, C_7 should be equal to C_m. The execution time C_e is therefore equal to:

$$C_e = C_1 + C_2 + C_4 + C_6 + C_8 + 3*C_m + 4*C_x \qquad (19.1)$$

To determine the system response time, it is also necessary to consider other tasks that could execute during the time when the system must respond to the external event. Consider the other tasks in Fig. 19.1. Assume that Monitor Auto Sensors (C_{10}) is periodically activated every 100 milliseconds; it could therefore execute three times in the space of 250 milliseconds. Monitor Shaft Rotation (C_{11}) is activated once every shaft rotation and therefore could execute up to 25 times during this time, assuming a maximum shaft rotation rate of 6000 rpm; that is, activated once every 10 msecs. Finally, Determine Distance and Speed (C_{12}) is activated periodically once every quarter of a second and therefore executes once. Every time another task intervenes, there could be two context switches, assuming that the executing task is pre-empted, and then resumes execution after completion of the intervening task. These three tasks could therefore impose an additional 58 context switches.

The total CPU time for these three tasks C_a, including system overhead, is given by:

$$C_a = 3 * (C_{10} + 2*C_x) + 25 * (C_{11} + 2*C_x) + (C_{12} + 2*C_x) \qquad (19.2)$$

The estimated response time to the external event has to be greater or equal to the total CPU time, which is the sum of the tasks in the event sequence, plus the CPU time for other tasks that execute during this period, including all system overhead. The total CPU time C_t is given by:

$$C_t = C_e + C_a \qquad (19.3)$$

TABLE 19.1 CRUISE CONTROL CPU TIMES

	CPU time (msec)		
Task	C_i	Periodic tasks $(C_i + 2*C_x)$	Event sequence tasks $(C_i + C_x + C_m)$
Cruise control interrupt (C_1)	1		
Monitor Cruise Control Input (C_2)	4		
Total Cruise Control Input ($C_1 + C_2$)	5		6
Cruise Control (C_4)	6		7
Auto Speed Control (C_6)	14	15	16
Throttle (C_8)	5	6	6
Message communication overhead (C_m)	1		
Context switching overhead (C_x)	0.5		
Monitor Auto Sensors (C_{10})	5	6	
Monitor Shaft Rotation (C_{11})	1	2	
Determine Distance and Speed (C_{12})	10	11	

Total CPU time used by tasks in event sequence = 35 msec

Estimates need to be made for each of the above timing parameters before the equations can be solved. The estimates are given in Table 19.1. Since the CPU is intended for real-time processing, it is assumed that context switching is relatively fast and carried out in 0.5 msec. Substituting for the estimated timing parameters from Table 19.1 in Eq. 19.1 results in an estimated value for C_e of 35 msec. Substituting for the estimated timing parameters in Eq. 19.2 gives an estimated value for C_a of 79 msec. From Eq. 19.3, the estimated total CPU time C_t is 114 msec, which is well below the specified response time of 250 msec.

It is possible to experiment with different values of the parameters to see how susceptible the estimated response time is to error. For example, if the context switching time were 1 msec instead of 0.5 msec, then C_e would increase to 37 msec and C_a would increase to 108 msec, giving a total CPU time C_t of 145 msec, an increase of 31 msec over the first estimate. This is still well below the specified response time of 250 msec.

19.3 Simulation Modeling

The performance analysis of the design described above could be used as a basis of a simulation model. The concurrent tasks would be explicitly simulated at a level of abstraction that reflects the response of each task to the inputs it receives and what outputs it generates. The performance parameters relating to task execution time and system overhead are parameters of the model, whose values would need to be estimated by the model builder. The model would output performance estimates of system response time and CPU overhead.

The model would need as input either a statistical distribution of system inputs or an event trace of expected system inputs. The accuracy of the model would depend to a large extent on the accuracy of the estimates of the timing parameters, as well as to how realistic the representation of the modeled input is.

19.4   Example of Performance Analysis Using Real-time Scheduling Theory

This section applies the real-time scheduling theory to the Cruise Control and Monitoring system. In applying the theory, consider first a steady state involving only the periodic tasks. After that, the driver-imposed aperiodic demands on the system are considered.

Consider the worst steady state case—the case of maximum CPU demand, with the car operating under automated control at the maximum shaft revolution rate. For the periodic tasks, consider the period of each task T_n, the CPU time required by the task C_n, and each task's CPU utilization, which is the ratio $U_n = C_n/T_n$. The CPU time for each periodic task includes the CPU time for two context switches. The steady state periodic tasks are described next, with the estimated timing parameters given in Table 19.2.

1. *Monitor Shaft Rotation.* It is assumed that Monitor Shaft Rotation is a periodic task. It is actually aperiodic, as it is activated by a shaft interrupt. However, the interrupt arrives on a regular basis as it arrives every shaft rotation, and so the task is assumed to behave as a periodic task. Assume a worst case of 6000 rpm, meaning that there will be an interrupt every 10 msecs, which therefore represents the minimum period of the equivalent periodic task. As this task has the shortest period, it is assigned the highest priority. Its CPU time is 2 msec, including two context switches of 0.5 msec each.

2. *Monitor Auto Sensors.* This task has a period of 100 msec and a CPU time of 6 msec, including two context switches of 0.5 msec each.

3. *Determine Distance and Speed.* This task has a period of 250 msec and a CPU time of 11 msec, including two context switches of 0.5 msec each.

4. *Perform Calibration.* This task has a period of 500 msec and a CPU time of 5 msec.

5. *Auto Speed Control.* Once activated, under automated control, this task executes

TABLE 19.2 CRUISE CONTROL AND MONITORING SYSTEM REAL-TIME SCHEDULING: PERIODIC TASK PARAMETERS

Task	CPU time C_n	Period T_n	Utilization U_n	Priority
Monitor Shaft Rotation	2	10	0.20	1
Monitor Auto Sensors	6	100	0.06	2
Determine Distance and Speed	11	250	0.04	4
Perform Calibration	5	500	0.01	6
Auto Speed Control	15	250	0.06	5
Throttle	6	100	0.06	3
Monitor Reset Buttons	5	500	0.01	7
Compute Average Mileage	20	1,000	0.02	8
Check Maintenance Need	15	2,000	0.01	9

periodically every 250 msec to compute the throttle value and has a CPU time of 15 msec.

6. *Throttle.* Once activated, under automated control, this task executes periodically every 100 msec to output the throttle position and has a CPU time of 6 msec.

7. *Monitor Reset Buttons.* This task has a period of 500 msec and a CPU time of 5 msec.

8. *Compute Average Mileage.* This task executes relatively infrequently with a period of 1 sec and a CPU time of 20 msec. It is not time critical.

9. *Check Maintenance Need.* This task executes even less frequently with a period of 2 sec and a CPU time of 15 msec. It is also not time critical.

The rate monotonic priorities of the tasks are assigned such that higher priorities are allocated to tasks with shorter periods. Thus the highest priority task is Monitor Shaft Rotation, which has a period of 10 msec. There are two tasks with a period of 100 msec, Throttle and Monitor Auto Sensors. Monitor Auto Sensors is always active while Throttle is only active under automated vehicle control. Monitor Auto Sensors is given the higher priority since an input it receives (e.g., brake pressed) may impact the throttle. Two tasks have a period of 250 msec: the higher priority is given to Determine Speed and Distance since it computes Current Speed that is then used by Auto Speed Control if it is active. The lowest priority task is Check Maintenance Need, which has the longest period.

From Table 19.2, the total utilization of the nine periodic tasks is 0.47, which is well below the theoretical worst-case upper bound of 0.69 given by the Utilization Bound Theorem. Therefore, according to the rate monotonic algorithm, all the tasks are able to meet their deadlines.

It should be pointed out that the access time to the shared data stores, which consists of just one read or one write instruction, is so small that the potential delay time due to one task blocking another is considered negligible. Cases where significant priority inversion delays can occur due to a lower priority task blocking higher priority tasks by accessing a shared data store are described in the real-time scheduling of the Robot Controller system and the Elevator Control system.

19.5   Example of Performance Analysis Using Real-time Scheduling Theory (RTST) and Event Sequence Analysis

19.5.1   Equivalent Aperiodic Task

Next, consider the case when the driver initiates an external event, either by using the cruise control lever or pressing the brake. This requires considering the tasks in the event sequence, as well as the periodic tasks. The first solution uses an equivalent aperiodic task to replace the four tasks in the event sequence.

It is necessary to consider the impact of the additional load imposed by the driver initiated external event on the steady state load of the periodic tasks. This is done by considering the impact of the tasks in the event sequence on the steady state analysis described above for the periodic tasks. The worst case is when the vehicle is already under automated control. If the car were not under automated control, then the Auto Speed Control and Throttle tasks would not be executing and thus there would be a lighter load on the CPU.

Consider an input from the cruise control lever. As described in the event sequence analysis, and shown in the event sequence diagram, the tasks required to process this input are Monitor Cruise Control Input, Cruise Control, Auto Speed Control, and Throttle. The CPU time to process this is given by Eq. 19.1. Although there are four tasks involved in the event sequence, they have to execute in strict sequence, since each task is activated by a message sent by its predecessor in the sequence. We can therefore assume, to a first approximation, that the four tasks are equivalent to one aperiodic task whose CPU time is C_e; that is, the CPU time of the four individual tasks plus message communication overhead and context switching overhead. The equivalent aperiodic task is referred to as the event sequence task.

From the real-time scheduling theory, an aperiodic task can be treated as a periodic task whose period is given by the minimum interarrival time of the aperiodic requests. Let the period for the equivalent periodic event sequence task be T_e. Assume that T_e is also the necessary response time to the driver's input. For example, if T_e is 250 msec, the desired response to the driver's input of pressing the brake or requesting to deactivate cruise control is 250 msec. For the equivalent periodic event sequence task, it is assumed that the driver can initiate external events at the rate of four per second, a truly worst and highly unlikely case. Nevertheless, if it can be shown that the system can support this worst case situation, then confidence in the system's performance will be high.

When assigning a priority to the event sequence task, the task is initially assigned its rate monotonic priority. Since the aperiodic event sequence task has the same period as two other periodic tasks, Auto Speed Control and Determine Distance and Speed, it is given the highest priority of the three. However, Monitor Shaft Rotation, Throttle, and Monitor Auto Sensors all have shorter periods and hence higher rate monotonic priorities than the event sequence task. The real-time scheduling parameters for this case, as well as the assigned task priorities, are given in Table 19.3 (Case 1).

Given the CPU estimates shown in Table 19.1 and then from Eq. 19.1, the CPU time C_e of the equivalent event sequence task is 35 msec. Given the equivalent period T_e is 250 sec, the task CPU utilization is 0.14. Since the total CPU utilization of the periodic tasks is 0.47, the total periodic and event sequence task CPU utilization is 0.61, which is below the worst case upper bound of 0.69 given by the utilization bound theorem. Consequently, the event sequence task can meet its deadline, as can all the periodic tasks.

It should be noted that we can treat the brake being pressed by the driver in the same way as an input from the cruise control lever. In the brake case, the tasks in the event sequence are Monitor Auto Sensors, Cruise Control, Auto Speed Control, and Throttle; the last three tasks are identical to those for a cruise control lever input. From Table 19.1, the estimated CPU time for Monitor Auto Sensors of 5 msec is the same as for Monitor Cruise Control Input. So the CPU time to process a brake press is similar to that for a cruise control input. Although the period for Monitor Auto Sensors is 100 msec, we assume that successive inputs from the real world occur at a maximum rate of four per second, and these inputs may be either brake inputs or cruise control lever inputs. The high sampling rate for Monitor Auto Sensors is to ensure that the brake or engine inputs are not missed.

TABLE 19.3 CRUISE CONTROL AND MONITORING SYSTEM REAL-TIME SCHEDULING: PERIODIC AND EVENT SEQUENCE TASK PARAMETERS

Task	CPU Time C_n	Period T_n	Utilization U_n	Priority (Case 1)	Priority (Case 2)
Monitor Shaft Rotation	2	10	0.20	1	1
Monitor Auto Sensors	6	100	0.06	2	3
Determine Distance and Speed	11	250	0.04	4	5
Perform Calibration	5	500	0.01	6	7
Auto Speed Control	15	250	0.06	5	6
Throttle	6	100	0.06	3	4
Monitor Reset Buttons	5	500	0.01	7	8
Compute Average Mileage	20	1,000	0.02	8	9
Check Maintenance Need	15	2,000	0.01	9	10
Event Sequence Task	35	250	0.14	4	2

Priorities: *Case 1* Rate monotonic priorities assigned

Case 2 Non-rate monotonic priorities assigned

We can therefore assume that the brake pressed case is similar to the cruise control lever input case, and treat both in the same way. Thus the event sequence analysis holds for an external event due to either a cruise control lever input or a brake input.

19.5.2   Assigning Non-rate Monotonic Priorities

One assumption and one approximation were made in the first solution. Consider first the assumption that all tasks can be allocated their rate monotonic priorities. A problem with giving the event sequence task its rate monotonic priority is that the task could potentially miss the cruise control interrupt if it has to wait for Monitor Shaft Rotation, Throttle, and Monitor Auto Sensors to execute. On the other hand, giving the event sequence task the highest priority means that Monitor Shaft Rotation would miss its deadlines because the CPU time for the event sequence task is 35 msec while the period of Monitor Shaft Rotation is 10 msec.

To avoid these problems, the event sequence task is assigned a lower priority than Monitor Shaft Rotation, but a higher priority than the Throttle and Monitor Auto Sensors tasks. This means that the event sequence task is given a higher priority than its rate monotonic priority, as shown in Table 19.3 (Case 2). Because of this, it is necessary to check each task explicitly to determine whether it meets its deadline.

The two highest priority tasks, Monitor Shaft Rotation and the event sequence task, have a combined utilization of 0.34 and so they will have no difficulty meeting their deadlines. Since the next highest priority tasks, Throttle and Monitor Auto Sensors, could both potentially get delayed by the event sequence task, a worst case analysis is required to show that they would not miss their deadlines, given that they each have a period of 100 msec.

Consider a worst case CPU burst over 100 msec with Monitor Shaft Rotation active ten times, the four tasks in the event sequence active once, as well as Throttle and Monitor Auto Sensors each active once. Monitor Shaft Rotation consumes 10*2 msec = 20 msec. The four tasks in the event sequence consume 35 msec. The Throttle and Monitor Auto Sensors tasks consume a further 6 msec each. The total CPU time consumed is 67 msec, which is less than the 100 msec period of Throttle and Monitor Auto Sensors. Thus all the tasks meet their deadlines.

It should be noted that although the overall CPU utilization is 61 percent, bursts of activity can lead to transient loads which are much higher. For example, in the 100 msec worst case CPU burst described above, the total utilization of the three steady state tasks and the one event sequence task is 67 percent, thereby still allowing lower priority tasks to execute. For example, if the next highest priority task, Determine Distance and Speed, were to also execute in this busy 100 msec, the CPU utilization would increase to 78 percent. Thus the real-time scheduling algorithm guarantees that all tasks can meet their deadlines no matter what sudden bursts of activity occur.

19.5.3 Detailed Analysis of Aperiodic Tasks

A more comprehensive analysis of the cruise control problem is obtained by treating each of the four tasks in the event sequence separately. The CPU parameters for each of the four tasks are shown in Tables 19.1 and 19.4, where each task has its context switching and message communication overhead added to its CPU time. In addition, the CPU time for the Monitor Cruise Control Input task is the sum of C_1 and C_2. All the tasks in the event sequence are treated as periodic tasks with a period equal to the minimum interarrival time of 250 msec. The only exception is Throttle, which is both in the event sequence and executes periodically with a period of 100 msec.

To ensure that tasks in the event sequence get a timely response they are assigned high priorities where possible. In particular, to respond to external interrupts quickly, the first task in the event sequence, Monitor Cruise Control Input, is assigned the second highest priority after Monitor Shaft Rotation. As its priority is higher than two tasks with a shorter period, Throttle and Monitor Auto Sensors, its assigned priority is above the rate monotonic priority. However the three other tasks in the event sequence are assigned their rate monotonic priorities. Throttle, which has a period of 100 msec, is allocated the fourth highest priority just below Monitor Auto Sensors, which has the same period. The other two tasks in the event sequence, Cruise Control and Auto Speed Control, both with the same period of 250 msec, are assigned the next two highest priorities.

To carry out a full analysis, it is necessary to apply the generalized real-time scheduling theory described in Chapter 11, where each task must be checked explicitly against its upper bound. This analysis is carried out using the Generalized Completion Time Theorem and is illustrated by the timing diagram shown in Fig. 19.2.

Monitor Shaft Rotation is the highest priority task with a period of 10 msec. Whenever it needs to execute, it pre-empts all other tasks to execute for 2 msec, so it

TABLE 19.4 CRUISE CONTROL AND MONITORING SYSTEM REAL-TIME
SCHEDULING: PERIODIC AND APERIODIC TASK PARAMETERS

Task	CPU time C_n	Period T_n	Utilization U_n	Priority
Monitor Shaft Rotation	2	10	0.20	1
Monitor Auto Sensors	6	100	0.06	3
Determine Distance and Speed	11	250	0.04	7
Perform Calibration	5	500	0.01	8
Auto Speed Control*	16	250	0.06	6
Throttle*	6	100	0.06	4
Monitor Reset Buttons	5	500	0.01	9
Compute Average Mileage	20	1,000	0.02	10
Check Maintenance Need	15	2,000	0.01	11
Monitor Cruise Control Input*	6	250	0.02	2
Cruise Control*	7	250	0.03	5

*Tasks in event sequence

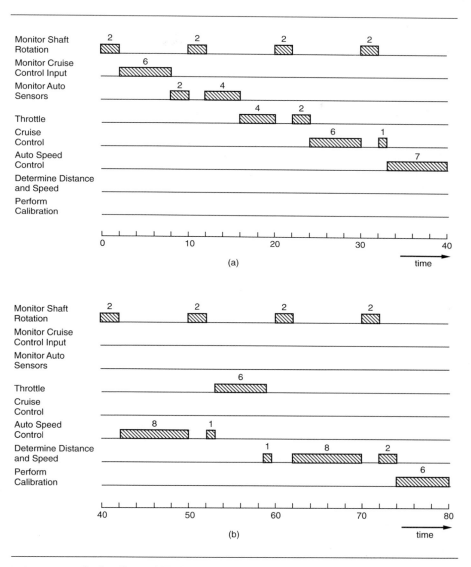

FIGURE 19.2 Cruise Control Timing Diagram

easily meets its deadline. Monitor Cruise Control Input is considered with the other
tasks in the event sequence, since it is important to determine that all four tasks
complete before the 250 msec deadline.

Consider the four tasks in the event sequence over the period T_e of 250 msec. As
before, the objective is to determine that the four tasks will complete execution before

the 250 msec deadline. It is necessary to apply the Generalized Utilization Bound Theorem and consider

a. Execution time for the tasks in the event sequence. The total execution time for the four tasks in the event sequence, $C_e = 35$ msec and $T_e = 250$ msec. Execution utilization = 0.14.

b. Pre-emption time by higher priority tasks with periods less than 250 msec, the period of the tasks in the event sequence. There are three tasks in this set. Monitor Shaft Rotation, with a period of 10 msec, can pre-empt any of the four tasks a maximum of 25 times for a total of 25*2 = 50 msec. In addition, Throttle and Monitor Auto Sensors, with periods of 100 msec, can each pre-empt the three lower priority tasks in the event sequence up to three times for a total of 3*(6 + 6) = 36 msec.

Total pre-emption time = 50 + 36 = 86.

Total pre-emption utilization = 0.2 + 0.06 + 0.06 = 0.32

c. Pre-emption by higher priority tasks with longer periods. There are no such tasks.

d. Blocking time by lower priority tasks. There are no such tasks.

Total elapsed time = Total pre-emption time + total execution time = 86 + 35 = 121 < 250.

Total utilization = pre-emption utilization + execution utilization = 0.32 + 0.14 = 0.46 < 0.69.

The total utilization of 0.46 is less than the Generalized Utilization Bound Theorem's upper bound of 0.69 and so the four tasks in the event sequence all meet their deadline.

To determine whether the two tasks with the shorter period of 100 msec meet their deadlines, it is necessary to check pre-emption and execution times during the 100 msec period.

a. Execution time for the two tasks, which are considered together because they have the same period. Total execution time = 6 + 6 = 12 msec. Execution utilization = 0.06 + 0.06 = 0.12.

b. Pre-emption time by higher priority tasks with periods less than 100 msec. The only task in this set, Monitor Shaft Rotation, can pre-empt 10 times during the 100 msec for a total pre-emption time of 10*2 = 20 msec. Pre-emption utilization = 0.2.

c. Pre-emption by higher priority tasks with longer periods. The only task in this set is Monitor Cruise Control Input, which could pre-empt once and execute for 6 msec. Pre-emption utilization = 0.06.

Total pre-emption utilization = 0.2 + 0.06 = 0.26.

Total utilization = pre-emption utilization + execution utilization = 0.26 + 0.12 = 0.38 < 0.69.

The total utilization of 0.38 is less than the Generalized Utilization Bound Theorem's upper bound of 0.69 and so the two periodic tasks with shorter periods both meet their deadline. A similar analysis for each of the lower priority periodic tasks shows that each of these tasks meets its deadline. The timing diagram shows two of these, Determine Distance and Speed, as well as Perform Calibration.

19.6   Design Restructuring

If the proposed design does not meet the performance goals then the design needs to be restructured. This is achieved by applying the task cohesion and task inversion criteria. In particular, the weaker forms of temporal cohesion (also referred to as temporal task inversion) and the other forms of task inversion, multiple instance task inversion and sequential task inversion, can be applied.

If there is a performance problem in the cruise control example, then one attempt at design restructuring is to apply sequential task inversion. Consider the case where the Cruise Control task sends a Speed Command message to the Auto Speed Control task, which in turn sends Throttle messages to the Throttle task. These three tasks may be combined into one task, the Inverted Cruise Control task, using sequential task inversion (shown in Fig. 14.25). This eliminates the message communication overhead between these tasks as well as the context switching overhead. Let the CPU time for the inverted task be C_i. Then:

$$C_i = C_4 + C_6 + C_8 \qquad (19.4)$$

The CPU time for the two tasks in the new event sequence C_e'' is now given by:

$$C_e'' = C_1 + C_2 + C_i + C_m + 2*C_x \qquad (19.5)$$

The message communication overhead is reduced from $3*C_m$ to C_m and the context switching overhead is reduced from $4*C_x$ to $2*C_x$. Given the estimated timing parameters times in Table 19.1 and substituting for them in Eqs. 19.4 and 19.5 results in a reduction of total CPU time from 35 msec to 32 msec. If the message communication and context switching overhead times were larger then the savings would be more substantial. For example, if C_m is 3 msec and C_x is 2 msec, then the total aperiodic CPU time would decrease from 47 msec to 37 msec.

20

Design of Distributed Applications

20.1   Introduction

This chapter describes how the CODARTS design method is extended to address the design of distributed concurrent and distributed real-time applications, which are applications that execute on geographically distributed nodes supported by a local area or wide area network. Typical applications include distributed real-time data collection and distributed real-time control applications.

The extension to CODARTS is called CODARTS/DA, or CODARTS for Distributed Applications. With CODARTS/DA, a distributed application is structured into subsystems. A subsystem is defined as a collection of concurrent tasks executing on one node. In particular, CODARTS/DA provides a set of criteria for structuring a distributed application into subsystems, which communicate by means of messages.

20.2   Distributed Processing Concepts

20.2.1   Introduction

A typical distributed processing environment is shown in Fig. 20.1, where several nodes are interconnected by means of a local area network. Each node consists of one or more processors with shared memory.

276

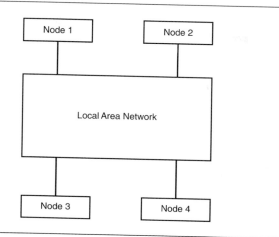

FIGURE 20.1 Distributed Processing Environment

A subsystem corresponds to a logical node. Thus, a subsystem is defined as a collection of concurrent tasks executing on one logical node. However, more than one subsystem (logical node) may execute on the same physical node. Thus the same application could be configured to have each subsystem allocated to its own separate physical node, or have all or some of its subsystems allocated to the same physical node. From now on in this chapter, the term "subsystem" will be used to refer to a logical node and the term "node" will be used to refer to a physical node.

One objective of CODARTS/DA is to design the application in such a way that the decision about mapping subsystems to physical nodes does not need to be made at design time, but is made later at system configuration time. To ensure this flexibility, it is necessary to restrict communication between tasks that are in separate subsystems to message communication.

Individual subsystems are designed using a design method for non-distributed concurrent systems, such as the DARTS, ADARTS, or basic CODARTS methods. Thus, tasks within the same subsystem, which by definition always reside on the same node, may use intertask communication and synchronization mechanisms that rely on shared memory.

With CODARTS/DA, no assumptions are made about the availability of a distributed data base. One of the objectives of CODARTS/DA is to structure the distributed application into relatively independent and autonomous subsystems, where any one subsystem may use a local data base if it needs to. Distributed access to the data is provided via server subsystems.

The remainder of this section considers different aspects of distributed processing environments and the support provided by distributed operating systems.

20.2.2 Distributed Kernel

In situations where a source task sends a message to a destination task, it should not
be necessary for the source task to know which node the destination task resides on.
Some commercial operating systems (e.g., VAX/ELN) provide a distributed kernel
that supports this transparent message communication capability. If such a capability
is not available, then a Distributed Task Manager (DTM) needs to be developed to
provide this transparency. The DTM is a layer of software that sits above the operating
system on each processor. It maintains a task name table, which relates task name to
node id. All intertask communication is routed via DTM.

Transparent message communication between distributed tasks is handled by
means either of a distributed kernel or distributed task manager. Figure 20.2 shows an
example of task communication using a distributed kernel. There is one instance of
the distributed kernel at each node. When a source task sends a message to a
destination task, the local kernel looks up the name table to determine where the
destination task resides. If the destination task resides on the same node as the source
task, then the local kernel routes the message directly to the destination task. For
example, a message from task B is routed directly to task C, since both tasks reside
on Node 1. If, on the other hand, the destination task resides on a remote node, the
local kernel sends the message to its counterpart kernel on the remote node. On
receiving the message, the remote kernel routes the message to the destination task
on that node. This is illustrated in this figure with task A, which resides on Node 1,
sending a message to task D, which resides on Node 2. The message request from task
A is handled by the local kernel on Node 1, which sends it to the remote kernel on
Node 2, from where it is routed to task D.

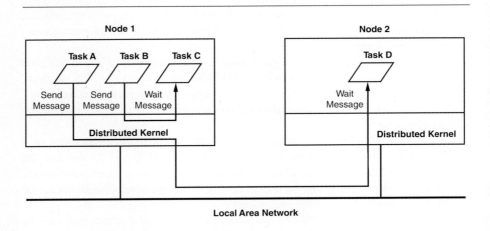

FIGURE 20.2 Message Communication between Distributed Tasks

It is assumed that as long as the network is operational, the message will arrive at the remote node. For example, if there is a parity error, then the network communication software, assumed here to be part of the distributed operating system software, will retransmit the message. However, if the remote node does not respond within a given timeframe, either because the network connection to the remote node is down or because the remote node itself is down, then the transmission will time out. In this case, the local kernel will receive a negative acknowledgement from the network communication software, indicating that the message was not received by the remote node. The local kernel will then return the negative acknowledgement to the source task. If the message does not arrive at the remote node, it is the responsibility of the source task to decide what to do, since the decision is application dependent. More information on distributed operating systems is given in [Nutt91, Tanenbaum92].

20.2.3   Remote Procedure Calls

Some distributed systems support remote procedure calls. A client subsystem on one node makes a remote procedure call to a server subsystem on another node. A remote procedure call is similar to a local procedure call, so the fact that the server is on a remote node is hidden from the client. The procedure called by the client, sometimes referred to as a client stub, takes the request and any parameters, packs them into a message, and sends the message to the server node.

At the server node, a counterpart server stub unpacks the message, and calls the appropriate server procedure (which represents the remote procedure), passing it any parameters. When the server procedure finishes processing the request, it returns any results to the server stub. The server stub packs the results into a response message, which it sends to the client stub. The client stub extracts the results from the message and returns them as output parameters to the client. Thus the role of the client and server stubs is to make the remote procedure call appear as a local procedure call to both the client and server.

20.2.4   Message Communication Using Ports

In some distributed systems, message communication between remote nodes is made even more loosely coupled by supporting ports. A task on one node does not send a message to an explicit destination task by name; instead, it sends the message to an output port. A destination task receives messages at its input ports. During system configuration, output ports are connected to input ports. This provides greater flexibility and greater potential for reuse since a task does not have to know explicitly who its producers and consumers are when it is designed. Such decisions are made later, and instances of the same task type can execute in different environments in different applications. An example of a distributed environment supporting ports and flexible configuration is CONIC [Kramer85, Magee89].

20.3   Steps in Designing Distributed Applications

There are three main steps in designing a distributed application consisting of subsystems that can be configured to execute on distributed physical nodes. The first step, **system decomposition,** structures the distributed application into subsystems that potentially could execute on separate nodes in a distributed environment. As subsystems can reside on separate nodes, all communication between subsystems is restricted to message communication. The interfaces between subsystems are defined. A set of subsystem structuring criteria is used for determining the subsystems.

The second step, **subsystem decomposition,** structures subsystems into concurrent tasks and information hiding modules. Since by definition, a subsystem can only execute on one node, each subsystem can be designed using a design method for non-distributed concurrent systems.

The third step is **system configuration.** Once a distributed application has been designed, instances of it may be defined and configured. During this stage, the subsystem instances of the target system are defined, interconnected, and mapped onto a hardware configuration. A set of subsystem configuration criteria is used for mapping the subsystem instances to physical nodes.

20.4   System Decomposition

20.4.1   Designing Configurable Distributed Subsystems

To manage the inherent complexity of large-scale distributed applications successfully, it is necessary to provide an approach for structuring the application into subsystems, where each subsystem can potentially execute on its own node. Communication between subsystems is by messages, so that subsystems can be mapped to different nodes. After performing this decomposition and carefully defining the interfaces between the subsystems, each subsystem can then be designed independently.

Two examples of distributed applications are used to illustrate the topics described in this chapter. Figure 20.3 shows a distributed Elevator Control System while Fig. 20.4 shows a distributed Factory Automation System.

In decomposing a distributed application into subsystems, the subsystem structuring criteria described in Chapter 13 are applied. These criteria relate to application (i.e., problem domain) specific characteristics. Additional criteria are needed to ensure that the subsystems determined during subsystem structuring are indeed capable of being mapped to distributed nodes.

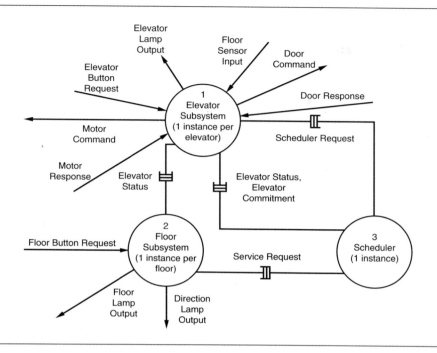

FIGURE 20.3 Distributed Elevator Control System

A distributed application needs to be designed with an understanding of the distributed environments it is likely to operate in. Although the actual mapping of subsystems to physical nodes is done later when an individual target system is instantiated and configured, it is necessary to ensure that the subsystems are designed so that they are configurable; that is, so that subsystem instances can later be effectively mapped to distributed physical nodes. Consequently, additional subsystem configuration criteria are required to help ensure that the subsystems are designed in such a way that instances of these subsystems can indeed be configured to run on distributed nodes. These criteria consider the characteristics of the distributed environment (i.e., the solution domain).

20.4.2   Distributed Subsystem Configuration Criteria

In a real-time and/or distributed environment, a service provided by a subsystem may be associated with a particular physical location or constrained to execute on a given hardware resource. In such a case, a subsystem is constrained to execute on the node at that location or on the given hardware.

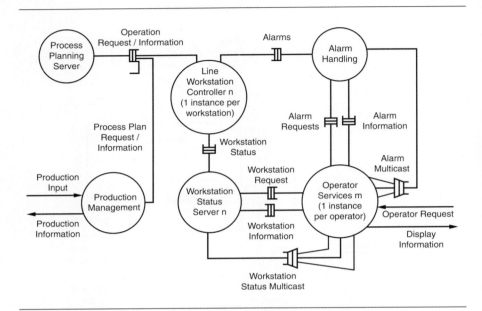

FIGURE 20.4 Distributed Factory Automation System

The distributed subsystem configuration criteria are provided to help ensure that configurable distributed subsystems are designed effectively. A subsystem can satisfy more than one of the following criteria.

1. *Proximity to the source of physical data.* In a distributed environment, the sources of data may be physically distant from each other. This criterion aims to provide proximity of the subsystem to the source of physical data. This ensures fast access to the data and is particularly important if data access rates are high.

2. *Localized autonomy.* With this criterion, the subsystem controls a given aspect of the system. It may receive some high-level commands from another node giving it overall direction, after which it provides the lower-level control, providing status information to other nodes, either on an ongoing basis or on demand.

   In both the cases of proximity to the source of physical data and localized autonomy, the subsystem is usually performing a specific site related service. Often the same service is performed at multiple sites. Each instance of the subsystem resides on a separate node, thereby providing greater local autonomy. Assuming a subsystem on a given node operates in relative independence of other nodes, then it can be operational even if other nodes are temporarily unavailable. Examples of subsystems that satisfy both of these criteria are the Elevator Subsystem (Fig. 20.3) and the Line Workstation Controller Subsystem (Fig. 20.4).

3. *Performance.* By providing a time critical function within its own node, better and more predictable subsystem performance can often be achieved. In a given distributed application, a real-time subsystem can perform time critical services at a given node, while other non–real-time or less time-critical services are performed elsewhere. Examples of subsystems that satisfy this criterion are the three Elevator Subsystems and the Line Workstation Controller Subsystem.

4. *Specialized hardware.* A subsystem may need to reside on a particular node because it supports special purpose hardware (e.g., a vector processor) or has to interface to special purpose peripherals, sensors, or actuators, which are connected to a specific node. Both the Elevator and Floor Subsystems interface to sensors and actuators.

5. *User interface.* With the proliferation of graphical workstations and personal computers, a subsystem providing a user interface may run on a separate node, interacting with subsystems on other nodes. This kind of subsystem can provide rapid response to simple requests supported completely by the node, and relatively slower responses to requests requiring the cooperation of other nodes. This kind of subsystem may require special purpose user I/O devices. The Operator Services and Production Management subsystems shown in Fig. 20.4 satisfy this criterion.

6. *Server.* A server subsystem provides a service for other subsystems. It responds to requests from client subsystems. However, it does not initiate any requests. Frequently, the server provides services that are associated with a data store or set of related data stores. Alternatively, the server may be associated with an I/O device or set of related I/O devices.

   A server subsystem may be allocated its own node because in the case of a data server it may support remote access to a centralized database or file store, and in the case of an I/O server, it is servicing requests for a physical resource that resides at that node. Examples of servers are File Servers, such as the Process Planning Server, and Line Printer Servers.

20.5 Defining Subsystem Interfaces

20.5.1 Introduction

As subsystems potentially reside on different nodes, all communication between subsystems is restricted to message communication. Message communication between two tasks in the same or different subsystems is generally handled in the same way. The main difference is that there is a possibility of a failure in message transmission when sending a message to a remote task. This section describes message communication between tasks in different subsystems.

20.5.2   Loosely-coupled Message Communication

With loosely-coupled message communication, the producer task sends a message to the consumer task and does not wait for a reply. The two tasks proceed asynchronously and a message queue may build up between them.

In a distributed environment there is an additional requirement that the producer needs to receive a positive or negative acknowledgement, indicating whether the message arrived at its destination or not. This is not an indication that the message has been received by the destination task, merely that it has safely arrived at the destination node. Thus some significant additional time may elapse before the message is actually received by the destination task.

There is a timeout associated with the Send Message request, so that a failure in message transmission will result in a negative acknowledgement being returned to the source task. It is up to the source task to decide how to handle this failure.

An example of loosely-coupled communication in a distributed environment is given in Fig. 20.3, where the Elevator subsystem sends Elevator Status messages to both the Floor and Scheduler subsystems.

20.5.3   Tightly-coupled Message Communication

First consider tightly-coupled message communication with reply. The producer task sends a message to the consumer task and then waits for a reply from the consumer. In this case the response may be a negative acknowledgement indicating that the destination node did not receive the message. This form of communication is typically between a client and a server, and is equivalent to the remote procedure call described earlier. If there is only one client and one server, then the tightly-coupled message communication with reply notation may be used. It is more often the case, however, that tightly-coupled message communication involves multiple clients and one server.

It should be noted that in distributed message communication, it is usually not necessary to support tightly-coupled message communication without reply. Communication between subsystems should be loosely coupled whenever possible; tightly-coupled message communication should only be used when a response is required.

20.5.4   Multiple Client/Server Message Communication

In the typical client/server situation, several clients request services from a server by sending messages to it. In this case, a message queue can build up at the server. The client can use tightly-coupled message communication and wait for a response from the server. Alternatively, the client can use loosely-coupled message communication, in which case the client can wait for messages from other sources in addition to the response from the server.

Whether the client uses loosely-coupled or tightly-coupled message communication with the server is application dependent and does not affect the design of the
server. Indeed it is possible for a server to have some of its clients communicating
with it using tightly-coupled message communication while others use loosely-coupled message communication. The design of server subsystems is described in more
detail later.

An example of multiple client/server message communication is shown in Fig.
20.5, where the server is the Process Planning Server, which responds to service
requests from multiple clients. The Process Planning Server has a message queue of
incoming requests from the multiple clients, together with a tightly-coupled response.
The server processes each incoming service request message on a FIFO basis and then
sends the message response to the client. The convention is often used to label the
tightly-coupled interaction between an individual client and server in the form of
request/response (e.g., Operation Request/Information).

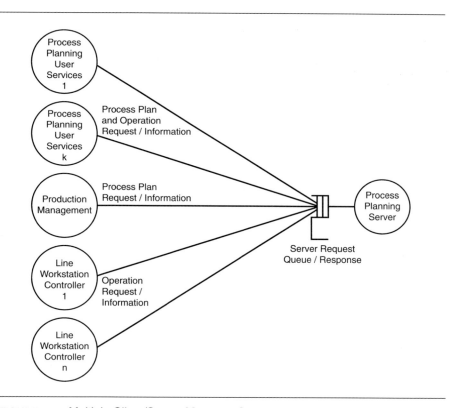

FIGURE 20.5 Multiple Client/Server Message Communication

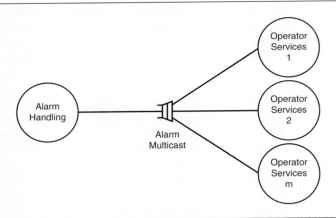

FIGURE 20.6 Group Communication

20.5.5 Group Message Communication

The message communication described so far has involved one source and one destination task. A desirable property in some distributed applications is that of group communication. This is a form of one-to-many message communication, where one message is sent by a sender to many recipients. Two kinds of group message communication (sometimes referred to as groupcasting) supported in distributed applications are broadcasting and multicasting.

With broadcast communication, a message is sent to all recipients, each of whom must then decide whether it wishes to process the message or discard it. In the case of multicast communication, tasks subscribe to a group and receive messages destined to all members of the group. Tasks can request to join or leave groups and can be members of one or more groups. A sender sends a message to the group without having to know who all the individual members are.

An example of multicast communication is shown in Fig. 20.6, where the Alarm Handling subsystem sends the same alarm message to all instances of the Operator Services subsystem who wish to receive messages of this type.

20.6 Subsystem Decomposition into Tasks

After determining the subsystems in the distributed application and defining the message interfaces between them, the next step is to design each subsystem. Each subsystem consists of one or more concurrent tasks. By definition all tasks within a given subsystem always execute on the same node.

A real-time subsystem is designed using a design method for non-distributed applications such as DARTS, ADARTS, or basic CODARTS. Thus each subsystem is decomposed into tasks as described earlier. Tasks within the same subsystem may, in addition to message communication, use event synchronization and communication via information hiding modules, which reside in shared memory.

20.7   Design of Server Subsystems

20.7.1   Introduction

Server subsystems play an important role in distributed applications. In a non-distributed application, a data store is encapsulated in a data abstraction module, which is an information hiding module. Tasks that need to access the data in the module call operations provided by the module.

In a distributed application, it is not possible for tasks on separate nodes to access a shared data store directly via a data abstraction module. It is therefore necessary for a data store that is accessed by more than one subsystem to be encapsulated in a single subsystem. The data store may be handled by a subsystem as part of a more general set of services it provides. Alternatively, the data store is managed by a server subsystem, whose role is to respond to client requests to read or update the data store.

A server subsystem provides a service for client subsystems. It receives message requests to read from or update the data store. It responds to these requests from client subsystems by sending message responses. It is also possible for a server subsystem to encapsulate a set of related data stores and provide services for all of them. A server subsystem does not initiate any requests for services from other tasks. There are two kinds of server subsystem to be considered, the Sequential Server Subsystem and the Concurrent Server Subsystem.

20.7.2   Sequential Server Subsystem

A Sequential Server Subsystem is designed as one task, which maintains a data store and responds to requests from client tasks to update or read data from the data store. The data store is encapsulated within a data abstraction module that provides service operations. When the Server Task receives a message from a client task, it calls the appropriate operation, as shown in Fig. 20.7.

The Server Task typically has a message queue of incoming service request messages. There is one message type for each service operation provided by the server. The main procedure of the Server Task unpacks the client's message and based on the message type calls the appropriate operation. The parameters of the message are used

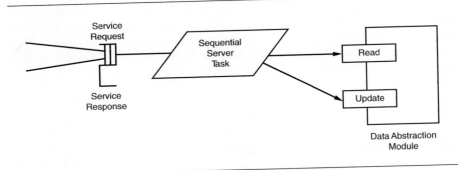

FIGURE 20.7 Software Architecture Diagram for Sequential Server Subsystem

as the parameters of the operation. The operation services the client's request and returns the appropriate response to the server task, which packs the response into a service response message and sends it to the client. The Sequential Server Task is equivalent to the server stub used in remote procedure calls.

20.7.3 Concurrent Server Subsystem

If the client demand for services is high, so that the server subsystem could potentially be a bottleneck in the system, an alternative approach is for the services to be provided by a Concurrent Server Subsystem and hence shared among several tasks. This assumes that improved throughput can be obtained by having concurrent access to the data store (e.g., if the data is stored on secondary storage). In this case, while one task is blocked waiting for some disk I/O operation to be completed, another task may use the CPU.

In a Concurrent Server Subsystem, several tasks may wish to access the data store at the same time, so access needs to be synchronized. The most appropriate synchronization algorithm to use is typically application dependent. Possible algorithms include the mutual exclusion algorithm and the Multiple Readers/Multiple Writers algorithm. In the latter case, multiple readers are allowed to access a shared data store concurrently. However, only one writer is allowed to update the shared data and only after the readers have finished.

The multiple readers/multiple writers solution applied to concurrent server subsystems is shown in Fig. 20.8. Each service is performed by one task. There may be several instances of a reader task. The Server Supervisor keeps track of all service requests, those currently being serviced and those waiting to be serviced. When it receives a request from a client, the Server Supervisor allocates the request to an appropriate reader or writer task to perform the service.

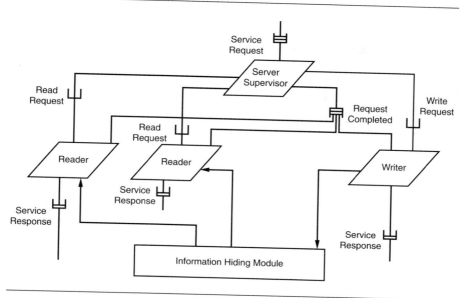

FIGURE 20.8 Concurrent Server Subsystem

For example, if the Supervisor receives a read request from a client, it allocates the request to an idle reader task and increments its count of the number of readers. It also passes the id of the client task to the reader, so that on completion the reader task can send a Service Response message directly to the client. The reader also notifies the Supervisor when it finishes, so that the Supervisor can decrement the reader count. If a write request is received from a client, the Supervisor only allocates the request to a Writer task when all readers have finished. This ensures that writer tasks have mutually exclusive access to the data. The Supervisor does not allocate any new read requests until the writer task has finished.

20.7.4   Distribution of Data

Both the sequential and concurrent server subsystems are single server subsystems; thus the data stores they encapsulate are centralized. In distributed applications, potential disadvantages of centralized servers are that the server could become a bottleneck and that it is potentially a single point of failure. A solution to these problems is data distribution. Two approaches to data distribution are the distributed server and data replication.

With the distributed server, data that is collected at several locations is stored at those locations. Each location has a local server, which responds to client requests for that location's data. This approach is used in the distributed Factory Automation System case study (Fig. 20.4), where manufacturing workstation status data is maintained at each location by a local Workstation Status Server, which responds to client requests from factory operators.

With data replication, the same data is duplicated in more than one location in order to speed up access to the data. It is of course important to ensure that procedures exist for updating the local copies of the replicated data so that the data does not get out of date. This approach is used in the Distributed Elevator Control System case study (Fig. 20.3), where each instance of the Elevator Subsystem (one per elevator) maintains its own local status and plan data store to keep track of where its elevator is and what floors it is committed to visit. In order for the Scheduler to select an elevator when a floor request is made, it needs to have access to the status and plan data for all the elevators. To expedite this, it maintains its own copy of each elevator's status and plan in an overall status and plan data store. This data is updated by elevator status and commitment messages from each instance of the Elevator Subsystem.

20.8 System Configuration

20.8.1 Configuration Issues

Once a distributed application has been designed, instances of it may be defined and configured. During system configuration, an instance of the distributed application, referred to as a target system, is defined and mapped to a distributed configuration consisting of multiple geographically distributed physical nodes connected by a network.

During this phase, decisions have to be made about what subsystem instances are required since some subsystems can have more than one instance; how the subsystem instances should be interconnected; and how the subsystem instances should be allocated to nodes.

During Target System Configuration, three activities need to be performed. First, **instances of the subsystems of the target system are defined.** For each subsystem type, where more than one instance can exist in a target system, it is necessary to define the instances desired. For example in the distributed Elevator Control System, it is necessary to define the number of elevators and numbers of floors required in the target system. It is also necessary to define one Elevator Subsystem instance for each elevator and one Floor Subsystem instance for each floor. Each Elevator Subsystem and Floor Subsystem instance must have a unique name, so that it can be uniquely identified.

For those subsystems that are parameterized, the parameters for each instance need to be defined. Examples of subsystem parameters are instance name (e.g., elevator id or floor id), sensor names, sensor limits, alarm names, etc.

Second, **interconnection of subsystem instances are defined.** The target system architecture defines how subsystems communicate with one another. At this stage, the subsystem instances are connected together. For example, in the Distributed Elevator Control Subsystem, each instance of the Floor Subsystem sends a Service Request message to the Scheduler subsystem. The Scheduler sends a Scheduler Request to individual instances of the Elevator Subsystems, so it must identify which Elevator it is sending the message to. Similarly, when an Elevator Subsystem instance sends an Elevator Status message to a Floor Subsystem instance, it must identify which Floor it is sending the message to.

Finally, the **subsystem instances,** which are logical nodes, **are mapped to physical nodes.** For example, two subsystems could be configured such that they each could run on a separate physical node. Alternatively they could both run on the same physical node.

20.8.2 Example of Target System Configuration

As an example of target system configuration, consider the Distributed Elevator Control System (Fig. 20.3). Each instance of the elevator subsystem (one per elevator) is allocated to a node to achieve localized autonomy and adequate performance. Thus the failure of one elevator node will not impact other elevator nodes. Each instance of the floor subsystem (one per floor) is allocated to a node because of proximity to the source of physical data. Loss of a floor node means that the floor will not be serviced but service to other floors is not impacted. The scheduler is allocated to a separate node for performance reasons, so it can rapidly respond to elevator requests. Loss of the scheduler node (hopefully temporarily) means that no new floor requests will be assigned to elevators, but that passengers on elevators will continue to be serviced until they arrive at their destinations.

20.8.3 Distributed Processing Environment

Certain decisions also need to be made concerning the distributed processing environment. Ideally this contains a distributed operating system, with a distributed kernel that provides transparent message communication between tasks. If this does not exist, a decision needs to be made about whether to develop a distributed task manager or not. If neither of these options is taken, then during detailed design and coding, it will be necessary to ensure that the node id of remote tasks is explicitly defined as part of the message to be sent. Tasks sending and receiving remote messages will need to interface directly with the network communication software.

21

Trends in Software Design Methods

This book reviewed a number of software design methods for concurrent and real-time systems. It also described two design methods, Ada-based Design Approach for Real-Time Systems (ADARTS) and Concurrent Design Approach for Real-Time Systems (CODARTS), which build on existing design methods. The methods were illustrated by means of several examples.

This chapter describes some current trends in software design methods. Many of these trends are not specific to design methods for concurrent and real-time systems. The trend most specific to real-time systems relates to the performance analysis of real-time designs.

21.1 Eclectic Design Methods

Greater efforts are likely to be made to incorporate concepts from different design methods and to integrate them to produce "eclectic" design methods. Efforts in this direction can be seen in Ada-based Design Approach for Real-Time Systems, Concurrent Design Approach for Real-Time Systems, and Entity Life Modeling [Sanden89]. Thus CODARTS integrates task structuring concepts from Design Approach for Real-time Systems with module and object structuring concepts from the Naval Research Laboratory Software cost reduction model and Object-Oriented Design methods, entity modeling from Jackson System Development, and the Real-time Structured Analysis notation. Entity Life Modeling integrates JSD concepts with information hiding and Ada tasking.

21.2   Domain Analysis and Design Methods

Much of the work in software reuse has been at the component level, where code components are reused or adapted by developers and then have to be integrated manually with the rest of the system that is being developed. Work is underway to develop reusable software architectures, also referred to as domain-specific software architectures.

Existing analysis and design methods are for the development of specific systems. In the future, domain methods are likely to be developed for specifying and designing families of systems [Parnas79, Lubars87, Gomaa93]. The method would guide users in developing a domain-specific software architecture, which would need to reflect the similarities and variations in the application domain. Individual target systems are then developed by tailoring the domain specific software architecture to the needs of an individual target system.

21.3   CASE Tools and Software Development Environments

Many existing computer assisted software engineering (CASE) tools for software specification and design methods are little more than graphical editors with some limited capability for checking for consistency among different components of a specification or design. Trends in software development environments [Dart87] are in the direction of making them support the entire software life cycle and orient them towards supporting specific software design methods incorporating the design heuristics of the design method.

21.4   Executable Specifications and Designs

CASE tools are being developed to allow specifications and designs to be executed and hence to allow designers to validate their designs. A good example of these tools is Statemate [Harel88a], which is based on the statecharts notation. Statemate allows a specification of the system to be developed that defines the functionality and behavior of the system. The specification may then be executed and checked for logical correctness.

21.5   Performance Analysis of Real-Time Designs

Software design methods for real-time systems need to be integrated closely with performance analysis techniques to allow real-time designers to analyze their designs from a performance perspective. Alternative designs could be evaluated and the designer then selects the best design to meet the system objectives.

Various performance analysis and modeling techniques could be used, including Petri net modeling, simulation modeling and real-time scheduling theory. One approach is to map the design into a Petri net model [Peterson81], whose performance can be analyzed using timed Petri net modeling techniques [Coolahan83]. Real-time scheduling is an approach that is particularly appropriate for hard real-time systems with deadlines that must be met as described in Chapters 11 and 19. There is currently considerable activity in this area, much of it at the Software Engineering Institute. The main objective is to extend the theory and make it practical for analyzing complex hard real-time systems.

21.6   Application of Knowledge-based Techniques

Many design methods use heuristics such as the DARTS task structuring criteria and the Structured Design module coupling and cohesion criteria. Heuristics are based on designer experience and are rules of thumb. Because of this, it is usually not possible to incorporate these heuristics into algorithms. However, knowledge-based tools could be developed that incorporate rules embodying these heuristics [Tsai88]. By doing so, a designer's assistant [Balzer83] could be provided to help the design team during architectural design.

21.7   Application of Formal Methods

Another growing trend in software specification and design methods is in the use of formal methods. A formal method uses a formal specification language; that is, a language with mathematically defined syntax and semantics. Good examples of some of the more mature formal methods are the Vienna Development Method (VDM) and Z. VDM has been successfully applied in the areas of programming language semantics and compiler construction. Methods that show promise for concurrent and real-time systems include temporal logic and Petri net based methods.

Formal methods for real-time systems are currently primarily at the research stage. An example of the successful use of formal methods on industrial projects in a different application domain is the Box Structured Information Systems Method [Mills86]. This uses formal methods in specification and design, and uses formal verification of specifications, designs, and code. A computer assisted software engineering tool with a formal basis is Statemate [Harel88a], which is based on finite state machine theory, and is used to assist in the development of real-time specifications.

PART FOUR

Case Studies

22

Cruise Control and Monitoring System Case Study

This chapter describes the ADARTS and CODARTS solutions to the Cruise Control and Monitoring system case study. The problem description is given in Chapter 4. In the ADARTS solution, the behavioral model is developed using RTSA, as described in Chapter 5. The ADARTS solution then continues with task structuring. The language independent architectural design is mapped to an Ada-based design. With the CODARTS solution, the behavioral model is developed using COncurrent Object-Based Real-Time Analysis (COBRA). The solution then continues with task structuring. In CODARTS, the step in which the design is mapped to Ada is optional.

22.1 Develop Environmental and Behavioral Models

22.1.1 Introduction

In this section, the environmental and behavioral models are developed using COBRA. The solution includes the system context diagram, a hierarchical set of data flow/control flow diagrams representing the subsystems, objects, and functions in the system, and state transition diagrams for all control objects.

22.1.2 Develop System Context Diagram

Figure 22.1 shows the system context diagram, in particular the external entities that the system has to interface to. Each external entity is represented by a terminator. The

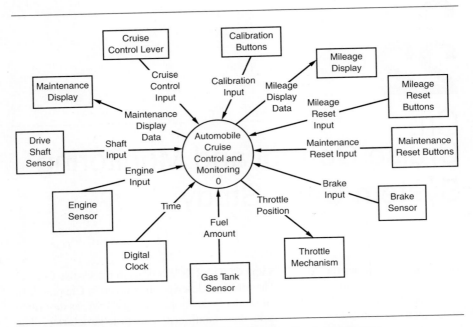

FIGURE 22.1 Cruise Control and Monitoring System Context Diagram

terminators correspond to I/O devices to which the system has to interface. Several of the terminators represent automobile input sensors (e.g., the cruise control lever for entering cruise control requests, the engine sensor for detecting when the engine is switched on and off, the brake sensor for detecting when the brake is pressed and released, and the various button sensors for detecting when the calibration, mileage reset, and maintenance reset buttons are pressed). One terminator represents an output actuator, the throttle mechanism, which controls the physical throttle. There are two output displays, the maintenance display and the mileage display.

There is a close correspondence between the external entities shown on the system context diagram and the external device I/O objects in the system. There should be one external device I/O object for each external entity. The external device I/O objects for this system are Cruise Control Lever, Brake, Engine, Throttle, Shaft, Calibration Buttons, Gas Tank, Mileage Reset Buttons, Maintenance Reset Buttons, Mileage Display, and Maintenance Display. It is assumed that the digital clock is supported by the system software.

22.1.3 System Decomposition

System decomposition into subsystems is based on the nature of service provided by the subsystem. Each subsystem performs a major service, which is relatively independent of the services provided by other subsystems.

In the Cruise Control and Monitoring system, an analysis of the problem indicates that there are two relatively independent and loosely-coupled subsystems: the Automobile Cruise Control subsystem and the Automobile Monitoring subsystem (Fig. 22.2). The Automobile Cruise Control subsystem is a real-time control subsystem, while the Automobile Monitoring subsystem provides data collection and analysis.

Furthermore, the interface between the two subsystems can be determined. Thus, the only data item needed by both subsystems is Cumulative Distance, which is computed by Automobile Cruise Control and used by Automobile Monitoring.

22.1.4 Behavioral Analysis

The decomposition of the Automobile Cruise Control subsystem follows the Behavioral Analysis approach described in Chapter 13. After an initial object determination, the emphasis is on the control and sequencing aspects of the subsystem. The control object, Cruise Control, is at the core of the subsystem and is defined by the state transition diagram shown in Fig. 22.3.

Using the Real-Time Structured Analysis notation, states are represented by rectangles, while labeled arrows represent state transitions. To the left of the slash is the input event that causes the state transition and an optional condition. To the right of the slash is the output event(s) that is generated when the transition occurs. The output event triggers (T), enables (E), or disables (D) a data transformation. The output events are numbered for conciseness, and preceded by a letter identifying the type of event.

E1   Enable "Increase Speed"
D2   Disable "Increase Speed"

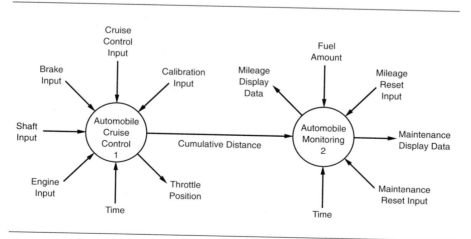

FIGURE 22.2 Decomposition into Subsystems

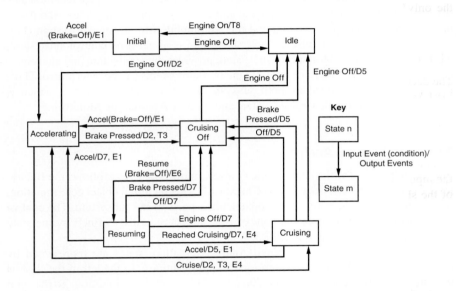

FIGURE 22.3 State Transition Diagram for Cruise Control Object

T3   Trigger "Selected Desired Speed"
E4   Enable "Maintain Speed"
D5   Disable "Maintain Speed"
E6   Enable "Resume Cruising"
D7   Disable "Resume Cruising"
T8   Trigger "Clear Desired Speed"

The different states of the car, from a cruise control perspective, are

□ *Idle.* In this state, the engine is switched off.

□ *Initial.* When the driver turns the engine on, the car enters Initial state. The car stays in this state as long as no attempt is made to engage cruise control. In Initial state, unlike Cruising Off state, there is no previously stored cruising speed.

□ *Accelerating.* When the driver engages the cruise control lever in the ACCEL position (transition Accel), the car enters Accelerating state and accelerates automatically, providing the brake is not pressed (condition Brake = Off).

□ *Cruising.* When the driver releases the lever (transition Cruise), the current speed is saved as the cruising speed and the car enters Cruising state. In this state, the car speed is automatically maintained at the cruising speed.

❑ *Cruising Off.* When the driver either engages the lever in the OFF position (Off transition) or presses the brake, cruise control is deactivated and the car returns to manual operation.

❑ *Resuming.* When the driver engages the lever in the RESUME position (transition Resume), and providing the brake is not pressed, the car automatically accelerates or decelerates to the last cruising speed. When the car reaches the desired speed, it enters Cruising state (transition Reached Cruising).

22.1.5   Decomposition of Automobile Cruise Control Subsystem

Following the behavioral analysis described in Section 13.8, the objects and functions required to directly support the cruise control aspects of the problem are shown on the data flow/control flow diagram (Fig. 22.4). At this stage, the analysis has been carried

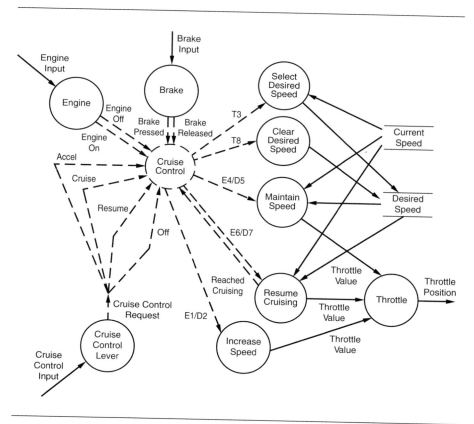

FIGURE 22.4 Initial Data Flow/Control Flow Diagram

out at one level of detail and in fact does not show all the services that this subsystem needs to provide. Thus the monitoring of shaft rotation in order to compute the Current Speed, which is stored in the data store, is not shown. In addition the calibration aspects of the problem are not shown.

A consolidation decision is therefore made to depict the Automobile Cruise Control subsystem as being composed of three aggregate objects, Automobile Control, Distance and Speed Measurement, and Calibration (Fig. 22.5). Each aggregate object is composed of related objects and functions. Most of the objects and functions from the data flow/control flow diagram (Fig. 22.4) are allocated to the Automobile Control aggregate object. The Current Speed data store, as well as all objects and functions required to compute the distance travelled and the current speed of the vehicle are allocated to the Distance and Speed Measurement aggregate object. All objects and functions related to calibration of the vehicle are allocated to the Calibration aggregate object. The Automobile Cruise Control subsystem shown in Fig. 22.2 is thus decomposed into the three aggregate objects shown in Fig. 22.5.

22.1.6 Decomposition of Automobile Control

Automobile Control is decomposed as shown on the DFD in Fig. 22.6. Three device input objects, represented by data transformations, monitor the automobile sensors. The Engine object reads the engine sensor and sends the Engine On and Engine Off event flows to Speed Control. The Brake objects reads the brake sensor and sends the Brake Pressed and Brake Released event flows to Speed Control. The Cruise Control

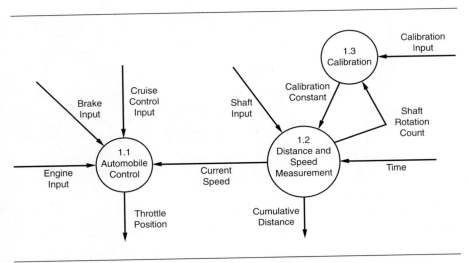

FIGURE 22.5 Decomposition of Automobile Cruise Control Subsystem

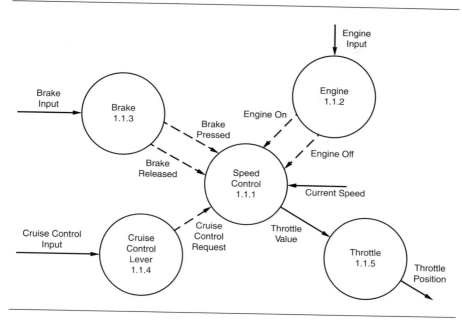

FIGURE 22.6 Decomposition of Automobile Control

Lever object reads inputs from the cruise control lever and sends these as Cruise Control Request event flows to Speed Control.

The aggregate object Speed Control computes the throttle value when cruise control is active and is decomposed further. Speed Control passes the throttle value to the Throttle object, which outputs the actual throttle position to the real-world throttle.

22.1.7 Decomposition of Speed Control

The aggregate object Speed Control is decomposed into the objects and functions shown in Fig. 22.7. The control object, Cruise Control, executes the state transition diagram (Fig. 22.3) and controls the functions shown on the DFD.

The functions on the DFD for Speed Control are triggered, enabled, or disabled at state transitions. A triggered transformation is a one-shot function. For example, Select Desired Speed is triggered when Cruise Control transitions into Cruising state. It then sets the Desired Speed, which is the speed the car is to cruise at, equal to the Current Speed. Clear Desired Speed clears this value.

A transformation that is enabled for the duration of the entire state is likely to be cyclic. For example, Maintain Speed is enabled when Cruise Control enters Cruising

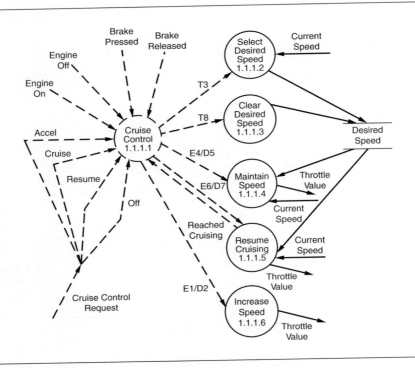

FIGURE 22.7 Decomposition of Speed Control

state and is disabled when Cruise Control leaves Cruising state. Thus Maintain Speed is active throughout Cruising state. It periodically reads Current Speed and Desired Speed, and adjusts the throttle value so that the cruising speed is maintained. Increase Speed is active during Accelerating state; it periodically adjusts the throttle value so that the speed of the vehicle is gradually increased. Resume Cruising is active in Resuming state; it periodically reads the Current Speed and Desired Speed data stores, and adjusts the throttle value so that the speed of the vehicle is increased or decreased to reach the cruising speed. When the cruising speed is reached, Resume Cruising sends the Reached Cruising event flow to Cruise Control.

22.1.8 Decomposition of Distance and Speed Measurement

The Distance and Speed Measurement aggregate object is decomposed into a DFD shown in Fig. 22.8. The device input object Shaft increments the Shaft Rotation Count, once for each rotation.

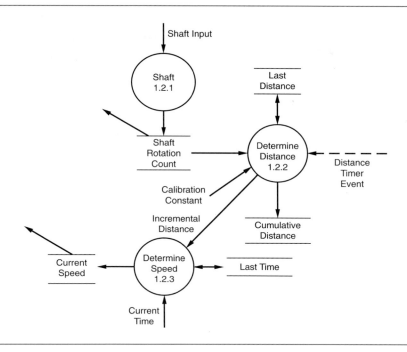

FIGURE 22.8 Decomposition of Distance and Speed Measurement

The Determine Distance function is activated periodically to compute the incremental distance travelled, given the current value of the Shaft Rotation Count, Last Distance (the value of the Shaft Rotation Count when incremental distance was last computed), and the Calibration Constant (the shaft rotation count per mile). Determine Distance then adds the Incremental Distance to the Cumulative Distance. The Determine Speed function receives the Incremental Distance and computes Current Speed given the incremental time.

22.1.9   Decomposition of Calibration

The Calibration aggregate object is decomposed into the DFD shown in ¨g. 22.9. Four transformations are required to compute the value of the calibration constant. The physical device I/O object, Calibration Buttons, reads the calibration buttons sensor and sends the Calibration Start and Calibration Stop event flows to the control object Calibration Control. Calibration Control is defined by means of the state transition diagram shown in Fig. 22.10.

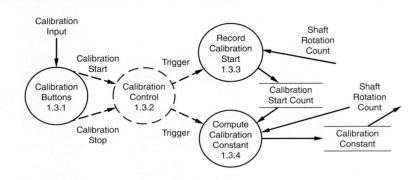

FIGURE 22.9 Decomposition of Calibration

When the driver pushes the Start Measured Mile Calibration button, Calibration Buttons sends the Calibration Start event flow to Calibration Control. Calibration Control then transitions from Not Measuring state to Measuring Mile state and triggers Record Calibration Start, which then reads the Shaft Rotation Count and stores it in Calibration Start Count.

When the driver pushes the Stop Measured Mile Calibration button, Calibration Buttons sends the Calibration Stop event flow to Calibration Control. Calibration Control then transitions back to Not Measuring state and triggers Compute Calibration Constant. Compute Calibration Constant then reads the Shaft Rotation

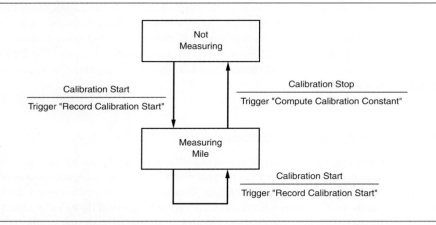

FIGURE 22.10 State Transition Diagram for Calibration Control Object

Count and the Calibration Start Count. It computes the difference, the shaft rotation count per mile, which is the Calibration Constant. As a safety check, if this count is not within predefined upper and lower limits, then the Calibration Constant is set to a default value.

22.1.10   Decomposition of Automobile Monitoring Subsystem

The Automobile Monitoring subsystem (Fig. 22.2) is decomposed into two smaller subsystems, Average Mileage and Maintenance, as shown in Fig. 22.11. The structure and behavior of these subsystems is determined using Non-state Dependent Behavioral Analysis.

The Average Mileage Subsystem computes and displays the average miles per gallon and average miles per hour. The Maintenance Subsystem determines whether maintenance is required on the car and if so lights up the maintenance display.

22.1.11   Decomposition of Average Mileage Subsystem

An example of applying Non-state Dependent Behavioral Analysis to the Average Mileage Subsystem is (Section 13.9) a scenario for Average MPG, which considers

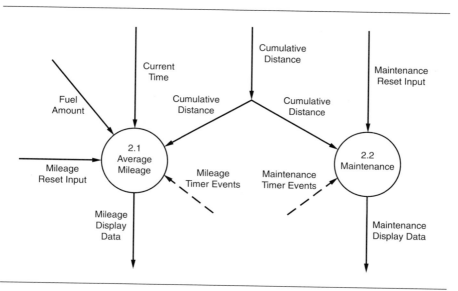

FIGURE 22.11 Decomposition of Automobile Monitoring Subsystem

the behavior of the system when the Average MPG reset button is pressed and periodically when the Average MPG is computed and displayed. The resulting DFD is shown in Fig. 22.12. Applying a similar behavioral analysis for Average MPH and superimposing that on the DFD of Fig. 22.12 results in the DFD for the Average Mileage Subsystem shown in Fig. 22.13.

22.1.12 Decomposition of Maintenance Subsystem

The Maintenance Subsystem is shown in Fig. 22.14. Three kinds of maintenance service are performed at regular intervals, oil filter, air filter and major service maintenance. Each is handled in a similar way.

For example, consider oil filter maintenance. On completing the oil filter service, the maintenance technician pushes the oil filter reset button. The Maintenance Reset Buttons device input object receives the Oil Filter Maintenance Reset input from the maintenance technician. It then sends an Oil Filter Reset event to Initialize Oil Filter, which then reads the current value of Cumulative Distance and stores it in the Miles

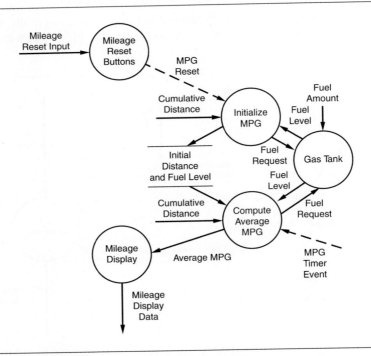

FIGURE 22.12 Initial Data Flow Diagram for Average MPG

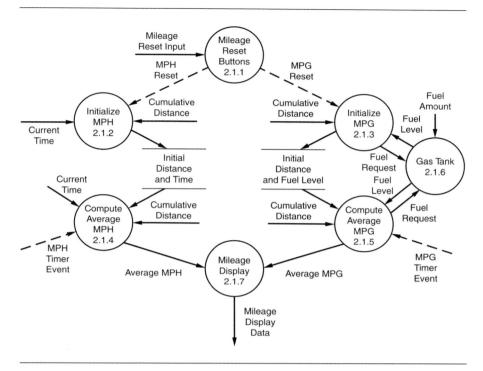

FIGURE 22.13 Decomposition of Average Mileage

at Last Oil Filter Maintenance data store. Check Oil Filter Maintenance periodically reads Cumulative Distance and compares it with the mileage value in the Last Oil Filter Maintenance data store to determine the distance travelled since the last service, and hence whether a new service is required. If it is, Check Oil Filter Maintenance sends an Oil Filter Status message to Maintenance Display, which outputs the message to the physical maintenance display.

22.2 Structure System into Tasks

22.2.1 Introduction

After developing the behavioral model using RTSA in ADARTS and COBRA in CODARTS, the next step in both ADARTS and CODARTS is to structure the system

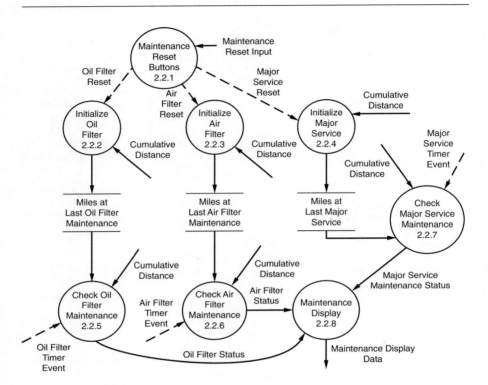

FIGURE 22.14 Decomposition of Maintenance

into concurrent tasks. With a hierarchical set of data flow diagrams, the decomposition from one level to the next does not necessarily coincide with the task boundaries. A solution to this problem is to piece together the leaf (lowest-level) transformations to form a detailed low-level data flow diagram before starting the task structuring activity. Since it is impractical to show this on a standard sheet of paper, the approach taken here is to analyze the leaf transformations on each data flow diagram and describe how the task architecture is derived. Each major subsystem is considered in turn, first the Cruise Control subsystem, then the Monitoring subsystem.

22.2.2   Define I/O Device Characteristics

Before proceeding further with the Task Structuring step, certain information needs to be obtained relating to the I/O devices, in particular whether the devices are asynchronous or not. For a passive I/O device, it is necessary to determine the frequency with which the device is polled.

Assume that the I/O devices for the Cruise Control and Monitoring system have the following characteristics. Passive input devices that need to be polled have their polling frequency in parentheses, while passive output devices that need to be updated have their update frequency in parentheses.

□ Asynchronous input devices: cruise control lever and drive shaft.

□ Passive input devices: brake sensor (100 ms), engine sensor (100 ms), gas tank sensor (on demand), calibration buttons (500 ms), mileage reset buttons (500 ms), maintenance reset buttons (500 ms).

□ Passive output devices: throttle (updated every 100 ms), mileage display (updated every second), maintenance display (updated every two seconds).

22.2.3   Determine Cruise Control Subsystem I/O Tasks

Following the guidelines, the I/O data transformations are considered first. For the Cruise Control Subsystem, this requires analyzing the DFDs. Consider the Automobile Control DFD, where four of the data transformations on this DFD represent device I/O objects and are not decomposed further.

The Cruise Control Lever object reads inputs from the cruise control lever. As the lever is an asynchronous input device, Cruise Control Lever is structured as an asynchronous device input task, as shown in Fig. 22.15. This task is activated by a cruise control interrupt when there is a new cruise control input. As the throttle is a passive output device, the Throttle object is structured as a periodic device output task, called Throttle, which outputs the throttle position to the real-world throttle actuator.

The brake and engine sensors are both passive input devices. Furthermore, they both need to be polled every 100 milliseconds. The Brake and Engine device input objects are therefore combined into a temporally cohesive periodic input task called Monitor Auto Sensors. This task is activated by a timer event every 100 msec.

Consider the Distance and Speed Measurement DFD (Fig. 22.16), in which there is one device input object, Shaft. The drive shaft is an asynchronous input device. Consequently, the Shaft object is structured as an asynchronous device input task that increments the Shaft Rotation Count every time it is activated. This task must also be a high priority task, since it is essential for it not to miss any rotations; otherwise there would be errors in the computations for Incremental Distance and Current Speed.

Consider the Calibration DFD (Fig. 22.17), in which there is one device input object, Calibration Buttons. The calibration buttons are passive and need to be polled every 500 milliseconds. Consequently Calibration Buttons could be structured as a periodic input task. However, before making a final decision, consider the other transformations that it interacts with.

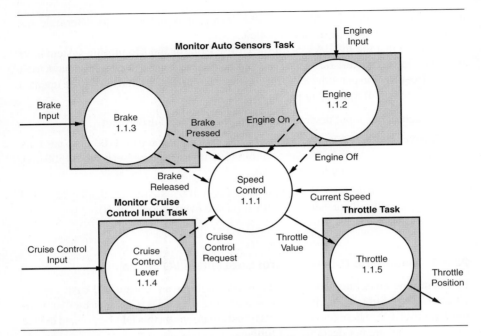

FIGURE 22.15 Cruise Control Subsystem: Device I/O Task Structuring

Calibration Control is a control object and therefore forms the basis of a control task. However Calibration Control can only be activated by an input from Calibration Buttons and cannot be active concurrently with it. Consequently, the two transformations can be combined into one task based on the sequential cohesion criterion. Furthermore, the functions Record Calibration Start and Compute Calibration Constant are triggered by Calibration Control and execute during the respective state transitions. Consequently, these two transformations can also be combined into the same task, Perform Calibration, based on control cohesion. The Perform Calibration task is periodically activated by a timer event because the calibration buttons are polled.

22.2.4   Determine Cruise Control Subsystem Control Tasks

Next the control objects (transformations) are considered, of which there are two in the Cruise Control Subsystem. Calibration Control was considered in the previous section. Now consider the Cruise Control control object, which is part of the Speed Control DFD shown on Fig. 22.18.

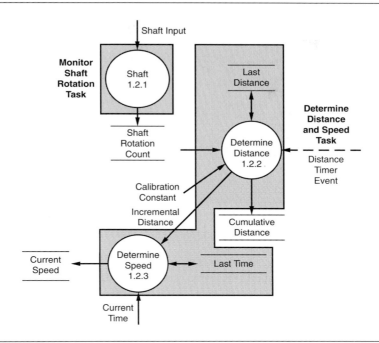

Shaft Input

Monitor Shaft Rotation Task

Shaft
1.2.1

Last
Distance

Determine Distance and Speed Task

Distance
Timer
Event

Shaft
Rotation
Count

Determine
Distance
1.2.2

Calibration
Constant

Incremental
Distance

Cumulative
Distance

Current
Speed

Determine
Speed
1.2.3

Last Time

Current
Time

FIGURE 22.16 Cruise Control Subsystem: Distance and Speed Task Structuring

The control object Cruise Control executes the cruise control state transition diagram. It is therefore structured as a separate high priority control task, so that state transitions appear to be instantaneous.

The functions all represent actions that are triggered, enabled, or disabled by state transitions. If a data transformation is triggered as a result of a state transition and performs a function that is executed during the state transition, then it may be combined with the control transformation into a task based on the control cohesion criterion. Based on this rationale, the transformations Select Desired Speed and Control Desired Speed, each of which is triggered and performs a function that is executed during the state transition, are combined with Cruise Control into a task, also called Cruise Control, according to the control cohesion criterion.

If, on the other hand, the data transformation is enabled and then runs cyclically until subsequently disabled, then it should be structured as a separate task, since both the control transformation and data transformation need to be active concurrently. The remaining three functions, Maintain Speed, Resume Cruising, and Increase Speed, are all enabled and disabled by state transitions. Since they execute concurrently with the Cruise Control task, they need to be in separate tasks. However, the execution of these

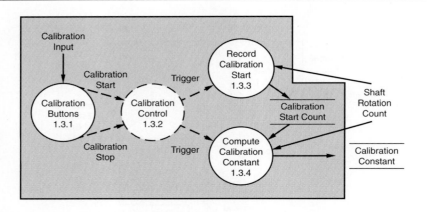

FIGURE 22.17 Cruise Control Subsystem: Perform Calibration Task

three transformations is mutually exclusive, since each one performs its speed control function in a different Cruise Control state. These three transformations may therefore be grouped into one task, Auto Speed Control, based on the sequential cohesion and functional cohesion criteria.

22.2.5   Determine Cruise Control Subsystem Periodic Tasks

Next, the data transformations that are executed periodically are considered. Consider the Determine Distance and Determine Speed periodic functions on Fig. 22.16. These transformations are activated periodically and could therefore be structured as separate periodic tasks. However, Determine Distance computes Incremental Distance, which is used by Determine Speed. Consequently the two transformations are grouped into one task based on the sequential cohesion criterion. This task, called Determine Distance and Speed, is also periodic since it is activated at regular intervals to compute distance and speed.

22.2.6   Draw Task Architecture Diagram

Once all the objects and functions on the data flow diagrams have been structured into tasks, a preliminary task architecture diagram is drawn, which shows the tasks identified during this phase (Fig. 22.19). At this stage, the task interfaces are still shown as they were on the data flow diagrams; that is, data flows, event flows, and data stores. Defining task interfaces is addressed later.

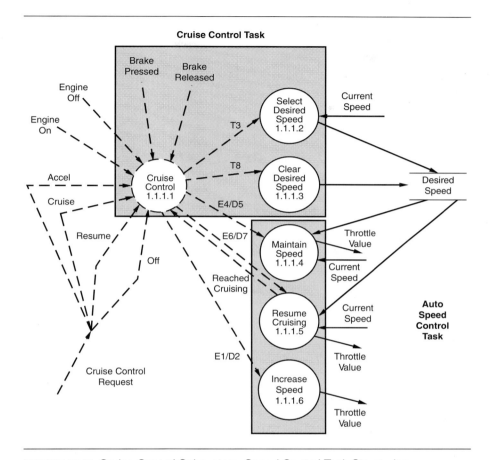

FIGURE 22.18 Cruise Control Subsystem: Speed Control Task Structuring

22.2.7   Determine Monitoring Subsystem I/O Tasks

Now consider the Monitoring Subsystem. As before, first consider the I/O tasks. Both the mileage reset buttons and the maintenance reset buttons are passive devices. Furthermore, they are polled with the same frequency, every 500 milliseconds. Consequently, the device input objects Mileage Reset Buttons and Maintenance Reset Buttons are combined into one task, Monitor Reset Buttons, based on the periodic input and temporal cohesion criteria.

Consider the transformations Initialize MPH and Initialize MPG (from Monitor and Display Averages) and the transformations Initialize Oil Filter, Initialize Air Filter, and Initialize Major Service (from Check Maintenance Need). They are also combined with the Monitor Reset Buttons task based on the sequential cohesion criterion. This

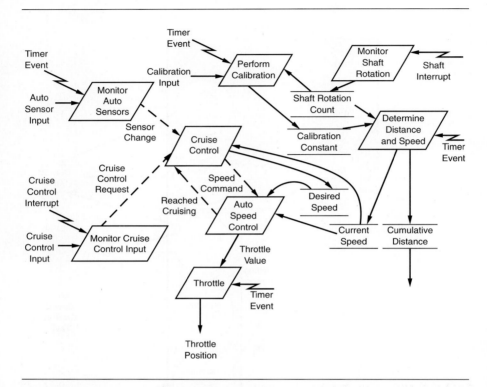

FIGURE 22.19 Preliminary Task Architecture Diagram for Cruise Control Subsystem

case is also an example of transformations on different diagrams being combined into one task. The transformations that compose the Monitor Reset Buttons task are shown on Fig. 22.20. The mileage and maintenance displays are passive output devices, and are therefore considered in the next section in conjunction with the transformations that use them.

22.2.8   Determine Monitoring Subsystem Periodic Tasks

As there are no control transformations in the Monitoring Subsystem, periodic tasks are considered next. Compute Average MPH and Compute Average MPG (from the Average Mileage Display DFD) are periodically executed. Thus they are candidates for periodic tasks. However, since it is necessary to update the mileage display every second, there is no reason for the two transformations that provide the display data to be allocated to different tasks. Consequently, Compute Average MPH and Compute Average MPG are combined into one task, Compute Average Mileage, based on the

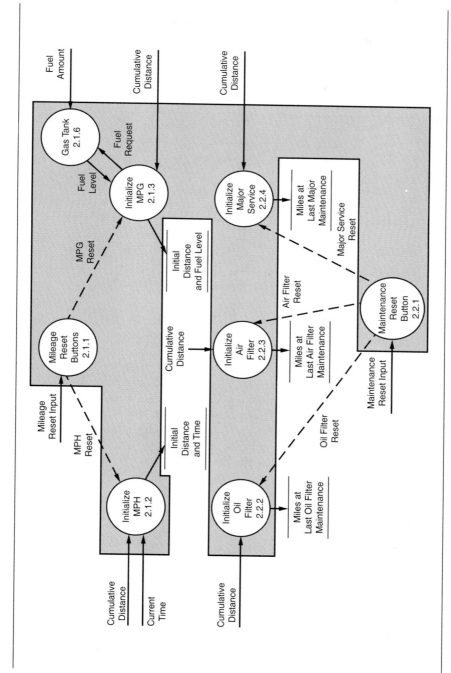

FIGURE 22.20 Monitoring Subsystem: Monitor Reset Buttons Task

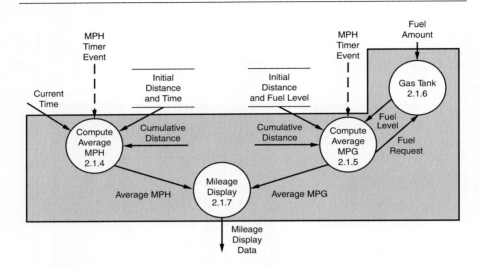

FIGURE 22.21 Monitoring Subsystem: Compute Average Mileage Task

temporal cohesion criterion. Furthermore, the Mileage Display device output object may also be combined with them based on the sequential cohesion criterion (Fig. 22.21), since the mileage display is passive.

For the same reason, three maintenance transformations, Check Oil Filter, Check Air Filter, and Check Major Service, are also structured as a periodic temporally cohesive task and combined with the device output object Maintenance Display (Fig. 22.22). The maintenance display is updated every two seconds. As it is updated less frequently than the mileage display, the Compute Average Mileage and Check Maintenance Need tasks are kept as separate tasks.

The preliminary task architecture diagram for the Monitoring Subsystem illustrates that all three tasks in this subsystem are periodic (Fig. 22.23). All task interaction in this subsystem is via the data stores.

22.2.9 Determine Task Interfaces

The next stage involves analyzing and defining task interfaces. Task interfaces are analyzed from the viewpoint of whether they are loosely or tightly coupled.

Consider the preliminary task architecture diagram for the Cruise Control subsystem (Fig. 22.19). There are three event flows that flow into the Cruise Control task. Since more than one event may arrive in quick succession and it is important not to miss any events, this interface should be loosely coupled. Furthermore, as it is important to maintain the sequence of these events, the task interface chosen is a FIFO message queue, called Cruise Control messages (Fig. 22.24).

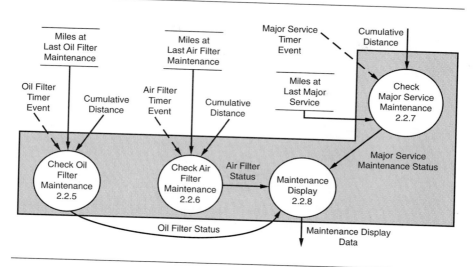

FIGURE 22.22 Monitoring Subsystem: Check Maintenance Need Task

On the other hand, consider the interface between Cruise Control and Auto Speed Control. Since the enabling or disabling of a speed command takes place during the state transition, it is desirable for Auto Speed Control to accept the command from Cruise Control without delay. The interface between these two tasks should therefore be tightly coupled. Since there is no response from Auto Speed Control to Cruise Control, the Speed Command interface is tightly coupled without reply. The interface between Auto Speed Control and Throttle is also tightly coupled without reply, since as soon as Auto Speed Control has computed a new Throttle Value, it should be accepted by the Throttle task.

The data stores that are accessed by more than one task are all mapped to information hiding modules. In the Monitoring Subsystem, the interfaces between the three tasks are all via data stores, which are mapped to information hiding modules (Fig. 22.25). This topic is addressed in more detail during the next step of the ADARTS and CODARTS methods, Module Structuring.

22.3   Structure System into Modules

22.3.1   Introduction

During the Module Structuring phase of ADARTS and CODARTS, the information hiding modules are determined. For those objects determined using COBRA in the

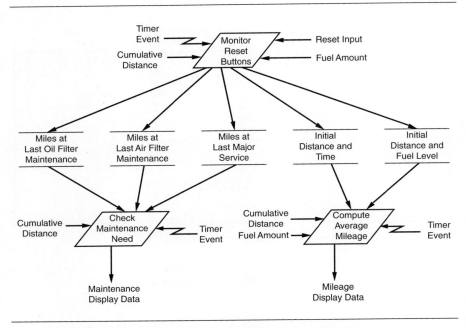

FIGURE 22.23 Preliminary Task Architecture Diagram for Monitoring Subsystem

Analysis and Modeling phase, there is a one-to-one mapping from the objects in the behavioral model to information hiding modules. All the functions determined in the RTSA behavioral model, and any remaining functions in the COBRA behavioral model, need to be mapped to information hiding modules. In addition, it is also necessary to define the operations for all the information hiding modules.

22.3.2 Define Device Interface Modules

A device interface module (DIM) hides the actual interface to the real-world device by providing a virtual interface to it. There is one DIM for each I/O device. During the analysis and modeling phase, the external device I/O objects are determined. Each external device I/O object is mapped to a DIM. In addition, it is necessary to determine the operations provided by each DIM. A data transformation representing an external device I/O object contains both the hidden physical interface to the device as well as the operations that read from and/or write to the device.

The DIMs in the Cruise Control and Monitoring system are

1. *Engine.* The Engine device input object in Fig. 22.26 is mapped to the Engine DIM, which hides how to interface to the engine sensor. It provides two opera-

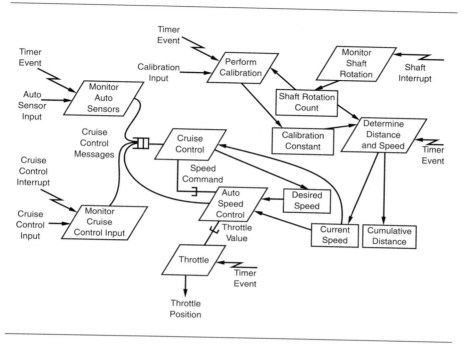

FIGURE 22.24 Task Architecture Diagram for Cruise Control Subsystem: Intertask
Communication

tions: Read, which reads the engine sensor; and Initialize, which initializes the
DIM's internal data structures and performs any necessary device initialization.

2. *Brake.* The Brake device input object in Fig. 22.26 is mapped to the Brake DIM,
which hides how to interface to the brake sensor. It provides two operations: Read,
which reads the brake sensor; and Initialize.

3. *Cruise Control Lever.* The Cruise Control Lever device input object in Fig. 22.26
is mapped to the Cruise Control Lever DIM, which hides how to interface to the
cruise control lever. It provides two operations: Read, which reads the cruise
control input; and Initialize, which initializes the DIM's internal data structures
and performs any necessary device initialization.

4. *Shaft.* The Shaft device input object on Fig. 22.27 is mapped to the Shaft DIM,
which hides how to handle shaft rotation inputs. It provides two operations: Read,
which reads the shaft input; and Initialize.

5. *Calibration Buttons.* The Calibration Buttons device input object on Fig. 22.28
is mapped to the Calibration Buttons DIM, which hides how to read inputs from
the calibration buttons. It provides two operations: Read, which reads the calibration input; and Initialize.

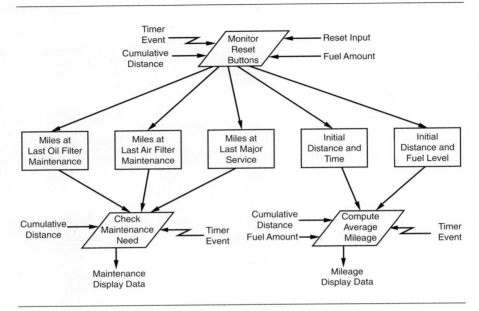

FIGURE 22.25 Task Architecture Diagram for Monitoring Subsystem: Intertask Communication

6. *Throttle.* The Throttle device output object on Fig. 22.26 is mapped to the Throttle DIM, which hides how to interface to the throttle. It provides two operations: Output, which outputs to the real-world throttle; and Initialize, which initializes the DIM's internal data structures and performs any necessary device initialization.

7. *Gas tank.* This DIM hides how to interface to the gas tank sensor. It provides two operations: Read, to read the gas tank fuel level (converted to gallons); and Initialize.

8. *Mileage Reset.* This DIM hides how to read inputs from the mileage reset buttons. It provides two operations: Read, to read the inputs from the mileage reset buttons; and Initialize.

9. *Maintenance Reset.* This DIM hides how to read inputs from the maintenance reset buttons. It provides two operations: Read, to read the inputs from the maintenance reset buttons; and Initialize.

10. *Mileage Display.* This DIM hides how to interface to the mileage display. It provides operations to Display MPG and Display MPH.

11. *Maintenance Display.* This DIM hides how to interface to the maintenance display. It provides operations to Display Oil Message, Display Air Message, and Display Service Message.

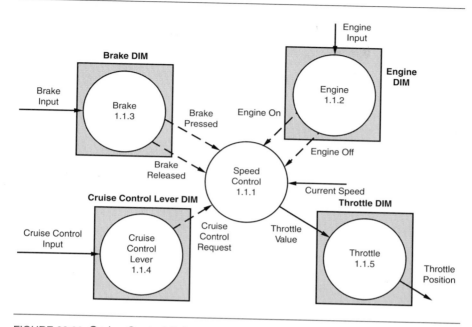

FIGURE 22.26 Cruise Control Subsystem: Device Interface Module Structuring

22.3.3 Define Data Abstraction Modules

Each data store forms the basis of a data abstraction module (DAM). The operations are identified by analyzing the transformations that access the data store.

1. *Shaft Rotation Count.* This DAM hides how the Shaft Rotation Count is updated (Fig. 22.27). It has operations to Update Shaft Rotation Count and Read Shaft Rotation Count. These operations are determined by examining the mini-specifications of the transformations that access the data store.

2. *Calibration.* This DAM hides how the Calibration Constant (Fig. 22.28) is computed. It provides three operations in the form of access procedures: Start Calibration, Stop Calibration, and Read Calibration Constant. Start Calibration corresponds to the data transformation Record Calibration Start, while the operation Stop Calibration corresponds to the data transformation Compute Calibration Constant. The operation Read Calibration Constant is determined by inspecting the mini-specification of Determine Distance (Fig. 22.27), which reads from the data store.

3. *Current Speed.* This DAM hides how the Current Speed (Fig. 22.27) is computed. It supports two operations, Update Current Speed and Read Current Speed. Update Current Speed corresponds to the data transformation Determine Speed,

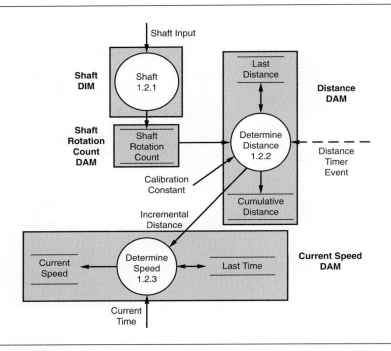

FIGURE 22.27 Cruise Control Subsystem: Distance and Speed Module Structuring

while Read Current Speed is determined by inspecting the mini-specifications of the data transformations in Fig. 22.29 which read from the data store (e.g., Maintain Speed).

4. *Desired Speed.* This DAM hides how the Desired Speed (Fig. 22.29) is maintained. It provides three operations in the form of access procedures: Select Desired Speed, Clear Desired Speed, and Read Desired Speed. Select Desired Speed and Clear Desired Speed correspond respectively to the similarly named data transformations. Read Desired Speed is determined by inspecting the mini-specifications of the data transformations, which read from the data store (e.g., Maintain Speed).

5. *Distance.* This DAM hides how distance is computed (Fig. 22.27). It maintains both the cumulative and incremental distance. It supports three operations: Compute Distance, Read Cumulative Distance, and Read Incremental Distance. Compute Distance corresponds to the data transformation Determine Distance. Read Cumulative Distance and Read Incremental Distance are determined by

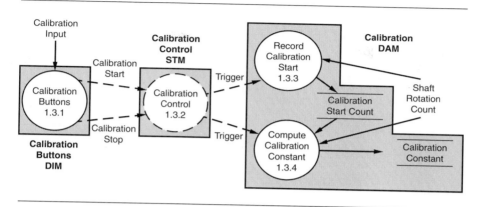

FIGURE 22.28 Cruise Control Subsystem: Calibration Module Structuring

inspecting the mini-specifications of the data transformations, which read from the data store.

22.3.4   Define State Transition Modules

State transition modules (STM) are determined from the control objects (transformations) in the behavioral model. For each state transition diagram that is mapped to a state transition table, there is a corresponding state transition module.

There are two control objects in the Cruise Control subsystem and none in the Monitoring subsystem. The Cruise Control STM encapsulates the Cruise Control state transition diagram. It provides two operations, Process Event and Current State, which are standard operations for STMs. Each action resulting from a state transition is supported by an operation. However, these operations are packaged into different information hiding modules, as shown in Fig. 22.29. The Calibration Control STM encapsulates the Calibration Control state transition diagram. It provides the same two STM operations, Process Event and Current State.

22.3.5   Define Function Driver Modules

Function driver modules (FDM) control a set of closely related outputs that are passed to virtual I/O devices. There are six FDMs.

1. *Speed Control.* The data transformations Increase Speed, Maintain Speed, and Resume Cruising (Fig. 22.29) are combined into a function driver module, Speed

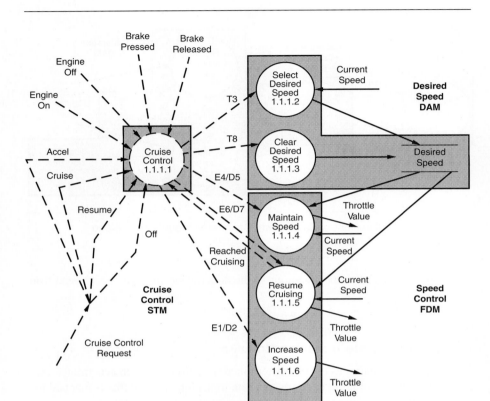

FIGURE 22.29 Cruise Control Subsystem: Behavior Hiding Module Structuring

Control, based on the fact that these functions all deal with automatic speed control and compute the throttle value, which is then passed to the throttle device. The module supports these three operations plus a fourth operation, Deactivate. Deactivate is implicit, since each of the three transformations is enabled and disabled by Cruise Control. Support for disabling the transformations is provided by the Deactivate operation.

2. *Average MPH.* This FDM hides how the average MPH is computed, which is then output to the mileage display. It supports two operations, Initialize MPH and Compute MPH, as determined by the two MPH transformations shown in Fig. 22.30.

3. *Average MPG.* This FDM hides how the average MPG is computed, which is

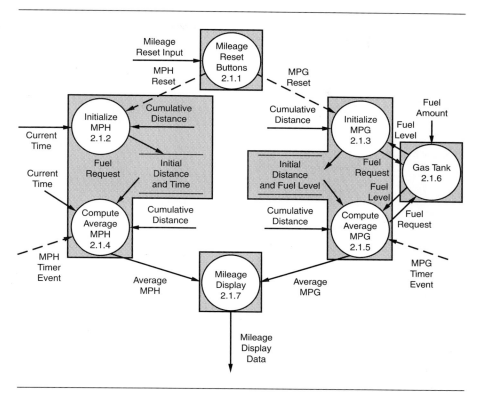

FIGURE 22.30 Monitoring Subsystem: Average Mileage Module Structuring

then output to the mileage display. It supports two operations, Initialize MPG and Compute MPG, as determined by the two MPG transformations shown in Fig. 22.30.

4. *Oil Filter Maintenance.* This FDM hides how oil filter maintenance checking is provided, including at what distance maintenance messages are output to the maintenance display. It supports two operations, Initialize Oil Filter and Check Oil Filter, as determined by the two Oil Filter transformations shown in Fig. 22.31.

5. *Air Filter Maintenance.* This FDM hides how air filter maintenance checking is provided, including at what distance maintenance messages are output to the maintenance display. It supports two operations, Initialize Air Filter and Check Air Filter, as determined by the two Air Filter transformations shown in Fig. 22.31.

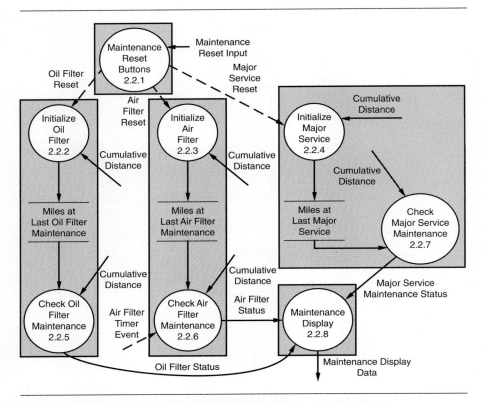

FIGURE 22.31 Monitoring Subsystem: Maintenance Module Structuring

6. *Major Service Maintenance.* This FDM hides how major service maintenance checking is provided, including at what distance maintenance messages are output to the maintenance display. It supports two operations, Initialize Major Service and Check Major Service, as determined by the two Major Service transformations shown in Fig. 22.31.

22.3.6   Determine Information Hiding Module Aggregation Hierarchy

Now that the information hiding modules have been determined from the behavioral model, an information hiding module aggregation hierarchy is developed in which these modules are categorized. Device interface modules and behavior hiding modules (in particular, data abstraction modules, state transition modules, function driver modules, and algorithm hiding modules) are determined from the behavioral model.

TABLE 22.1 INFORMATION HIDING MODULE AGGREGATION HIERARCHY

Device Interface Modules
   Engine
   Brake
   Cruise Control Lever
   Calibration Buttons
   Shaft
   Throttle
   Gas Tank
   Mileage Reset
   Maintenance Reset
   Mileage Display
   Maintenance Display

Behavior Hiding Modules
   Data Abstraction Modules
      Shaft Rotation Count
      Calibration
      Current Speed
      Desired Speed
      Distance
   State Transition Modules
      Cruise Control
      Calibration Control
   Function Driver Modules
      Speed Control
      Average MPH
      Average MPG
      Oil Filter Maintenance
      Air Filter Maintenance
      Major Service Maintenance

The module aggregation hierarchy for the Cruise Control and Monitoring system is shown in Table 22.1.

22.3.7   Use of Inheritance in Design

As described in Chapter 15, it is possible to design a Maintenance class with three subclasses: Oil Filter Maintenance, Air Filter Maintenance, and Major Service Maintenance. Using this approach, greater code sharing can be obtained than by designing them as separate modules. The generalization/specialization hierarchy is shown in Table 22.2.

The class Maintenance is defined with two operations, Initialize Maintenance and Check Maintenance. Initialize Maintenance is defined but Check Maintenance is

TABLE 22.2 GENERALIZATION/SPECIALIZATION HIERARCHY FOR
MAINTENANCE CLASS

Maintenance
    Oil Filter Maintenance
    Air Filter Maintenance
    Major Service Maintenance

deferred. Each subclass inherits the operation specification and body for Initialize Maintenance as well as the specification for Check Maintenance. It then defines the body of Check Maintenance, which is different for each kind of maintenance.

22.4   Integrate Task and Module Views

After determining the information hiding modules using the module structuring criteria, the next step is to determine the relationship between the tasks and the modules. In general, operations are executed by tasks but packaged with modules.

A software architecture diagram (SAD) shows the tasks and information hiding modules in a given system or subsystem. The operations of each IHM are explicitly shown. The tasks that call these operations are also shown with a line drawn from the task to the operation. The arrowhead shows the direction of the call from the task to the operation and hence represents control flow. For example, in Fig. 22.32, the Select Desired Speed and Clear Desired Speed operations of the Desired Speed IHM are called by the Cruise Control task, while the Read Desired Speed operation is called by the Auto Speed Control task.

Consider some examples of the relationship between tasks and modules. Consider the case of polled I/O in the Cruise Control subsystem (Fig. 22.32). The brake and engine sensors are polled. From a task structuring perspective, they are combined into a periodic temporally cohesive task, Monitor Auto Sensors. From a module structuring perspective, each device is mapped to a device interface module, Brake and Engine. The modules are embedded within this task, as no other tasks access their operations.

Consider an example from the Monitoring subsystem (Fig. 22.33). Compute Average Mileage is a periodic task that is temporally and sequentially cohesive. When activated by a timer event, it executes operations provided by two function driver modules. It calls the Compute MPH operation of the Average MPH module, which in turn calls the Display MPH operation of the Mileage Display device interface module, followed by the Compute MPG operation of the Average MPG module, which in turn calls Display MPG. The temporal cohesion is because Compute Average Mileage calls both Compute MPH and Compute MPG each time it is activated. The sequential

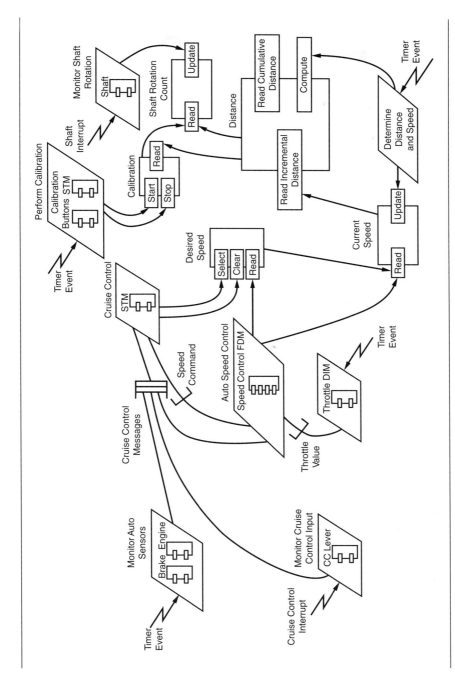

FIGURE 22.32   Software Architecture Diagram for Cruise Control Subsystem

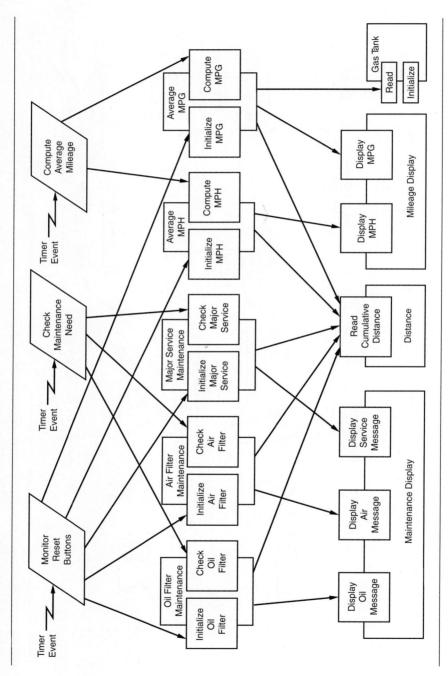

FIGURE 22.33 Software (and Ada) Architecture Diagram for Monitoring Subsystem

cohesion is because Compute MPH/MPG calls Display MPH/MPG. The modules are placed outside the task because their operations are called by more than one task.

22.5   Develop Ada-based Architectural Design

22.5.1 Introduction

At this stage, the design is language independent although compatible with Ada. Thus tasks and modules (packages) map directly to Ada. The next step in ADARTS is to develop an Ada-based design. This includes adding Ada-specific support tasks and defining Ada task interfaces.

Ada specific aspects of the design are shown in Ada architecture diagrams (AADs), as given in Fig. 22.34 for the Cruise Control subsystem. The AAD for the Monitoring subsystem is identical to the SAD.

22.5.2   Define Event Buffering Task

First message communication is addressed. A loosely-coupled message or event interface needs to be mapped to a message or event buffering task. Thus, a Cruise Control Event Buffering task is required to support the loosely-coupled message queue, which is used to pass events to the Cruise Control task. The Event Buffering task has two entries, Send Event and Receive Event.

The three producer tasks, Monitor Auto Sensors, Monitor Cruise Control Input, and Auto Speed Control, make unconditional entry calls to Send Event. The consumer task, Cruise Control, makes an unconditional entry call to Receive Event. The producers should not have to wait, providing the buffer does not get full. It is therefore important to ensure that the buffer is sufficiently large. It is acceptable for Cruise Control to make an unconditional entry call, since an input message needs to be available before a state transition can take place. Hence, if the buffer is empty it means that there is no work for Cruise Control to perform.

22.5.3   Define Tightly-coupled Task Interfaces

Tightly-coupled message interfaces are handled directly by an Ada rendezvous. Called tasks have entries that need to be defined. Thus the Auto Speed Control task has an entry Send Speed Command and the Throttle task has an entry Output to Throttle.

A possible design for the Auto Speed Control task is described as follows. It demonstrates in more detail the nature of the tightly-coupled message interface between Cruise Control and Auto Speed Control. The Auto Speed Control task has

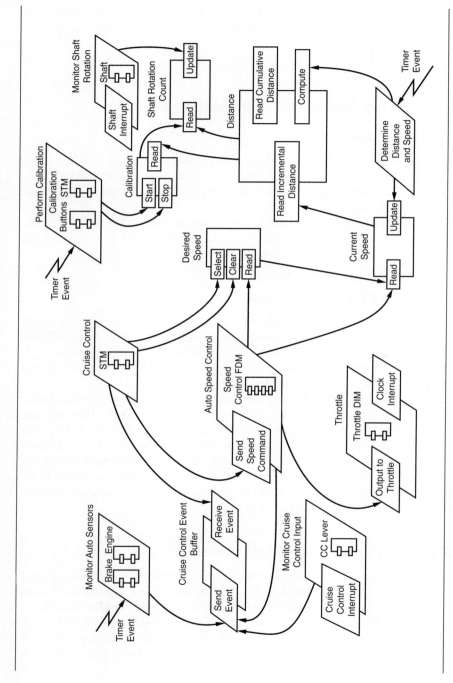

FIGURE 22.34 Ada Architecture Diagram for Cruise Control Subsystem

one entry point, Send Speed Command. Cruise Control makes an unconditional entry call to Auto Speed Control to pass the desired speed command to it. If Auto Speed Control is inactive, it makes an unconditional accept. Thus it is suspended until a speed command becomes available. On the other hand, Auto Speed Control may be active; for example, because it is maintaining the current speed. In this case, it periodically reads Current Speed and Desired Speed to determine whether a speed adjustment is needed. Since it also needs to be aware of whether a new speed command has arrived, it makes a timed accept, in which it either receives an entry call from Cruise Control or is awakened by a timer event and adjusts the speed.

22.5.4 Determine Synchronizing Tasks

Data abstraction packages, which are accessed by more than one task concurrently, must have properly synchronized access to the encapsulated data. As an example, consider the Shaft Rotation Count data abstraction package (DAP), which is accessed by three tasks. Synchronization of access may be achieved by having a task internal to the package. This synchronizing task allows multiple concurrent reads but only one write when no other reads are active.

An alternative approach is to use the pragma SHARED capability to ensure that reads or updates to the Shaft Rotation Count variable are indivisible and hence mutually exclusive. This alternative is possible because the package contains only one shared variable that is accessed by more than one task.

22.5.5 Define Interrupt Handling Entries

Tasks that receive interrupts from the external environment also need entries to handle these interrupts. Thus Monitor Cruise Control Input is an asynchronous device input task. It has an entry Cruise Control Interrupt, which is called by the hardware. Similarly the Monitor Shaft Rotation asynchronous device input task has an entry Shaft Interrupt. The Throttle task is a periodic device output task, which is activated by the real-time clock, to provide a more accurate measure of time, and has an entry Clock Interrupt.

22.6 Define System Subsets

In order to prepare for incremental software development, it is necessary to define system subsets. This allows subsequent detailed design, coding, and testing to proceed incrementally.

In the Cruise Control and Monitoring system, assume that the project manager decides that the Cruise Control Subsystem is more crucial and therefore should be developed first. Event sequence diagrams are used to determine the subsets of this subsystem to be developed.

Assume that the cruise control state of the car is in Initial state. The first case to be tested is that of the driver engaging the cruise control lever in the ACCEL position, resulting in controlled acceleration of the car. The second case to be tested is that of the driver pressing the brake. The sequence of internal events following each of these external events is given in an event sequence diagram (Fig. 22.35), which is based on a subset of the task architecture diagram.

Consider the case of the ACCEL cruise control input. The event sequence is as follows:

1. Cruise Control Interrupt arrives;

2. Monitor Cruise Control Input reads the ACCEL input from the cruise control lever;

3. Monitor Cruise Control Input sends a cruise control message to Cruise Control;

4. Cruise Control receives the message, executes its state transition diagram, and changes state from Initial to Accelerating;

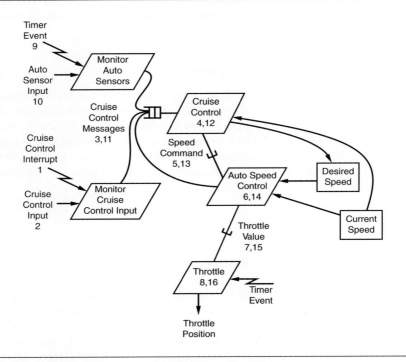

FIGURE 22.35 Event Sequence Diagram based on Task Architecture Diagram

5. Cruise Control sends an Increase Speed command message to Auto Speed Control;

6. Auto Speed Control executes the command and computes the throttle value;

7. Auto Speed Control sends a Throttle Value message to the Throttle task; and

8. Throttle computes the new throttle position.

This event sequence diagram shows that four tasks, Monitor Cruise Control Input, Cruise Control, Auto Speed Control, and Throttle, are required to support this first system subset. For the second case of the brake being pressed, an additional task is required, namely Monitor Auto Sensors. The event sequence 9–16, shown in Fig. 22.35, is derived in a similar way.

An event sequence diagram based on a subset of the Cruise Control subsystem AAD (Fig. 22.34) permits a greater degree of resolution in defining the subsets, showing the tasks and packages that need inclusion. The event sequence is refined as follows:

1. The Cruise Control Interrupt entry of the Monitor Cruise Control Input task is called by the hardware;

2. Monitor Cruise Control Input calls the Read Cruise Control Input access procedure of the Cruise Control Lever DIM to read the ACCEL input from the cruise control lever;

3. Monitor Cruise Control Input calls the Send Event entry of the Cruise Control Event Buffering task to buffer the cruise control request message to Cruise Control;

4. Cruise Control calls the Receive Event entry of the Cruise Control Event Buffering task to receive the message, executes its state transition diagram and changes state from Initial to Accelerating;

5. Cruise Control calls the Send Speed Command entry of the Auto Speed Control task;

6. Send Speed Command executes the Increase Speed command and computes the throttle value;

7. Auto Speed Control calls the Output to Throttle entry of the Throttle task to pass the Throttle Value; and

8. Output to Throttle computes the new throttle position.

By this means, the tasks and packages to be included in a given system subset are determined. The internals of those access procedures or entries that are not called in a given subset may temporarily be replaced by stubs. They will of course need to be provided in later subsets, as determined by subsequent event sequence diagrams. These event sequence diagrams can also be used to analyze the performance of the Cruise Control subsystem, as described in Chapter 19.

23

Robot Controller Case Study

23.1 Introduction

This case study is an example of using ADARTS with a behavioral model developed using Real-time Structured Analysis (RTSA). The example consists of a robot controller, which controls up to six axes of motion and interacts with digital sensors and actuators. For the purposes of this example, the case study has been substantially simplified from a real robot controller system design. However, it serves to illustrate the main concepts of ADARTS.

The robot controller controls the axes and digital I/O by executing a program, which is initiated from a control panel. The control panel consists of a number of push buttons and a selector switch for program selection (Fig. 23.1). The state transition diagram showing the different states of the robot controller is shown in Fig. 23.2. For simplicity, error conditions have been ignored.

When the POWER ON button is pressed, the system enters Powering Up state. On successful completion of the power up sequence, the system enters Manual state. The operator may now select a program using the Program Select rotary switch, which can be set to indicate the desired program number. When the operator presses RUN, this initiates execution of the program currently selected. The system transitions into Running state. The operator may suspend execution of the program by pressing STOP. The system then transitions into Suspended state. The operator may then resume program execution by pressing RUN. The system returns to Running state. To terminate the program, the operator presses END. The system now enters Terminating state. When the program terminates execution, the system returns to the Manual state.

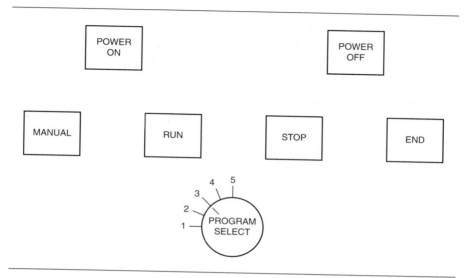

FIGURE 23.1 Robot Control Panel Layout

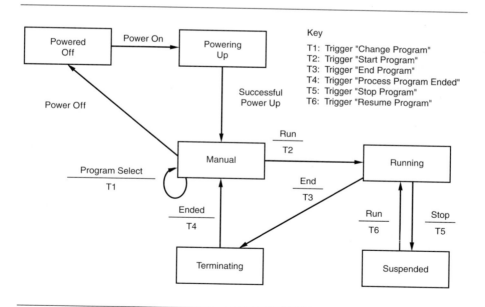

FIGURE 23.2 State Transition Diagram

23.2   Develop RTSA Specification

23.2.1   Develop System Context Diagram

The system context diagram is shown in Fig. 23.3. Following the guideline of using terminators to represent basic I/O devices, the robot sensors and actuators are shown as separate terminators. Similarly, the control panel buttons and switch terminator is separate from the control panel lights terminator. The whole system is shown as one data transformation called Perform Robot Control.

23.2.2   Perform Robot Control

As the robot controller example is comparatively small, it is not necessary to structure the system into subsystems. The overall data flow diagram for Perform Robot Control is shown in Fig. 23.4.

Each time the operator presses a button, the control panel input is read and validated by Process Robot Command. For simplicity, it is assumed that invalid user inputs are ignored. Process Robot Command sends valid robot commands to the appropriate transformation, either Interpret Program Statement or Generate Axis

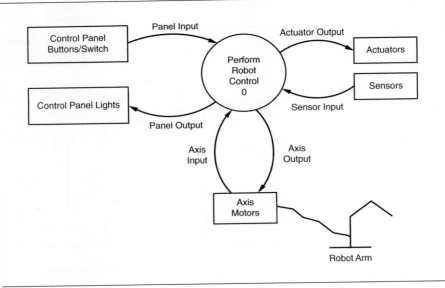

FIGURE 23.3 Robot Controller System Context Diagram

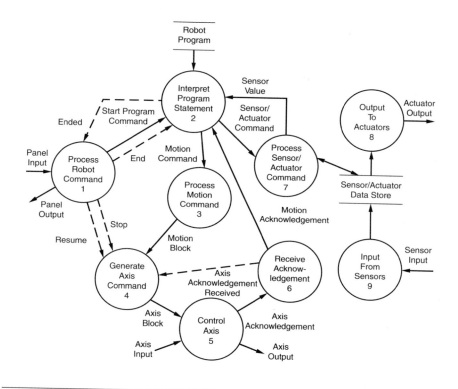

FIGURE 23.4 Overall Robot Controller System Data Flow Diagram

Command. In addition Process Robot Command also outputs the settings of the control panel status lights.

Process Robot Command passes the Start Program command to Interpret Program Statement, which starts interpreting the robot program. Interpret Program Statement executes arithmetic and logical statements directly. Motion and sensor/actuator statements require further processing. Interpret Program Statement sends motion commands to Process Motion Command and sensor/actuator commands to Process Sensor/Actuator Command.

Process Motion Command does some mathematical transformations on the motion data and passes a motion block to Generate Axis Command. Generate Axis Command converts the data to the required format for axis control and then passes an axis block to Control Axis. When the operator presses the STOP button, Generate Axis Command stops feeding axis blocks to Control Axis. When the operator presses the RUN button, Generate Axis Command resumes.

When Control Axis recognizes that the axis motion associated with an axis block has been completed, it sends an Axis Acknowledgement to Receive Acknowledgement. Receive Acknowledgement processes this acknowledgement and then passes it on as a Motion Acknowledgement to Interpret Program Statement. It also sends an Axis Acknowledgement Received event flow to Generate Axis Command.

Process Sensor/Actuator Command processes sensor/actuator I/O statements. For a sensor command, Process Sensor/Actuator Command reads current sensor values from the sensor/actuator data store (placed there by Input from Sensors). For an actuator command, it updates the sensor/actuator data store. Output to Actuators reads new actuator values from the sensor/actuator data store and outputs then to the external environment.

23.2.3 Process Robot Command

Figure 23.5 shows the data flow diagram that results from the decomposition of the Process Robot Command transformation, Read Panel Input receives inputs from the control panel. The inputs are sent as event flows to the control transformation Control Robot, which executes the state transition diagram. Control Robot checks that the input is valid given the current state of the system. Assuming the input is valid, Control Robot determines the new state and desired action from the state transition diagram. It then triggers the appropriate data transformation to perform the action.

Consider the case when the operator presses RUN and the system is in Manual state. When Control Robot receives a Run input event, it transitions to Running state and triggers Start Program. On the other hand, if the system is in Suspended state when Control Robot receives a Run input event, then Control Robot also enters Running state, but this time it triggers Resume Program. Thus the action performed, given the same input, is state dependent.

Start Program reads the Program Id, sends a Start Program command containing the program id to Interpret Program Statement, and sends a request to Output to Panel to switch the control panel Manual light off and Run light on. Resume Program sends a Resume event flow to Generate Axis Command, and sends a request to Output to Panel to switch the control panel Stop light off and Run light on.

23.3 Structure System into Tasks

After developing the RTSA specification, the next step is to structure the system into concurrent tasks. The task structuring criteria are applied to the leaf transformations. The transformations are mapped to tasks and a preliminary task architecture diagram is developed.

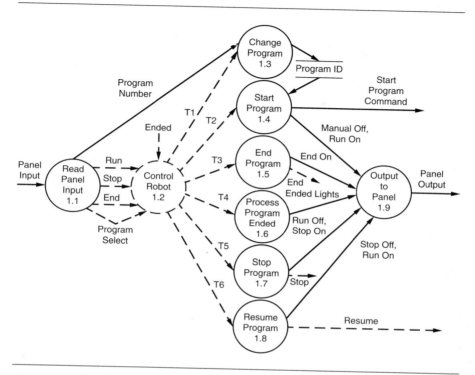

FIGURE 23.5 Data Flow Diagram for Process Robot Command

23.3.1   Determine I/O Tasks

First the I/O transformations are considered. The characteristics of the I/O devices are that the control panel buttons/switch and the control panel lights are both asynchronous I/O devices. Sensors and actuators are passive I/O devices and need to be polled. Each axis motor is an asynchronous I/O device.

Consider Fig. 23.6 first. As a first task structuring criterion, an asynchronous I/O device needs to be supported by an asynchronous device I/O task, since the task's effective speed is governed by the speed of the device it is interacting with. Consequently, the Read Panel Input transformation, which receives inputs from the control panel, is structured as a separate asynchronous device input task, the Control Panel Input Handler. Similarly the Output to Panel transformation is structured as a separate asynchronous device output task, the Control Panel Output Handler.

Other I/O transformations are shown in Fig. 23.7. Sensor/Actuator requests are processed by two tasks. The Input from Sensors transformation periodically scans the input sensors and so is structured as a separate periodic device input task, Process Sensor Input. Similarly, the Output to Actuators transformation is mapped to a periodic device output task, which periodically reads the Sensor/Actuator information hiding

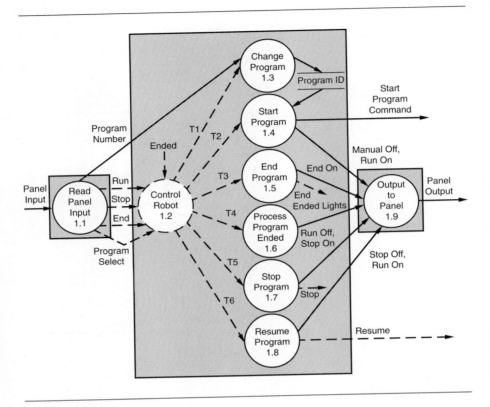

FIGURE 23.6 Task Structuring

module to determine if there are any new actuator outputs, and if so outputs the new values to the external environment. The two tasks have different periods and so are not combined.

Control Axis is structured as a separate time critical asynchronous device I/O task, the Axis Controller. In fact, there is one instance of the Axis Controller for every axis. Each instance of the Axis Controller runs on a separate processor.

23.3.2 Determine Control Tasks

A control transformation forms the basis for a control task. There is one control transformation in the system, Control Robot.

Control Robot triggers several data transformations. These transformations all execute during state transitions. Consequently, Control Robot and all the transformations it triggers may be grouped together (Fig. 23.6) into one task, the Robot Command Processor (RCP), according to the control cohesion task structuring criterion. Thus

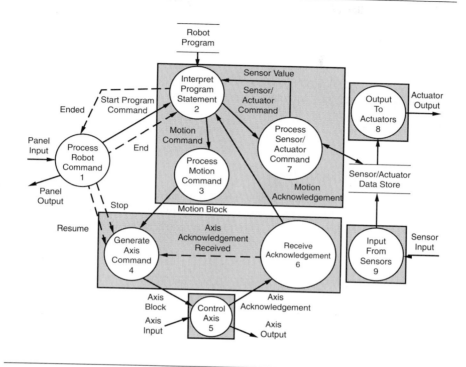

FIGURE 23.7 Task Structuring

after each control panel input is validated, the appropriate action is immediately processed.

23.3.3   Determine Asynchronous Internal Tasks

At this stage all I/O tasks and control tasks have been determined. There are no internal periodic transformations, so there are no periodic tasks. This remaining transformations, all on Fig. 23.7, are now considered. These are structured as internal tasks.

The data transformations Interpret Program Statement, Process Motion Command, and Process Sensor/Actuator Command represent a group of closely related functions, all Interpreter related. Furthermore, these transformations cannot execute concurrently because robot program statements are processed sequentially. Consequently, these transformations are grouped together to form one task, the Interpreter, according to the functional and sequential cohesion task structuring criteria.

Each time Generate Axis Command outputs an axis block to the Axis Controller, Receive Acknowledgement has to wait for an acknowledgement before Generate Axis

Command can output the next block. There is no advantage for the two transformations to execute concurrently. Therefore, the Generate Axis Command and Receive Acknowledgement transformations are grouped together into one task, the Axis Manager, according to the sequential cohesion task structuring criterion. In addition, the speed of these two transformations is dictated by the speed of the axes. Thus no other transformations can be combined with them into the Axis Manager task.

In the preliminary task architecture diagram (Fig. 23.8), all the tasks determined during Task Structuring are explicitly shown. However, at this stage the interfaces between the tasks are still DFD interfaces.

23.3.4   Define Task Interfaces

Once the tasks have been determined, the next step is to define the interfaces between the tasks. Panel input requests are queued up for the Robot Command Processor (RCP) by the Control Panel Input Handler. Thus the interface between the two tasks consists

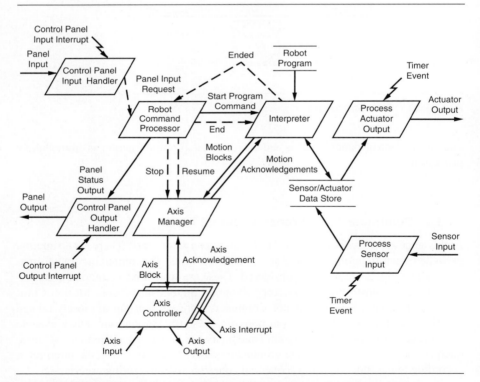

FIGURE 23.8 Preliminary Task Architecture Diagram: Data Flow/Control Flow Diagram Interfaces

of a loosely-coupled message queue. Similarly, panel status outputs are queued for the Control Panel Output Handler by the RCP and so this is also handled by a message queue (Fig. 23.9).

The RCP sends a Start Program message to the Interpreter identifying the program to be executed. The Interpreter handles all task communication and synchronization in its main procedure. Initially the Interpreter waits for the Start Program message from the RCP. On receipt of the message, it starts interpreting the robot program on a statement-by-statement basis.

For each motion command it interprets, the Interpreter generates a motion block and places it in the Motion Blocks message queue for the Axis Manager. Since some motion blocks imply a long move while others are short, the queue between the Interpreter and the Axis Manager acts as a buffer. When the Interpreter reads a sensor/actuator command, it needs to wait until axis motion has reached the desired position before executing the statement. Consequently the Interpreter waits for all outstanding Motion Acknowledgement messages from the Axis Manager before executing the sensor/actuator command.

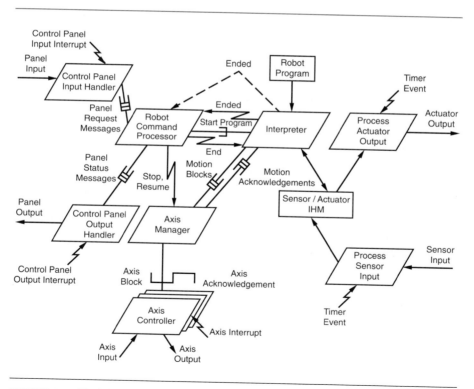

FIGURE 23.9 Task Architecture Diagram: Task Interfaces

After interpreting each program statement, the Interpreter checks whether an End event has been signalled by the RCP. When interpreting has been temporarily suspended, it waits for either an End event or a Motion Acknowledgement message. When End is signalled, it completes program execution and then signals Ended to the RCP.

The Axis Manager receives motion blocks from the Interpreter in its message queue. It also receives Stop and Resume event signals from the RCP. The Axis Manager handles all task synchronization in its main procedure. The Axis Manager waits for a motion block message from the Interpreter and is suspended if one is not available. When it receives the block, it tests to see if a Stop event has been signalled. If so, it waits for a Resume signal. If there is no Stop condition or if Resume was signalled, the Axis Manager sends the axis block to the Axis Controller and waits for an axis acknowledgement of block completion. The communication between the Axis Manager and the Axis Controller is an example of tightly-coupled message communication with reply.

A sensor/actuator data store is used to store the current values of the sensors. This data store is mapped to a Sensor/Actuator Information Hiding Module (SAIHM). When the interpreter processes an actuator output command, it updates the SAIHM. The Process Actuator Output task periodically reads the SAIHM for new Actuator Output. The Process Sensor Input task periodically scans the input sensors and when a change takes place updates the SAIHM. If the interpreter processes a sensor command, it reads the SAIHM for the current value of the sensor. Since access is made to the SAIHM by three tasks, access to it has to be synchronized by the IHM access procedures. In the revised task architecture diagram (Fig. 23.9), the task interfaces, in the form of messages, events, and information hiding modules, are explicitly shown.

23.4 Structure System into Modules

After the interfaces between the tasks have been defined, the next step is to structure the system into modules. First, device interface modules are determined. There is one DIM for each real-world device that the system has to interface to. These may be determined by analyzing the system context diagram:

1. *Control Panel Input DIM.* This DIM hides how to receive input from the control panel. It supports two operations (access procedures), Read Panel Input and Initialize.

2. *Control Panel Output DIM.* This DIM hides how to provide output to the control panel. It supports two operations, Write Panel Output and Initialize.

3. *Sensor Input DIM.* This DIM hides how to interface to the sensors. It supports two operations, Read Sensor Input and Initialize.

4. *Actuator Output DIM.* This DIM hides how to interface to the robot actuators. It supports two operations, Write Actuator Output and Initialize.

5. *Axis DIM.* This DIM hides how to interface to the axis motor. It supports two operations, Write to Axis and Read Axis Position.

Next, data abstraction modules are determined. There is one DAM for each data store. The sensor/actuator data store is mapped to the Sensor/Actuator DAM, as described in the previous section. The operations provided by the DAM are now determined. The Sensor/Actuator DAM supports four operations, Read Sensor, Update Actuator, Read Actuator, and Update Sensor, all of which are access procedures.

There is also a Robot Program DAM that encapsulates the robot program. It supports two operations, Read Next Statement and Initialize Robot Program.

There is one state transition module, the robot STM, which encapsulates the Control Robot state transition table, a tabular representation of the Control Robot state transition diagram. It supports one operation, Process Event.

When an input message or event is received, the Process Event operation is called with the robot input as a parameter. Process Event reads the state transition table, changes state if appropriate, and optionally returns an action to be performed. If the input is not valid for the current state (e.g., STOP is pressed while the system is in Manual state), the system does not change state and no action is returned. If the input is valid for the current state, then the system may change state and may optionally return an action to be performed. For example, if RUN is pressed while the system is in Manual state, the system transitions into Running state and returns the Start Program action.

The actions to be performed are encapsulated in a function driver module called the Command Handler, which has two operations, Process Robot Command and Send Panel Status.

23.5 Integrate Task and Module Views

Now that the tasks and information hiding modules have been defined, the next step is to determine the relationship between them. The software architecture diagram (Fig. 23.10) is developed to show this relationship.

Each IHM defined is explicitly shown, including its operations. The Sensor/Actuator DAM is external to the tasks as it can be accessed concurrently by three tasks, the Interpreter, Process Sensor Input, and Process Actuator Output. The operations of the DAM must ensure mutually exclusive access to the sensor/actuator data hidden by the DAM.

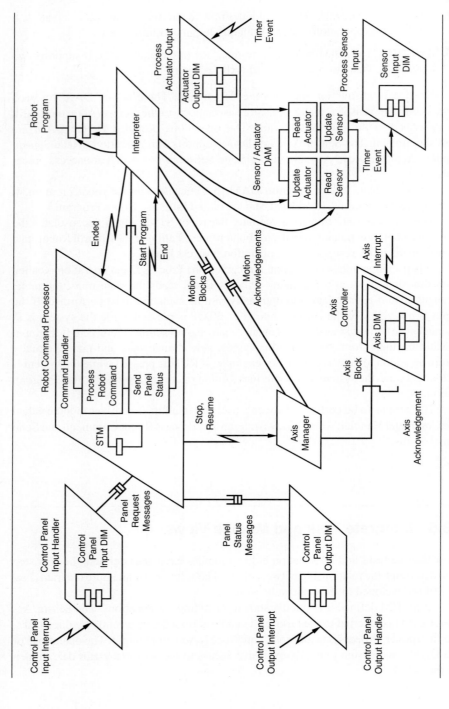

FIGURE 23.10 Software Architecture Diagram for Robot Controller System

23.6   Develop Ada-based Architectural Design

In the next step of ADARTS, the design is mapped to Ada as shown in the Ada architecture diagram (Fig. 23.11). First, Ada support tasks are introduced. Each loosely-coupled message queue is mapped to a message buffering task. Consequently four message buffering tasks are introduced: Robot Command Buffer for buffering Panel Request messages, Panel Status Buffer for buffering Panel Status messages, Interpreter Message Buffer for buffering interpreter commands from RCP and motion acknowledgements from the Axis Manager, and Motion Block Buffer for buffering motion block messages. The tightly-coupled message interface between the Axis Manager and the Axis Controller is mapped directly to an Ada rendezvous.

The Axis Manager supports two entries for the Stop and Resume events from RCP. It attempts to read the next motion block from the motion block buffer by calling the Receive entry. It then does a conditional accept on the Stop entry. If RCP is not waiting at the rendezvous, then the Axis Manager processes the motion block and sends it to the Axis Controller by making the Send Axis Block entry call. If RCP is waiting at the Stop rendezvous, then the Axis Manager accepts the call, and does an unconditional accept on the Resume entry. When RCP makes the Resume entry call, the Axis Manager is activated and processes the motion block. Thus, the Axis Manager waits at the Resume rendezvous while the robot controller is in Suspended state.

A synchronizing task is nested inside the Sensor Actuator DAM to ensure that access to the sensor/actuator data is mutually exclusive.

23.7   Real-time Scheduling in Robot Controller System

Real-time scheduling in the robot controller system starts after the task architecture has been developed. A time-critical aspect of the robot controller is rapid and accurate linear motion. A major issue is that linear motion in cartesian space does not correspond to proportional moves in robot joint space. Consequently a coordinate transformation algorithm is required, which is computationally intensive, for converting the coordinates of a point in linear space to joint coordinates. For any given linear move, several joint positions have to be computed, the more frequently this is done the more accurate the linear move. For the robot applications required, such as welding, sealing, and spray painting, the system engineers have determined that an axis block containing a joint position has to be sent to each Axis Controller, one for each joint, in not more than 75 msec.

In considering the real-time scheduling of the robot controller system, three scenarios will be considered: **steady state, robot startup,** and **robot stopping** scenarios. The scenario involving the fewest tasks is the steady state scenario, which is considered first.

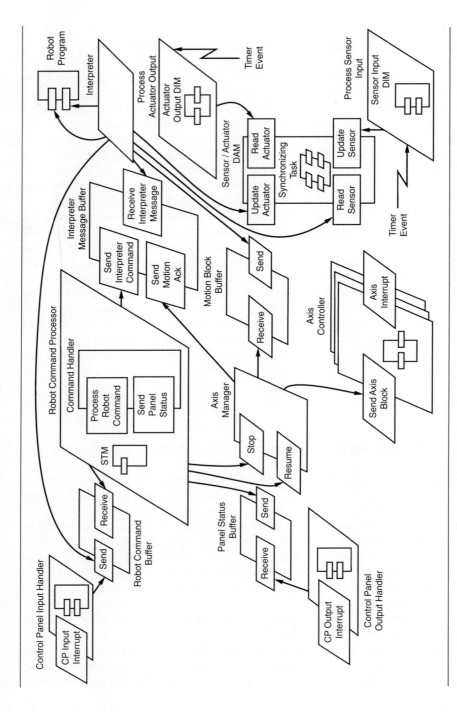

FIGURE 23.11 Ada Architecture Diagram for Robot Controller System

In the **steady state scenario,** the Intepreter task is interpreting the rob program and sending motion commands to the Axis Manager task. The Interpreter quired to interpret the robot program at a rate of one instruction every 125 msec ich is assumed to be the period of the task. Given that the Axis Manager is perting a computationally intensive time critical coordinate transformation, it must set axis block to the Axis Controller every 75 msec. This hard deadline is used as xis Manager's period.

There are six instances of the Axis Controller, one for each axis. As th s Controller tasks are extremely time critical, needing to issue an axis output e msec, each Axis Controller task executes on its own dedicated processor. By this, it is not necessary to consider the Axis Controller in this analysis.

In addition to the Intepreter and Axis Manager tasks, two periodic I/O task also active during this scenario, namely Process Sensor Input and Process Actu Output.

Table 23.1 shows the CPU time C_n, the period T_n, and the utilization U_n for ea of these four tasks. Assign the tasks their rate monotonic priorities, so that A Manager has the highest priority of these four tasks. It is often the case that comput tionally intensive tasks are not time critical and can have a lower priority. This i clearly not the case with the Axis Manager task which is time critical and is therefore given the highest priority.

Given the task parameters in Table 23.1, the utilization of these four tasks is 0.51, which is less than the Utilization Bound Theorem's worst case upper bound of 0.69. Although the tasks have been assigned their rate monotonic priorities, there is an additional check required to determine whether priority inversion due to synchronized access to the Sensor/Actuator IHM causes a problem. This does not impact the Axis Manager task which will therefore meet its deadline.

Consider the other three tasks, Process Actuator Output, Process Sensor Input, and the Interpreter, which all access the IHM. Process Actuator Output could be blocked by either of the lower priority tasks, Process Sensor Input or the Interpreter. The worst case for Process Actuator Output is being blocked by the Interpreter task

TABLE 23.1 ROBOT CONTROL SYSTEM REAL-TIME SCHEDULING
TASK PARAMETERS

Task	CPU time C_n	Period T_n	Utilization U_n	Priority
Process Actuator Output (1, 2, 3)	5	80	0.06	4
Process Sensor Input (1, 2, 3)	4	100	0.04	5
Interpreter (1, 2)	10	125	0.08	6
Axis Manager (1, 2, 3)	25	75	0.33	3
Control Panel Input Handler (2, 3)	2	50	0.04	1
Robot Command Processor (2, 3)	5	50	0.10	2
Control Panel Output Handler (2, 3)	5	500	0.01	7

Shown in parentheses are the scenarios each task participates in: 1 = steady state scenario; 2 = robot startup scenario; 3 = robot stopping scenario as it has a er CPU time of 10 msec. Process Actuator Output executes for 5 msec, although n also be pre-empted by the Axis Manager for 25 msec.

The worst case elapsed time = pre-emption time + execution time + blocking time = 5 + 10 = 40 msec. This is less than Process Actuator Output's period of 80 ms us Process Actuator Output will meet its deadline.

onsider Process Sensor Input, which could be pre-empted by both the Axis Man nd the Process Actuator Output tasks for a total pre-emption time of 30 mse uld also be blocked by the Interpreter task for 10 msec and it executes for 4 m

total worst case elapsed time = pre-emption time + execution time + blocking ti 0 + 4 + 10 = 44 msec. This is less than Process Sensor Input's period of 100 hus Process Sensor Input will also meet its deadline.

in this scenario, the Axis Manager and the Interpreter tasks execute according r rate monotonic priorities and are not blocked by lower priority tasks, this is is sufficient to show that all four tasks in the steady state scenario will meet deadlines.

n the second scenario, the **robot startup scenario,** the operator presses the Run n on the robot control panel to start the robot program. The Control Panel Input dler task is activated to process the operator input and send a message to the Robot mmand Processor task, which then determines from the state transition table that tart Program message must be sent to the Interpreter. The Interpreter initializes the ogram and then starts interpreting it. It starts sending motion blocks to the Axis lanager. A panel output message is also sent to the Control Panel Output Handler sk.

In addition to the four tasks involved in the first scenario, there are three more tasks taking part in this scenario. In the worst case, it is assumed that operator inputs can arrive every 50 msec. The equivalent periods for the Control Panel Input Handler and Robot Command Processor tasks are the worst case interarrival times. As these periods are shorter than those of the other tasks, they are allocated the highest priorities. Of the two, the Control Panel Input Handler is given the highest priority so that it can react quickly to interrupts.

In this case, the total CPU utilization of the seven tasks is 0.66, which is less than the Utilization Bound Theorem's upper bound of 0.69. However, an additional check is required since the Axis Manager is initially blocked waiting for a message from the Interpreter. Consider the tasks in the event sequence.

When a control panel button is pressed, as the Control Panel Input Handler and Robot Command Processor tasks have the highest priorities, they will execute for 2 and 5 msec respectively. These CPU times include context switch times, message communication, and event synchronization times. The total CPU time for these two tasks is 7 msec. Thus these two new tasks easily meet their deadline of 50 msec.

The next task to execute in the event sequence is the Interpreter, although it may be pre-empted once by each of Process Sensor Input and Process Actuator Output. The total execution time for these three tasks is 19 msec. Axis Manager is blocked until it receives the first motion block, after which it executes for 25 msec.

The total CPU time for these six tasks is 51 msec. This is less than Axis Manager's period of 75 msec. Thus all six tasks, including the four tasks from the first scenario, are able to complete execution before the first deadline of 75 msec and can therefore meet their deadlines. In fact, there is also time for the Control Panel Output Handler to process the panel output message before the end of this period.

In the third scenario, the **robot stopping scenario,** the operator presses a Stop button on the robot control panel to stop the robot. The Control Panel Input Handler task is activated to process the operator input and send a message to the Robot Command Processor task, which then determines from the state transition table that a Stop event must be sent to the Axis Manager. After processing the previous motion block, the Axis Manager task checks to see if a Stop message has been sent and immediately sends a Stop axis block to each Axis Controller task. A panel output message is also sent to the Control Panel Output Handler task.

As before, the total CPU utilization of the seven tasks is 0.66, which is less than the Utilization Bound Theorem's upper bound of 0.69. However, there is an interesting blocking case to consider before it can be determined whether the Axis Manager can meet its deadline.

When a control panel button is pressed, as before, the Control Panel Input Handler and Robot Command Processor tasks, having the highest priorities, execute first for 2 and 5 msec respectively. As the Axis Manager is the next highest priority task, it executes next. The worst case occurs if the Axis Manager has just started processing a motion block, in which case 25 msec will elapse before it checks its inputs again to determine if a message or event has arrived. This can be considered a form of blocking. Assume it takes the Axis Manager only 5 msec to process the Stop event.

Total elapsed time = pre-emption time + execution time + blocking time = 7 + 5 + 25 = 37 msec < 75 msec, the Axis Manager's period.

It takes 1 msec for the axis block to arrive at the Axis Controller and two further msec to issue the Stop Axis output to the axes. Thus the total time from the time the operator presses the Stop button to the time the Stop Axis command is issued to the axes is 40 msec.

The total elapsed time of 40 msec is within the 50 msec deadline of the Control Panel Input Handler and Robot Command Processor tasks. Thus the Axis Manager will meet its deadline. Note that in this transient case, the Axis Manager executes twice during its period. A quick check shows that this does not adversely affect the other lower priority tasks.

This analysis has shown that giving the tasks their rate monotonic priorities ensures that they always meet their deadlines. However, as the Axis Manager is CPU intensive, the Process Sensor Input and Process Actuator Output tasks are less responsive than they would be if they had higher priorities than the Axis Manager. A further analysis, left to the reader, shows that giving the two I/O tasks higher priorities than the Axis Manager would not cause the latter to miss its deadlines.

24

Elevator Control System Case Study

1 Introduction

This case study consists of an Elevator Control System that controls one or more elevators. The system has to schedule elevators to respond to requests from passengers at various floors and control the motion of the elevators between floors. This case study uses the COBRA method for the analysis and modeling of the system. It presents contrasting designs. The same behavioral model is mapped, in one case, to a non-distributed ADARTS/CODARTS design and, in another case, to a CODARTS/DA distributed design. Both designs are presented and their performance is analyzed.

24.2 Develop Environmental and Behavioral Models

24.2.1 Develop System Context Diagram

Figure 24.1 shows the system context diagram, in particular the external entities that the system has to interface to. Each external entity is represented by a terminator. For each elevator, there is a set of elevator buttons (a passenger presses a button to select a destination), a set of elevator lamps to indicate the floors to be visited by the elevator, an elevator motor, which is controlled by commands to move up, move down, and stop, and an elevator door, which is controlled by commands to open and close the door. For each floor, there are up and down floor buttons, which are pressed by

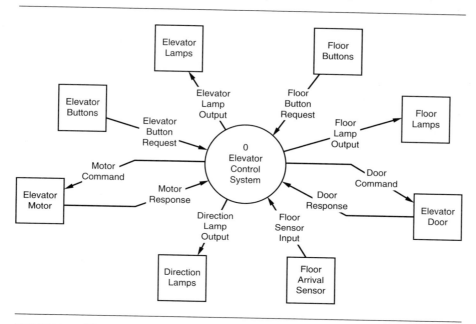

FIGURE 24.1 Elevator Control System: System Context Diagram

passengers needing to travel on an elevator, and a corresponding pair of floor lamps to indicate the directions that have been requested.

At each floor for each elevator, there are a pair of direction lamps to indicate whether an arriving elevator is heading in the up or down direction. For the top and bottom floors, there is only one floor button, one floor lamp, and one direction lamp per elevator. There is also a floor arrival sensor at each floor in each elevator shaft to detect the arrival of an elevator.

The hardware characteristics of the I/O devices are that the elevator buttons, floor buttons, and floor arrival sensors are asynchronous; that is, an interrupt is generated when there is an input from one of these devices. The other I/O devices are all passive. The elevator and floor lamps are switched on by the hardware, but must be switched off by the software. The direction lamps are switched on and off by the software.

24.2.2   Decompose System into Subsystems

The decomposition of the system into subsystems is based on the nature of service provided by the subsystem. An analysis of the problem indicates that there are three relatively independent and loosely-coupled subsystems. These are the Elevator, Floor, and Scheduler subsystems. The Elevator subsystem is a real-time control subsystem while the Floor subsystem is a data collection subsystem. Both subsystems are aggregate objects. There is one instance of the Elevator subsystem for each real-world elevator and one instance of the Floor subsystem for each real-world floor.

With multiple elevators, it is necessary to coordinate the activities of the elevators; in particular, when a floor request is made, it has to be serviced by a specific elevator. A real-time coordination subsystem, the Scheduler, is therefore needed. The Scheduler decides which elevator should service a given floor request.

The decomposition of the elevator system into the three subsystems is shown in the top level data flow/control flow diagram (Fig. 24.2). There are three data transformations corresponding to the three major subsystems. The Floor subsystem handles all floor related services, accepting inputs from the floor buttons external entities, and passing outputs to the floor lamps and direction lamps external entities.

The Elevator subsystem handles all elevator related services. It receives elevator button requests and sets elevator lamp outputs. It receives floor arrival sensor inputs informing it that the elevator is approaching the next floor. It sends start and stop motor commands to the motor external entity, and open and close door commands to the door external entity. It sends elevator status to the multiple instances of the Floor subsystem.

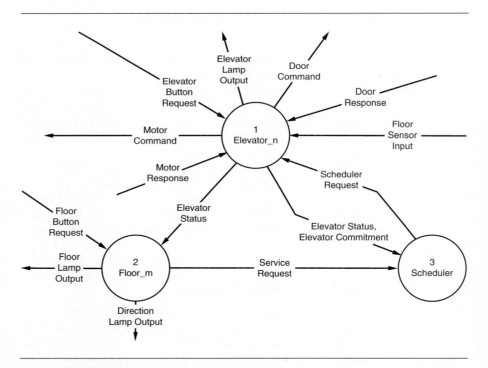

FIGURE 24.2 Decomposition into Subsystems

Passenger requests from within a given elevator have to be handled by that elevator. However, a floor button request, made by a person waiting at a floor to get on an elevator, needs to be scheduled. The instance of the Floor subsystem for that floor sends this Service Request to the Scheduler, which uses a scheduling algorithm to decide which elevator should handle the request. The Scheduler Request is then sent to the selected Elevator aggregate object. The Scheduler receives Elevator Status and Elevator Commitments from each elevator identifying where each elevator is and what floors it is planning to visit. The Scheduler uses this information in deciding which elevator should handle a given floor request.

The two subsystems that correspond to aggregate objects, the Elevator and Floor subsystems, are decomposed further, as described next.

24.2.3 Decomposition of Elevator Subsystem

State Transition Diagram. Since the Elevator subsystem is a state-dependent subsystem, the state transition diagram is developed first. There is one state transition diagram for each elevator, showing all the states and transitions for that elevator (Fig. 24.3). The state transition diagram is executed by a control object, Elevator Control, which controls the movement of the elevator. Thus, there is one instance of the Elevator control object and one instance of the state transition diagram for each elevator. The states of an elevator are

1. *Elevator Idle.* The elevator is stationary at a floor and there is no outstanding request for it. An elevator is idle with the door open.

2. *Door Closing to Move Up.* An elevator enters this state when it starts closing the door in order to satisfy a request for it to visit another floor further up.

3. *Door Closing to Move Down.* An elevator enters this state when it starts closing the door in order to satisfy a request for it to visit another floor further down.

The Door Closing to Move Up and the Door Closing to Move Down states are different because the input events, Up Request and Down Request, causing the transitions into these states are different. The output events when leaving the states, Up and Down, are also different.

4. *Elevator Starting.* An elevator enters this state when the door has closed and it is waiting for the motor to start moving the elevator up or down.

5. *Elevator Moving.* An elevator enters this state when it has started its journey up or down.

6. *Elevator Stopping.* This state is entered when the elevator is approaching a floor and this is a floor where the elevator has to stop.

7. *Elevator Door Opening.* This state is entered when the elevator has stopped at a floor and the door is opening.

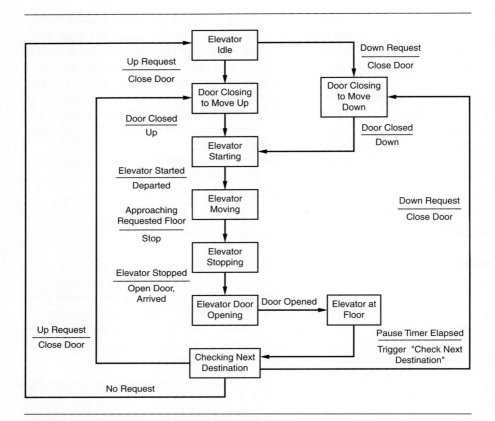

FIGURE 24.3 Elevator Control State Transition Diagram

8. *Elevator at Floor.* This state is entered when the elevator door has opened.

9. *Checking next Destination.* In this state, the next destination is checked: up, down, or remain at this floor.

Elevator Aggregate Object.   The Elevator subsystem is an aggregate object. Each elevator aggregate object is composed of several device I/O objects: n Elevator Button objects, n Elevator Lamp objects, one Motor object, one Elevator Door object, and one Floor Arrival Sensor object. It should be noted that each elevator aggregate object is composed of the same constituent set of objects.

The Elevator subsystem is decomposed as shown in the data flow/control flow diagram in Fig. 24.4. Along with the objects shown in Fig. 24.4, there is the aggregate object, Elevator Control and Management, which is decomposed further as shown in Fig. 24.5. The control object, Elevator Control, is defined by means of the state transition diagram shown in Fig. 24.3. Check This Floor and Accept New Request are

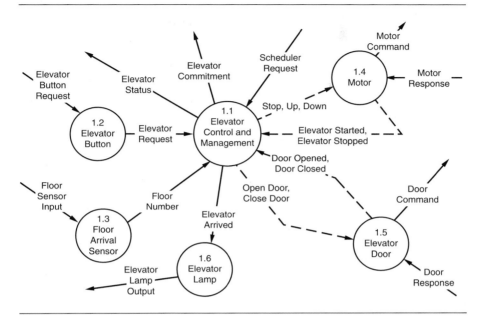

FIGURE 24.4 Decomposition of Elevator Subsystem

asynchronous functions. Check Next Destination and Update Status are asynchronous state-dependent functions.

Behavioral Analysis.   Now consider the behavioral aspects of this subsystem; in particular, the interaction of the Elevator Control object, as defined by the state transition diagram, and the objects and functions it interacts with. An event sequencing scenario is considered, in which an elevator is initially in Elevator Idle state and it is dispatched upwards to service a request.

Elevator Button (Fig. 24.4) receives elevator button requests and sends each Elevator Request to Accept New Request (Fig. 24.5). Whenever Accept New Request receives an Elevator Request or a Scheduler Request, it updates the Elevator Status and Plan data store. It checks the status of the elevator, and if the elevator is busy, it does nothing further. On the other hand, if the elevator is idle, and if the request is for a different floor, it sends either the event flow Up Request or Down Request.

Assume that the elevator is idle. Assume further that the Scheduler request is for a floor at a higher level, so Accept New Request sends an Up Request event flow to Elevator Control. In this case, the elevator transitions to Door Closing to Move Up state (Fig. 24.3), and the Close Door output event flow is sent to the Elevator Door object (Fig. 24.4), which in turn sends a command to the door external entity to close the door. When the door response is received by the Elevator Door object, it sends the Door Closed event floor to Elevator Control.

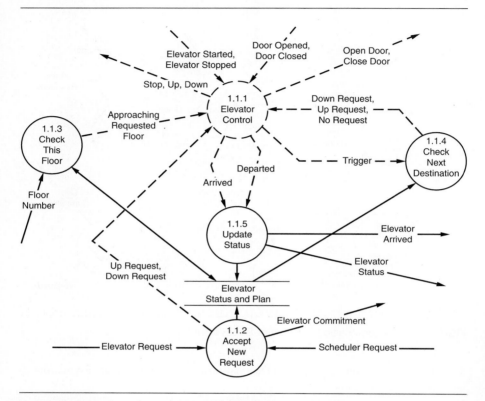

FIGURE 24.5 Decomposition of Elevator Control and Management

This results in the elevator transitioning to Elevator Starting state (Fig. 24.3). The Up output event flow is sent to the Motor object (Fig. 24.4), which in turn sends a command to the motor external entity to move upwards. When the motor response is received by the Motor object it sends the Elevator Started event flow to Elevator Control. As a result, Elevator Control transitions to Elevator Moving state. The Departed event flow is sent to Update Status, so that it can update the Elevator Status and Plan data store.

When the elevator approaches a floor, Floor Arrival Sensor receives an input from the floor arrival sensor, and sends the floor number to the Check This Floor asynchronous function (Fig. 24.5). Check This Floor reads the Elevator Status and Plan data store, and if it determines that the elevator is due to stop at this floor, it sends the Approaching Requested Floor event flow. The elevator transitions to Elevator Stopping state (Fig. 24.3) and sends the Stop output event flow to the Motor object (Fig. 24.4). After sending the Stop command to the real-world motor, Motor receives the motor response and sends the Elevator Stopped event flow. The elevator then transitions to Elevator Door Opening state. The Open Door output event flow results in the

Elevator Door object sending an Open Door command to the real-world door. Upon receiving the Door Response, the Elevator Door object sends that the Door Opened event flow and the elevator transitions to Elevator at Floor state.

Elevator Control pauses for passengers to get on and off the elevator. When the pause timer expires, it transitions to Checking Next Destination state and triggers the data transformation Check Next Destination.

Check Next Destination (Fig. 24.5) checks the Elevator Status and Plan data store to determine what the elevator should do next. It sends one of three responses: the No Request event flow (in which case the Elevator transitions to Elevator Idle state), the Up Request event flow (in which case the Elevator transitions to Door Closing to Move Up state), or the Down Request event flow (in which case the Elevator transitions to Door Closing to Move Down state).

24.2.4 Decomposition of Floor Subsystem

The Floor Subsystem is an aggregate object and consists of two floor buttons (up and down requests), two floor lamps, and two direction lamps per elevator. The number of floors is usually different from the number of elevators, but each floor has the same constituent objects. The top and bottom floors only have one of each object.

The decomposition of the Floor Subsystem is shown in a data flow/control flow diagram (Fig. 24.6), and consists of three data transformations. The Floor Button object receives Floor Button Requests from the floor button external entity and sends

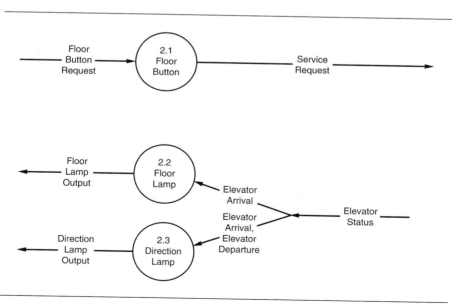

FIGURE 24.6 Decomposition of Floor Subsystem

these on as Service Requests. The Floor Lamp and Direction Lamp objects receive Elevator Status messages. Floor Lamp uses the Elevator Arrival message to send the switch off Floor Lamp Output to the floor lamp external entity. Direction Lamp uses the Elevator Arrival and Elevator Departure messages to send switch off and switch on Direction Lamp Outputs to the direction lamp external entity. The Elevator Arrival and Elevator Departure messages have parameters indicated whether the elevator is moving up or down.

24.3   Structure System into Tasks

Initially consider the case where the Elevator Control System is to be mapped to either a single CPU or tightly-coupled multiprocessing environment (i.e., with shared memory).

A key aspect of this solution is that the Elevator Status and Plan data store is accessible to all elevators and the Scheduler, so that one centralized repository of data may be used. This solution does not work in a loosely-coupled distributed system, where there is no shared memory.

To structure the system into tasks, it is necessary to analyze all the leaf data and control transformations on the data flow/control flow diagrams and apply the task structuring criteria. This will be performed by analyzing each of the data flow/control flow diagrams in turn. Two cases are considered, a single elevator control system and a multiple elevator control system.

Each subsystem is considered in turn. The Elevator and Floor subsystems are considered in the next two sections. The Scheduler, which is a also a leaf data transformation, is structured as a subsystem consisting of one asynchronous task. It performs a specific function, namely selecting the most appropriate elevator to handle a floor request, and is activated on demand, in particular when it receives a Service Request. In the single elevator case, the Scheduler degenerates into a trivial task.

24.3.1   Determine Elevator Subsystem Device I/O Tasks

Consider the Elevator data flow/control flow diagram (Fig. 24.4). Start with the device I/O objects. Elevator Button is structured as a separate task, Monitor Elevator Buttons (Fig. 24.7), based on the asynchronous device input task structuring criterion. Using task inversion, one task is designed to handle all the buttons rather than one task per button. Monitor Elevator Buttons is activated by the arrival of an interrupt when any of the elevator buttons is pressed. It then reads the Elevator Button input and sends the request so that it can be ready to service the next interrupt. Floor Arrival Sensor

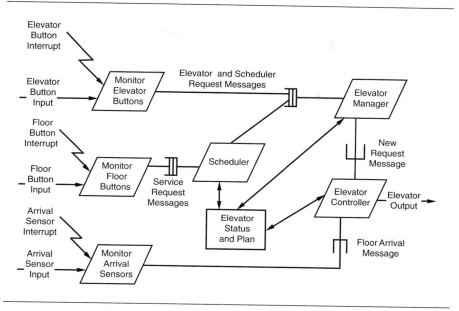

FIGURE 24.7 Task Architecture Diagram for Single Elevator Control System

is structured as an asynchronous device input task, Monitor Arrival Sensors, for the same reason.

Consider the other device I/O objects. These are all device output objects, which are activated by the control object, Elevator Control, and interact directly with the external environment, namely the motor, door, and elevator lamps.

It is given that all these devices are passive—that is, they do not generate I/O interrupts—so asynchronous output tasks are not required. Each output request is executed on demand, so a periodic output task is not required. Furthermore, the calling task always has to wait for the output request to complete. In this case, the device output object does not need to be structured as a separate task; it is combined with the calling task according to the control cohesion criterion. For example, if the Elevator Controller initiates the Close Door action, it waits for the Door Closed response since the elevator cannot start until the door has been closed.

24.3.2   Determine Elevator Subsystem Internal Tasks

Consider the Elevator Control state transition diagram shown in Fig. 24.3. This is a case of a control object, which is represented by a state transition diagram. During the analysis and modeling phase, the control aspects of a real-world elevator entity are mapped to a control object, Elevator Control (Fig. 24.5). In the case of multiple elevators, the control of each elevator is independent, and this is modeled by having one Elevator Control object for each elevator. During task structuring, each Elevator Control object is mapped to a separate Elevator Controller task (Fig. 24.8). Each task executes the state transition diagram for that elevator.

Consider whether any of the data transformations in Fig. 24.5 should be combined with the Elevator Controller task or alternatively, whether they should be structured as separate tasks. Two kinds of data transformations are illustrated, state-dependent and non-state dependent transformations. There are two non-state dependent data transformations, Check This Floor and Accept New Request. There are two state dependent data transformations, Check Next Destination and Update Status. Consider each of these data transformations in turn.

Check This Floor receives the floor number when Elevator Controller is inactive (it is in Elevator Moving state). A state change only takes place if Check This Floor determines by reading the elevator plan that the elevator should stop at this floor, in which case it generates the Approaching Requested Floor event flow. This, in turn, causes Elevator Control to transition to Elevator Stopping state. Since this function must always precede executing the state transition, Check This Floor may be combined with Elevator Control according to the sequential cohesion task structuring criterion.

Check Next Destination is triggered by Elevator Control as a result of the elevator transitioning into the Checking Next Destination state. Elevator Control then waits for a response from Check Next Destination. Since Check Next Destination is state dependent and the two transformations cannot execute in parallel, Check Next Destination is combined with Control Elevator according to the control cohesion task structuring criterion. Update Status may also be combined with Elevator Control, based on the control cohesion task structuring criterion, because it only executes during state transitions.

Accept New Request, however, executes asynchronously with the Elevator Controller task since a request for the elevator could come at any time while the Elevator Controller is executing. Consequently, Accept New Request is structured as a separate asynchronous task called the Elevator Manager. It is activated asynchronously by either an Elevator Request or a Scheduler Request. It executes relatively independently of the Elevator Controller task. The only interaction between the two tasks is when the elevator is in Idle state and a new request arrives. In that case, the Elevator Manager awakens the Elevator Controller task.

In summary, for the single elevator case, the Elevator subsystem is structured into four tasks, Monitor Elevator Buttons, Monitor Arrival Sensors, the Elevator Manager, and the Elevator Controller, as shown on the Task Architecture Diagram in Fig. 24.7. The case of the multiple elevator system is shown on the Task Architecture Diagram in Fig. 24.8, where there are several instances of the Elevator Controller task. Each instance of the Elevator Controller task is identical, executing its own copy of the state transition diagram.

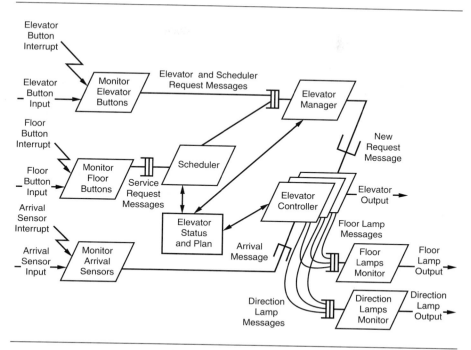

FIGURE 24.8 Task Architecture Diagram for Multiple Elevator Control System

24.3.3   Determine Floor Subsystem Tasks

The Floor subsystem (Fig. 24.6) is structured as follows. Floor Button is structured as a separate task, Monitor Floor Buttons, based on the asynchronous device I/O and task inversion task structuring criteria. It is activated by an interrupt, handles the interrupt, and then sends the Service Request so that it can be ready to handle the next interrupt.

The floor lamps and direction lamps are passive output devices. The device I/O objects that output to these devices are therefore candidates for combining with the calling task (Elevator Controller) according to the control cohesion criterion. This is indeed the solution for the single elevator case.

However, in the case of multiple elevators, there are multiple instances of the Elevator Controller task that may all be attempting to send requests concurrently to the floor lamps and direction lamps. In this case, it is necessary to have a resource monitor task for each device, to ensure that output requests are handled sequentially. Thus in the multiple elevator case, there needs to be a Floor Lamps Monitor task and a Direction Lamps Monitor task (Fig. 24.8). The Floor Lamps device output object is mapped to the Floor Lamps Monitor task. The Direction Lamp device output object is mapped to the Direction Lamps Monitor task.

24.3.4   Define Task Interfaces

Consider how the task interfaces are derived. First consider the data flows, which are shown on the data flow/control flow diagrams. These are mapped to either loosely-coupled or tightly-coupled message communication. It is only necessary to consider the interfaces between objects/functions that are mapped to separate tasks.

The data flow interface between Elevator Button (Fig. 24.4) and Accept New Request (Fig. 24.5) is mapped to a loosely-coupled message communication interface between the Monitor Elevator Buttons task and the Elevator Manager task (Figs. 24.7 and 24.8). This ensures that Monitor Elevator Buttons does not get held up, and hence does not miss any interrupts, when it sends a message to the Elevator Manager (which also receives Scheduler Request messages in the same queue). Since the Scheduler will often be busy when a message is sent, the data flow interface between Floor Button (Fig. 24.6) and the Scheduler (Fig. 24.2) is also mapped to a loosely-coupled message communication interface between the Monitor Floor Buttons task and the Scheduler task.

The data flow interface between Floor Arrival Sensor (Fig. 24.4) and Check This Floor (Fig. 24.5) is mapped to a tightly-coupled message communication interface between Monitor Arrival Sensors and the Elevator Controller task. The reason for this is that when Monitor Arrival Sensors sends the Floor Arrival message, the Elevator Controller is always inactive (as it is in Elevator Moving state) and so Monitor Arrival Sensors should not be held up for a significant period of time.

The event flow interface between Accept New Request and Elevator Control (Fig. 24.5) is mapped to tightly-coupled message communication interface between the Elevator Manager and the Elevator Controller. There are two event flows that the Elevator Manager can send, Up Request or Down Request, and so a message is used to carry the identity of the event flow. The interface is tightly coupled since the Elevator Manager only sends a message to the Elevator Controller if the latter is idle and needs to be woken up.

In the multiple elevator case, there is also the interface between the Elevator Controller task and the two resource monitor tasks, Floor Lamps Monitor and Direction Lamps Monitor. Update Status (Fig. 24.5) sends Elevator Status (floor and direction) data flows to both Floor Lamp and Direction Lamp (Fig. 24.6). This is mapped to a Floor Lamps Messages interface between Elevator Controller and the Floor Lamps Monitor. The interface is loosely coupled to allow multiple instances of Elevator Controller to send messages to Floor Lamps Monitor without being held up. The interface between the Elevator Controller and the Direction Lamps Monitor is also handled by loosely-coupled message communication (Fig. 24.8).

Consider the data stores that are accessed by more than one task and how they should be mapped to information hiding modules. The data store, Elevator Status and Plan, is mapped to an information hiding module of the same name, which is accessed by the multiple instances of the Elevator Controller task, the Elevator Manager task, and the Scheduler.

24.3.5   Discussion of Alternative Task Architectures

The main differences in the task architectures between the single elevator case (Fig. 24.7) and the multiple elevator case (Fig. 24.8) is in the multiple instances of the Elevator Controller task and the introduction of the two resource monitor tasks. In the multiple elevator case, another possible architecture is to have one instance of the Monitor Elevator Buttons, Monitor Arrival Sensors, and Elevator Manager tasks in addition to the Elevator Controller task for each elevator. In a single CPU environment, this solution is avoided because of the additional system overhead.

However, in a multiprocessing environment there could be one CPU for each elevator, which would have one instance of each of the Elevator Controller, Monitor Elevator Buttons, Monitor Arrival Sensors, and Elevator Manager tasks. The Scheduler, Monitor Floor Buttons, Floor Lamps Monitor, and Direction Lamps Monitor tasks would execute on a separate CPU. In the case of multiple CPUs with shared memory, the Elevator Status and Plan IHM would reside, as before, in the shared memory.

If there is no shared memory between the processors, then the Elevator Status and Plan IHM cannot be accessed directly by the tasks. The solution to the Distributed Elevator Control System problem is described later.

24.4   Structure System into Modules

24.4.1   Define Device Interface Modules

A device interface module (DIM) hides the actual interface to the real world device by providing a virtual interface to it. There is one DIM for each I/O device. Each device I/O object is mapped directly to a DIM. The operations provided by a DIM are determined by considering the functions each object needs to support.

The DIMS are:

1. *Elevator Buttons.* This DIM hides how to interface to the elevator button sensors. It provides two operations: Read, which reads the elevator button sensors, and Initialize.

2. *Floor Buttons.* This DIM hides how to interface to the floor button sensors. It provides two operations: Read, which reads the floor button sensors, and Initialize.

3. *Arrival sensors.* This DIM hides how to interface to the floor arrival sensors. It provides two operations: Read, which reads floor arrival sensors, and Initialize.

4. *Motor.* This DIM hides how to interface to the elevator motor. It provides Up, Down, and Stop operations, as determined by the Up, Down, and Stop event flows that the Motor object receives.

5. *Door.* This DIM hides how to interface to the elevator door. It provides operations to Open and Close, as determined by the Open Door and Close Door event flows that the Elevator Door object receives.

6. *Elevator Lamps.* This DIM hides how to interface to the elevator lamps. It provides an operation to Clear an elevator lamp. It is given that the hardware sets the elevator lamp, and so it is not required to provide a Set Elevator Lamp operation in software.

7. *Floor Lamps.* This DIM hides how to interface to the floor lamps. It provides an operation to Clear a floor lamp. It is given that the hardware sets the floor lamp, and so it is not required to provide a Set Floor Lamp operation in software.

8. *Direction Lamps.* This DIM hides how to interface to the direction lamps. It provides operations to Set a direction lamp and Clear a direction lamp.

24.4.2 Define Data Abstraction Module

Each data store forms the basis of a data abstraction module (DAM). The one major data abstraction module is the Elevator Status and Plan module. In order to determine the operations of the DAM, it is necessary to analyze the data transformations that access the data store (Fig. 24.5). The TADs show that there are three different tasks that access the DAM: the Scheduler, the Elevator Manager, and the Elevator Controller tasks (multiple instances of this task in the multiple elevator case). The Scheduler reads the plan and status of each elevator in order to select an elevator to service an outstanding floor request. This function (which is part of the mini-specification for the Scheduler data transformation) is mapped to an operation called Select Elevator. The Elevator Manager encompasses the Accept New Request data transformation, which updates the Elevator Plan and checks to see if the elevator is idle. This function is mapped to an operation Update Plan. The Elevator Controller task includes two data transformations that access the Elevator Plan, Check This Floor, and Check Next Destination. Each of these transformations is mapped to an operation of the DAM.

The operation New Floor incorporates the Check This Floor data transformation. It is called with a floor number and elevator id as parameters, determines whether the elevator should stop at this floor or not, and updates the status and plan for that elevator accordingly. The operation Check Destination incorporates the Check Next Destination data transformation. It checks in which direction the elevator should travel next and updates the status; if there are no outstanding requests, it sets the status to idle.

24.4.3 Define State Transition Module

There is one state transition module, the elevator STM, which encapsulates the state transition diagram (table). It supports two operations, Process Event and Current State. The elevator STM is maintained within the Elevator Controller task. Since there are multiple instances of this task, there will also be multiple instances of the STM, one for each elevator.

24.5   Integrate Task and Module Views

Now that the tasks and information hiding modules have been defined, the next step is to determine the relationship between the tasks and the modules. The software architecture diagram (Fig. 24.9) is developed to show this relationship. Each IHM defined is explicitly shown, including its operations.

The IHMs for each elevator are placed inside the Elevator Controller task. These are the State Transition Manager and the DIMS for the passive I/O devices supporting each elevator—Door, Motor, and Elevator Lamps. The DIMS for passive I/O devices supporting multiple elevators (Direction Lamps and Floor Lamps) are placed outside the Elevator Controller task. Each DIM for an asynchronous I/O device is placed inside the asynchronous device I/O task supporting that device. For example, the Elevator Buttons DIM is placed inside the Monitor Elevator Buttons task.

In the software architecture diagram for the multiple elevator control system (Fig. 24.10), a resource monitor task is used to ensure sequential access to the Direction Lamps and Floor Lamps DIMs, which support multiple elevators. Thus the Direction Lamps Monitor receives Direction Lamp messages from the Elevator Controller tasks requesting it to set or clear a given direction lamp. It calls the Set or Clear operation of the Direction Lamps DIM, passing the elevator and floor numbers (which it receives in the message) as parameters.

24.6   Develop Ada-based Architectural Design

In the next step of ADARTS, the design is mapped to Ada. In the Ada Architecture diagram, Ada support tasks are introduced first. Consider the single elevator case first. Each loosely-coupled message queue is mapped to a message buffering task. Consequently two message buffering tasks are introduced (Fig. 24.11): Elevator and Scheduler Request Buffer for buffering the Elevator and Scheduler Request message queue, and Service Request Buffer for buffering the Service Request message queue.

The tightly-coupled message interface between Monitor Arrival Sensors and the Elevator Controller is mapped directly to an Ada rendezvous. The tightly-coupled message interface between the Elevator Manager and the Elevator Controller is also mapped directly to an Ada rendezvous. Consequently, the Elevator Controller supports two entries, New Request, which is called by the Elevator Manager, and Pending Floor Arrival, which is called by Monitor Arrival Sensors.

A synchronizing task is placed inside the Elevator Status and Plan DAM to ensure that access to the data maintained by the module is mutually exclusive. The task has four entries, one for each of the four operations maintained by the DAM. The Elevator Status and Plan data store is nested within the synchronizing task.

The three asynchronous device input tasks all have entries that are called by the

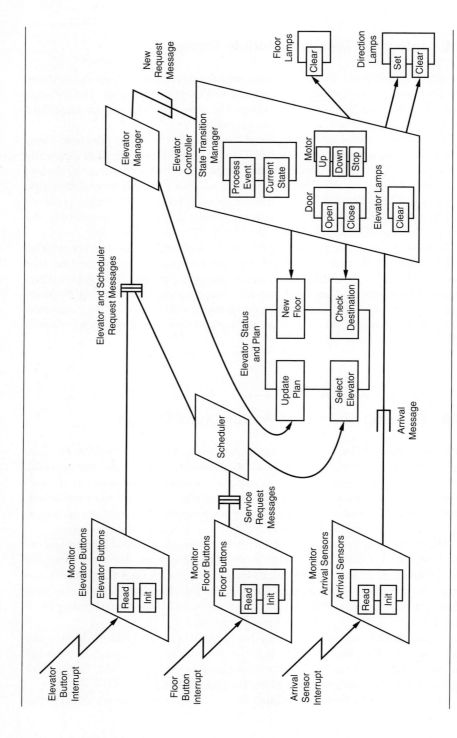

FIGURE 24.9 Software Architecture Diagram for Single Elevator Control System

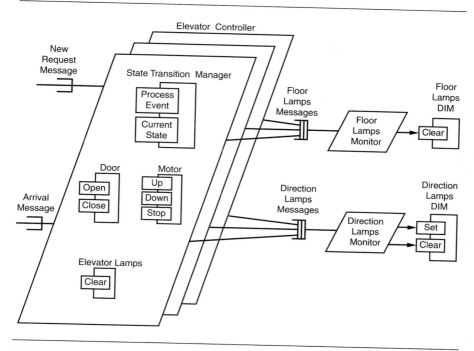

FIGURE 24.10 Software Architecture Diagram for Multiple Elevator Control System

hardware. These are Elevator Button Interrupt, Floor Button Interrupt, and Arrival Sensor Interrupt.

In the multiple elevator control system, to avoid excessive tasking overhead, the multiple instances of the Elevator Controller are mapped to one task, also called the Elevator Controller, using task inversion (Fig. 24.11).

24.7   Distributed Elevator Control System

24.7.1   Overall System Architecture

In the distributed elevator control system, the physical configuration consists of multiple nodes interconnected by a local area network. In a distributed configuration, it is necessary to enforce the rule that all communication between distributed subsystems is only by means of messages. The overall system architecture (Fig. 24.12) shows multiple instances of the Elevator Subsystem (one instance per elevator), multiple instances of the Floor Subsystem (one instance per floor), and one instance of the

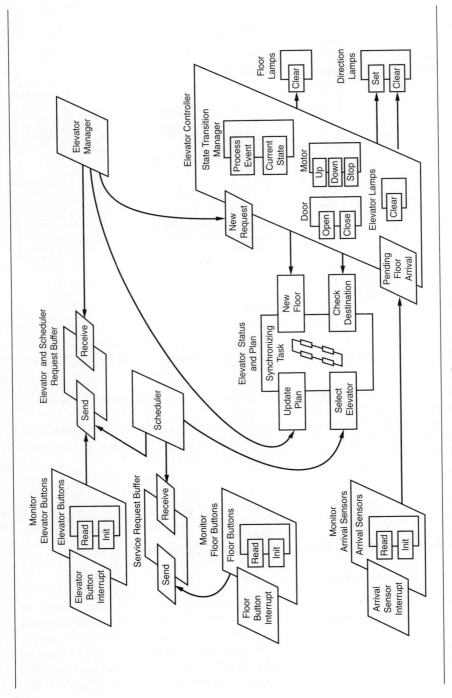

FIGURE 24.11 Ada Architecture Diagram for Elevator Control System

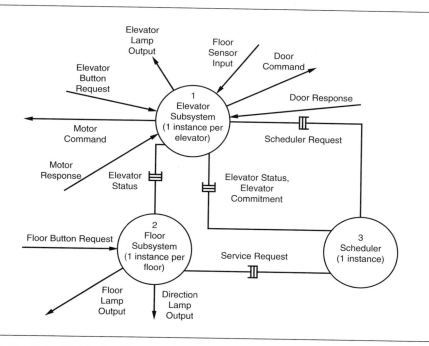

FIGURE 24.12 Distributed Elevator Control System: Overall Architecture

Scheduler Subsystem. All communication between the subsystems is via loosely-coupled message communication.

As there is no shared memory in a distributed configuration, it is not possible for the Scheduler Subsystem and the multiple instances of the Elevator Subsystem to access the Elevator Status and Plan data store directly, as in the previous solutions. A solution to this problem is to embed the Status and Plan DAM in a Server task. Instead of calling an operation of the DAM, a client task would send a message to the Status and Plan Server task. However, with this solution, there is the potential danger of this server becoming a bottleneck, as it has several clients, namely the Scheduler and the multiple instances of the Elevator Manager and Elevator Controller tasks. Instead, an alternative solution is the use of replicated data, with each instance of the Elevator Subsystem maintaining its own local copy of the Elevator Status and Plan DAM.

24.7.2 Structure of Elevator Subsystem

In the distributed solution to this problem, each instance of the Elevator Subsystem is composed of one instance of each of the Elevator Controller, Monitor Elevator Buttons, Monitor Arrival Sensors, and Elevator Manager tasks. In addition, each instance of the Elevator Subsystem also maintains its own local copy of the Elevator Status and Plan DAM.

In the task architecture diagram for the Elevator Subsystem (Fig. 24.13), the Elevator Manager task receives Elevator Request messages from Monitor Elevator Buttons and Scheduler Request messages from the Scheduler subsystem. It sends Elevator Commitment messages to the Scheduler. The Elevator Controller sends Elevator Status messages to both the Floor and Scheduler subsystems.

The subsystem software architecture diagram (Fig. 24.14) shows the IHMs and how they are accessed by the tasks. The design of the IHMs is generally similar to the non-distributed solution. The only difference is that the Local Elevator Status and Plan DAM is simpler than the centralized solution, as it only supports one elevator and does not need a Select Elevator operation.

During target system configuration, each instance of the Elevator Subsystem is typically mapped to an elevator node. Thus each elevator node can execute independently of the other nodes.

24.7.3   Structure of Floor Subsystem

Each instance of the Floor subsystem has one instance of each of the Monitor Floor Buttons, Floor Lamps Monitor, and Direction Lamps Monitor tasks (Fig. 24.15). Thus there is one task for each kind of I/O device.

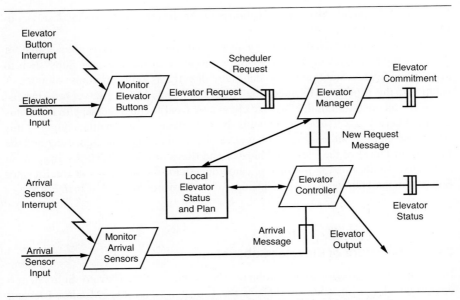

FIGURE 24.13 Task Architecture Diagram for Distributed Elevator Subsystem

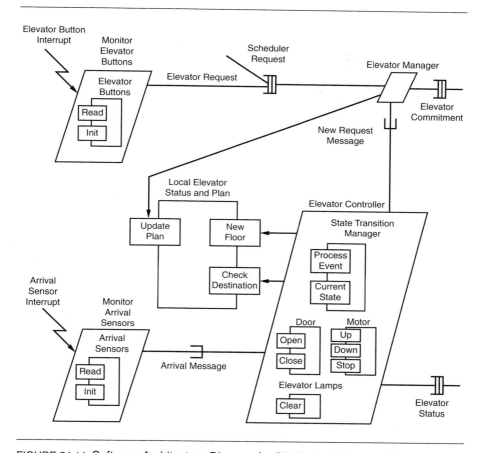

FIGURE 24.14 Software Architecture Diagram for Distributed Elevator Subsystem

The tasks in the Floor subsystem are similar to the non-distributed solution, except that there are multiple instances of them, one per floor. Monitor Floor Buttons sends Service Request messages for this floor to the Scheduler. Both the Floor Lamps Monitor and Direction Lamps Monitor receive Elevator Status messages for this floor from the multiple instances of the Elevator Controller task. In the subsystem software architecture diagram (Fig. 24.16) there is one instance of each DIM for each floor.

24.7.4 Structure of Scheduler Subsystem

There is one instance of the Scheduler subsystem, which consists of two tasks and one IHM (Fig. 24.17). The IHM is the Overall Status and Plan DAM, which contains the

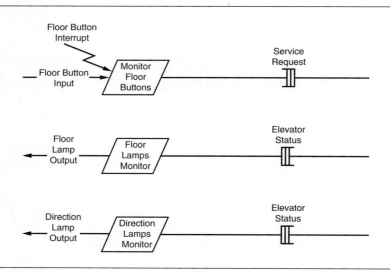

FIGURE 24.15 Task Architecture for Distributed Floor Subsystem

current status of each elevator and the plan for each elevator of what floors it is planning to visit.

At any given node, both the Elevator Controller and Elevator Manager access the local Status and Plan DAM. However, in order for the Scheduler subsystem to know what each elevator's status and plan is, each instance of the Elevator Controller sends status messages to the Scheduler to report on the elevator's arrival at and departure from each floor. In addition, the Elevator Manager sends the Scheduler commitment messages, which identify the floors the elevator is planning to visit. There are two kinds of commitment messages. The first, notification messages, originate because a passenger in the elevator pressed an elevator button; these messages inform the Scheduler of the floors that this elevator will visit for this reason. The second, acknowledgement messages, are responses from the Elevator Subsystem to the Scheduler Request messages sent by the Scheduler requesting the elevator to move to certain floors to pick up passengers.

The Scheduler Subsystem is structured into two tasks, the Elevator Status and Plan Server task and the Elevator Scheduler task. The former task receives the status and commitment messages and updates the overall Status and Plans DAM. The Elevator Scheduler task receives the Service Request messages from the multiple instances of the Monitor Floor Buttons tasks. Every time it receives a Service Request message, it checks to see if an elevator is due to visit the floor in question. If not, it selects an elevator and sends a Scheduler Request message to the Elevator Manager task for that elevator. The Overall Status and Plan DAM has operations to Update

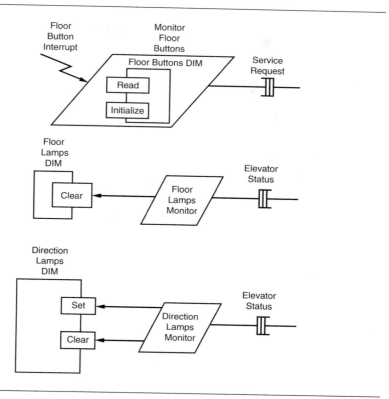

FIGURE 24.16 Software Architecture Diagram for Distributed Floor Subsystem

Status and Update Plan, as well as the operation to Select Elevator (Fig. 24.18). The Elevator Status and Plan Server task calls Update Status when it receives a status message. It calls Update Plan when it receives a commitment message.

24.7.5 Target System Configuration

During target system configuration the subsystems (Fig. 24.12) are mapped to physical nodes. One possible physical configuration is that there is one node for each instance of the elevator subsystem (one node per physical elevator), one node for each instance of the floor subsystem (one node per physical floor), and one node for the Scheduler subsystem. Thus, if there are n elevators and m floors, this physical configuration would require n + m + 1 physical nodes.

Another possible configuration is that all the instances of the Floor Subsystem

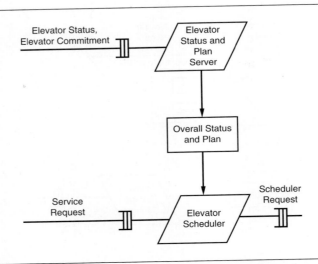

FIGURE 24.17 Task Architecture Diagram for Distributed Scheduler Subsystem

are mapped to one node. In that case, a possible optimization is for each of the tasks to handle the I/O devices for all floors instead of just one floor. Thus Monitor Floor Buttons would monitor the buttons for all floors instead of one floor. Similarly, Floor Lamps Monitor would handle floor lamps for all floors and Direction Lamps Monitor would handle the direction lamps for all floors. This configuration would not require a change in the task architecture of the Floor subsystem. However, the device interface modules would need to handle all lamps instead of just the lamps for one floor. The Scheduler subsystem could continue to be mapped to a separate node, or it could be mapped to the same physical node as the Floor subsystems. In the latter case, this physical configuration would require n + 1 physical nodes.

24.8 Performance Analysis of Non-distributed Elevator Control System

24.8.1 Performance Analysis Scenario

This section describes applying real-time scheduling theory to analyze the performance of the non-distributed version of the Elevator Control system prior to considering the distributed version in the following section. It is necessary to consider one specific

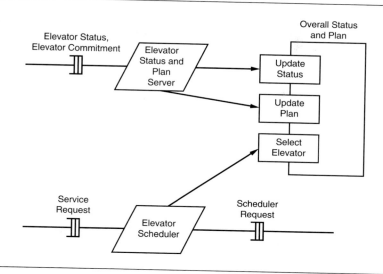

FIGURE 24.18 Software Architecture Diagram for Distributed Scheduler Subsystem

configuration of the Elevator Control system and then analyze the worst-case situation for it by applying the real-time scheduling theory. Consider a building with ten floors and three elevators. Hence there are three instances of the Elevator Controller task. Assume the following worst-case scenario:

a. Elevator button interrupts arrive with a maximum frequency of 10 times a second, which represents a minimum interarrival time of 100 msec. It is assumed that this is a busy period with several passengers on each elevator going to different floors. Since there are 10 floors and three elevators, there are a total of thirty buttons that could be pressed. This worst case scenario assumes that all 30 buttons are pressed within three seconds!

b. Floor button interrupts arrive with a maximum frequency of 5 times a second, which represents a minimum interarrival time of 200 msec. Since there is an Up and a Down button at each floor, except for the top and bottom floors where there is only one button, there are a total of 18 floor buttons. This means that in the worst case all 18 buttons could be pressed within 3.6 seconds.

c. All three elevators are in motion and arrive at floors simultaneously. This is interpreted to mean that the three floor arrival interrupts arrive within 50 msec of each other. This is actually the most time critical aspect of the problem, since when a floor interrupt is received, the Elevator Controller has to determine whether the elevator should stop at this floor or not.

24.8.2   Event Sequences

Consider first the following event sequences for the non-distributed system, as shown in Fig. 24.19:

a. Floor arrival event sequence (Period = T_a):

   1a. Monitor Arrival Sensors receives and processes interrupt.

   2a. Monitor Arrival Sensors sends Arrival Message.

   3a. Elevator Controller receives message and checks the Elevator Status and Plan data store to determine whether the elevator should stop or not. Invokes Stop Motor operation if it should stop.

b. Elevator button pressed event sequence (Period = T_b):

   1b. Monitor Elevator Buttons receives and processes interrupt.

   2b. Monitor Elevator Buttons sends Elevator Request message.

   3b. Elevator Manager receives message and records destination in Elevator Status and Plan data store.

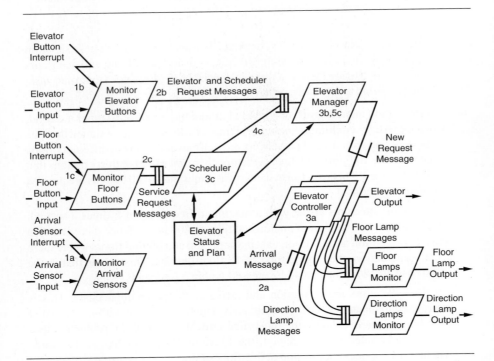

FIGURE 24.19 Event Sequence Diagram for Non-distributed Elevator Control System

c. Floor button pressed event sequence (Period = T_c):

  1c. Monitor Floor Buttons receives and processes interrupt.

  2c. Monitor Floor Buttons sends Service Request message.

  3c. Scheduler receives message, interrogates Elevator Status and Plan data store to determine whether an elevator is on its way to this floor. Assume not, so that the Scheduler selects an elevator.

  4c. The Scheduler sends a Scheduler Request message to the Elevator Manager task of the selected elevator.

  5c. Elevator Manager receives message and records destination in Elevator Status and Plan data store.

Although none of the tasks in the Elevator Control system are periodic, the aperiodic tasks are treated as periodic tasks with a period equal to the minimum event interarrival time.

24.8.3   Priority Assignments

The task parameters for the non-distributed Elevator Control system are shown in Table 24.1. Every task's CPU time includes the context switching time, a maximum of two context switches per task. Message handling overhead has been divided equally between the sender and receiver tasks. The periods of all the tasks in a given event

TABLE 24.1   NON-DISTRIBUTED ELEVATOR CONTROL SYSTEM: REAL-TIME SCHEDULING TASK PARAMETERS

Task	CPU time C_n	Period T_n	Utilization U_n	Assigned Priority
a) *Floor Arrival Event Sequence*				
Monitor Arrival Sensors	2	50	0.04	1
Elevator Controller	5	50	0.10	4
b) *Elevator Button Press Event Sequence*				
Monitor Elevator Buttons	3	100	0.03	2
Elevator Manager (Case b)	6	100	0.06	5
c) *Floor Button Press Event Sequence*				
Monitor Floor Buttons	4	200	0.02	3
Scheduler	20	200	0.10	6
Elevator Manager (Case c)	6	200	0.03	
Other Tasks				
Floor Lamps Monitor	5	500	0.01	7
Direction Lamps Monitor	5	500	0.01	8

sequence are the same time, since it is the arrival of the external event that initiates the event sequence. The Elevator Manager task is treated as if it were two separate tasks since it appears in two different event sequences. Its period is 100 msec in the first case, the activation frequency of Monitor Elevator Buttons, and 200 msec in the second case, the activation frequency of Monitor Floor Buttons.

It is also observed that since the periods of the three asynchronous device input tasks (all interrupt driven) are multiples of each other it is possible for these three tasks to be ready to be activated at virtually the same time. Since interrupts must be handled quickly so as not to be missed, the three interrupt handling tasks need to be processed ahead of all other tasks and are therefore assigned the highest priorities. Doing this violates the rate monotonic priority assignments since, for example, although Monitor Floor Buttons has a longer period than Elevator Controller, it is assigned a higher priority than it.

The interrupt driven tasks execute at a higher priority than the other tasks in the event sequence. Because of this, the tasks in a given event sequence cannot be treated as one equivalent task having the same period, as was done initially for the cruise control example in Chapter 19. Instead, they are treated as separate tasks having the same period.

Consider the priorities that should be assigned to the tasks by the designer. Apart from the three interrupt driven device input tasks, tasks are allocated their rate monotonic priorities. The interrupt driven Monitor Arrival Sensors task is allocated the highest priority, which is also its rate monotonic priority. However, the interrupt driven Monitor Elevator Buttons and Monitor Floor Buttons tasks are given the second and third highest priorities, which violates the rate monotonic assumptions. Elevator Controller is given the next highest priority according to the rate monotonic assignment because it has the shortest period. Although Elevator Manager is in two event sequences, it is given a priority according to its shorter period.

24.8.4   Real-time Scheduling for Non-distributed Environment

Adding up the task utilizations from Table 24.1 gives a total utilization of 0.4, which is well below the worst case utilization bound of 0.69 given by the Utilization Bound Theorem. However, because the rate monotonic priorities are violated, it is necessary to carry out a more detailed real-time analysis, as described in Chapter 11.

The analysis is done for each event sequence, since it is the elapsed time to complete each event sequence that is critical, rather than the elapsed time of each individual task. In the analysis it is necessary to consider pre-emption by tasks with a higher priority as well as blocking due to tasks with a lower priority.

Pre-emption is due to tasks in other event sequences, which have both a shorter period and a higher priority. These tasks are liable to pre-empt more than once. Pre-emption can also come from higher priority tasks with longer periods; for example, higher priority interrupt driven tasks from event sequences with longer periods. These tasks can only pre-empt once. Lower priority task blocking time is due to lower priority tasks acquiring resources, in this case the Elevator Status and Plan data store, required by higher priority tasks.

The real-time scheduling analysis for each of the event sequences is given next. The analysis is carried out using both the Generalized Utilization Bound Theorem and the Generalized Completion Time Theorem. The latter is also illustrated by the timing diagram in Fig. 24.20 in which the worst case is assumed of all three external interrupts arriving simultaneously.

a. *Floor arrival event sequence.* Tasks in event sequence: Monitor Arrival Sensors and Elevator Controller. From Table 24.1, it is given that the period of this event sequence = T_a = 50 msec.

□ Execution time for tasks in event sequence: 2 msec for Monitor Arrival Sensors followed by 5 msec for Elevator Controller giving a total execution time C_a of 7 msec. Execution utilization $U_e = C_a/T_a = 7/50 = 0.14$.

□ Pre-emption by higher priority tasks with longer periods: Both Monitor Elevator Buttons and Monitor Floor Buttons can pre-empt Elevator Controller. Possible 3 msec from Monitor Elevator Buttons to handle elevator button interrupt plus 4 msec from Monitor Floor Buttons to handle floor button interrupt.

Total pre-emption time $P_a = 3 + 4 = 7$ msec. Pre-emption utilization $U_p = P_a/T_a = 7/50 = 0.14$.

□ Blocking time from lower priority task: Possible 20 msec from Scheduler in critical section accessing data store can block Elevator Controller.

Total worst case blocking time $B_a = 20$ msec.

Worst case blocking utilization $U_b = B_a/T_a = 20/50 = 0.40$.

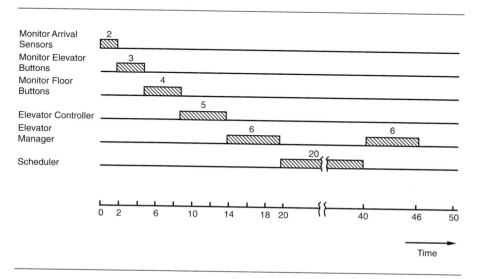

FIGURE 24.20 Elevator Control System Timing Diagram

Total elapsed time = Execution time + Pre-emption time + worst case Blocking time = $C_a + P_a + B_a = 7 + 7 + 20 = 34$ msec < period of 50 msec.

Total Utilization = Execution Utilization + Pre-emption Utilization + worst case Blocking utilization $U_e + U_p + U_b = 0.14 + 0.14 + 0.40 = 0.68$ < worst case upper bound of 0.69.

According to both the Generalized Utilization Bound Theorem and the Generalized Completion Time Theorem, the tasks in the floor arrival event sequence can always meet their deadlines.

b. *Elevator button press event sequence.* Tasks in event sequence: Monitor Elevator Buttons and Elevator Manager. From Table 24.1, it is given that the period of this event sequence = $T_b = 100$ msec.

□ Execution time for tasks in event sequence: Monitor Elevator Buttons for 3 msec followed by Elevator Manager for 6 msec, giving a total execution time $C_b = 3 + 6 = 9$ msec. $U_e = C_b/T_b = 0.09$.

□ Pre-emption by higher priority tasks with shorter periods: Monitor Arrival Sensors and Elevator Controller (pre-empts Elevator Manager) can each execute twice during the 100 msec period, giving a pre-emption time of 14 msec.

□ Pre-emption by higher priority task with longer period: Possible 4 msec from Monitor Floor Buttons to handle floor button interrupt (pre-empts Elevator Manager).

Total pre-emption time $C_p = 14 + 4 = 18$. Pre-emption utilization $U_p = C_p/T_b = 18/100 = 0.18$.

□ Blocking time from lower priority task: Possible 20 msec from Scheduler in critical section accessing data store (blocks Elevator Manager). Total worst case blocking time $B_b = 20$ msec. Worst case Blocking utilization $U_b = B_b/T_b = 0.20$.

Total Elapsed Time = Execution time + Pre-emption time + Worst case Blocking time = $9 + 18 + 20 = 47$ msec < period of 100 msec.

Total Utilization = $U_e + U_p + U_b = 0.09 + 0.18 + 0.20 = 0.47$ < worst case upper bound of 0.69.

According to both the Generalized Utilization Bound Theorem and the Generalized Completion Time Theorem, the tasks in the elevator button press event sequence can always meet their deadlines.

c. *Floor button press event sequence.* Tasks in event sequence: Monitor Floor Buttons, Scheduler and Elevator Manager (appears in two event sequences). From Table 24.1, it is given that the period of this event sequence = $T_c = 200$ msec.

□ Execution time for tasks in event sequence: Monitor Floor Buttons executes once for 4 msec, followed by Scheduler, which execute once for 20 msec. This is followed by Elevator Manager, which executes once for 6 msec.

Total execution time $C_c = 4 + 20 + 6 = 30$ msec. $U_c = C_c/T_c = 0.15$.

□ Pre-emption by higher priority tasks with shorter periods: Monitor Arrival Sensors and Elevator Controller (pre-empts Elevator Manager and Scheduler) can each execute four times for a total of 28 msec. Monitor Elevator Buttons and Elevator Manager (pre-empts Scheduler) can execute twice for a total of 18 msec. Total pre-emption time $C_p = 28 + 18 = 46$ msec. $U_p = C_p/T_c = 0.23$.

❑ Blocking time: Note that blocking due to access of the data store by other tasks has already been taken into account, so there is no additional blocking time.

Total elapsed time = Execution time + Pre-emption time + worst case Blocking time = 30 + 46 + 0 = 76 msec < period of 200 msec.

Total Utilization = $U_e + U_p$ = 0.15 + 0.28 = 0.43 < worst case upper bound of 0.69.

According to both the Generalized Utilization Bound Theorem and the Generalized Completion Time Theorem, the tasks in the floor button press event sequence can always meet their deadlines.

24.9 Performance Analysis of Distributed Environment

24.9.1 Performance Analysis Scenario

The above example shows that the single processor system can handle the three elevator, 10 floor case satisfactorily. However, it is clear that as the number of elevators and floors increases, the CPU load will grow and the system will eventually get overloaded. For example, to handle six elevators and 20 floors, it can be assumed that to a first approximation the utilization would double to 0.8. Repeating the analysis for the worst case floor arrival event sequence shows that deadlines would sometimes be missed. With 12 elevators and 40 floors, the required CPU utilization is 1.2, which is obviously impossible to achieve with a single CPU configuration.

Consider instead the distributed solution (Fig. 24.21), where there is one node per elevator, one node per floor, and one scheduler node. Assume that the same processors are used, so that task execution times do not change and that in addition there is a deterministic local area network whose capacity is 100 MBaud.

Consider the 12 elevator and 40 floor scenario. The load on each individual elevator node and each individual floor node should be less than that on the single CPU of the centralized scenario. However assume that the arrival rates do not change, an extremely unlikely worst case. The task parameters for the Distributed Environment are given in Table 24.2. The CPU utilization for the Elevator Subsystem is 0.23, while the CPU utilization for the Floor Subsystem is 0.04, suggesting that one floor node could easily handle more than one floor.

The node which needs to be analyzed in more detail is the Scheduler node, since this represents a potential bottleneck. With four times as many floors, it is assumed that the Scheduler task's period is shortened by a factor of 4 from 200 msec to 50 msec. Assume that the Elevator Status and Plan Server (Fig. 24.17), which receives

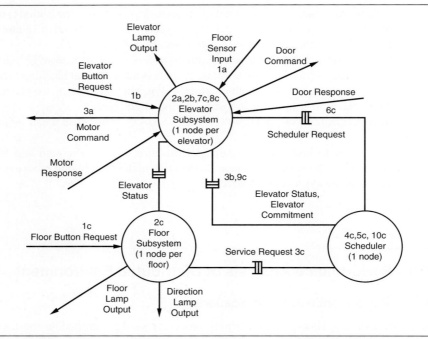

FIGURE 24.21 Event Sequence Diagram for Distributed Elevator Control System

messages from the multiple instances of the Elevator subsystem, has a period of 10 msec and an execution time of 2 msec to update the Status and Plan data store. From Table 24.2, the Scheduler node utilization is 0.6, which is below the upper utilization bound of 0.69 given by the Utilization Bound Theorem.

24.9.2 Real-time Scheduling for Distributed Environment

Consider the three critical event sequences described in the previous section and illustrated in Fig. 24.21 for the distributed configuration:

a. *Floor arrival event sequence.* This event sequence is handled entirely by tasks in the Elevator subsystem (Fig. 24.14). Tasks in event sequence: Monitor Arrival Sensors and Elevator Controller. Period of event sequence = T_a = 50 msec.

◻ Execution time for tasks in event sequence: 2 msec for Monitor Arrival Sensors followed by 5 msec for Elevator Controller giving a total execution time C_a of 7 msec. $U_e = C_a/T_a = 7/50 = 0.14$.

◻ Pre-emption by higher priority tasks with longer periods: Possible 3 msec from Monitor Elevator Buttons to handle elevator button interrupt. Pre-emption time C_p = 3 msec. Pre-emption utilization $U_p = 3/50 = 0.06$.

TABLE 24.2 DISTRIBUTED ELEVATOR CONTROL SYSTEM: REAL-TIME
SCHEDULING TASK PARAMETERS

Task	CPU time C_n	Period T_n	Utilization U_n	Assigned Priority
Elevator Subsystem				
Monitor Arrival Sensors	2	50	0.04	1
Elevator Controller	5	50	0.10	3
Monitor Elevator Buttons	3	100	0.03	2
Elevator Manager	6	100	0.06	4
Floor Subsystem				
Monitor Floor Buttons	4	200	0.02	1
Floor Lamps Monitor	5	500	0.01	2
Direction Lamps Monitor	5	500	0.01	3
Scheduler Subsystem				
Elevator Status and Plan Server	2	10	0.20	1
Elevator Scheduler	20	50	0.40	2

□ Blocking time from lower priority task: Possible blocking of 6 msec from Elevator Manager. Total worst case Blocking time B_a = 6 msec. Worst case blocking utilization $U_b = B_a/T_a = 6/50 = 0.12$.

Total elapsed time = Execution time + Pre-emption time + worst case Blocking time = 7 + 3 + 6 = 16 msec < period of 50 msec.

Total Utilization = $U_e + U_p + U_b$ = 0.14 + 0.06 + 0.12 = 0.32 < worst case upper bound of 0.69.

According to both the Generalized Utilization Bound Theorem and the Generalized Completion Time Theorem, the tasks in the floor arrival event sequence can always meet their deadlines. The utilization is less than in the centralized case, as there are fewer tasks in the Elevator subsystem.

b. *Elevator button press event sequence.* This event sequence is also handled entirely by tasks in the Elevator subsystem. Tasks in event sequence: Monitor Elevator Buttons and Elevator Manager. Period of event sequence = T_b = 100 msec.

□ Execution Time for tasks in event sequence: Monitor Elevator Buttons for 3 msec followed by Elevator Manager for 6 msec, giving a total execution time of 9 msec. $U_e = 0.09$.

□ Pre-emption by higher priority tasks with shorter periods: Monitor Arrival Sensors and Elevator Controller (pre-empts Elevator Manager) can each execute twice during the 100 msec period, giving a total pre-emption time of 14 msec. $U_p = 0.14$.

□ There is no blocking time since all the tasks in the Elevator subsystem have already been accounted for in considering the pre-emption time and execution time.

Total elapsed time = Execution time + Pre-emption time = 9 + 14 = 23 msec < period of 100 msec.

Total Utilization = $U_e + U_p$ = 0.09 + 0.14 = 0.23 < worst case upper bound of 0.69.

According to both the Generalized Utilization Bound Theorem and the Generalized Completion Time Theorem, the tasks in the elevator button press event sequence can always meet their deadlines. Once again, the utilization is less than in the centralized case.

24.9.3 Distributed Event Sequence

The Floor button press event sequence (event sequence c in Fig. 24.21) spans more than one distributed subsystem, since it requires tasks from all three subsystems to participate in processing it. Although the overall CPU utilization of each node has been shown to be adequate, the overall elapsed time is still a concern. It is necessary to apply the real-time scheduling theory to each of the nodes in turn, given the task parameters of Table 24.2. The period of this event sequence = T_c = 200 msec.

Consider first the Floor Subsystem (Fig. 24.15):

1c. Monitor Floor Buttons receives and processes interrupt. Monitor Floor Buttons is the highest priority task in this subsystem, so there is no possibility of pre-emption. There is also no possibility of blocking. Execution time = C_f = 4 msec.

2c. Monitor Floor Buttons sends message. Message processing overhead for preparing message to be sent over network, C_m = 1 msec.

Total elapsed time in Floor Subsystem $E_f = C_f + C_m$ = 4 + 1 = 5 msec.

Consider next the network transmission delay:

3c. Service Request message is sent over the network to the Scheduler subsystem. Assume the size of the message, including all header information required by the communication protocol, is 25 bytes or 200 bits. Given the network capacity of 100 MBaud, the transmission delay D_t is 200/100,000 = 2 msec.

Consider next the Scheduler subsystem (Fig. 24.17):

4c. Elevator Scheduler task receives message. Assume 1 msec delay for receiving and processing message sent over network, C_m = 1 msec.

5c. Elevator Scheduler interrogates Overall Status and Plan data store to determine whether an elevator is on its way to this floor. Assume not, so that the Elevator Scheduler selects an elevator and sends a Scheduler Request message to the Elevator Manager. C_s = 20 msec. Assume 1 msec delay for preparing message to be sent over network, C_m = 1 msec.

Possible blocking time for access to data store by Elevator Status and Plan Server $B_s = 2$ msec.

Worst case elapsed time in Scheduler subsystem $E_s = C_m + C_s + C_m + B_s = 1 + 20 + 1 + 2 = 24$ msec.

Consider next the network transmission delay:

6c. Scheduler Request Message is sent over the network to the Elevator subsystem. As before, transmission delay $D_t = 2$ msec.

Consider next the Elevator subsystem (Fig. 24.13):

7c. Elevator Manager receives and processes message. $C_m = 1$ msec. It then records destination in Local Elevator Status and Plan data store. $C_e = 6$ msec.

8c. Elevator Manager sends Elevator Commitment message to Scheduler subsystem. Message preparation time $C_m = 1$ msec. Execution time: Elevator Manager executes once for $C_m + C_e + C_m = 1 + 6 + 1 = 8$ msec.

There are several possible delays in the Elevator subsystem:
□ Pre-emption time: Monitor Arrival Sensors and Elevator Controller can each execute once for a total of 7 msec. Monitor Elevator Buttons and Elevator Manager (handling Elevator Button message) can execute once for a total of 9 msec. Total pre-emption time = 7 + 9 = 16 msec.
□ Blocking time: Note that blocking due to access of the data store by other tasks has already been taken into account, so there is no additional blocking time.

Worst case elapsed time in Elevator Subsystem E_e = Execution time + Total Pre-emption time = 8 + 16 = 24 msec.

There is an additional 2 msec network transmission delay (event 9c on Fig. 24.21) and worst case $E_u = 23$ msec to update the Overall Status and Plan data store by the Elevator Status and Plan Server (event 10c).

Having considered each of the three subsystems as well as network transmission delays, the worst case elapsed time to process a Floor button press = Floor subsystem elapsed time E_f + Transmission Delay D_t + Scheduler subsystem elapsed time for scheduling E_s + Transmission Delay D_t + Elevator subsystem elapsed time E_e + Transmission Delay D_t + Scheduler subsystem elapsed time for updating $E_u = 5 + 2 + 24 + 2 + 24 + 2 + 23 = 82$ msec.

The total worst case elapsed time to service the Floor button press event sequence is thus estimated to be 82 msec. It should be noted that this is well below the required response time of 200 msec. Even if the network transmission delay was 10 msec instead of 2 msec for each message, the overall elapsed time would only increase to 98 msec.

25

Distributed Factory Automation System Case Study

25.1 Problem Description of Factory Automation System

As an example of using the CODARTS extension for Distributed Applications (CODARTS/DA) design method for the design of a distributed application, a factory automation problem is considered. In a high volume/low flexibility assembly plant, manufacturing workstations are physically laid out in an assembly line (Fig. 25.1). Parts are moved between workstations on a conveyor belt. A part is processed at each workstation in sequence. Since workstations are programmable, different variations on a given product may be handled. Typically, a number of parts of the same type are produced, followed by a number of parts of a different type.

Each manufacturing workstation has an assembly robot for assembling the product, and a pick-and-place robot for picking parts off and placing parts on the conveyor. Each robot is equipped with sensors and actuators. Sensors are used for monitoring operating conditions (e.g., detecting part arrival), while actuators are used to switch automation equipment on and off (e.g., switching the conveyor on and off).

The manufacturing steps required to manufacture a given part in the factory, from raw material to finished product, are defined in a process plan. The process plan defines the part type and the sequence of manufacturing operations. Each operation is carried out at a manufacturing workstation.

The processing of new parts in the factory is initiated by the creation of a work order by a human production manager. The work order defines the quantity of parts required for a given part type.

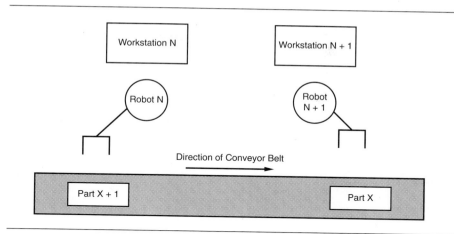

FIGURE 25.1 Factory Automation System

25.2   System Decomposition

The system context diagram (Fig. 25.2) shows the external entities that interface to the system. Three of the external entities represent different categories or types of user who interface to the system; in particular the Process Engineer, Production Manager, and Factory Operator. The other two external entities are the Assembly Robot and the Pick-and-Place Robot, each of which is controlled by a robot controller. Each robot controller has its manufacturing operations; that is the information about the robot programs to be executed, downloaded from the Factory Automation system. The Assembly Robot and Pick-and-Place Robot interface to the Factory Automation System by means of messages.

Figure 25.3 shows the decomposition of the Factory Automation system into subsystems based on the COBRA subsystem structuring criteria. The Process Planning subsystem is decomposed further (Fig. 25.4) into a Process Planning Server subsystem and a Process Planning User Services subsystem.

The Process Planning User Services subsystem interfaces to a class of user (the process engineer), providing the user with a set of services for creating, updating, and reading process plans. There is typically more than one instance of the Process Planning User Services subsystem, one for each process engineer.

The Process Planning Server subsystem maintains all process plans and operations. As data stores must be local to a subsystem, the Process Plans and Operations data stores are encapsulated within the Process Planning Server subsystem. As a server subsystem, it receives service requests from other subsystems and must respond to them. The process plans and operations are updated by the process engineers via the

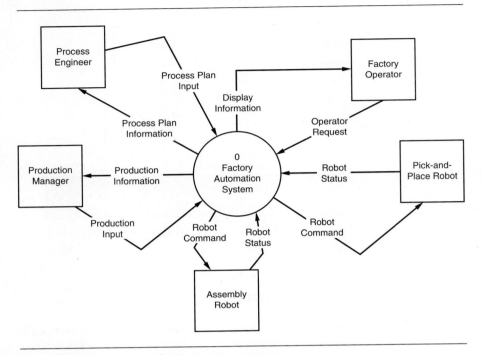

FIGURE 25.2 Factory Automation System Context Diagram

Process Planning User Services subsystem. Requests for information about process plans and operations come from the multiple instances of the Line Workstation Controller subsystem (Fig. 25.5) and Production Management.

Production Management (Fig. 25.3) is a user services subsystem. A production manager creates a work order to meet a customer need. When a work order is released to the factory, Production Management sends a Start Part message to the Part Processing subsystem identifying the part id and number of parts required.

The Alarm Handling subsystem is also a server subsystem. The alarms data store is encapsulated within the Alarm Handling subsystem. If an alarm condition is detected during part processing, an alarm is sent to Alarm Handling. The Operator Services subsystem is a user services subsystem; there is one instance of this subsystem for each operator. An operator can request to view the current status of one or more workstations. Operators may also view and acknowledge alarms.

The Part Processing subsystem is decomposed, as shown in Fig. 25.5, into a Receiving Workstation Controller, Line Workstation Controller, Shipping Workstation Controller, and Workstation Status Server. The Receiving Workstation Controller, Line Workstation Controller and Shipping Workstation Controller are real-time control subsystems that interface to the robot controllers and control the processing of each part. The Workstation Status Server is a Server subsystem.

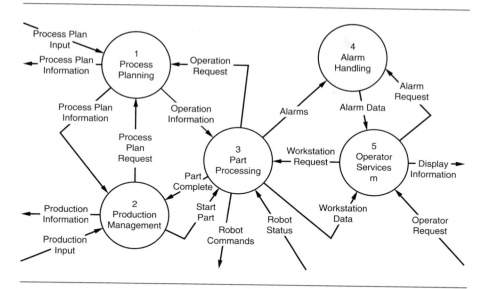

FIGURE 25.3 Data Flow Diagram for Factory Automation System

There is one instance of the Line Workstation Controller subsystem for each manufacturing workstation, and the instances are connected in series. When the Receiving Workstation Controller receives the Start Part message from Production Management, it starts the processing of the parts identified in the message. For each part to be assembled, it ensures that a piece of raw material of the appropriate type is obtained and is ready to be loaded onto the conveyor belt.

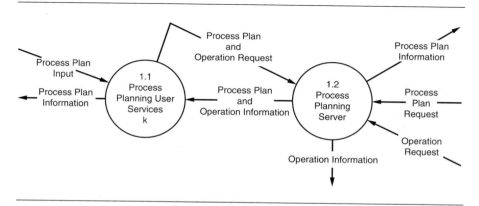

FIGURE 25.4 Decomposition of Process Planning

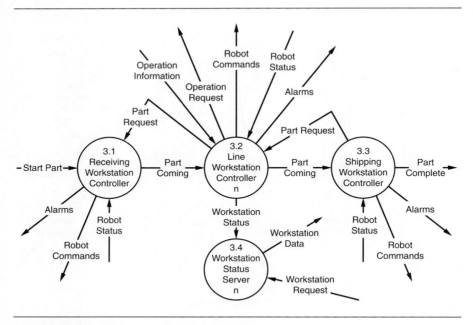

FIGURE 25.5 Decomposition of Part Processing

A just-in-time algorithm is used in the factory. This means that a workstation only requests a part when it is ready to process it, so that parts do not pile up at a workstation. When a workstation completes a part, it waits for a message from its successor workstation requesting the part. When the message is received, the Workstation Controller sends the Place command to the Pick-and-Place robot to place the part on the conveyor. Next, the Workstation Controller sends a Part Coming message to the successor workstation and a Part Request message to the predecessor workstation. The Receiving Workstation Controller maintains a count of the remaining number of parts for a given work order. The Shipping Workstation Controller controls the removal of each finished part from the conveyor belt in preparation for shipping, after which it sends a Part Complete message to Production Management.

25.3   System Architecture

25.3.1   System Structure

In mapping the COBRA behavioral model to a distributed architecture, it is necessary to ensure that configurable distributed subsystems are designed; that is, subsystems capable of being effectively supported in a distributed environment. It is therefore necessary to apply the distributed subsystem configuration criteria described in Chapter 20. The actual decisions for a given application are made later at system configuration time.

In a distributed environment, each subsystem potentially executes on its own physical node and all communication between subsystems is by means of messages. The distributed architecture is shown in Figs. 25.6, 25.7, and 25.8. Figure 25.6 shows the overall architecture while Fig. 25.7 shows the decomposition of the Part Processing subsystem and Fig. 25.8 shows the decomposition of the Process Planning subsystem.

In Fig. 25.7, there is one instance of each of the Receiving and Shipping Workstation Controllers subsystems and several instances of the Line Workstation Controller subsystem. Each of these subsystems is an autonomous subsystem that performs a specific site related service. Each subsystem is able to operate independently for a significant period of time, so it can be operational even if other nodes are temporarily unavailable. As these are real-time control subsystems, having them on separate nodes ensures that predictable subsystem performance can be achieved.

There are several server subsystems, each of which can potentially operate on its own node. There is one instance of each of the Process Planning Server and Alarm Handling subsystem. Best performance is likely to be achieved by allocating each server its own node, so that it can respond promptly to client requests. The Process Planning Server is part of the Process Planning subsystem and is shown in Fig. 25.8.

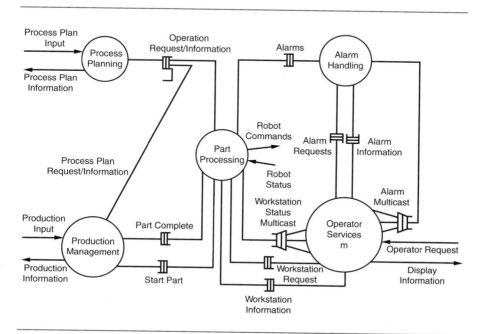

FIGURE 25.6 Factory Automation System Decomposition

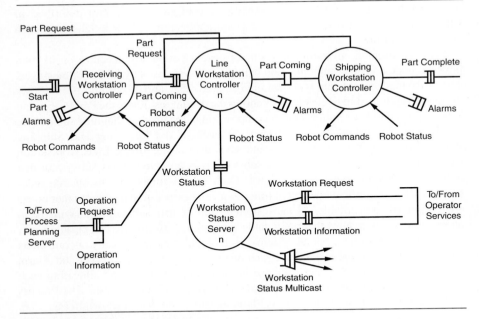

FIGURE 25.7 Decomposition of Part Processing

For the Workstation Server, one option is to have one server for the whole system. Another more decentralized option is to have one instance of this subsystem per workstation, in which case each instance of the Workstation Server could be assigned to the same node as the corresponding Workstation Controller. The reasons for this are that there is relatively high message traffic between the Workstation Controller

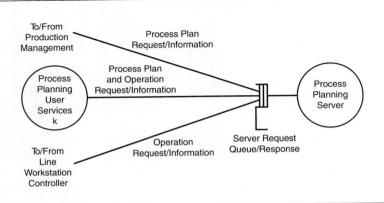

FIGURE 25.8 Decomposition of Process Planning

and Workstation Status Server subsystems, and there is likely to be enough capacity on each workstation node to support both subsystems.

Finally, there are several user interface subsystems, each of which could potentially be allocated its own node. These are Production Management (one instance), Process Planning User Services (one instance per process engineer), and Operator Services (one instance per operator). This allows rapid response to user inputs, with relatively slower response when interacting with the server subsystems.

25.3.2   Message Communication Between Subsystems

Consider the message communication interfaces between subsystems. Most message communication in distributed environments is loosely coupled. An example of loosely-coupled message communication is between Part Processing and Alarm Handling. Alarms are sent from the different workstations to Alarm Handling. When a new alarm message is received by Alarm Handling, it multicasts the alarm to all instances of the Operator Services subsystem that are registered to receive that type of alarm.

An example of Multiple Client/Single Server message communication is shown in Fig. 25.8 where the server is the Process Planning Server, which responds to service requests from multiple clients. The Process Planning User Services subsystem (of which there are typically multiple instances) sends new and updated process plans and operations to the server. The server responds to requests for operation information from the multiple instances of the Workstation Controller subsystem and to requests for process plan information from the Production Management subsystem.

Next consider an example of Multiple Client/Multiple Server message communication. At each workstation, there is a Workstation Status Data Store and a Workstation Status Server task, which encapsulates the data store. The data maintained by the Workstation Status Server task is updated via messages sent by the local Line Workstation Controller subsystem.

Clients of the Workstation Status Server task (i.e., the multiple instances of the Operator Services subsystem) often need to receive data from several workstations concurrently (e.g., a factory status display needs status information from each workstation in the factory). An Operator Services subsystem makes a request for workstation status by sending a message to the appropriate Workstation Status Server task, which responds with that workstation's data. Since Operator Services may send workstation requests to several workstation servers, it uses loosely-coupled message communication so that it can receive workstation responses in any order.

It is also desirable for a factory display to be updated either periodically or whenever there is a change in status, without the Operator Services subsystem having to send an explicit message request each time. This is addressed by multicast message communication. The Operator Services subsystem sends a message to the Workstation Status Server requesting to join that workstation's client group, which consists of all instances of the Operator Services subsystem that wish to receive this workstation's status. The Workstation Status Server sends Workstation Status multicast messages on an ongoing basis to each member of its client group. An Operator Services Subsystem has to inform the Workstation Status Server explicitly when it no longer wishes to receive status messages by sending it a Leave Workstation User Group message.

25.4   Design of Line Workstation Controller Subsystem

Each subsystem is designed using CODARTS. In this section, the design of two subsystems is described. The Line Workstation Controller is an example of a real-time control subsystem, while Alarm Handling is an example of a concurrent server subsystem.

25.4.1   Behavioral Analysis

There are multiple instances of the Line Workstation Controller subsystem, one for each factory workstation. The first step in using CODARTS to design the Line Workstation Controller subsystem is to develop a COBRA behavioral model. The data flow diagram for the Line Workstation Controller subsystem is shown in Fig. 25.9. Since this is a state-dependent subsystem, a state transition diagram is developed for the subsystem, as shown in Fig. 25.10.

The state transition diagram is executed by the control object, Workstation Control, which is represented by a control transformation. Figure 25.9 also shows two device I/O objects, Assembly Robot Interface and Pick-and-Place Robot Interface. In addition there are two subsystem interface objects, the Predecessor and Successor Workstation Interface objects.

Figure 25.10 shows that at workstation startup (an internal event), the workstation transitions into the Awaiting Part from Predecessor Workstation (PWS). As a result of the state transition, Workstation Control triggers the Predecessor Workstation Interface object to send a Part Request message. When a Part Coming message is received from the Predecessor Workstation, the Predecessor Workstation Interface object sends a message to the Process Planning server to request the manufacturing operation for this workstation. The operation defines the robot program names and parameters. Upon receipt of the operation information, the current part and operation data are stored in the Current Operation data store. Predecessor Workstation Interface then sends the Part Sent event flow to Workstation Control. This causes the workstation to transition to Part Arriving state.

A sensor attached to the pick-and-place robot controller detects that the part has physically arrived at the workstation. This robot status is sent to the Pick-and-Place

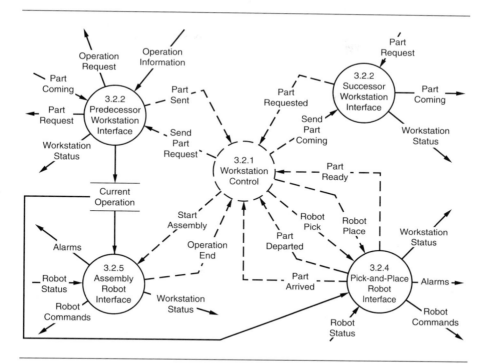

FIGURE 25.9 Line Workstation Controller Data Flow Diagram

Robot Interface object, which sends the Part Arrived event flow. Workstation Control transitions to Robot Picking state and triggers the Pick-and-Place Robot interface object, which reads the operation from the data store and downloads a Robot Pick command to the pick-and-place robot controller.

The pick-and-place robot controller then picks the part off the conveyor and places it in the workstation, resulting in Part Ready being sent. Workstation Control transitions to the Assembling Part state and triggers the Assembly Robot Interface object to send the start assembly operation to the assembly robot controller.

During part assembly, the assembly robot sends robot status information up to the Assembly Robot Interface object, which updates the Workstation Status and sends alarm messages if necessary. On completion of the assembly operation, Assembly Robot Interface sends the Operation End event flow.

If a Part Request message has already been received from the successor workstation (SWS), then Workstation Control transitions immediately to Robot Placing state. Otherwise, Workstation Control transitions into Awaiting Part Request from Successor Workstation. Upon receipt of the Part Requested event flow from the Successor Workstation Interface, it transitions into Robot Placing state. In either case, during the transition to Robot Placing state, Workstation Control triggers the Pick-and-Place

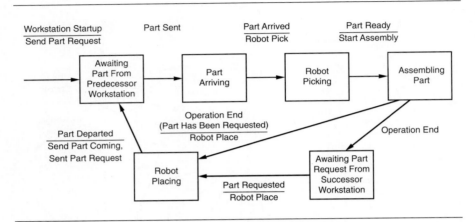

FIGURE 25.10 Workstation Control State Transition Diagram

Robot Interface object to place the part onto the conveyor. When the part has departed, Workstation Control triggers Successor Workstation Interface to send a Part Coming message to the SWS and triggers Predecessor Workstation Interface to send a Part Request message to the PWS.

25.4.2   Task Structuring

Next, the tasks in the Line Workstation Controller subsystem are determined by applying the task structuring criteria. By definition, executing the state transition diagram is a purely sequential activity. Consequently, the control object Workstation Control is mapped to a control task called Control Part Processing.

Transformations, which either send events to the control object or are controlled by the control object and are constrained not to execute in parallel with the control object, may be combined with it according to the sequential and control cohesion task structuring criteria. Such transformations are the Predecessor and Successor Workstation Interface objects, which only execute at state transitions either because they trigger a particular event which initiates a state transition or because they are activated as a result of a state transition. Thus these two objects are combined with Control Part Processing according to the sequential and control cohesion task structuring criteria.

The Pick-and-Place Robot Interface object is mapped to an asynchronous device I/O task, the Pick-and-Place Robot Interface task, since it needs to interface directly to the robot controller and to interact with it asynchronously. Similarly the Assembly Robot Interface object is structured into the Assembly Robot Interface task according to the asynchronous device I/O task structuring criterion. Both the Pick-and-Place

Robot Interface and Assembly Robot Interface tasks must be active concurrently with Control Part Processing, as they are continually monitoring the external environment and generating workstation status and alarm messages where necessary.

The task architecture diagram for the Workstation Controller and Workstation Status Server subsystems is shown in Fig. 25.11, which shows that the Control Part Processing task uses messages for communicating with tasks in other subsystems; that is, the predecessor and successor workstations as well as the Workstation Status Server and Process Planning Server. The Current Operation data store is encapsulated in the Control Part Processing task. Messages sent to the Pick-and-Place Robot Interface and Assembly Robot Interface tasks includes operation data from this data store.

It can be seen from this figure that Control Part Processing has one input message queue, in which it receives Part Coming and Part Request messages from other workstation controller subsystems, in addition to Robot Acknowledgements and Operation End messages from other tasks in the same subsystem. It also has tightly-coupled communication with the Process Planning Server.

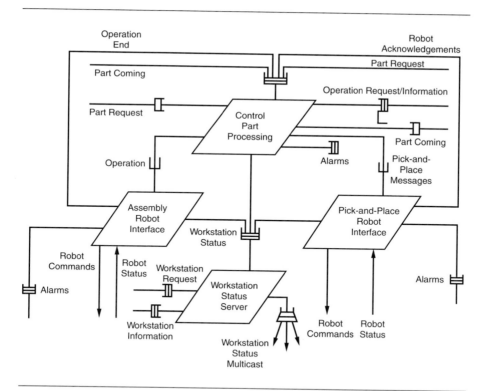

FIGURE 25.11 Task Architecture Diagram for Line Workstation Controller and Workstation Status Server Subsystems

25.5   Design of Alarm Handling Subsystem

The Alarm Handling subsystem is a server subsystem. The services provided are Read Alarm List, Request Registration, Acknowledge Alarm, and Process Alarms. The Read Alarm List service is a reader only service while the others are writer services. Alarm Handling is designed as a concurrent server subsystem (Fig. 25.12) to provide improved throughput. Each of the services is implemented as a task. Receive Alarm Requests is the server supervisor task. Because of the number of writer tasks, synchronization of access to the Alarms data store is achieved by means of mutual exclusion.

There are multiple instances of the Read Alarm List task. Read Alarm List returns the outstanding alarms to the client. Request Registration adds or removes a client to or from the list of clients who wish to be informed when an alarm of a particular type is received. Process Alarms adds new alarms received from workstations to the Alarm List and removes old alarms from the Alarm List. It also multicasts these alarms to all clients who have registered for alarms of this type. Acknowledge Alarm processes alarm acknowledgement request messages indicating that an operator has taken some action in response to an alarm.

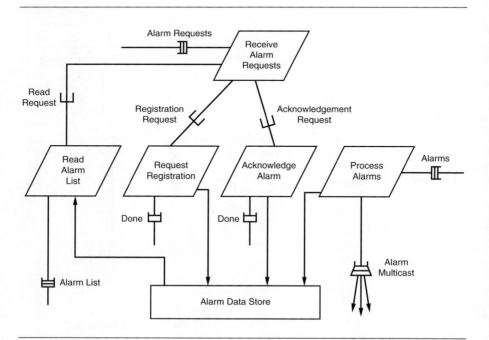

FIGURE 25.12 Task Architecture Diagram for Alarm Handling Subsystem

25.6 System Configuration

Consider the system configuration of the Factory Automation System. The distributed design can be mapped to different target system configurations dictated by the size of the factory, the number of users, expected throughput, and hardware availability.

Further decisions need to be made to configure individual target systems. The number of workstations needs to be defined. Parameters of parameterized subsystems need to be defined such as workstation id, alarm, and sensor names. Subsystem instances need to be connected together and allocated to physical nodes.

Consider first a highly distributed configuration. Each instance of the Workstation Controller subsystem, together with its companion Workstation Status Server subsystem (for line workstations) is allocated to a separate physical node to achieve localized autonomy and adequate performance. Thus the failure of one workstation node does not immediately impact other workstation nodes, although part throughput is delayed. Each instance of the Process Planning User Services, Production Management, and Operator Services subsystems, is allocated to a user interface node. The Alarm Handling and Process Planning Server subsystems are mapped to server nodes.

An alternative less distributed configuration is to allocate the Process Planning subsystems and Production Management to a multi-user interactive node. Even greater centralization could be achieved by adding the Alarm Handling and Operator Services Subsystems to the interactive node. In this scenario, only the workstation controller subsystems would have their own nodes.

Each system configuration selected needs to be analyzed from a real-time scheduling perspective, to ensure that it can meet its performance requirements. An example is given next for an individual workstation node.

25.7 Real-time Scheduling

A real-time scheduling analysis is carried out of the tasks on the Workstation node, since this is the most time critical node in the system. This node contains four tasks (Fig. 25.11), three from the Workstation Controller subsystem (the Control Part Processing task, the Pick-and-Place Robot Interface task, and the Assembly Robot Interface task), and one from the Workstation Status Server subsystem (a task of the same name).

An analysis of the processing required for one part, referred to as a cycle, shows that Control Part Processing receives seven messages during a cycle. It receives one message from the predecessor workstation, one from the successor workstation, one from the Process Planning Server, three from the Pick-and-Place Robot Interface task, and one from the Assembly Robot Interface task. The Pick-and-Place Robot Interface receives five messages in a cycle, the Pick and Place messages from Control Part

TABLE 25.1 DISTRIBUTED FACTORY AUTOMATION SYSTEM: REAL-TIME
SCHEDULING TASK PARAMETERS ON WORKSTATION NODE

Task	CPU time C_n	Period T_n	Utilization U_n	Priority
Control Part Processing	6	143	0.04	1
Pick-and-Place Robot Interface	10	200	0.05	3
Assembly Robot Interface	10	500	0.02	4
Workstation Status Server	15	143	0.11	2

Processing as well as three robot status messages from the robot controller. The Assembly Robot Interface task receives two messages, one from Control Part Processing and one from the robot controller. The Workstation Status Server receives six status messages from Control Part Processing so that it can keep track of the workstation status. In addition assume it receives one operator request each cycle.

The analysis therefore needs to consider the length of a part processing cycle. As a workstation interacts with several external electromechanical entities such as robots and conveyors, a cycle is comparatively slow—assume as a worst case a cycle of one second, which is so pessimistic it is physically impossible.

A preliminary real-time scheduling analysis indicates is shown in Table 25.1. In this table, each task's period is derived by dividing the cycle time of one second by the number of messages it receives. This analysis indicates a total CPU utilization of 0.22, which is well below the worst case utilization bound. Thus there is no need to do a more detailed analysis of the kind described for the distributed Elevator Control System. A more detailed analysis would take into account message transmission delays to and from the Process Planning Server, an event sequence analysis, and rate monotonic priority inversion issues if the two Robot Interface tasks were assigned higher priorities than the Workstation Status Server.

APPENDIX   Teaching Considerations

A.1   Prerequisites

The material in this book may be taught in different ways depending on the time available and the knowledge level of the students. This appendix describes possible academic and industrial courses that could be based on this book.

A prerequisite of these courses is an introductory course on software engineering covering the software life cycle, and the main activities in each phase of the life cycle. This prerequisite course would cover the material described in introductory books on software engineering such as Fairley [Fairley85], Pressman [Pressman91], Sage and Palmer [Sage90], or Sommerville [Sommerville92].

A.2   Suggested Academic Courses

The following academic courses could be based on the material covered in this book:

1. A senior undergraduate or graduate-level course on design methods with special emphasis on the design of concurrent and real-time systems.

2. A variation on the above course is to survey several of the design methods but to teach one in more detail (e.g., CODARTS), such that students can solve a substantial problem using the method.

3. A senior undergraduate or graduate-level course on real-time systems. In this case, the material in this module could be preceded by other topics in real-time system development as described in, for example, [Allworth87] and [Burns89].

4. An advanced graduate-level course on software design methods for concurrent and real-time systems that could follow an earlier course providing an introduction to software design. In this case, the material in Parts I and II of the book could be covered in the introductory course, with the material in Parts III and IV of the book covered in the advanced course. Both courses, particularly the advanced course, should have a design lab as a component of the course.

5. A design lab course is held as a follow up course to the design methods course in which the students work in groups to develop a solution to a substantial real-time problem using one of the methods. In this case, students could also implement all or part of the system.

In courses 1, 2, and 4, students should already be familiar with concurrent processing concepts, which would typically be covered in an introductory operating systems course. In course 2, concurrent processing concepts could be taught as part of the real-time systems course.

A.3 Suggested Industrial Courses

The following industrial courses could be based on the material covered in this book:

1. Survey of software design methods for concurrent and real-time systems. This would largely use the material in Parts I and II of this book, with Part III taught at the same level of detail as Part II. This course could be run at any length from one to five days, depending on the level of detail covered. In the longer versions of the course, a design lab should be held where students work in teams on a design exercise.

2. A course on one design method. Concepts are presented from Part I, a brief survey of the other methods from Part II is given, and then the selected design method is taught in greater detail. For example, if CODARTS is taught, then parts III and IV would be used for the bulk of the course. The design lab would concentrate on the selected design method. This course could be run at any length from one to five days, depending on the level of detail covered.

A.4 Worked Examples

It is difficult, if not impossible, to teach courses on software design without worked examples of the design methods. It is especially instructive if the same example can be used to illustrate each of the methods. The author has used an example of an Automobile Cruise Control and Monitoring System to illustrate each of the real-time software design methods.

The suggested approach for using the worked examples is to first present a given method and then to follow this by illustrating the method using the example of applying the method to the Cruise Control problem.

A.5   Design Exercises

As part of the course, students should also work on one or more real-time problems, either individually or in groups. Whether one or more problems are tackled depends on the size of the problem and the length of the course. However, sufficient time should be allocated for students to work on the problems since this is the best way for the students to really understand the method.

Real time problems not described in this book that may be used are:

- Buoy system [Booch86];
- Home-heating system [Booch91, Hatley88];
- Automated Teller Machine system [Rumbaugh91];
- Flexible Manufacturing system [Sanden93];
- Air-traffic control system [Nielsen88, Sanden93].

Possible approaches are:

1. Work on one problem throughout the course using one of the methods. This has the advantage that students get an in-depth appreciation of one of the methods.
2. Divide the class up into groups. Each group uses a different method to solve the same problem. Time is allocated at the end of the course for each group to present their solution. A class discussion is held on the strengths and weaknesses of each method as found in applying them to the problem.
3. Work on the same problem using each of the methods. Class discussions are held after each method so that students can compare their solutions.
4. A design lab course is held as a follow up course to the design methods course in which the students work in groups to develop a solution to a substantial real-time problem using one of the methods. In this case, students could also implement all or part of the system.

Glossary

AAD   Ada Architecture Diagram

Abstract Data Type (ADT)   A data type defined by the operations that manipulate it, thus hiding its representation details.

Abstract Interface Specification   A specification that defines the external view of the information hiding module, that is, all the information required by the user of the module.

Abstraction   A view of a problem that extracts the essential information relevant to a particular purpose and ignores the remainder of the information [IEEE83].

Active Component   In analysis, an active object or function. In design, a task.

Active Object   An autonomous object that initiates actions of its own. A concurrent task.

Ada Architecture Diagram (AAD)   A graphical notation showing a network of concurrent tasks and packages (information hiding modules), explicitly showing the operations provided by the packages, as well as task and package interfaces.

Ada-based Design Approach for Real-Time Systems (ADARTS)   A design method oriented towards the design of Ada-based real-time systems, although the first four steps are language-independent.

ADARTS   Ada-based Design Approach for Real-Time Systems

ADT   Abstract Data Type

Aggregate Object   A compound object composed of a group of related objects that work together in a coordinated fashion.

AHM   Algorithm Hiding Module

Algorithm Hiding Module (AHM)   An information hiding module that hides an algorithm used in the application domain.

Algorithm Object   An object that encapsulates an algorithm used in the problem domain.

Analog Data   Continuous data that can in principle have an infinite number of values.

Aperiodic Task   A task that is activated on demand. [See asynchronous task]

413

Asynchronous Device I/O task   A task that interfaces to an I/O device and is activated by interrupts from that device.

Asynchronous Function   A function activated on demand by another object or function to perform some action.

Asynchronous I/O device   An I/O device that generates an interrupt when it has produced some input or when it has finished processing an output operation.

Asynchronous State-Dependent Function   A function that is activated by a control object to perform a given action.

Asynchronous Task   A task that is activated on demand.

Behavior Hiding Module   A module that hides the behavior of the system as specified by a function defined in the requirements specification.

Behavioral Analysis   A strategy to help determine how the objects and/or functions within a system or subsystem interact with each other.

Behavioral Model   A model that describes the responses of the system to the inputs it receives from the external environment.

Binary Semaphore   A boolean variable that is only accessed by means of two atomic operations, Wait and Signal, usually used to enforce mutual exclusion.

Black box specification method   A specification that describes the externally visible characteristics of the system

Box Structured Information Systems Method   A method that uses a formal approach in specification and design, and uses formal verification of specifications, designs and code.

Calling Hierarchy   A calling hierarchy of operations provided by information hiding modules.

CASE   Computer Assisted Software Engineering

CFD   Control Flow Diagram

Class   An object type, hence a template for objects. An implementation of an abstract data type.

Class diagram   A diagram that is used in OOD to show the relationships between classes in the logical design of a system.

Cleanroom Software Development   An approach that uses the Box-Structured Information Systems Method for design and verification, and statistical usage testing for testing.

COBRA   COncurrent Object-Based Real-Time Analysis

CODARTS   COncurrent Design Approach for Real-Time Systems

CODARTS/DA   The extension to the CODARTS method for designing distributed applications.

Cohesion   In Structured Design, a criterion for identifying the strength or unity within a module. In DARTS, [See Task Cohesion Criteria]

Completion Time Theorem   A real-time scheduling theorem that states that for a set of independent periodic tasks, if each task meets its first deadline when all tasks are started at the same time, then the deadlines will be met for any combination of start times.

Component   In analysis, an object or function. In design, a task or information hiding module (IHM).

Component Interface Specification   [Also known as abstract interface specification.] A specification that defines the externally visible view of a component.

Computer Assisted Software Engineering (CASE) tool   A software tool supporting a software engineering method or technique.

Concrete Entity   An entity that exists in the real-world and has some physical attributes.

COncurrent Design Approach for Real-Time Systems (CODARTS)   A software design method for designing concurrent, real-time, and distributed applications.

COncurrent Object-Based Real-Time Analysis (COBRA)   An analysis and modeling method for concurrent and real-time systems that uses the same notation as RTSA but an alternative approach for analyzing and modeling the problem domain.

Concurrent task   [See Task]

Context Diagram   The highest level data flow diagram in a Structured Analysis, RTSA or COBRA specification that defines the boundary between the system to be developed and the external environment.

Continuous Data   Data that flows without interruption.

Control Cohesion   A task structuring criterion where a control object (transformation) is combined with the functions it controls into a task.

Control flow (Also known as event flow.)   A binary signal or multi-valued discrete signal that carries no data.

Control Flow Diagram (CFD)   A graphical notation showing the control (event) flows between data and control transformations.

Control Object   An active abstract object in the problem domain that has different states and controls the behavior of other objects and functions. A control object is defined by means of a finite state machine.

Control Specification   A specification that describes the behavior of the system in terms of decision tables, state transition tables, state transition diagrams and/or process activation tables.

Control Task   A task that executes a state transition diagram (mapped to a state transition table).

Control Transformation   A control object or function that is defined by means of a state transition diagram.

Coupling   A criterion for determining the degree of connectivity between modules.

Critical Section   The section of a task's code that must be executed mutually exclusively.

DAM   Data Abstraction Module

DARTS   Design Approach for Real-Time Systems.

DARTS/DA   An extension to the DARTS method for designing real-time applications.

Data Abstraction   An approach for defining a data structure or data type by the set of operations that manipulate it, thus separating and hiding the representation details.

Data Abstraction Module (DAM)   An information hiding module that hides the contents and internal structure of a data store. The data is accessed indirectly by means of access procedures or functions.

Data Abstraction Object   An object that models an abstract entity in the application domain that needs to be "remembered."

Data Dictionary   A collection of the names of all data items used in a software system, together with relevant properties of those items [IEEE83]. Defines the contents of all data flows, event flows, and data stores in the system.

Data Flow   The data that is passed between a source transformation and a destination transformation or to/from the external environment.

Data Store   A repository of data, usually shown on a Data Flow Diagram.

Data Transformation   A graphical notation for a function or object on a data flow or a data flow/control flow diagram.

Dataflow/Control Flow Diagram   A graphical notation showing a network of related data transformations and control transformations, and the data flow and event flow interfaces between these transformations.

Dataflow Diagram (DFD)   A graphical notation showing a network of related data transformations and the data flows between these transformations.

Deadlock   A case where two or more tasks are suspended indefinitely because each task is waiting for a resource acquired by another task.

Design Strategy   An overall plan and direction for performing a design.

Design Approach for Real-Time Systems (DARTS)   A software design method for concurrent and real-time systems that emphasizes structuring the system into concurrent tasks.

Design Concept   A fundamental idea that can be applied to designing a system.

Design Method   A systematic approach for creating a design. It helps identify the design decisions to be made, the order in which to make them, and the criteria used in making them.

Design Notation   A graphical, symbolic, or textual means of describing a design.

Device Interface Module (DIM)   An information hiding module that hides the characteristics of an I/O device and presents a virtual device interface to its users.

DFD   Dataflow Diagram

DIM   Device interface module

Disable Event Flow   An internal control signal that deactivates a previously enabled data transformation.

Discrete Data   Data that arrives at specific time intervals and so is similar to a message.

Distributed Kernel   A nucleus of an operating system that supports distributed applications.

Distributed Processing Environment   A system configuration where several geographically dispersed nodes are interconnected by means of a local area or wide area network.

Enable Event Flow   An internal control signal that activates a data transformation, which remains active until subsequently deactivated by a disable event flow.

Entity Structure Diagram (ESD)   A diagram used in Jackson System Development (JSD) to show the structure of a real world entity, in the form of the time ordered sequence of events received by it.

Entity-Life Modeling   A software design method for concurrent and real-time systems based on JSD, which maps directly to Ada.

Environmental Model   A model that defines the external entities that the system has to interface to, and the inputs to and outputs from the system.

Environment Simulator   A tool that models the inputs arriving from the external entities that interface to the system, and feeds them to the system being tested.

ESD   Event sequence diagram

Event   In Event Sequence Diagram, an external or internal stimulus used for synchronization purposes. It can be an external interrupt, timer expiration, internal signal, or internal message.

Event   In event flows or event synchronization, an external or internal signal that carries no data.

Event Flow   A discrete signal that has no data value.

Event Sequence Diagram (ESD)   A diagram that identifies the sequence of execution of components that are required to process an external event. Event sequence diagrams can be used with data flow diagrams, state transition diagrams, task architecture diagrams, software architecture diagrams, or Ada architecture diagrams.

Event Synchronization   Control of task activation by means of signals. Three types of event synchronization are possible: external interrupts, timer expiration, and internal signals from other tasks.

Event Trace   A time-ordered description of each external input and the time at which it occurred. Used in simulation models or environment simulators.

Extended Computer Module   An information hiding module that hides the characteristics of the hardware/software interface that are likely to change.

External Event   An event from an external entity, typically an interrupt from an external I/O device.

FDM   Function Driver Module

Finite State Machine (FSM)   A conceptual machine with a given number of states and transitions, which are caused by input events. A FSM is usually represented by a state transition diagram or state transition table.

Formal Method   A method that uses a formal specification language, i.e., a language with mathematically defined syntax and semantics.

FSM   Finite State Machine

Function Driver Module (FDM)   An information hiding module that controls a set of closely related outputs to a virtual I/O device.

Functional Cohesion   A task cohesion criterion where one or more closely related functions that cannot execute concurrently are grouped into a task.

Hardware Hiding Module   An information hiding module that is either an extended computer module or a device interface module (DIM).

I/O Task Structuring Criteria   This category of the task structuring criteria addresses how I/O transformations are mapped to I/O tasks and when an I/O task is activated.

IHM   Information hiding module

Incremental Software Development   An iterative approach to developing software in stages.

Informal Information Hiding Module Specification   An informal specification that defines the external view of the information hiding module, including its operations.

Information Hiding   The concept of encapsulating software design decisions in modules in such a way that the module's interface reveals only what its users need to know; thus each module is a "black box" to the other modules in the system (adapted from [IEEE83]).

Information Hiding Module (IHM)   A module that is structured according to the information hiding concept. The module hides some aspect of the system and is accessed by means of access procedures or functions.

Information Hiding Module Hierarchy   A tree-structured categorization of information hiding modules, also referred to as the module structure.

Information Hiding Module Structuring Criteria   [See module structuring criteria]

Inheritance   A mechanism for sharing and reusing code between classes.

Internal Event   A signal used for a synchronization between two active software components, e.g., tasks.

Internal Task Structuring Criteria   This category of the task structuring criteria addresses how internal transformations are mapped to internal tasks and when an internal task is activated.

Jackson Structured Programming (JSP)   A program design method where the structure of the program is based on the input and output data structures.

Jackson System Development (JSD)   A software design method that models the behavior of real world entities over time.

JSD   Jackson System Development

JSD Network Diagram   A diagram that shows all the components in a JSD design and the interfaces between them.

JSP   Jackson Structured Programming

Leaf-level Data Transformation   The lowest level components that are defined in SA, RTSA, and COBRA by means of mini-specifications.

Loosely-coupled Message Communication   A producer task sends a message to a consumer task and does not wait for a response; a message queue could potentially build up between the tasks.

Mathematical Model   A mathematical representation of a system.

Message Buffering Task   An Ada support task used to provide loosely-coupled message communication between Ada tasks.

Mode Determination Module   An information hiding module that hides a mode determination table defined in the SRS.

Modularity   The extent to which software is composed of discrete components such that a change to one component has minimal impact on other components [IEEE83].

Module   In Structured Design, usually a function or procedure. In NRL, ADARTS, and CODARTS, an [information hiding module].

Module Guide   The document that describes the information hiding module hierarchy in the NRL method.

Module Hierarchy   A hierarchical categorization of information hiding modules.

Module Structuring Criteria   The criteria for determining the information hiding modules in the system.

Multiple Instance Task Inversion   An optimization technique where all identical tasks of the same type are replaced by one task which performs the same service.

Multiple Readers / Multiple Writers algorithm   A solution involving multiple reader tasks that may access a data store concurrently, while writer tasks have mutually exclusive access.

Mutual Exclusion   Only allowing one task to have access to shared data at a time, often enforced by means of binary semaphores.

Naval Research Laboratory Software Cost Reduction Method (NRL)   A software design method for real-time systems that emphasizes information hiding.

Node   In a distributed environment, each node consists of one or more processors with shared memory.

NRL   Naval Research Laboratory Software Cost Reduction Method

Object   An instance of a class. An object is an information hiding module that contains both data and operations on that data.

Object Diagram   Diagram used in Object-Oriented Design (OOD) to show the objects in the system and to show how the objects interface to each other.

Object-Oriented Design   A software design method based on the concept of objects, classes, and inheritance.

OOD   Object-Oriented Design

Operation   An access procedure or function provided by an object or information hiding module.

Package   An Ada implementation of an information hiding module.

Passive Component   In analysis, a passive object or data store. In design, an information hiding module.

Passive I/O device   A passive (synchronous) I/O device does not generate an interrupt on completion of an input or output operation. The input from a passive input device needs to be read either on a polled basis or on demand.

Passive Object   An object that has operations that are invoked by active objects. [See active objects]

Performance Model   An abstraction of the real computer system behavior, developed for the purpose of gaining greater insight into the performance of the system, whether the system actually exists or not.

Periodic Function   A function that is activated at regular intervals to perform some action.

Periodic I/O task   A task that interfaces to a passive I/O device and polls the device on a regular basis.

Periodic State-Dependent Function   A function that is activated by a control object to perform some action that needs to be done at regular intervals. The function is activated on entry into a state, and deactivated on leaving a state.

Periodic Task   A task that is activated periodically (i.e., at regular, equally spaced intervals of time) by a timer event.

Petri Net   A dynamic mathematical model, with a graphical notation consisting of places and transitions, used for modeling concurrent systems.

Priority Message Queue   A queue where each message has a priority associated with it. The consumer always accepts higher priority messages before lower priority messages.

Process (Concurrent Processing)   Same as **task.**

Process (Structured Analysis)   A function of the system, also called transformation, bubble.

Pseudocode   A form of structured English.

Queuing Model   A mathematical representation of a computer system that is used to analyze contention for limited resources and for predicting system performance.

Rate-Monotonic Algorithm   A real-time scheduling algorithm that assigns higher priorities to tasks with shorter periods.

Real-Time Structured Analysis (RTSA)   An analysis and modeling method for real-time systems.

Real-time   Pertaining to the processing of data by a computer in connection with another process outside the computer according to time requirements imposed by the outside process. This term is also used to describe systems operating in conversational mode, and processes that can be influenced by human intervention while they are in progress [IEEE83].

Real-time Scheduling Theory   A theory for priority-based scheduling of concurrent tasks with hard deadlines. It addresses how to determine whether a group of tasks, whose individual CPU utilization is known, will meet their deadlines.

Regression Model   A statistical performance model of a computer system constructed by applying least squares fitting techniques to the performance data.

Resource Monitor Task   A task that ensures sequential access to a resource.

RTSA   Real-Time Structured Analysis

RTSAD   Real-Time Structured Analysis and Design

SAD   Software Architecture Diagram

SCD   System Context Diagram

SD   Structured Design

SDM   Software Decision Module

Sequential Cohesion   A task structuring criterion in which transformations that perform operations in a sequential order are mapped to a task (as used in DARTS/ADARTS/CODARTS).

Sequential Task Inversion   An optimization technique where tasks are combined such that the producer task calls an operation provided by the consumer rather than send it a message.

Simulation Model   An algorithmic representation of a system reflecting system structure and behavior, which explicitly recognizes the passage of time, hence providing a means of analyzing the behavior of the system over time.

Software architecture diagram (SAD)   A graphical notation showing a network of concurrent tasks and information hiding modules, explicitly showing the operations provided by the modules. Intertask interfaces, in the form of message communication and event synchronization, are also shown.

Software Decision Module (SDM)   An information hiding module that hides a software design decision that is likely to change.

State Transition Diagram (STD)   A graphical representation of a finite state machine in which the nodes represent states and the arcs represent transitions between them.

State Transition Module (STM)   An information hiding module that hides the contents of a state transition table.

State Transition Table (STT)   A tabular representation of a finite state machine.

STD   State Transition Diagram

SRS   Software Requirements Specification

STM   State Transition Module

Structure Chart   A diagram used in Structured Design and DARTS to show how a program or task is decomposed into modules, where a module is typically a procedure or function.

Structured Design (SD)   A design method used for functionally decomposing a program into modules and defining the interfaces between them.

STT   State Transition Table

Synchronizing task   An Ada support task used to synchronize access to data maintained by a data abstraction package.

System Context Diagram (SCD)   [See context diagram]

System Value Module   An information hiding module that computes a set of values, some of which are used by more than one function driver module.

TAD   Task Architecture Diagram

Task [Also concurrent task, process]   A task represents the execution of a sequential program or a sequential component of a concurrent program. Each task deals with a sequential thread of execution; there is no concurrency within a task.

Task Architecture Diagram (TAD)   A graphical notation showing a network of concurrent tasks and their interfaces, in the form of loosely-coupled and tightly-coupled message communication, event synchronization, and information hiding modules.

Task Behavior Specification (TBS)   A specification that describes a concurrent task's interface, structure, timing characteristics, relative priority, event sequencing logic, and errors detected.

Task Cohesion Criteria   This category of the task structuring criteria addresses whether and how transformations should be combined into concurrent tasks.

Task Interface   This is usually a message, event, or an information hiding module.

Task Inversion   An optimization concept that originated in JSP, whereby the tasks in a system can be combined in a systematic way.

Task Priority Criteria   This category of the task structuring criteria addresses the importance of executing a given task relative to others.

Task Structuring   A stage in system design where the objective is to structure the system into concurrent tasks and define the task interfaces.

Task Structuring Criteria   A set of heuristics for assisting a designer in structuring a system into concurrent tasks.

TBS   Task Behavior Specification

Temporal Cohesion   A task structuring criterion that groups transformations, which are not sequentially dependent but are activated by the same event, into a task.

Temporal Task Inversion   The case where two or more periodic, periodic I/O and/or periodic temporally cohesive tasks are combined into one task for optimization purposes.

Terminators   External entities that the system has to interface to, typically shown on a system context diagram.

Tightly-coupled Message Communication   The case where a producer task sends a message to a consumer task and then immediately waits for an acknowledgement.

Tightly-coupled Message Communication With Reply   The case when a producer task sends a message to a consumer task and then waits for a reply.

Tightly-coupled Message Communication Without Reply   The case where a producer task sends a message to a consumer task and then waits for acceptance of the message by the consumer.

Timed Petri Nets   A Petri Net that allows finite times to be associated with the firing of transitions.

Timer Event   A stimulus used for the periodic activation of an active component, e.g., task.

Timing Diagram   A diagram that shows the time-ordered execution sequence of a group of tasks.

Transaction Analysis   A design strategy used for mapping a dataflow diagram to a structure chart.

Transform Analysis   A design strategy used for mapping a dataflow diagram to a structure chart.

Transformation   A function or object on a dataflow/control flow diagram developed using Real-Time Structured Analysis or COBRA. [See data transformation]

Trigger Event Flow   An internal control signal that may originate from the external environment, or be generated by a data transformation or control transformation.

User Role Object   An object that models a sequence of related actions performed sequentially by a user.

User Role Task   A task that executes a sequence of user actions.

Uses Hierarchy   A hierarchy of operations (access procedures or functions) provided by the information hiding modules.

Utilization Bound Theorem   A real-time scheduling theorem that states the conditions under which a set of n independent periodic tasks scheduled by the rate monotonic algorithm will always meet their deadlines.

Annotated Bibliography

[Agresti86] Agresti, W. W., *New Paradigms for Software Development.* (Los Alamitos, CA: IEEE Computer Society Press, 1986).
A very good collection of papers covering critiques of the conventional software life-cycle model, prototyping, operational specification, and transformational implementation.

[Alford85] Alford, M., "SREM at the Age of Eight: The Distributed Computing Design System," *Computer,* Vol. 18, No. 4, April 1985, pp. 36–46.
Provides a good overview of the DCDS method.

[Allworth87] Allworth, S. T., and R. N. Zobel, *Introduction to Real-Time Software Design,* Second Edition. (New York: Springer Verlag, 1987).
A good introductory book on real-time system design, although much of the discussion is concerned with detailed design issues. Also good coverage of the MASCOT notation and hardware interfacing issues.

[Balzer83] Balzer R., et al., "Software Technology in the 1990s: Using a New Paradigm," *IEEE Computer,* November 1983.
Advocates a revolutionary paradigm for software development using a transformational approach.

[Basili75] Basili, B. R., and A. J. Turner. "Iterative Enhancement: A Practical Technique for Software Development." *IEEE Transactions Software Engineering SE-1,* 4 (Dec. 1975), pp. 390–396.
One of the first papers to advocate the incremental development approach to software engineering.

[Beilner72] Beilner, H., and G. Waldbaum, "Statistical Methodology for Calibrating a Trace-Driven Simulator of a Batch Computer System," in *Statistical Computer Performance Evaluation,* ed. W. Freiberger (New York: Academic Press, 1972).
Describes a semi-automated methodology based on several statistical methods for calibrating a performance model of a computer system.

[Beizer84] Beizer, B., *Software System Testing and Quality Assurance.* (New York: Van Nostrand, 1984).
A comprehensive introduction to the field of software testing, covering all its stages.

[Bic88] Bic, L., and A. C. Shaw, *The Logical Design of Operating Systems.* (Englewood Cliffs, N.J.: Prentice Hall, 1988).
A good reference book on operating systems.

[Boehm76] Boehm, B., "Software Engineering," *IEEE Transactions on Computers,* December 1976.
A classical paper on the waterfall model of the software life cycle.

[Boehm81] Boehm, B., *Software Engineering Economics.* (Englewood Cliffs, N.J.: Prentice Hall, 1981).
A detailed reference on software cost estimation using the basic, intermediate, and detailed COCOMO cost estimation models.

[Boehm88] Boehm, B., "A Spiral Model of Software Development and Enhancement," *IEEE Computer,* 21 (5), 61–72, May 1988.
Describes the spiral software life cycle model with its emphasis on risk analysis at several stages in the life cycle.

[Booch86] Booch, G., "Object-Oriented Development," *IEEE Transactions on Software Engineering,* February 1986.
This paper presents an overview of Object-Oriented Design, as viewed in the Ada world; that is, with emphasis on information hiding but not inheritance. The paper also outlines how a Structured Analysis specification can be mapped to OOD. This paper is also included in [Booch87b].

[Booch87a] Booch, G., *Software Engineering with Ada,* Second Edition. (Menlo Park, CA: Benjamin Cummings, 1987).
Describes the Ada programming language and its use, with particular emphasis on the features of the language that support large scale software system development, such as packages, tasks, and generics.

[Booch87b] Booch, G., *Software Components with Ada.* (Menlo Park, CA: Benjamin Cummings, 1987).
This book presents a large collection of Ada packages that form the basis of a software reuse library. It advocates a "software by composition" approach to software development.

[Booch91] Booch, G., *Object-Oriented Design with Applications.* (Menlo Park, CA: Benjamin Cummings, 1991).
A comprehensive book on one version of the Object-Oriented Design method with several detailed case studies.

[Brackett89] Brackett, J., "Software Requirements." *SEI Curriculum Module SEI-CM-19.* Software Engineering Institute, Carnegie Mellon University, Pittsburgh, Pa., 1989.
An excellent introduction to software requirements in a format intended primarily for educators.

[BrinchHansen73] Brinch Hansen, P., *Operating System Principles,* (Englewood Cliffs, N.J.: Prentice Hall, 1973).
A classical book on operating systems, although now somewhat dated.

[Britton81] Britton, K., R. Parker, and D. Parnas, "A Procedure for Designing Abstract Interfaces for Device Interface Modules," *Proceedings, Fifth International Conference on Software Engineering,* March 1981.
Describes the application of the information hiding concept to the design of device interface modules.

[Brooks75] Brooks, F., *The Mythical Man-Month.* (Reading, Mass.: Addison-Wesley, 1975).
A true classic covering the problems that are frequently encountered in developing and managing large-scale software systems, based on the author's actual experience managing the development of IBM's OS/360 operating system.

[Bruyn88] Bruyn, W., R. Jensen, D. Keskar, and P. Ward, "ESML: An Extended Systems Modeling Language," *ACM Software Engineering Notes* Vol. 13, No. 1, January 1988, pp. 58–67.
This paper presents the basic features of the Extended Systems Modeling Language (ESML), an attempt to merge the Ward/Mellor and Boeing/Hatley approaches to Real-Time Structured Analysis.

[Budgen88] Budgen, D., "Introduction to Software Design," *SEI Curriculum Module SEI-CM-2.* Software Engineering Institute, Carnegie Mellon University, Pittsburgh, Pa.
A very good introduction to software design in a format intended primarily for educators.

[Buhr84] Buhr, R., *System Development with Ada.* (Englewood Cliffs, N.J.: Prentice Hall, 1984).
This book presents a design-oriented introduction to Ada, with special emphasis on concurrent processing. Introduces a graphical design notation, the structure graph, that has gained widespread acceptance in the Ada community.

[Burns89] Burns, A., and A. J. Wellings, *Real-time Systems and Their Programming Languages.* (Reading, Mass.: Addison-Wesley, 1989).
An excellent book providing a comprehensive description of real-time systems and issues involved in programming these systems.

[Cameron86] Cameron, J., "An Overview of JSD," *IEEE Transactions on Software Engineering.* February 1986.
A clear summary of JSD. As the method has evolved, the steps described are slightly different from [Jackson83]. The method is illustrated by means of a detailed library example. This paper is also included in [Cameron89].

[Cameron89] Cameron, J., *JSP and JSD: The Jackson Approach to Software Development,* Second Edition. (Los Alamitos, CA: IEEE Computer Society Press, 1989).
A collection of articles and papers describing JSP and JSD and illustrating these methods using a range of examples of reasonable size and complexity. Covers the latest developments in JSD and has some interesting papers on JSD applied to real-time systems included, as well as papers addressing mapping JSD specifications to MASCOT and Ada. Also includes a comparison of JSD with OOD.

[Chen76] Chen P., "The Entity Relationship Model—Towards a Unified View of Data," *ACM Transactions on Database Systems,* 1 (1), 9–36, 1976.
An often-quoted paper that introduces Entity Relationship Modeling, which is widely used in logical database design, Structured Analysis, and Object-Oriented Analysis.

[Coad91] Coad, P., and E. Yourdon, *Object-Oriented Analysis.* (Englewood Cliffs, N.J.: Prentice Hall, 1991).
A popular introductory book on Object-Oriented Analysis. Provides a useful description of object structuring criteria.

[Coad92] Coad, P., and E. Yourdon, *Object-Oriented Design.* (Englewood Cliffs, N.J.: Prentice Hall, 1992).
A concise and somewhat limited view of Object-Oriented Design.

[Cobb90] Cobb, R. H., and H. D. Mills, "Engineering Software under Statistical Quality Control," *IEEE Software,* November 1990.
An interesting paper describing the Cleanroom Engineering approach to software development with its emphasis on formal verification and statistical usage testing.

[Cochran&Gomaa91] Cochran, M., and H. Gomaa, "Validating the ADARTS Software Design Method for Real-time Systems," *Proceedings ACM Tri-Ada Conference,* San Jose, Calif., October 1991.
Describes the validation exercise carried out applying ADARTS to a real-world real-time problem, and the lessons learned.

[Coolahan83] Coolahan, J., and N. Roussopoulos, "Timing Requirements for Time-Driven Systems Using Augmented Petri Nets," *IEEE Transactions on Software Engineering,* September 1983, pp. 603–616.
This paper describes extensions to Petri Nets to handle timing requirements for real-time systems.

[Cooling91] Cooling, J. E., *Software Design for Real-time Systems.* (London: Chapman and Hall, 1991).
A broad perspective on real-time systems, including languages and operating systems for real-time systems, development tools, and software life cycle aspects. Includes chapters on program design concepts, diagramming methodologies in software design, and software analysis and design: methods, methodologies, and tools.

[Courtois71] Courtois, P. J., F. Heymans, and D. L. Parnas, "Concurrent Control with Readers and Writers," *Communications ACM,* Vol. 10, October 1971, pp. 667–668.
An early version of the multiple readers/multiple writers algorithm.

[Dart87] Dart, S., R. Ellison, P. Feiler, and N. Habermann, "Software Development Environments," *IEEE Computer,* Vol. 20, No. 11, pp. 18–28.
An excellent introduction to and survey of software development environments.

[Davis88] Davis, A., "A Comparison of Techniques for the Specification of External System Behavior," *Communications ACM,* Vol. 31, No. 9, pp. 1098–1115, September 1988.
A summary of [Davis90].

[Davis90] Davis, A., *Software Requirements: Analysis and Specification.* (Englewood Cliffs, N.J.: Prentice Hall, 1990).
An excellent survey and comparison of different requirements analysis and specification techniques. Includes data flow diagrams, finite state machines, Petri Nets, and statecharts.

[DeMarco78] DeMarco, T., *Structured Analysis and System Specification.* (Englewood Cliffs, N.J.: Prentice Hall, 1978).
A very popular book on Structured Analysis, although a more up-to-date treatment of the subject is given in [Yourdon89].

[Dijkstra68] Dijkstra, E. W., "Co-operating Sequential Processes," in F. Genuys (ed.), *Programming Languages,* (New York: Academic Press, 1968, pp. 43–112).
A classical paper which first introduced the concept of concurrent processes and process synchronization using semaphores. Illustrated by means of several examples.

[Fagan76] Fagan, M., "Design and Code Inspections to Reduce Errors in Program Development," *I.B.M. Systems Journal,* Vol. 15, No. 3, 1976.
A comprehensive description of formal inspections, a more systematic approach to design and code reviews.

[Fairley85] Fairley, R., *Software Engineering Concepts.* (New York: McGraw Hill, 1985).
One of the best textbooks on software engineering available. Describes the basic concepts and major issues in the field. Contains a chapter on design that covers fundamental design concepts, design notations, and design methods.

[Faulk88] Faulk, S. R., and D. L. Parnas, "On Synchronization in Hard Real-time Systems," *Communications ACM,* March 1988.
A detailed description of how concurrent tasks are supported in the NRL method.

[Freeman83a] Freeman, P., "The Context of Design," in [Freeman83c].
An interesting discussion of the role of software design in software development.

[Freeman83b] Freeman, P., "The Nature of Design," in [Freeman83c].
An interesting discussion of what software design is; it also surveys different design methods and reviews fundamental design activities.

[Freeman83c] Freeman, P., and A. I. Wasserman, eds. *Software Design Techniques,* Fourth Edition. (Los Alamitos, CA: IEEE Computer Society Press, 1983).
A wide-ranging collection of papers on software design covering basic concepts, analysis and specification, architectural design, detailed design, and management issues.

[Gane79] Gane, C., and T. Sarson, *Structured Systems Analysis: Tools and Techniques.* (Englewood Cliffs, N.J.: Prentice Hall, 1979).
A popular book on Structured Analysis, although a more up-to-date treatment of the subject is given in [Yourdon89].

[Gehani84] Gehani, N., *Ada Concurrent Programming.* (Englewood Cliffs, N.J.: Prentice Hall, 1984).
A good book on concurrency in Ada. Several examples are covered, including the multiple readers/writers problem.

[Glass83] Glass, R. L., ed. *Real-time Software.* (Englewood Cliffs, N.J.: Prentice-Hall, 1983).
An interesting and varied collection of papers and articles on real-time software.

[Goldberg83] Goldberg, A., and D. Robson, *Smalltalk-80: The Language and Its Implementation.* (Reading, Mass.: Addison-Wesley, 1983).
A detailed reference on Smalltalk-80.

[Gomaa77] Gomaa, H., "A Hybrid Simulation/Regression Modelling Approach for Evaluating Multiprogramming Computer Systems," in *Computer Performance,* Ed. K. M. Chandy and M. Reiser, (Amsterdam: North Holland, 1977).
Describes regression models and hybrid simulation/regression models used for evaluating the performance of computer systems.

[Gomaa78] Gomaa, H., "The Calibration and Validation of a Hybrid Simulation/Regression Model of a Batch Computer System," *Software, Practice and Experience,* Vol. 8, No. 1, 1978. Describes how the statistical methodology described in [Beilner72] was used for the calibration and validation of a hybrid simulation/regression trace-driven performance model.

[Gomaa81a] Gomaa, H., "Prototyping as a Tool in the Specification of User Requirements," *Proceedings of the Fifth International Conference on Software Engineering,* 1981. Describes how prototyping may be used to assist in the Requirements Specification process with a detailed case study.

[Gomaa81b] Gomaa, H., "A Hybrid Simulation/Regression Model of a Virtual Storage Computer System," *The Computer Journal,* November 1981. Describes how the hybrid simulation/regression modeling approach was extended and applied to a virtual storage system.

[Gomaa82a] Gomaa, H., "The Impact of Rapid Prototyping on Specifying User Requirements," *Proceedings of the ACM Workshop on Rapid Prototyping,* April 1982. Describes a prototyping based method for requirements specification and gives an example of its use.

[Gomaa82b] Gomaa, H., "A Partially Automated Method for Testing Interactive Systems," *Proceedings IEEE Conference on Computer Software and Applications (Compsac) Conference,* Chicago, Il., November 1982. Describes a method for combined black box/white box testing of a concurrent interactive system, including a detailed description of developing scripts for automated functional testing.

[Gomaa84] Gomaa, H., "A Software Design Method for Real-time Systems," *Communications ACM,* September 1984. This was the first paper to describe the DARTS design method. The method is illustrated by means of an example of a robot controller system. A later version of the method is given in [Gomaa87]. The task structuring criteria are refined in this book.

[Gomaa86a] Gomaa, H., "Software Development of Real-time Systems," *Communications ACM,* July 1986. This paper describes how DARTS is used in a software life cycle context for real-time systems. The paper also describes the use of event sequence diagrams to assist in incremental development.

[Gomaa86b] Gomaa, H., "Prototypes—Keep Them or Throw Them Away?", *State of the Art Report on Prototyping,* Pergamon Infotech Ltd., 1986. This paper points out the differences between throw-away prototyping and evolutionary prototyping and the need for very different approaches in applying these techniques.

[Gomaa87] Gomaa, H., "Using the DARTS Software Design Method for Real-time Systems," *Proceedings of the Twelfth Structured Methods Conference,* Chicago, August 1987. This paper describes how DARTS may be used in conjunction with Real-Time Structured Analysis. The robot controller example [Gomaa84] is updated to reflect this.

[Gomaa89a] Gomaa, H., "A Software Design Method for Distributed Real-time Applications," *Journal of Systems and Software,* February 1989. This paper extends DARTS to address the design of distributed real-time applications. The new method, DARTS/DA is illustrated by means of a factory automation example.

[Gomaa89b] Gomaa, H., "Structuring Criteria for Real-time System Design," *Proceedings of the Eleventh International Conference on Software Engineering,* May 1989.
Describes the task and module structuring criteria used by different real-time design methods including RTSAD, NRL, OOD, and DARTS. Integrates the task structuring criteria of DARTS with the information module structuring criteria of NRL and OOD into a new method called ADARTS.

[Gomaa89c] Gomaa, H., "A Software Design Method for Ada-based Real-time Systems," *Proceedings of ACM Washington Ada Symposium,* June 1989.
A description of the ADARTS method with particular reference to Ada-based real-time systems.

[Gomaa93] Gomaa, H., "A Reuse-oriented Approach for Structuring and Configuring Distributed Applications," *IEE/BCS Software Engineering Journal,* March 1993.
This paper describes an approach for developing reusable specifications and architectures from which target systems are generated.

[Harel87] Harel, D., "Statecharts: A Visual Approach to Complex Systems," *Science of Computer Programming,* 1987.
A description of the basic concepts of Statecharts, illustrated by means of a detailed example of a digital watch. A broader perspective on statecharts is given in [Harel88b].

[Harel88a] Harel, D., et al. "STATEMATE: A Working Environment for the Development of Complex Reactive Systems." *Proceedings of the Tenth International Conference on Software Engineering.* (Los Alamitos, CA: IEEE Computer Society Press, 1988), pp. 496–506.
A good overview of the Statemate tool. Also describes how statecharts have been incorporated into Statemate.

[Harel88b] Harel, D., "On Visual Formalisms." *CACM* Vol. 31, No. 5 (May 1988), pp. 514–530.
This paper describes a number of important issues concerning design representation. The paper discusses general issues as well as presenting a good introduction to statecharts, illustrated by the digital watch example.

[Hatley88] Hatley, D., and I. Pirbhai, *Strategies for Real-time System Specification.* (New York: Dorset House, 1988).
A comprehensive description of the Boeing/Hatley approach to Real-Time Structured Analysis. The method is illustrated by means of several examples including the cruise control system and home heating system.

[Heninger80] Heninger, K., "Specifying Software Requirements for Complex Systems: New Techniques and Their Applications," *IEEE Transactions on Software Engineering,* SE-6, 1, January 1980, pp. 2–13.
An overview of the NRL black-box Requirements Specification method with examples from the A7-E aircraft project.

[Hoare74] Hoare, C. A. R., "Monitors: An Operating System Structuring Concept," *Communications ACM,* Vol. 17, No. 10, October 1974, pp. 549–557.
A classical paper on operating systems that introduces the monitor concept.

[Hoare85] Hoare, C. A. R., *Communicating Sequential Processes.* (Englewood Cliffs, N.J.: Prentice Hall, 1985).
This book describes a formal method for specifying communicating sequential processes.

[HOOD89] "HOOD User Manual." Issue 3.0, WME/89-353/JB, HOOD Working Group, European Space Agency, December 1989.
Describes the Hierarchical Object-Oriented Design Method. There is also a HOOD Reference Manual published by the same agency.

[IEEE83] *IEEE Standard Glossary of Software Engineering Terminology.* ANSI/IEEE/Std729-1983, Institute of Electrical and Electronic Engineers, 1983.
This IEEE standard provides definitions for many of the terms used in software engineering.

[Jackson75] Jackson, M., *Principles of Program Design.* (New York: Academic Press, 1975).
The original source book on JSP, although JSP is also covered in detail in [Cameron89].

[Jackson83] Jackson, M., *System Development.* (Englewood Cliffs, N.J.: Prentice Hall, 1983).
The original source book on JSD. A more current version of the method is given in [Cameron86] and [Cameron89]. The book is rather difficult to read as the description of the method is intertwined with three worked examples. The elevator example has been extracted and included in [Sanden89].

[Kato87] Kato, J., and Y. Morisawa, Direct Execution of a JSD Specification, *Proceedings of IEEE Compsac,* Tokyo, October 1987.
Describes a tool to support the execution of JSD specifications.

[Kelly87] Kelly J., "A Comparison of Four Design Methods for Real-time Systems," *Proceedings of the Ninth International Conference on Software Engineering,* March 1987.
Provides a framework for comparing real time design methods. Uses this framework to compare RTSAD, PAMELA, OOD, and NRL methods.

[Kleinrock75] Kleinrock, L., *Queueing Systems, Volume 1.* (New York: John Wiley & Sons, 1975).
The classical reference on queueing theory for analyzing and predicting computer system performance.

[Kramer85] Kramer, J., and J. Magee, "Dynamic Configuration for Distributed Systems," *IEEE Transactions on Software Engineering,* April 1985.
A very interesting paper describing the CONIC distributed programming environment, with its separation of the development of distributed software components from the specification of distributed system configurations consisting of predefined components.

[Lamb88] Lamb, D. A., *Software Engineering: Planning for Change.* (Englewood Cliffs, N.J.: Prentice Hall, 1988).
This book provides a very good introduction to many of the ideas of David Parnas that formed the basis of the NRL method.

[Lehoczy89] Lehoczy, J. P., L. Sha, and Y. Ding, "The Rate Monotonic Scheduling Algorithm: Exact Characterization and and Average Case Behavior," *Proceedings of IEEE Real-time Systems Symposium,* San Jose, CA, December 1987.
Presents an in-depth mathematical analysis of the rate monotonic scheduling algorithm, including a mathematical formulation of the Completion Time Theorem.

[Liu73] Liu, C. L., and J. W. Layland, "Scheduling Algorithms for Multiprogramming in Hard Real-Time Environments," *Journal ACM,* Vol. 20, No. 1, January 1973. Also in [Stankovic88].
The classical reference on real-time scheduling. Includes the mathematical analysis and proof of the Utilization Bound Theorem.

[Lubars87] Lubars, M. D., and M. T. Harandi, "Knowledge-based Software Design Using Design Schemas," *Proceedings of the Ninth International Conference on Software Engineering,* March 1987.
An interesting paper addressing a promising area of research, namely domain modeling.

[Magee89] J. Magee, J. Kramer, and M. Sloman, "Constructing Distributed Systems in Conic," *IEEE Transactions on Software Engineering,* June 1989.
A later paper on the CONIC distributed programming environment, which separates the development of distributed software components from the specification of distributed system configurations consisting of predefined components.

[Martin85] Martin, J., and C. McClure, *Structured Techniques for Computing.* (Englewood Cliffs, N.J.: Prentice Hall, 1985).
A wide-ranging survey of several diagramming techniques and design methods. Compares JSP, Structured Analysis/Design and Warnier/Orr method. The book is oriented towards information systems.

[McCabe85] McCabe, T., and G. Schulmeyer, "System Testing Aided by Structured Analysis: A Practical Experience," *IEEE Transactions on Software Engineering,* Vol. SE-11, No. 9, September 1985, pp. 917–921.
Describes an approach for deriving system test cases from a Structured Analysis specification.

[McCracken82], McCracken, D., and M. Jackson, "Life Cycle Concept Considered Harmful," *ACM Software Engineering Notes,* Vol. 7(2), pp. 28–32.
A brief note advocating an evolutionary prototyping approach to software development.

[Meyer87] Meyer, B., "Reusability: The Case for Object-Oriented Design," *IEEE Software,* March 1987.
An excellent paper describing the benefits of inheritance in Object-Oriented Design. Illustrated by means of a detailed example of an airline reservation system. The material is covered in more detail in [Meyer88].

[Meyer88] Meyer B., *Object-Oriented Software Construction.* (Englewood Cliffs, N.J.: Prentice Hall, 1988).
A comprehensive description of designing object-oriented systems using inheritance in addition to information hiding. Several examples are given using the object oriented programming language Eiffel.

[Mills86] Mills, H. D., R. C. Linger, and A. R. Hevner, *Principles of Information Systems Analysis and Design.* (New York: Academic Press, 1986).
A comprehensive description of the Box-Structured Information System design method.

[Myers78] Myers, G., *Composite/Structured Design.* (New York: Van Nostrand Reinhold, 1978).
An early book on the Structured Design method by one of its developers. The book introduces the information hiding concept as a module cohesion criterion, something still not done in later books, e.g. [Page-Jones88].

[Myers79] Myers, G., *The Art of Software Testing.* (New York: John Wiley, 1979).
A good introduction to the field of software testing, covering all stages of software testing.

[Nielsen88] Nielsen, K., and K. Shumate, *Designing Large Real-Time Systems with Ada*. (New York: McGraw Hill, 1988).
A detailed book for those interested in developing Ada-based real-time systems. Addresses many Ada-specific issues. The design method is based on DARTS [Gomaa84]. Several detailed case studies include the robot controller example [Gomaa84] and an air traffic control system.

[Nutt92] Nutt, G., *Centralized and Distributed Operating Systems*. (Englewood Cliffs, N.J.: Prentice Hall, 1992).
A good up-to-date book on operating systems with about half the book devoted to distributed operating systems, a topic of growing interest and importance.

[Orr77] Orr, K., *Structured Systems Development*. (Englewood Cliffs, N.J.: Prentice Hall, 1977).
This book describes a data structured approach to software design based on the Warnier method, in which the program structure is based on the data structure of the output.

[Page-Jones88] Page-Jones, M., *The Practical Guide to Structured Systems Design*, Second Edition. (Englewood Cliffs, N.J.: Prentice Hall, 1988).
Probably the most readable of the books on Structured Design. Also has an overview of Structured Analysis. However, the book does not cover recent developments in design methods. Unfortunately, unlike [Myers78], it views information hiding as a design heuristic rather than a module cohesion criterion.

[Parnas72] Parnas, D., "On the Criteria for Decomposing a System into Modules," *Communications ACM*, December 1972.
A classical paper that introduces the concept of information hiding as a software design criterion.

[Parnas74] Parnas, D., "On a 'Buzzword': Hierarchical Structure," *Proceedings of IFIP Congress 1974*. (Amsterdam: North-Holland Publishing Company, 1974), pp. 336–339.
An infrequently referenced paper that describes in more detail the interesting view that a software system consists of three orthogonal structures: the information hiding module structure [Parnas84], the uses structure [Parnas79] and the concurrent task structure [Faulk88]. A paper that should be read by all system designers, particularly those who believe that the same structuring criteria may be used for tasks and information hiding modules.

[Parnas79] Parnas, D., "Designing Software for Ease of Extension and Contraction," *IEEE Transactions on Software Engineering*, March 1979.
An important paper that describes the uses structure, a hierarchy of operations provided by modules, and how this structure may be used for determining subsets and extensions of a software system.

[Parnas84] Parnas, D., P. Clements, and D. Weiss, "The Modular Structure of Complex Systems," *Proceedings of the Seventh IEEE International Conference on Software Engineering*, Orlando, Florida, March 1984.
A very important paper that describes the application of the information hiding concept to the design of a complex real-time system. Detailed example of the onboard flight program for the A7-E aircraft.

[Parnas85] Parnas, D., and D. Weiss, "Active Design Reviews: Principles and Practices," *Proceedings of the Eighth IEEE International Conference on Software Engineering,* London, England, September 1985.
An interesting paper that advocates a highly participatory role by design reviewers.

[Parnas86] Parnas, D., and P. Clements, "A Rational Design Process: How and Why to Fake it," *IEEE Transactions on Software Engineering,* Vol. SE-12, No. 2, February 1986.
A clear overview of the NRL method that also describes the rationale behind it and stresses the importance of documentation throughout the life cycle. Several aspects of the method are described in more detail in other papers, e.g., [Parnas84].

[Peterson81] Peterson, J., *Petri Net Theory and the Modeling of Systems.* (Englewood Cliffs, N.J.: Prentice-Hall, 1981).
An excellent reference book on Petri nets, providing a readable treatment of the subject, with many examples.

[Peterson91] Peterson J., A. Silberschatz, and P. Galvin, *Operating System Concepts,* Third Edition. (Reading, Mass.: Addison-Wesley, 1991).
A very good reference book on operating systems.

[Pressman91] Pressman, R., *Software Engineering: A Practitioner's Approach,* Third Edition. (New York: McGraw-Hill, 1991).
A very good introduction to software engineering. Also has chapters on several design methods including Structured Analysis and Design, DARTS, Object-Oriented Design, and JSD.

[Prieto-Diaz87] Prieto-Diaz, R., "Domain Analysis for Reusability," *Proceedings of COMPSAC'87,* 1987.
An interesting paper that presents an approach to analyzing application domains.

[Renold89] Renold, A., "Jackson System Development for Real-time Systems," in [Cameron89].
A good description of how JSD may be used for designing real-time systems. Also includes a comparison of JSD with Structured Analysis/Design and DARTS.

[Rumbaugh91] Rumbaugh, J., M. Blaha, W. Premerlani, F. Eddy, and W. Lorensen, *Object-Oriented Modeling and Design.* (Englewood Cliffs, N.J.: Prentice Hall, 1991.)
One of the best books on Object-Oriented Analysis and Modeling. Gives a comprehensive treatment of both information modeling and statecharts applied to object modeling.

[Sage90] Sage, A. P., and J. D. Palmer, *Software Systems Engineering.* (New York: John Wiley & Sons, 1990).
An interesting book that takes a systems-based approach to software development, with considerable discussion of software quality, software reliability, development environments, integration, maintenance, management, and cost analysis.

[Sanden89] Sanden, B., "An Entity Life Modeling approach to the Design of Concurrent Software," *Communications ACM,* March 1989.
Describes a variation on JSD that addresses the design of concurrent and real-time systems, and also maps directly to Ada. Illustrates the method by comparing it to JSD using Jackson's elevator example [Jackson83].

[Sanden93] Sanden, B., *Software Systems Construction.* (Englewood Cliffs, N.J.: Prentice Hall, 1993).
A comprehensive and interesting book describing the construction of sequential and concurrent programs in Ada using an approach based on Jackson System Development and Jackson Structured Programming.

[SEI93] Carnegie Mellon University Software Engineering Institute, "A Practioner's Handbook for Real-Time Analysis—Guide to Rate Monotonic Analysis for Real-Time Systems," Kluwer Academic Publishers, Boston, 1993.
A comprehensive and detailed handbook on applying real-time scheduling to analyze the performance of real-time systems, with many examples.

[Seidewitz89] Seidewitz, E., "General Object-Oriented Software Development with Ada: A Lifecycle Approach," *Journal of Systems and Software,* February 1989.
An interesting paper on the GOOD method, describing its application of entity-relationship modeling to help identify objects in the problem domain.

[Sha90] Sha, L., and J. B. Goodenough, "Real-time Scheduling Theory and Ada," *IEEE Computer,* Vol. 23, No. 4, April 1990. Also *CMU/SEI-89-TR-14,* Software Engineering Institute, Pittsburgh, Pa., 1989.
A very readable and informative paper on a complex and highly relevant topic in real-time system design. An excellent introduction to real-time scheduling theory.

[Shlaer88] Shlaer, S., and S. Mellor, *Object-Oriented Systems Analysis.* (Englewood Cliffs, N.J.: Prentice Hall, 1988).
A rather narrow view of object-oriented analysis concentrating on semantic data modeling. However, the treatment given is readable though somewhat introductory.

[Simpson79] Simpson, H., and K. Jackson, "Process Synchronization in MASCOT," *The Computer Journal,* Vol. 17, No. 4, 1979.
An early paper on MASCOT, concentrating on the concurrent task synchronization aspects of MASCOT.

[Simpson86] Simpson, H., "The MASCOT Method," *IEE/BCS Software Engineering Journal,* Vol. 1, No. 3, 1986, pp. 103–120.
A more recent paper on MASCOT that covers the extensions and notation for MASCOT 3.

[Smith90] Smith, C. U., *Performance Engineering of Software Systems.* (Reading, Mass.: Addison-Wesley, 1990).
A comprehensive and practical book on the performance analysis and modeling of software systems, with numerous examples.

[Sommerville92] Sommerville, I., *Software Engineering.* (Reading, Mass.: Addison-Wesley, 1992).
A comprehensive and up-to-date treatment of software engineering.

[Sprunt89] Sprunt, B., J. P. Lehoczy, and L. Sha, "Aperiodic Task Scheduling for Hard Real-time Systems," *The Journal of Real-time Systems,* Vol. 1 (1989), pp. 27–60.
Describes the extensions to real-time scheduling theory to address aperiodic tasks in addition to periodic tasks.

[Stankovic88] Stankovic, J. A., and K. Ramamritham, *Hard Real-time Systems.* (Washington, D.C.: IEEE Computer Society Press, 1988).
A wide-ranging collection of papers covering the specification, design, and analysis of real-time systems, with particular emphasis on real-time languages, real-time operating systems, architecture and hardware, communication, real-time scheduling, and fault tolerance.

[Stroustrup86] Stroustrup, B., *The C++ Programming Language.* (Reading, Mass.: Addison-Wesley, 1986).
A comprehensive reference book on this object-oriented language.

[Tai91] Tai, K. C., Carver, R. H., and Obaid, E. E., "Debugging Concurrent Ada Programs by Deterministic Execution," *IEEE Transactions on Software Engineering,* January 1991.
Presents an interesting approach to testing concurrent systems.

[Tanenbaum92] Tanenbaum, A. S., *Modern Operating Systems.* (Englewood Cliffs, N.J.: Prentice Hall, 1992).
A comprehensive and up-to-date book on operating systems covering both traditional and distributed operating systems.

[Tsai88] Tsai, J., and J. Ridge, "Intelligent Support for Specifications Transformation," *IEEE Software,* November 1988, pp. 28–36.
Presents a knowledge-based approach for mapping data flow diagrams to structure charts.

[Ward85] Ward, P., and S. Mellor, *Structured Development for Real-time Systems,* Four Volumes. (Englewood Cliffs, N.J.: Prentice Hall, 1985).
A comprensive treatment of the Ward/Mellor approach to Real-Time Structured Analysis and Design.

[Ward86] Ward, P., "The Transformation Schema: An Extension of the Data Flow Diagram to Represent Control and Timing," *IEEE Transactions of Software Engineering,* Vol. SE-12, No. 2, February 1986.
An overview of Real-Time Structured Analysis with some refinement and terminology changes in the notation of [Ward85].

[Wegner87] Wegner, P., "Dimensions of Object-based Language Design," *Proceedings of ACM OOPSLA,* 1987.
An interesting paper giving a comprehensive taxonomy of languages supporting objects. Provides a clear overview of object-oriented concepts and how they are supported by object-oriented languages.

[Wegner90] Wegner, P., "Concepts and Paradigms of Object-Oriented Programming," *OOPS Messenger,* ACM Press, Vol. 1, No. 1, August 1990.
A comprehensive and updated version of [Wegner87] also addressing the important issues of concurrency in Object-Oriented Programming.

[Wirfs-Brock90] Wirfs-Brock, R., B. Wilkerson, and L. Wiener, *Designing Object-Oriented Software.* (Englewood Cliffs, N.J.: Prentice Hall, 1990).
A useful book on designing object-oriented programs.

[Yourdon79] Yourdon, E., and L. Constantine, *Structured Design,* Second Edition. (Englewood Cliffs, N.J.: Prentice Hall, 1979).
The classical text on Structured Design, although somewhat dated and not as readable as [Page-Jones88].

[Yourdon89] Yourdon, E., *Modern Structured Analysis.* (Englewood Cliffs, N.J.: Prentice Hall, 1989).
Probably the most comprehensive and up-to-date book on the popular Structured Analysis method. Includes material on the real time extensions to Structured Analysis and entity-relationship modeling. There are also two detailed case studies.

[Zave84] Zave, P., "The Operational Versus the Conventional Approach to Software Development," *Communications ACM,* February 1984.
This paper advocates an alternative approach to software development in which a problem-oriented executable operational specification is developed, followed by a transformation phase that results in an implementation-oriented specification. A characteristic of the operational specification is that, in order to be executable, it freely interleaves requirements (external behavior) and internal structure.

Bibliography by Subject Matter

GENERAL SOFTWARE ENGINEERING

Agresti86
Balzer83
Basili75
Boehm76
Boehm81
Boehm88
Brooks75
Chen76

Dart87
Fagan76
Fairley85
Harel87
Harel88a
Harel88b
IEEE83
Lubars87

Martin85
McCracken82
Pressman91
Prieto-Diaz87
Sommerville92
Sage90
Tsai88
Zave84

CONCURRENCY

Bic88
BrinchHansen73
Courtois71

Dijkstra68
Gehani84
Hoare74

Hoare85
Peterson81
Peterson91

REAL-TIME SYSTEMS

Alford85
Allworth87

Burns89
Glass83

Stankovic88

DISTRIBUTED SYSTEMS

Kramer85
Magee89

Nutt92
Tanenbaum92

SOFTWARE REQUIREMENTS AND PROTOTYPING

Brackett89
Davis88

Davis90
Gomaa81a

Gomaa82a
Gomaa86b

SOFTWARE TESTING

Beizer84	Gomaa82b	Myers79
Cobb90	McCabe85	Tai91

PERFORMANCE ANALYSIS

Beilner72	Gomaa81b	SEI93
Coolahan83	Kleinrock75	Sha90
Gomaa77	Lehoczy89	Smith90
Gomaa78	Liu73	Sprunt89

DESIGN CONCEPTS AND METHODS

General Software Design

Budgen88	Freeman83c	Orr77
Freeman83a	Gomaa93	Parnas72
Freeman83b	Mills86	Parnas74

Real-time Design

Buhr84	Kelly87	Simpson79
Cooling91	Neilsen88	Simpson86

RTSAD

Bruyn88	Myers78	Ward86
DeMarco78	Page-Jones88	Yourdon79
Gane79	Ward85	Yourdon89
Hatley88		

DARTS/ADARTS

Cochran&Gomaa91	Gomaa87	Gomaa89b
Gomaa84	Gomaa89a	Gomaa89c
Gomaa86a		

JSD and Extensions

Cameron86	Jackson83	Sanden89
Cameron89	Kato87	Sanden93
Jackson75	Renold89	

NRL Method

Britton81	Lamb88	Parnas85
Faulk88	Parnas79	Parnas86
Heninger80	Parnas84	

Object-Oriented Analysis, Design, and Programming

Booch86
Booch87a
Booch87b
Booch91
Coad91
Coad92

Goldberg83
HOOD89
Meyer87
Meyer88
Rumbaugh91
Seidewitz89

Shlaer88
Stroustrup86
Wegner87
Wegner90
Wirfs-Brock90

Index

WHERE THE SUN SHINES BRIGHTER

Nicola, a young mother, is black-mailed into moving to France with Oliver, her son, for the sake of his inheritance. Full of reservations as she leaves behind her long-term friend Andrew, she must also face Henri, her interfering ex-father-in-law. Nicola finds getting to know her French relatives and making a life for herself and Oliver a challenge. And, attracted to Gilles Bongars, working nearby, how will she react to Andrew's plan to start a new life in France with her?

Books by Jennifer Bohnet
in the Linford Romance Library:

CALL OF THE SEA

JENNIFER BOHNET

WHERE THE SUN SHINES BRIGHTER

Complete and Unabridged

LINFORD
Leicester

First published in Great Britain in 2006

First Linford Edition
published 2007

British Library CIP Data

Bohnet, Jennifer
  Where the sun shines brighter.—
  Large print ed.—
  Linford romance library
  1. Love stories
  2. Large type books
  I. Title
  823.9'2 [F]

  ISBN 978–1–84617–870–2

Published by
F. A. Thorpe (Publishing)
Anstey, Leicestershire

Set by Words & Graphics Ltd.
Anstey, Leicestershire
Printed and bound in Great Britain by
T. J. International Ltd., Padstow, Cornwall
This book is printed on acid-free paper

Urgent Matters

The letter landed on the doormat, sandwiched between the final telephone demand and some junk mail. Nicola saw the French stamps and frowned. Communication from France was usually restricted to Christmas and birthday cards for Oliver.

The letter, however, was addressed to *Madame Nicola Jacques* in Henri's distinctive handwriting.

Chère Nicola, it read. *You will come to La Prouveresse immédiatement. We have matters of urgence to discuss — things to settle. Bring Oliver. Henri.*

Nicola sighed. The letter, with its clipped English sentences and French words, conjured up an immediate picture of her ex-father-in-law. He wrote English the same way as he spoke it — short and sharp.

Whatever the reasons behind this

1

order to visit. Henri would have regarded her feelings in the matter as being of little importance. He'd decided her presence was needed, and so the command was issued.

Gazing out of the kitchen window as she waited for her coffee to percolate, Nicola considered the reasons for this unexpected demand. Was the old man feeling guilty about his treatment of her and Oliver over the past few years? Did he want to make amends?

Whatever it was, it made no difference. She had no intention of obeying the summons and rushing across to France. That part of her life had ended years ago.

These days, she had her own life to lead — a different life from the one she'd experienced when she was married to Marc Jacques . . .

'Morning, Mum.' Oliver rubbed the sleep from his eyes before kissing her on both cheeks. Marc had always greeted her like that every morning and, as a small boy, Oliver had

2

determinedly copied his daddy. Now, it was a natural part of his own morning routine.

'Want some toast?' Oliver asked, slotting two slices of bread into the machine.

'Not right now, thanks,' Nicola said, eyeing Henri's note.

'Who's the letter from?'

'Papa Henri,' Nicola replied, pushing it across the table to Oliver. She watched him read it.

'Any idea why he wants us to go?' Oliver asked.

Nicola shook her head.

'After all this time? No.'

'Are we going?'

'No, we're not.'

There was silence as Oliver read over the letter again.

'Actually, Mum, I wouldn't mind going. Oh, not because Papa Henri has summoned us, but . . . ' He paused. 'Dad was talking about taking me at the end of the year — when he got back from his latest mission. I'd like to see where he grew up, and get to know Papa Henri.'

Nicola was silent. In the thirteen years since Oliver was born they'd been to visit Marc's family twice — once, when Oliver was a baby, to show him off to his French relatives, and again, just before his fifth birthday.

At the time of the last visit, Nicola had hoped that these family occasions would become a regular feature of their lives, and that Marc would be reconciled with his father.

But, within weeks of Oliver starting school, Marc had taken a decision that would alter the course of their lives for ever.

After Oliver's birth, life had settled into as much of a routine as Marc would allow. Marc craved excitement — a way out of the dull routine. He was always urging Nicola to be spontaneous, reminding her that, 'Routine is the death knell for spontaneity.'

Nicola's protests that a routine paid the bills were always met with a Gallic shrug and a smile.

The fact that Marc was one of the kindest people she'd ever met made Nicola forgive him a lot of things when they were first married. But in the end, it was his very kindness and concern for other people that destroyed their own relationship.

His decision to join a relief agency for a sixth-month tour in a Third World country was the catalyst. From then on, all of Marc's energies went into humanitarian work, and he was away for weeks at a time.

Nicola got used to coping on her own, while Oliver adapted to his daddy working in different countries. Nicola always tried to make life as normal as possible during Marc's absences, and together, they looked forward to the times when he did come home.

She grew accustomed to their strange lifestyle and accepted that it was the way things had to be. The next shock came a year or two later.

Marc, arriving home for a few weeks,

elected to sleep in the spare bedroom, and told Nicola he wanted a divorce.

In vain, Nicola had protested.

'But *I* don't. Why can't we just let things stay as they are? OK, it's not ideal, but it's worked for the last few years.'

Marc had shaken his head sadly.

'Nicola, you're a great mother to Oliver and I know you want more children. But I'm no use as a father or a husband — it isn't fair on either of you. I love you both, so I'm letting you go.'

She remembered staring at him in disbelief. She'd thought they were happy. Perhaps their lifestyle was a little strange, but it was working. She still loved Marc, but now he was saying that because he loved her, he wanted a divorce.

Nicola couldn't see the logic in his argument at all. But Marc had been adamant. And, as always, he got his way.

At first Nicola found it hard to believe that they weren't still married.

Everything went on as normal. Marc continued with his humanitarian work wherever he was needed and back home, she and Oliver got on with their daily lives — Oliver at school, Nicola at the garden centre.

Marc was away for longer and longer periods, but when he was in the UK he always lived with them.

It took five years, but eventually Nicola recovered from her hurt and started to enjoy life once more. She didn't, as Marc had hoped, remarry and have more children, but she did go out with Andrew, a long-time mutual friend who was more than willing to fill the gap Marc had left in her life.

Oliver accepted his long-distance relationship with his father as the way things were. It usually took him a couple of days to get used to having him around when Marc returned from his work, but on the whole, their relationship was good.

Marc's absence from everyday involvement in their lives had certainly cushioned the initial impact of his death six months ago. There had been an accident — the Jeep he was travelling in had overturned.

It had happened just two weeks into a spell of duty that was scheduled to last for several months, so Oliver hadn't been expecting to see his dad for some time. But Nicola still worried that he was hurting inside, because, this time, Marc was not coming home.

Before his very first job in Ethiopia, Marc pinned a large map of the world to the kitchen wall with little pins stuck in it to show Oliver where he was working.

Every year, Marc would hang a calendar next to the map and write in all his destinations, his departure dates and his homecoming dates. Over the years it had become something of a ritual.

Last week, when Nicola had torn off the old monthly page, Marc's handwriting and the message, *See you both on the 17th* had confronted her. Written in anticipation some months ago, it took her breath away.

Her first thought had been for Oliver. How would he react to a message like this? She couldn't just rip a whole month out. She needed the calendar to put appointments and reminders on.

She'd been standing there wondering what to do when Oliver had arrived home from school. He'd taken one look at the calendar, scrambled in his schoolbag, found his black felt tip pen and obliterated his father's message before running out of the kitchen; Nicola had seen the tears welling up in his eyes.

The next day she'd scoured the shops for a new calendar, finally tracking one down in the local charity shop. Marc's calendar of African tribal leaders and orange sunsets was replaced by one of cute puppies and fluffy kittens.

The map of the world was still on the wall, though, with a red marker pinned into Colombia. When she'd said she was going to take it down Oliver had asked her to leave it.

'The kitchen wouldn't be the same without it,' he'd said.

* * *

'Mum? Are you OK? You were miles away.'

Nicola poured herself another coffee and tried to bring her thoughts back to the present.

'I'm fine. Just thinking.' She leaned over and pinched a piece of toast from Oliver's plate.

'So you'd like to visit Papa Henri?'

'Yes. Spending half-term in France would be good.'

Nicola sighed as she looked at Oliver.

'Don't expect him to be the perfect grandfather, will you? If he was, he wouldn't have ignored us for so long. I just know there's more to this sudden demand to visit than a simple desire to be reconciled with us.'

Oliver shrugged.

'Well, it's only a visit. I know I

10

probably won't be the grandson he wants. Besides, it's not just him, is it? There's the *tantes* as well.'

The mention of the *tantes* made Nicola smile. They were Henri's twin sisters. She and Tante Giselle had had fun together on the couple of occasions they'd met. Even Tante Odette had unbent enough to cuddle baby Oliver.

'OK,' Nicola said. 'I'll write and tell Papa Henri we can't come *immédiatement* as he demands, but we will come at half-term.'

Preparing for the Guests

Giselle smoothed the quilt over the freshly-made bed. She'd used the best linen for Nicola, linen that she'd washed and dried the old-fashioned way across a bed of wild herbs before folding it carefully and placing it in the old *armoire*.

Now, as the smell of lavender wafted through the room, she could scarcely believe this longed-for visit was about to happen.

Glancing out through the small window, set high in the eaves, Giselle could see Henri walking slowly along the old olive grove terrace at the back of the farm.

Forty acres of olive trees to the south of the house now grew La Prouveresse's commercial crop, but Henri maintained that this small terrace, planted by their great-grandfather, still bore the best olives. Only oil from those particular olives was used in their kitchen.

Giselle watched her brother for a few moments. He'd visibly aged in the last few months. Yet, at sixty-five, there was still something in the set of his shoulders that reminded her of the kind-hearted boy he'd been when they were growing up.

Always ready for mischief and getting his twin sisters into scrapes, he was the first to shoulder the responsibility and protect them when things went wrong.

He'd been ambitious in those days. Henri Jacques was really going to be someone when he grew up. The most famous saxophone player in the world, perhaps. But when his father had insisted that it was his duty, as the only son, to take over the farm and look after his sisters, he'd dutifully given up all ideas of living a musician's life.

He'd never understood his own son's refusal even to contemplate a life on the farm.

'I had to. What's so different for you?' he'd asked.

'I'm sorry, Papa. It's not the life I want. You of all people should understand that,' Marc had replied.

In vain, Henri had tried to change his mind.

'Only lucky people or fools get to live the life they want. The rest of us have to compromise.'

Josephine, Marc's mother, had been the peacemaker between them, telling Henri he couldn't keep Marc a prisoner. Things had changed in the twentieth century, and there were more opportunities for those who wanted to see the world. And perhaps once he'd seen some of it, their son might well be back.

Reluctantly, Henri had agreed to Marc spending a year travelling on the condition that, when the twelve months were up, he would return to work on the farm.

But when Josephine died shortly after Marc's eighteenth birthday, Henri had insisted that Marc return home for good immediately.

Within six months, Marc had said he couldn't take any more. The country life was smothering him.

The last bitter row ended when Henri put his foot down once and for all.

'If you don't stay and do your duty, I'll cut you off,' he'd challenged.

Marc had sighed.

'Papa, I'm sorry but I can't.' The next day, Marc had gone.

It was four years before he returned, bringing Nicola and baby Oliver to La Prouveresse for a short holiday. It was a holiday that soothed away some of the old hurts, but failed to heal the rift completely.

Giselle knew that for the past twenty years Henri had been living with the hope that Marc would one day regret leaving the farm and return for good. But that dream was gone.

★ ★ ★

As Henri reached the end of the olive terrace and half jumped, half slithered down the jutting-out rocks that served as steps back to level ground, Giselle closed the bedroom shutters.

Making a mental note to place a fresh vase of flowers on the dressing-table, she hurried downstairs to make Henri's morning coffee.

'*Ça va?*' she asked automatically as he opened the kitchen door.

'Everything's fine,' Henri answered, wiping the mud off his boots on the old olive oil filter that served as a back door mat.

Giselle poured his coffee.

'Just think,' she said, 'only one more day and Nicola and Oliver will be here. I find it hard to believe they're coming.'

Henri gave an irritated look.

'It's taken them long enough. Can't for the life of me see why they didn't come when they got my letter two months ago.'

'Henri, you know why. Nicola works and Oliver has school. It had to be half-term. Besides, you should think yourself lucky they're coming at all. Personally, I wouldn't have been surprised if they'd refused. Nicola must be wondering what sort of reception she's likely to get after all these years.'

Henri shrugged his shoulders but didn't answer his sister.

'I've made up the bed in Marc's old room for Oliver. And before you say anything, it's about time that room was used again.'

Henri looked at Giselle, his face expressionless.

'When Nicola and Oliver leave, I'm thinking of turning it into a sewing-room.'

'We'll see about that,' Henri replied, and he opened his 'Nice Matin' newspaper to the sports page, effectively shutting up his sister.

Giselle sighed and fetched her workbox from the dresser. Ten minutes with the crochet hook as she drank her coffee would serve to calm her down.

They both glanced up as Odette

opened the kitchen door. Giselle wore a smile of welcome on her face for her twin sister, whilst Henri sighed in irritation as the draught rustled his paper.

'Sylvie says you haven't forgotten you're taking her out tonight, have you?' Odette said as she started to put the shopping away.

'No,' Henri answered sharply as he stood up. 'Although why I need another woman bossing me around when I've got you two is beyond me. I'm off to the barn to check the sheep.' The door closed behind him.

Trouble

Giselle and Odette looked at each other and smiled. They'd both agreed years ago that their friend, Sylvie Traille, widow and grandmother, was good for Henri. It was to Sylvie he had turned when the news about Marc had arrived.

The twins had done their best to comfort him, but it had been Sylvie who'd stopped him giving up completely. They suspected, too, that Sylvie had had a hand in Henri finally writing and inviting Nicola and Oliver to visit.

Family unity was important to Sylvie and she'd always told Henri he was wrong to disown Marc.

'Did Sylvie have much else to say?' Giselle enquired.

Odette nodded.

'Raoul's in trouble with the villagers. You know the land on the edge of the village he inherited from old Dominic

19

last year? Well, he's decided he wants to sell it and the village is up in arms about it.

'They're accusing him of selling his inheritance and giving newcomers and foreigners the opportunity to buy 'their' inheritance. One or two are even moaning about the fact they can't get their stuff there any more.'

Giselle laughed.

'Nobody's bought any stuff from there since the *supermarché* was built five years ago!'

Once, the smallholding had been a thriving *pépinière*, the main source of plants, vegetables and fruit for the village, but now its land lay overgrown and neglected. The small cottage, empty for over a year, was in urgent need of some care and attention.

'I know,' Odette agreed. 'Raoul's been looking for a tenant but nobody wants to take it on. Ten acres is too big for most people to garden, but it's not really big enough for commercial purposes. He says he's got no option but to sell. Besides, he needs the money for something else.'

'Any idea what?' Giselle asked.

Odette shook her head.

'Some investment he wants to make in town is all he's told Sylvie. He asked her to mention the *pépinière* to Henri, although why he should think Henri needs any more land is beyond me. There's enough work up here for the three of us without taking on another ten acres a kilometre down the road.'

'True,' Giselle agreed. 'There used to be a couple of good olive trees on that land, though. Some citrus, and vines, too, if I remember. It would be a shame if it's all grubbed up and built on.'

Odette glanced at her.

'Sounds as if you'd like to save it.'

Giselle shook her head.

'It's too late for me to take on something like that.' She paused. 'But I do wonder, if Henri and Sylvie were ever to get married, where you and I would go?'

'All Set for Tomorrow?'

Nicola folded Oliver's favourite black T-shirt, unplugged the iron and went through to his bedroom with the last of his clothes.

Refusing to use a suitcase, Oliver had dragged one of Marc's old rucksacks out of the attic. Its pockets and pouches were already filled with the essentials of Oliver's life — his CD player, a travel game, the baseball cap Marc had brought back from Mexico, and his camera.

One of the smaller pockets held a notebook and Nicola could see the edge of a black and white photo sticking out between the pages. Nicola knew, without looking, it was the photo of Marc that usually stood on Oliver's bedside table.

Nicola heard the door slam.

'I'm upstairs, in your room,' she called out.

'What's for tea?' Oliver demanded as he threw his schoolbag and then himself on to the bed. 'I'm starving.'

'Nothing new there then,' Nicola teased. 'Andrew's coming for supper, so I've made spaghetti bolognese.'

'That'll be ages,' Oliver moaned. 'Can I have a cheese sandwich for now?'

'Finish packing first and then I'll make you one,' Nicola negotiated.

As she zipped her suitcase closed and Oliver did the last buckle up on his rucksack, Andrew arrived, complete with his own suitcase and a bottle of wine.

To Nicola's relief, he'd agreed to move in for the week to look after the house and the cat.

Nicola finished cooking supper and opened the wine as Andrew challenged Oliver to a quick game of chess on the computer. Andrew had been a part of his life for so long that Oliver treated him more like a big brother than a friend of his mother's.

'You all set for tomorrow?' Andrew

asked, as Nicola handed him a glass of wine.

She nodded.

'And you're sure you don't mind taking us to the airport at the crack of dawn? We could always get a taxi.'

'Don't be silly! I wish I was coming with you, though.'

Nicola didn't answer. Meeting Marc's family for the first time in years would be difficult enough without the added complication of taking another man along with her.

Later, after supper and with Oliver in his room, Andrew pulled out the sofa bed and Nicola fetched the quilt. As they companionably made up the bed, Andrew glanced at her.

'Nicola, I was wondering whether you could ever see me as anything other than a good friend?' he asked, looking at her thoughtfully.

Nicola, concentrating on shaking the duvet, didn't look up.

'I do already,' she replied. 'You're my best friend.'

As the silence between them deepened, she finally looked up at Andrew and realised he was struggling for words.

'I know how hard it's been for you all these years. This Marc business has been difficult, to say the least. But now you're free to love again — and I want it to be me you love.'

There was another pause.

'I'd like to think that you and I have a future together.'

Nicola was silent for several seconds before going over to Andrew and kissing him gently on his cheek.

'Oh, Andrew, what can I say?'

'Say you'll at least think about me while you're away in France. Think about us being more than best friends?'

'It's not just me though, is it? There's Oliver to consider,' Nicola said with a sigh.

'I like Oliver,' Andrew replied. 'And I think he likes me — I can't see a problem there. I know I could never replace Marc in his affections, but together we could give him a proper family life. Maybe even a brother or sister . . .'

Gently, he took Nicola in his arms.

'Please promise to think about us — about moving our friendship on to another level. The thing is, I can't imagine a life without the two of you in it.'

★　★　★

As the plane swooped down low over the Mediterranean to land at Nice Côte d'Azur airport, Nicola took a deep breath. Whatever happened during the course of the next few days, she must remember she was here purely for Oliver's sake.

This was a chance for him to meet his grandfather and his other French relatives, to give him the opportunity to try to build some sort of relationship with them.

She decided that she must put all feelings of resentment about the way

Henri had treated Marc and her over the years out of her mind.

Waiting for their luggage to show up on the carousel, Nicola felt a pang of dismay. She suddenly realised she hadn't made any arrangements for the journey out to La Prouveresse. She'd been so concerned with getting them to France that she'd forgotten the farm was an hour's drive inland from Nice.

'Welcome Back!'

As she and Oliver walked through to the arrivals lounge, she saw the back of a man who seemed vaguely familiar. When the man turned, smiled and held up a small placard reading, *Jacques family*, she recognised Marc's old schoolfriend immediately.

Nicola sighed with relief. Henri had at least sent someone to meet them, even if she would have preferred it to be someone other than Raoul Traille.

'Nicola! Welcome back.' As Raoul kissed her cheeks, Nicola tensed before remembering this was the normal French greeting, nothing more.

'It's been a long time,' Raoul said, looking at her. 'But you haven't changed a bit. I didn't need this.' He threw the placard into a bin.

Smiling, he turned and gravely shook the hand Oliver had shyly extended.

'Welcome to France, Oliver. I was your father's best friend at school, so I'm the one to talk to if you want to hear about all the mischief he got up to.'

As Raoul took her suitcase and led them outside to his car, Nicola decided to break the silence.

'Is Henri all right? To be honest, I'd forgotten about having to get from here to the farm. I suppose I'd expected him to meet us.'

'You know Henri,' Raoul replied, 'he's not much of a traveller. Nice is just that bit too far from the farm for him and the old rattle-trap he calls a car. When he heard I was going to be down here today he assumed I'd have no objection to meeting you. He was right, of course.'

The road out of Nice into the country was busy, but this didn't stop Raoul from pointing out places of interest to Oliver. Nicola, sitting in the back seat, closed her eyes. She'd forgotten how maniacal French drivers could be.

Oliver was fascinated by the mediaeval villages he glimpsed way up in the mountains, but not so keen on the horseshoe bends on the minor road leading to La Prouveresse.

'Scary,' was his verdict, as Raoul stopped for him to look over a deep abyss with nothing between them and the edge.

The village was quiet as they drove through, not yet fully awake after its lunchtime siesta. Initially, it still seemed to Nicola to be a typical sleepy French village, unaltered from her memories of eight years ago.

Bougainvillea still climbed rampant over the ruined castle that had once stood guard above the narrow streets while oleander bushes and tall plane trees lined the pavements.

The smell of strong coffee still wafted out from the café. Opposite the station, the old men of the village were gathering for their afternoon game of *boules*.

It wasn't until Raoul pointed out the

new bridge at the end of the village that she realised the village had suffered and changed in recent years. Torrential rains five years ago had swept away the gently curved fifteenth century bridge, eroded the banks of the river and left tonnes of stones in the riverbed.

Now a modern bridge carried the road through the village across the river. Ancient houses on either side of the river had been demolished, with stark concrete retaining walls in their place to keep the river at bay.

The village fountain still stood, unscathed, in the square. The square itself, with its restaurant tables and bright parasols, hadn't changed. Nicola even thought she recognised the brown dog asleep in front of the entrance to L'Oliveraie restaurant and hotel.

Driving out through the village, Nicola could feel herself tensing. Two more minutes and they would reach the farm.

She glanced at the derelict *pépinière* as they passed it, remembering how different it had looked on her last visit.

'That place looks sad. Such a waste.'

'Don't you start. The whole village is on at me about it,' Raoul said.

'When Old Dominic left it to me, I decided I didn't want to live there, but I can't find anyone to rent it. So I've said I'm going to sell it and invest the money in something. But, according to the village, I should keep it. I had hoped Henri might buy it, but he's not interested.'

Raoul changed down a gear and negotiated the driveway entrance to La Prouveresse carefully.

'I think it's time Henri did something about this track,' he groaned, trying to avoid potholes.

'No wonder they don't get many visitors up here.' He stopped the car in front of the farmhouse and turned to face Nicola.

'*Voilà!* We arrive. If you want, I can come in with you,' he offered. 'Help ease things along?'

Nicola shook her head.

'Thanks for the offer, Raoul, but we'll be fine. Henri has invited us, so it's not as if we're unwelcome. Come on, Oliver, let's introduce you to your grandfather.'

As Raoul disappeared back down the lane with a sharp toot of the horn, Tante Giselle ran down the steps at the side of the house and flung her arms around Nicola.

'*Bonjour*, Nicola, *et mon petit* Oliver!'

Petit Oliver dwarfed Giselle by at least ten inches but smiled good-naturedly as she hugged him.

'Come on in. Odette is waiting,' she cried.

The farmhouse kitchen was warm and inviting as Giselle took them inside. Odette hugged them both and offered them a cup of coffee.

'Or tea? We have some tea especially for you.'

'A cup of tea would be nice,' Nicola said. 'Is Henri working outside?'

'Tsh,' Giselle replied, shrugging her

shoulders. 'One minute he is here waiting and the next, he disappears.'

She looked at Oliver.

'I think he'll be in the barn. Go and ask him if he wants a cup of tea and a slice of *gâteau*. The barn is just across the back yard,' she said, gesturing out through the kitchen window towards a large stone building.

Oliver looked at Nicola uncertainly.

'Shall I come with you?' she asked.

Before Oliver could answer, Giselle gently touched her arm.

'*Non*, Nicola. It's better they meet alone, I think,' she said quietly.

'It's OK, Mum.' Taking a deep breath, Oliver opened the back door and went in search of his grandfather.

★　★　★

A sharp draught of air blew into the barn, snatching at wisps of straw bedding and lifting them haphazardly towards the rafters.

Carefully, Oliver closed the old

wooden door and stood for a few seconds, listening to the contented bleating of the sheep.

He could see Henri in the far corner, his back towards him, carefully measuring food into buckets. Philly, Henri's old collie, sleeping on a pile of discarded oil filter mats under the work bench, thumped her tail in welcome before getting up and ambling towards him.

'*Bonjour, Oliver*,' Henri said without turning.

'*Bonjour*, Papa Henri. *Comment ça va?*' Oliver said shyly.

Henri put one last scoop of food into a bucket, straightened up and slowly turned to face Oliver.

'*Tu parles français*, Oliver?'

Oliver shook his head.

'Not really. Dad taught me a bit but I'm not very good at it. You speak English though, so that's OK,' he said, smiling at his grandfather.

'Can I help you feed the sheep?'

Silently, Henri handed him a bucket

and indicated he should pour its contents into one of the hoppers. Together, they moved around the enclosure until all the hoppers were filled.

'Did your father ever talk to you about La Prouveresse?' Henri asked, bending down to secure a food sack.

Oliver nodded.

'Dad used to tell me about growing up on the farm. He thought it was brilliant. He said there was always stuff to do, but mostly it was good fun.'

Henri was slightly taken aback. Marc had never mentioned this.

As he put the last empty bucket down near the food sacks, Oliver went on.

'Tante Giselle sent me to tell you tea and *gâteau* are ready in the kitchen. Mum's waiting there, too,' he said, looking at Henri.

'Come on then. We'd better get back or I'll be in trouble for keeping you out here,' Henri said with a sigh.

Nicola looked up as they entered the

kitchen together, feeling some of the tension leave her body. Oliver had got over the first hurdle of meeting Papa Henri safely.

Tante Giselle poured the tea as Henri greeted Nicola. Tentatively, she responded to the unexpected hug that accompanied the customary cheek-kissing.

'Thank you for inviting us, Henri. Oliver has been really looking forward to it,' she said.

Henri shrugged his shoulders but sent an affectionate glance in Oliver's direction.

'Tomorrow, I show Oliver all over La Prouveresse.'

'And the urgent matter you mentioned in your letter?' Nicola asked.

'Later,' Henri said. 'It will keep.'

A Proper Family

The holiday passed in a blur of activity. One evening the *tantes* pulled a box of old family photos out of the loft and spent hours poring over them. There had been a Jacques family at La Prouveresse for nearly two hundred years and Oliver was fascinated by the history of the farm.

Henri took him out and about, too, proudly introducing him to everyone he met as '*Mon petit garçon* from *Angleterre.*'

Nicola was pleased for Oliver. At least he would feel like he had a proper family now — even if he would only see them occasionally.

On the afternoon of their last day, Nicola pushed open the old wrought iron gates that led into the small paved area where lunch was eaten most days in summer. She stood amongst the weathered, painted furniture, pots of lavender and rosemary and the trailing geraniums that tumbled down the stone wall. Looking out over the countryside, she took a deep breath of fresh air — this was one of her favourite places on the farm.

When Giselle and Odette had confessed they didn't have the time to do more than just keep this *petit jardin* tidy and accessible, Nicola had resolved she'd make it nicer for them.

So one day, when the *tantes* were busy working on the farm and Henri had taken Oliver off somewhere, she'd gone outside with the secateurs and started to tame the overgrowth. Looking around, she was pleased with her efforts.

Just the trailing geraniums to cut back and then all the plants would be ready for the summer months. As she worked she hummed happily to herself and thought about the holiday.

Oliver had certainly enjoyed himself, and she'd had a much-needed rest.

There had been a good feeling about the whole week, and no antagonism from Henri. He just seemed very happy — in his own grumpy way — to be back in touch with them.

The only thing that bothered her was the fact that Henri still hadn't spoken to her about the urgent matter that had prompted the visit in the first place. Had it simply been a ploy to get her and Oliver out there?

'Join Me?'

'You like working in the garden, Nicola?'

Nicola turned, startled. Henri was sitting at the wooden table, a carafe of rosé wine and two glasses in front of him.

She wondered how long he'd been sitting there watching her.

'Yes. It's my occupation.'

'Ah. I'd forgotten. Marc told me once, you 'ave a certificate in . . . 'orticulture, yes?'

In spite of herself, Nicola smiled at his pronunciation.

'Yes,' she replied.

'Will you join me in a glass of wine?' Henri asked. 'To celebrate your good 'oliday and to 'elp us discuss things.'

Without waiting for a reply he poured two glasses.

Nicola sipped her cold wine and

waited. So there were matters to discuss, after all.

'I have decided to make Oliver my heir,' Henri said.

Nicola looked at him.

'Oh, Henri. That's very generous of you. Have you told Oliver?'

'*Non*. It's not necessary at the moment. You and I will make the arrangements. Then we tell him.'

'I'm sorry, Henri, but I don't see where I come into all of this. You simply have to make a will leaving La Prouveresse to Oliver, give it to your *notaire*, and when the time comes, he informs Oliver.'

Henri looked at her.

'However, there is a condition he has to obey before I make my will.'

Nicola waited. Of course, with Henri, there would always be conditions. He hadn't mellowed that much.

'If Oliver is to inherit La Prouveresse, he has to come to France to live now.'

Nicola looked at Henri, stunned.

'But he can't — he's a child. He lives

with me in England.'

'If he's going to inherit the farm he has to live here. He's half French. He should learn to speak the language.'

'And you expect me to give up my life in England and bring him to live out here?'

Henri shrugged.

'He's a Jacques. He belongs here. And he's old enough to come on his own. Giselle and Odette would happily look after him. You don't have to come. Of course, you can visit whenever you like,' he added as an afterthought.

'And what if Oliver doesn't want to come?' Nicola retaliated.

'He will,' Henri answered confidently. 'He's really enjoyed this week. He has a feel for the farm — unlike his father.'

'But a holiday is different from living here permanently. No. I'm sorry, Henri, but I can't agree to your condition. If, in a few years, when Oliver has finished school, you still want to make him your heir, he'll be old enough to talk things through with you and decide for himself.'

Nicola put her glass on the table and stood up. Henri put out a restraining arm.

'The offer is for now, Nicola,' he said quietly. 'I shan't make it again. If you refuse and leave,' he shrugged, 'you will have thrown away your son's inheritance. Then I shall tell him about your refusal to safeguard his future. I wonder what his reaction will be.' And he turned and walked away.

After Henri had left, Nicola tried to carry on with her gardening, but her mind was in turmoil. After a few minutes, she threw the secateurs into the basket and leaned against the wall, gazing unseeingly at the view.

What an impossible situation.

Was she right to refuse Henri's offer so swiftly? Should she at least have discussed it with Oliver?

No, she couldn't place such a momentous, life-changing burden on a thirteen-year-old. It was a decision she had to make on her own.

But what would Oliver's reaction be when Henri told him she'd turned down La Prouveresse on his behalf? Would he listen when she pleaded she'd done it for the best? Or would he accuse her of being selfish, and not wanting to give up her own life in England?

Was that why her immediate reaction to Henri's offer had been no? She'd dismissed it as moral blackmail and refused even to consider it.

Wherever he lived, Oliver still had at least another five years' schooling ahead of him. And there was no way she'd allow Oliver to come to France without her. The house would have to be sold, her job at the garden centre given up . . .

Fleetingly, she wished she could talk to Andrew. He'd be able to help her make sense of things. Andrew. She smiled ruefully to herself.

Nicola had missed him this week, more than she'd thought possible. She'd even decided to tell him that she was ready for their relationship to move on when she got back to England.

But moving to France would make that impossible.

Dimly, in the distance, Nicola heard the village church clock striking the hour. She had to go in and get ready.

Sylvie had insisted that Henri book a table tonight and treat everyone to a farewell dinner at L'Oliveraie. Perhaps she'd get a chance to talk to Henri privately — persuade him to change his mind.

She forced herself to smile normally at Oliver as he came running into the garden.

'Mum? Papa Henri told me to come and find you. He said you might have some news for me. Have you?'

Any News?

'Mum, are you ready? We're all leaving for the restaurant in ten minutes,' Oliver said, running into the bedroom.

'Oh, and Papa Henri said you might have some news for me about our next visit. Have you?'

Nicola sighed. Trust Henri to start applying the pressure so early.

'No, I'm not ready, and no, I don't have any news about our next visit,' she said with slight impatience.

As she took her dress off the hanger she realised she shouldn't have snapped.

'I'll be five minutes. Have you washed your face and hands? Your hair certainly needs combing. You can't go to the restaurant looking scruffy . . . '

She watched as Oliver grabbed her comb and ran it through his hair. Nicola hesitated slightly, then brought up the dreaded subject once more.

'So, Papa Henri wants you to visit again?'

Oliver nodded.

'He says I can come any time — on my own if I want. I wouldn't like to leave you behind, though. Not until I'm much older, anyway.'

Silently, Nicola clipped her earrings into place and picked up her jacket and bag. At least she now knew Oliver wouldn't want to move to France on his own. But would he want to live in France permanently?

She glanced at him. Should she discuss Henri's 'condition' with him? No — she couldn't place such a momentous, life-changing burden on a thirteen-year-old boy. It was a decision she had to make on her own.

A sharp toot of a car horn made them both jump.

'Come on, Mum. Papa Henri will be cross if we're late!' Oliver ran down the stairs ahead of her.

Nicola followed slowly. It had been Sylvie's idea for Henri to treat them all to a farewell dinner, and it had promised to be a fun occasion. But now Nicola was dreading the next two or three hours. Henri was sure to try to bully a decision out of her . . .

★   ★   ★

L'Oliveraie Restaurant was almost full when Henri ushered his party inside. Sylvie, Raoul and Claudine were already sitting at the large table reserved for the Jacques family in front of a picture window.

After much laughter, hand shaking and air kissing with everyone they knew in the restaurant, Nicola found herself sitting between Tante Giselle and Claudine, Sylvie's daughter.

Henri, to her relief, was at the other end of the table, Sylvie on one side of him and Oliver on the other.

'Nicola, I'm so pleased you brought Oliver for half-term,' Tante Giselle said quietly. 'We will keep in touch now, *oui*?'

'If Henri has his way we'll be doing more than that, won't we?' Nicola answered, fiddling with her wine glass.

Tante Giselle looked at her.

'What do you mean?' she asked.

'This inheritance business,' Nicola replied softly. 'Surely Henri has told you his plan?'

Tante Giselle shook her head.

'*Non*. Henri can be very secretive at times. You will have to tell me.'

Nicola bit her lip. Why hadn't Henri told the *tantes*? The farm was their home, after all. It wasn't her place to tell them. But looking at Tante Giselle's concerned face, she felt the need to confide in her.

'Henri wants Oliver to inherit La Prouveresse, but he's insisting that, to do so, he has to come and live in France now.'

Tante Giselle was silent as Nicola continued.

'I can't decide what to do. If we stay in England, he loses his inheritance, and I get the blame. Why can't Henri just make Oliver his heir without this ridiculous residency clause?'

'Do you think living in France would be that bad?' Tante Giselle asked quietly.

Nicola shook her head and smiled.

'It would be better in lots of ways. But I can't let Henri run Oliver's life the way he tried to do with Marc. It wouldn't be fair.'

Tante Giselle patted her arm in a comforting gesture as she looked across the table at Oliver, who was talking happily to Henri.

'Only you can decide what is best for both of you, Nicola. All I can say is that it would be lovely to have you both here and . . . ' she leaned forward to whisper conspiratorially in her ear ' . . . I promise to help you keep Henri in his place.'

'Thanks, Giselle,' Nicola said with a smile. 'By the way, I think somebody over there is trying to attract your attention.'

As Giselle went to talk to her friend

at another table, Claudine spoke.

'It's nice to see you again, Nicola. Do I gather you're thinking of coming to live in France?'

Nicola put her finger against her lips.

'Shh. I've not decided and I haven't even mentioned it to Oliver yet. There are a few obstacles in the way.' She took a sip of her wine. 'How are you, Claudine?'

'I'm fine, thank you. I'm coming back to live in the village soon. My husband's just got a job in Nice so he's going to commute.'

On the two occasions the two women had met years ago, a tentative friendship had been formed, but the distance between them had kept it from developing.

'Well, if you do decide to come and live in France, we will get together. Is one of the obstacles a boyfriend, by any chance?' Claudine asked gently.

Nicola nodded. She had been missing Andrew a lot this week; his gentle sense of humour, the way he looked after her. When she got back she'd intended to tell him that she was ready for their relationship to move on, but coming to live in France would make that impossible.

Before she could say any more to Claudine, she saw Henri getting to his feet to propose a toast.

'Please raise your glasses to my grandson, Oliver. Wherever he lives, and whatever he does, may his future be filled with the happiness and prosperity he deserves.'

He looked directly at Nicola as he raised his glass, as though daring her to challenge his words. But instead, she smiled brightly at him, took a sip of wine and promised herself that, before the evening was over, she would try to talk to him privately.

A Plan

The idea came to Nicola in the middle of the sleepless night that followed the farewell dinner. At five o'clock, she decided to get up and investigate its possibilities.

Quietly, she crept down through the house and silently closed the door behind her. Outside, the sky had a rose hue as dawn began to filter over the mountains.

Despite the early hour, the air was warm, and Nicola felt a surge of well-being as she made her way down the farm drive before taking the short cut across the field towards the village.

Three minutes later, she was pushing open the old wooden back gate of the *pépinière*. The nameplate *Le Jardin de Dominic* had lost a screw and was hanging lopsidedly.

An overgrown path wound its way

past some outbuildings and round the side of the cottage before linking up with the main path that finished between two oleander bushes on either side of the front door.

Nicola wandered slowly around, deep in thought. Last night, when she'd finally managed to corner Henri on his own, he'd flatly refused even to consider settling for seeing Oliver during the school holidays.

'*Non*, Nicola. He comes to live in France or loses his inheritance. There's plenty of room at La Prouveresse for both of you if you decide to accompany him.'

'Oliver is definitely not moving over here on his own, Henri. He's far too young. If he comes, I come, too.'

Henri had shrugged.

'I'm sure we can all live together in harmony. You will let me have your decision before you leave, *oui*?' And Henri had returned to Sylvie, leaving Nicola seething at his arrogance.

Shortly afterwards, the party at the

restaurant had broken up and they'd returned to the farm. Nicola and Oliver said goodnight to everyone and went to their rooms. As Oliver was getting ready for bed, Nicola had popped her head round the door.

'So, you've enjoyed the week?'

'It's been brilliant, Mum. I'm really glad we came. Papa Henri can be a bit grumpy but I think he likes me.'

'Oh, I'm sure he does,' Nicola replied.

'We talked about Dad a bit,' Oliver said, glancing at her.

'Papa Henri says he wishes they'd been able to talk to each other more — got to know one another better. He said he doesn't want to make the same mistakes with me as he did with Dad.'

Nicola processed this information silently.

Oliver brushed his teeth vigorously before continuing.

'He says that he'll always be willing to listen and try to help if I've got a problem. Although, with us in England

and him here in France, I can't see how he could ever be much help; can you?'

Nicola watched her son's face grow thoughtful.

'We are coming back though, aren't we, Mum?' he asked, looking anxiously at Nicola. 'It's been fun. I really like France.'

It was a perfect opening for Nicola to say, 'Enough to live here?' but Oliver had already put his headphones on to listen to a favourite CD before he went to sleep.

Now, as she walked around the neglected smallholding in the early morning light, she considered the future, consoling herself with the thought that at least Oliver had said he liked France. If her idea did prove to be feasible, hopefully he would be pleased.

Nicola kicked some soil loose before bending down and running it through her fingers. The remains of the old garden layout were still visible in places through the overgrowth. Close to the back of the cottage, Nicola traced the outline of the old flower-beds, still defined by their original terracotta edging stones.

There were a number of old earthen-ware pots standing on the paved terrace near the cottage's kitchen door. Nicola visualised how they must have looked in the past, filled with lavender and rosemary, the flowers scenting summer days with perfume.

Two small interlocking ponds, where water had once tumbled soothingly over a rocky waterfall, were visible from the terrace. Tall lily plants seemed to be thriving in the marshy, silted-up ground.

Second Thoughts

Nicola imagined sitting on the terrace in the cool of a summer evening, listening to the frogs and watching the dragonflies flitting over the surface of the pond.

Against a boundary wall, a dilapidated greenhouse gave cover to an ancient vine, its trunk twisted and thick with age. Shrivelled grapes hung in bunches from its leafless stems. Nicola's fingers itched to pull them off, to tidy the vine up, ready for a new growing season.

She stood for a moment in the topmost corner of the garden, visualising the smallholding's position in relation to the village.

From there, she had a good view of the village and the surrounding area. Visible through the trees on the opposite side of the road was the campsite by the small river that wound its way down through the gorge towards the Mediterranean.

Nicola stood, listening to the faint, early morning sounds of the village. The noisy shutters of the *boulangerie* were being pushed up, letting the smell of baking baguettes waft out. Already, the inevitable aroma of fresh coffee from the café was drifting towards her on the light breeze.

A few cars passed the front of the cottage, en route to Nice. But one or two were going in the opposite direction towards the village — including Raoul's.

Idly, Nicola wondered where he'd been so early — or had he been out all night?

She made her way back towards the cottage and the outbuildings, cautiously pushing open the first door she came to.

Inside were the remnants of an old life: rusty garden implements, a bicycle, a wrought-iron garden table and chairs, a large leather trunk, damp cardboard boxes beginning to spill their contents.

One corner of the building had obviously served as a workshop. A bench with a vice and some old tools still stood in one corner. The other outbuilding had clearly been used for animals. The feeding trough was still attached to the wall and there was a small chicken coop in there. Broken bales of straw and hay littered the floor.

Deep in thought, Nicola pulled the door closed. Everything was so run down. It would take weeks, even months, to clear the land and produce anything. Both buildings were in need of urgent maintenance — drainpipes were falling off walls and windows were broken. Nicola bit her lip in frustration.

The idea that, in the middle of the night, had seemed so feasible and exciting, seemed silly and unattainable as the early morning sun began to creep up.

The pink glow was beginning to fade from the stone-built cottage in places, and Nicola could see that a number of the terracotta roof tiles were broken. The pale green paint was peeling off the shutters. Structurally, though, she knew it was sound. All it needed was some loving care and attention.

She was trying to rub some of the grime off one of the downstairs cottage windows in an attempt to see in when Raoul suddenly appeared.

'Want to look inside?' he asked, holding out a large iron key.

'How did you know I was here?'

'I noticed you when I was driving home.' He inserted the key into the lock.

'Are you going to tell me why you are wandering around here?' he asked.

Nicola didn't answer his question immediately.

'You're out and about early,' she said instead.

Inside, the cottage smelled musty and dark but, as Raoul pulled one of the downstairs shutters open, the early morning sunlight streamed through.

Now Nicola could see through to the kitchen that ran the width of the cottage and into the two rooms on either side of the small hallway. A few pieces of furniture were still in place in the rooms, and there was an ancient stove in the kitchen.

As she explored the ground floor, Nicola began to feel excited again. Despite its unkempt appearance, the cottage had a good feel about it.

'You and Henri seemed a bit distant last night,' Raoul said unexpectedly.

Nicola turned away and started to climb the steep stairs to look at the bedrooms without answering.

'Your mother was worried when you left the party early last night,' she commented instead, attempting to avoid Raoul's observation.

Raoul gave a shrug.

'She knew where I was going.'

Nicola wanted to ask where, but she knew it was none of her business.

Upstairs, the rooms were as dirty and dusty as those on the ground floor, and the small, old-fashioned bathroom with its stained bath and sink was uninviting. But there was a wonderful view of the mountains from the main bedroom.

As they stood, side by side, looking out at the snow-capped mountains, Raoul sighed.

'Nicola, it's six o'clock in the morning. Why are we standing in an empty cottage looking at the view?'

Nicola, deep in thought, turned slightly and looked at him.

'Would you sell this place to me? Or possibly rent it initially?'

'Of course,' Raoul replied instantly. 'But why would you want it?'

Nicola shrugged non-committally.

'I've been thinking it might be better for Oliver to grow up in France — to have his family around.'

'Has Henri been putting the pressure on?' Raoul asked shrewdly.

Nicola nodded.

'Just a bit.' She looked at him, and then impulsively decided to tell him the truth.

'He's Your Son'

'Between you and me, he wants to make Oliver his heir on the condition that he comes to live in France — with or without me.'

'Don't let him take over, Nicola.' Raoul said quietly. 'Oliver's your son. Henri smothered Marc when he was young, too. He may have learned from that mistake but, knowing Henri, it won't stop him from trying to interfere in Oliver's life in much the same way.'

'I know.' Nicola sighed. 'And that's the main reason I'd want a place of our own — if we come.' She glanced around. 'At least this place would give me something to do — getting the house done up and sorting the garden. Eventually, it could give me an income if I grow produce to sell.'

She began to make her way back downstairs.

'Anyway, I don't know if I can afford it yet. How much are you asking? It may be out of my price range — I gather you've got some secret investment in mind for the money?'

There was a short silence before Raoul spoke.

'As you've been so honest with me, I'll tell you something in confidence, too,' he began. 'Do you remember your last visit with Marc when I'd just been involved in a terrible tragedy skiing off piste?'

Nicola nodded. She could recall it well. The whole village had been shocked by the accident that killed a young married man from a nearby village. At the time, Raoul had been working at the ski resort, and subsequent investigations had placed most of the blame on him for failing to take the necessary safety measures.

Nicola remembered being struck by Raoul's almost casual acceptance of the situation. Whilst he'd acknowledged he had been at fault, he'd seemed somewhat detached.

It was the main reason she'd never really taken to him in the past. She couldn't understand how he could continue skiing off piste as if nothing had happened; as if he didn't care that a man had died.

'Didn't he leave a widow and a young child?' Nicola asked, wondering why Raoul had decided to mention the tragedy now.

'Marie and Luc. He's fourteen now,' Raoul explained.

He looked at her thoughtfully.

'I decided I would use the profits from this place to set up a trust fund for Luc. I don't need the money — and it would give him a better start in life.'

Nicola was stunned. So there was a softer, secret side to Raoul Traille, after all.

'That's incredibly generous of you, Raoul. How much were you hoping to raise?' she asked.

Deal?

When Raoul told her the figure he had in mind Nicola realised that selling her house in England would give her enough to buy it and have some left over to live on while she did the place up.

'Is that the correct market price?' she asked in disbelief. 'Not a special price for me?'

'It's the price in the estate agent's window,' Raoul replied. 'You can check it. I'm even open to offers on it.'

Nicola shook her head.

'No. The price seems fair enough, particularly in view of what you hope to do with the money.'

Raoul nodded and held his hand out.

'Would you like to shake on it now? I can withdraw it from the estate agent's today.'

Nicola took a deep breath and looked around at the unkempt rooms. She had hoped to return to La Prouveresse to think about it — not be pressurised into making a decision this morning. But, somehow, she had the feeling this place was right for her and Oliver.

She could picture them living here — making a new life for themselves — while securing Oliver's inheritance.

'The thing is, it may take some time to sell my house in England. I don't know how quickly I shall have the money.' She hesitated.

'Not a problem,' Raoul said, still extending his hand. 'I know the money will arrive.'

'Can you do me a favour and keep this to yourself for a couple of hours?' she said, slowly holding out her own hand.

'I need to talk to Oliver and Henri before the news becomes general knowledge.'

As Raoul's hand enveloped hers, he smiled.

'*D'accord!* It's a deal. Let's go and seal it with a coffee and a fresh croissant. I'm starving.'

Decisions

Tante Odette looked up from the stove where she was preparing breakfast as Nicola pushed the door open and walked into the kitchen.

'*Tiens*, Nicola! You're out and about early. You couldn't sleep?'

'A bit too much wine last night, I think,' she replied. 'Thought a walk in the fresh air might clear my head.' She helped herself to coffee from the pot.

She needed to talk to Henri and Oliver before she told anybody else what she'd really been up to.

'Is Henri around?' she enquired nonchalantly.

'Over in the barn as usual,' Tante Odette replied without looking up.

'Shall I take him a cup of coffee?' Nicola asked.

Tante Odette glanced at her but said nothing, simply filling the mug Henri used for his morning coffee and handing it to her.

In the barn, Henri was struggling to look at the feet of a ewe as Nicola walked in.

'*Bonjour*,' he grunted.

Nicola sat on a bale of straw waiting for him to finish, wishing she'd brought her own coffee.

Finally, Henri let the animal go and straightened up to look at Nicola.

'So, you've decided?' he asked.

Nicola nodded as she handed him his coffee.

'I can't throw Oliver's inheritance away before he's old enough to decide what he wants to do — so I will bring him to live in France. But . . . ' she held her hand up as Henri went to speak ' . . . I have a condition or two of my own.'

Henri looked at her, his eyes hard and expressionless. Nicola tried to ignore the way her heart was thumping. She had to stand up to him from the beginning if things were to have any chance of working out.

'I agree there is no point yet in telling Oliver he is to inherit the farm, but I want it in writing that Oliver is to be your heir. No changing your mind on a whim and disowning him, Henri, if Oliver does something to upset you once we are here.'

She paused for a second or two, expecting Henri to say something. When he didn't, she continued.

'I also want you to understand there is to be no interfering in his day-to-day life like you did with Marc. You are Oliver's grandfather — not his father.'

'Anything else?'

'Just one more thing. Raoul has agreed to sell Le Jardin de Dominic to me. Oliver and I will live there and not up here, at La Prouveresse.'

From the look on his face Nicola knew that this last piece of information had come as an unexpected blow.

'Oh, there's no need for that,' Henri said with a brash tone. 'There's plenty of room up here.'

'There's every need, Henri,' Nicola insisted. 'I know Oliver will spend a lot of time up here with you and the *tantes*, but we need our own space, too.'

Nicola paused and generously tried to soften the blow a little.

'There's also the small point that the farm may be Oliver's future — but it isn't mine. If I'm to give up everything in England, I need a home and a life of my own over here.'

There was silence whilst they eyed each other warily. Finally, Henri spoke.

'I'm not saying you're right about not moving into La Prouveresse, but I can see your point,' he said grudgingly.

'In the meantime, I'll get my *notaire* to draw up the necessary papers to make Oliver my heir.' He hesitated before wiping his hand on his trouser leg and holding it out towards Nicola.

'Thank you, Nicola. I know we both want what is best for Oliver. I hope you will be happy living here, in France.'

Nicola gave an uncertain smile as she shook his hand. She just hoped she wasn't making the biggest mistake of her and Oliver's lives.

Bon Voyage!

'How long before we come back then, Mum?' Oliver asked as he wriggled himself into the window seat and fastened his belt.

Nicola shrugged.

'A couple of months at the earliest, I should think. There's so much to arrange.'

Snapping her own seat belt shut, she closed her eyes and thought of how much she had to do in the coming weeks.

'I hope we're back in time to help Papa Henri with the olives. He promised I could drive the tractor!' Oliver enthused.

Nicola opened an eye.

'He did? We'll have to see about that.'

Inwardly, she was furious with Henri. How dare he! Tractors were far too dangerous to let inexperienced thirteen-year-old boys loose in the driving seat.

As Oliver clamped his headphones over his ears and disappeared into his own noisy world, Nicola reflected upon the last twenty-four hours and the major, life-changing decision she'd taken.

Oliver had hailed the news of their move to France with a whoop of delight. Nicola only hoped he would still feel the same when it came to having to say goodbye to all his friends.

The *tantes* had both been delighted when she'd told them the news.

'It will be so nice to have a boy around the farm again,' Odette had said, gently patting Nicola on the arm.

Tante Giselle had exuberantly hugged both Nicola and Oliver in turn.

'*Hourra!*' she'd said, clapping her hands excitedly. 'I'm so glad you've decided to come. And there was me thinking I'd turn Marc's old room into a sewing-room. Now, instead, I'll decorate it for Oliver.'

Gently, Nicola had interrupted.

'No, Giselle. I expect Oliver will spend a lot of time up here when he's not at school, but he's not going to be living on the farm. I'm buying Le Jardin de Dominic from Raoul.'

Once the *tantes* recovered from their initial surprise, both agreed that Nicola was probably doing the right thing in keeping her independence.

'Anyway,' Tante Giselle said, 'Le Jardin is so close — it's almost a part of the farm!'

'But Nicola, *la petite maison* of Le Jardin is in a terrible state. It will be impossible for you to live there. We will clean it before you come back and then help you decorate it, *oui*?' Tante Odette had said worriedly.

'Oh, I couldn't ask you to do that,' Nicola said.

'You're not asking — we're offering!' Tante Giselle had stated firmly. 'Besides, we are so pleased you are coming to live in France.'

She wiped the tears from her eyes before enveloping Nicola in another tight hug.

The *Tantes*

Recalling the scene in the kitchen, Nicola smiled. She didn't have the slightest doubt that, between them, the *tantes* would have her new home scrubbed and beaten into shape before she and Oliver returned.

They were a funny pair, the *tantes*, nearly sixty and still sharing the same large bedroom at the top of the farmhouse that they'd had as children. These days, they did most of the routine work on the farm, as well as looking after Henri.

Tante Giselle hadn't married or left La Prouveresse, but Tante Odette had married a Parisian, leaving home when she was twenty. She returned a mere five years later for reasons Nicola had never discovered.

From what she'd gathered from Marc years ago, there had been some kind of scandal that was never discussed. Funny, really; Tante Giselle was the noisy, extrovert twin and yet it was Odette — the quiet, reserved one — who was the centre of a family secret.

Once the stewardess had passed through with the buffet trolley, Nicola settled down with a notebook to make a list of the things she would need to organise. By the time the plane landed, she'd filled six pages.

Wheeling their luggage out through the arrivals hall, Nicola was pleased to see Andrew waiting. As he spotted them, his face lit up with a huge smile.

It was good to see him again, she thought to herself. But how on earth was she going to tell him the news about Le Jardin de Dominic? She knew he was going to hate the idea.

It was Oliver, however, who broke the news as they pushed their luggage trolley through the carpark.

'Guess what, Andrew? Mum's had this absolutely brilliant idea. She's going to sell the house, move to France and buy a smallholding!'

'I Can Explain'

Nicola closed her eyes in dismay. How could she have forgotten to tell Oliver not to mention the move? She'd wanted to break the news to Andrew herself, gently.

Andrew turned to look at Nicola wearing an expression of bewilderment.

'Tell me Oliver's joking?' he pleaded quietly. The look on Nicola's face told him that it was no joke.

'But what about us? I thought you were going to think while you were away — about us becoming more of a couple? Don't we even get to discuss this move together?'

'Andrew, I can explain. But not now. Not here,' Nicola said, attempting to calm him down.

He turned away without a word and began to stack the luggage into the boot of the car. Meanwhile, Nicola climbed inside, praying that Andrew wouldn't try to discuss things on the way home. She simply couldn't talk about it in front of Oliver.

If moving to France meant that her relationship with Andrew was going to be sacrificed, she at least owed him the truth. But Andrew had to understand that Henri had given her no choice.

The journey home was quiet, the atmosphere strained. Oliver, realising that his news had upset Andrew, retreated behind his earphones, and Nicola sat silently, not daring to look at him.

Once home, Oliver disappeared up to his room and Nicola pulled the present she'd bought Andrew out of her case. But he refused to take it.

'No, Nicola. Not until you tell me what's going on,' he said sadly. 'Why are you moving to France? Are you expecting me to come with you, or are you about to walk out of my life? I need to know — what exactly are your feelings towards me?'

'What Is Going On?'

The rain on Tuesday evening did nothing to lift Nicola's spirits as she prepared supper for herself and Andrew.

Oliver was spending the evening with a friend and so she and Andrew had a rare couple of hours to themselves. Andrew had suggested taking her out to dinner but, as she knew he intended to 'talk this French business through', she had opted for home territory.

She knew the evening was going to be difficult. Andrew had only spoken to her once after he'd rejected the present she'd bought him in France, demanding to know exactly how she felt about him.

When she'd shaken her head, refusing to discuss things with Oliver within earshot, he'd turned and left.

'I'll ring you,' he'd said. That was two days ago.

Tonight he was sure to demand answers to these questions, and she doubted he would be happy with the ones she was going to supply.

Nicola bit her lip. It was a shame, but she'd be glad when the evening was over and things had been sorted — one way or another.

Unusually, Andrew rang the doorbell when he arrived and waited for her to open the door. Normally he let himself in.

'Hello, Nicola. How are you?' he asked as he shook the rain from his coat.

'I'm fine,' she said. She attempted to give him her usual welcome kiss, but Andrew had already moved away from her into the hallway.

She sighed.

'Supper will be about ten minutes. Would you like a glass of wine?'

'What I'd really like, Nicola, is to know what is going on,' he said bluntly.

Nicola poured two glasses of wine and silently gave one to Andrew.

'I'm sorry Oliver blurted out the news before I had a chance to explain what had happened in France. Oliver doesn't know the real reason behind our move either, so what I'm about to tell you is in confidence.'

Andrew raised an eyebrow in surprise.

'So, how did you justify uprooting him?' he challenged.

Nicola shrugged.

'I told him that we'd have a better life over there. I'm hoping he will accept that,' Nicola replied.

'And the real reason?'

'Henri wants Oliver to inherit the farm. But to do so he has to move to France and spend the rest of his childhood there, with or without me.'

Andrew waited for her to finish.

'Initially, I told Henri there was no way I'd even consider his demand. Then he threatened to tell Oliver I had thrown his inheritance away — that I, alone, was responsible for depriving him of the farm.'

There was a silence and Nicola sighed.

'I couldn't discuss it with Oliver — he's too young to bear such a burden. I don't see that I have any choice but to uproot us and go to France — whatever the cost to me personally,' she added quietly.

'And will there be a cost to you personally?'

Nicola turned away, trying to fight back her tears.

'Yes, of course there would.'

Andrew continued to look at her, his face expressionless.

'And the smallholding you're buying?'

'Le Jardin de Dominic,' Nicola said.

'That's my independence from Henri. I refused to live on the farm. Besides, I'm going to need a life of my own over there.'

She glanced at Andrew, a small smile on her lips.

'You know I've always wanted a smallholding. Moving to France will at least give me that.'

Andrew took a sip of his wine.

'And where were you hoping I'd fit into all this? Did you even think about me, about us, before Henri issued his ultimatum? Did our relationship even cross your mind?'

'I thought about you a lot while I was away,' Nicola said slowly. 'I really missed you. I'd made my mind up that, yes, it was time for our relationship to move up a gear, as you suggested. The last thing I want to do is hurt you or lose what we have.'

'But?' Andrew said.

Nicola took a deep breath.

'I don't want to walk out of your life, as you've accused me of doing, but there's going to be the little matter of over a thousand miles between us for the next few years. I wish . . . ' she stopped and brushed a stray tear away ' . . . there was another way to safeguard Oliver's inheritance — but there isn't.'

Andrew looked at her.

'Tell me something, Nicola. If we'd

87

been a couple before you went to France would you still be talking of leaving me for a new life in another country?'

Nicola hesitated.

'It would have been different — an even harder decision. Hopefully we'd have gone together.' She paused. 'But, yes. I'd still have to go. Oliver's needs come first with me, and always will,' she added quietly.

'Nothing I can do or say is going to change your mind?'

Nicola shook her head.

'I'm so sorry, Andrew. I have to move to France with Oliver. But surely we can stay friends? Keep in touch? You will come to visit us?'

'Oh, Nicola.' Andrew sighed. 'I've said I can't imagine my life without you in it, but the truth is I don't know if I can handle just the occasional glimpse. It will always remind me of what might have been. I don't think I have the strength to cope with that. A clean break when you leave is probably the best option, as difficult as it may be . . .'

An Offer

The sun was shining as Giselle drove the ancient farm van down the driveway, past Henri and Odette who were busily pruning the vines in the small *vignoble*. She tooted the horn cheerfully before turning left and making her way down to the village.

The village square was busy with the small mid-week market. Giselle hummed absently to herself as she locked the van and began to make her way towards the stalls. A couple more weeks and Nicola and Oliver would be here. Life was beginning to look up!

Happily, she wandered around looking at the various stalls before buying the things she needed, including the cheese and lamb for supper. Passing a stall where a young potter had made a display of terracotta dishes, she bought a small oval one. She'd promised to show Nicola how to make potato gratin, and it would be ideal.

Finally, she stopped to chat with her friend who ran the soap stall and treated herself to a bar of her favourite, lavender.

'*Trois, s'il vous plait*,' she said. She knew Odette liked it, and she'd put the other one in the bathroom at Le Jardin when they'd finished clearing it.

Placing the soaps in her bag, she said her goodbyes, turning away just in time to catch a glimpse of Raoul hurrying past on the other side of the square.

Giselle got the distinct feeling Raoul had seen her and was avoiding her. She watched thoughtfully as he disappeared into the café. Why had he ignored her?

She was very fond of Raoul and he was invariably pleased to see her whenever they bumped into each other. He'd spent a lot of time up at La Prouveresse as a boy with Marc and he always called her Tante Giselle, kissing and hugging her every time they met.

For a second or two, Giselle was

tempted to wander over to the café and say hello, but decided she didn't have the time — she had to get to the *supermarché* before it closed for lunch. Besides, she was probably imagining things. Raoul was just too busy to stop. Giselle pushed the thought out of her mind and tried to concentrate on the rest of her shopping.

Soon, her basket was full and she joined a queue at the checkout, glad to put it down on the floor while she waited to be served.

'You're having a grand cleaning session up there at La Prouveresse by the looks of it, Giselle.'

Turning, Giselle smiled at Sylvie.

'*Non*. It is for Le Jardin de Dominic. Tomorrow Odette and I clean it, ready for Nicola and Oliver.'

Sylvie frowned.

'But Raoul says they are going to live at the farm, after all. At least until Henri has had all the building work done.'

'*Pardon*?' Giselle said. 'What are you

talking about, Sylvie? I didn't know Nicola had asked Henri to organise any building work at Le Jardin.'

There was a short pause before Sylvie went on, clearly embarrassed.

'Raoul's selling Le Jardin to Henri, not Nicola. Apparently Henri made him an offer he couldn't refuse.'

'I bet he did,' Giselle said under her breath. 'Sylvie, please excuse me. I have to go home.' Furiously, Giselle pushed her way out through the queue leaving behind her shopping.

Odette was in the kitchen when Giselle burst in.

'Where is he?' She demanded.

Odette looked up in surprise from the sauce she was stirring.

'In the barn, I think. What's wrong, Giselle?'

But Giselle had gone, slamming the kitchen door behind her.

So Cross

'I am so cross with you, Henri Jacques — why can't you stop meddling?'

Henri glanced up briefly from the piece of machinery he was working on before he shrugged.

'You've heard, then? It's just a business deal. Le Jardin virtually borders La Prouveresse — it seems stupid not to join the two together. The extra ten acres will be useful. And with the field next to it being developed, it's a good investment.'

'And Nicola and Oliver? What were you planning for them?'

'I thought they could live up here while the cottage is renovated, then I'd rent it to them — if they still want it, that is. They might want to stay up here with us by then . . . '

Giselle regarded her brother thoughtfully.

'Now, you listen to me, Henri. In the first place, I know why Nicola has agreed to bring Oliver to live here.' She paused. 'I've been feeling guilty ever since she told me, but the thought of having Oliver here is so exciting and wonderful that I didn't say anything to her. Perhaps I should have.'

Henri remained unresponsive as Giselle went on.

'I take it you didn't intend to tell Nicola before she got here? You meant simply to present her with a fait accompli when she had nowhere to go? Well, Henri, it won't work. You can't control their lives when they get here. Have you learned nothing from the past?'

Giselle sighed. She'd been hoping that Henri would respond to her last remark, but he was silent. She moved closer to her brother.

'I'm looking forward to them coming as much as you. But if you don't stop this ridiculous business deal with Raoul and let him sell Le Jardin de Dominic to Nicola as agreed, I shall telephone Nicola and tell her some of the home truths you conveniently omitted to mention during her visit. Then the whole thing will be off, anyway. We'll all continue to live our separate lives and you'll never get to know your grandson properly.'

There was a long silence as Giselle and Henri stared at each other. Henri was the first to turn away, his shoulders dropping.

'Do we understand each other, Henri?'

Henri nodded.

'*Oui.*'

'Good. And one more thing. Odette and I plan to start cleaning Le Jardin tomorrow in preparation for Nicola and Oliver. There's no reason now why we shouldn't do that, is there?' she asked quietly.

'I'm sure Nicola will be very grateful to you both,' Henri said avoiding his sister's gaze.

'I'm sure she will, too,' Giselle

replied. 'Now, you have a phone call to make, and I think Odette will have lunch ready.'

Henri covered the machine he'd been working on and they both returned to the farmhouse. On the way, a thought troubled Giselle.

Nicola might be grateful for the cleaning of Le Jardin de Dominic, but Henri's decision to deceive her and Oliver was another matter. She could only hope that Nicola would forgive her for playing a part in it . . .

*　*　*

Nicola watched thoughtfully as the *For Sale* sign was replaced by one with *SOLD* emblazoned across it in large letters. There was no going back now.

The new owners wanted to take possession at the end of the month — that gave her just three weeks to get everything packed and organised before she and Oliver left for France.

Hopefully everything was going to

plan in France, too. The last time she'd spoken to Raoul he had been quite distant and wasn't able to confirm many details.

He couldn't even give her a date for signing the contract, so it looked as if they were going to have to live up at La Prouveresse for a week or even two when they arrived. That would please the *tantes* — and Henri, of course.

Nicola was packing up the latest box of books ready to go to the charity shop when the telephone rang.

'*Allô*, Nicola? It's Giselle. How are you?'

'Hello, Giselle, I'm fine, thanks. Nothing wrong, is there?' Nicola asked, somewhat surprised.

'*Non*. I just wondered if you had a date for your arrival yet?'

'I think it will be about the twenty-eighth. The only problem is, I haven't heard anything about Le Jardin. The last time I spoke to Raoul he simply said it was all in hand and that, in France, these things take time.'

'*Oui*, they do,' Giselle agreed. 'And there was a small local problem, but that has now been dealt with. I think Raoul expects the papers to be ready at the end of the month so that date is perfect! Odette and I have cleaned the cottage, but you will stay up here with us for a day or two, yes?'

'Please, Giselle, if it's not a problem. The furniture won't be arriving until a couple of days after we do. Do you know anything about the problem with Le Jardin?' she asked curiously.

'Some local red tape,' Giselle said. 'You know how we French love paperwork! I'm sure Raoul will explain the delay when he sees you.'

Nicola was about to ask how Henri and Odette were when Oliver rushed in, slamming the door behind him and running upstairs to his room.

'Giselle, I'm so sorry, I've got to go. I'll talk to you again very soon.'

'What's the Matter?'

Oliver's bedroom door was firmly closed when Nicola went upstairs. She hesitated before knocking gently.

'Can I come in?' she asked quietly.

Oliver was lying on his bed, hands clasped behind his head, trying not to cry.

'What's the matter?' Nicola said, sitting on the bed.

'Everything! I don't want to go to France any more,' he said, jumping up off the bed and going to look out of the window. 'And you can't make me,' he went on, turning to face her defiantly.

'Oliver, I'm afraid I can,' she said. 'But what's suddenly happened to bring this on? Only a few weeks ago you were really excited at the thought of living in France.'

Oliver shrugged.

'I thought it would be exciting living

where Dad grew up, but all my friends are here. Besides, they've thrown me out of the school band. Mr Wilkinson said there was no point in me even going to rehearsals now that I'm leaving. He gave my place to Josh and he can't play for toffee.

'And Chloë won't come roller-skating with me any more because, oh . . . just because. And why don't we see Andrew any more? I miss him. I won't have any friends in France.'

Nicola sighed. She'd been waiting for Oliver to realise what moving to France would really mean — changing schools, giving up his after-school activities, leaving his friends behind . . . all this as well as having to adapt to a new country and a strange language when they got there.

'Well, Mr Wilkinson has a point. We're leaving in three weeks, and Josh will need to practise with the band. I'm sure there will be a school band for you to join in France — perhaps even better than the one here. As for Chloë, if you tell her she can come for a holiday once we're settled in, she'll start counting the days.'

Nicola paused.

'You'll be able to introduce her to all your new friends in your French school. We'll work out an itinerary — show her all the sights.'

'I still don't want to go,' Oliver muttered in protest.

Nicola bit her lip.

'I'm afraid not going is no longer an option. The house is sold and I'm buying Le Jardin de Dominic from Raoul. Oliver, I know it will be a big change for both of us — a real challenge — but it should be good, too.'

'Why do we have to go over there to live? Even Dad didn't want to live there, and it was his home.'

Nicola smothered a sigh.

'I've told you, Papa Henri suggested it and, having considered everything, I think it's the right thing to do. We'll have a better life in France. You'll get to know your relations and learn another language, and I'll be able to run a smallholding — something I've always wanted to do.'

'But why can't you do that here? At least you'd have Andrew to help you.'

'Things are too expensive,' Nicola said. 'Besides, Andrew's got his own life to lead. While we're on the subject, though, why don't you e-mail him and ask if he'd like to come to supper tonight?'

'If you want,' Oliver said sullenly. 'I'm not very hungry.'

'Not even for a pizza?' Nicola coaxed. 'Now, e-mail Andrew and find out if he'd like to come for supper. I'm going to do some more packing.'

Determined

Back downstairs, she made herself a cup of coffee and sat sipping it thoughtfully. Oliver's worries had re-opened all her own doubts over the move.

He was right; Marc had never wanted to return to France to live.

'The family would suffocate me, particularly my father,' he'd always said. 'You wouldn't believe how patriarchal these old French families can be. No, I'm definitely better off here.'

Well, she wouldn't let the Jacques family suffocate her and Oliver. She was determined to make a success of this new life and safeguard Oliver's inheritance. She'd also make sure she kept her own independence — particularly from Henri.

They'd still come back to England frequently to visit her relatives. Not that she had many now — just her cousins down in Devon. And she doubted that Andrew would want them to visit after the events of late.

Pensively, she looked out of the window. Since the evening Andrew had advocated a clean break when she finally moved, they'd only spoken on the telephone once or twice. She realised he was trying to distance himself from both her and Oliver in an effort to make the break easier, but she missed him. She'd asked him to come round a couple of times but he'd made his excuses.

Hopefully he'd accept Oliver's invitation to come for supper.

The phone rang later that afternoon.

'Nicola, it's Andrew. Listen, Oliver has just invited me to supper and I wanted to check . . . '

'Please come, Andrew,' Nicola interrupted. 'Oliver needs to see you. He's not very happy at the moment and he's missing you not being around. So am I,' she added quietly.

There was a short silence at the other end of the line before Andrew agreed.

'Is seven-thirty all right?' he asked.

'Thanks. And, Andrew?' Nicola paused. 'Let yourself in.'

Oliver was still upstairs when Andrew arrived clutching a bunch of flowers and a box of chocolates.

'Peace offering,' he said, handing them to her. 'I'm sorry I haven't been in touch. I've been trying to sort things out in my mind.'

He looked at her before gently taking her in his arms.

'Nicola, I hate the thought of you going to France. I also hate the fact that you will no longer be a part of my everyday life — but I can't bear the thought of losing contact with you altogether. I don't think a clean break is possible. Please may I have visiting rights in your new life?'

'I'd like that,' Nicola said with a smile. 'And I know Oliver will, too.'

A wry smile flitted across Andrew's

face as he pulled her closer and kissed her.

'A couple of weeks to settle in and then I'll be the first guest at Le Jardin de Dominic, OK?'

Goodbye

Nicola and Oliver stood and watched as the furniture van disappeared down the road and out of sight. She put her arm around her son's shoulders.

'Just think, the next time we see that, we'll be in France,' she whispered.

'You do think they'll look after Frisby properly, don't you?' Oliver asked anxiously.

'Of course. Bill the foreman told me he loves cats. He's got one even older than Frisby at home, and I've given them lots of her favourite food. I suspect she'll eat and sleep all the way down — that's much nicer than being put in the noisy hold of a plane. Come on, let's get our things. Andrew will be here any moment.'

'It's strange to think we'll never come back here, isn't it?' Oliver said unexpectedly.

Nicola looked at him but didn't say anything. And, as they dragged their suitcases to the front door, Oliver looked thoughtful.

'Are you sad at leaving this house, Mum?'

Nicola nodded.

'A bit. Your dad and I were very happy here in the beginning. You were born here.' She glanced at Oliver and saw that he was close to tears.

'You know, Oliver, the bricks and mortar aren't important. It's the memories we take with us. And we've both got some happy memories of this house, haven't we?'

Oliver nodded.

'Yes. And once we've left, I won't keep expecting Dad to walk through the door — even though I know he's never coming back.'

'Oh, Oliver, come here,' Nicola said, putting her arms around him and hugging him tight.

'I miss him, too, and I do understand. This new life in France will be good, you'll see. We'll make some more happy memories together.'

A toot from a car horn made them both jump and they looked up to see Andrew striding up the garden path.

'Hi! Give me a hand with the luggage, Oliver, while your mum locks up — then we'll be off.'

Once at the airport, Andrew waited with them until they'd checked in and Nicola had their boarding passes.

'Before you go, please listen to me, both of you,' Andrew began. 'Nicola, if things don't work out for any reason, you know my home is there for both of you. And Oliver, any time you want to see United play, I'd be more than happy to have you stay and take you.' He gave Oliver a hug and Nicola a kiss.

'I'm going to miss you both so much.'

Nicola swallowed hard. She hated goodbyes.

'Things will be fine, Andrew. We'll miss you, too, but you're coming over next month,' she said, trying not to cry.

She turned to Oliver.

'Right, our adventure starts here. Let's go.'

Nicola smiled a final goodbye at Andrew before turning away quickly so he shouldn't see the tears that were starting to fall down her cheeks. She held Oliver's hand tightly as they both walked through the security gate and on into the departure lounge.

'Welcome Back!'

It was late evening when they landed in Nice and Nicola and Oliver were glad to see Raoul waiting for them in the arrivals hall.

'Welcome back to France,' he said, kissing Nicola on the cheek and shaking Oliver's hand. Taking the luggage trolley from Nicola, he waited for the automatic doors to open and then led them towards his car.

'Claudine sends her best wishes, by the way. She was planning on coming down with me to meet you — to give you a proper welcome to France — but she's not feeling too good this evening.'

'Oh, nothing serious, I hope,' Nicola said.

Raoul shook his head.

'No, I don't think so. Anyway, she said she'd be up to see you at the farm tomorrow.'

Outside, the air was warm and scented with the smell of the eucalyptus trees that lined the carpark. Nicola took a deep breath. It was so different from the wet weather they'd left behind.

'Is everything progressing OK with Le Jardin?' she asked as they began the drive out to La Prouveresse.

'*C'est bon,*' Raoul answered. 'The *notaire* says the papers will be ready for signing this weekend and then Le Jardin de Dominic will be yours.'

'Good,' Nicola said. 'By the way, what was the little local problem that held everything up?'

Henri

Raoul hesitated.

'Henri,' he muttered.

'Henri? But it's nothing to do with him . . . ' Nicola said as realisation dawned. She should have known Henri would interfere. He hadn't liked it when she'd refused to live up at La Prouveresse with him and the *tantes*.

'He tried to stop you selling to me?'

'*Oui*. He really put the pressure on for a while and then I got a phone call saying it was all off and I had to sell to you after all.'

'But Raoul, we'd shaken on the deal. Why didn't you at least ring me and tell me what was going on?'

There was a long silence and Nicola wondered if he was going to answer her question. Eventually, he shrugged.

'To be honest, Nicola, I didn't know what to do. Henri kept insisting that

you and Oliver belonged on the farm
— that he would see you all right. He
was talking about making the house
nice before you moved in. Besides, I
kept hoping he would change his mind
and eventually, he did.

'I think Tante Giselle had a hand in
that, mind you,' he added thoughtfully.
'She's not spoken to me for some time.'

Nicola sat watching the lights of
passing cars flash by. She might have
guessed Henri would try to interfere at
this early stage, but at least Tante
Giselle had somehow managed to put a
stop to his scheming.

'Raoul, are you absolutely certain
that the papers will be ready for me to
sign this weekend? I won't be able to
rest until I know for sure that Le Jardin
de Dominic is mine.'

'Absolutely,' Raoul said. 'There is just
one more thing, though.'

'What now?'

'Last week the council gave themselves permission to develop the field
next to Le Jardin. If you don't want to

go ahead with the purchase because of it, I'd understand.'

Nicola sighed. She suddenly felt very tired. The last few weeks had been physically and emotionally draining and now the last thing she needed was to find there were problems with Le Jardin de Dominic before they'd even moved in.

'What sort of development? A block of apartments? Houses?'

Raoul shook his head.

'Nothing like that. They're planning a tourist information centre with 'A Taste Of The Countryside' shop. It won't be that big — a single storey building with a small carpark at most.'

Nicola was silent. She'd liked the fact that Le Jardin didn't have any close neighbours but, being set back off a main road, wasn't isolated, either. Having a tourist information office next door would inevitably mean people coming and going and more noise from cars.

'What exactly is this shop going to

sell?' Nicola asked.

'It promotes and sells produce from the local area,' Raoul said. 'Like honey, olive oil, wine, apple juice, soap, pottery — anything that is from around here.'

'So if I can get Le Jardin functioning as a *pépinière* again, I might have a market right on my doorstep?' Nicola said thoughtfully.

'*Oui*,' Raoul said, glancing at her. 'It could be good for you.'

'Can I look at the plans anywhere?'

'If you like, I'll take you down to the Hôtel de Ville tomorrow and explain them to you,' Raoul said enthusiastically.

'Henri will also be able to tell you more — he might even know when they plan to start building. He's on the town council, and hoping to become mayor one day.'

★   ★   ★

Nicola was silent. Right now she was so cross with the way Henri had tried to buy Le Jardin from under her that she was determined not to ask him for anything. It would be difficult enough, accepting his hospitality for the next few days.

The sooner she could sign the completion papers for Le Jardin de Dominic and start their independent French lives, the better!

It's Yours!

'*Merci beaucoup, Madame Jacques, la pépinière* is now yours. I hope you and your son will be very happy there.' The *notaire* pushed the keys across the table to Nicola.

As she placed them carefully in her bag, Nicola felt an overwhelming sense of relief. Four days after arriving in France, Le Jardin de Dominic was finally hers. She and Oliver could begin their lives in their new home.

She glanced at Henri, who'd insisted upon accompanying her to the lawyer's office.

'Just to help. Your French is not up to the legal phrases, is it?' was all he'd said when she'd questioned the necessity of him coming.

Nicola had to admit that her limited French was not good enough for all the official forms she'd had to fill in since arriving in France. But she couldn't help feeling that Henri was looking after his own interests in some way.

Going through the paperwork in the lawyer's office had felt very much like the point in the church marriage service where the vicar asks if there are any objections. Until she'd actually signed, Nicola kept expecting Henri to intervene in some way.

Now, he moved to her side as they left the office to walk back to the car.

'*Voilà*! You have your smallholding. I, too, hope you and Oliver will be happy there.'

'Thank you, Henri,' Nicola said quietly, hoping that he meant what he said.

'Good doing business with you, Nicola,' Raoul said, shaking her hand. 'If you have any problems or if I can help in any way, just give me a ring,' he added.

Before Nicola could say anything in reply, Henri cut in abruptly.

'Now she's here, she's got the family for that.'

Nicola tried not to let her resentment show. Henri hadn't shown much family loyalty to them in the past, but now that she and Oliver were living in France, it was obvious that the renowned Henri Jacques's possessive streak was going to resurface.

Raoul glanced at Henri sharply before turning to Nicola.

'Well, you know where I am anyway,' he said.

Nicola looked at them in turn.

'I appreciate the help I've had from both of you, but I've got to stand on my own two feet. I did it in England, so there is no reason why I shouldn't do it out here.'

Henri ignored her remarks.

'Well, I've work to do back at the farm,' he said, before striding off in the direction of his car.

Raoul smiled.

'You'll soon pick the language up — you could always find yourself a night-time language tape. Now, can I give you a lift back to Le Jardin?'

'Thanks, but I left Oliver at La Prouveresse,' Nicola replied. 'Henri is taking me back there to collect him so I'd better catch him up. After lunch, Oliver and I are going to paint the kitchen at Le Jardin before the furniture arrives tomorrow. I can't believe how quickly the time has gone since I arrived. There's been so much to organise.'

As they hurried towards Henri in the carpark, a large Land-Rover swished past them before parking at the far end.

'Ah, Nicola. Somebody you need to meet!' Holding her arm, Raoul led her purposefully over towards the man who was getting out of his car.

Nicola glanced at him suspiciously.

'Raoul, what are you doing?' She hesitated.

Raoul laughed. Standing to one side, Nicola watched as he and the man greeted each other enthusiastically with much hugging and handshaking.

The man's sultry Mediterranean looks and dark, bohemian hairstyle seemed at odds with his business-like suit and shiny leather shoes.

As she watched and waited for Raoul to introduce her, something tugged at Nicola's memory. Was it possible she already knew this man?

Amid the torrent of quickly spoken French, Nicola caught the occasional word.

'*Anglaise*. Henri. Le Jardin de Dominic.'

Raoul was clearly explaining who she was before he turned.

'Nicola, meet Gilles Bongars. He's the surveyor in charge of the new 'Taste Of The Countryside' centre.'

'*Enchanté, madame.*' The hand that shook Nicola's was strong, and held her fingers in a tight grip before releasing them.

'You'd like me to discuss the proposals with you?'

Nicola nodded.

'Please,' she replied.

Both Raoul and Henri had gone over the building plans with her in the mayor's office yesterday, but she was still unsure about certain things. Perhaps Gilles would be able to answer some of her questions.

'I'll be on site this afternoon at four o'clock. We'll meet then?'

'Thank you,' Nicola said. 'I'll look forward to it.'

'So shall I, *madame*,' Gilles answered seriously before bidding goodbye to them both.

Henri tooted his car horn impatiently and Nicola turned quickly to Raoul.

'Goodbye, and thank you. I hope Luc appreciates what you've done for him.'

Raoul shrugged his shoulders.

'I hope so, too. I'll bring him to meet Oliver soon, if you'd like? They're about the same age.'

It was nearly lunchtime when Henri and Nicola arrived back at La Prouveresse. Henri went straight to the barn to get the tractor and tools ready for an afternoon working in the olive groves and Nicola made her way to the kitchen.

Both the *tantes* were there — Odette busy preparing lunch and Giselle sitting at the large wooden table with Oliver, going through the contents of a shoebox. They glanced up with welcoming smiles as Nicola walked in.

'Hi, Mum. Is Le Jardin de Dominic ours now?' Oliver asked.

Nicola waved the keys in the air triumphantly.

'Yes! So this afternoon you and I are painting the kitchen. What have you got there?' she asked curiously, looking at the motley collection of things lying on the table.

'Some of Dad's things. The *tantes* have given them to me. Look, Dad had a catapult — and there's a diary he kept the year he turned fourteen. I'm not sure whether I ought to read that or not,' Oliver said worriedly.

'I expect he thought it was going to be private for ever and ever. I've got another photo of him now, too

— skiing. Tante Giselle has said she'll take me skiing next winter, if I want.'

Nicola glanced across at Giselle.

'You still ski?' she asked.

'*Oui*, of course,' Giselle said. 'These days I have plenty of padding if I fall!' She laughed, as she glanced down at her ample figure.

Home Sweet Home

Nicola inserted the large key into the front door lock of Le Jardin de Dominic and took a deep breath before turning it. Her next step would carry her across the threshold of her new life.

Once inside, she quickly opened the shutters, allowing the sunlight to come streaming in. The *tantes* had done a great job of cleaning the place and the musty smell of a neglected cottage had been replaced by the sweet scent of cleaning materials and bunches of dried lavender and rosemary.

Before she set about starting to paint the kitchen, Nicola wandered around visualising where the furniture would go when it arrived the next morning.

Humming happily to herself, she began to paint the long wall a shade the tin described as 'sunshine yellow'. The noise of the tractor at La Prouveresse two fields away drifted down towards her and she glanced out of the kitchen window.

Oliver had begged to be excused from decorating duties that afternoon, saying he wanted to work with Henri in the olive grove. Much to Oliver's disappointment, Nicola had made Henri promise he wouldn't let him anywhere near the tractor driving seat.

She knew it was early days, but Oliver's relationship with his grandfather seemed to be developing along the right lines. So far, Henri hadn't overstepped any of the boundaries she had in place to stop him interfering in Oliver's life.

Moving into Le Jardin would inevitably put some distance between themselves and Henri as they made friends and settled into their new lives. Hopefully, there would soon be other influences outside of the farm — and Henri — competing for Oliver's attention.

As she neared the end of the kitchen

wall, Nicola heard a car door slam and, seconds later, the noise of the old-fashioned iron knocker on the front door was echoing around the empty house.

Cautiously, she opened the door to find Claudine standing there clutching a plant pot.

'First Visitor'

'Hi! Raoul said I'd find you here this afternoon. I wanted to be your first visitor. Can't stay long as I have to get to the school but I just thought I'd welcome you to your new home. This needs to go outside.'

As instructed, Nicola placed the potted grapefruit plant on the yet to be cleaned patio beneath the kitchen window.

'The blossoms will smell wonderful,' Claudine said. 'I love the wall colour,' she added as they walked back into the kitchen.

'You don't think it's too bright?' Nicola asked anxiously. As the paint dried, it looked far more garish than she'd envisaged.

Claudine shook her head.

'*Non. C'est bon*. It's cheerful. Besides, it will soon fade. Where's Oliver?'

'Helping Henri,' Nicola replied. 'Speaking of Oliver and schools, I have to sort something out for him. Where do I start?'

Claudine frowned.

'*Difficile*. He's thirteen, isn't he? Well, it would have to be Nice for a senior school. How about the English school there? At least that way his lack of French won't be a problem. I could get you the number,' she offered.

'The schools finish soon for two months,' she went on. 'Why not reserve Oliver a place and let him have an extra-long summer holiday this year? He can start a new school year in September. He'll probably have made a few friends in the village by then, too.'

'That's a wonderful idea,' Nicola said slowly. 'It's been a hard year for him. Three months will give him a chance to come to terms with things — settle in here and then get on with his education. Thanks, Claudine.'

'Well, I must dash,' she said with a smile. 'Oh, I have a message from

Raoul, before I forget. He's arranged for two men to come and help shift furniture tomorrow morning. They'll be here at nine o'clock.'

Claudine leaned forward to give Nicola the customary kisses.

'*Bonne chance* in your new home, Nicola.'

Standing in the doorway of Le Jardin de Dominic, waving goodbye to Claudine, Nicola saw Gilles Bongars's Land-Rover pull up next door.

As she stood there dithering, Gilles raised a hand in acknowledgment and smiled at her. There was nothing else for it, she would have to go and meet the elegant Monsieur Bongars in her work clothes.

Carefully pulling the front door closed behind her, Nicola began to make her way across to the neighbouring field. Hopefully Gilles would be able to supply answers about the new development.

★   ★   ★

'Would you like a cup of coffee?' Nicola offered as she and Gilles walked into the kitchen of Le Jardin. 'Odette insisted on bringing me a flask after lunch. I'm afraid there's only water, otherwise. I'm not equipped for entertaining yet, as you can see.' She indicated the empty kitchen with her hands.

'A glass of water would be fine,' Gilles replied, giving a warm smile. 'When do you get to move in properly?'

'Tomorrow, I hope,' Nicola said excitedly as she poured the water. 'Are you sure you don't mind taking a look at the cottage? I feel I've imposed enough on your time already.'

For the past hour, Gilles had walked her around the site next door, explaining what was going where and patiently answering all of her questions.

Apparently, although building work would begin in about a month, Gilles didn't expect the centre to be open for business for at least another six.

'It will take time to organise and set

up the farmers' co-operative as well as getting the handicraft producers together. And finding the right people to run the place won't be easy. Because it's going to be a tourist information centre as well, staff will have to speak at least two languages.'

One of Nicola's biggest worries had been the amount of extra traffic the place would generate, but Gilles couldn't see that being a problem.

Finally, it seemed that all her questions had been answered.

'Thank you so much for taking the time to explain things to me,' she said. 'I'll leave you to get on with your work now.' Nicola held out her hand to say goodbye.

Gilles hesitated fractionally before taking it in his.

'I was so sorry to hear about Marc's death. I knew him slightly — when we were both growing up. I'm sure you and your son must miss him.'

There was a short silence before Nicola replied.

'Marc divorced me several years ago but we remained good friends. We do both miss him.'

'It's hard when someone you've been close to is no longer around,' Gilles said. 'For whatever reason.' He released her hand before looking over at Le Jardin. 'You've got a lot of work on your hands with that place.'

'I'm beginning to realise that.' Nicola laughed. 'Perhaps you can recommend a good builder?'

When she mentioned the improvements she was hoping to make at the cottage, he immediately offered to help.

'It's not a problem,' Gilles said, despite Nicola's protests. 'I'm happy to help. What exactly are you thinking of doing?'

'Well, first I'd like to know if it's possible to knock a wall down and incorporate the small outbuilding into the cottage as an extra room. I'd also like to do something with the attic.'

'You'd better show me around, then,' he said with a smile. 'I'll just fetch my measure from the car.' With that Gilles disappeared back outside.

When he reappeared, he was holding a small basket of flowers.

'I thought you'd like these,' he said, smiling shyly at her. 'A small house-warming present — to wish you *bonne chance* with your new life.'

'Thank you,' Nicola said. 'That's so kind of you.'

'This is the first time I've been in the cottage,' Gilles said, looking around. 'It's certainly got lots of atmosphere and I love those beams! Right, is this the wall you want to take down?' he asked, tapping a small hammer against it.

Nicola nodded.

'I'll just take a look in the outbuilding but I don't see a problem,' Gilles said. 'It's not a supporting wall.'

For some time Gilles wandered around downstairs, measuring, tapping and making notes. Finally, Nicola stood with him on the upstairs landing and pointed out the attic hatch.

Standing on the old rickety table that had been left in the small bedroom, Gilles managed to lift the hatch and haul himself up into the attic.

'Hey, it's good up here. It already has a floor — and there's plenty of headroom.'

Moments later, a dusty but smiling Gilles jumped down and rejoined her on the landing.

'You'll need to do something about access, but two windows back and front in the roof and *voilà*! You will have a room under the stars.'

'As easy as that?' Nicola said, smiling back at him — his enthusiasm was so infectious. Suddenly she realised why Gilles had seemed so familiar that morning when Raoul had introduced them. He reminded her of Marc.

He had the same dark Latin looks, the same charm and the same enthusiasm for life.

'I will draw up the plans and submit them for you, yes?' Gilles asked as he followed Nicola downstairs.

'Are you sure it's no trouble?' Nicola demurred.

'For me, it's a little job. No problem. I can bring the plans next week for you to see before I submit them. OK?'

'OK, and thank you very much, Gilles.' Looking at him, standing there covered in dust, Nicola laughed. 'You have a cobweb in your hair,' she said.

'Cobweb?' Gilles looked at her, puzzled, as he put his hand up to his head.

'A spider's web from the attic — here, let me get rid of it for you,' she said, reaching up and carefully brushing it away.

'How Are You?'

'Mum, did you know there's an orange tree in the garden?' Oliver asked as he helped Nicola to clear the garden of old junk later that same evening.

Already there was a large pile by the front gate — the remains of an iron bedstead, rotten window-frames, a pushchair and an ancient lawnmower amongst other rubbish waiting for the council to come and collect.

'Really?' Nicola said absently, still thinking about the visit Gilles Bongars had paid to Le Jardin earlier.

'Where?'

'Up by the back boundary wall. I think there's a lemon tree there, too.'

'And we've got the grapefruit tree that Claudine gave us as well. Looks like we're going to have a real orchard — let's hope they all produce lots of fruit.'

Nicola glanced at Oliver. He'd been rather quiet all evening and she was about to ask him if there was something on his mind when they heard the shrill ring of the newly connected telephone.

'I'll get it,' Oliver said, running towards the cottage. 'It's Andrew,' he called out a few seconds later.

Making her way through to the sitting-room, Nicola could hear Oliver telling Andrew about the things he'd been doing on the farm and that he wasn't going to school until September.

'Well, he seems happy. How about you? Missing me, I hope?' Andrew said when she finally got hold of the receiver.

'Yes to both questions!' Nicola said. She'd been too busy moving into Le Jardin and organising things to miss anyone or anything in the last few days, but she didn't want to upset Andrew by telling him that. Besides, she really was pleased to hear from him.

'How are you?' she went on. 'Still coming out here at the end of the month?'

'I can't wait,' Andrew said. 'Might have some exciting news by then, too.' Refusing to divulge any more information, he hurriedly changed the subject. 'You'll have to wait and see. Now, tell me how things are going out there. Is Henri behaving himself? The furniture is due tomorrow, isn't it?'

'Things are just fine,' Nicola replied, going on to tell him about the events of the past few days and the fact that a 'Taste Of The Countryside' centre was to be built next door.

'Sounds as if you'll have an outlet for all your stuff straight away,' Andrew said.

'Look, I'd better go. I'll ring again before I come over, so if there is anything you want me to bring, just let me know. Take care. Love you. Speak soon.'

It was only as she replaced the receiver that Nicola realised that while she'd talked about the new centre and the plans the surveyor was drawing up for Le Jardin, she hadn't mentioned Gilles Bongars to Andrew. But then, why should she?

A Surprise

Oliver was in the kitchen helping himself to a biscuit from one of the numerous packets Tante Odette had placed in the ancient kitchen cupboard.

'Mum, it's Dad's birthday next week. He'd have been forty-two, wouldn't he?' he said unexpectedly.

'Yes,' Nicola answered, looking across at Oliver. With all the business of moving to France she'd completely forgotten about Marc's upcoming birthday.

She'd always made a special occasion out of Marc's birthday, whether he was home or not. She'd known he'd be celebrating wherever he was in the world and had wanted Oliver to be able to join in, even at a distance. But surely Oliver wouldn't be expecting that this year?

'Things are very difficult now,

Oliver,' Nicola said gently. 'I don't think celebrating Dad's birthday this year . . . ' Her voice trailed away. She didn't know what to say.

Oliver looked at her.

'I know nothing will bring Dad back. But do you think, just this year, we could have a special tea up at La Prouveresse with Papa Henri and the *tantes*? And maybe Raoul could come, too, because he was his best friend.'

There was a pause before Oliver continued.

'I like being in the places where he used to be and talking to people who knew him and can tell me about him. I do miss him.'

Nicola nodded slowly.

'Fair enough. I'll ask the *tantes*. Now come here and give me a hug.'

As she held Oliver, Nicola fought to keep the tears at bay.

'Your dad would be so proud of you,' she said.

Forty-eight hours later, Nicola, standing in the chaos that was the sitting-room of Le Jardin de Dominic, was glaring at Henri and his companion.

'Henri, whatever possessed you to do this without checking with me first?' Nicola shouted.

'I didn't know I needed permission to give my grandson a present,' he retorted.

'It all depends on the present,' Nicola snapped back. 'Have you told him about it?'

'*Non*. It's a surprise.'

'Well, that's something, I suppose.'

Nicola took a deep breath to try and steady herself. After the traumas of the last few days she didn't need this added hassle with Henri.

The furniture van had had a puncture on the *autoroute*, and it was twelve hours late arriving at Le Jardin, throwing everything and everybody behind schedule. Nicola and Oliver had been forced to spend an extra night up at the farm instead of moving into Le Jardin.

The two men Raoul had arranged to help with the furniture couldn't come at the new time and, despite both Giselle and Odette spending the day at Le Jardin to help with the unpacking, there were still boxes everywhere waiting to be unpacked.

Tonight was going to be the first night they would sleep in their new home and Nicola had been desperately searching for the box of bed linen when Henri arrived with his inopportune present.

If only he'd waited until they were a bit more settled before springing this on her. The thing was, she quite liked the look of Henri's companion, but she needed to make him understand that he'd overstepped the mark.

'So, what's the story behind this present?' Nicola asked wearily.

Before Henri could answer, Oliver came running downstairs.

'Can I Keep Her?'

'*Bonjour*, Papa Henri! Oh, you've got a new dog. What's its name?' Oliver knelt down by its side to stroke it.

'Mischief,' Henri said with a defiant look at Nicola. 'And she's not my dog! I got her for you. But your *maman* says you can't have her.'

'No, I didn't,' Nicola protested. 'I just said I wished you'd asked me first.'

'There was no time. The vet was about to take her to the refuge. The couple who owned her are leaving the country and can't take her with them. She's eleven months old.'

'Can I keep her, Mum?' Oliver pleaded.

Feeling she was being coerced into making a decision, Nicola sighed.

'It's a big responsibility, Oliver. She'll need walking, grooming, training. And what about Frisby?' she said.

'Oh, they'll get used to each other,' Oliver replied confidently. 'She's never been afraid of dogs. Oh, please let me keep Mischief. I promise to look after her.'

'If it's a problem having her here, I can keep her up at the farm and Oliver can come up there to . . . ' Henri began.

'No,' Nicola interrupted Henri firmly. 'If Mischief is going to be Oliver's dog then she will live down here with us.'

She knew Henri was trying to make her look like the disapproving mother.

'I can keep her then?' Oliver asked excitedly.

Nicola nodded.

'Thanks, Mum! I'll take her to meet Frisby right now.' Holding Mischief's lead, he ran from the room.

'We now have a cat and a dog, Henri. Oliver doesn't need any more pets or surprise presents, OK?' Nicola said.

'Now, if you'll excuse me, I still have this place to sort out.' She moved towards the box of linen she'd just spotted in the far corner.

The rest of the day passed in a blur of unpacking. Nicola discovered there was a distinct lack of cupboard space in the cottage.

It was nine o'clock before she decided that she'd had enough. The rest could wait until tomorrow.

Earlier, Oliver had pulled the ancient table out of the outbuilding, scrubbed it clean and placed it on the patio outside the kitchen. Impulsively, Nicola decided it was warm enough to eat their first meal at Le Jardin outside and she threw a bright cloth over the table.

Tante Odette had made them up a supper picnic basket with one of her special chicken flans and a *tarte au citron*. There was some crisps and lemonade for Oliver and a small bottle of La Prouveresse wine for Nicola.

'You won't have time to cook,' Odette had said as she insisted on leaving the hamper in the kitchen. 'And you must eat.'

Now, as she and Oliver sat and ate their supper under a darkening sky, Nicola was grateful for Odette's thoughtfulness. She hadn't realised how hungry she was and, judging by the way Oliver was tucking in, he was enjoying supper, too.

Taking a sip of wine, Nicola felt herself relax finally after the rigours of the past few weeks. She'd got them both here into their new home. She closed her eyes in an attempt to set the moment in her memory.

Oliver sat with Mischief at his feet while one or two bats began to flit around the eaves of the cottage. Whatever happened in the future, she must remember this quiet moment as the real beginning of their new life.

'Mum.' Oliver's whisper sounded urgent and Nicola came back to reality with a jolt. 'Mum, I think there's someone at the top of the garden with a torch. I can see a light.'

Worriedly, Nicola opened her eyes. Intruders on their first night in Le

Jardin? Surely Mischief should be growling? But Mischief seemed oblivious to any unwanted guests. She was still sitting happily at Oliver's feet, ready to pounce on any crumbs.

Apprehensively, Nicola looked around the garden. Oliver was right. There was a flashing light over near the boundary wall. On a second look, she noticed there was one by the back gate and another one by the olive tree.

'Oh, Oliver. It's not an intruder. We've got fireflies. Aren't they wonderful?'

Together they watched as more and more lights began to weave and dance around the garden. They appeared to be everywhere.

'It's like having fairies at the bottom of the garden dancing to an invisible orchestra,' Nicola whispered. Even Oliver was enthralled by the show they were being treated to.

The display went on for nearly fifteen minutes before slowly fading to leave just half a dozen in solitary splendour before they, too, disappeared and the garden was deserted.

'Wow,' Oliver said. 'That was amazing.'

It was indeed, Nicola thought as she began to clear away the supper things. A wonderful, unexpected welcome to their new home and surely a good omen for the future? She could only hope so.

Marc's Birthday

It wasn't yet midday, but the heat from the sun shining in a cloudless blue sky was already intense as Nicola made her way slowly up the drive to La Prouveresse.

Stopping to look back at the view, she could just make out the roof of Le Jardin, now partially obscured by the leaves on the trees. Standing there, deep in thought, Nicola breathed in the beauty of her surroundings, realising that the stillness which engulfed the Provençal countryside in summer was beginning. Soon, it would be too hot to work outside in the midday sun.

Oliver had already been busy giving Henri a hand harvesting the hay and stacking it high in the barn. Now, the shorn fields were turning brown under the heat of the sun and Nicola watched the swallows wheel and dart for the tiny insects hovering above the small stream that ran alongside.

Taking one last look, she turned and walked the remaining fifty yards to the farmhouse. Henri was in the kitchen with the *tantes* when she pushed open the kitchen door.

'*Bonjour*, Nicola,' Giselle said. 'You've finished the unpacking?'

'More or less,' Nicola replied. 'But I guess I won't be completely settled until after the alterations are done and I can put things in their permanent places.'

She glanced across at Henri.

'Has Oliver mentioned this weekend to you? Marc's birthday?'

The *tantes* shook their heads and Henri glanced at her sharply.

'*Non.*'

'The thing is, I've always made the day special for Oliver whether Marc was at home or not. Usually he was away.' Nicola paused. 'Oliver obviously realises that this year is different, but he still wants to do something on the day.'

She took a deep breath before continuing.

'He'd like to have a special meal up here and share your memories of Marc. I know it's painful for everyone, but I think Oliver really needs to remember his dad's birthday this year.'

It was Henri who broke the silence that followed her words.

'Morbid, if you ask me,' he said. 'Marc's dead and gone. Nothing is going to alter that. Oliver needs to get on with his life.'

'I think that's what he is trying to do,' Nicola replied slowly. 'Coming to live here, where Marc was born and grew up, has simply made him want to know more about his father. He wants to learn about things that he would have learned from Marc in the course of a proper lifetime relationship — things that will help to keep his memory alive.'

Nicola looked at the *tantes*.

'You've already helped so much by talking about his father to him, and giving him that box of Marc's things.'

Nicola turned to Henri. 'You know, it might help you to talk about Marc, too, and remember him in a positive way.'

Henri regarded her stonily.

'I remember Marc in my own way. I don't find it necessary to be for ever talking about him.'

It was Tante Giselle who broke in.

'Henri, we have so many more memories of Marc than Oliver. It can't be wrong to share them with him. I think a special dinner on Sunday celebrating Marc's life is a good idea.'

Ignoring Henri's mutinous face, Giselle spoke directly to Nicola.

'It's so good having you both living here, and if there is anything I can do to help make you and Oliver happy in your new life, I will. We all know it wasn't an easy decision for you to come and live in France, don't we, Henri?' she said, turning directly back to her brother.

For several seconds, a hush fell over everyone in the kitchen. It was Henri who broke the silence when, to Nicola's surprise, he looked at Giselle and nodded.

'*Oui*. Arrange what you like,' he said, before opening the kitchen door and disappearing across the yard towards the old olive terrace.

'*Voilà*! It is arranged,' Giselle said. 'Dinner on Sunday will be dedicated to the memory of Marc.'

'You can all come down to Le Jardin if it would make it easier,' Nicola said hesitantly. 'I know Oliver wanted it to be up here in Marc's old home, but if it's going to cause resentment . . . ' Her voice trailed away anxiously.

'*Non*. We will have it here,' Giselle said. 'I promise you Henri will come round to the idea. Now, what shall we have to eat? Marc's favourite was roast lamb with rosemary and garlic. Shall we cook that?'

Walking back down to Le Jardin an hour later, Nicola thought about Henri's sudden decision to acknowledge Marc's birthday at the weekend and Giselle's conviction that all would be well on the day.

It was as though Tante Giselle's softly spoken words had managed to melt Henri's hard exterior.

Fleetingly, Nicola wondered what sort of hold Giselle could possibly have over her brother, before deciding that it was no concern of hers. The main thing was Oliver would be able to talk about Marc on his birthday, with people who had known and loved him.

Perhaps she, too, would learn something new about the man she'd married all those years ago.

⋆   ⋆   ⋆

As Nicola opened the back gate to Le Jardin, Gilles Bongars drove in through the main entrance.

'*Bonjour*, Nicola. I have the plans to show you before I submit them to the mayor. You have the time to look? I'm meeting with him in an hour.'

'Come on in,' Nicola said, unlocking the front door.

'Raoul has taken Oliver to meet Luc, so I am on my own for lunch. Would you like to join me? Nothing fancy — just salad and tuna.'

'Thank you,' Gilles replied.

Once she'd looked at the plans for altering the house and thanked him for producing them so quickly, Gilles gave her a hand organising lunch. They sat down companionably to eat on the terrace under the shade of a large parasol.

'You are enjoying your new life here in France? Do you think things will work out for you?' he asked as he poured water into their glasses.

'Early days yet, but I think it's going to be OK. My biggest worry is Oliver. I hope he can come to terms with Marc's death and be happy here — it's the most important thing.'

'You are lucky to have Giselle and Odette nearby, and Henri, too, of course. At least you're not completely alone in a strange land.'

Nicola didn't like to tell Gilles that

Henri was proving to be one of her biggest problems as he continued.

'Although, even having family around can be difficult in times of bereavement,' he added thoughtfully. 'They don't always understand that sometimes, it is necessary to let the grief out. Relatives can smother your natural emotions with good intentions simply to encourage you to get on with your life.'

Nicola glanced at him. Clearly, Gilles had experienced some tragedy in his life, too.

He looked at her sadly.

'One day, I will tell you how I know this — but not today.

'Now,' he said, standing up, 'I must go. Thank you for the food. Will you allow me to return the favour next week? There's a little restaurant in the next village where I often have lunch . . . '

'I'd love to, thank you,' Nicola replied quickly.

Watching Gilles drive away, she

thought about the sadness she'd glimpsed in his eyes when he'd spoken about the need to let grief out. Whatever had happened in his life, it had clearly made him receptive to the unhappiness of others.

Deciding it was silly to try to do too much to the house before the alterations were done, Nicola concentrated on attempting to get the garden and land near the house into some sort of order over the next few days.

Oliver gave her a hand and together, they pulled weeds, pruned bushes and cleaned out the silted-up pond. Oliver also pulled the old bicycle out of the shed and offered to restore it for her.

'It'll be useful for shopping in the village,' he said. 'The basket will hold quite a lot. I can use it, too — until you get me a bike again,' he added with a cheeky grin.

After all their hard work, the garden was already beginning to look better and Nicola was pleased with their efforts. Next week, she intended to bribe Oliver into giving her a hand digging the land at the top of the holding.

Bad News

On Saturday afternoon, they were about to walk into the village to cheer on Henri, who was playing with the local *boules* team in an inter-village competition, when the telephone rang. It was a distraught Andrew on the other end.

'Nicola, we need to talk.'

'Andrew! I'm just on my way out. What's so urgent it can't wait? You'll be here in two weeks.'

'Is there any point in me coming over?' Andrew demanded belligerently.

'Yes, of course there is,' Nicola said, slightly taken aback. 'Oliver and I are really looking forward to seeing you. We've got all sorts of things planned.'

'Before I come, I need to know how you feel about me — about us. I can't go on without knowing, particularly after the news I've just had.'

'What news, Andrew?'

'You know I told you I might have something exciting to tell you? Well, I have, but it's not what I expected.'

There was a pause.

'Instead of being promoted I've been made redundant.'

Even though he was miles away, Nicola could sense Andrew's bitterness.

'I've got a golden handshake but the fact remains that I'm unemployed as of the end of this week. All I need now is for you to tell me that you've decided we don't have a future together. I can't go on not knowing one way or the other.'

'Andrew,' Nicola said gently, 'I don't know whether we've got a future together, but I do know how much I am looking forward to seeing you. Oliver is, too. As for the redundancy, try thinking of it as an opportunity for you to do something new.'

She took a deep breath.

'Why don't you come over here earlier and stay for longer than a week?

That way you'll have time to relax and think about your future properly. We can also talk things through together, then.'

Even as she made the offer, Nicola felt her heart sink. Did she really want Andrew coming to stay for an indefinite time, pressurising her into making decisions?

'I want my future to be your future and I want to talk about it now,' Andrew answered crossly, ignoring her offer.

'Andrew, I haven't got time for this right now,' Nicola pleaded.

'When will you ever have time for me, Nicola?'

Nicola was silent. She was no closer to knowing her true feelings about Andrew than she'd been before she left England. For the past few weeks she'd been so busy she'd barely had time to give him more than a passing thought.

Diplomatically, she decided to leave the question unanswered.

'I'm sorry, Andrew, but I've promised

to take Oliver into the village. We're already late and I have to go. We'll do all the talking you want when you get here,' she said firmly. 'Now, cheer up and go and organise a flight. Ring me later and tell me when you're coming so I can arrange for you to be met.'

Nicola frowned as she replaced the phone and switched on her answering machine. Andrew was clearly in a state. She could only hope that he'd manage to come to terms with his redundancy before he arrived for his holiday.

Knowing he was coming to France to talk and sort things out, once and for all, would make things difficult. The leisurely visit she had been looking forward to had suddenly taken on an ominous quality.

He was obviously expecting her to make a decision soon and the choice facing her was stark: either a commitment to advancing their relationship or finishing it altogether.

Nicola sighed. Why couldn't they just

remain friends? Why did things have to change?

By the time she and Oliver finally walked to the village, the game of *boules* was well under way.

Giselle and Odette, who were watching Henri and his team from the edge of the ground, were soon instructing Oliver in the finer points of the game. Nicola, sitting on one of the wrought iron benches under the shade of the leafy plane trees, allowed her thoughts to drift.

It was so pleasant just sitting there, listening to the rhythmic clunk of the over-thrown balls hitting the board at the end of the playing range. She doubted she'd ever understand the rules of *boules*, but Oliver seemed to be catching on quickly.

Listening to his happy laughter, she began to relax. It might be early days yet but, despite the problems, she was beginning to believe that she had done the right thing in moving to France.

It had given her the smallholding

she'd always dreamed of and Oliver the chance of growing up in beautiful countryside, surrounded by his family. The only thing she worried about was her relationship with Andrew.

At A Distance

Nicola sighed inwardly to herself as Andrew re-entered her mind. As relationships went, it had hardly been ideal. Stuck for years at the 'best friends' stage rather than moving on . . .

But that had been her own decision. Her feelings had been swamped by memories of Marc and how much she'd loved him, and they'd ensured she'd kept Andrew at a distance.

Perhaps if she'd tried harder to get her life back on track after she and Marc had separated, she and Andrew would already be more than good friends. And Andrew's declaration of love in the weeks before she moved to France had come far too late for her.

If she was honest with herself, insisting that she had to obey Henri and come to France for the sake of Oliver's inheritance had provided her with the ideal excuse to run away from a situation she wasn't ready to face up to . . .

Mischief stirred at her feet and barked as Oliver came running over to them, jolting her out of her reverie.

'Mum, Grandpa Henri says I can have Dad's *boules* set if I'm going to learn to play. He says he'll look it out and give it to me tomorrow evening.'

Tomorrow evening: the dinner party at La Prouveresse to celebrate Marc's birthday. Oliver was looking forward to it so much, but Nicola had had reservations ever since she mentioned it to Giselle and Odette.

'About tomorrow evening — you won't expect too much, will you, Oliver?' Nicola said. 'People, particularly Papa Henri, may not have the same fond memories of your dad that you do. They might remember a different side of him.'

'I know that, Mum. I just want to hear about some of the things he did when he was growing up. There are all sorts of things in his diary that he never mentioned to me,' Oliver said.

'So, you've been reading his diary then?'

He nodded.

'I decided Dad wouldn't mind me reading it — even though it's a private thing. It's not as if I'm going to show it to everyone.'

Oliver looked at Nicola.

'You didn't say what Andrew wanted earlier. Is he still coming to see us?'

Nicola nodded.

'Yes. Probably earlier than expected, too.' And she explained about Andrew losing his job.

'How long is he going to stay?' Oliver asked.

'I've no idea,' Nicola replied. 'It depends on lots of things. He might have to return home quickly for job interviews.' She shrugged. 'He might even decide to stay for the summer.'

'If you two get married he won't want us to go back to England with him, will he?' Oliver asked anxiously.

'Whatever makes you think we might get married?' Nicola said, stunned by the unexpected question.

'Andrew asked me once if I'd mind if you married him.'

'He had no business asking you,' Nicola said, inwardly furious with Andrew. There was a slight pause before she spoke again.

'And would you?'

Oliver shook his head.

'No. I like Andrew. He doesn't try to boss me around — he's more like a friend. But I like it here, too. I definitely wouldn't want to go back. So, if you do get married, Andrew will have to come here to live.'

The Party

On Sunday evening, when Nicola and Oliver were walking up to La Prouveresse, they could hear voices and soft music drifting in the air from the *petit jardin*. The *tantes* had spent the day turning the small area into a perfect dinner party setting.

The weathered wooden table had been covered with a gaily patterned Provençal cloth and laid with the best china and glasses. To Oliver's obvious delight, a small case containing six steel *boules* balls had been placed on his chair.

'Thank you, Papa Henri. I'll take great care of them. Was Dad a good player?'

'Yes, he played for the junior village team. He was one of the best,' Henri said sternly.

Giselle and Odette had persuaded

172

Henri to weave some fairy lights in among the bougainvillea and candles were already flickering away in terracotta pots.

Nicola glanced at Henri, trying to gauge the mood he was in. His face was impassive as he silently handed her a glass of wine before turning away to greet Sylvie, Raoul and Claudine. She sighed.

Hopefully the others would be forthcoming with their memories and Henri would relax as the evening wore on. Even if he didn't contribute, surely listening to others talking about his son would help him — whether he realised it or not.

It was Raoul who started things off as they all enjoyed the first course of smoked salmon and salad.

'Do you remember cooking salmon the first time Marc and I got back from a weekend's camping and fishing up in the mountains?' he asked Giselle.

She nodded.

'*Oui*. It was delicious! Marc said it

had taken a long time to catch.'

Raoul nodded.

'Mmm. We'd spent most of the day with the others and caught nothing, so we went out at midnight and caught it in another river.'

'*Imbéciles*!' Henri said. 'If you'd been caught, it would have been me paying the fine.'

Raoul shrugged.

'We were ten. It was an adventure. We didn't stop to think about the consequences — and it wasn't as if we did it again. It was the only time I ever knew Marc to do something he shouldn't.'

Raoul looked at Henri.

'Besides, in those days all Marc wanted was to please you. We only did it because he'd promised to bring you a salmon.'

Henri absorbed this information silently.

It was Giselle who broke the tension.

'Marc was never one to make idle promises. You always knew if Marc said he'd do something, he would — and usually with lots of enthusiasm. He was such a kind boy.'

'He was so good with the animals, too,' Odette said. 'Except for that rogue ram we had one year.'

As Nicola listened to Odette and the others reminiscing and laughing about the ram that had butted everything and everybody, her own memories of Marc began to filter back.

★　★　★

How happy they'd been in the beginning; what hopes they'd had for the future. How overjoyed they were at the birth of Oliver. Then, other memories began to drift into her mind.

She remembered her unhappiness as Marc began to distance himself from her, getting more and more involved in his humanitarian work, and her inability to understand why he had to sacrifice their personal happiness.

She glanced across at Oliver as he laughed at something Raoul said, before whispering to Giselle.

'The Marc I knew and loved could also be incredibly selfish. He always wanted things done his way.'

'I see he took after his father there, then,' Giselle replied quietly as she placed the roasted leg of lamb on the table.

'The Jacques men have always been stubborn, too,' she added in a louder voice, looking at Henri, who ignored her remark.

'I've been reading Dad's diary,' Oliver said to Raoul. 'He mentions you a lot. You were best friends for a long time, weren't you?'

Raoul nodded.

'Practically from the day we were born until the day he left La Prouveresse. He didn't even tell me he was going . . . ' Raoul said, a sad glint in his eye.

'He did write to me when he met your *maman*. He wanted me to be best man at the wedding.'

He glanced across at Nicola.

'Your mother looked beautiful. It was a great wedding. I thought they would be together for ever . . . ' He shook his head.

So did I, Nicola thought, taking a sip of her wine.

Henri, at the far end of the table muttered something. Nicola could only make out the words, 'Didn't invite me.' And, biting her lip, she wished she could reply that he wouldn't have come anyway.

But there was no point in antagonising Henri over something that had happened a long time ago.

'Will I get to meet Cousin Pascal one day?' Oliver asked conversationally as he helped himself to some of his favourite sauté potatoes.

'Dad says in his diary he took him sailing a couple of times down at Antibes.'

Complete silence greeted Oliver's remark, but he'd certainly caught everybody's attention. The silence lengthened.

Oliver looked at Nicola.

'What have I said?' he asked quietly.

Nicola shrugged, bewildered. Pascal wasn't a name she could ever remember Marc mentioning, so she didn't have any idea to why it had caused such obvious unease among certain Jacques family members.

Odette was looking visibly shaken and Nicola intercepted a concerned look Giselle gave her sister before finally breaking the silence.

'No, Oliver, you won't meet Pascal. He lives in Paris and we lost touch with him years ago.'

At the mention of Paris, Nicola suddenly wondered if Oliver had unwittingly stumbled across somebody involved with Odette's hidden past. She remembered what Marc had once told her.

'Tante Odette was quite a girl in her youth. I don't know the full story, but apparently, years ago, she had to leave Paris in a hurry.'

Now, watching the colour slowly

return to the cheeks of the middle-aged woman sitting opposite her, trying to imagine her as a young wife, Nicola could only speculate about the secrets that this reserved French woman could be harbouring.

Whatever they were, she hoped that the unexpected mention of Pascal hadn't brought back too many unhappy memories. Both the *tantes* had been so kind; she'd hate to hurt either of them.

It was Claudine who brought everybody's thoughts firmly back to Marc.

'Does anyone remember the band Marc played in and I sang with?' She glanced at her brother. 'I know you do, because you were upset they wouldn't let you join in. You made my life a misery for months.'

'Listening to Marc practising drums in the barn made our life a misery, too,' Henri said dryly. 'The noise was deafening at times. But when he improved, we used to play the occasional piece of jazz together. I remember enjoying that,' he added quietly.

'I was in a band back home . . . in England,' Oliver said. 'I really enjoyed it. I hope I can join one here.'

He looked at his grandfather.

'I've never heard you play the sax. Dad told me you were really good. Do you still play?'

Henri shook his head.

'*Non*,' he replied.

Oliver hesitated.

'You won't teach me to play it then?' he asked quietly.

Henri looked at him and sighed.

'*Peut-être*. If I ever find my saxophone again.'

Oliver, taking his grandfather's words as a definite, was overjoyed.

'Great. I'll help you look for it!' he said.

Nicola smiled and shook her head in amusement. Oliver was getting more and more like Marc every day. Not just in looks but also in the way he reacted to people. Getting his own way was a skill that Marc had possessed in abundance.

'I remember going to jazz evenings down in Nice,' Claudine said. 'Great fun. Marc always reckoned none of the saxophone players were anywhere near as good as you, Henri.'

Raoul laughed.

'You two really did go and listen to the jazz then? I always thought it was just a ruse for you to spend time together away from family.'

Claudine nodded.

'It was, but the jazz was too good to miss. Oh, and those romantic late-night strolls along the Promenade des Anglais. I wouldn't have missed them for anything. But, even then, Marc was planning to leave.'

She fiddled with her wine glass and took a long drink before glancing at Nicola and continuing.

'I lived in hope that he would either change his mind — or at least ask me to go with him. *Mais, non.*' She shrugged.

'And when he returned, he was a married man. Did you know I was his first ever girlfriend?' she asked unexpectedly, looking across at Nicola.

Nicola shook her head.

'No, he never said. But I know he was very fond of you. He wanted us to meet and hoped we'd be friends.'

'Young love, eh?' Claudine said before taking a sip of her wine.

Just then, Sylvie placed a plate of food in front of Claudine and started to talk in rapid French.

Nicola couldn't understand all the words Sylvie said to her daughter, but the action spoke for itself. Enough was enough.

'Long Ago'

When Nicola had said to the *tantes* that remembering Marc's birthday would be hard for everyone, she hadn't bargained on just how painful the experience would be for her personally.

She'd thought she'd mastered her feelings about Marc but, here she was, feeling jealous over what had clearly been a teenage romance, long before the two of them had even met.

Absently, Nicola took a bread roll from the basket and broke a piece off as she tried to rationalise her thoughts.

'Ah, Nicola, it was all a long time ago,' Odette said quietly, placing a comforting hand on her arm.

Nicola looked at her in surprise. Giselle was usually the first with sympathy, not Odette.

'If Marc had really loved Claudine, he would have come back for her, but it was you he loved and married. Enjoy the memories of the good times you had together.' Odette paused.

'Sometimes it is hard to look at things dispassionately and get on with life — particularly when you've been hurt by rejection. Believe me, Marc's love for you and Oliver was one of the mainstays of his life.'

Nicola smiled weakly but, before she could say anything, Oliver, who had overheard the quiet conversation, broke in resentfully.

'If he loved us so much, why did he leave us? If he hadn't, he wouldn't have died. We didn't drive him away like Papa Henri did.' He glared at his grandfather angrily.

'I don't care what any of you say,' he shouted. 'Dad should have lived with us more.'

Brushing tears away from his eyes, Oliver turned and ran out of the *petit jardin*.

Instinctively, Nicola rose to follow him, but Henri stopped her.

'*Non*, Nicola. It is time I had words with my grandson. I will go alone.'

'Don't Worry'

Nicola watched in silence as Henri left the *petit jardin* to find Oliver. There was little point in asking him to take it easy with Oliver. She knew Henri would deal with the situation in his own way, whatever she said. Nicola could only hope and pray he wouldn't make things worse.

Giselle, ever practical, stood up and began to clear the table.

'Odette has made Marc's favourite fruit salad for dessert. I will fetch it.' She disappeared into the lengthening shadows, towards the farmhouse.

'Nicola, please don't worry. Henri will be gentle with Oliver, I promise you.' Sylvie's quiet voice broke into Nicola's thoughts.

Nicola looked at Sylvie uncertainly. 'Gentle' wasn't a word she'd normally associate with Henri.

'I'm beginning to think this dinner party was a bad idea,' Nicola said wearily.

'I know I've learned more about Marc's life than I really expected.' And she glanced across the table to where Raoul was talking quietly to Claudine.

She turned back to Sylvie then.

'As for Oliver, these memories have simply stirred up all his negative feelings again — just when I was beginning to think he'd come to terms with everything. I dread to think what he's accusing Henri of now.' Nicola shook her head worriedly.

Sylvie smiled encouragingly.

'Deep down, Henri has a very big heart. He will be hurting for Oliver as well as himself. If they can just talk about their feelings to each other it will help both of them so much,' she said.

'This whole Marc business has hurt Henri just as much as Oliver.' She sighed. 'Maybe more,' she added, glancing at Nicola. 'He realises he was to blame for a lot of the bad feeling between him and Marc. His biggest regret is that he will never be able to tell Marc he is sorry.'

Sylvie watched as Giselle placed the fruit salad and large cheeseboard on the table.

'Since you and Oliver came to live here, Henri has begun to live again — Oliver is his new purpose in life,' she said.

'But that isn't necessarily a good thing,' Nicola protested. 'He'll try and control him like he did with Marc.'

'*Non*.' Sylvie shook her head. 'This time he knows he must tread gently. He already listens more and tries not to insist his is the only way to do things.' She smiled at Nicola.

'Believe me, Henri is not the same as he was. Oh, he's still stubborn but he's changed — hasn't he, Giselle? He knows he mustn't repeat the mistakes of the past.'

Giselle nodded as she began to serve the fruit salad.

'*Oui*. He still likes to have the last

word if he can but he's getting used to not having it.' She laughed.

'Having you both here has really made a difference, Nicola — to all our lives,' Giselle added quietly. 'Perhaps I shouldn't say this, but I think Marc treated you very shabbily over the last few years and I'm glad you didn't reject the rest of us and refuse to bring Oliver to live here.'

'You know I couldn't do that, Giselle,' Nicola said, looking at her. 'Staying in England wasn't an option in the end.'

'Nicola, there's something I ought to tell you,' Giselle said quietly. 'The thing is . . .'

'Listen!' Sylvie interrupted urgently. 'Is that what I think it is?'

Everybody stopped talking to listen as the mournful notes of a saxophone drifted towards them on the warm night air. As they listened, the tentative notes became stronger and, within minutes, Gershwin's famous 'Summertime' was filling the air.

'Henri's found his saxophone after all these years,' Giselle said with tears in her eyes. 'I'm so pleased! He was always more content when he could lose himself in his music.'

As the notes of 'Summertime' died away, other haunting tunes followed and everyone fell silent, listening to the impromptu concert. Finally, as the bats started to flit around the roofs of the outbuildings illuminated by the moon, the music stopped.

A few minutes later, Henri and Oliver arrived back in the *petit jardin* side by side, Henri with his arm around Oliver's shoulder and Oliver carrying his grandfather's saxophone.

All signs of tears had disappeared from Oliver's face, but Nicola could see he was still rather subdued. Resisting the urge to put her arms around him — which she knew would embarrass him — she simply smiled.

'Are you OK?' she asked.

Oliver nodded.

'Papa Henri and I had a long chat

about Dad — and other stuff.' There was a short pause before he continued.

'Mum, can I change my name? Papa Henri says, as I'm growing up in France now, I should use the French version of my name. It just means putting in an extra 'i' and pronouncing it differently — I'd really like to do it . . . '

★   ★   ★

In an effort to keep her mind off the painful memories that the dinner party had opened up, Nicola threw herself into work at Le Jardin for the next few days.

She was determined to try and dig a vegetable plot and clean out the small greenhouse at the top of the field before Andrew arrived.

There was also the question of getting the small bedroom in the cottage in a habitable condition for Andrew. The only piece of furniture in there at the moment was the old sofa bed she'd brought from England. At the very least the room needed some drawers and hanging space for clothes.

When Giselle and Odette heard her problem, they offered her a small wardrobe and dressing table.

'They're just rotting away in the barn — much better to be used,' Giselle said. 'I'll get Henri to bring them down.'

Giselle came to Le Jardin with Henri, sitting on the back of the tractor clutching a rolled-up rug.

'I thought this might be useful, too,' she shouted.

Henri unloaded the furniture and climbed back on the tractor.

'I've got to get it back. The vétérinaire is due.'

He looked at Giselle.

'Don't forget,' he muttered, and disappeared back up the lane to La Prouveresse in a cloud of tractor exhaust.

Nicola looked at Giselle and sighed.

'Don't forget what?' she asked.

Giselle shrugged helplessly.

'I've told him it's none of our business but, well, you know Henri.' Giselle paused before continuing. 'He wants to know how close you are to this man Andrew. Oliver has spoken about him a lot. Henri thinks you might be planning to marry him.'

'Why didn't Henri ask me himself? He's not usually so diffident about sticking his nose in.'

'He's trying hard not to upset you by asking questions. He thought it would be better if I asked you, instead.' Giselle laughed nervously. 'But you don't have to tell me if you don't want to. And I don't have to tell Henri, either,' she said seriously.

'Andrew is an old friend, Giselle. He was around to pick up the pieces when Marc insisted on us divorcing. When Marc was killed he was very good with Oliver.' Nicola was quietly reflective. 'He hasn't actually proposed to me yet, but I know he wants to marry me. He's even asked Oliver how he'd feel about it, can you believe?'

'And you? Do you want to marry him?'

'I don't know, Giselle. I am very fond of Andrew, but whether I love him enough for marriage, I honestly don't know. I suspect, though, the pressure is going to be on for a decision during the next couple of weeks.'

Giselle was silent, concern etched on her face.

'You must do what is best for you, Nicola. No-one else — not even Oliver. Follow your instincts and things will work out in the end. Now, shall I give you a hand getting these things upstairs, *oui*?'

It was only after Giselle had left that Nicola remembered she hadn't asked her what it was she had been about to tell her at the dinner party.

Whatever it was, it couldn't be that important, she reasoned; otherwise, she was certain Giselle would have remembered to mention it . . .

Coffee With Claudine

Early the next morning, Claudine telephoned. 'Fancy meeting for a coffee in the village café?'

'I'd love to,' Nicola replied. 'I have to get back sharp, though. I'm having lunch with Gilles Bongars and he's picking me up at twelve thirty,' she went on.

'In that case, see you in half an hour. We can't have you being late for a date with the gorgeous Gilles,' Claudine said, laughing.

'It's not a date,' Nicola protested. 'It's simply a thank you for the lunch I gave him last week.'

'Oh, a regular date?' Claudine teased. 'See you soon.'

Nicola smiled as she put the phone down. A date, indeed. She knew it was only Gilles returning her earlier hospitality.

Cycling into the village, Nicola was surprised by the number of people who already recognised her as a local.

'*Bonjour, Madame* Jacques,' they said happily.

She wandered around the small market before making her way across the town square, towards the coffee shop.

Claudine was already seated at one of the pavement tables with an empty cup in front of her. Smiling, she raised a hand in greeting as she saw Nicola.

'Coffee, or a glass of rosé?' she asked.

'Water, I think,' Nicola replied. 'It's too hot for coffee and too early for wine. For an Englishwoman, anyway,' she added, glancing around and seeing half carafes of wine on nearly every table.

Claudine ordered water and another coffee.

'How's Oliver after his upset at the party?' she asked.

'You mean Olivier, as he now seems

196

determined to be called?' Nicola said, laughing.

'He's a bit quiet, still. I managed to get him to apologise to Henri — although he's still insisting he meant every word.'

'Do you know what Henri said to him?'

Nicola shook her head.

'No, not really. I think he explained that we all make mistakes and everyone has regrets in their lives.' She gave a resigned shrug. 'At least they're still talking. Henri does seem to be making a real effort with him. He's even giving him saxophone lessons now, much to Oliver's delight!'

Nicola took a sip of her coffee.

'Raoul said he knew of a car that was for sale, so Henri and Oliver have gone off together to give it the once-over,' she explained. 'I hope the trip turns out OK — in more ways than one. I really need a car, but I also need Oliver and Henri to have a good relationship . . . '

'I'm sure Oliver will come to terms

with things soon. He's young and has so much to look forward to here. And Henri, well, he must have learned something from all the mistakes he made with Marc.'

'I certainly hope so,' Nicola said. 'Claudine, can I ask you something? Do you know who Pascal is? I didn't want to ask Giselle or Odette — they were clearly upset on Sunday at the mention of his name. And I wouldn't dream of asking Henri.'

'Pascal, the man who used to take Marc sailing?' Claudine asked.

Nicola nodded.

'I'm just curious,' she said. 'Marc obviously enjoyed the time he spent with him, but the mere mention of his name seemed to throw everybody into a state.'

'I remember his visits because I was envious of Marc going sailing — but I don't know much about him. He was some sort of relation by marriage to Odette, I think. Possibly her brother-in-law? He only came that once. You'd need to talk to Mum. She knows everybody's darkest secrets,' Claudine said as she pushed her empty coffee cup away.

'Nicola, I want to apologise for my behaviour on Sunday evening.'

Nicola shook her head.

'Claudine, there's no need . . . '

'There's every need. I would like us to be friends and I can't allow the shadow of Marc to come between us.'

Claudine fiddled with her gold chain necklace as she continued.

'I was nineteen and absolutely devastated when Marc left. But the truth is, deep down, I knew that Marc didn't really love me. Oh, we had some great times together but, if I'm truthful, the love was all on my side — not his. Teenage infatuation, I guess.'

Nicola was quiet, realising how hard it was for Claudine to talk to her about this.

Claudine hesitated.

'You know, Phillipe and I have had a few problems recently. That's one of the reasons we came back here to live — to try and work things out between us with a less stressful lifestyle.

'I'm afraid I'd had a bit too much wine on Sunday and with everybody talking about Marc it somehow made my teenage dreams seem more real than the present.'

'Claudine, I don't know what to say except that I hope you and Phillipe work it out.'

Claudine smiled.

'Things are definitely better. Luckily, he didn't witness my behaviour on Sunday.' She looked at Nicola apprehensively.

'You won't . . . ?'

'Of course not,' Nicola said quickly. 'The whole thing is forgotten.'

Even as she reassured Claudine, though, she was wondering about her own feelings. That rush of jealousy she'd experienced when she'd heard Claudine and Marc had been teenage sweethearts was still there, and still hurting.

Just what was it going to take for her to forgive and, more importantly, forget Marc, and learn to love again? Perhaps coming here to live hadn't been such a brilliant idea after all . . .

'A Nice Man'

'So, you're lunching with Gilles Bongars?' Claudine said, breaking into Nicola's thoughts. 'He's a nice man. Single, too,' she added with a smile.

'Claudine, stop it. It's just lunch. Anyway, talking of which, I'd better get back to Le Jardin.' As Nicola stood up, an idea popped into her head.

'Would you and Phillipe like to come to supper one evening next week? An old friend is visiting from England. I'd like you to meet him.'

'That sounds wonderful! Let me know which evening and I'll make sure Phillipe is home early.'

Cycling home, Nicola tried to put thoughts about Andrew's impending visit out of her mind. Since his last phone call when he'd been so upset, she'd started to worry about his visit to Le Jardin.

A depressed and belligerent Andrew wouldn't make for an easy guest. Hopefully he would have calmed down before he arrived and they could discuss their relationship calmly. If not, she was in for a difficult time.

Sighing, she put the bicycle away in the shed and went to get ready for her lunch with Gilles, determined not to let her worries overshadow the treat of being taken out to lunch.

The restaurant where Gilles had booked a table was a few kilometres up the road from Le Jardin, but it seemed to exist in a time warp.

From the moment she walked over the drawbridge and under the arch into the ancient moated village, Nicola was fascinated by the place. Tall, thin sixteenth century houses lined narrow lane after narrow lane, occasionally opening out into a small square.

Window-boxes, with their tumbling red, white and pink geraniums, clung precariously to sills and narrow alleys were ablaze with colourful flowers.

'A Magical Place'

The restaurant was situated on the main square where a large chestnut tree gave welcome shade and the sound of water from an old fountain soothed as it tinkled into its granite trough.

'What a magical place,' Nicola said as they took their places at one of the tables outside.

'After lunch, we can take a stroll in the hidden mediaeval gardens, if you like,' Gilles replied.

'But will we have time? When do you have to be back at work?' Nicola asked.

Gilles shook his head.

'Today I made sure I kept the afternoon free,' he said, smiling at her.

The popular restaurant was busy with a mixture of tourists and locals enjoying the good food and chat. Several people stopped by their table to say hello to Gilles and shake Nicola's hand vigorously when he introduced her.

Gilles smiled apologetically.

'It is because of my job. Everybody wants me to be their friend!'

Nicola laughed.

'I'm sure it's more than that.' She laughed.

The restaurateur came to the table and took their order personally, promising Nicola she was in for a treat when she chose *daube de boeuf à la Provençale*, the *plat du jour*.

They shared a small carafe of wine and laughed companionably at the antics of a small child at a nearby table.

'Do you have any children?' Nicola asked.

Gilles shook his head.

'*Non*. I've never married and I've always thought children needed to be a part of a proper family. Sadly, I've only ever met one person I wanted to spend my life with,' he added quietly.

Nicola took a reflective sip of her wine.

'In an ideal world I would agree about children, but it doesn't always work like that,' she said, looking at him sadly.

'Oh, Nicola, I'm so sorry. I didn't mean to upset you. I know sometimes things go wrong however hard you try personally.' And he reached out to cover her hand with his, a gesture Nicola found strangely comforting.

As they lingered over their coffees, Gilles broke the silence.

'I have two tickets for a big band concert a week on Saturday. Would you like to come with me? I could pick you up at about six; we'd drive down to Nice, have dinner and then go to the concert. I couldn't promise to get you home before one, though.'

'Thank you,' Nicola said, taken aback. 'It sounds like fun. I'm sure the *tantes* would enjoy having Oliver for the evening — ' Nicola broke off mid-sentence as she remembered Andrew's visit.

'You already have plans for that

evening?' Gilles asked, disappointment in his voice.

Nicola shook her head.

'No. It's just that I have a friend coming to stay later this week.' She smiled at Gilles. 'But I'm sure the *tantes* won't mind entertaining an extra person for the evening.'

How Andrew would react to her going to a concert with Gilles was another matter . . .

★   ★   ★

The temperature was in the nineties as Nicola made her way up to La Prouveresse late on Friday afternoon. She was glad of the slight breeze that was gently stirring the leaves of the eucalyptus trees. Henri had arranged for her new car to be delivered next week and she needed to pay him.

At the bottom of the drive as she stopped to cool in the shade before continuing, she spotted a letter in the mailbox. Clearly *La Poste* had made a late delivery and the *tantes* hadn't been down in the heat to collect the mail.

She glanced at the letter curiously. Addressed to Henri, it had a Parisian postmark and the address of a firm of lawyers stamped across it.

Knowing that Henri used a local firm of lawyers, Nicola couldn't help wondering what the letter might be as she lifted it out of the box.

As she strolled slowly up the drive she could see Henri and Oliver walking back from the small La Prouveresse vineyard.

The farmhouse was deserted when Nicola reached it and she found Giselle and Odette sitting in the shade of the *petit jardin*, sharing a jug of iced home-made lemonade.

'Nicola, you will join us, yes?' Giselle handed her a glass.

'When does your friend arrive?' Odette asked.

'Tomorrow afternoon,' Nicola replied.

'*Bon.* Will you bring him for supper? Sylvie will be here, too.'

'Thanks. I thought we could go to the fête in the village on Sunday. Are you going?'

'*Oui*, of course,' Giselle and Odette chorused together.

'Even Henri will go — it's a tradition.'

The mention of Henri reminded Nicola why she was visiting.

'Will you give this to Henri for me, please? It's the Euros for my car,' she explained as she fished in her bag for the envelope containing the money.

'Oh, and this was in the box as I came up.'

Giselle frowned as she took the letter and saw the postmark.

'Another one,' she said, before glancing at her sister. At that moment, Henri and Oliver arrived and Giselle silently passed the letter to her brother.

He brushed aside the offer of a glass of lemonade as he opened the letter and read its contents.

'Your past is catching you up, Odette. You'd better ring them,' he said curtly.

'Find out what it's all about once and for all. I don't want them turning up here.'

'Can't you ring them for me, Henri?' Odette asked anxiously as she read the letter.

'After all, it's you they've written to asking for information about my whereabouts. Can't you find out why they want me to contact them? Then I'll ring them.'

Odette bit her bottom lip anxiously before looking at her sister.

'You don't think they'll send me to prison, do you?' she asked.

★ ★ ★

'Andrew should be here by about five o'clock.' Nicola said. 'I hope you won't be too late back.'

'We won't,' Oliver promised. 'Raoul says we should be back by six o'clock at the latest.'

Nicola had hoped both she and Oliver would be at home to greet

Andrew when he arrived, but then Raoul had said he and Luc were spending the day in Nice and would Oliver like to join them?

'A bit of skateboarding along the Promenade des Anglais while I see to some business and then lunch. You're welcome to come, too,' Raoul had added, looking at Nicola.

'There are lots of good shops in town. And I know a nice little bistro . . .'

Tempting though the offer was, Nicola felt she had to say no. She couldn't risk not being back in time for Andrew's arrival. He had already telephoned to say he was hiring a car, so not to worry about meeting him.

Having waved goodbye to Raoul and the boys, Nicola fetched Mischief's lead and set off for the village. She needed a baguette and some basil for the tomato salad she was planning to make and the dog needed a walk before the day became too hot.

Once she was back at Le Jardin,

211

Nicola spent the rest of the morning in the garden, sowing the newly dug vegetable plot with some early winter vegetables and beginning a small herb garden to the side of the kitchen.

At one o'clock, deciding it was too hot to work outside, she retreated indoors out of the heat for lunch and the luxury of a short siesta in the cool of her bedroom.

'I've Missed You'

The slamming of a car door woke her with a jolt, and a quick glance at the bedside clock told her that she'd slept the afternoon away.

'You weren't in bed, were you?' Andrew said, laughing, when she opened the front door. 'You look as if you've just got up.'

'Oh, you know, when in France, do as the locals do,' Nicola answered lightly, running her hand through her hair in an effort to tidy it.

'A short siesta when it's hot works wonders. How are you? It's lovely to see you.' She leaned forward to give him a welcome kiss on the cheek.

But Andrew had other ideas and pulled her against him in a tight embrace.

'Oh, Nicola, I can't tell you how much I've missed you,' he said, planting a gentle, undemanding kiss on her lips.

When he released her, Nicola stayed in the circle of his arms for a few seconds, her arms around his neck, surprised by how happy she felt.

This was the Andrew she remembered of old. The belligerent Andrew bellowing down the telephone at her, demanding answers she couldn't give, had apparently been left behind in England.

'Where's Oliver?' he asked.

'He's gone out for the day with a friend. He'll be back in about an hour or so. Come on in and I'll give you the grand tour.'

Showing Andrew upstairs to his room, Nicola was full of apologies because it was so small.

'Gilles expects the plans to be passed soon, then I can get the builders in to convert this into another bathroom and the attic into two more bedrooms,' she explained as she opened the bedroom door.

'I hope you'll be comfortable in here,'

she said, going across to the window. 'You've got a wonderful view of the mountains.'

'I'll be fine,' Andrew assured her. 'So, tell me, who is Gilles?'

'A friend who offered to help me with the plans for this place. He's actually the local surveyor in charge of the new 'Taste Of The Countryside' building next door.'

Just as Nicola was debating whether to mention her Saturday night outing with Gilles, Oliver slammed the back door and bounded up the stairs, throwing himself at Andrew. As Mischief decided it would be fun to do the same, chaos prevailed for a few minutes.

Back downstairs, as she made tea for them all, Andrew and Oliver had a lively discussion about the new striker that United had signed. Andrew was amazed that Oliver was so up to date with his information before realising he was permanently on the internet.

'I bet you e-mail Chloë every day,

too,' Andrew teased. 'You'll have to get your mum an e-mail address so she can write to me. Although, if things work out, we should be together a bit more.' He glanced across at Nicola. 'But we'll talk about that later. Right now, I want to hear all about your new life.'

By the time Oliver had told him about his new friend, Luc, and how Papa Henri had found Mischief for him and Nicola had given him a quick tour of Le Jardin de Dominic's land, it was time to walk up to La Prouveresse for supper.

As Oliver ran ahead, Nicola tried to warn Andrew about the kind of welcome he could expect from the Jacques family.

'The *tantes* are lovely. They'll make you feel welcome whatever. As for Henri, well . . . he'll probably be fine, too. But, on the other hand, he could be rude. Sylvie is going to be there and she keeps him in check most of the time, so hopefully . . . '

'Is Henri still trying to run your life?'

Andrew interrupted.

Nicola shook her head.

'Not really, although he does like to know what's going on down to the last detail — and soon lets me know if he doesn't approve. The *tantes* and Sylvie reckon he's changed recently.'

'And how does he treat Oliver?' Andrew asked, concerned.

'They spend a lot of time together. Thankfully he's not trying to tell Oliver what he should do as much as I feared he might — but he still has his moments,' Nicola said, looking down.

As they neared the top of the drive, they were surprised to see the *tantes*, Henri and Sylvie standing in a huddle gazing down the valley. Henri had the binoculars to his eyes and was muttering away in rapid French under his breath.

'It's the first of the summer fires,' Giselle explained as she pointed across the valley. 'Fortunately, it doesn't appear to be a serious one.'

A thin column of black smoke was

rising from the forest that lay five or six kilometres above the village. They watched silently as a plane dumped its cargo of water before turning away to clear air space for the next one.

It was some time before Henri lowered his binoculars.

'I think they've managed to control it. Mind you, the firemen will be there all night dampening things down. The trouble is, everything is so dry,' he said.

'Does it happen often?' Andrew asked.

'Too often. People don't think.' Henri glared at Andrew as though he was personally responsible.

'This is Andrew,' Nicola said quickly and introduced everyone.

'Shall we eat?' Giselle said. 'Supper is almost ready. Oliver, can you help me carry things to the table, please?'

Stunned

Conversation around the table was general and, mainly in deference to Andrew, in a mixture of French and English. Nicola was surprised by how good Andrew's French was.

'I've been taking lessons since you left,' he explained.

'What do you do in England?' Henri asked.

'I've been working in the construction industry,' Andrew replied. 'But I've just been made redundant.' He glanced at Nicola before continuing. 'It seems an ideal opportunity to re-think my life. Perhaps re-train and do something completely different. Anyway, I've decided to take a year off. My redundancy money is enough to live on, if I'm careful. I thought I might spend time over here, if that's all right with you?' he said quietly, looking at Nicola.

'I'll have to return to the UK briefly at the end of this holiday but then I'll be back to live with you, here, in France.'

There was no doubting Oliver's delight at this news. But Nicola, although she smiled warmly at Andrew, was inwardly stunned. Was he hoping to move into Le Jardin with them? And, more importantly, was he expecting her to welcome him with open arms?

Last Night

It was Sunday morning, and unusually, Nicola was awakened by the noise of traffic going past Le Jardin de Dominic. Sleepily, she glanced at the bedside clock. It was 6.30 a.m.

Lying still and listening, as the sound of the church bell added its sombre bass peal to the early morning sounds, she remembered it was the day of the fête. And that Andrew was sleeping in the next room . . .

Nicola sighed. Andrew. His news last night about moving to France had been totally unexpected. It had left her reeling at the hidden implications behind it.

Walking home from La Prouveresse last night, she'd tried to tell him, as gently as she could, that he couldn't move in with her and Oliver.

'It's purely a practical consideration,'

she'd said, trying to soften the blow.

'There really isn't enough room. And once the plans are passed and the builders start knocking down walls, we might have to return to La Prouveresse — Giselle suggested it only the other day.'

Andrew was silent for a few moments and Nicola could sense his hurt. As she went to open the back gate leading to Le Jardin, Andrew put his hand out and stopped her.

'Do you like having me here, Nicola?' he asked.

'Yes, of course I do, Andrew,' Nicola replied. 'But the fact remains that you can't move in with me when you return from England. Le Jardin just isn't big enough. You have to find somewhere else to live — your own place.'

Andrew looked at her silently.

'So, I suggest you spend the rest of your holiday looking for somewhere,' Nicola went on determinedly. 'That's if you are serious about moving out here,' she added.

'Oh, I'm serious,' Andrew said slowly. 'Although I had hoped you'd be a bit happier about having me around again . . . '

Nicola looked at him and tried to banish the guilty feelings about her lack of enthusiasm, but before she could say anything, Andrew spoke again.

'And afterwards? When the alterations to Le Jardin are finished and there is room — will there still be a problem having me around?'

Nicola sighed.

'Andrew, there won't be a problem. I enjoy your company. It will be fun having you here . . . ' She hesitated. 'It's just that it would be too easy to slip into being regarded as the local 'English couple' — and neither of us would be free to meet other people and create new, independent lives here.'

'And is that what you want, Nicola? An independent life? No ties?'

'No — and yes,' she said. 'The only person I have to worry about is Oliver; otherwise, I can please myself — do what I want. It's been a long time since I've been able to do that without feeling guilty.'

Andrew looked at her sadly before drawing her towards him.

'Oh, Nicola, what is going to become of us?'

It was a question Nicola didn't know the answer to, and she'd mutely shaken her head. So, when she didn't respond to the touch of Andrew's lips against her forehead, he'd released her and she'd slipped out of his arms to run into the house.

Now, as the early morning sunlight streamed into her bedroom, she took a deep breath and, pushing back the bedclothes, got up.

Hopefully Andrew wouldn't be brooding about their argument and they could enjoy their day at the fête without last night looming over them like a black cloud.

More of an agricultural show than an ordinary fête, the festivities were in full swing by the time Nicola and Andrew arrived to join in the fun.

Traffic had been banished from the village for the day and the narrow streets were crammed with stalls and stands of every description. Making their way slowly along the crowded streets, soaking up the atmosphere and marvelling at the variety of goods on display, Nicola was amazed at how the village had transformed itself for the fête.

It seemed, too, that all the local farmers and their livestock had come to the village for the day. Flocks of sheep were being auctioned off down in the marketplace and all around there was the sound of animals.

Two large Percheron horses were giving rides to excited children and the shooting range set up near the edge of town was a definite hit with the teenagers.

Already, the smell of cooking hung in the air as the *socca* and roast chicken vans opened for business, while stalls full of locally produced cheeses added their own unmistakable brand of aromas to the feasts on offer.

Unsure

With so much to do and see, the day passed quickly and it was soon time for the afternoon parade of prize-winning animals. Nicola, Andrew and Giselle fought their way through the crowds to get a good view as a smiling Oliver led Henri's prize-winning ewe around the show ring.

'Oliver certainly seems to have settled down well,' Andrew said, with a proud look. 'He's much more confident in himself. He's grown, too — taller than you these lays!'

Nicola nodded.

'Moving here has definitely helped him put things in perspective, although I think he misses Marc more than he lets on.'

Giselle agreed.

'But he and Henri are helping each other sort their feelings out.'

She glanced at Nicola.

'Are you still thinking of sending Oliver to the English school in September? His French as improved so much I'm sure he'd be able to cope with a normal French school. I know Henri would like him to go to Marc's old school,' Giselle added quietly.

Nicola didn't answer straight away, Oliver had already hinted that he would like to go to Marc's old school with his friend, Luc, but she wasn't sure. Luc, from the little she'd seen of him, was fast developing into a teenage rebel, and she was beginning to worry about his influence on Oliver.

'We'll see,' she said finally. 'It's still a few weeks before the final decision has to be made.'

A Phone Call

Up at La Prouveresse on Tuesday morning, Giselle pounded dough on the kitchen table, her thoughts elsewhere. These days, she rarely made bread, saying that the *boulangerie* needed the business, but there was nothing quite so satisfying as kneading dough. This morning, she needed the physical relief she always got from ten minutes of pummelling the olive bread into shape.

Henri was on the telephone, talking in a low voice edged with caution. Standing at the sink washing up, Odette was casting anxious glances at him.

'*D'accord.* Hold on and I will ask my sister if she will speak to you now.'

Odette gasped at his words and turned pale as Henri looked at her.

'Relax,' he said gently. 'Nobody wants to put you in jail — but you do have a decision to make . . . '

Both Odette and Giselle looked at him and waited.

'These lawyers in Paris are acting for the Bois family. They say it would be in your best interests to talk to them. They have some information about Pascal . . . ' Henri paused briefly before continuing. 'But they will only tell you in person.'

'Pascal? Is he . . . dead?' Odette whispered.

Henri shook his head.

'*Non.*'

There was a short silence before Henri spoke again.

'Odette, you don't have to talk to them if you don't want to. I will tell them your decision is no and that you want no further involvement with the Bois family. They have assured me the matter will end there.'

'Have you any idea what they want to tell me?' Odette asked quietly.

Henri shook his head.

'*Non.* Now, are you going to talk to

them?' He held the phone out to her.

Slowly, Odette moved across the kitchen and took the receiver from Henri.

'*Bonjour*. This is Odette Bois speaking. I understand you have something to tell me . . . '

★ ★ ★

When the *For Sale* sign went up at the campsite opposite Le Jardin later in the week, Andrew could hardly contain his excitement.

'Come on, let's go and look,' he said, taking hold of Nicola's hand and pulling her across the road.

'You told me I had to find somewhere of my own. Well, perhaps this is it.'

'It's very run-down,' Nicola said doubtfully.

'Is there a house on the site?' Andrew asked enthusiastically.

'Yes, but I don't know whether it's habitable. The old lady who owns it apparently moved into the village years ago.'

'It could be a good investment, even if it does need a lot of renovation,' Andrew said, trying to see through the overgrown hedge that bordered the land.

'Somehow, I can't see you running a campsite,' Nicola said carefully.

'Oh, I don't know — I like people and it would certainly be a challenge sorting it out.' He glanced at Nicola. 'You could help me,' he said quietly. 'A joint project.'

Nicola shook her head.

'I've got enough on my hands with Le Jardin at present. The campsite challenge would have to be your own.'

There was a short silence before Andrew spoke softly.

'Are we ever going to do anything together, Nicola?'

When she didn't answer, he turned away.

'Well, I'm going to have a look anyway. Are you coming?'

Hesitantly, Nicola accepted his help to climb over the padlocked gate. Did Andrew have to turn everything into a question about their relationship? All week he had been dropping not-so-subtle hints about his feelings and their future together.

A short, overgrown track led them towards some derelict outbuildings, an old-fashioned shower block and a building that had once been the campsite café. Various narrow footpaths disappeared into the undergrowth, where the remains of several caravans could be seen.

Despite the heat, Nicola shivered.

'This place makes me feel uneasy,' she said. 'I don't like it here. I'm going home.'

'Well, will you be all right to go back by yourself? I'd like to explore a bit more, and find the house,' Andrew said. 'I'll see you later, if that's OK.'

Dismay

He set off down one of the footpaths, leaving Nicola to make her own way down the drive.

As she crossed the road towards Le Jardin she saw Gilles Bongars waiting for her.

'Gilles, how lovely to see you. Have you got time for a coffee?'

'Thank you,' he replied. 'Nicola, I've come today to tell you that the plans for Le Jardin have been passed, but now I also have to apologise.' He looked across towards the 'Taste Of The Countryside' site.

Nicola followed his gaze and saw with dismay that most of the fence separating Le Jardin from the building site had been destroyed.

'I am very sorry. The driver of the bulldozer made a mistake. On Monday I will have men here to repair the fence.'

'Please don't worry, Gilles. These things happen.' Nicola smiled. 'Now, come on in and I'll make some coffee — you can tell me what I should do now that the plans have been passed.'

They were sitting in the kitchen with the plans spread out on the table when Andrew returned. Within minutes of Nicola introducing them, the two men had found a common rapport because of their joint interest in the building industry.

When Andrew mentioned he'd been across the road looking at the campsite as a possible project for when he moved to France, Gilles immediately asked if he'd like a second opinion.

'I remember when it was busy all summer. But even then the house needed some major maintenance,' he said.

'There's not much of the house left now — most of the roof has gone and one of the walls,' Andrew said. 'It needs demolishing and a new one built. Would planning be difficult, do you think?'

Gilles shrugged.

'I shouldn't think so,' he said. 'I'm picking Nicola up tomorrow evening. Why don't I come a bit earlier and we can go over and have a good look before you make any decisions?'

'Thanks,' Andrew said. 'I'd appreciate that.' He glanced across at Nicola.

'You didn't say you were going out tomorrow. Where are the two of you off to, then?'

'A concert in Nice,' Gilles answered easily. 'I'd ask you to join us, but I'm afraid the tickets sold out weeks ago.'

'If it's any consolation, Giselle and Odette are really looking forward to spoiling you and Oliver tomorrow evening,' Nicola said quickly. 'Giselle is making some of her famous duck and orange pâté for supper,' she added, inwardly praying that Andrew wouldn't create a scene in front of Gilles.

To her relief, he simply smiled.

'Sounds delicious,' he said, before starting to study the plans that were still spread out on the table.

'Guilty'

As promised, Gilles arrived in time the next afternoon for Andrew to take him across to the campsite for an in-depth inspection.

Oliver had already left for La Prouveresse when they returned.

'The *tantes* are expecting you any time,' Nicola told Andrew as she picked up her handbag and prepared to leave. 'Enjoy your evening.' She smiled. 'I'll see you in the morning.'

'I'm sure we will,' Andrew replied. 'You look very nice, by the way.' He leaned forward to give her a kiss on the cheek. 'You enjoy yourself, too.'

Sitting at Gilles's side as they drove out of Le Jardin, Nicola couldn't help but feel slightly guilty at leaving Andrew.

Perhaps she should have told Gilles that she wasn't free this evening after all. There would have been other concerts.

'We have a slight change of plan,' Gilles said, interrupting her thoughts.

'The restaurant I wanted to take you to was full so we'll dine at my apartment instead. I'll cook for you.' Gilles glanced at Nicola anxiously.

'Is that OK? I *can* cook, you know,' he assured her. 'It won't be a takeaway.'

Relaxed

Gilles's apartment was delightful. Situated at the top of a faded, shuttered building in the heart of the old town, it was traditionally furnished and, with its four rooms, larger than Nicola had expected.

There were several silver-framed photos placed on the shelves in the alcove by the wood-burning stove. One was of a middle-aged couple smiling as they sailed a yacht. Nicola took them to be Gilles's parents. Idly she wondered about the identity of the attractive girl laughing into the camera in another photo.

'My twin sister,' Gilles said, catching her glance.

'I didn't know you . . . '

'She died the day after that photo was taken,' Giles said briefly. 'Twenty years ago.'

' 'Sorry' is such an inadequate word, isn't it?' Nicola said quietly.

Gilles nodded.

'It still hurts, but life does go on.' He opened the door. 'Now, why don't you wait out here? I'll just be a few moments.' He gestured her to go through.

Standing on the rooftop terrace as Gilles attended to things in his kitchen, Nicola took in the views.

In one direction she could see the harbour with the Mediterranean beyond and, in the other direction, the range of mountains that formed the Maritime Alps.

'What breathtaking views,' she said, as Gilles handed her a glass of sparkling wine. 'It must be magical when it's dark and all the lights are switched on.'

Gilles nodded.

'I often come up here at the end of a difficult day and simply stand and stare. It seems to recharge the batteries somehow.'

The dinner he'd prepared was simple

and delicious — salmon and rocket salad for starters, *daube de boeuf à la Provençale* — 'I know you'd like that,' Gilles had said with a laugh — followed by chocolate mousse and coffee.

By the time they left to walk the short distance to the concert hall, they were totally relaxed in each other's company. Crossing the busy Rue de Notre Dame, Gilles took Nicola's hand, and continued to hold it until they reached the theatre.

'It's Been Lovely'

It was late when the concert finished but, as they emerged into the night, Nicola was amazed by how many people were still out enjoying themselves.

Sitting at one of the many pavement cafés, she lazily watched the late-night world of Nice go by.

Bars were thronged with people while music from discos and jazz clubs drifted on the still-warm night air. The locals mingled happily with the holiday-makers, and there was even a game of *boules* going on down one of the side streets.

The drive home through the quiet and deserted countryside passed quickly. Coming to a stop outside Le Jardin, Gilles glanced across at Nicola.

'I have enjoyed this evening. I hope you have, too?'

'It's been lovely. Thank you, Gilles. I'm only sorry you have such a long drive home again.'

Gilles shrugged.

'Not a problem.' There was a pause before he went on. 'May I ask you something?'

'Of course,' Nicola said, as she got out of the car.

As Gilles came to stand next to her, he hesitated.

'You and Andrew. Are you . . . a couple?'

'We're old friends. He helped me through a difficult patch in my life, and I am very fond of him. But no, as much as Andrew would like us to be, we're not a couple,' Nicola replied quietly.

'So, if I ask you out again, he will not be angry with me?'

Nicola giggled at his bashful manner.

'No, I'm sure he'd be happy for me,' she replied.

'Good.' And Gilles leaned forward, kissing her on the cheek.

'Sleep well. I'll see you soon,' he said.

Getting ready for bed, Nicola thought about the evening — and Gilles. She'd really enjoyed herself and hoped that Gilles meant what he'd said about asking her out again.

As for Andrew, she hoped she'd convinced him that she wanted to remain friends for now. But how he'd react to her seeing Gilles again, she couldn't tell.

★   ★   ★

Nicola stirred irritably and tried to shrug off the hands that were shaking her violently.

'Go away. It can't possibly be time to get up yet,' she said, determinedly clutching the duvet around her.

'Mum! Wake up!' Oliver shouted. 'There are wild boar in the garden. They're ruining everything. Andrew needs your help.'

Nicola sat bolt upright.

'How did they get in?'

'The fence is down, remember?'

243

Oliver said. 'Come on!'

Once downstairs, Nicola pulled on her wellingtons and struggled to make sense of the scene before her.

'How long do you think they've been in here?' she asked Andrew.

'Long enough to ruin your vegetable garden and dig up your flower-beds,' he said, shining the torch through the garden to show her some of the devastation the animals had already caused.

'Right now, they are at the top of the garden, rooting around under the trees. As far as I can see there are two adults and three or four babies,' he said.

'The adults are pretty aggressive. Probably our best plan is to try to herd them back towards the building site, and hope they don't attack us.'

'But there's nothing to stop them coming straight back,' Nicola said, dismayed.

'Papa Henri has an electric fence he doesn't use — shall I ring him?' Oliver asked.

'Yes, please,' Nicola said. 'Although I suspect he's going to be less than pleased to be woken up at half-past three!'

'It's an emergency! He'll understand,' Oliver replied confidently.

And he was right. Henri drove down with the electric fence and stayed to help Andrew erect it.

'No point in chasing them off until it's up. They'll only come straight back,' he said. 'I don't know what Gilles Bongars was thinking of, not getting that fence put back up yesterday. He should have known the boars would be in here *tout de suite*.'

Once the two strands of wire were in place, the four of them began the nerve-racking task of chasing the boars out of the garden.

'Concentrate on the adults,' Henri said. 'But be careful. They will protect the babies.'

It took an hour before all the wild boar were out of the garden and the electric fence had been switched on to keep them out. Nicola sighed with relief as she watched them disappear in the darkness into the field behind the building site.

'Thanks, Henri. A cup of coffee before you go home?'

'No, thanks.' Henri shook his head. 'I'll have something stronger when I get back. Don't forget to ring Bongars later — he should at least be told what's happened.'

'Night, Mum. I'm going back to bed,' Oliver said sleepily.

Nicola looked at Andrew.

'I'm going to make myself some hot chocolate, and possibly an early breakfast. I'm starving. Would you like anything?'

'Please,' Andrew said, following her into the kitchen. 'I want to talk to you about something, too.'

'How was your evening?' Nicola asked.

'Great. The *tantes* were on good form. They really made me feel part of the family. Giselle says she'll take me

246

skiing this winter — if I'm not too busy.'

Nicola smiled.

'So, what did you want to tell me?'

'I've decided to buy the campsite,' Andrew said.

Nicola was quiet for a few seconds.

'Are you sure? It's the first place you've looked at. There may be something better on the market. Please don't rush into things, Andrew.'

She shrugged thoughtfully.

'I doubt that the campsite is going to have a lot of people interested in it. Le Jardin had a habitable house, and look how long it was empty.'

'But this is a business opportunity, with land,' Andrew insisted. 'It's different. Besides, there's nothing else in the neighbourhood on the market. I talked to Raoul about it — and Gilles. They both said it was a good opportunity and I should snap it up — especially as I need something close to Le Jardin,' he added.

Nicola looked at him as he continued.

'If our friendship is going to be given the chance of developing, there's no point in buying something miles away . . . '

'I'll Miss You'

On Wednesday morning, Nicola and Oliver were standing on the doorstep of Le Jardin preparing to say goodbye to Andrew.

Secretly, Nicola was relieved at how well Andrew's holiday had gone in the end. Once he'd decided he was going to buy the campsite, the last few days of his visit had been taken up with meetings and seemingly never-ending French bureaucracy.

The question of their relationship had been temporarily pushed aside — but Nicola knew it was only a matter of time before Andrew would once again start to ask questions about their future together.

'I hope you don't mind, but I've left a few things in the chest of drawers in my room.' Andrew's voice brought her back to reality. 'It seems silly taking all my stuff, especially as I'll be returning with all my worldly goods in a week or two.'

Stifling a sigh, Nicola agreed that it was silly for him to take everything away again. But he'd obviously forgotten that the building work on Le Jardin was due to start before he returned, and that the room would have to be cleared . . .

'Right then, I'm off,' Andrew said, ruffling Oliver's hair by way of saying goodbye.

Turning, he took Nicola in his arms and held her tightly.

'Thanks for having me to stay. Just a few more weeks and I'll be down here permanently.' And he kissed her tenderly before getting in his car and winding down the window.

'Don't work too hard while I'm away,' he called out. 'And try to miss me a little bit — I know I'll miss you.'

Nicola bit her lip as Andrew started the car and drove away. She knew she was going to be too busy working to miss him. The weeks until his return were likely to be her most stressful yet at Le Jardin.

Not only did she have to get the house ready for the builders, but there was now the question of restoring the garden after the onslaught from the wild boar.

Thankfully, an apologetic Gilles had organised for the fence to be mended first thing on Monday morning, so that the garden was secure again.

Oliver had already given Nicola a hand replanting the plants that had survived being rooted out and left by the boars, but there was still a lot to be done — including setting up a vegetable plot again.

That had to be her first priority if she was to have fresh produce to sell when the 'Taste Of The Countryside' centre opened its doors.

'We Need To Talk'

As Andrew's car disappeared from view, Giselle arrived.

'Oh, I've missed saying goodbye,' she said ruefully. 'I'd hoped to be in time.' She sighed. 'Still, he'll be back soon, *oui*?'

Nicola nodded.

'This time next month the campsite will be his. Although where he's going to live whilst he builds a house is anyone's guess.'

'Oh, he's organised a mobile home to be delivered. Didn't he tell you?' Giselle said. She looked at Nicola shrewdly. 'Are you not looking forward to Andrew coming to live here?'

Nicola sighed.

'Not really. I think he's moving here for all the wrong reasons. I know he says he's fed up with his old way of life and that he wants a challenge, but I'm worried he expects me to play an important part in his new life — and I'm not ready for that yet . . . '

'Other people's expectations are not always easy to deal with, are they?' Giselle said quietly. 'Nicola, I need to talk to you.'

Nicola glanced at her in surprise. Giselle, normally the most level-headed of women, was agitatedly playing with the silver cross that she wore around her neck. Clearly she had something serious on her mind.

'Shall we go indoors?' Nicola asked, wondering what it could be.

A Shock for Nicola

It wasn't until they were both seated at the patio table that Giselle, glancing apprehensively at Nicola, spoke.

'You are happy here in France, aren't you, Nicola? You don't regret coming here? You don't long to go back to *Angleterre*?'

Nicola didn't answer immediately. She'd been so busy settling in that she honestly hadn't given the question of whether she was happy much thought. Her main concern had always been whether Oliver was happy — not herself.

But now, as she thought about Giselle's question, she nodded.

'Yes, I am happy here. And no, I don't long to go back to England.'

'Good,' Giselle said, visibly relaxing. 'Odette and I love having you and Oliver here. It's made such a difference to our lives. I'd have hated it if you weren't happy, too.'

Nicola looked at Giselle questioningly and waited. There had to be more to Giselle wanting to talk to her than just making sure she was happy in her new life.

'I've been feeling guilty ever since you bought this place,' Giselle said, gesturing around her. 'And there is something I must tell you before you hear it from somebody else.'

Nicola watched Giselle hesitate.

'You see, Nicola, there's a little fact that Henri conveniently forgot to tell you when he blackmailed you into coming to live in France . . . You didn't have to come here after all!'

The Truth

'Henri! I want a word with you about Oliver's inheritance.' Nicola's voice, even to her own ears, sounded brusque and rude. But she didn't care — she was furious with Henri and determined to tell him exactly how she felt.

Henri, on his way to the barn, stopped and turned to look at Nicola.

'Giselle told you, didn't she?' he said. 'I thought it would happen eventually. She never was one to keep her mouth shut where the truth was concerned.'

'I wish she'd opened it before,' Nicola snapped. 'It would have saved a lot of misunderstanding and deceit.'

'My guess is that you wouldn't be here at all,' Henri said slowly. 'If you'd known the truth, you'd never have come to France in the first place. Even when you agreed to come, you weren't exactly thrilled at the prospect.'

Nicola looked at him crossly.

'I wasn't thrilled at being blackmailed into making the decision. Forcing me to come here was bad enough, but basing it on a downright lie is even worse. It makes a complete farce of our being here.'

There was a short silence before Henri spoke.

'I didn't lie about wanting Olivier to grow up here, getting to know his French family.

'And the truth is, if you'd known the way French inheritance laws work — that Olivier, as my only direct descendant, would inherit La Prouveresse, whatever I did — you would never have even considered coming here to live, would you?'

Nicola was thoughtful, but Henri didn't give her the chance to say anything.

'I'd have seen Olivier a couple of times a year, if I was lucky,' he went on, shaking his head. 'I wanted more than visiting rights. I also wanted a chance to try to heal the rift I'd created between us.'

There was silence as Henri looked at her.

'Well, now you know, Olivier inherits La Prouveresse whatever happens. So you can pack up and return to England. I can't expect you to stay; not now you know the truth. Isn't that what you've come to tell me?'

Before Nicola could answer, he turned and walked into the barn, closing the door firmly behind him.

She gazed after him, exasperated. Trust Henri to make sure he had the last word by walking away from the argument. It would serve him right if she did sell up and go back to England.

She sighed. Her initial anger, when Giselle had told her the truth about the blackmail, had faded somewhat. But she had been determined to confront Henri over his lie, although the fact that he didn't seem the least bit repentant was disconcerting.

And was he really expecting her to

leave everything she'd been working on over the last few months and return to England?

Hesitantly, Nicola turned and knocked on the kitchen door of La Prouveresse. She had a suspicious feeling that Giselle had been avoiding her ever since telling her the truth about Henri, and she needed to put things right between them.

Both the *tantes* were pleased to see her, though, even if Giselle did look a bit wary.

'I've just spoken to Henri,' Nicola said quietly. 'And I told him I knew the truth about Oliver's inheritance.'

Giselle glanced at her quickly.

'Nicola, I feel so guilty about this whole affair.'

'Please don't, Giselle,' Nicola said quietly. 'If anybody should feel guilty, it's Henri, but he doesn't seem to have a guilty feeling in his body. He didn't even attempt to apologise.'

Giselle looked down at her feet as Nicola went on.

'He also seems to expect me to hot-foot it back to England, taking Oliver with me, now that I know the truth.'

Giselle gasped suddenly.

'You're not going back, are you?'

Nicola shook her head.

'No. But knowing that I can leave without Oliver losing his inheritance is a big relief,' she said. 'This way, I have a safety net if things don't work out at Le Jardin — and I know where I stand with Henri, finally.'

'Have you told Olivier what Henri did?' Giselle asked.

'No.' Nicola shook her head. 'He didn't know the real reasons behind us coming to France, so there was no point. He and Henri are building a good relationship — I wouldn't want to spoil that.'

'Henri means well,' Odette said slowly. 'It's just that sometimes he goes the wrong way about it.'

Nicola smiled sardonically.

'That's true.'

A Visit

For the next few days Nicola was busy, clearing up the mess caused by the wild boars that had invaded her garden and planting some new stock in the salad and vegetable plots she was trying to establish. On top of that, she needed to start preparing the house for the builders.

Oliver boxed up the things in his bedroom and gave his mother a hand clearing out the shed next to the kitchen.

Raoul, who called in unexpectedly at Le Jardin to see how things were going, found himself helping them move a bed into the small room downstairs where Nicola intended to sleep while the building work was going on. Oliver had already decided he was going to live up at La Prouveresse until his new room was ready.

Afterwards Nicola poured them all cold drinks and they went out on to the patio.

'Thanks for that,' Nicola said to Raoul. 'Now, to what do I owe the honour of this visit?'

'Have you decided which school Olivier will be going to yet?' Raoul asked unexpectedly.

Nicola looked crossly at Oliver.

'Have you been moaning to Raoul?'

Oliver looked sheepish, but Raoul sprang to his defence.

'Not moaning, exactly,' he said. 'Olivier just mentions it every time he sees me.' He laughed.

'But seriously, Nicola, you will have to make a decision soon — school starts in less than ten days.'

Nicola sighed.

'I know,' she said.

'Mum, I really want to go to the French school — not the English one down in Nice,' Oliver pleaded.

'Oh, Oliver, I'm not sure. I know your French has come on by leaps and bounds, but will you understand lessons like science in French? Some subjects are hard enough to understand without struggling with the language.'

'Papa Henri and the *tantes* will help me translate things, if there's something I don't understand,' Oliver said confidently.

'I know, Oliver, but they were at school a long time ago,' Nicola said. 'They won't be familiar with the sort of work you can expect to be doing.'

'I still think I'll cope,' Oliver said stubbornly. 'Anyway, Luc will help me, too. So please — I really want to go to Dad's old school.'

Raoul looked at Nicola.

'Why not let him go for a term and see how he gets on? If it doesn't work out, then in January you can send him down to Nice.'

'I suppose I'm going to have to let you at least try the French school,' Nicola said slowly, turning to look at Oliver. 'I suspect, though, you're going to find it a lot harder than you expect.'

Oliver punched the air with his fist.

'Yes! Thanks, Mum. I'm going to e-mail Luc.' The kitchen door banged behind him as he ran indoors.

'Don't worry,' Raoul said. 'Everyone will help, and you can always ring me.' He glanced at Nicola before continuing.

'Olivier's school wasn't the only reason I called in,' he said quietly. 'I need some advice.' He paused. 'And I thought, with the experiences you've had, you would be the best person to ask.'

A Trip to Nice

The 'Taste Of The Countryside' building next door was progressing rapidly and Gilles was there almost daily as the hot summer days slowly passed.

Invariably, his visits were early morning ones and Nicola got used to Gilles knocking on the door of Le Jardin, holding fresh croissants, just as she was putting her breakfast coffee on. The mornings he didn't appear, she missed him, and the days seemed strangely long. He'd become a really good friend.

The day before the builders arrived to start on Le Jardin, Nicola and Claudine drove to Nice for a shopping expedition. Oliver, who'd spent the night at his friend Luc's, was catching the train from Luc's village and meeting them there. Buying his school clothes and equipment was top priority.

'Are you sure you want to drive?' Claudine asked as she settled herself into Nicola's car. 'We could always take my car.'

Nicola shook her head.

'No, thanks. I need to get used to driving here. But I'm relying on you to navigate for me when we get to Nice. I don't know my way around there!'

By the time Nicola was negotiating the narrow one-way streets of Nice, Claudine had filled her in on all the gossip from the village — and given her some surprising news of her own.

'I'm pregnant.' She smiled. 'Isn't it wonderful?'

'Congratulations!' Nicola said. 'Is Phillipe pleased?'

Claudine nodded happily.

'He's thrilled, too. He's always said he wanted children. The only person who doesn't seem happy for me is my brother. Raoul is strangely quiet these days.'

'I think he's got problems of his own,' Nicola said quietly.

Claudine looked at her.

'Has he been talking to you?'

Nicola nodded.

'He asked my advice, as an outsider,' she added quickly, not wanting to hurt her friend. 'He seemed to think I would know how to solve his problem.'

'And did you?'

'Not really,' Nicola said, wondering how much she could say to Claudine without breaking Raoul's confidence. 'My experiences with Marc and Oliver were different from . . . '

'Ah!' Claudine interrupted. 'It's Marie, isn't it? She's turned him down again.' She sighed. 'Every year he asks her to marry him — and every year she says no. Did Raoul want you to have a word with her?'

'No,' Nicola said quietly. 'Raoul's problem is Luc. Marie has said she will marry Raoul — once he and Luc have a better relationship. He wanted my advice on how he could establish the sort of relationship Oliver and Andrew have. At the moment Luc doesn't really want to communicate with Raoul.'

There was a short silence while Nicola concentrated on parking.

'Oliver told me that Luc has simply turned his mind against Raoul and is determined not to approve of his mother marrying him.'

'So, what advice did you give to Raoul?'

'What could I say, other than give it time?' Nicola sighed. 'But I do feel sorry for Marie, stuck in the middle.'

'Yes, you're lucky that Olivier has accepted Andrew so well,' Claudine said thoughtfully. 'When you two finally get married . . .'

'Hey! I've not accepted his proposal yet,' Nicola protested. 'You make it sound like a foregone conclusion.'

'But that's why Andrew is moving over here, isn't it? So you two can marry and build a new life together. That's what he told Phillipe the night we came to dinner.'

Nicola gazed at her in dismay. Andrew had clearly not been listening when she'd told him she wanted to keep her independence.

When he returned next week she was going to have to talk to him again. Somehow, she had to find a way of making him accept the fact that she was happy with her current, single status.

Another Life

Three days after the builders started work on Le Jardin de Dominic, the noise and the dust became too much for Nicola and she joined Oliver, who was staying up at La Prouveresse.

Giselle and Odette were delighted to have them both at the farm again. Even Henri went out of his way to be affable and make Nicola feel welcome — and no mention was made again of her returning to England.

After supper, Henri usually went down to Sylvie's for a couple of hours, leaving the *tantes* and Nicola to do their own thing until bedtime. Nicola enjoyed those evenings sitting around the old wooden table in the farmhouse kitchen with the *tantes* listening to the muted sounds of Oliver practising his saxophone.

'Do you ever wish you'd moved away

from the village and lived different sorts of lives?' she asked curiously one evening.

Both the sisters looked at her for several seconds without replying and then, to Nicola's dismay, Odette got up and left the room.

'I'm sorry,' Nicola said, looking at Giselle. 'It's none of my business. I shouldn't have asked. Now I've upset Odette . . . '

Giselle smiled at her.

'Do you know the saying *Bien dans sa peau*?'

'Happy in my skin?' Nicola said, slowly translating the words.

Giselle nodded.

'Yes. I'm content enough with the way things are. A husband and children of my own would have been good, but it was not to be — the children part, anyway. You never know, I might still find a husband!'

She laughed then, gathering her thoughts.

'But Odette, now, she's not really

been happy in her skin since she returned from Paris.' Giselle looked at Nicola thoughtfully. 'Did Marc ever tell you about Odette's past?'

Nicola shook her head.

'Only that she was once married and lived in Paris. I don't think he ever knew the truth behind her return to La Prouveresse; he was very young at the time.'

'When she became a widow, Henri forced her to return,' Giselle said quietly. 'He didn't approve of what she was doing in Paris and insisted she came home. Pascal . . . '

'Pascal,' Odette interrupted, coming back into the room, 'begged me to stay.'

Moving across to Nicola, Odette handed her a black and white photograph.

'This is me, in another life — a long time ago. And to answer your question, yes, I do wish I'd lived a different life.'

As Nicola looked at the photograph, she knew she would never have

272

recognised Odette as being the woman in it.

The young, pretty brunette standing in the arms of a handsome man and laughing happily up at him was clearly in love with life and the man holding her. The camera had captured perfectly the look of love that the couple were sharing.

'Your husband was very handsome,' Nicola said gently.

There was a short pause.

'*Non*, Nicola. That's not my husband. It is his brother, Pascal,' Odette said, sadly brushing away a tear as she took the photograph back from Nicola.

★　★　★

Nicola had been hoping that she and Oliver would be back down in Le Jardin before Oliver's first day at his new school. Oliver's school term, however, started before the builders had even finished knocking down any of the walls!

'*Bonne chance*, Olivier!' Henri said gruffly as Oliver gulped down his croissant and picked up his school bag before dashing out of the kitchen and down the farm drive to catch the school bus.

Nicola had offered to drive him to school on the first day but Oliver had declined, saying he'd prefer to go by himself on the bus.

Nicola was pleased he was so keen to start a new phase of his life, but she couldn't help feeling sad that another chapter of her own life was over.

Walking slowly down to Le Jardin as the school bus disappeared from view, Nicola found herself remembering Oliver's first day at primary school. She'd felt bereft that day, too, but Marc had been at her side back then.

After Oliver had vanished excitedly into the school building, Marc helped dry her tears and had taken her out for the day. But so much had changed since then. Today, she was on her own. Nicola smothered a sigh and tried to stop the tears from coursing down her cheeks.

Oliver would be fourteen soon. Today was just another step on his way to becoming an adult. It was only a matter of a few more years before he'd be off to university, finding his own way in life, not needing her on a daily basis any more . . .

Memories

'*Bonjour*, Nicola. Are you all right?' Gilles's gentle voice broke anxiously into her reverie.

Nicola jumped with surprise. She'd been so deep in her own thoughts that she'd arrived at the back gate of Le Jardin without noticing her surroundings, unaware that Gilles was waiting for her by his car.

Now, looking miserably at Gilles, she nodded and struggled to speak normally.

'I'm fine really, thanks. It's just that Oliver going off to his new school brought back a few memories and also made me think about the future. How uncertain everything in life can be.' Nicola smiled tremulously at Gilles through her tears.

'Oh, Nicola, *ma petite*, come here.' Gilles pulled her towards him, wrapping his arms around her tightly. He held her silently for a moment before talking.

'Have you had breakfast?'

'No. I couldn't eat anything — I was more nervous than Oliver.'

'Come on then, get in the car. What you need is a strong cup of coffee,' Gilles said, opening the door.

Within minutes, Nicola found herself sitting at the village café, a large coffee and a plate of croissants in front of her.

'This is so kind of you,' she said, looking at Gilles. 'I'm really grateful for the company, too. I've missed our early morning breakfasts recently,' she added shyly.

'Me, too,' Gilles said. 'I don't like to see you unhappy, Nicola.' He slowly reached across the table and took her hand in his.

'I know there is nothing I can do about today — it's one of life's personal milestones for Olivier and you.' He looked at Nicola, his eyes serious. 'Olivier will be fine — and so will you.

As for the future — who knows what it will bring?'

He paused thoughtfully before continuing.

'I realise we haven't known each other very long and I don't want to presume anything too soon, but already we seem to have something special between us. Please, if I can help in any way at any time, just ask. Promise?'

Nicola smiled through the tears that were threatening to start again at his kind words.

'I promise. Thanks, Gilles.'

He smiled and squeezed her hand tightly.

'Now, I have to spend a couple of hours in Monaco today. Why don't you come with me?'

A Special Friendship

Nicola sat at one of the terrace tables of the Café de Paris, sipping coffee and watching the world go by while Gilles attended his business appointment in an office somewhere along the Avenue de Grande-Bretagne.

Remembering the comforting hug Gilles had given her that morning, and his earlier words about their special friendship, Nicola felt a small glow of happiness spread through her body. She was so lucky to have met him.

Nicola watched as a group of teenagers posed close to three vintage sports cars parked at the foot of the casino steps. She smiled to herself as the souvenir photographs were taken.

A glamorous woman leaving the Hôtel de Paris opposite and stepping into a waiting limousine took her attention. Surely it was . . .

'Seen anyone famous then?' Gilles teased as he greeted her with a customary kiss on both cheeks. He placed his briefcase on the table and ordered a coffee.

Nicola shook her head.

'Nobody that I can put a name to,' she said. 'But it's been fun watching.'

'I thought we'd have lunch up in the old town of Monaco,' Gilles said. 'We'll take a taxi up to the Place d'Armes and then walk up the ramp way to the Palais de Monaco. The views out over the Principality are spectacular.'

Walking hand in hand up the gentle incline towards the palace, Gilles pointed out some of the well-known landmarks and gave Nicola a potted history of the small country.

After watching the changing of the guard on the courtyard outside the palace, the cool interior of Monaco Cathedral provided a welcome respite.

They lunched in the hidden court-yard of a small restaurant and, as they lingered over coffee, a girl went from table to table selling single stem red roses. Everyone, with the exception of Gilles, declined to buy a bloom.

Wordlessly, he presented his chosen rose to Nicola, leaning across to kiss her gently as he did so. Nicola blushed as a ripple of applause broke out at his romantic gesture.

'Gilles, that was lovely,' Nicola said as they began to make their way back down to the harbour through the terraced gardens beneath the palace. 'I can't thank you enough for turning this into such a memorable day.'

Gilles put his arm around Nicola's shoulders and squeezed her tightly.

'I hope you and I have many more memorable days together,' he said quietly. 'Now, I want you to meet some special people and then I'll drive you home.'

Five minutes later, Gilles ushered Nicola into one of the large luxurious apartment blocks overlooking the Port of Monaco. The concierge looked up briefly with a welcoming smile.

'*Bonjour*, Monsieur Bongars,' he said, before the lift took them up to the eleventh floor.

Standing in the elevator, Nicola suddenly felt apprehensive at the thought of meeting people who lived in such opulent surroundings, however special they might be to Gilles. And why was it so important to him that she met them?

She was about to ask Gilles to explain when the lift stopped.

Gilles pulled the safety door aside and pushed open the outer door to reveal a spacious apartment. Turning, he took hold of her hand.

'Come on in,' he said. 'I want you to meet my parents.'

Laurent and Stephanie Bongars were charming and made Nicola feel more than welcome once she'd got over her initial surprise.

'We're so pleased to meet you,' Stephanie said with her perfect English accent. 'Gilles has told us so much about you.'

Nicola smiled as she shook hands with them both.

'I'm delighted to meet you, too!' she said, slightly taken aback.

'Come, let's sit out on the balcony,' Laurent said. 'We'll have some tea.'

'Sorry, Papa, we can't stay,' Gilles said. 'Nicola has to get back for her son, Olivier. But I couldn't bring her to Monaco and not introduce you to each other. I promise we'll return soon.'

Oliver was already in the kitchen of La Prouveresse when Nicola got back late that afternoon. The *tantes* and Henri had been keen to know the details of his first day at school.

Nicola stifled her pangs of guilt about not being home for his return.

'How did it go then?' she asked.

Oliver nodded, his mouth too full of baguette to speak for a second or two.

'OK. I'm in Luc's team for football. And there is a school band. The teachers seem all right, too,' he added as an afterthought.

'Did you understand the lessons?'

Nicola said anxiously.

'Mostly,' Oliver answered. 'Papa Henri's going to help me with my biology homework later. Where have you been?'

'I was in Monaco with Gilles,' Nicola said, ignoring the speculative look Henri threw in her direction. 'I had a lovely day.'

'Andrew called earlier,' Giselle said. 'His departure has been delayed. He's going to be a couple of days late getting here.'

'That's a pity,' Henri said. 'The co-operative can take our grapes on Monday. I was hoping he'd be here to help us pick.'

'I can help!' Oliver enthused.

Before Henri could answer, Nicola put her foot down.

'No. You'll be at school.'

Oliver looked at his grandfather, disappointment in his face.

'We'll need your help when we do the olives,' Henri said. 'It's a bigger job and it goes on for days.'

Oliver seemed to perk up at that thought.

For the next few days Nicola helped Giselle and Odette prepare the extra food that would be required on the day of the *vendange*.

Traditionally, lunch was given to all the neighbours who came to help pick the grapes, although it was mainly Sylvie, Raoul and Claudine who provided the extra hands.

'The vineyard is so small now it takes hours rather than days to pick the fruit. But it's still an excuse for a social get-together,' Giselle had said.

A Visitor

On Monday at noon, Nicola placed a hand in the small of her aching back and slowly stretched. It had been a long morning spent out in the open with the hot sun beating down. Her hair under her straw hat was soaked with sweat but, at last, the row of vines Henri had given her was clipped bare of grapes.

Taking a swig from her almost empty water bottle, Nicola glanced along the vines to see how the others were doing.

Giselle and one of the neighbours were working companionably along the far vine. They, too, would soon be finished. And Raoul and Sylvie were already walking towards the trailer with their last full baskets.

Henri was waiting by the tractor, ready to drive the harvest back up to La Prouveresse and then down to the co-operative.

Nicola emptied the contents of her basket into the trailer and began to make her way back to the farmhouse to give Odette a hand with lunch.

Just as she reached the farmyard, she was surprised to see a man getting out of a car parked in front of the barn.

'*Bonjour, monsieur.* Can I help you?' Nicola enquired.

The stranger turned at the sound of her voice.

'*Bonjour, madame.* I am here to see Odette Bois. On official business,' he added quietly.

'Is she expecting you?'

The man shook his head.

'No. But I am sure she will see me, once she knows I am here.' He handed Nicola a card.

Nicola smothered an exclamation as she looked at the name on the card. She glanced up at the man.

'I'm not sure — '

'Please, just tell her Pascal is here . . . '

'He's Here?'

Leaving Pascal standing by his car, Nicola made her way slowly into the farmhouse. She could hear the others returning from the vineyard, and the tractor and trailer chugging up through the field and on down the drive to the village. Nicola wished Giselle would arrive — she'd know what to do.

Odette was standing by the stove carefully stirring the soup in preparation for lunch.

'*Bonjour*, Nicola. Is it finished?'

'Yes. Everybody is on their way up. Henri has decided to take the trailer straight down to the co-operative and he told us not to wait for him.'

'Tch, Henri — he's always the same. Why can't he come with the others?' Odette's smile faded as she glanced up at Nicola and saw the serious look on her face.

'There is something wrong?'

Silently, Nicola held out the card Pascal had given her. She watched the colour drain from Odette's face as she read the name.

'He seems to think you'll see him.'

'He's here?' Odette whispered.

Nicola nodded.

'He's waiting outside. If you want, I can go and tell him you're not here.'

Odette shook her head, a smile slowly creeping over her face.

'No. I would like to see him. But privately,' she said.

Biting her lip, she looked at Nicola.

'What shall I do?'

Nicola thought quickly.

'You stay here and I'll go and tell Pascal to drive down to Le Jardin — you can join him there. Here, take my back door key. The builders will have gone to lunch in the village, so it should be quiet.'

Nicola pressed her house key into Odette's palm and quickly ran outside to give Pascal his instructions before anyone else arrived in the farmyard.

Pascal looked at her anxiously as she urged him to leave.

'You are sure Odette will come?' he asked.

'I promise,' Nicola said. 'Now go, before any of the family arrive.'

There was no sign of Odette when Nicola got back to the kitchen — just her discarded apron on the table and the soup bubbling away noisily on the range. Two minutes later, as Nicola sliced up a baguette, Odette reappeared.

'How do I look?'

Nicola smiled.

'Beautiful,' she said.

Odette had changed from her working clothes into a pale blue dress, and her hair was pinned into a loose chignon. Her eyes were sparkling and her whole demeanour was transformed. She was clearly looking forward to this unexpected meeting.

'Thanks, Nicola.'

'Are you sure you don't want me to

come with you?' Nicola asked. 'Or Giselle?'

Odette shook her head.

'No. This is something I have to do on my own. I'll see you later.' The kitchen door closed behind her.

Thoughtfully, Nicola carried on putting the finishing touches to lunch. Giselle was the first to arrive and looked surprised to see Nicola on her own.

'Where's Odette?'

Quickly, Nicola explained about Pascal's arrival and Odette's desire to see him by herself.

'Thank goodness Henri didn't meet him in the yard,' Giselle said, relieved.

'Why does Henri dislike Pascal so much?' Nicola asked curiously. 'And why did Odette insist on seeing him on her own?'

Giselle sat down at the table and gave a heavy sigh.

'Oh, Nicola it's a long story, but basically, Pascal was — is — the love of Odette's life.'

'But she's his brother's widow,' Nicola said.

Giselle nodded.

'That, too.'

As she took a breath, about to explain things to Nicola, they both heard voices coming across the farmyard.

'We'll talk later. In the meantime, not a word to anyone, while we have lunch . . . '

In the Past

Walking down the farm drive before cutting across the field that would bring her out at the rear of Le Jardin de Dominic, Odette tried to compose the thoughts that were racing around her mind.

When the lawyers had said they were writing to her about Pascal Bois, just knowing that he was still alive had been enough to make her heart skip a beat or two. Now, the prospect of meeting him again was almost unbearable.

It was thirty years since they'd last seen each other. Thirty years of pointlessly wishing things could have been different.

If only she'd had the courage of her convictions and had listened to her heart, not Henri. She remembered how, the last time Pascal had visited, he'd charmed everyone. He'd taken Marc sailing and then begged her to return to Paris with him.

She'd hidden her broken heart from everyone except Giselle when Pascal finally accepted her refusal and left. If she'd returned to Paris with him, how different her life would have been. Odette sighed. But it was far too late for regrets.

Now, as she opened the back gate of Le Jardin, she could only hope that Pascal had forgiven her for turning him away. Could this unexpected visit possibly be heralding in a future where they would be in contact again?

Pascal heard the click of the gate and turned, smiling in relief when he saw her.

'I wasn't sure you'd come,' he said quietly.

'How could I refuse?'

She felt like a young girl again, her heart skipping a beat as she studied his face, still familiar after all these years. She looked at him wordlessly. He was leaning heavily on a walking stick.

'A logging accident, about twenty years ago,' Pascal said, following her gaze. 'The leg didn't heal as it should, but then nobody expected me to live after the accident.'

Odette's eyes opened wide in distress.

'I didn't know you'd had an accident.'

Pascal shrugged.

'It happened in Canada. I didn't see any point in telling you.' He regarded her silently. 'It was the worst time of my life.'

Odette bit her lip as she looked at him mutely.

It was Pascal who broke the reflective silence that had surrounded them.

'You look wonderful,' he said.

'Thank you.' Odette smiled. 'You look well, too.'

She hesitated before asking the all-important question.

'Pascal, why are you here?'

Pascal looked at her steadily for several seconds.

'Before the lawyers started to write official letters, I wanted to see if, like me, you had any regrets about the past?'

Odette's barely perceptible nod seemed to give him the courage to continue.

'Could we talk and maybe give ourselves a second chance? Or is it too late?' Pascal asked.

Odette swallowed hard, before slowly moving closer to him.

'I've never forgiven myself for sending you away and hurting you. Perhaps the time is finally right for us to put the past behind us and look to the future.'

Odette reached up and gently kissed Pascal, and he, in turn, drew her towards him in a tight embrace, as if he never intended to let her go again . . .

★ ★ ★

Once everybody had finished lunch and Nicola and Giselle were on their own in the kitchen clearing up, Giselle began to tell Nicola the complex tale of Odette and Pascal.

'All Odette ever wanted was to get married and have a family. When she met and married Albert Bois she thought she was going to live happily ever after.'

Giselle sighed, looking pensive.

'The reality when she moved to Paris was very different. Albert was a few years older than her, set in his ways and, well, let's just say Odette realised she'd made the biggest mistake of her life. But, in those days, women were expected to accept their lives.'

Thoughtfully, Giselle put the clean crockery on the dresser.

'It didn't help matters when she and Pascal realised how they felt about each other.' She glanced at Nicola.

'In the end, she told Henri what was going on and said she wanted to leave Albert and come home. There was to be no question of divorce — she simply couldn't take any more and needed to get away from the situation.'

'And Pascal? How did he feel about her leaving?' Nicola asked.

'Deeply upset and hurt. He wanted them to leave together — emigrate to another country and start a new life. But Odette said no. She felt she'd spend her life looking over her shoulder, waiting for them to be discovered.

'There was nothing Pascal could say or do. He just had to accept her decision, although it made them both unhappy for years.'

'Why did he return when Marc was a boy?' Nicola asked.

'Albert had died and Pascal came to tell Odette she was finally free — and to ask her to marry him.'

'She obviously said no,' Nicola said. 'But why?'

Henri's Orders

'Henri went berserk when he heard what was going on and told her there was no way she could marry Pascal.'

'But why not? She was a widow.'

'In those days, to marry your husband's brother wasn't looked upon kindly,' Giselle said. 'In the eyes of the Church — and Henri — it was morally wrong.'

'So, Henri made Odette give up Pascal and her dreams to stay here?' Nicola shook her head in disbelief.

'Yes. He said it was her own fault she'd married the wrong brother in the first place and it was too late to change things. He insisted she had to forget the Bois family and get on with her life — without Pascal.'

'Henri has a tendency to interfere in people's lives, doesn't he?' Nicola said ruefully.

'He always thinks he knows best,' Giselle agreed. 'Right now, I'm wondering how he's going to receive the news that Pascal has returned.' She glanced at Nicola. 'I'm curious, too — how did Odette react?'

Nicola smiled.

'She was shocked initially, but happy. I'd say she was really looking forward to seeing him.'

Giselle sighed.

'Well, I don't suppose for one moment Henri will be pleased to see him. And I hope I'm not the one who has to tell him about our unexpected visitor . . .'

Nicola was still in the kitchen talking to Giselle when Henri returned from the co-operative, still unaware that Odette had a visitor.

'I'm going down to Le Jardin to check on the builders,' Nicola said quickly. 'Then I'm going to meet Oliver off the school bus. I'll see you later.'

She mouthed an apology at Giselle before she left. There was no way she wanted to be involved in the rekindling of an old family feud.

Now, standing by the bus stop in the village waiting for the school coach, Nicola wondered where Odette and Pascal were. There had been no sign of them at Le Jardin earlier.

'What are you doing here, Mum?' Oliver asked, jumping off the coach.

'I thought we might go for a pizza in the village,' Nicola said. 'Just you and me. We can talk about what you want for your birthday next month, if you like? And then I've got to go to the campsite and wait for Andrew's mobile home to arrive.'

'Will he be here soon?'

'Some time in the next two days, I think,' Nicola replied.

'He'll be phoning soon if you'd like a word with him.'

Oliver shrugged his shoulders indifferently.

'I'll talk to him when he gets here. Mum?' He looked at Nicola uncertainly.

'I don't want a party or anything for my birthday, just Luc and maybe a couple of the other guys to supper.'

He waited while Nicola ordered their pizzas and drinks before continuing.

'I'd really like a scooter, though.'

'No way,' Nicola said instantly. 'You're far too young!'

'No, I'm not!' Oliver protested. 'It's not like it is in England, Mum. You can have a scooter here when you're fourteen!'

'No,' Nicola said firmly. 'I'm not even going to consider it. The roads around here are far too dangerous. All the boys I've seen riding scooters don't have any road sense.'

'I wouldn't be that stupid,' Oliver muttered. 'You let me ride a bicycle on these 'dangerous' roads.'

Nicola was silent. She tormented herself with worry every time Oliver was out on his bike. He didn't go far — just into the village and up to the farm — but she was always on tenterhooks when he was out.

'And that's as far as I'm prepared to go, because I trust you to be sensible. As soon as you're old enough, you can learn to drive.'

'But that's years away,' Oliver grumbled.

'Well, it's all that's on offer,' Nicola said, exasperated.

She looked at Oliver as he began to eat his pizza, a sullen look on his face. Was this the beginning of those dreaded teenage years all her friends warned her about?

Nicola sighed. At least Andrew would be here soon. He could usually jolly Oliver out of himself.

'When you get back to La Prouveresse, Odette's old friend from Paris, Pascal, might be there,' Nicola said in an effort to start Oliver talking to her again.

'You know, the Pascal that your dad mentioned in his diary?'

'Do you think he'll take me sailing like he did with Dad?' Oliver asked excitedly.

'I doubt it. He's a lot older now. Besides, I'm not sure how long he'll be staying. If I know Papa Henri, it won't be long.'

Thoughtfully, Nicola sipped her drink, wondering whether Henri and Pascal had come face to face.

After their pizza, Oliver went back to the farm to make a start on his homework, while Nicola travelled to the campsite to await the arrival of Andrew's mobile home.

Nicola stood waiting for the low-loader to manoeuvre its ramps into position for the home to be gently eased on to the pitch Andrew had prepared. She glanced up across the valley.

La Prouveresse was clearly visible from where she stood, and Pascal's car was slowly travelling up towards the farmhouse. Fleetingly, Nicola wondered how things were progressing.

The mobile home was soon in position and Nicola closed the gate to the campsite before making her way across the road to Le Jardin.

She'd decided to give the Jacques family a bit more time to sort themselves out before she returned to La Prouveresse and the inevitable atmosphere there was sure to be between Odette and Henri.

The phone was ringing as she let herself into Le Jardin.

'Has it arrived?' Andrew asked anxiously.

'Yes, it's ready and waiting for you. I've got the keys. How far down are you?'

'Just outside Bordeaux. I can't go too fast with this van, even on the *autoroute*, but I should hopefully be with you tomorrow, before it gets dark. How are things with you? Oliver all right? Henri?'

Nicola laughed.

'Henri is Henri. Not only have I discovered he blackmailed me into moving down here using outright lies, I now hear he made poor Odette reject the love of her life. I'll tell you all about it when you get here.'

'What do you mean — downright lies?'

'Oh, because of the complexity of French law Oliver inherits the farm anyway. I'll explain later.'

Nicola heard a sharp intake of breath down the phone.

'So, we needn't have uprooted ourselves and moved to France at all?'

'No, it appears that I didn't have to come here,' she said. 'But I'm glad I did, and I hope you will be happy here, too, Andrew. Just remember, nobody twisted your arm to come here — it's what you wanted to do. I'll see you tomorrow.'

Nicola sighed as she replaced the receiver. Hopefully, rebuilding his house and preparing the campsite for visitors would keep Andrew busy and happy for the next few months. Otherwise, she could see problems ahead.

It was starting to rain as Nicola walked back up to La Prouveresse and the gentle breeze of earlier had turned into a fierce wind. Nicola could hear the ominous sound of thunder rumbling away in the distance, and the occasional flash of lightning lit up the mountains behind the farm.

Giselle was alone in the kitchen when Nicola quietly opened the kitchen door and peered round hesitantly, not wanting to walk into a Jacques family row.

'Ah, Nicola, come on in out of the rain,' Giselle said. 'Thank goodness we picked the grapes today. They've just given out a severe weather warning for later this evening.'

'It's bad enough out there already,' Nicola said. 'I can't believe how quickly the weather has changed. Where is everybody?' she asked, hanging her coat up to dry near the range.

'Olivier's still doing his homework in his room. Henri's in the barn, and Odette's gone out for dinner with Pascal.'

'Have Henri and Pascal come face to face yet?' Nicola asked, concerned.

'Yes, but it's no use asking me what was said,' Giselle said. 'They both disappeared into the barn and Henri stayed there when Pascal left.'

'Has Odette at least told you why Pascal is here?'

Giselle nodded.

'He's seventy soon and says the biggest regret of his life is his relationship with Odette. He wanted to see if she had any regrets, too, and if, perhaps, there was any chance, at this late stage of their lives, of them starting again.'

Giselle grinned broadly at Nicola.

'I haven't seen Odette looking so happy in years,' she added. 'She's promised to tell me everything when she gets back tonight.'

'Is Pascal staying here?' Nicola asked.

'No.' Giselle shook her head. 'I did offer, but he didn't think it was a good idea. He's booked himself into an *auberge* in the village for a few days. He's returning to Paris at the weekend.'

A loud clap of thunder overhead

made both women jump and Giselle moved across the kitchen to pull the curtains just as a flash of lightning illuminated the figure of a man running across the farmyard. It was Henri.

'Can I give you a hand preparing supper?' Nicola said. 'Or shall I disappear to my room for a bit? Let you and Henri talk in private?'

'Supper's all ready,' Giselle said. 'Give Olivier a call and then you can help me serve. Disappear, indeed! Henri and I have had enough private talk for one day!'

The next morning, the wind and the rain showed no sign of stopping and Nicola decided working indoors at Le Jardin was her best option for the day.

The builders had almost finished the major structural alterations — even the wooden spiral staircase was in position, giving access to the new bedroom and bathroom. Downstairs, the wall dividing the sitting-room from the adjoining outbuilding had been knocked down and a window fitted into the old doorway.

Most of the rubble had been removed already and the builders had promised the rest would be gone before they started to plaster the walls. Hopefully it would only be another week before they finished and then she and Oliver could move back.

There was a quiet knock on the back door before it opened. It was Gilles.

'*Bonjour*, Nicola,' he said.

She turned, a welcome smile on her face.

'Dreadful weather,' Gilles went on. 'The roads are starting to flood and there were already some minor land-slides in the gorge when I drove up this morning. Still, the *météo* said the worst should be over by this evening.

'Oh, sorry,' he said, leaning forward to kiss Nicola on the cheek and managing to shower her with rain from his wet hair.

'It's looking good,' he went on, glancing around.

Nicola nodded.

'Now I've got to start thinking about paint colours and looking for some furniture. I want a dresser on that wall for starters. In England, I would normally head for the nearest auction or second-hand shop. Is there something similar here?'

'There are big warehouses in Nice, and smaller ones in Antibes. Let me know when you're ready, and I'll take you.'

Nicola smiled her thanks.

'Feel like braving the elements and coming across to 'A Taste Of The Countryside'?' Gilles asked. 'They're doing the finishing touches to the inside fittings. I can offer you a cup of hot coffee, too.'

A Day Out

Once inside the new wooden building, Nicola looked around as Gilles poured her a coffee.

'When do you think it'll be open for business?' she asked.

'The co-operative have appointed a liaison officer to start work at the end of the month. She'll get things organised quickly. Don't forget to register with her so you can sell your produce. The official opening is pencilled in for the first week in January.'

Nicola looked slightly worried.

'What with the boars digging up and trampling over everything, and now this weather, my crops are way behind schedule. I'm beginning to think I'll never have anything to sell,' she said ruefully, taking her coffee.

'Are you and Olivier doing anything next Sunday?' Gilles asked. 'There's a motorbike scramble in the next valley and I wondered if you'd like to go for a day out? It would give me a chance to get to know Olivier better,' he added quietly.

'That's very kind of you, Gilles, but I'm not sure that anything to do with motorbikes is a good idea at the moment,' Nicola replied. 'I've refused to buy him one for his birthday so, of course, I'm now the world's worst mother!'

'Well, we could always go canoeing instead,' Gilles suggested. 'The rivers should be running well after this deluge. I'd love the chance to spend some time with Olivier — and for him to get to know me,' he added.

'All right! Just so long as I can stand on the edge and watch,' Nicola said. 'Personally, I'm not a canoe person — it's much too close to the water for me!'

* * *

Pulling into the tollbooth at the Nice exit on the *autoroute*, Andrew heaved a sigh of relief. Two more hours and he should reach the campsite.

Torrential rain and wind had made the last hundred kilometres of driving treacherous. Winding the window down to hand his money to the cashier, an icy blast of wind filled the van. As Andrew took his change, a *gendarme*, his face red with cold, peered in through his window.

'Your destination, please, *monsieur*?'

'I'm picking up the N202,' Andrew said. 'Heading up towards Digne for about sixty kilometres.'

'There's been some rock falls on that road — and the weather's not good past Touet-sur-Var.' The *gendarme* pointed in the direction of a small group of lorries waiting by the side of the road.

'If you really can't wait, I suggest you tag on to the end of that convoy — they're making their way to the 202 as well. My advice to all of you would be to park up overnight and continue the journey tomorrow.'

Andrew glanced across at the lorries.

'I really want to get home this evening, so I think I'll join the convoy,' Andrew said.

The *gendarme* shrugged.

'Take care, then — and be prepared for road blocks and diversions. *Bonne chance*!'

Andrew wound the window up and rubbed his tired eyes before putting the van into gear and moving off to take his place at the back of the slow-moving line of traffic.

Thirty kilometres later, he noticed the lorries turning into the carpark of a roadside café. Andrew hesitated before following. He glanced at his watch. It was 7.30 p.m.

The conditions hadn't been as bad as he'd feared and the road blocks and diversions the *gendarme* had warned about hadn't materialised. Now the rain was easing slightly and there was very little traffic about, so driving wasn't as difficult.

He'd have a quick cup of coffee, phone Nicola to give the approximate time of his arrival, then set off on the last thirty kilometres.

With any luck he'd be having supper with Nicola and Oliver up at La Prouveresse by ten.

★ ★ ★

Nicola and Giselle were in the kitchen companionably preparing supper when Andrew rang. Henri had gone down to the village to have supper with Sylvie — and Odette and Pascal still hadn't returned from their day out!

Giselle answered the phone, handing it over to Nicola with a smile.

'Hi, I've just stopped for a coffee. The weather's not too bad so it shouldn't take me too long to do the last stretch. I reckon I should be with you in about an hour — an hour and a half at the most,' Andrew said, a hint of tiredness in his voice.

'I've put a small gas heater on in the

316

mobile home so it should be nice and cosy for you. And there's some bedding down there, although Giselle says you're more than welcome to stay up at the farm tonight after supper.'

'Thanks, but I'm really looking forward to my first night down on the campsite,' Andrew replied. There was a short pause before he continued.

'Nicola, I'm sorry if I upset you yesterday. You obviously made the right decision for you and Oliver in moving to France and, despite all the problems of the last few weeks, I am glad I'm joining you. The truth is, I'm looking forward so much to seeing you and Oliver — and to sharing your lives again.'

'I'm looking forward to you being here, too,' Nicola said.

'We've had some good times together over the years, haven't we?' Andrew said. 'Hopefully we can build on them. I don't mean to crowd you, but you know how I feel about you.'

'I know,' Nicola said gently. 'But

we're just going to have to see how things go. Let's get you settled in and then worry about our relationship, OK? By the way, there's a bottle of champagne in the fridge ready to celebrate your arrival. See you soon!'

Thoughtfully, she replaced the receiver. Andrew had sounded so positive and upbeat. It had been like talking to the old Andrew again and she was surprised to realise just how much she was looking forward to having him around on a daily basis.

Just then, a loud clap of thunder made her jump.

'Sounds as though the storm is hanging around the valley,' Giselle said. 'I hope it doesn't delay Andrew too much.'

Homeward Bound

The weather took a turn for the worse soon after Andrew left the café. Sighing to himself, he peered tiredly through the rain-bombarded windscreen. It looked as though this last hour of driving was going to be the most difficult of the whole journey. The rain was so heavy now that the wipers were struggling to cope.

With the van headlights highlighting debris littering the road from minor rock falls, Andrew carefully negotiated his way along the mountain road through the gorge. Some of the crumbling rock face was hung with giant nets to stop any major falls before they hit the ground, but as Andrew drove slowly up through the valley, they seemed hopelessly inadequate.

Large boulders and smaller rocks were scattered all over the road. In amongst the stones and gravel were rock plants which had been torn by their roots from the precipice above.

Just as Andrew braked for the dangerous bend that would take him on to the final homeward stretch, a loud rumble of thunder and flash of forked lightning across the valley to his right momentarily took his attention . . .

★ ★ ★

'So, where do we go from here?' Pascal asked quietly. He and Odette were dining at L'Oliveraie restaurant in the village. Their original plan had been to go farther afield, but the evening's bad weather had made that impossible.

Knowing the news of her 'gentleman friend from Paris' was probably all round the village by now, Odette had suggested somewhere local.

'As long as you are prepared for everyone to want to meet you,' she'd warned him anxiously. 'They will want to know what is happening between us.'

'*Bien*,' Pascal had said, shrugging. 'It is time everyone knew the truth about us.'

And people couldn't have been nicer to them. All evening, friends of Odette kept coming across, wanting to be introduced to the attractive man by her side.

Now, as they lingered over their coffee, she regarded Pascal seriously. She, too, had been wondering about the future, knowing that Pascal was due to return to Paris after the weekend.

'I've told Henri what I want to happen,' Pascal continued quietly.

Odette looked anxiously at him. Henri had been avoiding her since Pascal's unexpected arrival. Giselle had said she'd tried to talk to him, but that he'd simply changed the subject.

'What did he say?'

'That you must do what you consider to be best.'

'I can't believe that Henri is being so reticent.' Odette glanced up at Pascal. 'What exactly did you tell him?'

'That you and I were not going to lose touch with each other ever again.' Pascal reached across the table and took her hand in his. 'That the world had moved on and there was no reason why we shouldn't marry.'

Odette's eyes widened.

'I can imagine Henri's reaction to that.'

'He was surprisingly quiet. I think Henri has mellowed a lot since I last knew him.'

'Marc's death was a terrible blow to him,' Odette said quietly.

'Deep down, he always hoped Marc would return. The fact that they were estranged when he died is something that Henri has had difficulty coming to terms with.'

She stirred her coffee thoughtfully.

'Having Nicola and Olivier living here has made a huge difference to him. Henri dreads the thought of history repeating itself — he adores Oliver.'

'He's a nice lad,' Pascal said. 'From the little I've seen of him, he's a lot like

Marc.' He squeezed her hand gently.

'But you haven't answered my question. Now Henri is leaving it up to you, shall we do what we should have done years ago and get married?'

Odette swallowed hard, trying to stop the tears that were threatening.

'I can't believe that, after all this time, you and I are getting a second chance,' she said, shaking her head. 'It's like a dream. Promise me I won't wake up tomorrow and you'll have disappeared.'

'Odette, believe me, this is for real — for the rest of our lives.

'I take it you do want to marry me?'

'More than anything,' she cried.

'Now, where shall we live? Down here? Paris? Or somewhere completely new to both of us?'

'I'd love to spend some time in Paris,' Odette said. 'But I don't think I could live there permanently. I'm a real countrywoman these days. Could we live down here and go for frequent visits — or would you find being so close to Henri a problem?'

Pascal shook his head.

'*Non*. I think Henri and I have both gained tolerance as we've aged. I've got a small apartment in Paris which I think you'll like, so we just need to find something down here. Tomorrow we will go to the estate agent's and . . . '

'Tomorrow we will tell everybody our news,' Odette interrupted gently. 'Somehow I don't think Giselle will be surprised — but I think Henri may have something to say.'

The wind finally blew the storm away overnight and everything was calm early the next morning as Nicola stumbled down the drive and across the road to the campsite.

Blinded by the tears that were coursing down her cheeks, she struggled for several moments before inserting the key into the door of Andrew's mobile home.

The heater she'd plugged in yesterday afternoon to warm the place for

Andrew's arrival was still switched on, filling the small space with muggy air. Absently, she bent down and switched it off before slowly looking around.

Everything appeared normal. She wandered through into the kitchen area. Provisions she'd bought in the village shop still stood on the small work surface.

Coffee, tea, biscuits, a packet of pasta, salt, kitchen paper. She knew without looking that there was milk, butter, cheese, eggs and vegetables in the small fridge. She'd placed it all there only a day ago — alongside the champagne to toast Andrew's arrival and his new life in France.

Miserably, she opened the door leading to the small bedroom. Was it only two days ago that she and Oliver had brought the boxes with the few clothes and possessions Andrew had left behind and arranged them in his new home?

She took a sweater out of a drawer and hugged it against her.

Hoping to make the place feel a bit more like home, she'd put a framed photograph of the three of them on the shelf by the window. She'd found it in one of Andrew's boxes when she was unpacking.

Clutching the sweater and the photo to her, she collapsed on to the settee and stared blindly out of the window.

Last night, when the *gendarme* had knocked on the door of the farmhouse, she'd struggled to accept what he was telling her. That morning, in Andrew's deserted mobile home, the truth finally began to sink in.

Andrew was dead. He'd been killed instantly when his van had skidded off the road, the police said.

Nicola looked at Andrew's happy smiling face staring out at her from the photograph. He'd been so looking forward to starting his new life in France. And she knew he'd been hoping, too, that their relationship would take a significant leap forward.

Andrew had stubbornly refused to accept her reluctance to commit to him. He loved her and was convinced that, given time, she would return this love.

'It's All My Fault'

A gentle knock on the door startled her.

'May I come in?' Gilles asked quietly. 'Henri said I might find you here.'

Nicola smiled tremulously at him.

'Hi. You're out and about early.'

'I heard about the accident and wanted to be with you.'

'Thank you,' Nicola said. She glanced at him tearfully. 'I just feel so guilty. All I can think about is the fact that he was coming here to be with me and . . .' She paused. 'If I'm honest, I'd already decided I didn't love him enough to marry him, but I didn't want to hurt him. I cowardly thought that once he was here things would slip into place and he'd realise we weren't meant to be a couple.

'If only I'd told him, he wouldn't have bought the campsite and he wouldn't have been driving on that road. He'd still be alive. It's all my fault for being so selfish.'

'Stop right now,' Gilles said sternly, taking her into his arms and holding her tightly.

'You are torturing yourself over something that you cannot possibly be responsible for. Andrew was the one who decided to move to France and buy the campsite. He was the one who thought that his life here in France would be better.' Gilles hugged her.

'I know from what you've told me that Andrew hoped you'd return his love, but I also believe that you brushed his advances away enough times for him to get the message that your love for him wasn't the same as his for you. It's not your fault he didn't accept your feelings. Please don't blame yourself for anything.'

Gilles pressed his lips gently against her forehead.

'How has Olivier taken the news?'

'Badly. He's lost his father and now a man he regarded almost as an older brother, all in the space of a few months.'

Gilles continued to hold her tightly for several silent moments.

'We'll just have to make sure he knows we're here for him. I remember when my sister died. I just couldn't cope; my poor parents were beside themselves with grief and worry.'

He looked thoughtfully at Nicola.

'The next few weeks will be hard — for both of you — but promise me you'll let me help in any way I can.'

As Nicola mutely nodded her thanks, Gilles took her hand.

'Now, come on, let's get you out of here.'

A Sad Time

For the next few days, Nicola found that the only way to stop brooding about Andrew and the accident was to try to keep busy.

Oliver had been surprisingly willing to return to school.

'Moping around here isn't going to help either of us,' Nicola had said gently. 'I know it's hard, but we both need to keep our lives as normal as possible.'

A week later, Andrew's funeral was held in the tiny village church.

Nicola was amazed at the number of people who came to pay their last respects to this Englishman they'd barely known. Wreaths and bunches of flowers covered the ground as Andrew was laid to rest in the small cemetery just west of the village.

Standing there, listening to the priest

intoning the words of the service, Nicola found thoughts of Marc, as well as Andrew, filling her mind.

Now, as the priest said a benediction for Andrew, Nicola found herself including Marc in her prayers. It was a final goodbye to two men she had loved in such different ways.

★   ★   ★

Two days after the funeral, Nicola was down at Le Jardin to see the builders off. Wandering around, assessing the cleaning and decorating she had to do before moving back, Nicola felt nothing but tiredness. The pleasure she'd been expecting to feel in her newly finished home simply wasn't there.

Standing in her newly enlarged bedroom, looking out over the garden, she sighed. There was more work to be done out there. Next door she could see Gilles's car parked beside the 'Taste Of The Countryside' building. Briefly, she thought about wandering across to see him.

'Nicola?' Claudine's voice floated up the stairs.

'Great transformation,' she said, looking around. 'I suppose you can't wait to start decorating and getting it the way you want.'

Nicola smiled ruefully.

'I'm not sure I've got the enthusiasm right now,' she said. 'Anyway, how are you?'

Claudine smiled happily.

'I'm fine. I wonder whether you'd like to come to Nice with me tomorrow?'

'I should really make a start here but another day won't make much difference. Perhaps I can find some paint for the sitting-room. Plus it's Oliver's birthday next week, so I need inspiration. Yes, a couple of hours in town would be good.'

'How is Olivier?' Claudine enquired.

'He spends all of his spare time practising the same mournful tune on his saxophone over and over again.

Henri spends a lot of time in the barn with him.'

Nicola was thoughtful for a moment.

'I'm hoping that next week's birthday tea will be the beginning of getting Oliver back into doing other things. At the moment he doesn't even want to see Luc or play *boules* with the village lads.'

Organising his birthday treat was proving difficult. Oliver had simply shrugged when asked what he wanted to do on the day. When Nicola pressed him on what present he would like, he sighed.

'You know what I want. If I can't have a motorbike I don't want anything.'

As well as organising a birthday tea at La Prouveresse, Nicola bought a computer game for Oliver.

Now was not the time to take him to task for his rudeness — she could only hope that he'd slowly start to work through his grief.

Oliver's Present

Henri was in the kitchen at La Prouveresse, talking to Giselle and Odette, when Nicola returned from her day in Nice. Opening the kitchen door, Nicola heard Odette's happy voice.

'Pascal will be back at the weekend and we're going to see the priest to arrange the wedding. We were thinking near Christmas. We both hope you will give us your blessing,' she added quietly.

Odette turned to Nicola.

'Do you think Olivier would like to be a witness?'

'Congratulations,' Nicola said, hugging her. 'I'm so glad everything is finally working out for you. And yes, I'm sure Oliver would love to be a witness.'

'Nicola, I want a word with you,' Henri said, ignoring her words. 'It's about Olivier.'

'Is he all right?' Nicola asked quickly. 'Where is he?'

'In the barn, practising, as usual,' Henri answered shortly. 'But I am worried about him. He's not a happy boy.'

'I know that.' Nicola sighed. 'Unfortunately, there's nothing I can do to alter recent events.'

Henri looked at her sternly.

'I want to get him a bike for his birthday.'

'No, Henri,' Nicola said.

'The lad really needs something good to happen in his life.'

'Oh, and you call buying him something dangerous like a motorbike good?'

'*Non*. But I thought I could get him a trials bike. That way, he could ride it on the farm and have lots of fun, but it wouldn't be legal for him to take it on the road. Could you live with that compromise?'

Nicola gazed at Henri in surprise. He was actually talking to her before doing something that might upset her.

'Yes, an off-road bike could be the answer. But where will we find one so close to his birthday?'

'I've already got it,' Henri said sheepishly. 'It's hidden in the store room. I just thought I'd better check with you first. I didn't want you accusing me of deceiving you again.'

Nicola gazed at him in disbelief and then she laughed.

'Oh, Henri. Trust you to do things the wrong way round!'

'Happy Birthday!'

Nicola woke early on the morning of Oliver's birthday and lay for a few moments listening to the sounds of the farm and thinking about the future. Living up at La Prouveresse was so easy; over the last week or two since Andrew's accident the *tantes* had comforted her and taken charge of everyday things. It would be all too easy to stay here and let Giselle carry on spoiling her.

Nicola sighed. The time was coming when she simply had to return to Le Jardin and get on with her own life once again. Oliver, too, needed to get back into a normal routine.

Starting to get dressed, she resolved that next week she'd get to grips with the decorating and move things back into Le Jardin.

Hearing Oliver and Henri's voices as

they came out of the store room, Nicola crossed to the window and watched Oliver pushing his new trials bike across the farmyard.

Henri opened the gate into the field and, once inside, Oliver kickstarted the machine. Nicola watched anxiously as he began to rev the gears before jumping on the saddle and attempting to steer the bike across the rough terrain.

Henri somehow managed to run alongside him for the first fifty yards or so, shouting instructions before stopping and watching as Oliver wobbled his way across the field and back again.

Opening the window, Nicola leaned out and called to him.

'Well done, Oliver — and happy birthday!'

By the time everybody had gathered for his birthday tea later in the day, Oliver was confident enough to demonstrate his skills up and down the farm drive.

After tea, watching him chase Luc

with a paintballing gun — Gilles's birthday present — Nicola began to feel optimistic that perhaps the healing process had started.

'It's so good to hear Oliver laughing again,' she said quietly to Gilles, who was standing by her side.

'Yes,' he agreed, glancing at her. 'But how are you coping, Nicola? I was talking to the manageress at 'A Taste Of The Countryside' yesterday and she mentioned you hadn't signed up yet. The opening ceremony isn't that far off, and I know she wants to invite all the producers.'

'It's on my 'things to do' list,' Nicola said. 'I've promised myself that this week I will start to get my life back on track.' She smiled wanly at Gilles.

'I've really neglected the garden recently. The weeds are unbelievable! Still, spending time sorting out the garden will be good for me.'

'I can give you a hand a couple of evenings if you like,' Gilles offered. 'But only on the condition that you let me take you and Olivier out to supper afterwards.'

'Thanks,' Nicola said gratefully. 'The *tantes* have already offered to give me a hand getting the house ready to decorate — but I might need you to help us move the furniture!'

'You just have to ask.' Gilles smiled.

As they stood companionably side by side, watching Oliver and Luc playing around, Gilles's hand sought hers and held it tightly. Strangely comforted by the gesture, Nicola happily entwined her fingers with his.

The next morning, after Oliver had left for school, Nicola was determined to make a start on getting things back to normal before her resolve weakened, and so she made her way down to Le Jardin.

Both Giselle and Odette had promised to join her mid-morning to help with cleaning the house, so Nicola made a beeline for the neglected garden. Two hours later, she was pleased with her efforts.

The weeds in the vegetable plot had been banished and she had a small basket full of baby carrots, garlic, a few lettuces and some freshly dug potatoes. The *tantes* arrived as she was walking towards the house to put the produce in the kitchen.

'We've brought a flask of coffee and some sandwiches for lunch,' Giselle announced cheerfully.

'And we met the postman,' Odette said, handing Nicola an official-looking letter.

Andrew's Legacy

Nicola frowned when she saw the English postmark. It was from Andrew's solicitors. She'd been in constant touch with them over the funeral arrangements and costs and she was sure she'd done everything that was necessary for them. Slowly, she opened the letter.

'Nicola, whatever's the matter?' Giselle sounded anxious. 'You've gone very pale.'

Nicola looked up.

'Apparently I'm Andrew's sole beneficiary. He's left me everything — including the campsite.'

There was a short silence as the *tantes* regarded her.

'I don't know what to do,' Nicola said finally.

'I've got more than enough on my plate with Le Jardin. I really don't want to run a campsite as well.'

She gave a sigh.

'But it seems so unfeeling just to give up on it. Andrew had such dreams for the place. I feel guilty enough over things already without . . . '

'Nicola, you've got to stop blaming yourself for Andrew's death,' Odette interrupted sternly. 'I'm sure it's the last thing he'd want you to do. I know he'd want you to get on with your life and be happy.'

'There's no rush for a decision, is there?' Giselle asked. 'These things always take time to sort out. It will be the New Year before all the paperwork is sorted.'

'You're both right,' Nicola said. 'I'll put off making a decision until next year. See how I feel then.'

'Actually, Nicola, I've just had an idea,' Odette said quickly.

'Would you rent it to Pascal and me? You know we've been looking for somewhere down here. The campsite would make an ideal base for us. It's close enough to everybody, and yet private, too. We could even rebuild the house.'

Excitedly, she turned to Nicola.

'In fact, rather than rent it — you could sell it to us!'

Moving On

'Are you sure you want this place?' Nicola asked, looking anxiously at Odette and Pascal. 'You'd be taking on a lot. I'll understand if you've changed your minds.'

It was late afternoon and they were standing outside the mobile home on the campsite.

'It's perfect for us,' Pascal said. 'Close enough to everyone — but far enough away to let us lead our own lives. And rebuilding the house will give me something to do — a challenge for my retirement.'

'The lawyer in the UK dealing with Andrew's affairs is aware you want to buy the place and he's preparing all the legal documents for the transfer,' Nicola explained.

'But I'm quite happy if you want to make a start before it becomes official

346

in the New Year. And Gilles said if you need any help working out plans and getting planning permission, just ask.'

'I appreciate that,' Pascal said. 'I'd like to use the mobile home as a base before the wedding.'

'Have you set a date yet?' Nicola asked.

'The twenty-third of December,' Pascal replied.

'Five o'clock at the town hall and half-past five at St Joseph's,' Odette added. 'And supper afterwards at the château. I still can't quite believe it,' she added, smiling happily at Pascal.

'How is Gilles?' Pascal asked, turning back to Nicola.

'Fine. I've left him helping Oliver. They're decorating Le Jardin this afternoon. I promised them both a special supper, so I'd better get back. Please, take the keys and treat the place as yours from now on,' she said, placing them in Pascal's palm.

Pensively, Nicola made her way up the drive to the main road. It was such a short time since Andrew had excitedly cajoled her into looking at the campsite, full of plans for it and his future.

With a sigh, she pulled the wooden gate closed behind her. In addition to her own grief, Andrew's death had created all sorts of complications and difficulties in her life. The campsite was one — Oliver was another.

Since the accident he'd become more and more withdrawn and bad tempered, disappearing to ride around the farm on his trials bike for hours rather than spending time with her or the *tantes*.

Nicola, knowing how he'd looked up to Andrew and realising he was having difficulty coming to terms with the double blow that life had dealt him, was loath to tell him off. But the time was rapidly coming when she would have to say something about his behaviour.

He was being particularly aggressive towards Gilles. Nicola sighed. Life would be much easier if only Oliver could bring himself to accept Gilles's increasing presence in their lives.

She'd really had to insist he stayed to give them a hand with the decorating today. Hopefully they hadn't come to blows during her short absence.

To her relief, all seemed calm when she went into the house.

'Hey, it's looking good,' she said, glancing into the sitting-room where Gilles was up a ladder painting the ceiling and Oliver was putting the finishing touches to the walls.

'It should be dry enough to put the furniture back in place tomorrow,' Gilles said. 'Then you can move in again.'

Nicola smiled ruefully.

'I was hoping to be down here for the weekend, but the *tantes* are going to Paris tonight with Pascal on a shopping expedition so Oliver and I are staying with Henri for a few more days. Next week we're definitely moving back in,' she said determinedly.

'Are you going to register with 'A

Taste Of The Countryside' now the house is finished?'

'I'm not sure,' Nicola replied. I think Oliver and I will just enjoy the place for a little while on our own.' She glanced at him and smiled.

'It's been good staying up at the farm, but now we need to spend some time together, and get on with our lives.'

'Can I go out on my bike now you're back?' Oliver demanded grumpily, banging the lid back on a paint pot.

Nicola gazed at him, exasperated.

'Supper's at half past eight up at La Prouveresse. Don't be late.'

'Will he be there?' Oliver jerked his head in Gilles's direction.

'Oliver, that is extremely rude. Apologise at once.' Nicola stared at her son in disbelief. 'How dare you speak like that? And yes, Gilles will be joining us for supper.'

Sullenly, Oliver glanced towards Gilles and apologised, but then, to Nicola's distress as he left the room they both heard him mutter under his breath.

'You should stay away from my mother anyway — all the men she likes die.'

In the silence that followed the slamming of the door, Gilles slowly climbed down the ladder. And as the tears began to fall down Nicola's face, he gently took her in his arms and held her tightly as she sobbed against his shoulder.

'Maybe Oliver has a point. They always say these things come in threes and . . . '

Gilles silenced her with a kiss.

'Don't be silly, Nicola, I couldn't stay away from you and Olivier now if I tried. And I don't want to. Since I met you, my life has taken on a whole new meaning. All I want to do is take care of you.'

He paused and stroked her cheek gently.

'Olivier will accept my presence eventually. At the moment, though, I think he's not only sad and angry about his father and Andrew — he's also frightened to make friends with me in case he gets hurt again.'

Nicola sighed.

'He's grown up so much this past year, but I suppose, deep down, he's still just a bewildered young boy.'

Gilles nodded.

'Try not to worry. He won't drive me away, I promise. Next time I'm alone with him I'll try to reassure him. Now, how about some food? I'm starving. I don't think I can wait until suppertime.'

'That's something you both have in common, anyway.' Nicola laughed. 'Oliver is always hungry. Come on then, let's go up to La Prouveresse and see the *tantes* and Pascal on their way. I'll make you a sandwich before I start preparing supper.'

'Where's Oliver?'

The *tantes* were preparing to leave for their Parisian trip when Nicola and Gilles walked into the kitchen.

'We'll be gone for three days,' Giselle said. 'Odette should find a dress easily in that time. I, however, might have a problem.' She looked ruefully down at her curvaceous body.

'*Haute couture* is not known for being available in large sizes and I really would like something that little bit special,' she said wistfully.

Nicola smiled sympathetically.

'Do you have any particular colour in mind?'

'Odette thinks she'll go for ivory and she wants me in something similar. I fancy a bit more colour, but we'll see.'

After waving goodbye to the *tantes* and Pascal, Nicola made Gilles a sandwich and then started to prepare supper. He gave her a hand setting the table.

'The cheeseboard looks a bit bare,' he said. 'Is there any more?'

'There's a fresh baguette and some brie in the pantry,' Nicola said, concentrating on making the sauce for the salmon.

Gilles shook his head.

'Can't see it. Just a small piece of Cantal and some Roquefort. No bread either, just some biscuits.'

'That's strange. Giselle is normally so organised — she never runs out of anything. Oh, well, we'll just have to make do for tonight. I'll go shopping in the morning.'

Nicola turned as the kitchen door slammed closed, expecting to see Oliver, but it was Henri.

'Oliver not with you?' she said. 'I told him to be back in time for supper and it'll be ready soon.'

'I haven't seen him since this afternoon when he went whizzing off on his bike,' Henri answered.

'He'll be here soon — Mischief will see to that. She'll be wanting her own food.'

But Oliver hadn't turned up by the time supper was ready and Nicola went out to the *petit jardin* to ring the bell that hung there. Once used to summon the farm workers for meals, it could be heard even in the distant fields. Oliver knew its sound and had always been back at the farm within ten minutes of the bell being rung.

But not this evening.

Anxious

'He wouldn't have gone on the road with his bike, would he?' Nicola asked anxiously.

Henri shook his head.

'Give him another ten minutes and then I'll go and look for him.'

'But where should we start looking?' Nicola said.

'I think I might have an idea where he's gone,' Henri admitted.

Nicola glanced at him sharply.

'He's been asking me questions about La Chambre du Roi.'

Nicola looked at him, puzzled.

'It's a small cave that the locals named after the more famous one up in the mountains. It's about a kilometre or so the other side of the copse.' Henri paused.

'It was a favourite place of Marc's. He would go there whenever he needed to sort things out in his mind. He said it was a healing place. There are wonderful panoramic views. There's also a spring and a small pond . . . '

'A pond?' Nicola interrupted.

'Still pretty dried up at the moment, I suspect, after the hot summer,' Henri said reassuringly.

'Olivier has been talking about the place since I told him about it. I promised to take him there but I've been so busy, I kept telling him later. My guess is he's gone to find the place for himself.'

'Can you give me directions?' Nicola reached for her coat.

'*Non*, Nicola. I will go. I'll take the tractor and go by road. It will be quicker,' Henri said.

'I'll stay with Nicola,' Gilles said quietly. 'Unless you want me to come with you?'

'*Non, merci*.' Henri shook his head. 'It's best if you stay here.'

Gilles reached into his pocket and handed Henri his mobile phone.

'Here, take this and ring when you get there. If he's not there we'll phone the *gendarmerie* and start to organise a search of the area.'

Nicola bit her lip at the mention of the *gendarmerie*. Gilles put his arm around her.

'Try not to worry. Henri's convinced that he'll find Olivier.'

★　★　★

Sitting in the entrance to the cave, Oliver carefully broke the baguette into pieces and spread the brie with his pocket knife as Mischief watched him hopefully.

'Here you go, girl. This will have to keep you going until we get back.' And he divided the pieces between them.

As he ate, Oliver looked around him. Just knowing that it was one of his dad's favourite places made him feel good. He'd spent some time exploring the cave and had found the initials *MJ* carved into the slab of rock near the back of the cave, a discovery which, to his surprise, had made him cry.

He glanced up at the night sky. He should really have left for home before now. It was going to be difficult retracing his steps in the dark. Fleetingly, he felt a twinge of guilt, for he knew that his mother would be worried. But perhaps she hadn't missed him yet; she had Gilles for company.

Oliver thought about the ride home — the bike didn't have lights and there was no comforting moon in the sky yet. It would be easier to go home by road but, having promised Nicola he wouldn't take his bike on the road, he knew he had no choice but to return cross-country.

Below him, open countryside gave way to olive terraces and, lower down, the vineyards with their old cottages. Beyond that, the distant stone walls and the ochre-coloured roofs of the village had disappeared from view.

Now, Oliver watched as the occasional headlight from a car driving through a distant village flashed between the buildings.

The rutted track he'd ridden along had merged into the shadows of the fields it skirted. Owls preparing to start out on their nightly supper hunt screeched from the high branches of the overhanging oak trees. Bats flew above his head, in and out of the cave.

Standing up, Oliver gave the last piece of baguette to Mischief and looked apprehensively in the direction of home. But, before he could kickstart his bike, Mischief cocked an ear and whined softly.

Oliver heard the noise then, too — the rhythmic chug of a tractor engine that seemed to be getting closer. Glancing down towards the track again, he saw headlights slowly approaching.

Peering into the darkness, Oliver finally recognised his grandfather. As Henri stopped the tractor, Mischief finished her bread before dashing off in a frenzy of barking to greet Henri and his dog, Meg.

'*Bonsoir*, Olivier,' Henri said quietly. 'Are you all right?'

Oliver nodded and waited as Henri took the mobile phone Gilles had given him out of his pocket. He hesitated.

'Do you know how to use this?' Henri asked.

'Yes,' Oliver replied.

'Better phone your mother, then,' Henri said, handing him the mobile. 'Tell her you are all right and you'll be home soon.'

Oliver could hear the relief in his mother's voice when she answered the phone.

'Thank goodness,' she said. 'Gilles and I have been so worried about you.'

'I'm sorry,' Oliver said. 'Papa Henri is giving me a ride home on the tractor. See you soon.'

The Truth

As Oliver helped Henri tie the bike on to the tractor, his grandfather glanced at him.

'Any particular reason for coming out here today?'

Oliver shrugged his shoulders.

'Nope. Just wanted to see the place. I didn't mean to worry Mum. Is she very cross?'

Henri shook his head.

'Not cross, just concerned. Gilles was worried, too.'

'I wasn't very nice to Gilles earlier,' Oliver said quietly.

'I know Mum thinks I don't like him, but I do. It's just that . . . ' he bit his lip ' . . . Dad's gone — and now Andrew. Why can't we just be us for a while — with you and the *tantes*, of course. We don't need anyone else,' he added, looking at Henri.

362

Henri sighed.

'Life has been hard for your mother. She didn't really want to come to France after your papa died, and things haven't been easy for her.'

He paused before continuing.

'She always told me she needed a life and friends of her own, as well as the Jacques family, if she was going to be happy here.'

'But it was her idea to move to France! She said we'd have a better life over here with family around. And she's got Le Jardin . . . ' Oliver protested.

Henri shook his head.

'*Non*, Olivier. It was my idea. I insisted you came.'

He paused, searching for words.

'I think it's time you knew the truth. You see, *mon petit garçon*, one day La Prouveresse will be yours and I wanted you to grow up here, get to know it. I accused your mother of denying you your birthright if she didn't move to France. I made her believe that if you didn't come I'd disinherit you.'

He glanced at Oliver.

'But I was lying. You're my direct descendant and you inherit, whatever I do — or don't do.'

'Does Mum know that now?'

'Yes.'

Oliver was quiet for several seconds.

'So, she could decide to return to England?' He glanced anxiously at Henri. 'You don't think Mum is planning on doing that, do you? I don't want to go back. I really like living here.'

'I think your mother also likes living here now things are settling down. And having Gilles as a special friend is helping.'

Henri was silent as he pulled the rope securely around the bike and tied the final knot to the tractor framework.

'Talk to your mother, Olivier — you'll find you're still her number one concern. But she needs Gilles in her life, too.'

'Papa Henri, have you got a torch in the tractor?'

Henri nodded.

'May I show you something, then, before we leave?'

Oliver turned and led his grandfather over to the rock at the back of the cave.

'Look, I found Dad's initials.' And he shone the torch over the weathered *MJ* carved into the stone. Directly beneath it were two smaller, freshly cut letters, *OJ*.

Oliver glanced anxiously at his grandfather.

'I won't get into trouble for that, will I? I just wanted to be somewhere permanently with Dad.'

Henri put his arm around Oliver and held him tight.

'I miss him, too, Olivier, but together we will keep his memory alive.'

Changes

'I now declare 'A Taste Of The Countryside' open.' The mayor cut the red ribbon with a flourish and pushed open the door. A smatter of applause broke out before everyone moved into the building to sample the wine and other produce on offer.

Nicola, walking around with Gilles, looked at the variety of foodstuffs that the area produced. Seeing it all gathered together in one place was amazing. Honey, olive oil, wine, lavender, apple juice, poultry, cheeses, preserves — the choice seemed endless.

Nicola's own small offerings of fresh herbs and some other plants were quickly snapped up.

'I think that next year, when you have Le Jardin de Dominic really organised, you will have a good outlet for your produce,' Gilles said.

'I hope so,' Nicola said. 'Now the house is finished I can concentrate on the garden — something I'm really looking forward to.'

Next to the tourist information corner with its leaflets and maps, there was also a colourful display of local artists' work, from paintings and photographs of the area, to bowls and sculptures made from olive wood.

'Do you think Odette and Pascal would like one of these?' Nicola said, picking up a large salad bowl complete with olive wood servers.

It was just two days before the wedding and she still had to find a suitable present.

'Good idea,' Gilles answered. 'Will you excuse me for a while? I have to go and talk to someone about a survey. Shouldn't take long, then we can collect Olivier and join my parents for lunch.'

Nicola was still looking at the salad bowl when Giselle joined her.

'If you are thinking of buying it for Odette and Pascal,' Giselle began, 'I know Odette would love it. She was casting covetous looks at the one we have up at the farm but I told her hands off!'

'In that case, I'll definitely get it for her — unless you want to?' Nicola hesitated.

'I've already got them something else,' Giselle replied.

'Have they decided where they're going after the wedding?' Nicola asked.

'The plan is for them to spend the night at the château after the reception, a couple of days over Christmas at La Prouveresse and the campsite — which, by the way, they are going to rename Moulin du Roc. And then on the twenty-eighth they're off on their honeymoon.'

Nicola smiled, taking in all that Giselle had just said.

'And before you ask, not even Odette knows where they're going. Pascal has simply promised her somewhere exotic!'

'Lucky lady,' Nicola said. She glanced

at Giselle curiously. 'But it's not only Odette's life that is about to change. How do you feel about living up at the farm without her after all these years?'

Nicola paused and smiled.

'Not to mention coping with Henri on your own . . . '

Giselle laughed.

'Actually I've decided to make some changes in my life, too,' she said. 'Get involved with more things outside the farm for a start.'

She looked around her before leaning towards Nicola.

'Some of the villagers feel women should have a bigger say in the running of things,' she whispered. 'I've been asked to consider standing for *maire*.'

'Won't you be in competition with Henri?' Nicola asked.

Giselle smiled as she shook her head.

'Funnily enough, when I told him I was thinking of standing, he said he'd decided not to stand for *maire* after all, and wished me *bonne chance!*'

'Well, if it's what you want, I hope you win the election,' Nicola said. 'And don't forget, any time you feel lonely up at the farm, or Henri gets to you, you know where I am. Mind you, the amount of time Oliver has been spending up at La Prouveresse with you, I suspect you'll be glad of some peace and quiet.'

'Don't be silly, I adore having you both around,' Giselle said quietly. 'I'm just so pleased that things are finally starting to sort themselves out. Olivier seems a lot happier these days.'

Nicola nodded.

'I think he is. He's certainly less moody and seems to have accepted Gilles, too, which is a relief. They were huddled together yesterday in the sitting-room making a list or something. Wouldn't tell me what they were up to — just looked very guilty and said it was a secret!'

'Your friendship with Gilles also seems to be flourishing, *oui?*' Giselle said, looking at her quizzically.

Nicola blushed. But before she could say anything, Gilles returned and it was time to leave for their lunch date with his parents and Oliver.

Wedding Bells

'Oliver, are you ready? We're going to be late if we don't leave now!'

'I've just got to get something from the shed,' Oliver said, running down the stairs and out of the back door. 'Can you give me a hand, please, Gilles?'

Nicola sighed exasperatedly.

'Patience, *ma cherie*,' Gilles said. 'I'll see you at the car. Would you open the boot, please?' He closed the back door behind him.

Before locking the cottage door, Nicola glanced around. Le Jardin was, finally, exactly how she'd imagined it could be.

Now, with the Christmas tree and the other seasonal decorations in place, the sitting-room was ready for their first Christmas in France. And it was a Christmas that promised to be as family orientated as she'd always dreamed it should be.

On Christmas Eve she and Oliver were joining everyone up at La Prouveresse for the all-important French family celebration evening meal. Giselle had been planning the menu for weeks — including the traditional thirteen desserts.

'Why thirteen?' Nicola had asked when Giselle roped her in to help make some.

'The idea is you have a small taste of each one and it's supposed to help protect you through the coming months. Thirteen represents Christ and the disciples.'

'Well, it certainly makes our plum pudding look a bit boring.' Nicola had laughed as she prepared some candied fruit under Giselle's expert guidance.

On Christmas Day everybody, including Gilles who was spending Christmas Eve with his parents, was coming to Le Jardin for lunch. Nicola sighed happily as she locked the door. For the first time in years she was looking forward to Christmas.

Watching as Oliver and Gilles appeared clutching an assortment of tin cans, boots and balloons between them, Nicola giggled.

'So this is what you two have been plotting. I hope Odette and Pascal are ready for this quaint English custom.'

She glanced at her watch.

'They should be at the Hôtel de Ville by now. Come on, we don't want to be late for the church ceremony.'

Although Odette had originally wanted Oliver to be a witness, when she discovered he was too young she and Pascal decided that just Henri and Giselle would witness the civil ceremony. Oliver could sign the church registry with them instead.

'It is the church service that is really important for me,' Odette said. 'And for that I want all my family there.'

Nicola caught her breath as Gilles drove into the village. The Christmas decorations were all switched on, lending a magical quality to the place in the half-light of the late afternoon.

A canopy of small white twinkling lights hung across the square, gently swaying in the breeze. Ropes of fairy lights had been wound around the trunks of the trees and up into their bare branches and a large silver star hung at the entrance to the market.

The words of 'Silent Night' floated on the air from a group of carol singers gathered around an accordion player by the Christmas tree in the square.

Villagers were beginning to gather in small crowds waiting for the bride and groom to make their appearance from the Hôtel de Ville.

The smell of lilies on the altar of St Joseph's wafted out through the open doors and Father Lapine, standing in the porch, smiled benevolently at the gathering crowds.

Nicola, Gilles and Oliver made their way to the steps of St Joseph's to wait with Sylvie and Claudine, and were soon joined by Raoul, Marie and Luc.

As Raoul kissed Nicola on the cheek

in greeting, he whispered in her ear.

'Marie and I are engaged.'

'Oh, I'm so pleased for you,' Nicola said. 'Luc is better then? He accepts you more?'

Raoul shook his head sadly.

'*Non*. But . . . ' He looked at Nicola apologetically.

'It was really Andrew's accident that brought things home to Marie. She finally saw that we'd wasted too many precious years feeling guilty.'

'Things will work out with Luc, I promise,' Nicola said gently. 'Is there anything I can do to help?'

'Thanks,' Raoul said. 'Olivier seems to be a beneficial influence, so if you and Gilles can keep up the good work, it should rub off on to Luc!'

Nicola glanced across at Oliver, who was laughing at something Gilles had said. Looking at her son in the smart suit Pascal had insisted on buying him for the wedding, Nicola felt a surge of pride coupled with hope for the future.

A cheer broke out on the opposite

side of the square and Pascal and Odette appeared, hand in hand, in the doorway of the Hôtel de Ville, with Henri and Giselle behind them.

As people clapped and cheered, the accordion player moved across the square towards them, playing as he walked.

Odette, radiant in her heavily embroidered dress, held Pascal's hand tightly as she smiled at the crowd of well-wishers.

The notes of the song faded away, and were replaced by a jazzed-up version of 'The Wedding March' as the musician beckoned the happy couple to follow him in a dance around the square. Then, slowing the beat down to the more sedate, traditional march, he led them back to St Joseph's for their church dedication service.

Surrounded by family and friends, Odette and Pascal mounted the steps and entered the quiet sixteenth century church where Father Lapine welcomed them and began the service.

Nicola, standing between Gilles and Oliver, brushed a tear away in happiness as she watched Odette finally making her vows to the man she had always loved.

Gilles looked at Nicola lovingly as he squeezed her tight.

'Do you think Olivier would agree to be best man at our wedding — or would you rather he gave you away?' he whispered.

As his words sank in, Nicola turned and smiled at him.

'We will have to ask him which he'd rather do,' she answered softly, as her own tears of happiness started to flow.

THE END